Programming and Problem Solving with Delphi

Mitchell C. Kerman

Addison
Wesley
Longman

Boston   San Francisco   New York
London   Toronto   Sydney   Tokyo   Singapore   Madrid
Mexico City   Munich   Paris   Cape Town   Hong Kong   Montreal

Executive Editor: *Susan Hartman Sullivan*
Editorial Assistant: *Andy Smith*
Managing Editor: *Pat Mahtani*
Production Supervision: *Diane Freed*
Cover Design: *Regina Hagen*
Cover Image: *Photodisc*
Composition/Interior Design: *Pre-Press Company, Inc.*
Copyeditor: *Jill Hobbs*
Proofreader: *Judy Strakalaitis*
Manufacturing Coordinator: *Caroline Fell*

Access the latest information about Addison-Wesley titles from our World Wide Web site: http://www.aw.com/cs

Many of the designations used by manufacturers and sellers to distinguish their products are claimed as trademarks. Where those designations appear in this book, and Addison-Wesley was aware of a trademark claim, the designations have been printed in initial caps or all caps.

The programs and the applications presented in this book have been included for their instructional value. They have been tested with care but are not guaranteed for any particular purpose. The publisher does not offer any warranties or representations, nor does it accept any liabilities with respect to the programs or applications.

Library of Congress Cataloging-in-Publication Data
Kerman, Mitchell C.
    Computer programming fundamentals with applications in Delphi/Mitchell C. Kerman p. cm.
ISBN 0-201-70844-2 (pbk.)
    1. Computer programming. 2. Delphi (Computer file) I. Title.

QA76.6.K464 2002
005.26'8—dc21   2001022966

2345678910—CRS—0302

To Janet, Charles, and Jessica
for making my world a much happier place
(and showing me that carbon is a more important element than silicon . . .)

Contents

5 Decision Structures 121

6 Repetition Structures 149

7 Text Files 171

10 Data Structures 257

11 Binary Files 339

12 Sorting and Searching 357

16 Additional Delphi Components 453

17 Advanced Delphi Programming 507

Appendices

A. Computer Arithmetic and Number Systems 553

B. ASCII (ANSI) Character Values 573

C. Object Pascal Programming Standards 575

D. Customizing the Delphi Integrated Development Environment 579

Preface

This book is an introductory-level computer science, programming, and problem-solving textbook. The book is geared toward undergraduate-level computer science courses. It assumes that students only have a rudimentary knowledge of computer operations (Windows 9x/ME/NT/2000), but assumes no prior knowledge of computer programming. The text uses Borland Software Corporation's Delphi and Object Pascal as the development environment and computer language to present programming fundamentals, concepts, example programs, programming assignments, and projects. It contains enough material for a two-semester sequence of computer science classes.

The main objective of this text is for students to attain a solid foundation in computer programming fundamentals and to exercise these fundamental skills using Delphi and Object Pascal. In this manner, a student can master one development environment (Delphi) and programming language (Object Pascal) and then easily learn others.

Why Delphi?

Borland's Delphi traces its roots to the Pascal programming language. Pascal was created in 1971 by Niklaus Wirth as an introductory computer programming language. Pascal was widely accepted and used as the language of choice in the computer science curricula of many universities (both nationally and internationally). Due to its speed and versatility, it was also used extensively in the commercial sector.

Turbo Pascal is Borland's very popular version of the Pascal language. With the developments of the Windows operating system and object-oriented programming, Borland naturally extended its Turbo Pascal product into Turbo Pascal for Windows and Object Pascal for Windows. Borland's Delphi is the next step in the evolution of the Pascal programming language. In essence, it is Object Pascal with a visual development environment for the Windows operating system. It is designed for the rapid development of Windows-based applications.

In recent years, C++ and Java have competed with Pascal as the primary language taught in introductory computer science courses. Like Borland's Turbo Pascal, Delphi has a large following and is widely used in industry because it offers the syntactically easy language of Object Pascal coupled with compiled program speeds that rival those of C++. This textbook bridges the gap between industry and academia, bringing Pascal back to its roots in the academic environment.

Purpose of This Book

Few modern introductory programming texts adequately address general programming methodology. Many of these texts focus on the nuances and package-specific features offered by a program development environment rather than on establishing a foundation of solid programming techniques and a general understanding of the common control structures available in most high-level languages. Additionally, these texts tend to be lengthy and to intimidate many students. This book rectifies this situation by introducing control structures in general terms and then describing their Object Pascal implementation. Although this text is concise in comparison to others on the market, it provides a *complete* introduction to programming fundamentals and demonstrates sound programming practices. Advanced, package-specific features of Delphi are introduced after programming fundamentals have been presented and mastered.

Although Delphi offers many outstanding features, there are a few hurdles that a student new to programming must overcome. First, there is the overhead involved with learning Delphi's integrated development environment (IDE). As with any Windows-based programming platform, familiarity with the IDE is required before a student can learn and practice computer programming skills. This is much like learning any other Windows application. Second, beginners often become confused as to the differences between the controls in the user interface they design and the programs they write to work with these controls.

This text rises to each of these challenges. A quick but thorough introduction to the Delphi IDE is the focus of Chapter 2. More advanced IDE concepts appear later in the text. The intent is for the student to start programming right away, and Chapter 2 introduces the first program. Furthermore, the differences between a program and a user interface are emphasized throughout the text to avoid confusion between the two. Finally, the text promotes proper programming practices; we identify the possible programming pitfalls, show examples of them, and present ways to avoid making them.

Outstanding Features

Among this book's features, the most prominent are that it:

- Assumes no prior knowledge of computer programming.
- Stresses computer programming fundamentals. Students attain a solid foundation in computer programming and master basic programming skills that are applicable to any computer language.

- Uses Delphi, an Object Pascal-based programming platform that is widely used in the corporate sector.
- Includes chapters and appendices that cover such topics as computer history and the evolution of computer programming languages, computer arithmetic and number systems, object-oriented programming, advanced Delphi programming, and databases.
- Covers Windows-based programming concepts, such as object liking and embedding (OLE), dynamic data exchange (DDE), and ActiveX components.

Pedagogical Features

This text offers numerous features to aid instructors and enhance student learning:

Chapter Objectives. Each chapter begins with a list of chapter objectives, stating the concepts that the student will learn and the tasks that will be performed by the conclusion of the chapter.

Definition Boxes. Definition boxes define the most important terms within the chapter and compare and contrast key terms.

Syntax Boxes. Boxed inserts highlight important concepts and Delphi syntax, allowing students to quickly locate key information within the text.

Code Callouts. Important points and key concepts in program source code are explained in code callout boxes.

Programming Keys. Programming keys provide tips and warnings to aid the beginning programmer.

GUI Design Tips. Graphical user interface (GUI) design tips are presented throughout the text, providing guidelines for and enhancing student understanding of proper GUI design.

Real-World Examples. Examples in the text are drawn from real-world problems in business, math, science, and engineering. The exercises and programming projects at the end of each chapter are geared toward these real-world problems as well.

Case Studies. Case studies appear throughout the text, providing the student with insight into how the concepts presented apply to real-world situations.

Chapter Summaries. Each chapter concludes with a summary that provides the student with an indispensable study aid. Each chapter summary is divided into sections appropriate for that chapter, as follows:

- *Key Terms.* This section provides a glossary of terms presented in the chapter.
- *Keywords.* Delphi keywords introduced in the chapter are listed according to their applicability.
- *Key Concepts.* This section summarizes the concepts and Delphi syntax introduced in the chapter.

Review Questions. Each chapter has review questions, allowing students to test their recall and understanding of the material presented.

Chapter Problems. Each chapter contains problems to test student mastery of the material.

Programming Projects. Programming projects allow students to combine already mastered material with the new concepts presented in the chapter.

Online Supplements. A Web site provides an instructor's manual containing the answers to the review questions, chapter problems, and programming projects. This manual is for instructors only. It is available through your Addison-Wesley sales representative or by sending an e-mail message to aw.cse@awl.com.

CD-ROM. The companion CD-ROM contains the Standard edition of Delphi 5 and all coded examples from the text.

Style Conventions

This book uses the following style conventions:

```
Object Pascal statements and program text appear in monospace
font. Words that the reader types also appear in this font.
```

Statements containing generic names that may be changed by the programmer are italicized.

Names of keys appear in all capital letters (e.g., ENTER key).

Italics are used for emphasis and for variables within equations.

To the Student

Welcome, and congratulations on your decision to learn computer programming with Delphi. Whether you are a novice or an expert programmer, this text is designed for you. Programming fundamentals are stressed in the initial chapters to prepare you for the advanced topics that are covered in the later chapters. The chapters are organized so that they introduce specific concepts and build on them as you progress. Access to a computer with Delphi 5 installed is desirable so that you will be able to try examples presented in the text. Working through examples and getting the intended results from the computer is without question the best method of reinforcing the programming techniques presented. If you are not math savvy, don't worry: the most advanced mathematics in the text requires only a knowledge of basic algebra. Overall, I encourage you to experiment with Delphi; experimentation and discovery is a major part of the learning process.

The CD-ROM packaged with the text contains Delphi 5 Standard, a fully-functional version of Delphi. You can install this version on your home computer so that you can work on your programs both at home and in your school's computer lab.

Finally, I envy you, the student: You are about to embark on an enjoyable and rewarding journey into the world of computer programming. Bon voyage!

To the Instructor

This text was written to fill a very large void in the available literature. Few books concerning Delphi are truly introductory programming texts. Most are trade books or books for advanced programmers. This text revitalizes Object Pascal and brings Delphi into the academic realm.

Presently, there is dissension in the industrial and academic communities over the preferred methodology for teaching an introductory programming class. Essentially, there are two schools of thought. The first school believes in a fundamentals-first approach, introducing constants, variables, decision structures, and loops before advancing to object-oriented programming. The second school, on the other hand, believes in introducing objects as a fundamental structure. Because both approaches have potential advantages and disadvantages, this text is designed with flexibility of presentation in mind. The main flow of the text follows the first school but objects and object-oriented programming may be introduced earlier by covering Chapter 15 along with Chapter 4.

This text contains enough material for a two-semester sequence of introductory and advanced programming with Delphi. The chapters cover the following topics:

- Chapter 1 introduces computer history and the evolution of computer programming languages.
- Chapter 2 describes the Delphi development environment and guides students through writing their first program.
- Chapter 3 introduces problem solving, algorithm design, flowcharts, pseudocode, and the program development cycle.
- Chapter 4 describes the elements of programming, such as data types, constants, and variables.
- Chapter 5 explains relational operators, Boolean operators, and decision structures.
- Chapter 6 introduces repetition structures.

- Chapter 7 discusses text file input and output.
- Chapter 8 describes structured programming concepts.
- Chapter 9 stresses the importance of error-proofing and debugging source code.
- Chapter 10 covers data structures. It introduces arrays, records, user-defined data types, pointers, linked lists, stacks, queues, deques, priority queues, heaps, and trees.
- Binary file input and output is the topic of Chapter 11.
- Sorting and searching are covered in Chapter 12.
- Chapter 13 describes database fundamentals and database programming.
- Chapter 14 introduces recursion concepts.
- Chapter 15 introduces object-oriented programming.
- Chapter 16 describes additional Delphi components not discussed in previous chapters.
- Advanced Delphi programming: Chapter 17 covers topics such as ActiveX programming, multiple forms and multiple document interface (MDI) forms, random numbers, graphics, object linking and embedding (OLE), dynamic data exchange (DDE), and Internet programming.
- Appendix A describes computer arithmetic and number systems, including binary, octal, and hexadecimal.
- Appendix B shows the ASCII table.
- Object Pascal Programming Standards are listed in Appendix C.
- Appendix D describes how to customize the Delphi integrated development environment.
- Appendix E discusses distributing your Delphi programs.
- Appendix F lists the Object Pascal reserved words.
- Visual Basic programmers should refer to Appendix G for a discussion of the migration from Visual Basic to Delphi.

Recommended Coverage

The recommended coverage of the text depends on the length of the class and the type of students being taught. The recommendations are split according to both of these criteria. Because later chapters build on concepts presented in earlier ones, we recommend covering the chapters in the order listed.

Computer Science and Engineering Students:

First Semester: Chapter 1, Appendix A, Chapters 2, 3, 4, 5, 6, 7, 8, 9, and the beginning of Chapter 10.

Second Semester: The remainder of Chapter 10 and Chapters 11, 12, 13, 14, 15, 16, and 17.

Note: Instructors who introduce objects as a fundamental data structure should cover Chapter 15 along with Chapter 4 in the first semester.

Business and Other Majors:

First Semester: Chapters 1, 2, 3, 4, 5, 6, 7, 8, 9, and the beginning of Chapter 10.

Second Semester: The remainder of Chapter 10 and Chapters 11, 12, 13, 15, 16, and 17.

Note: Instructors who introduce objects as a fundamental data structure should cover Chapter 15 along with Chapter 4 in the first semester.

Acknowledgments

As with any undertaking of this magnitude, there are always a large number of people to thank upon its completion. First, I would like to thank both Borland Software Corporation and Addison-Wesley (AW) for giving me the opportunity to write this book. Many heartfelt thanks go to Jane Allen, Rebecca Cavagnari, Kari Gallant, Karen Giles, Ben Riga, and Danny Thorpe of Borland Software Corporation and Susan Hartman Sullivan, Michael Hirsch, and Andy Smith of AW. The AW production staff is second to none, and I could not have written this text without their help. I appreciate the outstanding work of my managing editor, Pat Mahtani; book project manager, Diane Freed; copyeditor, Jill Hobbs; proofreader, Judy Strakalaitis; and the designers, artists, and compositors at Pre-Press Company, Inc. Additionally, I extend many thanks to Claire Collins, formerly of Borland Software Corporation, and Lisa Kalner, formerly of AW.

The reviewers provided excellent recommendations for improving the text. You have my sincerest appreciation:

Myron Berg	Dickinson State University
Dr. Guillermo A. Francia, III	Jacksonville State University
Taskin Kocak	University of Central Florida
Thomas Theobald	Borland Software Corporation
Jodi L. Tims, Ph.D.	St. Francis College
Richard B. Warnock	Salt Lake City Community College

Finally, I must extend a great deal of gratitude, appreciation, love, and affection to my wife and children for sacrificing time with me while I wrote this text.

Mitchell Kerman

April 2001

Chapter 1

An Introduction to Computers and Computer Science

Chapter Objectives

In this chapter you will:

- Learn about the history of modern computers
- Become acquainted with the different types of computer systems
- Learn the difference between hardware and software
- Become familiar with the microcomputer hardware block diagram and the six components of a typical microcomputer system
- Learn about the different types of computer memory
- Gain an understanding of binary numbers and learn related terminology
- Learn the differences between machine language, low-level languages, and high-level languages
- Learn the difference between compilers and interpreters

A Brief History of Computers

In their early history, humans used their fingers for counting. This fact explains why we use the base 10, or decimal, number system. Eventually, humans discovered that other objects, such as pebbles and sticks, could aid in counting. In the Stone Age, for example, wolf bones were used as tally sticks. These bones are the oldest known computing devices.

Many consider the first true computing devices to be the ancient counting tables and tablets known as **abaci.** The word **abacus** (plural *abaci*) is derived from the Greek *abax*, meaning "table or board covered with dust." Evidence of these devices dating from as early as 3000 B.C. has been found in the Tigris-Euphrates Valley and from as late as 5 B.C. in Egypt. The early abacus consisted of grooves carved into a stone or clay tablet. Pebbles were slid along these grooves from one side of the tablet to the other to represent numbers. This system allowed for easier counting and aided in simple calculations like addition and subtraction. Around A.D. 12, the modern abacus first appeared in China. It consists of a wood frame containing several columns of beads threaded on strings or wires (Figure 1.1). The modern abacus is an extremely useful computing tool; in fact, it is still used in certain parts of the world today.

The following timeline presents a brief history of the computing devices and innovations that led to the development of modern-day computers and shaped the computer industry:

1600s

Circa 1600—John Napier, the inventor of logarithms, invents a hand-held device to assist with multiplication and division operations. The device is known as Napier's rods or Napier's bones.

FIGURE 1.1   The Abacus

FIGURE 1.2   Pascal's Adding Machine
Reproduced by permission from IBM. Copyright 2001 by International Business
Machines Corporation.

1622—Using Napier's logarithms as a base, William Oughtred invents the
slide rule. Oughtred's slide rule was circular in shape.

1623—William Schickard creates the first mechanical calculator. Blaise Pascal,
the creator of the famous triangle, invents a mechanical adding machine with
an automatic carry function (Figure 1.2).

1673—Gottfried Leibniz builds a multiplication machine.

1800s

1820—Thomas de Colmar invents the arithometer.

1822—Charles Babbage, a British mathematician and engineer, designs the
difference engine (Figure 1.3).

1833—Babbage designs the analytical engine. Although the mechanical version of his design was never built, it contained all of the components of the
modern computer. That is, it had units for input, output, memory, arithmetic,
logic, and control. The design used punched cards to communicate algorithms to the engine, and numbers were stored on toothed wheels that served
as memory. Babbage's design had a great influence on the development of
computers, and he is known as the "father of the computer."

1854—George Boole, a self-taught British mathematician, invents a system for
symbolic and logical reasoning. This system, known as Boolean algebra, is
later used as the basis for computer design.

1890—The first punched cards are used to read information into a computing
machine.

FIGURE 1.3   Babbage's Difference Engine
Reproduced by permission from IBM. Copyright 2001 by International Business Machines Corporation.

1920s

1924—The Forms Tabulating Company, started in 1896, becomes the C-T-R (Calculating-Tabulating-Recording) Company in 1914. In 1924, C-T-R Company changes its name to International Business Machines (IBM).

1925—Vannevar Bush invents the large-scale differential analyzer.

1930s

1935—Konrad Zuse develops the Z-1 computer.

1936—John Vincent Atanasoff, a mathematician and physicist at Iowa State University, and John Berry, Atanasoff's graduate assistant, develop the first electronic digital special-purpose computer, known as the Atanasoff-Berry computer. This computer uses vacuum tubes instead of the less efficient relays for storage and arithmetic functions.

1937—Alan Turing, a British mathematician, develops the theoretical "Turing machine," laying the foundation for the development of general-purpose programmable computers. Turing is also famous for breaking the German "Enigma" code during World War II, thereby allowing Allied forces to decipher secret German messages.

1939—Bell Labs develops the complex number calculator.

1940s

1943—The Colossus Mark I decrypting computer is built.

1944—The Harvard Mark I computer is developed.

1945—Grace M. Hopper finds a moth fused to a wire of the Mark I computer, causing the machine to malfunction. She originates the term "debugging" for the process of finding and removing errors.

1946—Two electrical engineers, John Mauchley and J. Presper Eckert, build ENIAC (Electrical Numerical Integrator And Calculator), the first large-scale, fully electronic, general-purpose digital computer, at the University of Pennsylvania. ENIAC uses 18,000 vacuum tubes for storage and computation, weighs 30 tons, and occupies an area of 1500 square feet. ENIAC can perform 300 multiplications of two 10-digit numbers per second; by comparison, the Mark I performs only one multiplication every three seconds. ENIAC is shown in Figure 1.4.

1947—Three physicists, John Bardeen, Walter Brattain, and William Shockley, invent the transistor at Bell Labs. The transistor replaces the vacuum tube and revolutionizes computer design because it is smaller, lighter, cooler, and more

FIGURE 1.4 ENIAC
Photo courtesy of Unisys Corporation.

reliable. Additionally, the first stored-program computer, the Manchester Baby, is developed this same year.

1950s

1951—The UNIVAC (Universal Automatic Computer) is delivered to the U.S. Census Bureau.

1953—IBM develops its first computer, the IBM 701 EDPM.

1957—John Backus and team members develop the FORTRAN (FORmula TRANslation) programming language, a compiled language useful in the scientific and academic communities.

Late 1950s—Grace M. Hopper pioneers the development and use of COBOL (COmmon Business-Oriented Language), a programming language for the business community that uses English-like phrases. The LISP (LISt Processor) language is also developed.

1960s

1960—The ALGOL (ALGOrithmic Language) programming language is created.

1964—John G. Kemeny and Thomas E. Kurtz, two professors of mathematics at Dartmouth College, develop the BASIC (Beginners All-purpose Symbolic Instruction Code) language. The first computer "mouse" and "windows" are also developed in this year. Additionally, IBM introduces the System 360 (Figure 1.5), its first "family of computers."

1967—The first computers using integrated circuits are built.

1968—Intel Corporation is founded.

1969—Work begins on ARPAnet, a precursor of the modern-day Internet.

1970s

1971—Intel Corporation develops the first microprocessor. The floppy disk is also created this year. Niklaus Wirth develops the Pascal programming language, named for the French mathematician Blaise Pascal.

1973—Ethernet, the first local area network (LAN), is developed.

1974—The Scelbi and the Mark-8, the first "personal computers," are introduced.

1975—Paul Allen and Bill Gates found Microsoft Corporation. Stephen Wozniak and Stephen Jobs found Apple Computer Corporation and sell the Apple I in kit form. IBM mass-produces its first personal computer, the IBM 5100. The MITS Altair 8800 personal computer is introduced.

1976—Apple Computer introduces the Apple II.

1977—Radio Shack introduces the TRS-80.

1978—Dan Bricklin and Dan Fylstra write Visicalc, the first spreadsheet program, and found Software Arts.

FIGURE 1.5   IBM System 360
Reproduced by permission from IBM. Copyright 2001 by International Business Machines Corporation.

1980s

1981—IBM introduces the IBM PC, a personal computer (Figure 1.6). Microsoft releases MS-DOS version 1.0.

1984—The Apple Macintosh (Figure 1.7) debuts.

1985—Microsoft releases its first version of Windows. Intel creates the 80386 microprocessor.

1989—Intel introduces the 80486 microprocessor.

1990s

1992—Intel introduces the Pentium microprocessor.

1996—Intel introduces the Pentium Pro microprocessor.

1997—Intel introduces the Pentium II microprocessor.

1999—Intel introduces the Pentium III microprocessor.

FIGURE 1.6   IBM PC
Reproduced by permission from IBM. Copyright 2001 by International Business Machines Corporation.

FIGURE 1.7   Apple Macintosh
Photo courtesy of Apple Computer, Inc.

FIGURE 1.8   Motorola PowerPC 740 Microprocessor
Copyright of Motorola. Used by permission.

Based on the preceeding timeline, there have been four generations of electronic computers:

1940 to 1950	First generation	Computers use vacuum tubes
1950 to 1964	Second generation	Computers use transistors
1964 to 1971	Third generation	Computers use integrated circuits
1971 to Present	Fourth generation	Computers use microprocessors

Figure 1.8 shows a picture of one such microprocessor, Motorola's PowerPC 740.

Types of Computers

Computers are classified according to their power, size, and cost. Computer power does not refer to power in the electrical sense but rather to other factors affecting the machine's computational capability, such as speed and storage capacity. **Mainframes** are large, powerful computers that cost hundreds of thousands—if not millions—of dollars. They perform calculations very quickly and have massive amounts of storage capacity. **Minicomputers** are smaller than mainframes, with costs ranging from tens of thousands to hundreds of thousands of dollars. They are typically not as fast as mainframes and have smaller storage capacities. **Microcomputers,** the smallest computers, are the machines most commonly purchased by the general public and are usually referred to as **personal computers** (PCs). Microcomputer costs usually range from hundreds to thousands of dollars. With advancing technology, the power available in today's microcomputers rivals that provided by the minicomputers and mainframes of just a few years ago.

This book introduces computer programming concepts using examples in Delphi, a program development environment that uses the Object Pascal programming language. Delphi is produced by Borland Software Corporation and works under the Microsoft Windows operating system on IBM-compatible PCs. Thus this text focuses on microcomputer systems, although the computer programming fundamentals presented here apply to programming any computer system, from a thousand-dollar PC to a multimillion-dollar mainframe.

Components of a Typical Microcomputer System

> Computer **hardware** consists of the physical components of a computer system.

The **hardware,** or physical components, of a microcomputer system consists of six elements (Figure 1.9):

1. The **central processing unit (CPU)** is the computer's "brain."

   The CPU or **microprocessor** (often abbreviated μP) resides on the computer's **motherboard** (primary circuit board). A microprocessor is an integrated circuit (or chip) that performs the computer's main functions. It contains a small amount of internal memory, or **registers,** as well as the **arithmetic logic unit (ALU),** which performs all mathematical and logical operations.

2. A monitor is a **display device** that allows you to see information. The monitor is also referred to as a display or **cathode ray tube (CRT).**

3. The CPU receives information from **input devices.** The most common input devices are the keyboard and mouse, but other input devices include game controllers, microphones, scanners, and digital cameras.

4. The CPU sends information to **output devices.** A monitor is the most common output device; without it, it would be difficult to interact with the computer. Another output device is a printer, which allows the computer to print information on paper, producing a hard copy. Speakers, yet another output device, allow you to hear sounds and music produced by the computer, provided that a sound card is installed.

5. Just like humans, computers store information in **memory.** The two types of computer memory are **read-only memory (ROM)** and **random access memory (RAM).** As the name implies, ROM is read-only; it consist of permanent memory where the computer's instruction set resides. No instructions can be added or written to ROM. Furthermore, ROM is not erased when the computer is shut down; instead, it is permanently retained, or

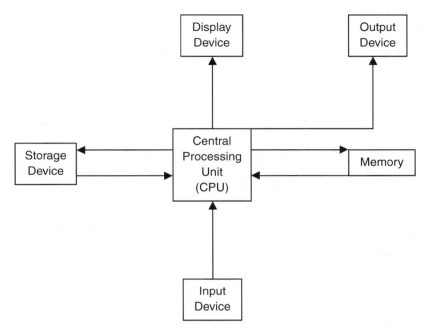

FIGURE 1.9   Hardware of a Typical Microcomputer System

hardwired, in the computer. For this reason, ROM is also known as non-volatile memory. RAM, on the other hand, is the computer's workspace or temporary memory. It is where computer programs reside and store information. Unlike ROM, RAM is volatile memory that is erased when the computer shuts down.

6. Because RAM is erased when the computer's power is turned off, we need a place to keep our programs. **Storage devices** allow programs to be saved for easy retrieval at some other time. Storage devices may be classified as either removable or nonremovable media. Hard disks are nonremovable media that contain massive amounts of storage space. Floppy disks are removable media that offer significantly less storage capacity than do hard disks. Recent advances in technology have, however, blurred the distinction between floppy disks and hard disks. Zip disks, for instance, are removable media that can store the equivalent of about 70 floppy disks. CD-ROM (compact disc read-only memory) drives are removable media, read-only storage devices that allow you to install programs from a CD (compact disc), run programs on CD, or listen to music CDs. Recordable CD (CD-R) and re-recordable CD (CD-RW) drives are also available. The most recent technology is the DVD (digital video disc), which is expected to replace CD-ROM drives because of its incredible storage capacity.

Computer **software** consists of the computer programs or applications that run on a computer.

In contrast to computer hardware, computer **software** consists of the applications or programs that you buy or write to work on the computer. Typical software applications include word processors, spreadsheets, databases, programming languages, and games. An **operating system** is the software that allows you to easily operate your computer. It controls the CPU's interactions with all of the other components in the computer system. Windows 98, for example, is an operating system that provides a readily understandable **graphical user interface (GUI)**.

The Binary Number System

Although numerous computer languages exist, internally computers understand only the base 2, or **binary,** number system. People, unlike computers, use the **decimal** number system, or base 10, which comes more naturally to humans because we first learned to count using our 10 fingers. The binary system consists of only two digits, 0 and 1. In computer terms, these two digits translate to a switch being either open or closed. When a switch is open (binary value of 0), it does not allow electrical current flow; thus the switch is off and no signal is present. When the switch is closed (binary value of 1), it allows electrical current flow; thus the switch is on and a signal is present. The use of 0 and 1 to represent the absence and presence of a signal, respectively, is purely a matter of convention.

1001 1100_2 is an example of a binary number. For clarity, we subscript the number with a 2 to indicate that it is a binary number rather than 10,011,100 (ten million eleven thousand one hundred) in decimal. Each 0 or 1 in this number is called a **bit,** meaning *binary dig*it. Computers group and store information in series of eight bits, with each series called a **byte.** Continuing with the food consumption theme, computer programmers humorously say that when you take half a byte, you have a **nibble,** or four bits. This humor is lost when you combine two bytes to get a **word.**

Storage and memory capacities are measured in bytes. Common units include the kilobyte, megabyte, and gigabyte. A **kilobyte (KB)** is 1024 (2^{10}), or approximately 1000, bytes. Similarly, a **megabyte (MB)** is 1,048,576 (2^{20}) bytes, and a **gigabyte (GB)** is 1,073,741,824 (2^{30}) bytes.

As a programmer and computer user, you should be aware that not all numbers can be exactly represented on a computer. A computer uses a finite number of bits to store any number. The real number system, however, is continuous; between any two real numbers lies an infinite number of other real numbers. For instance, how many real numbers lie between 1.01 and 1.02? Start counting: 1.011, 1.0101, 1.01001, 1.010001, 1.0100001, and on and on. Unfortunately, because computers represent numbers through a finite number of bits, they can represent only a finite number (albeit a very large number) of real numbers. As a consequence, computers and mathematical operations performed on computers are subject to **round-off errors** due to their imprecise representation of numbers. Such errors and the computer representation of real numbers are discussed in detail in Appendix A.

The Evolution of Computer Programming Languages

Because computers truly understand only binary information, people first programmed them in binary fashion. Programs written in binary code are called **machine language** programs. Programming in machine language proved both time-consuming and error-prone, however, so programmers developed **assembly language.** In assembly language, programmers write code using **mnemonics,** or symbolic instructions that are easily memorized and understood by humans. For instance, to load the 16-bit AX register (an internal register in the microprocessor) with the decimal value 157, a programmer need write only MOV AX, 157 rather than its machine language equivalent, 1011 1000 0000 0000 1001 1101. Once complete, an assembly language program is converted to machine language by an **assembler** so that the computer can execute it. Assembly language is called a **low-level language** because a direct (usually one-to-one) correspondence exists between the assembly language and machine language instructions.

As you can see, the trend is to make programming easier for humans. Why should we have to translate our instructions into binary when the computer can do it for us? As computer programming languages evolved along this philosophy, **high-level languages** were developed. High-level languages use English-like phrases as programming constructs; examples include BASIC, C, FORTRAN, and Pascal. Furthermore, many high-level languages are **general-purpose languages** that may be used to solve many types of problems.

The underlying goal of high-level languages was to make programs independent of the machine architecture and easily transportable among different platforms. Unfortunately, most failed miserably in this respect because different implementations of the languages were developed for specific machines. For instance, a Pascal program written on an IBM PC probably will not work on an Apple Macintosh without changing the original program, or **source code.** Java, a language developed by Sun Microsystems, was the first computer language designed to be truly platform independent. A Java program works the in same way and without modification on any machine that supports Java.

Most recent computer languages are object-oriented, which means that they support the creation and use of objects. These languages include C++, Java, Object Pascal, and Visual Basic. The object-oriented paradigm allows computer programs to more closely model the real world. It has a wide range of applications, including simulation and modeling.

High-level languages are either **compilers** or **interpreters,** with the difference reflecting how the actual program is executed.

Much like assembly language, a compiled language requires the source code to be translated to machine language by a compiler. In other words, the

> A **compiler** is a computer program that translates high-level source code into machine language and creates an executable file. An **interpreter** is a computer language that translates and executes the source code on an instruction-by-instruction basis.

source code is translated into machine language and an executable module is created. The computer then runs this executable module. The computer will not see any changes that you make to the source code until you recompile the program into a new executable module. Languages such as C, FORTRAN, and Pascal are compilers.

Interpreters, on the other hand, work much the same way as human interpreters. To help you understand a foreign language, an interpreter translates spoken words into your native tongue on a phrase-by-phrase or sentence-by-sentence basis. Similarly, an interpreter on a computer reads the source code one line or one statement at a time, translates the statement into machine language, and executes the machine language equivalent of the statement. With this approach, the computer will immediately see any changes that you make to the source code once you reexecute the program. The disadvantage is that interpretive languages execute code more slowly (and often significantly more slowly) than compiled languages do. BASIC is an example of an interpreter.

The Development of Delphi

Delphi traces its roots to the Pascal programming language. Named for the French mathematician Blaise Pascal, the Pascal language was created by Niklaus Wirth in Zürich, Switzerland, as an introductory computer programming language. Pascal encouraged the use of structured code and sound programming practices, instilling good habits in the novice programmer. As a result, the language was quickly adopted and soon became the language of choice in the computer science curricula of many universities, both in the United States and internationally. Due to its power, speed, and versatility, Pascal was also extensively used in the commercial sector.

Turbo Pascal is Borland's very popular version of the Pascal language. With the development of the Windows operating system and the emergence of object-oriented programming, Borland naturally extended its Turbo Pascal product into Turbo Pascal for Windows and Object Pascal for Windows. Borland's Delphi is the next step in the evolution of the company's Object Pascal programming platform.

"Delphi" was the code name for Borland's next-generation Object Pascal development environment. The designers chose it to emphasize the product's ability to connect to databases such as Oracle. Delphi was a city in ancient Greece where the Oracles of Apollo were consulted, hence the code name Delphi for the development environment. The name gained popularity, and the product was eventually marketed under the same name. Delphi encompasses the Object Pascal language and compiler, the visual development environment, database tools, and the Visual Component Library (VCL). The product vastly increases the speed with which Windows-based programs can be written. It is specifically designed for Rapid Application Development (RAD) of Windows programs.

Delphi 1 was released in February 1995. In March 1996, Delphi 2 was released; it was followed by version 3 in May 1997. Borland then sought to integrate its programming platforms with the Common Object Request Broker Architecture (CORBA), an emerging architecture for creating distributed applications. In mid-1997, Borland acquired Visigenic, the industry-standard supplier of Object Request Broker (ORB) technology. The CORBA-enabled Delphi 4 appeared in June 1998. The most recent update, Delphi 5, was released in August 1999. Delphi is a key product for Borland. Most of Borland's programming platforms share this visual development environment. Thus learning Delphi will familiarize you with other Borland products, such as C++Builder for C and C++ programming and JBuilder for Java programming.

Three editions of Delphi 5 exist: Standard, Professional, and Enterprise. The editions differ in terms of functionality, available components, and resources provided. The Standard edition allows for rapid visual development of Windows-based applications. The Professional edition provides all of the functionality of the Standard edition, plus development tools for building Web and database applications. The Enterprise edition offers a high-productivity development solution for Internet and distributed computing. All editions require the Windows operating system. You can use any edition of Delphi 5 with this textbook. Previous releases may also be used, but the figures in the book may not exactly match your computer screen in that case.

The Standard edition of Delphi 5 is packaged on the CD-ROM that accompanies this book. It allows the student to learn computer programming and write Object Pascal code, but it does not contain as many features or components as the Professional and Enterprise editions. Nevertheless, the Standard edition is a fully functional development environment that will allow you to write, test, debug, and compile your programs.

Summary

Key Terms

abaci—Ancient counting tables and tablets; the plural of abacus.

abacus—An ancient counting device still used in some parts of the world today. The word is derived from the Greek *abax,* meaning "table or board covered with dust."

arithmetic logic unit (ALU)—The part of a computer responsible for performing all mathematical and logical operations.

assembler—A program that converts assembly language into machine language.

assembly language—A low-level language that uses mnemonic instructions.

binary—The base 2 number system consisting of the digits 0 and 1.

bit—A binary digit; a 0 or 1.

byte—A group of eight bits.

cathode ray tube (CRT)—See *display device*.

central processing unit (CPU)—The "brain" of the computer. In a micro-computer, the CPU is a microprocessor.

compiler—A computer program that translates high-level source code into machine language and creates an executable file.

decimal—The base 10 number system consisting of the digits 0 through 9.

display—See *display device*.

display device—A specific type of output device that allows the operator to visually see information. Also called the display, monitor, or cathode ray tube.

general-purpose language—A computer language that may be used to solve many types of problems.

gigabyte (GB)—1,073,741,824 (2^{30}) bytes.

graphical user interface (GUI)—A user-friendly interface composed of both pictures (or icons) and words.

hardware—The physical components of a computer system.

hardwire—To permanently place or write into the computer hardware.

high-level language—A computer language that uses English-like phrases as instructions.

input device—A device from which the CPU receives information.

interpreter—A computer language that translates and executes the source code on an instruction-by-instruction basis.

kilobyte (KB)—1,024 (2^{10}) bytes.

low-level language—A language in which a direct (usually one-to-one) correspondence exists between its instructions and the related machine language instructions.

machine language—The native binary language of a computer.

mainframe—A large, powerful, high-speed computer with massive amounts of storage capacity and costing hundreds of thousands to millions of dollars.

megabyte (MB)—1,048,576 (2^{20}) bytes.

memory—Physical locations or addresses where a computer stores information.

microcomputer—The type of computer that is most commonly purchased by the general public; also known as a personal computer (PC). Costs usually range from hundreds to thousands of dollars.

microprocessor (μP)—An integrated circuit that performs the computer's main functions. The microprocessor contains registers and the arithmetic logic unit.

minicomputer—A computer that is typically not as fast as a mainframe and has a smaller storage capacity with a cost ranging from tens of thousands to hundreds of thousands of dollars.

mnemonic—Literally, a "memory aid."

mnemonics—Symbolic assembly language instructions that are easily memorized and understood by a programmer.

monitor—See *display device.*

motherboard—The primary circuit board in a microcomputer.

nibble—Half of a byte; a group of four bits.

operating system—Software that controls how the CPU interacts with all of the other components in the computer system.

output device—A device to which the CPU sends information.

personal computer—A microcomputer.

random access memory (RAM)—Volatile memory used as workspace by the computer's software programs. This memory is erased when the computer is turned off.

read-only memory (ROM)—Nonvolatile memory that contains the computer's permanent instruction set. This type of memory is read-only; data cannot be temporarily stored in this memory.

register—A memory location internal to a microprocessor.

round-off error—An error due to the imprecise representation of numbers on a computer.

software—Computer programs or applications.

source code—A program as written in its original language.

storage device—A device that allows programs and data files to be saved on storage media for easy retrieval at some later time.

word—Two bytes; a group of 16 bits.

Key Concepts

- Four generations of electronic computers characterized by the main components of the computers exist: vacuum tube, transistor, integrated circuit, and microprocessor-based machines.

- The three types of computer systems include mainframes, minicomputers, and microcomputers. These systems differ in terms of their power, size, and cost.

- Although this book focuses on programming microcomputer systems, the programming fundamentals presented here apply to programming any computer system.
- Hardware comprises the physical components of the computer system. The hardware block diagram of a typical microcomputer system classifies the hardware components into six categories.
- Computer programs and applications that run on a computer are software. The operating system is the most important software package on a computer; it controls the interactions of all computer components.
- The two types of computer memory are random access memory (RAM) and read-only memory (ROM). RAM is volatile memory used as workspace by a computer's software. This memory is erased when the computer is turned off. ROM is nonvolatile, read-only memory that contains the computer's permanent instruction set.
- People use the decimal number system, or base 10. Internally, computers understand only binary, or base 2, numbers. The binary number system contains only two digits, 0 and 1.
- Not all numbers can be exactly represented on a computer because numbers are stored using a finite number of bits. This problem can result in round-off errors.
- Computer programming languages evolved from machine language to low-level languages to the high-level languages of today.
- High-level languages can be either interpreters or compilers. A compiler converts the entire source code into an executable module, whereas an interpreter executes the source code on a line-by-line basis.
- Delphi is an advanced, Windows-based programming platform that evolved from Borland's Pascal.

Review Questions

1. Who is considered to be the "father of the computer"?
2. Which mathematician created a system of algebraic logic?
3. Name the three types of computer systems and explain the differences among them.
4. What is the difference between hardware and software? Give examples of each.
5. Draw a hardware block diagram for a typical microcomputer system.
6. What is the binary number system? Why is it important to understand this number system?
7. What is machine language? Why were low-level and high-level languages developed?

Problems

1. List the four generations of electronic computers and their respective years of inclusion.
2. List the six elements of microcomputer system hardware and describe the purpose of each element. Give examples of each element.
3. What are RAM and ROM? How do they differ?
4. Define the following terms:
   a. bit
   b. byte
   c. nibble
   d. word
   e. kilobyte
   f. megabyte
   g. gigabyte
5. What is the difference between a high-level language and a low-level language? Give examples of each.
6. What is the difference between a compiler and an interpreter? Give example languages for each.

Chapter 2

The Delphi Development Environment

Chapter Objectives

In this chapter you will:

- Become familiar with the operation of a graphical user interface (GUI), including the use of the mouse and icons

- Recognize the necessity of an easy, yet functional user interface

- Become familiar with the Delphi integrated development environment, including its menus, toolbars, and windows

- Become familiar with the "elementary" Delphi components

- Learn how to create a simple GUI

- Gain an understanding of the relationship between Delphi projects and forms

- Learn about the different Delphi file types

- Work with the Delphi editor by learning how to save, print, compile, and execute a program

- Become familiar with the Delphi help facility and online documentation

This chapter is designed to familiarize you with Delphi. It describes the Delphi program development philosophy and introduces the menus, toolbars, and windows that make up the Delphi **integrated development environment (IDE).** The chapter also introduces the "elementary" components that are used in combination to create a simple user interface.

The Delphi Design Philosophy

The Microsoft Windows operating system provides a simple **graphical user interface (GUI).** In this GUI, a user controls the operations of the computer by moving a **pointer** and selecting **icons.** An icon is a button with a picture, which may represent either a **program** (**application**) or **folder** (directory location). For instance, the [W] icon is associated with Microsoft Word 2000 word-processing software, the [ ] icon represents the Delphi development environment, and [ ] is the icon for a folder. The user controls the pointer by physically moving an input device, such as a **mouse.** To activate an icon, the user positions the pointer above the icon and then clicks the left mouse button twice (that is, **double-clicks** the left mouse button).

In such a graphical operating environment, it is also desirable to include a graphical, point-and-click interface in applications software. Prior to the introduction of object-oriented programming and the Windows operating system, creating such user interfaces required a great deal of programming effort. To simplify this lengthy programming chore, Delphi provides the programmer with a palette of user interface components that can be used to quickly design interfaces with point-and-click, drag-and-drop ease. To create a user interface, the programmer needs merely select the desired components from the palette and place them in the program. Thus Delphi is a platform for **rapid application development (RAD)** under the Windows operating system.

Why do we place so much emphasis on a program's user interface? The importance of a simple and appealing user interface should not be underestimated. Extremely useful and effective programs have failed miserably in the commercial market because their user interfaces were overly complicated. The bottom line is this: *Programs should make things easy for the user, not the other way around.* In other words, *a programmer should take any steps necessary to ensure that a program suits the customer's needs, in terms of both functionality and ease of use.* For this reason, maintaining a constant dialog between the programmer and customer is essential.

Delphi provides a perfect vehicle for accomplishing this task. It allows a programmer to easily design a user interface that satisfies the customer's requirements. Any modifications can be made on the fly until the customer is satisfied with the user interface.

Using Delphi

This section provides a rudimentary introduction to Delphi. As you'll soon see, Delphi displays a Windows-type screen known as a **form.** The boxes, buttons, sliders, and other **objects** that are typically found on these forms are called **components.** We describe Delphi's opening screen, menus, toolbars, and windows and then introduce the five "elementary" Delphi components that make up any simple user interface. Next, the text describes how to place, move, and size components in a user interface. Finally, it examines the Delphi help facility and online documentation.

> A **component** is an object in the user interface of a program or any object that may appear in the Delphi Component Palette.

In this chapter, you will also create your first program using Delphi. Along the way, you will learn about the Delphi editor and how to save, print, compile, and run (or execute) your programs.

The Delphi Opening Screen

When you initially start Delphi, the Borland Delphi "splash page" appears first. This splash page simply announces that the Delphi development environment is loading into the computer's memory. Delphi then begins a new **project.** By default, this project is an application; that is, the project consists of the files necessary to make an executable program (*.EXE file). Delphi has many different project types available, and the programmer may easily change the default project type (see Appendix D). This book focuses on creating standalone applications, however, so changing the default project type is unnecessary for our purposes. Other project types include control panel applications, Web server applications, **dynamic link libraries (DLLs),** ActiveX controls, and Active forms, just to name a few. You will work with ActiveX controls and Active forms in Chapter 17. Unless stated otherwise, you will initiate a new project by starting Delphi with a blank application as the default project type or by selecting `New Application` from the `File` menu of the menu bar.

The Delphi Screen Layout

Figure 2.1 shows the Delphi IDE default screen layout. Like most other Windows applications, this screen contains a **menu bar.** Additionally, the default layout contains six **toolbars** and three smaller windows. The toolbars are the **Standard toolbar, View toolbar, Debug toolbar, Custom toolbar, Component Palette,** and **Desktop toolbar.** The windows are the **Form window, Object Inspector** window, and **Code Editor** window.

The Delphi menu bar appears in Figure 2.2. It is a typical drop-down menu; that is, when the user selects a menu item, all of the options available for that menu item appear on a drop-down list. Figure 2.2 shows the drop-down list for

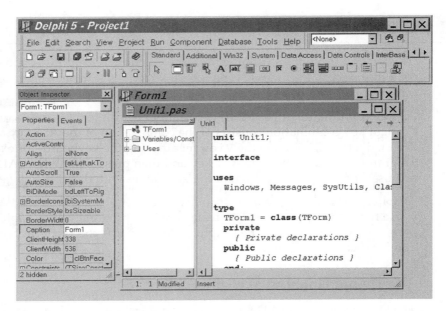

FIGURE 2.1 Delphi IDE Default Screen Layout

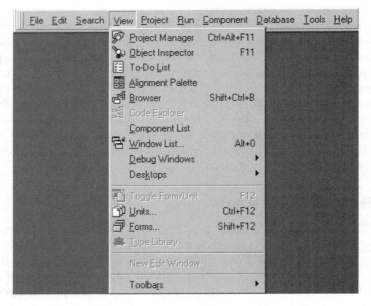

FIGURE 2.2 Delphi Menu Bar and View Menu

the `View` menu. Positioning the pointer over the desired menu heading and pressing the left mouse button activates the associated drop-down menu. To select an option from the drop-down menu, position the pointer over the desired menu option and press the left mouse button (that is, left-click on the option).

You may also use the keyboard to select menu items. On the menu bar, one letter in each menu heading is underlined. The underlined letter indicates the **shortcut key combination** (or *shortcut*) necessary to activate the drop-down menu. The shortcut key combination consists of the combination of the ALT key and the underlined letter. To activate the `View` menu using the keyboard, for example, the programmer holds down the ALT key and then presses the V key (ALT+V). This text uses the convention of combining key names with the plus sign (+) to denote shortcut key combinations. For example, "press ALT+E to activate the `Edit` menu" means that the programmer should hold down the ALT key and press the E key so that the `Edit` menu will appear.

On the `View` menu in Figure 2.2, notice that one letter of each menu option is underlined. With a menu active (dropped down), the programmer can press just the underlined key to activate the associated menu option. For instance, you can activate the `View` menu by pressing ALT+V and you can open the Project Browser by pressing the B key. Additionally, the `View` menu in Figure 2.2 lists shortcut key combinations to the right of their menu options. These shortcuts allow the programmer to perform a task without using the menu system. To quickly open the Project Browser without using the menus, for example, hold down the SHIFT and CTRL keys and press the B key (SHIFT+CTRL+B).

Rather than describe each menu heading and all of the related tasks and options in detail here, these items will be introduced as they are used in the text. When a reference to a menu and subsequent menu option is required, this text uses the following convention: `Menu Heading|Option`. You should then select the indicated `Menu Heading` from the menu bar and select the indicated `Option` from the associated drop-down menu. Try experimenting with these menus as a way of increasing your familiarity with the Delphi user interface. Don't worry—you cannot physically damage your computer by experimenting with Delphi.

As in most Windows-based applications, the toolbars in Delphi contain icons that provide a shortcut means of performing various tasks found on the menu bar. The 🖫 icon, for instance, means "Save" and can also be found in the `File` menu. To display the meaning of a toolbar icon, simply position the pointer on the icon and leave it there. After a few seconds, a description of the icon's function will appear. Once again, rather than providing a detailed description of each icon's function here, we will simply discuss the general purpose of each of Delphi's toolbars. You can then explore the toolbars by experimenting with them. If a particular toolbar is not visible, select `View|Toolbars` from the menu and choose the toolbar from the list. The toolbar will appear on your screen. Alternatively, you can right-click on the menu bar or on one of the visible toolbars. A drop-down list will appear that allows you to toggle the visibility of the toolbars. You can customize the toolbars to better suit your needs and personal preferences

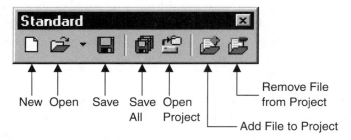

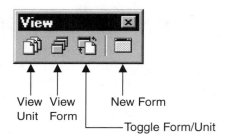

FIGURE 2.3   Standard Toolbar

FIGURE 2.4   View Toolbar

by selecting the `Customize...` option from this drop-down list or by selecting `View|Toolbars|Customize...` from the menu bar. Appendix D further describes how to customize the toolbars.

Figure 2.3 shows the Standard toolbar. This toolbar contains icons for executing common tasks, such as opening, saving, and creating Delphi projects and associated files.

The View toolbar (Figure 2.4) contains icons for creating new forms, viewing forms and code **units,** and toggling between a form and its code unit. This toolbar allows you to quickly switch between windows in the Delphi IDE.

The Debug toolbar (Figure 2.5) is used for interactive testing and debugging of your programs. It provides quick access to several Delphi debugger commands that are available on the Run menu. The Delphi debugger is a **design time** utility. That is, it can be used only inside of the Delphi development environment while you are working on the source code.

Figure 2.6 shows the Custom toolbar. By default, this toolbar contains a single button to access the Delphi online help facility.

The Component Palette (Figure 2.7) is a tabbed toolbar that provides quick access to common program components. These components are part of Borland's **Visual Component Library (VCL),** a collection of components that are organized in a hierarchical structure according to a parent–child relationship. Components serve as the building blocks for the GUI of every Delphi applica-

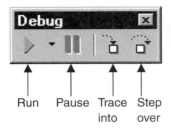

FIGURE 2.5   Debug Toolbar

Help Contents

FIGURE 2.6   Custom Toolbar

FIGURE 2.7   Component Palette

tion. Components that may appear on the screen at **run time** are known as **controls.** Controls form a subset of the VCL: Every control is a component, but not every component is a control.

The programmer can customize the desktop settings by using the Desktop toolbar (Figure 2.8). This toolbar contains a list of the available desktop layouts and allows the programmer to load and save different layouts. A desktop layout specifies the display, sizing, **docking,** and window placement options for the IDE. A selected layout remains in effect for all projects and is used the next time Delphi is started.

> **Design time** is the time when the program and user interface are being written in the Delphi IDE. **Run time** is the time when the compiled program (executable module) is executing or running.

A form is the default container for Delphi components. Essentially, it comprises the user interface of your program. In the Form window, you can edit the form, resize it, and place Delphi components on it. Figure 2.9 shows a sample Form window containing a blank form named `Form1`. If the Form window does not appear on your screen or if you would like to view a different form in the

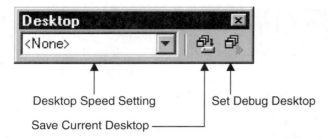

Desktop Speed Setting   Set Debug Desktop

Save Current Desktop ——————————

FIGURE 2.8   Desktop Toolbar

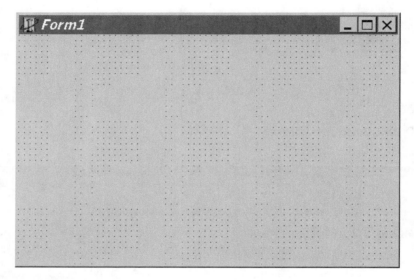

FIGURE 2.9   Form Window

project, select View|Forms... or press SHIFT+F12. Then, select the desired
form name in the View Form window and click the OK button. If no form names
appear in the View Form window, then the current project does not include any
forms. Select File|New Form to add a form to the project.

Delphi uses Object Pascal, an **object-oriented language** that is an extension
of standard Pascal. All components in Delphi are objects, and objects have various **properties** associated with them. A form, for instance, is an object in Delphi
and has certain properties, such as a name, caption, height, and width (the actual form property names are Name, Caption, ClientHeight, and Client-
Width, respectively). When you create a new component, Delphi automatically
assigns **default settings** to each of its properties. As you design your program
(that is, at design time), the Object Inspector window allows you to change a

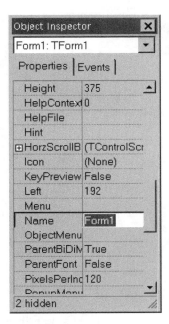

FIGURE 2.10   Object Inspector Window

component's properties by modifiying those properties' default settings. In the Object Inspector window, simply click on the property that you want to change and replace the current setting with the desired setting. Figure 2.10 shows an example of the Object Inspector for `Form1`. If the Object Inspector does not appear on your computer screen, you may display it by selecting `View|Object Inspector` or by pressing the F11 key.

The Code Editor is a full-featured text editor that allows you to view and edit the source code in your Delphi projects. Additionally, it provides powerful features to assist you in writing Object Pascal code. Each code unit of your Delphi project can be displayed on a different page tab within the Code Editor window or in a new Code Editor window. To open a unit within the Code Editor, select `View|Units...` or press CTRL+F12. Then, select the desired unit name from the View Unit window and click the OK button. Figure 2.11 shows the Code Editor window with two active page tabs, Unit1 and Project1.

In addition to the three windows that are shown by default, Delphi offers several other useful windows. In Figure 2.11, the **Code Explorer** window is located in its default position, inside the Code Editor window to the left of the active editor page tabs. In other words, this window is docked on the left side of the Code Editor window. The Code Explorer allows the programmer to easily navigate through the unit files. Its tree diagram shows all of the types, classes, properties, methods, global variables, and global routines that are defined in the code unit

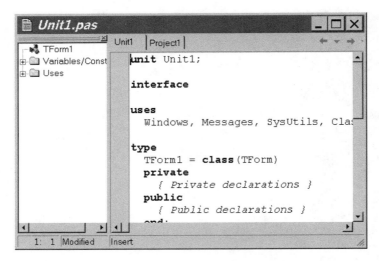

FIGURE 2.11   Code Editor and Code Explorer Windows

currently being edited in the Code Editor window. The Code Editor also lists the other units that are used by the unit currently being edited. Select View|Code Explorer to open the Code Explorer window if it is not already visible.

When you compile a project, the Delphi compiler may display warning and error messages in the **Messages window.** By default, the Messages window appears docked at the bottom of the Code Editor window. To view the Messages window, right-click on the Code Editor and select Message View from the pop-up menu. Double-clicking on a specific message in the Messages window displays the erroneous line (or lines) of source code in the Code Editor. Furthermore, right-clicking in the Messages window activates its pop-up menu. The Messages window also displays the search results when you select Search|Find in Files... from the menu bar.

The programmer can view the files that compose a Delphi project in the **Project Manager** window (Figure 2.12). In the Project Manager, projects may be arranged into **project groups,** where a project group consists of related projects or projects that function together as part of a multitiered application. In addition, this window allows you to easily navigate among the various projects and access each project's constituent files within a project group. Select View|Project Manager or press CTRL+ALT+F11 to open the Project Manager window.

To successfully complete a program, especially a large program, the programmer needs to perform many tasks. Delphi's **To-Do List** provides a built-in notepad that helps you organize these tasks. This list can prove extremely helpful in planning, programming, testing, and debugging large projects that are written by a team of programmers. Figure 2.13 shows an example To-Do List. Select

Project Manager
Project1.exe
New
Remove
Activate
Files
Path
ProjectGroup1
C:\Program Files\Borland\Delphi5\Projects
Project1.exe
C:\Program Files\Borland\Delphi5\Projects
Unit1
C:\Program Files\Borland\Delphi5\Projects
Unit1.pas
C:\Program Files\Borland\Delphi5\Projects
Form1
C:\Program Files\Borland\Delphi5\Projects

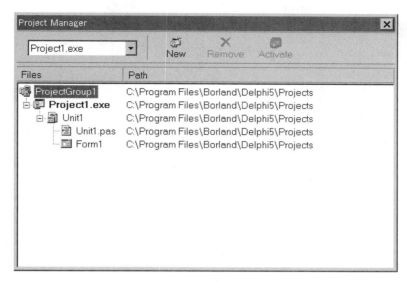

FIGURE 2.12 Project Manager Window

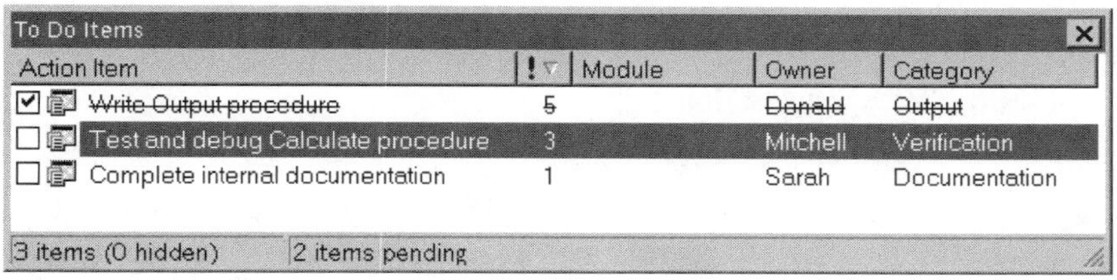

To Do Items
Action Item
!
Module
Owner
Category
Write Output procedure
5
Donald
Output
Test and debug Calculate procedure
3
Mitchell
Verification
Complete internal documentation
1
Sarah
Documentation
3 items (0 hidden)
2 items pending

FIGURE 2.13 To-Do List

Align

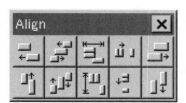

FIGURE 2.14 Alignment Palette

`View|To-Do List` from the menu bar to open this window. You can add, edit, and delete list items by right-clicking on the To-Do List window.

The **Alignment Palette** window (Figure 2.14) provides a rapid means of aligning components on a form. Select `View|Alignment Palette` from the menu bar to open this window.

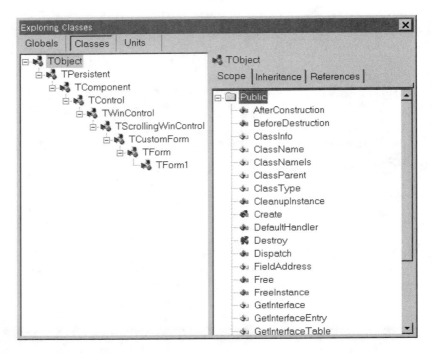

FIGURE 2.15 Project Browser

The **Project Browser** (Figure 2.15) lists the units, classes, types, properties, methods, variables, and routines that are declared or used in the current project. It arranges this information in a tree diagram. To open the Project Browser, select View|Browser or press SHIFT+CTRL+B.

To open the **Component List** (or **Components window**), shown in Figure 2.16, select View|Component List from the menu bar. This window shows an alphabetical listing of all components that are available in your version of Delphi and the VCL. You may add a component to your Delphi program by selecting the component from this window with either the keyboard or the mouse. When you use the mouse, the Component Palette provides a more rapid means of selecting

Programming Key: Delphi Tip

Use the Component Palette instead of the Components window to rapidly select components and place them in your applications.

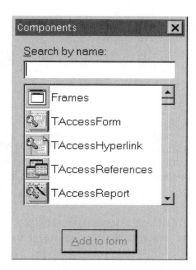

FIGURE 2.16   Component List

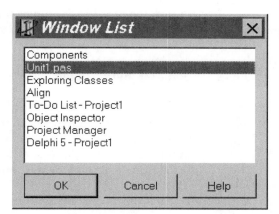

FIGURE 2.17   Window List

components and placing them in your applications, as it organizes the components according to their functions. For this reason, it is recommended that you use the Component Palette in lieu of the Components window.

The **Window List** allows you to quickly switch between windows in the Delphi IDE. If you have many windows open, it offers the easiest way to locate a window and make it active. Open the Window List by selecting `View|Window List` or pressing ALT+0. Then, select the desired window from the list and click the OK button. Figure 2.17 shows a sample Window List.

Delphi contains several windows that are associated with its built-in debugger. These windows are discussed in detail in Chapter 9.

Now that you are familiar with the Delphi IDE and the concept of Delphi components, let's look more closely at five "elementary" components that you will use throughout this text.

Elementary Components

The elementary components are not described as "elementary" because they are easier to use than other components but rather because they are generally used in more complex combinations to create a simple user interface for a program. The five elementary components are forms, **labels, edit boxes, memo boxes,** and **buttons.**

Of these five components, the form is the only object that does not appear in the Components window or on the Component Palette. To insert a new form into your project, select `File|New Form` or click the New Form button on the View toolbar. Similarly, to remove a form from your project, select `Project|Remove from Project...` on the menu bar or click the Remove File From Project button on the Standard toolbar. The Remove From Project window will then appear on the screen. In this window, you can select the unit and form files that you want to remove from your project. To select a contiguous group of files, you can left-click the first file and then SHIFT+left-click the last file in the group. Multiple files that are not grouped together may be selected by left-clicking the first file and CTRL+left-clicking the other files. Click the OK button to remove the selected files from your project.

When working in Delphi, you might envision yourself as a painter and the form as your canvas. You "paint" a user interface for your application by placing components on the form. Then, you alter the appearance of these components by changing their properties. Later, you will see the steps necessary to make your form interact with the user. Interactivity becomes possible when components on the form respond to the user's actions.

Most of the examples in this book use projects consisting of only one form. Chapter 17 discusses the creation of more complex projects that require the use of multiple forms. For now, our discussion will concentrate on the four other elementary components and the process of designing a simple user interface. The four elementary components described in the remainder of this section appear on the Standard tab of the Component Palette.

A Label

A label is a component used in an application to display text that the user cannot change. Follow the steps listed below to practice using the label component:

1. Start a new project by selecting `File|New Application`.
2. Place a label on the form. This task is accomplished by double-clicking the label icon in the Standard tab of the Component Palette.

3. Move the new label by **dragging** it to a new location on the form. With the mouse over the label, click and hold the left mouse button and then move the mouse to reposition the label. When the label is in the desired location, release the mouse button.

4. Change the `Name` property of the label to lblMyLabel. In the Object Inspector, click on the `Name` property and then type `lblMyLabel`. Make sure that you are changing the properties of the label and not the form. Verify this fact by ensuring that `Label1: TLabel` appears in the drop-down box at the top of the Object Inspector window. Press the ENTER key when you have finished typing.

5. Notice that the caption of the label changed so that it matches the label's name (lblMyLabel). Select the `Caption` property of the label in the Object Inspector, type `This is my first label!`, and press the ENTER key. The caption on the label will change as you type this text.

6. Change the background color of the label. Select the `Color` property and click on the arrow in the box. Use the scroll bar to find the yellow color, then click on it.

7. Change the label's font and text color. Select the `Font` property and click on the ellipses (the three dots). In the Font window, change the font to Arial, the style to Bold Italic, and the size to 20. Select the red color from the drop-down list, then click the OK button.

8. Add another label to the form. This time, single-click on the label icon in the Component Palette. Next, go to an empty space on the form in the Form window and click and hold the left mouse button. Drag the mouse, then release the mouse button. The new label will appear on your form in the exact size and position where you dragged the mouse.

9. Change the `Name` and `Caption` properties of this new label to lblAnother and Another Label, respectively.

10. Select the form by choosing Form1 from the drop-down list at the top of the Object Inspector window.

11. Change the `Name` and `Caption` properties of the form to frmLabelExample and Label Example, respectively.

12. Run this very rudimentary program by clicking the Run icon on the Debug toolbar, selecting Run | Run from the menu bar, or pressing the F9 key. A form similar to the one shown in Figure 2.18 should appear on your screen.

13. Stop the program by clicking the X in the upper-right corner of the form, selecting Run | `Program Reset` from Delphi's menu bar, or pressing CTRL+F2 with the Delphi window active.

Edit Box

An edit box contains text that is placed in the box either at design time or at run time. The `Text` property contains the text that will appear in the edit box, and

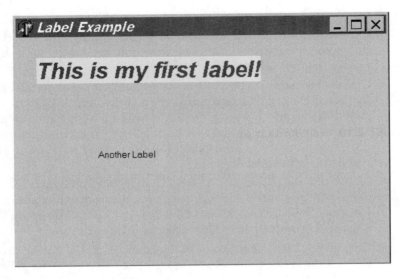

FIGURE 2.18   Label Example

the `MaxLength` property specifies the maximum number of characters that can be displayed or entered into the edit box. A `MaxLength` of 0 means that the program imposes no limit on the number of characters in the edit box. The `Font` property allows you to set the Font object properties for the edit box. If the `ReadOnly` property is set to True, the user will not be able to alter the data in the edit box at run time. Follow the steps listed below to practice using the edit box control:

1. Start a new project by selecting `File|New Application`.
2. Place an edit box control on your form. This task can be accomplished by double-clicking the edit box icon in the Component Palette.
3. Resize the edit box. Position the pointer on top of one of the "sizing handles" along the perimeter of the edit box, and click and drag the sizing handle using the left mouse button. When the edit box is the desired size, release the mouse button.
4. Move the new edit box by dragging it to a new location on the form. With the mouse over the edit box, click and hold the left mouse button and then move the mouse to reposition the edit box. When the edit box appears in the desired location, release the mouse button.
5. Change the `Name` property of the edit box to edtMyText. In the Object Inspector window, click on the `Name` property and then type `edtMyText`. Make sure that you are changing the properties of the edit box and not the form. Verify this fact by ensuring that `Edit1: TEdit` appears in the drop-down box at the top of the Object Inspector window.

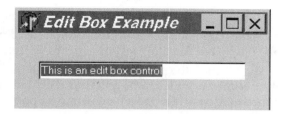

FIGURE 2.19   Edit Box Example

6. Select the `Text` property in the Object Inspector and type `This is an edit box control`. Press the ENTER key when you have finished typing. Notice that the text in the edit box changes as you type.

7. Change the color of the text in the edit box to blue. Click the plus sign (+) to the left of the `Font` property in the Object Inspector. The plus sign changes to a minus sign (–), and all Font object properties are listed below the `Font` property. Select the `Color` property and click on the arrow in the box. Use the scroll bar to find the blue color, then click on it.

8. Select the form by choosing Form1 from the drop-down list at the top of the Object Inspector window. Change the `Name` and `Caption` properties of the form to frmEditBoxExample and Edit Box Example, respectively.

9. Press the F9 key to execute this interface (which is really a program without any of your own code) and experiment with the edit box. The screen should appear as shown in Figure 2.19. With the program running, change the text in the edit box to read `This is MY edit box control`.

10. Click the X in the upper-right corner of the form to stop the program.

11. Change the `ReadOnly` property to True.

12. Press the F9 key to execute this interface again. Attempt to change the text in the edit box. Notice that it cannot be changed by the user while the interface is executing (that is, at run time).

13. Click the X in the upper-right corner of the form to stop the program.

Memo Box

A memo box can contain multiple lines of text. The `MaxLength`, `Font`, and `ReadOnly` properties of a memo box are identical to those of an edit box. The `Text` property contains all of the text in the memo box, but this property can be accessed only at run time. The `Lines` property contains the individual lines of text in the memo box; it may be accessed at both design time and run time. The `WordWrap` property indicates whether the text will wrap at the right margin or continue past the right end of the memo box. Practice using the memo box control by following the steps shown on the next page:

1. Start a new project by selecting `File|New Application`.

2. Place a memo box control on your form. This task can be accomplished by double-clicking the memo box icon in the Component Palette.

3. Resize the memo box. Position the pointer on top of one of the "sizing handles" along the perimeter of the memo box, and click and drag the sizing handle using the left mouse button. When the memo box is the desired size, release the mouse button.

4. Move the new memo box by dragging it to a new location on the form. With the mouse over the memo box, click and hold the left mouse button and then move the mouse to reposition the memo box. When the memo box appears in the desired location, release the mouse button.

5. Change the `Name` property of the memo box to memSample. In the Object Inspector window, click on the `Name` property and then type `memSample`. Make sure that you are changing the properties of the memo box and not the form. Verify this fact by ensuring that `Memo1: TMemo` appears in the drop-down box at the top of the Object Inspector window.

6. Select the `Lines` property and click on the ellipses (the three dots). The String List Editor window will appear on the screen. Replace the text in this editor so that it matches that shown in Figure 2.20. Click the OK button when you have finished typing.

7. Select the form by choosing Form1 from the drop-down list at the top of the Object Inspector window. Change the `Name` and `Caption` properties of the form to frmMemoBoxExample and Memo Box Example, respectively.

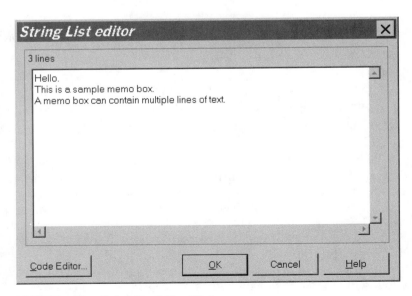

FIGURE 2.20   String List Editor Window

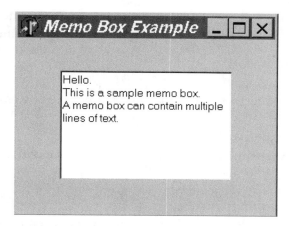

FIGURE 2.21   Memo Box Example

8. Press the F9 key to execute this program. The screen should be similar to Figure 2.21. Type some text on a new line in the memo box until it wraps around to the next line.

9. Click the X in the upper-right corner of the form to stop the program.

10. Use the Object Inspector to change the `WordWrap` property of the memo box (memSample) to False and the `ScrollBars` property to ssBoth.

11. Press the F9 key to execute this program. Continue to type text on a new line in the memo box until the text scrolls past the right end of the box. Add more lines of text until it scrolls past the bottom of the memo box.

12. Click the X in the upper-right corner of the form to stop the program.

Button

A button is used to begin, interrupt, or end a process. Typically, it initiates an action by executing a portion of code or an entire program. In other words, the user expects something to happen when he or she clicks a button. When a button is clicked with the mouse, it appears to be "pushed in." For this reason, buttons are also referred to as push buttons.

Buttons can be assigned shortcut key combinations. This assignment makes a combination of keyboard keys equivalent to clicking the button with the mouse. For example, try the following:

1. Start a new project by selecting `File|New Application`.

2. In the Object Inspector, change the `Name` and `Caption` properties of the form to frmButtonExample and Button Example, respectively.

3. Place a button control on the form (frmButtonExample). This task can be accomplished by double-clicking the button icon in the Component Palette.

4. Change the `Name` property of the button to btnMyButton. In the Object Inspector window, click on the `Name` property and then type `btnMyButton`. Make sure that you are changing the properties of the button and not the form. Verify this fact by ensuring that `Button1: TButton` appears in the drop-down box at the top of the Object Inspector window.

5. Change the `Caption` property of the button to `&Click Me`. Notice that the caption on the face of the button reads C̲lick Me.

6. Resize and reposition the button as desired.

7. Press the F9 key to execute this program. The screen should be similar to Figure 2.22.

8. Left-click the button. Notice that the button appears to be "pushed in" when it is clicked with the mouse.

9. Press ALT+C to activate the button via its shortcut key combination. Notice that the button does not appear to be indented when it is activated in this manner.

10. Click the X in the upper-right corner of the form to stop the program.

The caption of `btnMyButton` reads C̲lick Me and not `&Click Me`. The ampersand (&) in front of a character in the `Caption` property denotes the shortcut key combination. This character is underlined in the caption that appears on the face of the button, indicating the availability of a shortcut key to the user. At run time, the user activates the shortcut key combination by holding down the ALT key and then pressing the key associated with the underlined character. In this case, you would hold down the ALT key and then press the C key (ALT+C) on the keyboard (at run time). This key combination activates `btnMyButton`, although the button does not appear to be "pushed in" as it does when it is clicked with the mouse. To place an ampersand in the caption of a button, use a double ampersand (&&). For instance, setting the `Caption` property of `btnMyButton` to `This &&` `That` displays the caption `This & That` on the button, and no shortcut key is assigned to the button.

You have now created a few simple forms (and programs) in only minutes. Creating a Windows-based user interface using Delphi really is just that easy. You are now familiar with several commonly used properties of forms, labels, edit

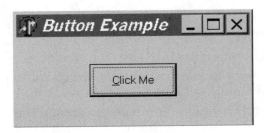

FIGURE 2.22   Button Example

boxes, memo boxes, and buttons. Don't be afraid to experiment with the different components and property settings. You can design some really creative interfaces.

Placing, Moving, and Sizing Components

As described in the previous examples, you can place a component on a form in two ways: by double-clicking or by using the click-and-drag technique. These methods work for all VCL components.

To reposition a component, simply click and drag the object to the desired position on the form. When the component appears in the desired location, release the mouse button. While you are repositioning a component, the object location (relative to the upper-left corner of the form) will appear underneath the mouse pointer. The unit of measurement is **pixels.**

To resize a component, select the component (left-click on the component) and then drag a sizing handle until the component reaches the desired size. Figure 2.23 shows an example of a memo box with sizing handles. While you are resizing a component, the object dimensions will appear underneath the mouse pointer. As with the location information, the unit of measurement for component size is pixels.

Accessing Additional Components

Many companies produce components and controls that you can purchase and use in your Delphi applications. Additionally, many components are available free of charge over the Internet. You can customize your Component Palette by installing third-party components and ActiveX controls or by creating and installing your own components and controls. These options appear under the Component menu on the Delphi menu bar. Also, you can rearrange the Component Palette by selecting `Component|Configure Palette...` from the menu. Appendix D discusses these topics in greater detail.

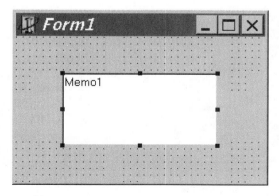

FIGURE 2.23   Memo Box with Sizing Handles

Component Naming Conventions

Throughout this text, we will use a prescript consisting of three lowercase characters as the naming convention for all Delphi VCL components. For instance, all label names are prescripted with `lbl`; thus a label that identifies the date is named `lblDate` rather than just `Date`. Similarly, edit boxes are prescripted with `edt`, memo boxes with `mem`, and buttons with `btn`. This convention allows a programmer to easily identify the type of a component based solely on its name.

Personalizing the Integrated Development Environment

Delphi allows you to modify the IDE by changing the environment, editor, debugger, and project options. The Tools menu provides access to the environment, editor, and debugger options, and the Project menu allows access to the project options. For instance, if you select `Tools|Environment Options...` from the menu bar, the Environment Options window shown in Figure 2.24 will appear on your screen. From this window, you can select tabs and options to modify the Delphi working environment. Appendix D describes how to customize the Delphi IDE.

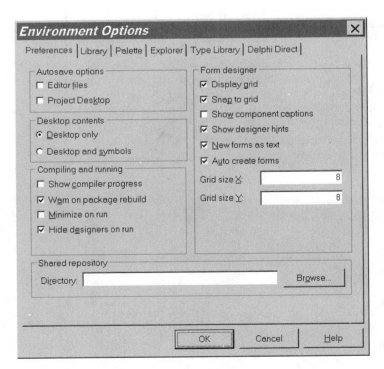

FIGURE 2.24   Environment Options Window

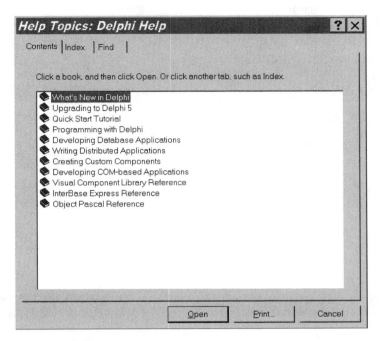

FIGURE 2.25 Delphi Help Window

Help and Online Documentation

Delphi contains an online, **hypertext** help facility. Its provides an easy and convenient reference for programmers. To start the Delphi help facility, select `Help|Delphi Help` from the menu or click the Help Contents icon on the Custom toolbar. The Delphi Help window, shown in Figure 2.25, will appear on the screen. In addition, Delphi provides help on the Delphi productivity tools (`Help|Delphi Tools`) and Windows programming (`Help|Windows SDK`). You should become familiar with these help facilities; they will prove to be invaluable as you become a more adept programmer.

Your First Program

Of course, this text would be incomplete without a Delphi version of the infamous "Hello, World!" program. This section provides the instructions necessary for you to create your first program and allows you to practice working with the Delphi interface and controls. Once again, don't be afraid to experiment. You cannot physically damage your computer by programming, experimenting, or playing with Delphi.

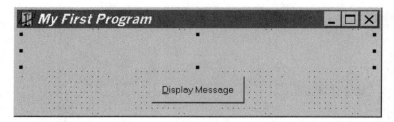

FIGURE 2.26   Form for Your First Program

Figure 2.26 shows the form used in our program. Notice that this form contains a label and a button. In the beginning chapters of this text, programming examples are highlighted by displaying the form in a figure. Accompanying each figure is a table that lists the components and properties that were changed from their default settings. The following table shows the components and property settings applicable to this program:

Component	Property	Setting
Form	Name	frmFirstProgram
	Caption	My First Program
Label	Name	lblMessage
	Caption	*Empty*
	Font	
	Name	Arial
	Size	26
	Style	
	fsBold	True
Button	Name	btnDisplayMessage
	Caption	&Display Message

Place a label and a button on the form, and then modify the component property settings to match those listed in this table. When your work is complete, your form should resemble Figure 2.26.

In later chapters, you will be more adept with the Delphi interface, so the form (or a sample program execution) will be shown in a figure accompanied by a listing of the program code. You are expected to determine what components and property settings are required by examining the form and reading the code. In those instances where property settings are unclear, a table (similar to the one above) will specify the desired settings.

Designing the user interface is the initial step in writing a program with Delphi. After you place the components on the form, you must specify the appropriate properties. That is, you must assign descriptive names and informative captions to your program's components. For example, the default name and caption for the first button on a form is Button1. You should always change it, because this name is uninformative to other programmers and the caption provides the user with no insight into the purpose of the button.

Programming Key: GUI Design Tips

Proper GUI design is an art form. The following guidelines are provided to assist you in designing simple, yet effective, user interfaces for your programs:

1. The interface should be easy to understand.
2. The interface should be visually pleasing.
3. Avoid "information overload." The interface should not be cluttered with too much information or too many controls. If the user must enter a large amount of information, consider using multiple forms, a menu system, or data files.
4. The "flow" of information and data entry on any form should be natural—either left-to-right or top-to-bottom.
5. The interface should guide the user through the data entry process.

After you design the form and change the default property settings, it is time to write the source code. Follow these steps:

1. Select the btnDisplayMessage button from the drop-down list at the top of the Object Inspector window.
2. Click the Events tab in the Object Inspector.
3. Select the OnClick event, type DisplayMessage in the box to the right of the event name, and press the ENTER key. The Code Editor window becomes active, and Delphi automatically places the headings for this **event handler** in the window. Do not worry about the meanings of these headings right now; they are explained in later chapters.
4. Type in the code listed in Figure 2.27 so that your code window matches it.

As you type in the code, notice that a pop-up menu appears when you type the period (dot separator) following lblMessage (Figure 2.28). This pop-up

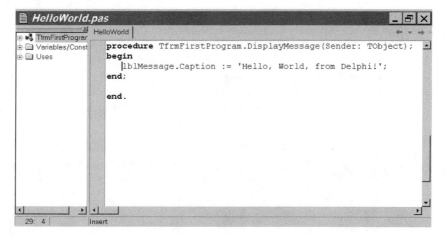

FIGURE 2.27   Code for Your First Program

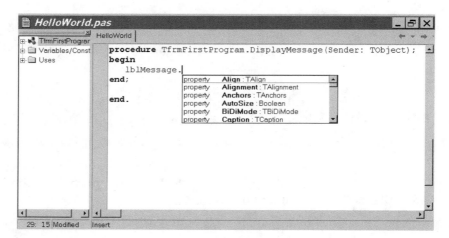

FIGURE 2.28   Delphi Code Completion Feature

menu lists the available **methods** and properties of the `lblMessage` label component. You may select the desired method or property from this pop-up menu by using either the mouse or cursor keys. Alternatively, you can begin to type in the desired method or property name, and Delphi will automatically scroll through the pop-up menu to find the method or property name matching the characters typed. Delphi will automatically complete the method or property name for you in the code when you press the space bar or ENTER key. This pop-up menu constitutes the **code completion feature** of Delphi's **Code Insight,** a set

FIGURE 2.29   Execution of Your First Program

of tools designed to help the programmer write source code. It can help you avoid the burden of typing in many cases. If you prefer that Delphi not pop up a menu of object "members" as you type in code, select `Tools|Editor Options...`, select the Code Insight tab, clear the check box next to Code completion, and then click the OK button.

When you finish typing in the code, run your program by clicking the Run button on the Debug toolbar, selecting `Run|Run` from the menu bar, or pressing F9. When you press ALT+D or click the `Display Message` button, you should see the message appear in the label, as shown in Figure 2.29.

As with any work that you do on a computer, you should intermittently save your programming work in case of a power outage or in the unlikely event that your computer crashes. It is especially important that you save your program before executing it in Delphi. Of course, you should always save finished copies of your programs so that you may modify them at a later date.

Programming Key: Delphi Highlight

Delphi's Code Insight includes five tools to aid the programmer:

1. *Code Completion* displays a list of available data types when you declare a variable or a list of properties and methods when you use an object. As you type the data type, property, or method, Delphi performs an incremental search of the drop-down list. By default, this list is sorted by scope. To display it in alphabetical order, right-click the drop-down list and select Sort by Name from the pop-up menu. Once you have located the desired item, press the ENTER key to select it and place it in your code.

2. *Code Parameters* displays a dialog of the names and types of the parameters for a function, method, or procedure. You can use it to view the required arguments for a function, method, or procedure as you enter it into your code.

3. *Code Templates* provides syntax templates for basic code constructs. Pressing CTRL+J in the Code Editor activates this feature and displays

a pop-up menu of the available templates. Additionally, you can type in the beginning of a statement and then press CTRL+J. If Delphi can resolve the statement, it will fill in the code with the applicable template. If Delphi cannot resolve the statement, it displays a list of those templates that most closely match the statement. To modify or add code templates, select the Code Insight tab under `Tools|Editor Options....`

4. *Tooltip Expression Evaluation* displays the value of a variable or expression as tooltip text during interactive debugging.

5. *Tooltip Symbol Insight* displays declaration information for any identifier in the Code Editor. A pop-up window lists the kind of identifier (procedure, function, type, constant, variable, unit, and so on) as well as the unit file and line number of its declaration.

Programming Key: Delphi Highlight

Another navigation feature in Delphi's Code Editor is bookmarks. Delphi permits 10 bookmarks in the Code Editor, numbered 0 through 9. To toggle a bookmark, position the cursor on the desired line of code, and then press SHIFT+CTRL+*number*, where *number* is one of the number keys 0 through 9. To jump to a numbered bookmark, press CTRL+*number*.

A Delphi project is composed of several different file types; the three main file types are **project files, unit files,** and **form files.** The project file (*.DPR) is the "main program"; it accesses the unit files and form files that compose the Delphi project. In this way, the project file ties together the various files that are associated with a specific project. At this point in your Delphi experience, a one-to-one relationship exists between unit files and form files: Each unit file has an associated form file, and vice versa. The form file (*.DFM) lists the objects on the form and the object property settings, and the unit file (*.PAS) contains the source code associated with the form.

You must save both the project and the forms for your Delphi application. When you save a form, both the unit file and form file are saved under the same name with the appropriate file extension. To save a form, select `File|Save` or `File|Save As...` on the menu bar, click the Save icon on the Standard toolbar, or press CTRL+S. To save the project file, select `File|Save Project As...` on the menu bar. To rapidly save all files associated with a project, select `File|Save All` on the menu or click the Save All icon on the Standard toolbar. Figures 2.30, 2.31, and 2.32 show the contents of the "Hello, World" project, unit, and form files, respectively.

```
program YourFirstProgram;

uses
  Forms,
  HelloWorld in 'HelloWorld.pas' {frmFirstProgram};

{$R *.RES}

begin
  Application.Initialize;
  Application.CreateForm(TfrmFirstProgram, frmFirstProgram);
  Application.Run;
end.
```

FIGURE 2.30   Project File

```
unit HelloWorld;

interface

uses
  Windows, Messages, SysUtils, Classes, Graphics, Controls, Forms, Dialogs,
  StdCtrls;

type
  TfrmFirstProgram = class(TForm)
    lblMessage: TLabel;
    btnDisplayMessage: TButton;
    procedure DisplayMessage(Sender: TObject);
  private
    { Private declarations }
  public
    { Public declarations }
  end;

var
  frmFirstProgram: TfrmFirstProgram;

implementation

{$R *.DFM}

procedure TfrmFirstProgram.DisplayMessage(Sender: TObject);
begin
    lblMessage.Caption := 'Hello, World, from Delphi!';
end;

end.
```

FIGURE 2.31   Unit File

```
object frmFirstProgram: TfrmFirstProgram
  Left = 192
  Top = 138
  Width = 544
  Height = 167
  Caption = 'My First Program'
  Color = clBtnFace
  Font.Charset = DEFAULT_CHARSET
  Font.Color = clWindowText
  Font.Height = -13
  Font.Name = 'MS Sans Serif'
  Font.Style = []
  OldCreateOrder = False
  PixelsPerInch = 120
  TextHeight = 16
  object lblMessage: TLabel
    Left = 6
    Top = 8
    Width = 523
    Height = 51
    Color = clBtnFace
    Font.Charset = ANSI_CHARSET
    Font.Color = clWindowText
    Font.Height = -43
    Font.Name = 'Arial'
    Font.Style = [fsBold]
    ParentColor = False
    ParentFont = False
  end
  object btnDisplayMessage: TButton
    Left = 200
    Top = 72
    Width = 137
    Height = 41
    Caption = '&Display Message'
    TabOrder = 0
    OnClick = DisplayMessage
  end
end
```

FIGURE 2.32   Form File

Programming Key: Delphi Tip

You can edit Delphi project, unit, and form files with any text editor or word processor. We highly recommend using the Delphi code editor and writing programs exclusively in the IDE. Attempting to write a Windows-based Object Pascal program outside of Delphi can be both time-consuming and error prone.

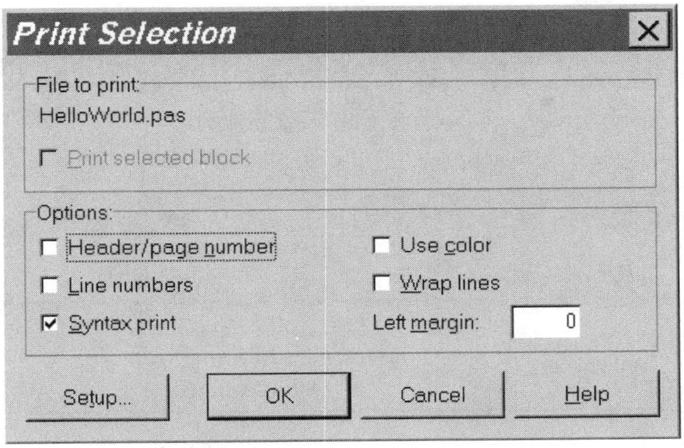

FIGURE 2.33 Print Selection Dialog Box

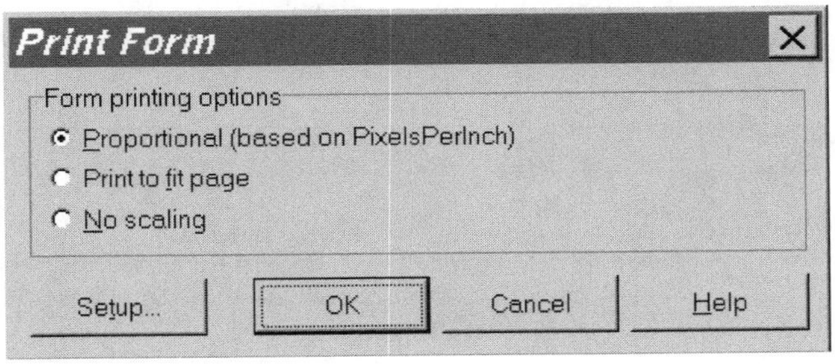

FIGURE 2.34 Print Form Dialog Box

To review your work, you can print out or obtain a **hard copy** of the active page tab in the Code Editor window or the active form. Delphi displays the appropriate print dialog box based on the currently active window. The Print Selection dialog (Figure 2.33) will print the source code in the Code Editor window, and the Print Form dialog (Figure 2.34) will print an image of the active Form window. To obtain a hard copy, select `File|Print...` on the menu.

A compiled program is an **executable module** (*.EXE file) that can be run without starting Delphi. You can compile your program by selecting `Project|Compile projectName` on the menu bar or by pressing CTRL+F9. To run (or execute) a compiled program outside of Delphi, find the associated *.EXE file using Windows Explorer (a file utility included with Windows). Double-click the program icon, and the program will execute.

> An **executable module** is a file that may be executed by the computer, also called a program file or EXE file.

Programming Key: Delphi Highlight

The main Delphi file types are summarized below:

File Extension	Description
DFM	Delphi form file
DPR	Delphi project file
PAS	Delphi unit file

In addition, Delphi generates various files in conjunction with its work in maintaining and compiling your projects. Most of these files are "transparent" to the programmer and never need to be considered, but they should not be deleted. The following table summarizes these file types:

File Extension	Description
CFG	Project configuration file that stores project configuration settings
DCI	Holds changes to Code Insight settings
DCT	Holds component template changes
DMT	Contains changes to menu templates
DOF	Delphi options file that contains the current settings for project options
DRO	Holds changes (additions) to the object repository
DSK	Holds desktop settings, such as open windows and window positions
RES	Contains project version and icon information
TDS	Holds the external debug symbol table
TODO	To-Do List file

Console Applications

Although Delphi is a RAD tool for Windows-based applications, this book would be remiss if it did not discuss console applications. Prior to the development of the Windows operating system, IBM-compatible PCs used a **disk operating system**

(DOS), such as Microsoft's MS-DOS or IBM's PC-DOS. DOS is a command-line–driven operating system, and it contains no graphical interface. The DOS interface is still available in the Windows operating system and can be accessed by selecting Start|Programs|MS-DOS Prompt from the Windows Start menu.

DOS-based programs are usually nongraphical, meaning that they normally contain text menus instead of icons. **Console application** is Delphi's name for a 32-bit Windows program without a graphical interface that executes in a console window (DOS window). It is the closest that Delphi gets to creating a true DOS-based program.

The following steps generate the "Hello, World" program as a console application:

1. Create a console application. Select File|New..., click the Console Application icon under the New tab of the New Items window, and click the OK button.

2. A Code Editor window opens on your screen. Notice that no Form window appears. Why? You are creating a console application, and this application type does not use forms.

3. Modify the text in the Code Editor window so that it matches Figure 2.35.

4. Press the F9 key to execute this program. The window in Figure 2.36 will appear on the screen.

5. Press the ENTER key to end this console application.

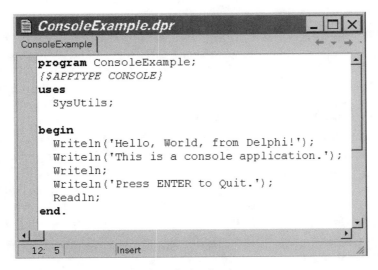

FIGURE 2.35 Code for Console Application

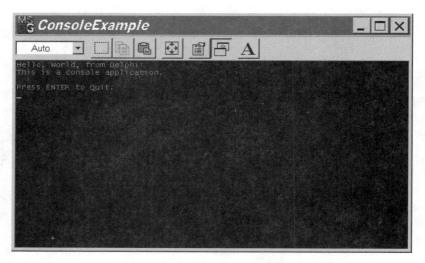

FIGURE 2.36   Execution of Console Application

Summary

Key Terms

Alignment Palette—A window that provides a rapid means of aligning components on a form.

application—See *program.*

button—A component used to begin, interrupt, or end a process. Typically, it initiates an action by executing a portion of code or an entire program.

code completion feature—The part of Delphi's Code Insight where a pop-up menu appears listing applicable properties and methods of an object; this feature allows the programmer to quickly complete a line of code.

Code Editor—A full-featured text editor in the Delphi IDE that allows the programmer to view and edit the source code of Delphi projects.

Code Explorer—A window in the Delphi IDE that allows the programmer to easily navigate through the unit files. It contains a tree diagram that shows all types, classes, properties, methods, global variables, and global routines that are defined in the code unit currently being edited in the Code Editor window.

Code Insight—In Delphi, a set of tools designed to help the programmer write source code.

component—An object in the user interface of a program or any object that may appear in the Delphi Component Palette.

Component List (Components window)—A window that shows an alphabetical listing of all components available in that version of Delphi and the VCL.

Component Palette—A tabbed toolbar that provides quick access to common program components.

console application—Delphi's name for a 32-bit Windows program without a graphical interface that executes in a console window (DOS window).

control—A component that may appear on the screen at run time. Controls form a subset of the VCL: Every control is a component, but not every component is a control.

Custom toolbar—By default, a toolbar that contains a single button to access the Delphi online help facility.

Debug toolbar—A toolbar that provides access to design time tools for interactive testing and debugging of programs.

default setting—The setting that Delphi automatically assigns to a property of an object.

design time—The time when the program and user interface are being written in the Delphi IDE.

Desktop toolbar—A toolbar that allows the programmer to customize the desktop settings.

disk operating system (DOS)—A command-line–driven operating system that contains no graphical interface, such as Microsoft's MS-DOS or IBM's PC-DOS.

dock—The act of placing one window inside of another and attaching it in a specific location.

double-click—The act of rapidly clicking a mouse button twice (typically the left mouse button).

dragging—The act of repositioning an object on the display by clicking the left mouse button on the object and holding the button while moving the mouse. The object then moves in accordance with the mouse movements.

dynamic link library (DLL)—A library file that may be added (or linked) to a program to provide additional functionality.

edit box—A component containing text that is placed in the box either at design time or at run time.

event handler—A subprogram that executes when an action or event occurs.

executable module—A file that may be executed by the computer; a compiled program or a program file.

folder—a directory location on a storage device.

form—The default container for Delphi components; a window or dialog box that appears in a program.

form file—A file that lists the objects on the form and the object property settings.

Form window—A Delphi window that displays the currently selected form. In this window, the form can be edited, resized, and have Delphi components placed on it.

graphical user interface (GUI)—A user interface that contains icons and is controlled via a pointing device such as a mouse.

hard copy—A printed or paper copy; a printout.

hypertext—"Active" text that contains links to definitions, explanations, examples, and related topics.

icon—A button that contains a picture.

integrated development environment (IDE)—In Delphi, a working environment that integrates all phases of the programming process, including editing, testing, and debugging.

label—A component used to display text that the user cannot change.

memo box—A component that can contain multiple lines of text.

menu bar—A group of words or headings typically located at the top of the screen. When the user clicks one of these words with the mouse, an associated drop-down menu opens.

Messages window—A window that displays the results of a search within a Delphi project as well as compiler warning and error messages.

method—A subprogram associated with an object. In general, a method alters an object's properties.

mouse—A hand-operated input device used to control the pointer location on the display. The mouse typically contains a mechanical ball to control the pointer position and left and right buttons to allow the user to make selections.

object—An item that has associated properties and methods.

Object Inspector—A Delphi window that allows the programmer to change component property settings at design time.

object-oriented language—A computer programming language that supports objects.

pixel—A picture element; one point on the screen; a measurement of screen resolution.

pointer—A position indicator on the display, typically in the form of an arrow. Pointers are necessary in GUIs.

program—A file that may be executed (or run) by the computer to perform a specific task; also called an application.

project—A program in Delphi. A project may contain one or more forms.

Project Browser—A window that lists the units, classes, types, properties, methods, variables, and routines that are declared or used in the current project.

project file—The main program of a Delphi project. It accesses the unit files and form files that compose the Delphi project.

project group—A group of related projects or projects that function together as part of a multitiered application.

Project Manager—A window that enables easy navigation among the various projects and each project's constituent files within a project group.

property—An attribute of an object.

rapid application development (RAD)—The program development philosophy for which Delphi was created; the process of designing, coding, testing, correcting, and distributing applications programs quickly.

run time—The time when the program is executing or running.

shortcut key combination—A "hot key" combination that performs a specific task when the associated keys are pressed simultaneously.

Standard toolbar—A toolbar that contains icons for common tasks, such as opening, saving, and creating Delphi projects and associated files.

To-Do List—A built-in notepad on which the programmer can organize tasks, goals, and milestones.

toolbar—A group of icons typically located below the menu bar. Many of these icons provide menu shortcuts by performing the same tasks as the menu items.

unit—A module of source code. Units promote structured programming and code reuse.

unit file—A file that contains the source code associated with its form.

View toolbar—A toolbar that contains icons for creating new forms, viewing forms and code units, and toggling between a form and its code unit.

Visual Component Library (VCL)—A collection of components that are organized in a hierarchical structure according to a parent–child relationship.

Window List—A window that allows the programmer to quickly switch between windows in the Delphi IDE.

Keywords

Properties

Caption	Name
Color	ReadOnly
Font	ScrollBars
Lines	Text
MaxLength	WordWrap

Key Concepts

- The Microsoft Windows operating system is a GUI, and programs designed for this environment are usually graphical in nature. Delphi is one of Borland's RAD tools for Windows-based programs.

- Delphi provides an IDE for the programmer. This environment consists of a menu bar, six toolbars, and three windows. The toolbars are the Standard toolbar, View toolbar, Debug toolbar, Custom toolbar, Component Palette, and Desktop toolbar. The windows are the Form window, Object Inspector window, and Code Editor window.

- Delphi has five "elementary" components that can be used to create a simple user interface: forms, labels, edit boxes, memo boxes, and buttons. With the exception of forms, all of these components are located on the Standard tab of the Component Palette.

- Delphi uses three main file types: project files, unit files, and form files. The project file contains the main program that accesses the unit files and form files that compose the Delphi project. A form file lists the objects on the form and the object property settings. A unit file contains the source code associated with its form.

- The Delphi help facility is a hypertext facility that provides online documentation and additional information about Delphi. It is an easy and convenient reference for programmers.

Review Questions

1. What is a GUI? Give an example.
2. Why is the user interface of an application so important?
3. Name and describe the toolbars and windows in the Delphi IDE.
4. Name and describe the five elementary Delphi components. Why do we call these components "elementary"?
5. How do you place components on a form? How do you move them? How do you resize them?
6. How can you modify the Delphi IDE?
7. Name and describe the three main file types that compose a Delphi project.
8. Where can you find additional information about Delphi?

Problems

1. What is a shortcut key combination? How does the programmer assign a shortcut key and on which component is it used? How does the user activate the shortcut key combination?
2. What is the purpose of the component naming conventions?
3. Create the following user interface in Delphi:

Component	Property	Setting
Form	Name	frmLabels
	Caption	Label Example
Label	Name	lblLastName
	Caption	*your last name*
Label	Name	lblFirstName
	Caption	*your first name*

4. Design a user interface with red, white, and blue labels. Each label caption should name its color in black text.
5. What is the purpose of the ReadOnly property in an edit box?
6. Create the user interface shown in Figure 2.37.

Component	Property	Setting
Form	Name	frmNameExample
	Caption	Enter Your Name
Label	Name	lblFirstName
	Caption	FirstName
Label	Name	lblLastName
	Caption	LastName
Edit Box	Name	edtFirstName
	Text	*blank*
Edit Box	Name	edtLastName
	Text	*blank*

7. Design a user interface with two command buttons. The first command button caption should say "Yes" and the second should say "No."

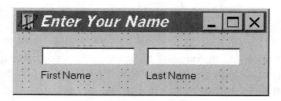

FIGURE 2.37   Problem 6

8. Modify the "Hello, World!" program to display the text "Hello, *your name.*" when the user clicks the "Display Message" button.

9. Modify the "Hello, World!" program. Change the button name to `btnDontClick` and the caption to `Don't Click Me`. The program should display the text "Please follow directions. Don't click the button!" when the user clicks the button.

10. Modify the "Hello, World!" program to display a message of your own choosing.

Chapter 3

Planning Your Program

Chapter Objectives

In this chapter you will:

- Be introduced to the problem-solving process
- Learn the definition of an algorithm
- Learn the meanings of common flowchart symbols
- Discover the advantages of pseudocode versus flowcharts
- Develop algorithms using both flowcharts and pseudocode
- Gain an understanding of the program development cycle

Now that you have been introduced to the Delphi development environment and learned how to create a simple program, it is time to create programs that solve larger, more complex problems. Large programs are often developed by a team of programmers. Such projects require a careful orchestration of the efforts of all programmers to complete the program successfully and promptly. Before a programmer begins writing source code for even a simple program, however, he or she must first plan the construction of the program. This planning phase constitutes a major part of the problem-solving process. This chapter introduces problem solving, algorithm design, and the program development cycle.

The Problem-Solving Process

Many problems in business, science, and engineering require you to analyze a given set of inputs in order to determine a solution. **Problem solving** is the process of taking a set of inputs, doing some calculations with these inputs, and then acquiring a result. Oftentimes, the most difficult aspect of problem solving is the transformation of the inputs into the desired result. If the result is incorrect (that is, cannot be verified by hand calculation or simply does not make sense), the problem-solving process must be repeated until the correct result is achieved. An **algorithm** is a "recipe" for problem solving. This series of steps, or method, converts the inputs for a specific problem into a meaningful output. Erroneous results usually indicate an incorrect algorithm that must subsequently be corrected. Figure 3.1 depicts the problem-solving process.

> An **algorithm** is a series of steps, or a method, for converting the inputs for a specific problem into a meaningful output. It is a "recipe" for problem solving.

Now let's think about how you solve problems. Suppose that you must plan a graduation party. How would you do it? The tasks that must be performed to hold such an event follow a logical order. First, you must send out the invitations and determine how many people will attend. Second, you need to assign specific people to bring certain items, such as plates, cups, drinks, and food. Third, you must find a place to hold the party. You may also want to hire a disc jockey or find a band to play music at the party. This sequence of necessary events continues. In your mind or on paper, you are creating a "laundry list" of the steps necessary to have a successful graduation party. In essence, you are creating an algorithm to plan a party.

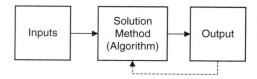

FIGURE 3.1   The Problem-Solving Process

Planning is the crucial first step in any problem-solving process. Like an architect who develops blueprints for a building before it is constructed, you should plan a solution method before you attempt to solve a problem. In terms of computer programming, you should create an algorithm before you sit in front of a computer and start writing code. Two popular tools that programmers use to develop algorithms and plan programs are **flowcharts** and **pseudocode.**

Programming Key: Tips

Solving large, complex problems is no trivial task, even on a computer. Complex problems often require large programs to solve them. Modular programming is a method of dividing a large program into smaller subprograms. Chapter 8 discusses this "divide-and-conquer" technique.

Flowcharts

Flowcharts are diagrams that show the "flow" of program events through time. In these diagrams, specific shapes represent different processes performed by the computer. For instance, a diamond represents a decision structure and a parallelogram denotes an input or output operation. Lines with arrows, called **flowlines,** connect the different shapes to show the sequence of events as the program progresses from start to finish. Many symbols are used in flowcharts, the most common of which are shown in Figure 3.2.

> A **flowchart** is a diagram that shows the flow of program events through time, with specific shapes representing different processes performed by the computer.

Appendix A includes several example flowcharts. The flowchart in Figure A.1, for instance, describes the algorithm to convert integer values from binary to decimal. Figure 3.3 shows a flowchart for a simple "cash register" program. This program allows a user to enter the prices for any number of products purchased and then computes the tax and total for the transaction.

Flowcharts are not as prevalent today as they were many years ago in the early days of computer science. Their popularity diminished rapidly for four main reasons:

- Flowcharts require a large investment of time to produce.
- Flowcharts are lengthy and not space efficient. A flowchart for a small program can easily extend to more than one page.
- Flowcharts are not easy to change or correct.
- Flowcharts do not specify the particular construct that a programmer should use for any individual loop or decision structure.

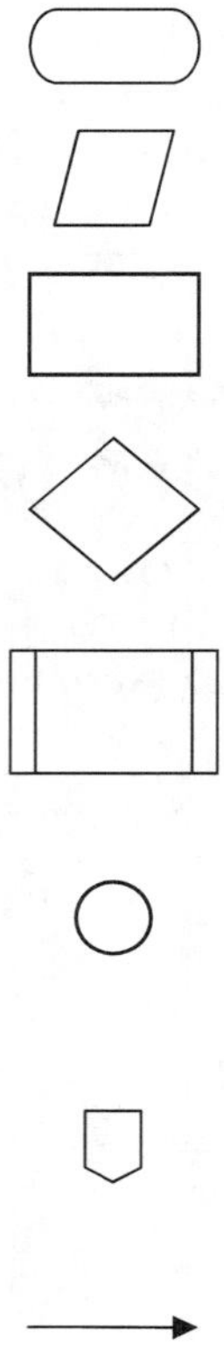

Terminator. Shows the starting and ending points of the program. A terminator has flowlines in only one direction, either in (a stop node) or out (a start node).

Data Input or **Output.** Allows the user to input data and results to be displayed.

Processing. Indicates an operation performed by the computer, such as a variable assignment or mathematical operation.

Decision. The diamond indicates a decision structure. A diamond always has two flowlines out. One flowline out is labeled the "yes" branch and the other is labeled the "no" branch.

Predefined Process. One statement denotes a group of previously defined statements. For instance, "Calculate m!" indicates that the program executes the necessary commands to compute m factorial.

Connector. Connectors avoid crossing flowlines, making the flowchart easier to read. They indicate where flowlines are connected. Connectors come in pairs, one with a flowline in and the other with a flowline out.

Off-Page Connector. Even fairly small programs can have flowcharts that extend several pages. The off-page connector indicates the continuation of the flowchart on another page. Just like connectors, off-page connectors come in pairs.

Flowline. Flowlines connect the flowchart symbols and show the sequence of operations during the program execution.

FIGURE 3.2   Common Flowchart Symbols

As an example, assume that you want to modify the cash register program to track the total number of customers, the total of all purchases, and the total taxes collected during one day. You could not accomplish this modification without rewriting (or redrawing) the entire flowchart, as shown in Figure 3.4. For this and other reasons listed previously, pseudocode has replaced flowcharts as the preferred method of describing algorithms.

Pseudocode

Pseudocode, as the name implies, is "false" code. It is similar to a high-level language in that it uses English-like phrases as statements. Each programmer uses his or her own pseudocode; consequently, no "standard" pseudocode exists.

Pseudocode offers several advantages relative to flowcharts and has become the most widely used program planning technique. Unlike flowcharts, pseudo-

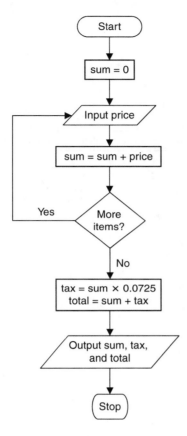

FIGURE 3.3 Flowchart for a Cash Register Program

code does not require a large amount of time to write, and it is extremely space-efficient. A programmer can simply focus on developing an efficient algorithm rather than worrying about creating a "clean" flowchart. Figure 3.5 contains an example of pseudocode for the cash register program.

> **Pseudocode** is "false" code consisting of English-like phrases used to develop or describe an algorithm.

Because pseudocode is a "false" high-level code, it is also easier to convert to actual program code than are flowcharts. The pseudocode specifies the programming constructs that the programmer should use for each loop and decision structure.

In addition, pseudocode is very easy to modify. The pseudocode for the cash register program in Figure 3.5 is easily converted into the pseudocode for the modified version of this program shown in Figure 3.6. Notice that the original pseudocode from Figure 3.5 is contained within the modified pseudocode in Figure 3.6.

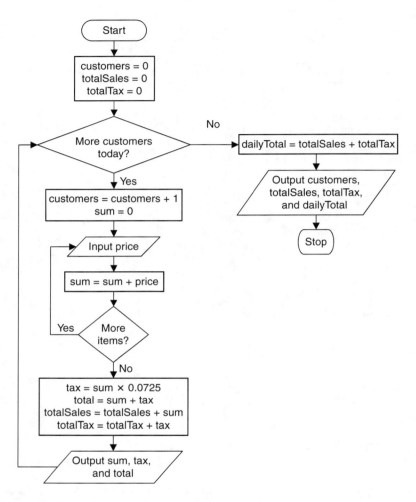

FIGURE 3.4   Flowchart for a Modified Cash Register Program

```
sum = 0
While More items do
    Input price
    sum = sum + price
End While
tax = sum × 0.0725
total = sum + tax
Output sum, tax, total
```

FIGURE 3.5   Pseudocode for a Cash Register Program

```
customers = 0
totalSales = 0
totalTax = 0
While More customers do
   customers = customers + 1
   ┌─────────────────────────┐
   ¦ sum = 0                 ¦
   ¦ While More items do     ¦
   ¦    Input price          ¦
   ¦    sum = sum + price    ¦     Original
   ¦ End While               ¦     Pseudocode
   ¦ tax = sum × 0.0725      ¦
   ¦ total = sum + tax       ¦
   ¦ Output sum, tax, total  ¦
   └─────────────────────────┘
   totalSales = totalSales + sum
   totalTax = totalTax + tax
End While
dailyTotal = totalSales + totalTax
Output customers, totalSales, totalTax, dailyTotal
```

FIGURE 3.6   Pseudocode for a Modified Cash Register Program

The Program Development Cycle

The development of a computer program is a lengthy and time-consuming process. To ensure that the final version of a program works correctly and is as error-free as possible, programmers follow the **program development cycle.** The program development cycle consists of six basic steps (Figure 3.7):

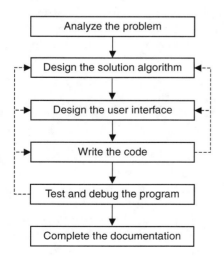

FIGURE 3.7   The Program Development Cycle

1. **Analyze the problem.** Clearly define the problem to ensure that it is fully understood. Determine the inputs and the required output.

2. **Design the solution algorithm.** Determine the relationship between the inputs and output. Write an algorithm to solve the problem and use a simple test case to validate your algorithm.

3. **Design the user interface.** Determine what a user of your program should see. Design the screen layout. Where will the user input data? Where and how (in what format) will the output be displayed? Is there a way to make data entry easier for the user? As discussed in Chapter 2, Delphi enables the programmer to quickly design a graphical user interface (GUI).

4. **Write the code.** Translate the algorithm into a computer programming language. In this book, we will translate our algorithms into Object Pascal using the Delphi development environment.

5. **Test and debug the program.** Testing is a means of finding errors in a program, and debugging is the process of correcting those errors. A **bug** is an error in a program. Rear Admiral Grace M. Hopper of the U.S. Navy originated this term in 1945 when she found that a moth fused to a wire on the Mark I computer caused the machine to malfunction. To get a program to work, you must **debug** it, or remove all the bugs.

6. **Complete the documentation.** Documentation consists of all materials that describe the program, its purpose, and its operation. Documentation may be internal or external. **Internal documentation** consists of comments that appear inside the program code. It allows someone unfamiliar with the program to read the code and understand what it does. **External documentation** includes flowcharts, pseudocode, program purpose statements, assumptions, design requirements, and input/output requirements. Commercial programs often provide user's manuals as documentation. The primary purpose of documentation is to allow someone other than the programmer to use the program and to modify the code if necessary.

∘ C ∘ A ∘ S ∘ E ∘ S ∘ T ∘ U ∘ D ∘ Y ∘

Debra is shopping at Kreider's Delicatessen & Market. Her house is located eight blocks away from the store. Debra wants to walk home, but she does not want to carry more than 10 pounds of groceries.

Debra's shopping list, which follows, indicates the amount of each item that she wants to purchase (in pounds). Debra has also prioritized her shopping list according to her desire for each product. The desirability of an item is rated on a point scale from 1 to 10, where 10 points denotes a highly desirable item and 1 point indicates a less desirable item.

According to Debra's shopping list, which items should she buy?

Item	Amount (lb)	Desirability (points)
Ambrosia salad	0.50	8
Bagels	2.00	5
Bologna	1.00	4
Cheddar cheese	1.00	4
Coleslaw	1.00	2
Cream cheese	0.50	4
Ham	1.00	10
Monterey Jack cheese	1.00	10
Potato salad	1.00	8
Roast beef	1.00	6
Salami	1.00	6
Sausage	2.00	3
Smoked salmon	1.00	9
Sourdough bread	0.50	7
Tuna salad	0.50	1

Restating this problem, Debra wants to maximize the desirability of the products purchased such that the total weight of her purchases does not exceed 10 pounds. She cannot purchase all of the items since the total weight is 15 pounds. To solve this problem, Debra uses the ratio of an item's desirability to its weight (points/pound ratio). The following table shows this ratio for each item:

Item	Ratio (points/lb)
Ambrosia salad	16
Bagels	2.5
Bologna	4
Cheddar cheese	4
Coleslaw	2
Cream cheese	8
Ham	10
Monterey Jack cheese	10
Potato salad	8
Roast beef	6
Salami	6
Sausage	1.5
Smoked salmon	9
Sourdough bread	14
Tuna salad	2

Debra acts in a greedy fashion and selects those items that give her the most points per pound as long as the addition of the item does not cause her to exceed the weight limit. Thus Debra's solution is a **greedy algorithm:**

Item	Amount (lb)	Desirability (points)
Ambrosia salad	0.50	8
Bologna	1.00	4
Cheddar cheese	1.00	4
Cream cheese	0.50	4
Ham	1.00	10
Monterey Jack cheese	1.00	10
Potato salad	1.00	8
Roast beef	1.00	6
Salami	1.00	6
Smoked salmon	1.00	9
Sourdough bread	0.50	7
Tuna salad	0.50	1
	10.00	77

Debra buys 12 items with a total weight of 10 pounds and total desirability of 77 points.

Summary

Key Terms

algorithm—A series of steps, or a method, for converting the inputs for a specific problem into a meaningful output; a "recipe" for problem solving.

bug—An error in a computer program.

debug—The process of removing errors from a computer program.

external documentation—Any paper documents that describe a program, including flowcharts, pseudocode, program purpose statements, assumptions, design requirements, input/output requirements, and user's manuals.

flowchart—A diagram that shows the flow of program events through time, with specific shapes representing different processes performed by the computer.

flowline—A line with an arrow that connects flowchart symbols to show the sequence of events during program execution.

greedy algorithm—An iterative algorithm that operates in a greedy fashion by choosing the item of greatest value in each step.

internal documentation—Comments that are written inside the program source code.

problem solving—The process of taking a set of inputs, doing some calculations with these inputs, and then acquiring a result.

program development cycle—A series of six basic steps in the process of developing a computer program.

pseudocode—"False" code consisting of English-like phrases used to develop or describe an algorithm.

Key Concepts

- The problem-solving process involves a sequence of steps intended to arrive at a result from a set of inputs.

- An algorithm is a method that identifies the steps necessary to solve a particular problem.

- Programmers commonly use flowcharts and pseudocode to formalize solution algorithms. Whereas flowcharts contain standard symbols to represent different computer operations, no such standard exists for pseudocode; each programmer develops his or her own pseudocode. Despite this lack of standardization, pseudocode is used more frequently than flowcharts because it is less time intensive, more space efficient, easier to modify, and closer to actual source code.

- Programmers follow a six-step program development cycle to ensure that a program is as error-free as possible. The last step of this cycle involves completing the program documentation, which consists of both internal and external documentation. Adequate documentation allows someone other than the programmer to use or modify the program.

Review Questions

1. What is the problem-solving process?
2. What is an algorithm?
3. Name the two tools commonly used by programmers to develop algorithms.
4. Name and describe the meaning of five different flowchart symbols.
5. What are the advantages of pseudocode over flowcharts?
6. State and describe the six steps of the program development cycle.

Problems

1. Create a flowchart for an algorithm to make a peanut butter-and-jelly sandwich.

2. From Problem 1, assume that you have two predefined processes named *MakeHalf* and *PutTogether*. *MakeHalf* can make half of the sandwich by inputting the slice of bread and either peanut butter or jelly. For instance, *MakeHalf*(slice1, jelly) puts jelly on slice1 of the bread. *PutTogether*(slice1, slice2) puts the two slices of bread together to create a whole sandwich. Rewrite your flowchart from Problem 1 to use these two predefined processes.

3. Write the pseudocode for Problems 1 and 2.

4. Create a flowchart for a program that determines the largest of three numbers using the following simple two-step method: (1) Compare the first number with the second number and select the larger of the two; (2) Compare the number chosen in step 1 with the third number and select the larger.

5. Write the pseudocode for Problem 4.

6. Develop a flowchart for a program that adds a series of user-entered numbers. The program should display the sum and terminate when the user enters 0.

7. Write the pseudocode for Problem 6.

8. Develop a flowchart for the game of *high–low*. The first player enters a number between 0 and 100. The second player then tries to guess the first player's number. If the number is lower than the guess, the computer responds "lower." If the number is higher than the guess, the computer responds "higher." The game ends when the second player correctly guesses the first player's number. The program should track the number of guesses and display this information before it terminates.

9. Write the pseudocode for Problem 8.

10. Given the amount of time it takes an automobile to travel a certain distance, we can compute the vehicle's *average velocity* using the following formula:

$$\text{Average velocity} = \text{distance} \div \text{time}$$

Create a flowchart for a program that computes the average velocity of a vehicle.

11. In Problem 10, it does not make sense to have a negative distance or a nonpositive time. Modify your flowchart from Problem 10 to "bulletproof" your program and prevent invalid entries for *distance* and *time*.

12. Write the pseudocode for Problems 10 and 11. Did it take you longer to write the flowcharts or the pseudocode? Which was easier to modify when converting your answer from Problem 10 into an answer for Problem 11?

13. The current inventory policy of the Ace Widget Shop is to place an order for 100 widgets with a widget supplier whenever the daily ending inventory reaches 30, provided that there are no outstanding orders that have not yet been received. Create a flowchart for a program that helps the Ace Widget Shop determine whether to place an order based on the following variables: beginning inventory, sales, ending inventory, reorder point, quantity delivered, and projected delivery date of last order placed.

14. Write the pseudocode for Problem 13.

15. Develop a flowchart for the dealer of a game of blackjack in which the dealer must continue to draw cards until the dealer's hand contains 5 cards or 16 or more points.

16. Write the pseudocode for Problem 15.

17. For any positive integer m, $m!$ is read "m factorial" and is defined as

$$m! = (m)(m-1) \ldots (2)(1), \text{ and } 0! = 1$$

Write a flowchart for a program that computes $m!$ for any positive integer m.

18. Write the pseudocode for Problem 17.

19. A *permutation* of size k is any *ordered* sequence of k objects taken from a set of n distinct objects, where $n \geq k$. The number of permutations of size k that can be constructed from the n objects is given by

$$_nP_k = \frac{n!}{(n-k)!}$$

A *combination* of size k is any *unordered* subset of k objects taken from a set of n distinct objects, where $n \geq k$. The number of combinations of size k that can be formed from n distinct objects is given by

$$_nC_k = \binom{n}{k} = \frac{n!}{k!(n-k)!}$$

Create a flowchart for a program that computes the number of permutations and combinations for given n and k values. You may use a predefined process to compute factorials.

20. Write the pseudocode for Problem 19.

Chapter 4

Elements of Programming

Chapter Objectives

In this chapter you will:

- Distinguish between variables and data types
- Learn how to declare, initialize, and use variables
- Learn about constants, including the difference between hard-coded and named constants
- Learn about operators, precedence rules, and common math and string functions
- Understand the concepts of scope and lifetime
- Discover the advantages and disadvantages of global variables
- Learn how to comment code and improve program readability
- Become familiar with methods of interactive input and output

Now that you have become familiar with the Delphi interface, it is time to turn your attention to learning the basics of computer programming. This chapter introduces several elements of programming that are common to most high-level languages, such as variables, constants, and data types.

Variables and Data Types

> A **variable** is a quantity that can assume any value. A computer variable is a named memory location that stores a value.

In mathematics, a **variable** is a quantity that can assume any value. A variable is easily recorded on paper by simply writing down its value, which can be of any size. On a computer, however, variables are stored in memory, which requires physical resources. Thus a computer variable is a named location in memory where values are stored. These values can change throughout a program's execution. Because a computer has limited physical resources, the memory allocated for storing a variable should be conserved to the maximum extent possible. This practice effectively limits the set of the values that the variable can assume, or the **range** of the variable. Assigning a **data type** to a variable limits the amount of memory that the variable consumes and informs the compiler how much memory should be reserved for the variable. Variables can assume any value within the limits of their assigned data types.

The type of information stored in a computer variable differs from the information contained by a mathematical variable. Whereas mathematical variables can contain only **numeric data** (numbers), computer variables may hold either numeric data or **character data** (letters and symbols as well as numbers). **Alphanumeric data** is a subset of character data that includes only numbers and letters (but no symbols). Thus two types of data can be stored in computer variables: numbers and characters.

These two types of data are treated differently when stored by the computer. Storage of character data is comparatively simple and requires only two data types: characters and strings. A **string** is a group of characters that the computer stores in a **string variable,** and a **character** is a string consisting of only one character (a string of length 1). Numeric variables, on the other hand, require more data types because numbers come in a variety of flavors. Numbers can be either **integer** or **real.** Because integers are numbers with no fractional components, they generally require less memory to store than real numbers. For this reason, it makes sense to use different data types to conserve memory if we know that a variable will hold only integer values.

For example, if you are certain that a value will be an integer between 0 and 255, you can assign the `Byte` data type to the variable. From our discussion of bits, bytes, and binary numbers (see Appendix A), it follows that the binary representation of 255 is $1111\ 1111_2$. As you can see, the binary representation of 255 includes eight digits (or bits). Because a byte consists of eight bits, we have no reason to use more memory space than a byte to store this value. Figure 4.1 lists the Object Pascal data types, memory requirements, and associated variable ranges. Several of these data types are common to many high-level languages, but they may differ in

Logical and Numeric Data Types

Data Type	Range	Format or Size	Significant Digits
Shortint	−128 to +127	signed 8-bit	
Smallint	−32768 to +32767	signed 16-bit	
Integer (or Longint)	−2147483648 to +2147483647	signed 32-bit	
Int64	-2^{63} to $+2^{63}-1$	signed 64-bit	
Byte	0 to 255	unsigned 8-bit	
Word	0 to 65535	unsigned 16-bit	
Longword (or Cardinal)	0 to 4294967295	unsigned 32-bit	
Boolean (or ByteBool)	True or False	1 byte	
WordBool	True or False	2 bytes	
LongBool	True or False	4 bytes	
Real48	2.9×10^{-39} to 1.7×10^{38}	6 bytes	11 to 12
Single	1.5×10^{-45} to 3.4×10^{38}	4 bytes	7 to 8
Real (or Double)	5.0×10^{-324} to 1.7×10^{308}	8 bytes	15 to 16
Extended	3.6×10^{-4951} to 1.1×10^{4932}	10 bytes	19 to 20
Comp	$-2^{63}+1$ to $+2^{63}-1$	8 bytes	19 to 20
Currency	−922337203685477.5808 to +922337203685477.5807	8 bytes	19 to 20

Character and String Data Types

Data Type	Maximum Length	Memory Required
Char (or AnsiChar)	1 ANSI character	1 byte
WideChar	1 Unicode character	2 bytes
ShortString	255 ANSI characters	2 to 256 bytes
Strin (or AnsiString)	2^{31} ANSI characters	4 bytes to 2 gigabytes
WideString	2^{30} Unicode characters	4 bytes to 2 gigabytes

FIGURE 4.1   Object Pascal Data Types

terms of memory requirements and the range of values that may be stored. Consult your compiler documentation for more specific information.

Examining Figure 4.1, we see that Object Pascal provides a variety of data types for storing the same type of data. Although these data types can effectively limit memory consumption by variables, this text uses the "standard" data types (`Integer`, `Real`, `Char`, `String`, and so on) in its example programs.

Naming, Declaring, and Using Variables

In most languages, variable names must begin with a letter and be followed by any number of alphanumeric characters. For instance, `A5` is a valid variable name, but `5A` is not. Additionally, some languages are **case sensitive,** such that `A5` and a5 are seen as being different variables. In any case, you should choose your variable names so that each variable is **self-commenting,** or describes its own contents. Someone reading your program will have no idea what a variable named A5 contains unless your code is carefully traced. By comparison, a variable named todaysDate is self-explanatory.

In Object Pascal, variable names must begin with a letter or the underscore (_) character. Any number of alphanumeric characters or underscores may follow the first character, but only the first 255 characters of the name are significant. Delphi's Object Pascal compiler is not case sensitive; it is **case insensitive.** For example, if you declare a variable named todaysDate and then use the variable todaysDATE within your program code, the compiler sees both names as the same variable. Rather than use underscores in variable names, this text uses lowercase letters for variable names, with an uppercase letter distinguishing the first letter of the second and subsequent words contained in the variable name. Thus todaysDate, totalSales, dailyTotal, and costOfGoodsSold are all examples of variable names that satisfy this naming convention.

To assign a data type to a variable, you **declare** the variable as a particular data type in your program. Object Pascal, like most other languages, requires that you explicitly declare variables. This policy serves several purposes:

- It allows other programmers who read your code to easily determine the type of data stored in the variables and the ranges of the variables.
- It provides greater control over the memory required by your program. You can save considerable memory space by assigning the data type with the lowest memory requirements to each of your variables (as long as each variable can still store its required value).
- It avoids the confusion that might otherwise arise when variables with the same name appear in different sections of your code.
- It encourages self-commenting variable names.

You use the **var** statement to declare and assign data types to variables in Object Pascal. This **keyword** tells the compiler the type of the variable, and the compiler then knows how much memory space to reserve for the variable. Thus a var statement is a **nonexecutable statement.** It is not compiled into executable code but rather provides necessary instructions to the compiler at **compile time.** The simplest form of the var statement is shown below:

> A **keyword** is a reserved word or symbol recognized as part of a programming language.

```
var variableName: DataType;
```

To declare a variable named myNumber as an integer variable, for example, you would use the following line of code:

```
var myNumber: Integer;
```

In this code, notice that the variable name is followed by a colon (:) and the data type is followed by a semicolon (;). This punctuation is part of the **syntax** (structure or grammar) of the `var` statement. In Object Pascal, the semicolon (;) is the **statement separator;** it separates one statement from another statement.

You can declare two or more variables of the same data type on a single line using a `var` statement. For instance,

```
var number1, number2: Integer;
```

declares two integer variables, `number1` and `number2`. The syntax for this form appears below. The portion in square brackets is optional and may be repeated any number of times. Thus you can declare several variables of the same data type on a single line.

```
var variableName[, variableName]: DataType;
```

Finally, you may use a single `var` statement to declare variables of different data types. That is, consecutive variable declarations do not have to repeat the `var` keyword. The general syntax of the `var` statement follows:

```
var
   variableName[, variableName]: DataType;
   [variableName[, variableName]: DataType;]
```

The following **code fragment,** or incomplete portion of source code, declares several variables:

```
var
    dollars:        Integer;
    cents:          Integer;
    cost:           Real;
    myMessage:      String;
```

Programming Key: Tips

In the preceding example code fragment, the variables `dollars` and `cents` are declared on two separate lines although they are of the same data type. To improve the readability of your source code, declare only one variable per line.

To assign values, Object Pascal uses an assignment operator (:=). The assignment operator := consists of a colon (:) immediately followed by an equals sign (=). Notice that no space appears between these two symbols. As an example, the following code fragment increments the count variable by 2:

```
count := count + 2;
```

In this code, it is important to realize that the := operator means "is assigned" rather than "is equal to" as in mathematics. If you were to give this "equation" to a mathematician, you would be told that it does not make sense. In mathematics, we would subtract the count variable from each side and end up with 0 = 2, which is incorrect. In computer science, however, this statement is perfectly valid. It is interpreted as "assign the value of count plus 2 to the count variable." *The rule for variable assignments is that the result from the expression on the right side of the := operator is stored in the variable that appears on the left side of the operator.* Thus, to assign a value of 1 to the count variable, we write count := 1, but never 1 := count, because we cannot assign the value of count to 1, a numeric constant. *In assignment statements, you can think of the := operator as an arrow pointing toward the left (←) that means "is assigned to."* In fact, many programmers use ← in their pseudocode rather than := to avoid confusion.

The code unit in Figure 4.2 declares and uses variables. Can you tell what this code does? What is the output? Compare your answer to the actual program output shown in Figure 4.2.

Programming Key: Tips

The := operator is used for variable assignment, with a variable appearing on the left side of the operator. An assignment statement is always of the form

```
variableName := expression;
```

In Figure 4.2, notice that the variable num is assigned the value 5 immediately after it is declared. That is, num is **initialized** to 5. After a variable is declared, it must then be initialized, or assigned an initial value. In Object Pascal and most other languages, after a variable is declared, it contains whatever "junk" value is residing in its assigned memory location. *We cannot overemphasize the importance of initializing variables before they are used.* In the code in Figure 4.2, for example, if we omit the line num := 5, then the output of the code is unpredictable and may no longer match that shown in the figure. Our program will no longer generate the desired output, because the code now has a **logic error** due to the omission of the variable initialization.

```
unit VariableEx;

interface

uses
  Windows, Messages, SysUtils, Classes, Graphics, Controls, Forms, Dialogs,
  StdCtrls;

type
  TfrmVariableExample = class(TForm)
    btnExample: TButton;
    memOutput: TMemo;
    procedure DoExample(Sender: TObject);
  private
    { Private declarations }
  public
    { Public declarations }
  end;

var
  frmVariableExample: TfrmVariableExample;

implementation

{$R *.DFM}

{Example variable declaration and use}
procedure TfrmVariableExample.DoExample(Sender: TObject);

var
 num: Integer;

begin
  num := 5;
  memOutput.Lines.Add(IntToStr(num));
  num := num + 1;
  memOutput.Lines.Add(IntToStr(num));
  num := num - 2;
  memOutput.Lines.Add(IntToStr(num));
  num := num + 3;
  memOutput.Lines.Add(IntToStr(num));
  num := num - 4;
  memOutput.Lines.Add(IntToStr(num));
  num := num + 5;
  memOutput.Lines.Add(IntToStr(num));
  num := num - 6;
  memOutput.Lines.Add(IntToStr(num));
end;

end.
```

Program Execution

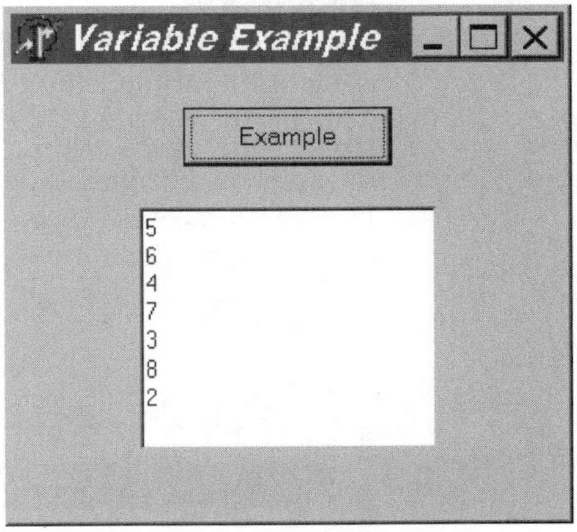

FIGURE 4.2 Example Variable Declaration and Use

Constants

A **constant** is a named item that retains a constant value throughout the execution of a program. It may be defined by any mathematical or string expression. At compile time, the compiler simply replaces the constant name with its associated value. A **numeric constant** refers to a number, or numeric literal; a **string constant** is a string literal. The number 7, for example, is a numeric constant, whereas "days per week" is a string constant. Numeric and string constants that are used explicitly within the source code in lieu of named constants are said to be **hard-coded** into the program. You can easily change a named constant when necessary by simply editing the line of source code that specifies the value for the constant. Hard-coded constants are not so easily changed; a programmer must alter every line of source code in which the constant is used to modify the program. Therefore, it is best to use named constants within your code to allow for easy future modifications.

Programming Key: Tips

To facilitate future modifications of your programs, consider using named constants for those constants that appear in two or more locations within your source code.

In Object Pascal, the **const** statement is used to define constants. Like the var statement, the const statement can be used to declare a group of constants. The general form of the const statement appears below:

```
const
  constantName = Expression;
  [constantName = Expression;]
```

As a style convention in this text, constants appear in all uppercase letters with subsequent words separated by underscores. The constant, DAYS_PER_WEEK, satisfies this style convention. Figure 4.3 displays a **code segment,** or portion of source code, that uses the const statement. This figure emphasizes the difference between named constants and hard-coded constants.

Which method is easier to read? Which is more descriptive and self-commenting?
If the constants are used throughout your code, which method is easier to change?

```
const
  MAX_WORK_WEEKS = 50;
  MAX_HOURS_PER_WEEK = 45;

var
  frmConstantsExample: TfrmConstantsExample;

implementation

{$R *.DFM}

{------------------------------------------------------------------------------
EXAMPLE USE OF CONSTANTS
------------------------
This code calculates the maximum yearly work hours for a particular business and
demonstrates the difference between hard-coded and named constants.
------------------------------------------------------------------------------}
procedure TfrmConstantsExample.MaxYearlyWorkHours(Sender: TObject);

var
  maxYrWkHrs: Integer;

begin
  {Using hard-coded constants}
  maxYrWkHrs := 50 * 45;
  memOutput.Lines.Add('Using hard-coded constants:');
  memOutput.Lines.Add('The maximum yearly work hours is ' +
                      IntToStr(maxYrWkHrs));
  memOutput.Lines.Add('');

  {Using named constants}
  maxYrWkHrs := MAX_WORK_WEEKS * MAX_HOURS_PER_WEEK;
  memOutput.Lines.Add('Using named constants:');
  memOutput.Lines.Add('The maximum yearly work hours is ' +
                      IntToStr(maxYrWkHrs));
end;
```

Program Execution

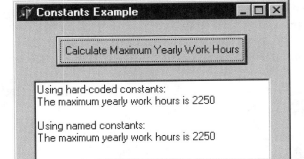

FIGURE 4.3 Example Use of Constants

> ### Programming Key: Delphi Highlight
>
> Delphi's Object Pascal compiler allows the programmer to create typed constants if desired. The general syntax to declare typed constants follows:
>
> ```
> const
>     constantName: DataType = Expression;
>     [constantName: DataType = Expression;]
> ```
>
> The behavior of typed constants depends on the compiler state, which compiler directives within the source code may alter (see Chapter 17). In the default {$J+} or {$WRITEABLECONST ON} compiler state, typed constants behave like initialized variables and can have new values assigned to them. If the {$J–} or {$WRITEABLECONST OFF} compiler directive is in effect, the values of typed constants cannot change at run time. Essentially, typed constants are read-only variables that operate similarly to true constants.
> We recommend using typed constants only for advanced programming.

Arithmetic Operators

Just as arithmetic **operators** denote specific operations to be performed in mathematics, equivalent operators are available that denote these operations on a computer. Addition, for instance, is denoted by the plus sign (+) both in mathematics and on a computer. Multiplication, however, is denoted by the times symbol ($\times$) in mathematics and by an asterisk (*) on a computer. Similarly, division uses the division symbol ($\div$) in mathematics but is denoted by a forward slash (/) on a computer. Such **binary operators** require two **operands,** where an operand is a value or expression that is used by an operator. Other operators, such as the negation operator, are **unary operators** that require only one operand. Figure 4.4 lists the Object Pascal arithmetic operators, the required operator types, and the data type of the resulting value. In this figure, the example column uses two variables, x and y, as operands for the various arithmetic operators.

> An **operator** is a symbol that denotes a specific operation to be performed. An **operand** is a value or expression that is used by an operator. A **unary operator** requires only one operand, and a **binary operator** requires two operands.

In Object Pascal, the result of a division operation (/) is always of the Extended data type, regardless of the data types of the two operands. For integer

Operation	Operator	Operand Types	Result Type	Example
Sign Identity	+ (unary)	integer, real	integer, real	+x
Sign Negation	– (unary)	integer, real	integer, real	–x
Multiplication	*	integer, real	integer, real	x * y
Division	/	integer, real	real	x / y
Integer Division	div	integer	integer	x div y
Modulo Division	mod	integer	integer	x mod y
Addition	+	integer, real	integer, real	x + y
Subtraction	–	integer, real	integer, real	x – y

FIGURE 4.4   Object Pascal Arithmetic Operators

variables x and y, for instance, x/y returns an Extended value. For the other arithmetic operators, the result is of type Extended whenever at least one operand is a real value; the result is of type Int64 when at least one operand is of type Int64; otherwise, the result is of type Integer.

You may not be familiar with the **integer division** and **modulo division** mathematical operations. Integer division, denoted by the **div** operator, is used to divide two integer values and return only the integer part of the quotient; any fractional portion is simply truncated or ignored. For example, the result of 5 div 2 is 2. Although 5 divided by 2 equals 2.5, only the integer part of the quotient, 2, is the result of integer division. The fractional part of the quotient is ignored. In other words, the value of x div y is the value of x/y rounded in the direction of zero to the nearest integer. Modulo division, denoted by the **mod** operator, is used to divide two integer values and return the integer remainder. For example, 5 mod 2 equals 1; that is, 5 divided by 2 equals 2 with a remainder of 1, which is the result of the modulo division. Mathematically, x mod y is equivalent to x − (x div y)*y.

Built-in Math Functions

Object Pascal includes many built-in mathematical functions. Figure 4.5 describes the most common of these functions.

Function	Returns
Abs(x)	Absolute value of x
Ceil(x)	Lowest integer greater than or equal to x
Exp(x)	Real value of e raised to the power of x, where e is the base of the natural logarithms
Floor(x)	Highest integer less than or equal to x
Frac(x)	Fractional part of x as an Extended data type
Int(x)	Integer part of x as an Extended data type
IntPower(base, exponent)	Extended value of base raised to the exponent power
Ldexp(x, p)	Returns $x \times 2^p$ as an Extended data type
Ln(x)	Natural logarithm of the real value x
LnXP1(x)	Natural logarithm of the real value $(x + 1)$
Log10(x)	The log base 10 of x
Log2(x)	The log base 2 of x
LogN(n, x)	The log base n of x
Max(x, y)	The greater of the two numeric values
Min(x, y)	The lesser of the two numeric values
Pi	3.1415926535897932385
Power(base, exponent)	$base^{exponent}$
Round(x)	The real value x rounded to the nearest whole number as an Int64 data type. If x is exactly halfway between two whole numbers, the result is always the even number.
Sqr(x)	The square of x (x^2)
Sqrt(x)	The square root of x ($x^{1/2}$)
Trunc(x)	Truncates the real number x to an integer value

FIGURE 4.5 Built-in Math Functions

Unlike most computer languages, Object Pascal uses a function to perform exponentiation rather than an operator. Typical computer exponentiation operators include the double asterisk (**) and the caret symbol (^). Object Pascal, however, reserves the use of the caret symbol for pointers (see Chapter 10).

String Operators and Built-in String Routines

Recall that a string is a group of characters. String literals are denoted by apostrophes, or single quotes. The following line of code assigns a value (a string literal) to today, a string variable:

```
today := 'Tuesday';
```

The **concatenation** operation, denoted by the plus sign (+), is the only string operation available in Object Pascal. Concatenation combines strings in the prescribed left-to-right order. Because the plus sign performs different operations depending on the context in which it is used, we call it an **overloaded operator.** The following code fragment demonstrates string concatenation:

```
weekendDays := 'Saturday' + ' and ' + 'Sunday';
```

Upon execution of this code, the variable weekendDays contains the string Saturday and Sunday.

In the preceding example, you may have noticed that the apostrophes are not part of the string. What if you want to define a string that contains the apostrophes? The following code fragment *does not work:*

```
weekendDays := ''Saturday and Sunday'';
```
⬅ This line of code does not work. It generates a syntax error.

This code fragment generates a **syntax error,** or an error in grammar or punctuation. Delphi's compiler does not understand the structure of this statement. It sees the first apostrophe immediately followed by a second apostrophe and interprets this sequence as the **null string** (or **empty string**), a string that contains no characters. The compiler then encounters the word "Saturday" and does not know how to interpret it because it does not recognize that it is part of a string. Fortunately, you have several ways to include apostrophes in your strings. Within a string, the compiler interprets a sequence of two apostrophes as one apostrophe in the string. The following code fragment therefore correctly assigns 'Saturday and Sunday' to weekendDays:

```
weekendDays := '''Saturday and Sunday'''
```
⬅ The first and last apostrophes delimit the string. Each pair of apostrophes within the string delimiters is interpreted as one apostrophe.

Another way to include apostrophes in a string is to use character values. This method also allows you to incorporate characters and symbols that are not readily available on your keyboard in your strings. Every character in the computer has an associated **ASCII** (American Standard Code for Information Interchange) value. Because Windows cannot display all ASCII (pronounced *ask-ee*) characters, it uses the more limited **ANSI** (American National Standards Institute) character set. For the most part, ASCII and ANSI (pronounced *ann-see*) character values are equivalent.

Object Pascal has two built-in functions to work with ASCII characters:

Chr(*n***)**   Returns the character whose ASCII value is *n*

Ord(*chr***)**   Returns the ASCII value (ordinal position) of the character *chr*

For example, Chr(65) returns the character A; conversely, Ord('A') returns the value 65. That is, the ASCII value for an uppercase A is 65. Appendix B lists the ASCII (ANSI) character values. The ASCII value for an apostrophe is 39, so we can rewrite our variable assignment as follows:

```
weekendDays := Chr(39) + 'Saturday and Sunday' + Chr(39);
```

This variable assignment is equivalent to the previous one; it assigns 'Saturday and Sunday' to weekendDays.

Programming Key: Tips

To use a nonkeyboard character in a string, you must first find the character's ASCII value (see Appendix B). You can then use the string concatenation operator (+) and the Chr function with the character's ASCII value to add this character to your string.

Programming Key: Delphi Highlight

Instead of using the Chr function and the string concatenation operator, Delphi's Object Pascal allows you to use **control characters** in a string. A control character consists of the # symbol followed by an integer value between 0 and 255, and it denotes the corresponding ASCII character. For instance,

```
myString := #72#101#108#108#111;
```

is equivalent to

```
myString := 'Hello';
```

As another example,

```
weekendDays := #39'Saturday and Sunday'#39;
```

is equivalent to both

```
    weekendDays := '''Saturday and Sunday''';
and
    weekendDays := Chr(39) + 'Saturday and Sunday' +
                   Chr(39);
```

Object Pascal also provides the necessary data types and functions to work with the **Unicode character set,** a character set in which each character is represented by two bytes. Thus a Unicode string consists of a sequence of two-byte words. This character set has the advantage of containing characters from foreign languages, making it possible to create applications for international use. Unicode characters and strings are also called **wide characters** and **wide strings,** respectively. The first 256 Unicode characters map to the ANSI character set. For

Function	Purpose
CompareStr	Compares two strings with case sensitivity
CompareText	Compares two strings by ordinal value without case sensitivity
Concat	Concatenates two or more strings into one string
Copy	Returns a substring of a string
IsDelimiter	Indicates whether a particular character in a string matches one of a set of delimiter characters
LastDelimiter	Returns the position of the last character in a string that matches any of the delimiter characters
Length	Returns the number of characters in a string
LowerCase	Returns a copy of a string in all lowercase letters
Pos	Returns the position of the first character in a substring that occurs in a specified string
QuotedStr	Returns a single-quoted version of a string
StringOfChar	Returns a string with a specified number of repeating characters
StringReplace	Returns a string with occurrences of one substring replaced by another substring
Trim	Removes leading and trailing spaces and control characters from a string
TrimLeft	Removes leading spaces and control characters from a string
TrimRight	Removes trailing spaces and control characters from a string
UpperCase	Returns a copy of a string in all uppercase letters
WrapText	Splits a string into multiple lines as its length approaches a specified size

Procedure	Purpose
Delete	Removes a substring from a string
Insert	Inserts a substring into a string beginning at a specified point
SetLength	Sets the length of a string
SetString	Sets the contents and length of the given string
Str	Converts a numeric variable to a string
Val	Converts a string to a numeric variable

FIGURE 4.6   Built-in String Routines

our purposes, however, the ANSI character set is sufficient. Consequently, this book does not use Unicode characters. Consult the Delphi online documentation for more information about Unicode characters and the creation of international applications.

Borland's Object Pascal offers a variety of built-in routines to manipulate strings, making it one of the best languages for working with strings. Figure 4.6 describes some of the most useful built-in string routines.

In Figure 4.6, we can see that the `QuotedStr` function provides yet another means of placing single quotes around a string. Once again, the following code fragment assigns 'Saturday and Sunday' to weekendDays:

```
weekendDays := QuotedStr('Saturday and Sunday');
```

Working with Strings

If the contents of a string variable should not exceed a certain length, we can declare that variable as a **short string.** Short strings may be used when the maximum length of the data in the string will not exceed 255 characters. The general syntax for dimensioning a short string follows:

```
var
    stringName: String[n];
```

Note that the variable *stringName* occupies $n + 1$ bytes of memory (from 0 to n), where bytes 1 through n contain the characters in the string, the zero-numbered byte contains the size of the string, and n is less than or equal to 255. The `ShortString` data type is equivalent to `String[255]`. The `String[n]` and `ShortString` data types exist primarily to provide backward compatibility with earlier versions of Delphi and Borland Pascal. An example of a short string appears in the following code fragment:

```
var
  myString: String[10];

begin
  myString := 'This is an example';
  memOutput.Lines.Add(myString);
end;
```

When this code executes, the string This is an appears in the memOutput memo box. Why?

The `String` data type is equivalent to the `AnsiString` type that implements **long strings,** or strings whose sizes are limited only by the amount of available memory. Rewriting the previous example using long strings, we have

```
var
  myString: String;

begin
  myString := 'This is an example';
  memOutput.Lines.Add(myString);
end;
```

When this code executes, the string `This is an example` appears in the mem-Output memo box.

Programming Key: Delphi Highlight

`String` was the first string data type used in Borland's Turbo Pascal and was originally implemented as a short string. The default {$H+} or {$LONG STRINGS ON} Delphi compiler directive defines the `String` data type to be equivalent to the `AnsiString` type. The {$H-} or {$LONGSTRINGS OFF} compiler state is useful for working with code from older versions of Delphi or Borland Pascal that use short strings by default. With this setting, you can locally override the meaning of the `String` type definition to ensure the generation of short strings. Alternatively, you can change the `String` variable declarations in the code to `String[255]` or `ShortString`, which are unambiguous and independent of the $H setting.

A string is really just an **array** of characters. In general, an array is an indexed collection of elements of the same data type (called the **base type**). Each character within a string has a unique index value. Figure 4.7 represents the structure of a sample string variable as an array of characters. Chapter 10 discusses array variables and their applications in greater detail.

> The **base type** is the data type assigned to all elements of an array. An **array** (or **array variable**) is an indexed collection of elements of a particular base type.

To access a particular character within any type of string variable, you can use the *stringName[i]* syntax, where *i* is the index

Assume that `myString` is a `String` variable and the following assignment is made:

```
myString:= 'This is an example';
```

The structure and contents of `myString` appear below:

Index	1	2	3	4	5	6	7	8	9	10	11	12	13	14	15	16	17	18
myString	T	h	i	s		i	s		a	n		e	x	a	m	p	l	e

FIGURE 4.7   Example String Variable Structure

of the character within the string (that is, you want to access the *i*th character in the string). The first character in a string variable has an index value of 1, the second character has an index value of 2, and so on. Note that *stringName[i]* is a character, so you can store it in a variable of any character or string type. Additionally, you can use it in assignment statements or as a parameter for a subprogram. The following example illustrates its use:

```
var
   myString: String;
   myChar:   String;
   aChar:    Char;

begin
   myString := 'This is an example';
   myChar := myString[12];
   myChar := UpperCase(myChar);
   aChar := myChar[1];
   myString[12] := aChar;
   memOutput.Lines.Add(myString);
end;
```

What is output in the memOutput memo box when this code executes? The correct answer is: This is an Example.

Programming Key: Tips

A string is a group of characters. On many occasions, a programmer may need to access an individual character within a string. For the string variable *stringName*, *stringName[i]* accesses the *i*th character of the string.

Precedence Rules

Expressions on a computer are not necessarily evaluated from left to right. Instead, operators follow certain **precedence rules** (also known as an **order of operations**), just as they do in mathematics. Figure 4.8 lists the precedence rules for Object Pascal's arithmetic operators. For instance, these rules ensure that we evaluate 10 – 3 * 2 as 4. Multiplication has a higher precedence than subtraction, so we first multiply 3 by 2, resulting in 6. The 6 is then subtracted from 10, giving the final answer of 4. As in mathematics, parentheses may be used to override the order of operations. Evaluation of (10 – 3) * 2 yields 14, for example, because we must evaluate 10 minus 3 first.

1. Identity (+) and negation (–)
2. Multiplication and division (*, /, div, mod)
3. Addition and subtraction (+, –)

When multiplication and division occur together in an expression, each operation is evaluated as it occurs from left to right. Likewise, when addition and subtraction occur together in an expression, each operation is evaluated in order of appearance from left to right.

Parenthetical expressions may be used to override predefined precedence rules.

FIGURE 4.8   Arithmetic Operator Precedence Rules (Order of Operations)

Typecasting and Type Conversion Functions

Object Pascal is a **strongly typed language,** meaning that it distinguishes among a variety of data types and uses specific rules and limitations to indicate which data types can be substituted in place of one another. The benefit of strong typing is that the compiler can treat data intelligently and validate source code more thoroughly, preventing hard-to-diagnose **run-time errors.** As an example of Pascal's strong typing, consider the following code fragment:

```
var
  myChar: Char;
  myByte: Byte;

begin
  myChar := 'A';
  myByte := myChar;
end;
```

> This code generates a compile-time error (or syntax error) because of Object Pascal's strong data typing.

The `Char` and `Byte` data types each require one byte of memory space to store variable values. The preceding code generates a syntax error because we cannot assign a variable of type `Char` to one of type `Byte` (or vice versa) due to Object Pascal's strong typing rules.

Oftentimes, the programmer may desire to perform an operation prohibited by Object Pascal's strong typing, as in the previous example. **Typecasting** is one mechanism used to circumvent the strong typing rules. Essentially, a typecast temporarily changes the data type of an expression. The general syntax for a typecast is *DataType*(`expression`). For example, `Integer('A')` casts the character `A` as an integer. Any variable can be cast to any type, provided that the memory requirements are the same and integers are not mixed with real numbers. To convert between the numeric types, you use the standard type conversion routines, such as `Int` and `Trunc` (discussed later in this section).

We can now correct our previous example as follows:

```
var
  myChar: Char;
  myByte: Byte;

begin
  myChar := 'A';
  myByte := Byte(myChar);
end;
```

> Byte(myChar) typecasts the character variable myChar as a Byte data type.

Typecasting cannot convert values between integers, real numbers, and strings. In contrast, type conversion routines allow you to convert variable values among the different data types. Figure 4.9 summarizes Object Pascal's type conversion routines.

The term **mixed-mode arithmetic** refers to an arithmetic expression that contains variables of different numeric data types. For example, the following code fragment contains no errors:

```
var
  num1:    Real;
  num2:    Integer;
  result:  Real;

begin
  num1 := 7.2;
  num2 := 3;
  result := num1 * num2;
end;
```

> num1 * num2 is a mixed-mode operation.

Function/Procedure	Purpose
CompToCurrency	Converts a Comp value to a Currency value
CompToDouble	Converts a Comp value to a Double value
CurrencyToComp	Converts a Currency value to a Comp value
CurrToStr	Converts a Currency value to a string
CurrToStrF	Converts a Currency value to a string using a specified format
DoubleToComp	Converts a Double value to a Comp value
Int	Returns the integer part of a real value
IntToStr	Converts an integer to a string
Round	Rounds a real value to the nearest integer value
Str	Converts a numeric variable to a string
StrToCurr	Converts a string to a Currency value
StrToInt	Converts a string that represents an integer (decimal or hex notation) to an integer value
StrToInt64	Converts a string that represents an integer (decimal or hex notation) to an Int64 value
Trunc	Truncates a real number to an integer value
Val	Converts a string to a numeric variable

FIGURE 4.9 Type Conversion Routines

In the preceding code, `num1` is a real number and `num2` is an integer. Thus `num1 * num2` is a mixed-mode operation. From Figure 4.9, we see that no explicit data type conversion routine is available to convert an integer to a real number. Such conversion routines are unnecessary because Object Pascal automatically **promotes** numeric variables with lower memory requirements to numeric variables with higher memory requirements. In other words, the type conversion between an integer and a real number is implicit. In this example, `num2` is promoted to a real number to perform the `num1 * num2` calculation, and the result of this calculation, 21.6, is then stored in the real variable `result`. If you attempt to carry out such a mixed-mode operation in another language, the data type promotion may not be automatic and an error will result. When possible, you should avoid mixed-mode arithmetic by using variables of the same data type in arithmetic expressions.

Scope and Lifetime

> The **scope** of an object refers to its availability, or visibility, to specific parts of a program, whereas its **lifetime** refers to the length of its existence in the computer's memory space.

The **scope** of an object refers to its availability, or visibility, to specific parts of a program. The **lifetime** of an object refers to how long the object exists in the computer's memory space. Both scope and lifetime are important programming concepts.

In Object Pascal, declarations and statements are organized into *blocks.* Blocks define the local namespaces (or scopes) for *labels* and *identifiers* within the source code. A block consists of a series of declarations followed by a **compound statement.** All declarations must occur together at the beginning of the block. The general syntax of a block follows:

```
declarations
begin
   statements
end
```

The `declarations` section can include declarations of variables, constants, types, procedures, functions, and labels in any order. Each program, function, and procedure consists of one block.

An identifier, such as a variable name, can be used only within its scope. The location of the identifier's declaration determines its scope. An identifier declared within a program, function, or procedure has a scope limited to the block in which it is declared, for example, whereas an identifier declared in the interface section of a unit has a scope that includes any other units or programs that use this unit. Identifiers with narrower scope—especially those declared in functions and

Location of Identifier Declaration	Extent of Scope
Declaration of a program, function, or procedure	From the point where it is declared to the end of the current block, including all blocks enclosed within that scope
Interface section of a unit	From the point where it is declared to the end of the unit, and to any other unit or program that uses that unit
Implementation section of a unit, but not within the block of any function or procedure	From the point where it is declared to the end of the implementation section; the identifier is available to any function or procedure within that implementation section
The name of a field in a record type	From the point of its declaration to the end of the field type definition
The name of a property or method in a class	From the point of its declaration to the end of the class type definition; also includes descendants of the class and the blocks of all methods in the class and its descendants

FIGURE 4.10   Scope Rules

procedures—are referred to as *local.* Identifiers with a wider scope are called *global.* Figure 4.10 summarizes the rules that determine the identifier scope.

Blocks allow you to use identifiers with the same name in different parts of a program. When one block encloses another, the former is called the *outer block* and the latter is called the *inner block.* If an identifier declared in an outer block is redeclared in an inner block, the inner declaration overrides the outer one for all unqualified (or nonspecific) occurrences of the identifier within the inner block. For instance, assume that the variable `myValue` is declared in the interface section of a unit and redeclared in a function named `Compute` within that unit. All unqualified occurrences of `myValue` in the `Compute` function block will then be governed by the local declaration.

As a variable is one type of identifier, its scope may be either local or global. A variable with a local scope is called a **local variable;** a variable with a global scope is called a **global variable.** We know the scope rules for these types of variables, but what about their lifetimes? When is the memory space for these variables allocated and deallocated? Local variables are available for use only within the subprogram in which they are declared. The variable is allocated memory space (or created) when the subprogram begins, and it is deallocated (or destroyed) when the subprogram ends. Global variables, however, are available to all parts of the program. They are created when the program begins and removed from memory when the program ends.

Figure 4.11 provides an example of variable scope and lifetime. In the figure, the integer variable `myValue` is declared as a global variable in the interface section of the `ScopeEx` unit and as a local variable in the `ShowScope` event handler in the implementation section of this unit. The global variable `myValue` contains the value 1, but the local variable contains the value 2. In the `ShowScope` event handler, the local variable `myValue` **shadows** the global variable of the same name. In other words, the compiler sees all references to the variable `myValue` as pertaining to the local variable in this event handler. To access the global variable `myValue` in the `ShowScope` event handler, you must use a **qualifier,** or an

```
unit ScopeEx;

interface

uses
  Windows, Messages, SysUtils, Classes, Graphics, Controls, Forms, Dialogs,
  StdCtrls;

type
  TfrmScopeExample = class(TForm)
    btnScopeExample: TButton;
    memOutput: TMemo;
    procedure ShowScope(Sender: TObject);
  private
    { Private declarations }
  public
    { Public declarations }
  end;

var
  frmScopeExample: TfrmScopeExample;
  myValue:         Integer;

implementation

{$R *.DFM}

procedure TfrmScopeExample.ShowScope(Sender: TObject);

var
  myValue: Integer;

begin
  myValue := 2;
  memOutput.Lines.Clear;
  memOutput.Lines.Add('In ScopeEx unit:');
  memOutput.Lines.Add('myValue = ' + IntToStr(ScopeEx.myValue));
  memOutput.Lines.Add('');
  memOutput.Lines.Add('In ShowScope event handler:');
  memOutput.Lines.Add('myValue = ' + IntToStr(myValue));
end;

{*****************************************************************************
Main Program for ScopeEx Unit
*****************************************************************************}
begin
  myValue := 1;
end.
```

Program Execution

```
Scope Example                    _ □ ×

        Run Scope Example

In ScopeEx unit:
myValue = 1

In ShowScope event-handler:
myValue = 2
```

FIGURE 4.11 Scope and Lifetime Example

identifier (or group of identifiers) that specifies another identifier. The general syntax of a qualified identifier follows:

qualifier1[.*qualifier2*].*identifier*

where *qualifier1* (and all subsequent qualifiers, such as *qualifier2*) qualify identifier. Thus ScopeEx.myValue is a qualified identifier for the global variable myValue.

Interactive Input and Output

Chapter 2 introduced Dephi's elementary components, such as buttons, edit boxes, and memo boxes. These components constitute the primary method of interactive input and output (I/O) used in this text. You may use edit boxes and memo boxes for both input and output, although this book uses edit boxes exclusively for input and memo boxes for output.

Since Delphi uses Object Pascal, an object-oriented language, all of the components in the VCL (such as buttons, edit boxes, and memo boxes) are objects. Objects have associated **methods** that act on them. Object Pascal, like most object-oriented languages, uses the *dot separator* to separate the object name from its methods and properties. An edit box named `edtExample`, for instance, has a `Text` property that contains the string found in the edit box. To clear the contents of `edtExample` in a program, you would write the following line of code:

```
edtExample.Text := '';
```

This line of code assigns the null string (empty string) to the `Text` property of the edit box `edtExample`. The null string is an apostrophe immediately followed by another apostrophe (nothing appears in between the apostrophes). This technique represents one way to clear the contents of an edit box. Another way to clear an edit box is to use its `Clear` method. That is, the following line of code can be used instead of the previous code to clear the contents of `edtExample`:

```
edtExample.Clear;
```

A memo box has methods that perform tasks associated with clearing the box and displaying lines of text in the box. For a memo box named `memBox`, two of the most important methods are as follows:

`memBox.Clear;`	Clear the contents of `memBox`
`memBox.Lines.Add(newline);`	Add *newline* to the `Lines` property of `memBox`

The example program in Figure 4.12 computes the square root of a number. In this program, the user inputs a number into an edit box (`edtInputNumber`). The user must then click the `Compute Square Root` button (`btnComputeSqrRt`) to have the program perform the calculation and display the output. The output is displayed in a memo box (`memOutput`).

GUI Design Tips

A GUI should lead the user through the data entry process. The `TabOrder` property specifies an order for the different components on a form. A `TabOrder` of 0 indicates the first control object, 1 indicates the second control object, and so on. The user can press the TAB key to move to the next component in the sequence.

Input boxes are another means of interactive user input, whereas message boxes allow for interactive output. Input and message boxes are not predesigned on the form by the programmer at design time but rather open separate windows when the code is encountered at run time. A simplified syntax for using input and message boxes appears below. Consult the Delphi online help facility for more information about input and message boxes.

```
stringVar := InputBox(caption, prompt, default);
```

Displays an input box with the given *caption*, *prompt*, and *default* response. User input is assigned to the string variable *stringVar*.

```
unit SquareRootEx;

interface

uses
  Windows, Messages, SysUtils, Classes, Graphics, Controls, Forms, Dialogs,
  StdCtrls;

type
  TfrmSquareRoot = class(TForm)
    edtInputNumber: TEdit;
    btnComputeSqrRt: TButton;
    memOutput: TMemo;
    lblInputNumber: TLabel;
    procedure SquareRoot(Sender: TObject);
  private
    { Private declarations }
  public
    { Public declarations }
  end;

var
  frmSquareRoot: TfrmSquareRoot;

implementation

{$R *.DFM}

procedure TfrmSquareRoot.SquareRoot(Sender: TObject);

var
  value:  Real;
  code:   Integer;
  result: String;

begin
  Val(edtInputNumber.Text, value, code);
  value := Sqrt(value);
  Str(value, result);
  memOutput.Lines.Add('The square root of ' + edtInputNumber.Text +
                      ' is ' + result);
end;

end.
```

Program Execution

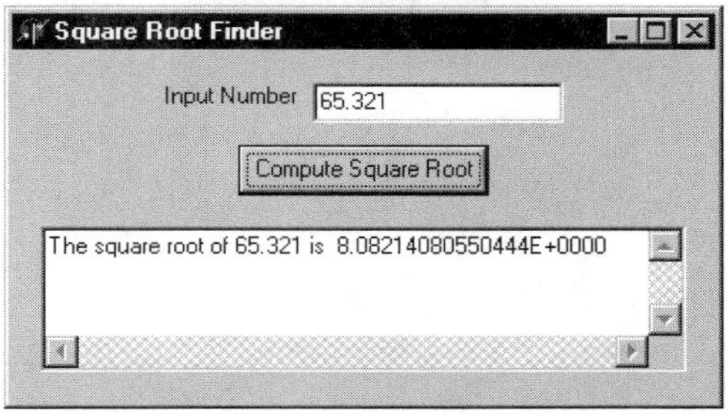

FIGURE 4.12 Square Root Finder

integerVar := Application.MessageBox(*message, caption,*
MB_OK);

Displays a message box with the given *message, caption,* and an OK button. The integer value 1 is returned when the user clicks the OK button.

```
unit SquareRootEx;

interface

uses
  Windows, Messages, SysUtils, Classes, Graphics, Controls, Forms, Dialogs,
  StdCtrls;

type
  TfrmSquareRoot = class(TForm)
    btnComputeSqrRt: TButton;
    procedure SquareRoot(Sender: TObject);
  private
    { Private declarations }
  public
    { Public declarations }
  end;

var
  frmSquareRoot: TfrmSquareRoot;

implementation

{$R *.DFM}

procedure TfrmSquareRoot.SquareRoot(Sender: TObject);

var
  value:  Real;
  code:   Integer;
  number: String;
  result: String;

begin
  number := InputBox('Input Number', 'ENTER A NUMBER', '0');
  Val(number, value, code);
  value := Sqrt(value);
  Str(value, result);
  result := 'The square root of ' + number + ' is ' + result;
  code := Application.MessageBox(PChar(result), 'ANSWER', MB_OK);
end;

end.
```

Program Execution

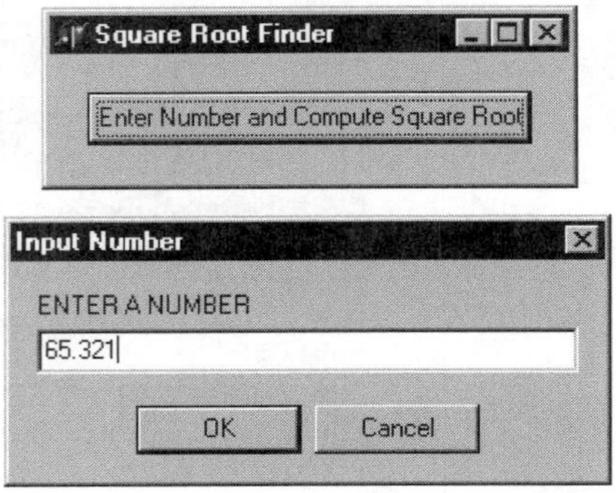

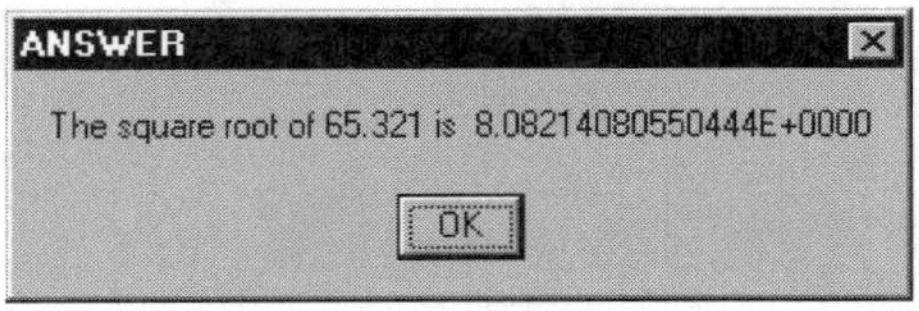

FIGURE 4.13 Modified Square Root Finder

The program in Figure 4.13 performs the same task as the program in Figure 4.12, but it uses input and message boxes. Note that the edit box and memo box are no longer needed on the form; the only object on the form is a button (btnComputeSqrRt).

Output Formatting Routines

As programmers, we desire to control the appearance and presentation of the output of our programs. Delphi provides several powerful, built-in formatting routines for displaying numeric and string data. Figure 4.14 lists the most common output formatting routines. Notice that many of these routines are repeated from earlier figures, as they serve more than one purpose.

Routine	Purpose
FmtStr	Assembles a formatted string using a specified format and an array of arguments
Format	Returns a formatted string assembled from a specified format and an array of arguments
LowerCase	Returns a copy of a string in lowercase
Str	Formats a string and returns it to a variable
Trim	Trims leading and trailing spaces and control characters from a string
TrimLeft	Trims leading spaces and control characters from a string
TrimRight	Trims trailing spaces and control characters from a string
UpperCase	Returns a copy of a string in uppercase

FIGURE 4.14   Output Formatting Routines

Both the FmtStr procedure and the Format function require the use of **format strings.** A format string is a combination of literal characters and format specifiers that indicate a desired format. Delphi's online help provides extensive information concerning format strings and format specifiers. Rather than reiterate this information here, let's look at a simple example:

```
Format('%10.2n', [6154.2287259]);
```

This function call returns the string '   6,154.23' (without the single quotes). Note that this string contains two leading spaces. The '%10.2n' format specifier means that the returned string has a fixed length of 10 characters with 2 digits appearing after the decimal point, and the string appears in numeric format with thousands separators (commas).

Ending a Program

Your programs should provide the user with a means of graceful termination. In other words, the user should not have to reboot (or restart) the computer to exit your program. Normally, Windows applications provide buttons in the title bar that enable the user to minimize and maximize the application window and close the application. These same functions may also be accessed through the system menu by left-clicking the icon in the upper-left corner of the application's title bar. Rather than relying on the system menu or the X button, you can create your own "exit" buttons in your programs. Also, you can write programs that end automatically once they complete their processing.

To exit an application, use the Terminate method of the Application object. Thus the following code exits an application: Application.Terminate. The example code segment shown below exits the application when the user clicks the Exit button:

```
{End the application when the user clicks the Exit button}
procedure TfrmExitExample.ExitProgram(Sender: TObject);
begin
  Application.Terminate;
end;
```

Program Readability

Programming is the ultimate means of self-expression on a computer. Like an artist who creates a beautiful painting, programmers often feel well-deserved pride and accomplishment in their work. Computer programming can also give you feelings of great power; the computer dances at your command. An artist's painting is worthless, however, unless other people have the opportunity to enjoy it. Like the artist conveying thoughts and emotions through canvas, a programmer communicates ideas through source code. Remember, a program not only is a means of informing the computer of your desires but also communicates your ideas to other people. Programmers clarify and explain source code by using comments. Just as a cookbook describes the details of a recipe with comments, you should add comments to your program.

Comments placed at the beginning of your source code should include the program title, program purpose or description, programmer's name, program version number, date programmed, and date last modified. Not every line of source code needs to be commented. In fact, you should use comment sparingly in your source code. Remember, the idea is to make your source code self-commenting by using descriptive names for objects, variables, constants, functions, and procedures. Place comments at the beginning of each function and procedure to describe its purpose, required parameters, and output. Furthermore, it is better practice to place comments before a large block of code to describe what the block as a whole does rather than comment each line of the code.

Indenting code and adding white space (blank lines) both greatly enhance program readability. Indenting code within control structures by two or three spaces is usually sufficient. As you will see, the examples in this book use indentation and white space to enhance readability. You should adopt a method of indentation and white space with which you are comfortable and that suits your programming style.

Delphi's Object Pascal compiler ignores comments and white space, except when the comments function as separators or compiler directives. Object Pascal offers several ways to construct comments. The syntax for comments follows:

```
{Text that appears between a left brace and a right brace
constitutes a comment}

(*Text that appears between a left parenthesis followed
by an asterisk and an asterisk followed by a right
parenthesis constitutes a comment*)

// Text between a double-slash and the end of the line
// constitutes a comment
```

A comment that contains a dollar sign ($) immediately after the opening { or (* is a compiler directive. For instance, {$WARNINGS OFF} directs the compiler not to generate warning messages. Compiler directives are introduced as necessary throughout this text and discussed in greater detail in Chapter 17.

As an aid to the programmer and to improve the readability of the source code, the Delphi code editor uses italics and a blue font color for comments.

Your Second Program

As your second program, you will create a temperature conversion program. The purpose of this program is to convert between temperatures measured in Fahrenheit and Celsius. The relationship between temperatures in Fahrenheit (°F) and Celsius (°C) is as follows:

$$°F = 32 + (9/5)(°C)$$

Figure 4.15 displays the form used in this program. This form contains one label, one edit box, two buttons, and one memo box. Create a form that contains these components and modify the component property settings to match those listed in the following table:

Component	Property	Setting
Form	Name	frmTempConv
	Caption	Temperature Conversion
Label	Name	lblTempData
	Caption	Enter a temperature
Edit Box	Name	edtTempData
	Text	*Empty*
Button	Name	btnFtoC
	Caption	Convert Fahrenheit to &Celsius
Button	Name	btnCtoF
	Caption	Convert Celsius to &Fahrenheit
Memo Box	Name	memOutput
	Lines	*Empty*
	ReadOnly	True
	ScrollBars	ssVertical

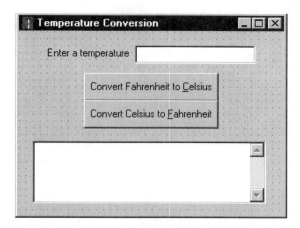

FIGURE 4.15   Form for the Temperature Conversion Program

Next, modify the event settings for the components in the Object Inspector window as follows:

Component Name	Event	Setting
btnFtoC	OnClick	ConvertFtoC
btnCtoF	OnClick	ConvertCtoF

Now, open the Code Editor window and type in the code so that it matches Figure 4.16.

After you type in the code, run your program by clicking the Run button on the Debug toolbar, selecting Run | Run from the menu bar, or pressing the F9 key. Enter the number 25 in the edit box and click the Convert Celsius to Fahrenheit button. The program informs you that 25.00°C is equivalent to 77.00°F. Now type 98.6 in the edit box and press ALT+C (the shortcut for the Convert Fahrenheit to Celsius button). Make sure that the program tells you the answer is 37.00°C, as shown in Figure 4.17.

Finally, convert any temperature that you desire. When have finished, click the X button in the upper-right corner of the program window.

```
{****************************************************************************
Temperature Conversion Program
------------------------------
This program converts temperatures between Fahrenheit and Celsius units

Applicable formulae:

F = 32 + (9/5)C
C = (5/9)(F - 32)
****************************************************************************}
unit TemperatureConversion;

interface

uses
  Windows, Messages, SysUtils, Classes, Graphics, Controls, Forms, Dialogs,
  StdCtrls;

type
  TfrmTempConv = class(TForm)
    edtTempData: TEdit;
    lblTempData: TLabel;
    btnFtoC: TButton;
    memOutput: TMemo;
    btnCtoF: TButton;
    procedure ConvertFtoC(Sender: TObject);
    procedure ConvertCtoF(Sender: TObject);
  private
    { Private declarations }
  public
    { Public declarations }
  end;

const
  DEGREE = Chr(176);

var
  frmTempConv: TfrmTempConv;

implementation

{$R *.DFM}
```

FIGURE 4.16   Source Code for the Temperature Conversion Program

```
{------------------------------------------------------------------------------
Convert temperature in edtTempData edit box from Fahrenheit to Celsius and
display the result in memOutput memo box.
------------------------------------------------------------------------------}
procedure TfrmTempConv.ConvertFtoC(Sender: TObject);

var
  code:      Integer;
  degreesF: Real;
  degreesC: Real;
  fromF:     String;
  toC:       String;

begin
  Val(edtTempData.Text, degreesF, code);
  degreesC := (5.0/9.0)*(degreesF - 32.0);
  Str(degreesF:6:2, fromF);
  Str(degreesC:6:2, toC);
  fromF := Trim(fromF + DEGREE + 'F');
  toC := Trim(toC + DEGREE + 'C');
  memOutput.Lines.Add(fromF + ' is ' + toC);
end;

{------------------------------------------------------------------------------
Convert temperature in edtTempData edit box from Celsius to Fahrenheit and
display the result in memOutput memo box.
------------------------------------------------------------------------------}
procedure TfrmTempConv.ConvertCtoF(Sender: TObject);

var
  code:      Integer;
  degreesF: Real;
  degreesC: Real;
  fromC:     String;
  toF:       String;

begin
  Val(edtTempData.Text, degreesC, code);
  degreesF := 32.0 + (9.0/5.0)*degreesC;
  Str(degreesF:6:2, toF);
  Str(degreesC:6:2, fromC);
  toF := Trim(toF + DEGREE + 'F');
  fromC := Trim(fromC + DEGREE + 'C');
  memOutput.Lines.Add(fromC + ' is ' + toF);
end;
```

FIGURE 4.16   *(continued)*

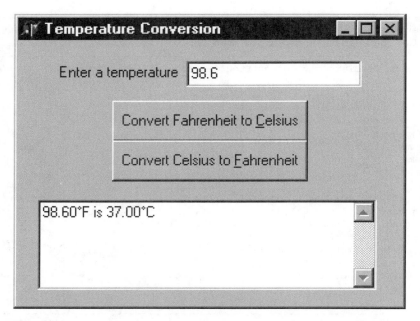

FIGURE 4.17   Sample Execution of the Temperature Conversion Program

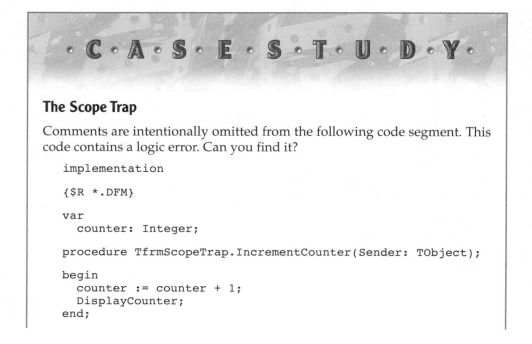

The Scope Trap

Comments are intentionally omitted from the following code segment. This code contains a logic error. Can you find it?

```
implementation

{$R *.DFM}

var
  counter: Integer;

procedure TfrmScopeTrap.IncrementCounter(Sender: TObject);

begin
  counter := counter + 1;
  DisplayCounter;
end;
```

```
procedure TfrmScopeTrap.ResetCounter(Sender: TObject);

begin
  counter := 0;
  DisplayCounter;
end;

procedure TfrmScopeTrap.SetTo1(Sender: TObject);

var
  counter: Integer;

begin
  counter := 1;
  DisplayCounter;
end;

procedure TfrmScopeTrap.DisplayCounter;

begin
  memOutput.Lines.Add(IntToStr(counter));
end;

{Unit Main}
begin
  counter := 0;
end.
```

This code contains a global variable named `counter`. The `Display-Counter` procedure prints the value of this variable in the `memOutput` memo box. The `SetTo1` event handler (incorrectly) contains a local variable also named `counter`. Thus, this event handler sets the local variable `counter` to 1, not the global variable. In summary, the value of the global variable `counter` is not affected by the `SetTo1` event handler. This type of mistake is common among novice programmers.

Summary

Key Terms

alphanumeric data—A subset of character data that consists of letters and numbers but no symbols.

ANSI—American National Standards Institute.

array (array variable)—An indexed collection of elements of the same data type.

ASCII—American Standard Code for Information Interchange.

base type—The data type for all elements of an array variable.

binary operator—An operator that requires two operands.

case insensitive—Refers to a program's inability to recognize a difference between uppercase and lowercase letters; not case sensitive.

case sensitive—Refers to a program's ability to recognize a difference between uppercase and lowercase letters.

character—A string consisting of only one character; a string of length 1.

character data—Data consisting of letters, numbers, symbols, or any combination thereof.

code fragment—An incomplete portion of source code.

code segment—A portion of source code.

compile time—The time when a program's source code is translated into machine language and an executable file is created.

compound statement—In Object Pascal, the statements appearing between the `begin` and `end` keywords.

concatenation—An operation that combines strings in a prescribed left-to-right order.

constant—A named item that retains the same value throughout the execution of a program.

control character—In Delphi, a sequence of the # symbol followed by an integer value between 0 and 255 that denotes the corresponding ASCII character.

data type—A keyword that describes the size of a variable and the range of values that it may contain.

declare—To associate a variable with a data type and reserve memory space for the variable.

empty string—See *null string*.

format string—A combination of literal characters and format specifiers that indicate a desired format.

global variable—A variable that is available to all parts of a program; a variable with global scope.

hard-coded—Refers to numeric constants and string constants that appear in a program's source code.

initialization—The process of assigning an initial value to a variable.

integer—A number with no fractional component.

integer division—A division operation that returns only the integer part of the quotient; any fractional portion of the quotient is simply truncated or ignored.

keyword—A reserved word or symbol recognized as part of a programming language.

lifetime—The length of an object's existence in the computer's memory space.

local variable—A variable that is available for use only within the subprogram in which it is declared; a variable with local scope.

logic error—An error in the logic of a program or algorithm.

long string—In Object Pascal, a string whose size is limited only by the amount of available memory.

method—A subprogram that is associated with an object. Typically, a method alters the properties of its associated object.

mixed-mode arithmetic—An arithmetic expression that contains variables of different numeric data types.

modulo division—A division operation that returns only the integer remainder.

nonexecutable statement—A statement that is not compiled into executable code, such as a comment or compiler directive.

null string—The string containing no characters; the string of length 0.

numeric constant—A number; a numeric literal.

numeric data—Data consisting of numbers.

operand—A value or expression used by an operator.

operator—A symbol that denotes a mathematical or string operation.

order of operations—See *precedence rules.*

overloaded operator—An operator that performs different operations depending on the context in which it is used.

precedence rules—A designated order of carrying out operations to evaluate an expression.

promote—To change a variable's data type to one that requires more memory space.

qualifier—An identifier or group of identifiers that specify another identifier.

range—the bounds or limits of a variable's possible values.

real (real number)—A number with a fractional component.

run-time error—An error that occurs while a program is executing or running.

scope—An object's availability, or visibility, to specific parts of a program.

self-commenting—Refers to a program element with a name that describes its contents or purpose.

shadowing—Refers to a local variable inhibiting the visibility of a global variable with the same name.

short string—In Object Pascal, a string that does not exceed 255 characters in length.

statement separator—A symbol that separates one statement from another statement.

string—A group of characters.

string constant—A string literal.

string variable—A variable that contains character data.

strongly typed language—A computer programming language that distinguishes among a variety of data types and imposes specific rules and limitations on the substitution of data types.

syntax—Structure or grammar.

syntax error—An error in the grammar or punctuation of the source code.

typecasting—A method of temporarily changing the data type of an expression to circumvent strong typing rules.

unary operator—An operator that requires only one operand.

Unicode character set—A character set in which each character is represented by two bytes.

variable—A quantity that can assume any value; a named memory location that stores a value.

wide character—A Unicode character.

wide string—A string of Unicode characters.

Keywords

Compiler Directives

{$H−} or {$LONGSTRINGS OFF}

{$H+} or {$LONGSTRINGS ON}

{$J−} or {$WRITEABLECONST OFF}

{$J+} or {$WRITEABLECONST ON}

{$WARNINGS OFF}

Data Types

AnsiChar	Byte
AnsiString	ByteBool
Boolean	Cardinal

Char	Real48
Comp	Shortint
Currency	ShortString
Double	Single
Extended	Smallint
Int64	String
Integer	WideChar
LongBool	WideString
Longint	Word
Longword	WordBool
Real	

Methods

Add	Terminate
Clear	

Operators

−	:=
*	div
/	mod
+	

Properties

Caption	ScrollBars
Lines	TabOrder
Name	Text
ReadOnly	

Routines

Abs	CurrToStr
Ceil	CurrToStrF
Chr	Delete
CompareStr	DoubleToComp
CompareText	Exp
CompToCurrency	Floor
CompToDouble	FmtStr
Concat	Format
Copy	Frac
CurrencyToComp	InputBox

Insert	Power
Int	QuotedStr
IntPower	Round
IntToStr	SetLength
IsDelimiter	SetString
LastDelimiter	ShowMessage
Ldexp	Sqr
Length	Sqrt
Ln	Str
LnXP1	StringOfChar
Log2	StringReplace
Log10	StrToCurr
LogN	StrToInt
LowerCase	StrToInt64
Max	Trim
MessageBox	TrimLeft
MessageDlg	TrimRight
Min	Trunc
Ord	UpperCase
Pi	Val
Pos	WrapText
Statements	
(* *)	const
//	end
{ }	var
begin	

Key Concepts

- Several elements of programming are common to all computer languages, including variables, constants, data types, scope and lifetime, and comments.

- A variable's value can change throughout program execution. A variable can contain either numeric or character data.

- Variables are assigned data types to limit the amount of memory they require and to inform the computer (and programmers) of the type of data they store. The var statement is used to declare variables:

```
var
  variableName[, variableName]: DataType;
  [variableName[, variableName]: DataType;]
```

- The programmer should explicitly initialize all variables by using the assignment operator (:=). In a variable assignment, the variable name must appear on the left side of the := operator:

```
variableName := expression;
```

- A constant maintains the same value throughout the program. Two types of constants exist: named constants and hard-coded (or literal) constants. The const statement allows the programmer to define named constants. Named constants are preferred because they are typically self-commenting and easier to change. The general syntax follows:

```
const
  constantName = Expression;
  [constantName = Expression;]
```

- Arithmetic and string operators provide the means to perform computations. All computations are performed in strict adherence to the operator precedence rules.

- Delphi contains a variety of built-in math functions and string routines, making it an extremely powerful and versatile programming platform.

- Every character in the computer has an associated ASCII (or ANSI) value. The Ord function returns the ASCII value of a character. The Chr function returns the character associated with a particular ASCII value.

- A short string is a string that does not exceed 255 characters in length. To dimension a short string, use the following syntax with the integer n less than or equal to 255:

```
var
  stringName: String[n];
```

- To access a particular character within a string variable, use the *stringName[i]* syntax, where i is the index of the character within the string. The first character in a string variable has an index value of 1, the second character has an index value of 2, and so on. *stringName[i]* contains a character, so it can be used as a character variable within a program.

- Object Pascal is a strongly typed language. Typecasting is one mechanism used to circumvent strong typing rules by temporarily changing the data type of an expression. The general syntax for a typecast is *DataType(expression)*. Additionally, data type conversion routines explicitly convert a variable value from one data type to another.

- Scope refers to the visibility of an object, whereas lifetime is the duration of an object's existence in the computer's memory space. For example, a variable's scope may be either local or global.

- Edit boxes and memo boxes are the primary means of interactive input and output in Delphi. To clear an edit box, use

```
edtBox.Text := '';
```

or

```
edtBox.Clear;
```

Methods for a memo box include

```
memBox.Clear;                    {Clear the contents of
                                  memBox}
memBox.Lines.Add(newline);       {Add newline to the
                                  Lines property of
                                  memBox}
```

- Input boxes and message boxes may also be used for input and output, respectively. To read data from an input box into *stringVar,* use

```
stringVar := InputBox(caption, prompt, default);
```

To output *message* to a message box with an OK button and a title of *caption,* use

```
integerVar := Application.MessageBox(message,
                  caption, MB_OK);
```

- Delphi provides several powerful, built-in formatting routines for displaying numeric and string data. These routines allow the programmer to control the appearance and presentation of the program output. Both the `FmtStr` procedure and `Format` function require the use of format strings. A format string is a combination of literal characters and format specifiers that indicate a desired format.

- Programs should provide a means of graceful termination. To exit an application, use the `Terminate` method of the `Application` object as follows:

```
Application.Terminate;
```

- Comments and white space can greatly improve the readability of code. Object Pascal offers several ways to construct comments:

```
{  comment  }
(* comment *)
// comment
```

Review Questions

1. What is a variable? How does it differ from a constant?
2. Why should you assign a data type to a variable?

3. Which statement do you use to declare variables? To declare constants?
4. Why is it important to initialize variables?
5. Which data types can contain numeric data? Character data?
6. What is the assignment operator? Give an example of its use.
7. What is the difference between hard-coded and named constants? Which are preferred and why?
8. What are integer division and modulo division? Which operators are associated with each?
9. Write the code to assign the letter "m" to the tenth character in the variable `myString`.
10. What is the purpose of typecasting?
11. The variable `myReal` contains the value 12.00. How can you assign the value in `myReal` to the variable `myInteger`?
12. What are scope and lifetime? How do they apply to variables?
13. State the advantages and disadvantages of global variables.
14. How do you clear an edit box? A memo box?
15. What are input boxes and message boxes?
16. Write the line of code that gracefully ends a program.
17. What can a programmer do to improve the readability of his or her code?
18. Why is it important to comment your code? How do you construct a comment in Object Pascal?

Problems

1. Change the program in Figure 4.12 to find the cube root of a number entered by the user. Use an edit box for input and a memo box for output.
2. Repeat Problem 1 using an input box for input and a message box for output.
3. Modify the program in Figure 4.16 to use an input box to input the temperature and a message box to display the result.
4. Write a program that allows the user to enter his or her first and last names in two separate edit boxes and then outputs the last name, a comma, and the first name on the same line in a memo box.
5. Write a program that allows the user to enter his or her first, middle, and last names in three separate edit boxes and then outputs the user's initials in a memo box.
6. Write a program that computes a vehicle's *average velocity* using the formula shown below, where *distance* and *time* are user inputs.

$$\text{average velocity} = \text{distance} \div \text{time}$$

7. *The Car Chase Problem.* A speeding car is traveling at x miles per hour. A police car in pursuit of the speeder is traveling at y miles per hour, where $y > x$. If the police car is initially a distance d away from the speeder, how long does it take the police car to catch the speeder and how far must the police car travel to do so? Write a program to solve this problem, where x, y, and d are user inputs. Remember to account for both cases: (1) the speeder is traveling toward the police car, and (2) the speeder is traveling away from the police car.

8. The speed of light, c, is approximately 3×10^8 meters per second. Write a program that prompts the user to input a time in seconds and then displays the distance that light travels during that time period.

9. Use your program from Problem 8 to find the approximate distance of a *light-year*, the distance that light travels in one year. Modify your program from Problem 8 to display the distance in feet, meters, kilometers, and miles. (That there are 3.28 feet per meter and 1.61 kilometers per mile.)

10. The *quadratic formula* can solve for the roots of a *quadratic equation* of the form $ax^2 + bx + c = 0$. The quadratic formula is shown below:

$$x = \frac{-b \pm \sqrt{b^2 - 4ac}}{2a}$$

Write a program that allows the user to input values for a, b, and c, and then displays the two roots of x. Do not worry about imaginary roots, and assume that the value of a is always nonzero.

11. The *normal distribution,* or *Gaussian distribution,* is the most important continuous probability distribution in statistics. The *probability density function (pdf)* of the normal random variable X, with mean μ and standard deviation σ, gives the probability that X is equal to some value x. It is defined as follows:

$$N(x, \mu, \sigma) = \frac{1}{\sigma\sqrt{(2\pi)}} e^{-(1/2)[(x-\mu)/\sigma]^2}$$

for $-\infty < x < +\infty$, where $-\infty < \mu < +\infty$ and $\sigma > 0$, π is approximately 3.14159, and e is approximately 2.71828. Write a program that displays the normal probability density for user-entered values of x, μ, and σ.

12. A *cumulative distribution function (cdf)* for a random variable X gives the probability that X is less than or equal to some value x. The cdf for the *exponential distribution* is defined as follows:

$$P(X \leq x; \lambda) = 1 - e^{-\lambda x}, \qquad x \geq 0$$
$$0, \qquad x < 0$$

Write a program that displays the cumulative probability of the exponential distribution for user-entered values of x and λ.

Programming Projects

1. Modify Problem 12 to solve for x, the point where the exponential cdf equals a value of y. The user should input the values of y and λ, and your program should then solve for x.

2. Beaumont High School has one laser printer that serves its entire computer lab (30 machines). The school is considering the purchase of an additional laser printer for the lab, but the administration would like to know the average waiting time for the current configuration. On average, the printer receives one print job every three minutes, and it has the capacity to print 30 jobs per hour. Write a program to find the average number of jobs in the print queue and the average amount of time that a student spends waiting for a printout. The applicable formulae appear below:

   λ = the average number of jobs received per time period (arrival rate)

   μ = the average number of jobs printed per time period (service rate)

   L_q = average number of jobs in the print queue = $\dfrac{\lambda^2}{\mu(\mu-\lambda)}$

   W = average time that a student spends waiting for a printout = $\dfrac{1}{\mu-\lambda}$

   How do the results change if the school replaces the laser printer with a high-speed model that has the capacity to print 45 jobs per hour?

Chapter 5

Decision Structures

Chapter Objectives

In this chapter you will:

- Become familiar with the relational and Boolean operators and the precedence rules for these operators

- Gain an understanding of Boolean expressions and the difference between complete and short-circuit Boolean evaluation

- Learn DeMorgan's laws and understand how they relate to both computer science and mathematics

- Expand and reduce Boolean expressions

- Use truth tables to evaluate and compare Boolean expressions

- Learn the two types of decision structures, the appropriate situations for their use, and ways to convert from one structure to the other

- Gain an understanding of sequential and nested statements

- Learn about programming style and programming standards

So far, you have seen that a computer executes program code sequentially from the beginning of the program to the end. Sometimes, however, a programmer wants the computer to execute specific code based on the presence (or absence) of certain conditions. This type of operation requires a programming construct formally known as a **decision structure.** All decision structures involve the comparison of two or more expressions.

Comparisons

To understand decision structures, you must first learn the various operators involved with creating such structures. A decision structure may consist of both **relational operators** and **Boolean** (or **logical**) **operators.**

Relational Operators

> **An expression** is a combination of keywords, operators, variables, and constants that yields a string, number, or object.

For any two expressions A and B of the same type, one of three conditions must exist: $A < B$, $A = B$, or $A > B$. Formally, an **expression** is a combination of keywords, operators, variables, and constants that yields a string, number, or object. Relational operators are used to compare expressions. As in mathematics, you can combine relational operators in computer programming to test whether $A \leq B$, $A \geq B$, or $A \neq B$. Figure 5.1 lists the Object Pascal relational operators and their mathematical counterparts. These relational operators are found in most high-level languages.

A relational operator that compares two expressions forms a **Boolean** (or **logical**) **expression,** which evaluates to be either True or False. The result of a Boolean expression that contains numeric expressions is self-explanatory. For instance, the Boolean expression 5 < 2 is False, whereas 5 > 2 is True. String expressions are evaluated according to the ASCII values of their characters. For example, "A" has ASCII value 65 and "a" has ASCII value 97, so the following Boolean expression is evaluated to be True:

```
'America' < 'america'
```

Another example is shown below. This time the Boolean expression is False. Can you see why?

```
'America' < 'AMERICA'
```

Relational Operator	Object Pascal	Mathematics
Less than	<	<
Less than or equal to	<=	$\leq$
Greater than	>	>
Greater than or equal to	>=	$\geq$
Equal to	=	=
Not equal to	<>	$\neq$

FIGURE 5.1   Object Pascal Relational Operators

A	B	A and B	A or B	not A	not B
False	False	False	False	True	True
False	True	False	True	True	False
True	False	False	True	False	True
True	True	True	True	False	False

FIGURE 5.2   Truth Table for and, or, and not Boolean Operators

Programming Key: Warning

Be careful when you are using relational operators with string expressions, as these expressions are evaluated according to their ASCII values. Results of these Boolean expressions are not intuitive.

Boolean Operators

Boolean operators are used to combine Boolean (logical) expressions. The three primary Boolean operators are and, or, and not. All other Boolean operators can be derived from these primary Boolean operators, but are beyond the scope of this text. To show the results of combining Boolean expressions with Boolean operators, you typically use **truth tables,** as shown in Figure 5.2.

A **truth table** displays the evaluation of a Boolean expression for all possible combinations of variable values.

As Figure 5.2 also shows, the and operator performs a **logical conjunction** of two expressions; the result is True only if *both* expressions evaluate to True. The or operator performs a **logical disjunction** of two expressions; the result is True if *either or both* expressions evaluate to True. Finally, the not operator performs a **logical negation** of an expression; the result is the opposite of the expression evaluation.

Programming Key: Delphi Highlight

The Delphi compiler supports two modes of evaluation for Boolean expressions: **complete evaluation** and **short-circuit** (or **partial**) **evaluation.** These evaluation modes apply to the and and or operators. In complete evaluation, each conjunct or disjunct is evaluated, even when the result of the entire expression is already determined. Given the expression A or B, for example, if A is True, then the result of the expression evaluation must be True. Nevertheless, the compiler requires the evaluation of expression B. Short-circuit evaluation, on the other hand, follows a strict left-to-right evaluation that stops once the result of the entire expression is determined. Using the A or

B example again, the expression is evaluated as True once A is known to be True; the compiler does not evaluate expression B.

Complete evaluation is useful when one operand is a function with side effects that alter the execution of the program. Short-circuit evaluation is usually preferred because it allows for faster execution of code and, in most cases, minimum code size. Short-circuit evaluation also allows the use of constructions that might otherwise result in illegal run-time operations. For example, consider the following Boolean expression:

```
(denom <> 0.0) and ((numer/denom) > 1.0)
```

If `denom` equals zero, then the first expression is False. Therefore, short-circuit evaluation would evaluate the entire expression as False. Complete evaluation, however, results in a run-time error because the second expression attempts a division-by-zero operation.

The default compiler state is `{$B—}` or `{$BOOLEVAL OFF}`, enabling short-circuit evaluation. To enable complete evaluation locally, use the `{$B+}` or `{$BOOLEVAL ON}` directive in your code. You can switch to complete evaluation on a project-wide basis by selecting `Project| Options...` and placing a check mark in the Complete Boolean evaluation box in the Syntax options frame of the Compiler tab.

Relational and Boolean Operator Precedence

All relational operators have equal precedence and are evaluated from left to right, in the order in which they appear. For the Boolean operators, `not` has the highest precedence, followed by `and`, and then `or`. When an expression contains operators of more than one type, mathematical operators are evaluated first, relational operators are evaluated next, and Boolean operators are evaluated last. You may insert parentheses to override the precedence rules or to improve program readability when the same expression includes operators of different types. Figure 5.3 provides an example.

Which of the following Boolean expressions is easier to read and evaluate?
Does this Boolean expression evaluate to True or False?

Without parentheses:

```
3 * 5 > 8 * 2 or 6 * 7 < 100 - 5 * 5
```

With parentheses:

```
((3 * 5) > (8 * 2)) or ((6 * 7) < (100 - (5 * 5)))
```

Answers: With parentheses; True

FIGURE 5.3   Use of Parentheses to Improve Program Readability When Using Operators of Different Types in the Same Expression

DeMorgan's Laws

DeMorgan's laws relate to the negation of Boolean expressions and Boolean operators. They are used to reduce or expand Boolean expressions into equivalent Boolean expressions. DeMorgan's laws have many applications in mathematics, probability, and computer science. In fact, a direct parallel can be drawn between these laws in set theory and computer science, as shown in Figure 5.4.

Expanding and Reducing Boolean Expressions

In practice, both DeMorgan's laws and Boolean algebra are used to expand and reduce Boolean expressions. The result of these operations often yields an expression in which the logic is clearer and easier to follow. This process is akin to the mathematical reduction of expressions. For instance, which is easier to

Set Theory	Computer Science
not(A $\cap$ B) = not(A) $\cup$ not(B)	not(A and B) = not(A) or not(B)
not(A $\cup$ B) = not(A) $\cap$ not(B)	not(A or B) = not(A) and not(B)

FIGURE 5.4   DeMorgan's Laws

$$A \wedge (B \vee C) = (A \wedge B) \vee (A \wedge C)$$

A	B	C	B or C	A and (B or C)	A and B	A and C	(A and B) or (A and C)
False	False	False	False	False	False	False	False
False	False	True	True	False	False	False	False
False	True	False	True	False	False	False	False
False	True	True	True	False	False	False	False
True	False	False	False	False	False	False	False
True	False	True	True	True	False	True	True
True	True	False	True	True	True	False	True
True	True	True	True	True	True	True	True

Equivalent Expressions

FIGURE 5.5 Use of a Truth Table to Confirm the Equality of Boolean Expressions

comprehend: $(6/3)^2 + 4^3 + (3.5 \times 2) + (5 \times 10) - 5^2$ or 100? Obviously, 100 is the preferred expression because it is easier to understand.

Many texts use a shorthand notation when writing Boolean expressions. In this section, we will use the customary shorthand notation when discussing examples of the expansion and reduction of Boolean expressions. The and operator is typically replaced by $\wedge$, and the or operator is replaced by $\vee$. The not operator is indicated by either a tilde (~) preceding the Boolean expression or a line above the Boolean expression. Here the tilde (~) serves as the not operator. Thus the expression A and (not B) translates to $A \wedge (\sim B)$ in this shorthand notation. Do not forget the precedence rules for Boolean operators, however. In the preceding example, the parentheses are not really necessary in either notation because not has a higher precedence than and, but they are added for clarity.

The expansion of a Boolean expression is relatively straightforward. An example follows:

$$A \wedge (B \vee C) = (A \wedge B) \vee (A \wedge C)$$

Figure 5.5 uses a truth table to confirm the equality of the expressions on both sides of the equals sign. To reduce this Boolean expression to its original form, we can simply "factor out" the A from each "term." Alternatively, we can continue to expand the expression and then logically reduce terms as shown below.

$(A \wedge B) \vee (A \wedge C) =$

$((A \wedge B) \vee A) \wedge ((A \wedge B) \vee C) =$

{first parenthetical expression reduces to A}

$A \wedge ((A \wedge B) \vee C) =$

{expand the second parenthetical expression}

$A \wedge ((A \vee C) \wedge (B \vee C)) =$

{expand this expression about A}

$(A \wedge (A \vee C)) \wedge (A \wedge (B \vee C)) =$

{first parenthetical expression reduces to A}

$$A \wedge (A \wedge (B \vee C)) =$$

$$\{A \wedge A \text{ evaluates to } A, \text{ so we get}\}$$

$$A \wedge (B \vee C)$$

Logical reduction is important in producing tighter (that is, more compact) code. We will employ logical reduction of expressions further in our discussion of decision structures.

Programming Key: Tips

How can we reduce the following Boolean expression:

```
(x = 10) or (x > 10)
```

The equivalent Boolean expression is simply `x >= 10`. The main point here is that the `<=`, `>=`, and `<>` operators are all combinations of two separate operators. The following table shows long Boolean expressions and their equivalent short expressions:

Long Expression	Equivalent Short Expression
`(x = 10) or (x > 10)`	`x >= 10`
`(x = 10) or (x < 10)`	`x <= 10`
`(x < 10) or (x > 10)`	`x <> 10`

Programming Key: Tips

In practice, we must often employ a combination of Boolean and mathematical logic to find equivalent expressions. This process may require negating relational operators as well as Boolean operators. Consider the following example:

```
(not((x > 5) or (x < 5))) or (not((y < 10) or (y =10 )))
```

By converting to equivalent short relational expressions, we obtain:

```
(not(x <> 5)) or (not(y <= 10))
```

Finally, by negating the relational operators, we find the simplified expression:

```
(x = 5) or (y > 10)
```

Decisions

Object Pascal contains two decision structures: **if** statements and **case** statements.

if Statements

In Object Pascal, if statements are very similar to subjunctive statements in English. For instance, consider the following subjunctive statement:

> If my average golf score is 10 or more strokes less than yours, then I will give you a 5-stroke handicap on our next game.

This statement can be directly translated into Object Pascal code as shown in the following code fragment:

```
handicap := 0;
difference := yourAverageScore − myAverageScore;
if (difference >= 10) then begin
  handicap := 5;
end;
```

In Object Pascal and most other high-level languages, if statements form the primary decision structure. The general form for a *simple* if statement, called an **if-then** statement, is shown below:

```
if condition then begin
  [statements;]
end;
```

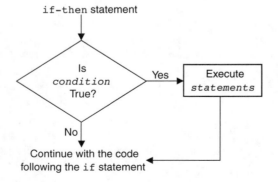

FIGURE 5.6 Flowchart for an if-then Statement

All of the statements between the `begin` and `end` keywords are executed only when *condition* is True, and *condition* must be a Boolean expression. Figure 5.6 displays a flowchart for an `if-then` statement.

An `if-then` structure that contains no statements to be executed when *condition* is True is called an **empty `if` statement.** Because they serve no practical purpose, empty `if` statements should be removed from the source code.

Programming Key: Tips

When the `then` clause of an `if-then` statement contains only one statement, a compound statement is unnecessary and the `begin` and `end` keywords may be omitted. For instance, we can rewrite the previous example as follows:

```
if (difference >= 10) then handicap := 5;
```

As a style convention, we recommend always using compound statements delimited by `begin` and `end` keywords in your code structures. This practice enhances the readability of the source code and prevents syntax errors when a programmer inserts an additional line of code into the structured statement. The Object Pascal Programming Standards (Appendix C) and the general syntax displayed throughout this text follow this style convention.

Some decisions require more complex structures than simple `if-then` statements. Consider modifying our subjunctive statement:

If my average golf score is 10 or more strokes less than yours, then I will give you a 5-stroke handicap on our next game. Otherwise, I will give you a 2-stroke handicap.

This example requires the more advanced **if-then-else** statement. The simple form of the `if-then-else` statement follows:

```
if condition then begin
    [statements1;]
end
else begin
    [statements2;]
end;
```

Simple `if-then-else` statement

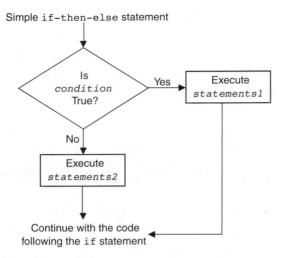

FIGURE 5.7   Flowchart for a Simple `if-then-else` Statement

Figure 5.7 shows a flowchart for the simple `if-then-else` structure. The code in *statements1* executes only when *condition* is True; *statements2* executes only when *condition* is False.

Our modified code using an `if-then-else` statement follows:

```
difference := yourAverageScore — myAverageScore;
if (difference >= 10) then begin
    handicap := 5;
end
else begin
    handicap := 2;
end;
```

Programming Key: Tips

In the preceding code, notice that the first line from the previous example (`handicap := 0;`) is missing. Initializing `handicap` to zero is now unnecessary because it is assigned a value in the `if-then-else` structure.

Notice that the opposing player is always given a minimum handicap of 2 strokes, even when the opposing player is a better golfer. We now modify the subjunctive statement one last time:

If my average golf score is 10 or more strokes less than yours, then I will give you a 5-stroke handicap on our next game. If it is between 7 and 9 strokes less than yours, then I will give you a 3-stroke handicap. If it is between 4 and 6 strokes less than yours, then I will give you a 2-stroke handicap. Otherwise, I will give you no handicap on our next game.

We must now use the following general form of the `if-then-else` statement:

```
if condition1 then begin
    [statements1;]
end
else if condition2 then begin
    [statements2;]
end
        .
        .
        .
else if conditionN then begin
    [statementsN;]
end
else begin
    [statementsX;]
end;
```

Figure 5.8 shows a flowchart for the general `if-then-else` structure. An `if` statement may include any number of `else if` clauses but may contain at most one `else` clause. In evaluating this `if` statement, *statements1* executes when *condition1* is True; *statements2* executes when *condition1* is False and *condition2* is True; *statementsN* executes when *conditionN* is True and all other preceding conditions (*condition1* through *condition{N-1}*) are False; *statementsX* executes only if all conditions (*condition1* through *conditionN*) are False.

Programming Key: Tips

In any `if` statement, at most one set of statements executes. The only statements executed in an `if` statement are those statements that follow the first condition that is evaluated to be True. Consequently, the order of the conditions is important and must follow logically.

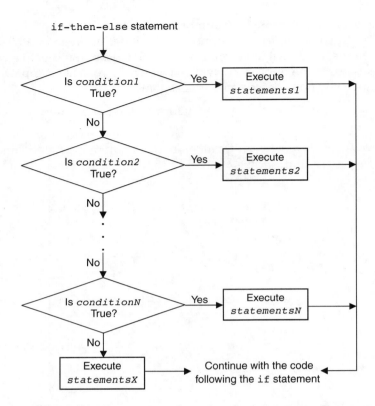

FIGURE 5.8   Flowchart for a General `if-then-else` Statement

In the modified code fragment shown next, only one assignment statement for `handicap` executes depending on the value of `difference`. Trace this code to be sure that you understand what happens when the value of `difference` is 15, 8, 4, and 1.

```
difference := yourAverageScore — myAverageScore;
if (difference >= 10) then begin
   handicap := 5;
end
else if (difference >= 7) then begin
   handicap := 3;
end
else if (difference >= 4) then begin
   handicap := 2;
end
else begin
   handicap := 0;
end;
```

In general, `if` statements that contain `else if` clauses can be written as **sequential** `if-then` statements. Once again, the order of the conditions is important and must be logically correct. The previous example can be rewritten using sequential `if-then` statements as follows:

> **Sequential statements** are statements or constructs that follow each other in sequence. In general, they consist of a sequential grouping of the same programming construct in the source code.

```
handicap := 0;
difference := yourAverageScore - myAverageScore;
if (difference >= 4) then begin
   handicap := 2;
end;
if (difference >= 7) then begin
   handicap := 3;
end;
if (difference >= 10) then begin
   handicap := 5;
end;
```

This code fragment performs the same operation as the code in the previous example, but a different number of statements is executed. When the value of `difference` is greater than or equal to 10, for example, the `if-then-else` structure performs only one comparison and two assignment operations (including assigning the value to `difference`), whereas the sequential `if` statements perform three comparisons and five assignments. In this case, the sequential `if` statements carry out almost three times as many operations as the `if-then-else` structure. The difference in the execution speed of each block of code may be negligible when this code is executed once or only a few times. If the code is repeated a large number of times, however, the `if-then-else` structure will execute substantially more quickly. Such factors are important in **code** (or **algorithm**) **optimization.**

In general, why does a programmer choose one structure over another if code optimization is not an issue? The main reason is the programmer's preferred **programming style.** Use whichever style you prefer, but maintain a consistent style throughout your source code.

> **Nested statements** are statements or constructs that appear within other statements or constructs. In general, a nested statement refers to a construct that appears in the same type of programming construct.

Additionally, in all of the preceding code fragments, notice how indentation improves the readability of the code. Keeping the `if`, `else`, and `end` keywords aligned is a common practice that is used to improve code readability.

Many programmers often **nest** `if` statements; that is, they place `if` statements within other `if` statements. An example of a nested `if` structure follows:

```
if condition1 then begin
   if condition2 then begin
     [statements1;]
   end
   else begin
     [statements2;]
   end;
end;
```

Programming Key: Tips

By always using compound statements within your `if` structures, you avoid a common difficulty that arises in connection with nested `if` statements. In a series of nested `if` statements containing fewer `else` clauses than `if` keywords, it may not be apparent to which `if` statement an `else` clause belongs. Consider the following example `if` statement (with compound statements purposely omitted):

```
if expression1 then if expression2 then statement1
else statement2;
```

There appears to be two ways to interpret this statement:

```
if expression1 then
   if expression2 then
     statement1
   else
     statement2;
```

or

```
if expression1 then
  if expression2 then
    statement1
else
  statement2;
```

The Delphi compiler sees this `if` statement in the first way. That is, this statement is considered equivalent to the following `if` structure with compound statements:

```
if expression1 then begin
  if expression2 then begin
    statement1;
  end
  else begin
    statement2;
  end;
end;
```

The rule is that each `else` is associated with the nearest available `if` keyword. To force the compiler to read our example in the second way, we must explicitly write the following:

```
if expression1 then begin
  if expression2 then begin
    statement1;
  end;
end
else begin
  statement2;
end;
```

This nested `if` statement is equivalent to the unnested `if` statement shown below. In this case, *statements1* executes when both *condition1* and *condition2* are True; *statements2* executes when *condition1* is True and *condition2* is False.

```
if (condition1 and condition2) then begin
  [statements1;]
end
else if (condition1 and not(condition2)) then begin
  [statements2;]
end;
```

Finally, the unnested `if` statement may be simplified as follows:

```
if (condition1 and condition2) then begin
  [statements1;]
end
else if condition1 then begin
  [statements2;]
end;
```

As shown above, we can remove the `and not(condition2)` portion of the Boolean expression from the `else if` clause. Why? Simply stated, this portion of the Boolean expression is redundant. Remember that conditions are checked sequentially in `if` statements. If *statements1* does not execute, then *condition1* and/or *condition2* must be False. When *condition1* is True, *condition2* must be False for *statements1* not to be executed. Thus we need check only whether *condition1* is True in the `else if` clause, as *condition2* is known to be False based on the order of the conditions.

Nesting or unnesting `if` statements is simply a matter of programming style. Use whichever method is most comfortable for you and easier for you to understand.

As a final note concerning `if` statements, recall the earlier discussion of reducing and expanding Boolean expressions. You should keep this idea in mind when writing `if` statements. Reduce or expand the Boolean expressions as necessary so that your `if` statements remain readable and easy to understand. Any `if` statements containing conditions that are difficult to understand should be adequately commented.

Programming Key: Tips

Novice programmers often write unnecessary `if` statements, and some programming shortcuts may be used to avoid this problem. The following code fragment is an unnecessary `if` statement:

```
if (A > B) then begin
  C := True;
end;
```

In this code, the Boolean variable C is assigned the value `True` if the value of variable A is greater than the value of variable B. This code fragment may also be written as a single line of code that performs the same operation:

```
C := (A > B);
```

In summary, assigning values to Boolean variables usually does not require an `if` statement.

`case` **Statements**

The `case` statement is another decision structure in Object Pascal. Every `case` statement can be converted into an equivalent `if` statement, but the reverse is not true; every `if` statement cannot be written as a `case` statement. Nevertheless, the `case` statement is an extremely versatile decision structure, and many other high-level languages include control structures equivalent to it. The general syntax of the `case` statement follows:

```
case selectorExpression of
   caseList1: begin
                 statements1;
              end;
   caseList2: begin
                 statements2;
              end;
               .
               .
               .
   caseListN: begin
                 statementsN;
              end;
   else begin
      statementsX;
   end;
end;
```

Here, `selectorExpression` is an expression that is compared to each `caseList` expression. It must be an expression of an **ordinal type,** (that is `Integer`, `Char`, or `Boolean`). Furthermore, each expression in a `caseList` must be an ordinal expression that can be evaluated at compile time. For instance, `12`, `True`, `4 — 9 * 5`, `'X'`, and `Integer('Z')` are all valid `caseList` expressions, but variables and most function calls are not. A `caseList` may also be a **subrange** having the form `firstExpr..lastExpr`, where `firstExpr` and `lastExpr` are ordinal expressions with `firstExpr ≤ lastExpr`. Finally, a `caseList` may be a list in the form `expr1, expr2, . . ., exprN`, where each `expr` is an ordinal expression or a subrange.

A `case` statement may have any number of `caseList` expressions, but at most one `else` clause. The execution of a `case` statement parallels that of the `if-then-else` structure. If `selectorExpression` matches any expression in a `caseList`, then the statements following that `caseList` execute, and control then passes to

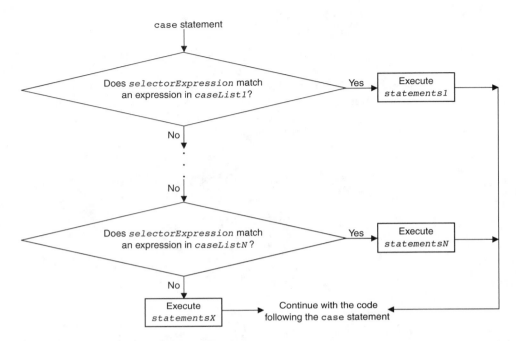

FIGURE 5.9   Flowchart for a `Case` Statement

the code following the `case` statement. If *selectorExpression* matches an expression in more than one *caseList*, only the statements following the first matched *caseList* expression execute. If *selectorExpression* does not match an expression in any *caseList*, then the statements following the `else` clause, *statementsX*, execute. Although an `else` clause is not required in a case statement, using one ensures that your code can handle unforeseen *selectorExpression* values. If *selectorExpression* does not match any *caseList* expression and no `else` clause is present, execution continues with the code following the `case` statement. Figure 5.9 shows a flowchart for the `case` statement.

You can nest `case` statements in the same manner that you nest `if` statements. Each nested `case` statement must have a matching `end` keyword.

Let's demonstrate the use of the `case` statement by converting the `if-then-else` statement in the golf handicap example into an equivalent `case` structure. First, we must make a few assumptions concerning the golf scores. Assume that the number of strokes for each hole is a minimum of one (for a hole-in-one) and a maximum of eight. The minimum score for an 18-hole round of golf is therefore 18 (1 stroke/hole × 18 holes) and the maximum score is 144 (8 strokes/hole × 18 holes). The maximum difference in golf scores for any two players is at most 126 (144 – 18). This difference can be positive or negative, depending on whether you are a better or worse golfer than your friend. The following code fragment implements the golf handicap example as a `case` statement and demonstrates the use of lists and subranges:

```
difference := yourAverageScore — myAverageScore;
case difference of
  4, 5, 6: begin
             handicap := 2;
           end;
  7, 8, 9: begin
             handicap := 3;
           end;
  10..126: begin
             handicap := 5;
           end;
  else begin
    handicap := 0;
  end;
end;
```

Notice that this code has a problem if our assumptions are invalid. For instance, what if your score is 64 and your friend's score is 192? According to this code, what handicap does your friend receive during the next game? The `if-then-else` structure did not require any assumptions concerning the golf scores, so it is not susceptible to this problem. We can fix this problem in our `case` statement simply by increasing the maximum possible difference in scores (say, from 126 to 500). Our code would then work correctly for all reasonable differences in golf scores. A programmer, however, needs to account for all possible input values, whether they are reasonable or not. The `if` statement is therefore more appropriate and foolproof if we do not wish to make assumptions concerning the input values (golf scores in this example). The error-proofing of code is discussed in Chapter 9.

Our discussion of decision structures concludes with a few questions. Given the following code fragment,

```
if (ave >= 0.90) then begin
  letterGrade := 'A';
end
else if (ave >= 0.80) then begin
  letterGrade := 'B';
end
else if (ave >= 0.70) then begin
  letterGrade := 'C';
end
else if (ave >= 0.60) then begin
  letterGrade := 'D';
end
else begin
  letterGrade := 'F';
end;
```

can you *directly* convert this `if` statement into a `case` statement? Why or why not? If not, can you employ any "tricks" to make the conversion?

Programming Style

Programming style—and your freedom in this respect—has been mentioned several times throughout this chapter. Often you may not have a choice among different styles when programming in an academic or commercial environment. Many companies and institutions adopt a set of **programming standards** to ensure that all of their programmers will follow the same programming style. Remember, you are not programming only for yourself, but also for other people. An institution may desire to modify your code long after you have left. The Object Pascal Programming Standards for this text appear in Appendix C.

GUI Design Tips

Radio buttons and check boxes are common Delphi interface components that are used in conjunction with decision structures. Radio buttons allow the user to select a single item from a list of several alternatives, whereas check boxes allow the user to select one or more items from a list. Chapter 16 provides more details on these controls.

The following example illustrates the use of radio buttons and check boxes in decision structures. Figure 5.10 shows a sample execution of this program.

Component	Property	Setting
Form	Name	frmGUITips
	Caption	RadioButton and CheckBox
Label	Name	lblGender
	Caption	Gender
Label	Name	lblDescription
	Caption	Description
RadioButton	Name	radMale
	Caption	Male
RadioButton	Name	radFemale
	Caption	Female
CheckBox	Name	chkIntelligent
	Caption	Intelligent

Component	Property	Setting
CheckBox	Name	chkEnthusiastic
	Caption	Enthusiastic
CheckBox	Name	chkFriendly
	Caption	Friendly
CheckBox	Name	chkHardWork
	Caption	Hard-working
Button	Name	btnEvaluate
	Caption	Evaluate
Memo Box	Name	memOutput
	Lines	*Empty*
	ReadOnly	True

Component Name	Event	Setting
btnEvaluate	OnClick	Evaluate

```
unit GUITipsEx;

interface

uses
  Windows, Messages, SysUtils, Classes, Graphics,
  Controls, Forms, Dialogs, StdCtrls;

type
  TfrmGUITips = class(TForm)
    lblGender: TLabel;
    radMale: TRadioButton;
    radFemale: TRadioButton;
    lblDescription: TLabel;
    chkIntelligent: TCheckBox;
    chkEnthusiastic: TCheckBox;
    chkHardWork: TCheckBox;
    chkFriendly: TCheckBox;
    btnEvaluate: TButton;
    memOutput: TMemo;
    procedure Evaluate(Sender: TObject);
  private
    { Private declarations }
  public
    { Public declarations }
  end;
```

```
var
  frmGUITips: TfrmGUITips;

implementation

{$R *.DFM}

procedure TfrmGUITips.Evaluate(Sender: TObject);
var
  none: Boolean;
begin
  memOutput.Clear;
  if radMale.Checked then begin
    memOutput.Lines.Add('You are a man.');
  end
  else if radFemale.Checked then begin
    memOutput.Lines.Add('You are a woman.');
  end
  else begin
    memOutput.Lines.Add('You did not enter your
  gender.');
  end;

  memOutput.Lines.Add('');
  memOutput.Lines.Add('You are:');

  none := True;
  if chkIntelligent.Checked then begin
    memOutput.Lines.Add('Intelligent');
    none := False;
  end;
  if chkEnthusiastic.Checked then begin
    memOutput.Lines.Add('Enthusiastic');
    none := False;
  end;
  if chkFriendly.Checked then begin
    memOutput.Lines.Add('Friendly');
    none := False;
  end;
  if chkHardWork.Checked then begin
    memOutput.Lines.Add('Hard-working');
    none := False;
  end;
  if none then begin
```

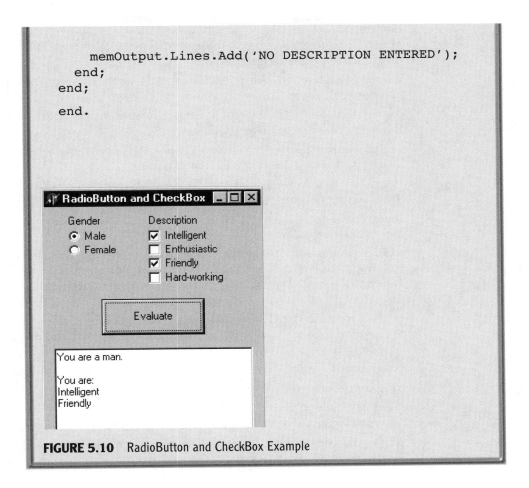

```
        memOutput.Lines.Add('NO DESCRIPTION ENTERED');
      end;
    end;

    end.
```

FIGURE 5.10   RadioButton and CheckBox Example

Summary

Key Terms

Boolean expression (logical expression)—An expression that evaluates to be either True or False.

Boolean operator (logical operator)—An operator used to combine Boolean (or logical) expressions.

code (algorithm) optimization—Writing fast and compact code (algorithms).

complete evaluation—A compiler mode of evaluation for Boolean expressions in which each conjunct or disjunct is evaluated, even when the result of an entire expression has already been determined.

decision structure—A programming construct that involves the comparison of two or more expressions and the conditional execution of statements based on the result of this comparison.

empty `if` statement—An `if` statement that contains no statements to be executed when the condition is True.

expression—A combination of keywords, operators, variables, and constants that yields a string, number, or object.

logical conjunction—A combination of logical expressions where the result is True only if both expressions evaluate to True.

logical disjunction—A combination of logical expressions where the result is True if either or both expressions evaluate to True.

logical negation—A logical expression where the result is the opposite of the expression evaluation.

nested statements—Statements or constructs that appear within other statements or constructs. Generally refers to a programming construct that contains the same type of programming construct within its executable statements.

ordinal type—A data type whose values can be ordered in sequence from the first value to the last value, such as `Integer`, `Char`, and `Boolean` data types.

programming standards—A set of rules regarding programming style.

programming style—A programmer's choice of constructs and use of nesting, white space, and comments.

relational operator—An operator used to compare expressions.

sequential statements—Statements or constructs that follow each other in sequence. Generally refers to a sequential grouping of the same programming construct in the source code.

short-circuit (partial) evaluation—A compiler mode of evaluation for Boolean expressions that follows a strict left-to-right evaluation that stops once the result of the entire expression is determined.

subrange—A subset of values of an ordinal data type.

truth table—A table that displays the evaluation of a Boolean expression for all possible combinations of variable values.

Keywords

Compiler Directives

```
{$B-} or {$BOOLEVAL OFF}
{$B+} or {$BOOLEVAL ON}
```

Operators

<	>=
<=	and
<>	not
=	or
>	

Statements

begin	if
case	of
else	then
end	

Key Concepts

- A decision structure allows the execution of specific code based on the presence or absence of certain conditions.
- Relational operators are used to compare expressions. In Object Pascal, the relational operators include less than (<), less than or equal to (<=), greater than (>), greater than or equal to (>=), equal to (=), and not equal to (<>).
- The comparison of two expressions using a relational operator forms a Boolean (or logical) expression. Boolean expressions are combined using Boolean operators, such as and, or, and not.
- The Delphi compiler supports both complete and short-circuit evaluation of Boolean expressions. In complete evaluation, each conjunct or disjunct is evaluated, even when the result of the entire expression has already been determined. Short-circuit evaluation follows a strict left-to-right evaluation that stops once the result of the entire expression is determined.
- An expression may combine the three different types of operators: arithmetic, relational, and Boolean. Precedence rules specify the order in which the operators in expressions will be evaluated. In Object Pascal, arithmetic operators are evaluated first, relational operators are evaluated next, and Boolean operators are evaluated last. Additionally, all relational operators have equal precedence and are evaluated in the order in which they appear from left to right. The not operator has the highest precedence among the Boolean operators, followed by and, and then or. Parentheses can be used to override these precedence rules. Using parentheses in an expression that contains operators of different types greatly enhances program readability.
- DeMorgan's laws relate to the negation of Boolean expressions and Boolean operators and have various applications in mathematics, probability, and

computer science. These laws may be used to reduce or expand Boolean expressions into equivalent expressions. We can show the equivalence of Boolean expressions either algebraically (by using algebraic logic) or by using a truth table.

- Two decision structures in Object Pascal are the `if` statement and `case` statement.

- The general syntax of the `if` statement follows:

```
if condition1 then begin
  [statements1;]
end
else if condition2 then begin
  [statements2;]
end
              .
              .
              .
else if conditionN then begin
  [statementsN;]
end
else begin
  [statementsX;]
end;
```

- The `case` statement has the following syntax:

```
case selectorExpression of
  caseList1: begin
               statements1;
             end;
  caseList2: begin
               statements2;
             end;
             .
             .
             .
  caseListN: begin
               statementsN;
             end;
  else begin
    statementsX;
  end;
end;
```

- Every `case` statement can be converted into an equivalent `if` statement, but not every `if` statement can be written as a `case` statement. This difference occurs because the `case` statement works only with ordinal data types.

- Oftentimes, control structures are nested, or one control structure is contained within another control structure. For example, one `if` statement may appear inside of another `if` statement. Indenting nested control structures and statements within control structures improves program readability.
- Programming standards are adopted by a company or institution to ensure that all programmers will follow the same programming style.

Review Questions

1. Name and give an example of the use of three relational operators.
2. Name the three primary Boolean operators.
3. What is the difference between complete and short-circuit evaluation of Boolean expressions?
4. What are precedence rules and why are they important?
5. State DeMorgan's laws.
6. List some methods of showing equivalence among Boolean expressions.
7. Describe the syntax and operation of the general `if` statement and the `case` statement.
8. Can every `if` statement be written as a `case` statement, and vice versa? Explain.
9. What is a nested control structure?
10. What are programming standards?

Problems

1. The exclusive or operator, denoted by `xor`, performs an exclusive disjunction. The Boolean expression `A xor B` evaluates to True when either A or B is True, but not both. Prove that `A xor B` is equivalent to `(~A ∧ B) ∨ (A ∧ ~B)`.
2. Write the program for Problem 4 in Chapter 3.
3. Modify the average velocity program from Problem 6 in Chapter 4 so that it checks the user's input. If the user enters a negative distance or non-positive time, the program should display the appropriate error message and then end.
4. Modify the quadratic formula solver from Problem 10 in Chapter 4 so that it checks the user's input. If the roots are imaginary or the value of *a* is zero, the program should display the appropriate message and then end.
5. Write a program that allows the user to input two strings and displays the string with the higher ASCII value in a memo box.
6. Write a program that allows the user to input two strings and displays the shorter string (the string of the least length) in a memo box.

7. Write a program that allows the user to input a number and then determines whether the number is positive, negative, or zero. The answer should be output to a memo box.

8. Write a program that allows the user to input a string and then determines whether the string begins with a number, symbol, space, uppercase letter, or lowercase letter. The answer should be output to a memo box.

9. Write a program that allows the user to input his or her name and then determines whether the user's name begins with a vowel or consonant. The answer should be output to a memo box.

Programming Projects

1. Write a program that determines the number of each type of coin to give as change for a user-entered amount. If the user enters $5.88, for instance, your program should output "3 Quarters, 1 Dime, and 3 Pennies" (do not be concerned with the dollar amount). The program should consider only quarters, dimes, nickels, and pennies. The objective of the program is to give change in the minimum number of coins possible.

2. Extend Project 1 to include dollar values in the change. If the user enters $5.88, for instance, your program should output "1 $5 Bill, 3 Quarters, 1 Dime, and 3 Pennies." The program should consider only $1, $5, $10, and $20 bills, plus quarters, dimes, nickels, and pennies. The objective of the program is to give change in the minimum number of bills and coins possible.

3. Our calendar—the Gregorian calendar—was introduced in 1582. Write a program that determines the day of the week for any date after 1582. Your program should do the following:
   a. Request the month and year as numeric inputs.
   b. Determine the number of days in the month and request the day as a numeric input. Ensure that the user input is valid. All years divisible by 4 are leap years, with the exception of those years divisible by 100 and not by 400. The years 1600 and 2000 are leap years, for instance, but 1700, 1800, and 1900 are not. If you are clever, you can test this condition using a single `if` statement.
   c. Use the following algorithm to determine the day of the week:
      ● Treat January and February as the thirteenth and fourteenth months of the previous year, respectively. Thus 1/10/1998 is treated as 13/10/1997. Similarly, 2/10/1998 becomes 14/10/1997.
      ● Let m, d, and y denote the month, day, and year, respectively. Compute w, where

$$w = d + 2^*m + \text{Int}((3/5)^*(m + 1)) + y + \text{Int}(y/4)$$

$$- \text{Int}(y/100) + \text{Int}(y/400) + 2$$

      ● Let the remainder of w divided by 7 denote the day of the week, where 0 is Saturday, 1 is Sunday, 2 is Monday, and so on.

Chapter 6

Repetition Structures

Chapter Objectives

In this chapter you will:

- Learn the operation and use of repetition structures, including `for`, `while`, and `repeat` loops

- Understand the major differences between the repetition structures and discover the appropriate situations for their use

- Convert between repetition structures

- Learn about accumulator and flag variables

- Become familiar with ordinal routines

Chapter 5 introduced decision structures, one type of flow control structure. This chapter discusses another structure to control program flow—the repetition structure.

Repetition

Oftentimes, an algorithm requires repeating a group of statements, which is commonly called *looping* by programmers. **Loops** allow for the repetition of code. Consider, for example, the following problem:

What is the sum of the integers from 1 to 100?

This problem is rather easy and quick to solve on a computer by using a loop, whereas it may take you a great deal of time to solve by hand. Fortunately, the great mathematician Carl Friedrich Gauss recognized that the sum of the integers from 1 to n is given by

$$\sum_{i=1}^{n} i = \frac{n(n+1)}{2}$$

In this equation, the Σ (sigma) denotes summation, so the variable i is summed from 1 to n. The formula on the right side of the equation allows us to quickly obtain the answer of 5050 for $n = 100$.

Object Pascal provides three repetition structures: **for loops, while loops,** and **repeat loops.**

`for` Loops

`for` loops are a **determinate** (or **definite**) **loop structure.** They can be used only when the programmer knows or can calculate the exact number of times that the loop must execute. The syntax of the *incrementing* `for` loop follows:

```
for counter := start to finish do begin
   [statements;]
end;
```

The variable `counter`, which is the **loop counter,** must be a local variable of any ordinal data type. The expressions `start` and `finish` specify the starting and ending values of `counter`, respectively, and must be **assignment-compatible** with `counter`. The value of `start` must be less than or equal to the value of

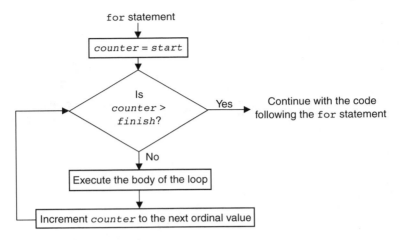

FIGURE 6.1   Execution of the Incrementing for Loop

finish for the statements inside of the loop (the **body of the loop**) to execute. After executing the body, the incrementing for loop automatically increments the value of *counter* by one (or one ordinal position). Control then returns to the top of the loop, and the value of *counter* is compared to *finish*. The body of the loop continues to execute as long as *counter* is less than or equal to *finish*. Figure 6.1 displays a flowchart of the incrementing for loop execution cycle.

For integer values of *start* and *finish*, the number of times that the incrementing for loop executes the body is easily computed as follows:

$(finish - start) + 1$ where $start \leq finish$

$0,$ where $start > finish$

The following code fragment uses an incrementing for loop to compute the sum of the integers from 1 to 100:

```
var
  counter: Integer;
  sum:     Integer;
begin
  sum := 0;
  for counter := 1 to 100 do begin
    sum := sum + counter;
  end;
end;
```

After this for loop executes, the variable sum contains the sum of the integers from 1 to 100, or 5050.

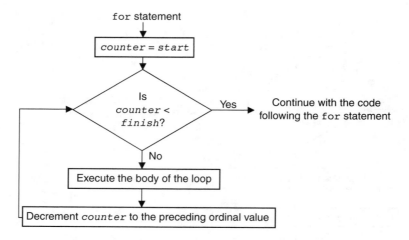

FIGURE 6.2   Execution of the Decrementing `for` Loop

In some situations, a program needs a loop counter to count down rather than count up. This case requires the use of the *decrementing* `for` loop, which has the following general syntax:

```
for counter := start downto finish do begin
  [statements;]
end;
```

As before, `counter` is the loop counter, and `start` and `finish` specify the starting and ending values of `counter`, respectively. For the decrementing `for` loop, however, the value of `start` must be greater than or equal to the value of `finish` for the body to execute. After the body executes, `counter` is automatically decremented by one (or one ordinal position), and the body of the loop continues to execute as long as `counter` is greater than or equal to `finish`. Figure 6.2 shows a flowchart of the decrementing `for` loop execution cycle.

For integer values of `start` and `finish`, the number of times that the decrementing `for` loop executes the body is easily computed as follows:

$(start - finish) + 1$ where $start \geq finish$

$0,$ where $start < finish$

As shown in the code fragment that follows, we can just as easily compute the sum of the integers from 1 to 100 using a decrementing `for` loop as we can with an incrementing one. By the commutative property of addition, we know that

$100 + 99 + 98 + \cdots + 1$ equals $1 + 2 + 3 + \cdots + 100$. Thus both loops arrive at the correct answer of 5050.

```
var
  counter: Integer;
  sum:     Integer;

begin
  sum := 0;
  for counter := 100 downto 1 do begin
    sum := sum + counter;
  end;
end;
```

A `for` loop that contains no statements within its body is an **empty loop.** Empty loops are commonly used to create **time delays** during program execution.

Just as with `if` statements, you can nest `for` loops. Each loop must have a unique variable name for its loop counter. The following code fragment uses nested `for` loops to display a multiplication table up to 12 × 12. The memo box memOutput displays the table.

```
{Display a 12 x 12 multiplication table}
var
  row:     Integer;
  col:     Integer;
  lineOut: String;
  product: String;

begin
  for row := 1 to 12 do begin
    lineOut := '';
    for col := 1 To 12 do begin
      Str((row * col):4, product);
      lineOut := lineOut + product;
    end;
    memOutput.Lines.Add(lineOut);
  end;
end;
```

The next example demonstrates the use of a character loop counter. Remember, the loop counter does not need to be an `Integer`; it may be of any ordinal type. Thus this code fragment is perfectly valid. It stores all lowercase letters in the string variable `alphabet`.

```
var
  letter:   Char;
  alphabet: String;

begin
  alphabet := '';
  for letter := 'a' to 'z' do begin
    alphabet := alphabet + letter;
  end;
end;
```

Our final example of `for` loops uses both integer and character loop counters. This code fragment displays a character design in a memo box.

```
const
  NUMLINES     = 10;
  DISPLAY_CHAR = 'I';
  SPACE        = ' ';

var
  lineOut:    String;
  lineNum:    Integer;
  letterNum:  Integer;
  letterVal:  Integer;
  letter:     Char;

begin
  memOutput.Clear;
  for lineNum := NUMLINES downto 1 do begin
    lineOut := '';
    for letterNum := 1 to lineNum do begin
      lineOut := lineOut + DISPLAY_CHAR;
    end;
    for letterNum := 1 to (2 * (NUMLINES - lineNum))
                    do begin
      lineOut := lineOut + SPACE;
    end;
    for letterNum := 1 to lineNum do begin
      lineOut := lineOut + DISPLAY_CHAR;
    end;
    memOutput.Lines.Add(lineOut);
```

```
    end;

  letterVal := 62;
  for lineNum := 1 to NUMLINES do begin
    lineOut := '';
    for letter := Chr(letterVal) to
                  Chr(letterVal + (2 * NUMLINES) - 1)
                  do begin
      lineOut := lineOut + letter;
    end;
    memOutput.Lines.Add(lineOut);
    letterVal := letterVal + 1;
  end;
end;
```

Upon executing this code fragment, the following character design appears in the memo box:

```
IIIIIIIIIIIIIIIIIII
IIIIIIIII  IIIIIIII
IIIIIIII   IIIIIII
IIIIIII    IIIIII
IIIIII     IIIII
IIIII      IIIII
IIII        IIII
III          III
II            II
I              I
>?@ABCDEFGHIJKLMNOPQ
?@ABCDEFGHIJKLMNOPQR
@ABCDEFGHIJKLMNOPQRS
ABCDEFGHIJKLMNOPQRST
BCDEFGHIJKLMNOPQRSTU
CDEFGHIJKLMNOPQRSTUV
DEFGHIJKLMNOPQRSTUVW
EFGHIJKLMNOPQRSTUVWX
FGHIJKLMNOPQRSTUVWXY
GHIJKLMNOPQRSTUVWXYZ
```

while **and** repeat **Loops**

The while and repeat loops are **indeterminate** (or **indefinite**) **loop structures.** That is, the programmer does not necessarily know how many times that the body of one of these loops will execute. You can also use while and repeat loops in place of `for` loops as determinate loop structures as well. Thus every `for` loop has equivalent `while` and `repeat` loops, but the reverse is not true.

The `while` and `repeat` loops of Object Pascal have comparable structures in most other high-level languages. The syntax of each of these loop structures appears below:

```
while condition do begin
   [statements;]
end;
```

```
repeat
   [statements;]
until condition;
```

where `condition` is a Boolean expression. A `while` loop executes the statements within its body as long as `condition` is True (while `condition` is True), whereas the `repeat` loop executes its body as long as `condition` is False (until `condition` becomes True). Figure 6.3 contains execution flowcharts of both loop structures. Unlike the `for` loop, the programmer must explicitly change the value of `condition`, the **controlling expression,** within the body of the loop; otherwise, an **infinite loop** (or **endless loop**) results.

In the preceding syntax, notice that the `begin` and `end` keywords delimit the body of the `while` loop but not the `repeat` loop. All statements appearing between the `repeat` and `until` keywords constitute the body of a `repeat` loop.

Aside from the loop-terminating conditions and syntax, another major difference distinguishes the two loop structures. A `repeat` loop executes the body of the loop at least once, whereas the `while` loop may never execute its body. Thus every `repeat` loop can be readily translated into a `while` loop, but translating in the reverse direction may require a little more work. The fact that the body of a `while` loop may never execute can be easily handled by using an `if` statement as a redundant check of the condition in the `repeat` loop structure. Notice that we call this `if` statement a redundant check. The lesson to be learned here relates to code optimization: In some situations, one loop structure is more appropriate than the other. In general, if the loop must execute at least once, a `repeat` loop is appropriate; otherwise, you should use a `while` loop.

As an example, we will translate the code to sum the integers from 1 to 100 into each of these loop structures:

```
{Using a while loop}
sum := 0;
count := 1;
while (count <= 100) do begin
  sum := sum + count;
  count := count + 1;
end;

{Using a repeat loop}
sum := 0;
count := 1;
repeat
  sum := sum + count;
  count := count + 1;
until (count > 100);
```

The variable sum is an **accumulator;** it sums, or accumulates, the final answer. Notice that these two code fragments are not strikingly different. In fact, only the loop structure changes and the terminating condition logically reverses. In this case, any loop structure (for, while, or repeat) works. Ultimately, the choice of loop structure is a matter of code optimization and programming style.

> An **accumulator** is a variable that sums values within a loop structure.

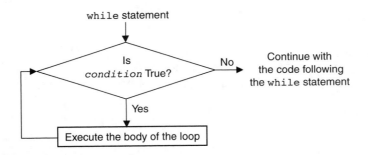

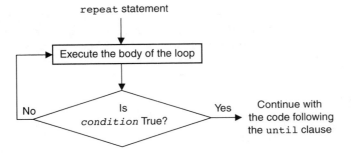

FIGURE 6.3 Execution of while and repeat Loops

Can you find a common programming error in the following code fragment?

```
var
  value: Integer;
begin
  value := 0;
  while (value <= 10) do;
  begin
    memOutput.Lines.Add(IntToStr(value));
    value := value + 1;
  end;
end;
```

The semicolon following the do keyword in the while statement creates an infinite loop. In effect, this statement really reads while (value <= 10) do {nothing};. Since value, the controlling expression, is initialized to zero and never changed in the body of the loop, an infinite loop results. To avoid this problem, always use a trailing begin keyword rather than one on the line after the while statement. The following code fragment corrects the error by using a trailing begin keyword:

```
var
  value: Integer;
begin
  value := 0;
  while (value <= 10) do begin
    memOutput.Lines.Add(IntToStr(value));
    value := value + 1;
  end;
end;
```

A flag is a variable (typically, a Boolean variable) that indicates the presence (or absence) of a condition.

Both while and repeat loops often use **flags.** A flag is a Boolean variable that indicates a condition. For instance, the following code fragment uses the flag variable correct to loop until the user enters either Yes or No:

```
var
  answer:  String;
  correct: Boolean;
```

```
begin
  repeat
    answer := InputBox('Yes or No',
                        'Enter your answer', '');
    answer := Trim(UpperCase(answer));
    correct := (answer = 'YES') or (answer = 'NO');
  until correct;
end;
```

Recall that the loop counter of a `for` loop may be of any ordinal data type. Translating a `for` loop with a non-integer loop counter into the equivalent `while` or `repeat` structure requires the program code to increment or decrement the loop control variable to the succeeding or preceding ordinal value, respectively. This task is accomplished using the ordinal routines shown in Figure 6.4.

As described in Figure 6.4, the `Inc` procedure increments an ordinal variable by a specified long integer value. By default, it increments the variable by one if no value is specified. `Inc(x)` corresponds to the statement `x := x + 1`, and `Inc(x, n)` corresponds to the statement `x := x + n`. In a similar manner, the `Dec` procedure decrements an ordinal variable by a specified long integer value. Thus `Dec(x)` corresponds to the statement `x := x − 1`, and `Dec(x, n)` corresponds to `x := x − n`. The main difference, however, is that `Inc` and `Dec` generate optimized code and are especially useful inside loops.

The following code fragment implements the alphabet example using a `while` loop; all lowercase letters are stored in the string variable `alphabet`. Implementing the equivalent `repeat` structure is left as an exercise for you.

```
var
  letter:   Char;
  alphabet: String;
begin
  alphabet := '';
  letter := 'a';
  while (letter <= 'z') do begin
    alphabet := alphabet + letter;
    letter := Succ(letter);
  end;
end;
```

Function	Purpose
Odd	Returns True if the argument is an odd number
Ord	Returns the ordinal value of an ordinal-type expression
Pred	Returns the predecessor of the argument
Succ	Returns the successor of the argument

Procedure	Purpose
Dec	Decrements an ordinal variable by 1 or *n*
Inc	Increments an ordinal variable by 1 or *n*

FIGURE 6.4 Object Pascal Ordinal Routines

In a `for` loop, the expressions *start* and *finish* are evaluated only once before the loop begins. Thus an incrementing `for` loop is almost—but not exactly—equivalent to the following `while` loop:

```
counter := start;
while (counter <= finish) do begin
  [statements;]
  counter := Succ(counter);
end;
```

The `while` loop reevaluates *finish* before each iteration, resulting in noticeably slower performance if *finish* is a complex expression. Additionally, any changes to *finish* within the body of the loop can affect the number of times that the loop executes.

As a final example of indeterminate loops, consider the password example shown below. This code fragment gives the user three attempts to enter the correct password (Borland). The loop ends when the user either enters the correct password or has exhausted his or her three tries. The decision structure that follows the loop determines which of these two events occurred. Note that the password is case sensitive.

```
const
  PASSWORD = 'Borland'; {Note: Password is case sensitive}
  MAX_TRY  = 3;
var
  tries:  Integer;
  passwd: String;
begin
  tries := 1;
  passwd := '';
  while (passwd <> PASSWORD) and (tries <= MAX_TRY)
  do begin
    passwd := Trim(InputBox('ENTER PASSWORD (Attempt '
            + IntToStr(tries) + ')',
            'What''s the password?', ''));
    Inc(tries);
  end;

  if (passwd = PASSWORD) then begin
    ShowMessage('You have the correct password' +
              '...ACCESS GRANTED');
  end
```

```
else begin
  Beep;
  ShowMessage('Incorrect password...ACCESS DENIED');
  Application.Terminate;
end;

ShowMessage('Welcome to my program...');

{The rest of your program goes here...}
end;
```

GUI Design Tips

Loops are often used to iterate through the contents of Delphi interface components, such as list boxes, combo boxes, group boxes, radio group boxes, and checklist boxes. These components are described in Chapter 16.

We can simplify the GUI Design Tip example in Chapter 5 by using a checklist box and a loop. A list box is a component that allows the user to select one or more items from a list. A checklist box is a scrollable list box in which each item has a check box next to it. Users can check or uncheck items in the list as desired.

Component	Property	Setting
Form	Name	frmGUITips
	Caption	CheckListBox
Label	Name	lblGender
	Caption	Gender
Label	Name	lblDescription
	Caption	Description
RadioButton	Name	radMale
	Caption	Male
RadioButton	Name	radFemale
	Caption	Female
CheckListBox	Name	cbxDescription
	Items	Intelligent; Enthusiastic; Friendly; Hard-working
Button	Name	btnEvaluate
	Caption	Evaluate

> The semicolons in the Items property of the checklist box indicate that these items are separated on different lines in the String List editor (that is, you should press ENTER after entering each item).

Component	Property	Setting
Memo Box	Name	memOutput
	Lines	*Empty*
	ReadOnly	True

Component Name	Event	Setting
btnEvaluate	OnClick	Evaluate

The code is modified as shown below, and Figure 6.5 displays a sample execution. Note that this code accesses the array elements of the Items property of the checklist box. Arrays and array operations are discussed in Chapter 10.

```
unit GUITipsEx;

interface

uses
  Windows, Messages, SysUtils, Classes, Graphics,
   Controls,
  Forms, Dialogs, StdCtrls, CheckLst;

type
  TfrmGUITips = class(TForm)
    lblGender: TLabel;
    radMale: TRadioButton;
    radFemale: TRadioButton;
    lblDescription: TLabel;
    btnEvaluate: TButton;
    memOutput: TMemo;
    cbxDescription: TCheckListBox;
    procedure Evaluate(Sender: TObject);
  private
    { Private declarations }
  public
    { Public declarations }
  end;

var
  frmGUITips: TfrmGUITips;

implementation

{$R *.DFM}

procedure TfrmGUITips.Evaluate(Sender: TObject);

var
  none: Boolean;
  desc: Integer;
```

```
begin
  memOutput.Clear;
  if radMale.Checked then begin
    memOutput.Lines.Add('You are a man.');
  end
  else if radFemale.Checked then begin
    memOutput.Lines.Add('You are a woman.');
  end
  else begin
    memOutput.Lines.Add('You did not enter your gender.');
  end;

  memOutput.Lines.Add('');
  memOutput.Lines.Add('You are:');

  none := True;
  for desc := 0 to (cbxDescription.Items.Count - 1)
  do begin
    if cbxDescription.Checked[desc] then begin
      memOutput.Lines.Add(cbxDescription.Items[desc]);
      none := False;
    end;
  end;
  if none then begin
    memOutput.Lines.Add('NO DESCRIPTION ENTERED');
  end;
end;

end.
```

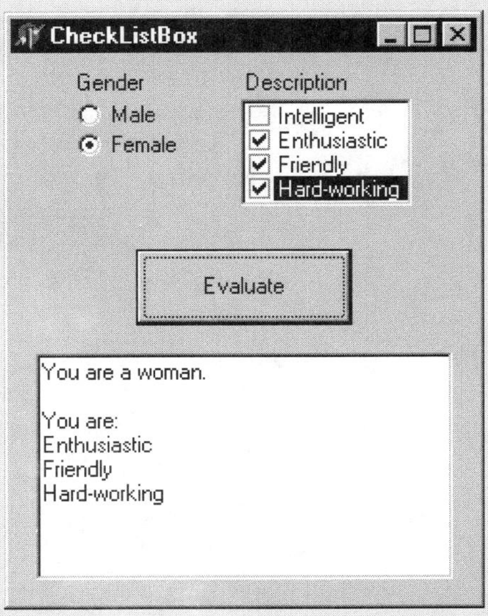

FIGURE 6.5 CheckListBox Example

· C · A · S · E · S · T · U · D · Y ·

GoodLook Cosmetics Company

Jean is a sales representative for the GoodLook Cosmetics Company. Each month, she is required to report sales figures for the different types of cosmetics sold. To calculate these amounts, she simply multiplies the sales price by the quantity sold for each item and then sums these products. Because the company offers an exceptionally large number of items, hand calculations are both time-consuming and error-prone. Jean needs a program that will allow her to enter the sales price and quantity sold for each item and then perform the calculations automatically.

Help Jean by writing a program to perform the required operations. First, develop an algorithm. Then, code your algorithm using Delphi. Compare your answer to Jean's code unit below.

```delphi
unit GoodLookCosmetics;

interface

uses
  Windows, Messages, SysUtils, Classes, Graphics, Controls,
  Forms, Dialogs, StdCtrls;

type
  TfrmGoodLook = class(TForm)
    btnEnter: TButton;
    memOutput: TMemo;
    procedure ComputeSales(Sender: TObject);
  private
    { Private declarations }
  public
    { Public declarations }
  end;

var
  frmGoodLook: TfrmGoodLook;
implementation
{$R *.DFM}

const
  PMESSAGE = 'Enter the product price ( <= 0 to stop)';
  QMESSAGE = 'Enter the (integer) quantity sold for item ';

procedure TfrmGoodLook.ComputeSales(Sender: TObject);
```

```
var
  price:     Real;
  code:      Integer;
  quantity:  Integer;
  count:     Integer;
  totalSales: Real;
  outMessage: String;
begin
  count := 0;
  totalSales := 0.0;
  repeat
    Inc(count);
    repeat
      Val(InputBox('Enter Price for Item ' +
                  IntToStr(count), PMESSAGE, ''), price,
                  code);
      if (code  0) then begin
        Application.MessageBox('Price must be a real ' +
                              'number!', 'PRICE ERROR',
                              MB_OK);
      end;
    until (code <> = 0);
    if (price > 0) then begin
      outMessage := QMESSAGE + IntToStr(count);
      repeat
        Val(InputBox('Enter Quantity', outMessage, ''),
            quantity, code);
        if (quantity <= 0) or (code <> 0) then begin
          Application.MessageBox('Quantity must be a ' +
                                'positive integer!',
                                'QUANTITY ERROR', MB_OK);
        end;
      until (quantity > 0) and (code = 0);
      totalSales := totalSales + (price * quantity);
    end;
  until (price <= 0);

  memOutput.Clear;
  memOutput.Lines.Add(IntToStr(count - 1) +
                     ' items entered.');
  memOutput.Lines.Add('Total Sales: $' +
                     Trim(Format('%8.2n', [totalSales])));
end;

end.
```

Summary

Key Terms

accumulator—A variable that sums values within a loop structure.

assignment-compatible—Refers to those expressions that may be assigned to a variable of a specific data type.

body of the loop (**body**)—The statements inside a loop structure.

controlling expression—A Boolean expression that controls the operation of a `while` or `repeat` loop.

determinate (**definite**) **loop structure**—A loop structure in which the programmer knows or can calculate the exact number of times that the body of the loop will execute.

empty loop—a loop structure that contains no statements within its body.

endless loop—See *infinite loop.*

flag—A variable that indicates the presence (or absence) of a condition; typically a Boolean variable.

indeterminate (**indefinite**) **loop structure**—A loop structure in which the programmer does not necessarily know or cannot calculate the exact number of times that the body of the loop will execute.

infinite loop—A loop structure that never terminates.

loop—A control structure used to repeat a group of statements until a certain condition is present (or absent).

loop counter—The loop control variable in a `for` loop.

time delay—Statements that cause a program to wait for a specific length of time before executing the remainder of the code; generally refers to an empty loop.

Keywords

Functions

Odd	Pred
Ord	Succ

Procedures

Dec	Inc

Statements

do	for
downto	repeat

MODULO

5 div 2 = 2

5 MOD 2 = 1

↓

5/2 = 2 remainder ①

```
to              while
until
```

Key Concepts

- Repetition structures provide an easy means of repeating groups of statements.
- The three repetition or loop structures in Object Pascal are `for` loops, `while` loops, and `repeat` loops. `for` loops are determinate loops; the programmer knows or can calculate the exact number of times that a loop of this type will execute. `while` and `repeat` loops, on the other hand, can be either determinate or indeterminate; the programmer does not necessarily know the number of times that one of these loops will execute. Therefore, every `for` loop has equivalent `while` and `repeat` loop structures, but every `while` and `repeat` loop cannot be written as a `for` loop.
- Two types of `for` loops exist: the incrementing `for` loop and the decrementing `for` loop. The loop counter counts up in the incrementing `for` loop, and it counts down in the decrementing `for` loop.

  The syntax of an incrementing `for` loop follows:

  ```
  for counter := start to finish do begin
    [statements;]
  end;
  ```

  The syntax of a decrementing `for` loop follows:

  ```
  for counter := start downto finish do begin
    [statements;]
  end;
  ```

- A `while` loop executes the statements within its body as long as *condition* is True (while *condition* is True), whereas the `repeat` loop executes its body as long as *condition* is False (until *condition* becomes True). Therefore, a `repeat` loop executes its body at least once, but the `while` loop may never execute its body.
- The syntax of a `while` loop follows:

  ```
  while condition do begin
    [statements;]
  end;
  ```

  The syntax of a `repeat` loop follows:

  ```
  repeat
    [statements;]
  until condition;
  ```

- If we precede the `repeat` loop with an `if` statement, we can convert every `while` loop into a `repeat` structure. Converting a `repeat` loop into a `while` loop requires less work and is relatively straightforward.
- An accumulator variable sums the numbers inside a loop to eventually arrive at a final answer. A flag variable is a logical (Boolean) variable that is used to indicate a condition.
- Ordinal routines provide a means of incrementing, decrementing, and determining the ordinal positions of ordinal values and variables.

Review Questions

1. Describe the syntax and operation of the `for`, `while`, and `repeat` loops.
2. Does every `for` loop have equivalent `while` and `repeat` loop structures? Why or why not?
3. Do every `while` loop and every `repeat` loop have equivalent `for` loop structures? Why or why not?
4. Can every `while` loop be written as a `repeat` loop? Why or why not?
5. Can every `repeat` loop be written as a `while` loop? Why or why not?
6. What is an accumulator variable? A flag variable?
7. Name and describe the purpose of the ordinal routines.

Problems

1. Modify the average velocity program in Problem 6 from Chapter 4 to validate the user's input. Force the user to input a non-negative distance and positive time by using loops.
2. Modify the quadratic formula solver in Problem 10 from Chapter 4 to validate the user's input. Force the user to enter a nonzero value of *a*. If the roots are imaginary, display a message indicating this case.
3. Write a program that allows the user to input a string in an edit box and prints the string in reverse order in a memo box.
4. A palindrome is a word or phrase that reads the same forward and backward. For example, "mom" and "dad" are both palindromes. Write a program that determines whether a user-entered string is a palindrome. Make sure that your program is not case sensitive. For instance, your program should recognize "Mom" and "MOm," and all other permutations of uppercase and lowercase letters, to be palindromes.
5. Write a program that converts a user-entered decimal number to its binary equivalent.

6. Write a program that converts a user-entered binary number to its decimal equivalent.

7. Write a program that adds 20 nonzero numbers entered by the user and displays their sum.

8. Modify the program from Problem 7 to add any quantity of nonzero numbers entered by the user. The input loop should end and the program should display the sum when the user enters a zero.

9. Given the rational function

$$f(x) = \frac{8x}{3x^2 + 5x + 2}$$

Write a program that computes the values of $f(x)$ when x varies between –5 and 5 with an increment of 0.5. Display x and corresponding $f(x)$ values in a table within a memo box.

10. Modify the program from Problem 9 to prompt the user for an x value and output the corresponding $f(x)$ value. The program should end when the user inputs a value of 100,000 for x.

11. Write a program that implements the cash register program from Chapter 3.

12. Write a program that implements the modified cash register program from Chapter 3.

Programming Projects

1. Write a program that determines the minimum number of each type of coin required to give change in any amount between 1¢ and 99¢. The program should consider only quarters, dimes, nickels, and pennies.

2. Modify the program in Project 3 from Chapter 5 to print a monthly calendar. The user should input the month and year as numeric inputs, and the program should output a calendar for that month and year.

3. A tickertape program is a program that scrolls a message across the screen, similar to the old-fashioned stock exchange tickertape machines. Write a tickertape program. The program should allow the user to enter a message and then scroll this message in a label on the form. The program should include buttons to start and stop the tickertape.

4. Write a program that mimics the operation of a typewriter. The program should allow the user to enter a message, and then the program should "type" this message in a memo box.

Chapter 7

Text Files

Chapter Objectives

In this chapter you will:

- Discover the need for data files
- Create a text file using the Delphi Code Editor
- Gain an understanding of text file input and output operations
- Create and use text files in Object Pascal
- Become familiar with text file routines and file management routines

Some computer programs are not very effective unless they have the ability to store and retrieve data. Consider a **personal information manager (PIM)** program that requires you to retype the names, addresses, and telephone numbers of your contacts each time that the program starts. Such a program would not be very useful. **File input and output (file I/O)** is the part of computer programming concerned with storing information to and retrieving information from **data files.**

> **File input and output (file I/O)** is the part of computer programming concerned with storing information to and retrieving information from data files.

Object Pascal recognizes three types of data files: text, typed, and untyped files. This chapter illustrates the use of text files, the most common of these data file types. Chapter 11 discusses the remaining two types of data files.

Text Files

> A **sequential file** is a file that is accessed from the beginning of the file to the end of the file (in sequence).

Text files (or **sequential files**) are accessed in order from the beginning of the file to the end of the file. The term **access** refers to both reading from the file and writing to the file. Thus the process of reading from or writing to a text file always starts at the beginning of the file and continues until the end of the file is reached; that is, it proceeds in sequence.

Creating a Text File with the Delphi Code Editor

A text file consists of ASCII text and can be edited using any text editor or word processor that supports saving files in ASCII format, such as the Delphi Code Editor or the Windows WordPad and Notepad accessories. As an example, let's create a text file with the Delphi Code Editor. Select `File|New...` from the Delphi menu bar to open the New Items dialog box. Next, select the Text icon on the New page of the New Items dialog as shown in Figure 7.1. Finally, click the OK button.

An empty page named `File1.txt` appears in the Code Editor window. Add the following lines to this page:

```
Anderson     73
Castor       82
Hartley      91
McGuire      89
Ramone       67
Swanson      78

          111
123456789012 Spacing guide
```

> Do not type these lines into the file. They merely serve as a spacing guide and indicate the positions of the characters in the file.

These lines contain the last names and first exam scores for six students in a computer programming class. Do not type the last two lines into the data file; they are

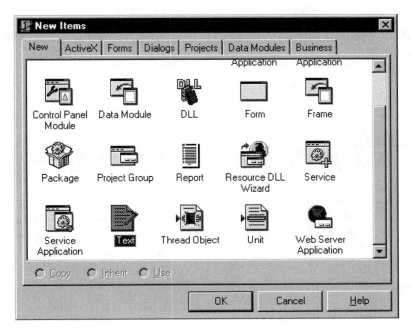

FIGURE 7.1   Creating a Text File with the Delphi Code Editor

simply a spacing guide to help as you type the characters into the file. Make sure that your spacing is correct, as it is important for the example later in this chapter. After typing the lines into the data file and verifying that all characters are in their proper positions, save the file. Select `File|Save As...` to open the Save As dialog box. Type in `exam1` as the file name, and select `Text file (*.txt)` from the Save as type list box. Click the Save button, and Delphi will save `exam1.txt` as an ASCII text file.

The `exam1.txt` file contains additional characters that are not visible in the Delphi Code Editor. These additional characters are known as **control characters, hidden characters,** or **escape characters.** If these control characters were visible, the `exam1.txt` file would have the following appearance:

```
Anderson     73<CR><LF>
Castor       82<CR><LF>
Hartley      91<CR><LF>
McGuire      89<CR><LF>
Ramone       67<CR><LF>
Swanson      78<CR><LF>
<EOF>
```

Each pair of pointed brackets and sequence of letters (`<letters>`) designates a control character. `<CR>` is a carriage return (ASCII value 13), and `<LF>` is a line feed (ASCII value 10). In much the same way that a typewriter works, a carriage return forces the output to begin at the left margin and a line feed moves the output to the next blank line. The end-of-file marker (<EOF>) prevents the cursor from moving past the end of the written text. For instance, if you move the cursor (the blinking position indicator) below the last line of text (containing the name Swanson) and then press the down arrow key, the cursor will not move down any further.

Working with Text Files

Now that you know how to create text files and understand their format, it is time to introduce the Object Pascal statements for text file I/O. Before we can access a file, we must **open** the file. Similarly, when we have completed our operations with the file, we should **close** the file.

To access a text file in Object Pascal, you first create a variable capable of referencing a text file. Declaring a variable of the `TextFile` data type creates a **file reference variable,** which in turn contains a **file pointer.** A file pointer is similar to the cursor in a text editor. That is, a cursor indicates the position within a file in a text editor, and a file pointer indicates the position in an open file. For an input file, the file pointer indicates the next data item to be read from the file. For an output file, the file pointer indicates the position of the next data item written to the file.

> The **file pointer** indicates the current read or write position in an open data file.

Next, we must associate the file reference variable with a data file using the **AssignFile** procedure. The syntax follows:

```
AssignFile(fileRef, fileName);
```

where *fileRef* is a file reference variable and *fileName* is a string expression. *fileName* can contain any valid Windows file name and can specify the **path** of the file, which indicates the disk drive and subdirectory where the file resides.

Finally, before we can access a data file, we must open it. A text file can be opened for either input or output, but not both simultaneously. The **Reset** procedure opens or reopens a text file for input, and the **Rewrite** and **Append** procedures open or reopen a text file for output. The syntax for these procedures follows:

```
Reset(fileRef);
Rewrite(fileRef);
Append(fileRef);
```

As before, *fileRef* is the file reference variable. Reset opens the existing data file whose name is associated with *fileRef* and sets the file pointer to the beginning of the file. If the file is already open, it is first closed and then reopened. A "file not found" run-time error results if no data file with the given name exists.

The Rewrite procedure creates a new data file whose name is associated with *fileRef* and sets the file pointer to the beginning of the file. If a data file of the same name already exists, it is deleted and a new, empty file is created in its place. If the file is already open, it is closed and then recreated. In summary, the Rewrite procedure either creates a new file or overwrites an existing one.

To add data to the end of a file, you use the Append procedure. Append opens the existing text file whose name is associated with *fileRef* and positions the file pointer at the *end* of the file. If the file is already open, it is closed and then reopened. If no data file with the given name exists, a "file not found" run-time error results.

Once a Reset statement opens a text file for input, data can be read from the file using the **Read** statement:

```
Read(fileRef, variable);
```

This statement reads the next piece of data indicated by the file pointer from the input file associated with *fileRef*, stores this information in *variable*, and then moves the file pointer to the next character in the input file. The data type of *variable* should match the type of data being read from the input file. If the data file consists of integers, for example, the data should be read into Integer variables. **Whitespace characters** (spaces and tabs) delimit numerical data in text files.

You can combine multiple Read statements into one statement. For example, consider

```
Read(myFile, variable1);
Read(myFile, variable2);
Read(myFile, variable3);
```

This group of statements reads three pieces of data from the file associated with the file reference variable `myFile`. This group of statements is equivalent to

```
Read(myFile, variable1, variable2, variable3);
```

Thus the general syntax of the `Read` statement is as follows:

> `Read(fileRef, variable1 [, variable2, ...]);`

Whereas the `Read` statement reads data item by item from a text file, the **Readln** statement reads only a specified number of data items per line. The syntax to read one data item into a variable follows:

> `Readln(fileRef, variable);`

This statement reads the next piece of data indicated by the file pointer from the input file associated with *fileRef,* stores this information in *variable,* and then moves the file pointer to the beginning of the next line of the input file.

The general syntax of the `Readln` statement follows:

> `Readln(fileRef, variable1 [, variable2, ...]);`

Unlike with the `Read` statement, we cannot combine `Readln` statements. For example,

```
Readln(myFile, variable1);
Readln(myFile, variable2);
Readln(myFile, variable3);
```

is significantly different from

```
Readln(myFile, variable1, variable2, variable3);
```

Do you see why? The first group of three statements reads one variable per line on three separate lines. The single statement reads three variables on the same line.

When a file is opened for output with the `Rewrite` or `Append` statement, data may be written to the file using the **Write** procedure. The general syntax appears below:

> `Write(fileRef [, expression[:minWidth[:decPlaces]]]);`

As before, *fileRef* is the file reference variable. The *expression* is an expression of any simple or string data type, whereas *minWidth* and *decPlaces* are integer expressions. The optional *minWidth* parameter specifies the minimum number of characters in the output of *expression*. If the length of *expression* is less than *minWidth*, then the Write procedure pads the left side of the output with blank spaces. All characters in *expression* are output when its length exceeds *minWidth*. For a real-type *expression*, the optional *decPlaces* parameter specifies the number of digits following the decimal point. Any number of expressions may be output with a single Write statement (including no expressions) by separating the expressions with commas. For example,

```
Write(myFile, 10:5, 10.47589:8:2);
```

outputs the following text to the file associated with myFile:

```
   10     10.48
```

The **Writeln** statement operates in the same way as Write does, except that it outputs a carriage return/line feed combination (<CR> <LF>) after all of its expressions are output. For instance,

```
Write(myFile, 'Hello ');
Write(myFile, 'and Good-bye');
Writeln(myFile);                         {Skip to next line}
Writeln(myFile, 'Hello ');
Writeln(myFile, 'and Good-bye');
```

outputs the following text:

```
Hello and Good-bye
Hello
and Good-bye
```

As with Read and Readln, you can combine Write statements but not Writeln statements. Thus you can rewrite the preceding example as follows:

```
Write(myFile, 'Hello ', 'and Good-bye');
Writeln(myFile);                         {Skip to next line}
Writeln(myFile, 'Hello ');
Writeln(myFile, 'and Good-bye');
```

Finally, when your program has finished working with a file, you should close the file. The **CloseFile** statement ends the association between a file reference variable and a data file, returning these resources to the system. For an output file, the CloseFile statement also writes the end-of-file character before it closes the file. The syntax of the CloseFile statement follows:

```
CloseFile(fileRef);
```

Text File Routines

Object Pascal includes two extremely important functions for working with text files: the **Eof** and **Eoln** functions. The Eof (end-of-file) function returns a Boolean value that indicates whether the end of an input file has been reached. Eof(*fileRef*) is True when the file pointer is beyond the last character of the file associated with *fileRef*. This function can be used in an indefinite loop structure to read data from an input file until the end of file is reached. The Eoln (end-of-line) function returns a Boolean value that indicates whether the file pointer is at the end of the current line. For an input file associated with *fileRef*, Eoln(*fileRef*) is True when the file pointer is at the end of the current line or Eof(*fileRef*) is True. The Eoln function can also be used in an indefinite loop structure for processing an input file character by character.

Figure 7.2 summarizes the text file routines available in Delphi's Object Pascal.

File Management Routines

Delphi also offers built-in file management routines for performing tasks such as creating directories and renaming files. Figure 7.3 describes Delphi's file management routines.

Function	Purpose
Eof	Tests whether the file pointer is at the end of the file
Eoln	Tests whether the file pointer is at the end of a line
SeekEof	Returns True if there is no more text (other than white space) in the file
SeekEoln	Returns True if there are no more characters (other than white space) on the current line

Procedure	Purpose
Append	Prepares an existing file for adding text to the end
AssignFile	Associates the name of an external file with a file variable
AssignPrn	Assigns a text file variable to the printer
CloseFile	Terminates the association between a file variable and an external file
Erase	Deletes a file
Flush	Empties the buffer of a text file opened for output
Read	Reads data from a file
Readln	Reads a line of text from a file
Reset	Opens an existing file
Rewrite	Creates and opens a new file
SetTextBuf	Assigns an I/O buffer to a text file
Write	Writes data to a text file
Writeln	Writes data and an end-of-line marker to a text file

FIGURE 7.2   Object Pascal Text File Routines

Function	Purpose
CreateDir	Creates a new directory
DeleteFile	Deletes a file from disk
DirectoryExists	Determines whether a specified directory exists
DiskFree	Returns the number of free bytes on a specified drive
DiskSize	Returns the size of a specified drive in bytes
FileDateToDateTime	Converts a DOS date-time value to TDateTime value
FileExists	Tests whether a specified file exists
FileGetAttr	Returns the file attributes of FileName
FileGetDate	Returns a DOS date-time stamp for a specified file
FileOpen	Opens a specified file using a specified access mode
FileRead	Reads a specified number of bytes from a file
FileSearch	Searches a specified DOS path for a file
FileSeek	Positions the current file pointer in a previously opened file
FileSetAttr	Sets the file attributes of a specified file
FileSetDate	Sets the DOS time stamp for a specified file
FileWrite	Writes the contents of a buffer to the current position in a file
FindFirst	Searches for the first instance of a file name with a given set of attributes in a specified directory
FindNext	Returns the next entry matching the name and attributes specified in a previous call to FindFirst
ForceDirectories	Creates all the directories along a directory path if they do not already exist
GetCurrentDir	Returns the name of the current directory
RemoveDir	Deletes an existing empty directory
RenameFile	Changes a file name
SetCurrentDir	Sets the current directory

Procedure	Purpose
ChDir	Changes the current directory
FileClose	Closes a specified file
FindClose	Releases memory allocated by FindFirst
GetDir	Returns the current directory for a specified drive

FIGURE 7.3   Object Pascal File Management Routines

Text File Example

An example code unit that uses text files for input and output appears below. This code uses the `exam1.txt` file created earlier in this chapter as an input file. It assumes that the `exam1.txt` file is located in the **root directory** (main directory) of drive C (that is, `C:\exam1.txt`). The code unit creates one output file in the root directory of drive C; `names.txt` is a data file consisting of all last names in `exam1.txt`. Figure 7.4 shows the program form after executing this code, and Figure 7.5 gives the contents of `names.txt`.

```
unit TextIOEx;

interface

uses
  Windows, Messages, SysUtils, Classes, Graphics, Controls,
  Forms, Dialogs, StdCtrls;

type
  TfrmTextIO = class(TForm)
    btnTextIO: TButton;
    memOutput: TMemo;
    procedure DoExample(Sender: TObject);
  private
    { Private declarations }
  public
    { Public declarations }
  end;

var
  frmTextIO: TfrmTextIO;

implementation

{$R *.DFM}

{Read the exam1.txt data file, display the data in the
memOutput memo box, and create the names.txt file that
contains the last names.}
procedure TfrmTextIO.DoExample(Sender: TObject);

var
  inFile:    TextFile;
  outFile:   TextFile;
  lastName:  String[10];
  examScore: Integer;

begin
  AssignFile(inFile, 'c:\exam1.txt');
  AssignFile(outFile, 'c:\names.txt');
  Reset(inFile);
  Rewrite(outFile);
  Writeln(outFile, 'Last Name');
```

```
    Writeln(outFile, '---------');
    memOutput.Clear;
    memOutput.Lines.Add('Student    Exam 1');
    memOutput.Lines.Add('-------    ------');
    while not(eof(inFile)) do begin
      Readln(inFile, lastName, examScore);
      Writeln(outFile, Trim(lastName));
      memOutput.Lines.Add(lastName + IntToStr(examScore));
    end;
    memOutput.Lines.Add('');
    memOutput.Lines.Add('C:\names.txt file created.');
    memOutput.Lines.Add('PROGRAM COMPLETE');
    CloseFile(inFile);
    CloseFile(outFile);
  end;

  end.
```

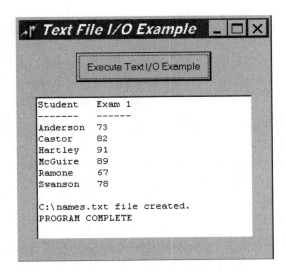

FIGURE 7.4 Form for Text File I/O Example

```
Last Name
---------
Anderson
Castor
Hartley
McGuire
Ramone
Swanson
```

FIGURE 7.5 Contents of names.txt

Programming Key: Warning

Errors in the formatting of input data files are often the cause of run-time file input/output errors. In particular, extra blank lines preceding the end-of-file marker are a common cause of such run-time errors. Before you debug your program, make sure that the input file appears in the required format.

Programming Key: Delphi Highlight

Oftentimes, text files consist of data in comma-separated format; that is, the text file contains data items that are separated (or delimited) by commas. The Borland Database Engine (BDE) contains an ASCII driver for dealing with such input. For instance, setting the `TableType` property of a table object to `ttASCII` indicates that the table's data file consists of comma-delimited ASCII text. Chapter 13 discusses the BDE, databases, and database applications.

GUI Design Tips

The drive combo box, directory list box, filter combo box, and file list box components allow the programmer to quickly design user interfaces to select drives, directories, file filters, and files. These components are located on the Win 3.1 page of Delphi's Component Palette, as described in Chapter 16.

The following example implements a simple disk explorer program in Delphi. Note that this project does not require any manual coding. Figure 7.6 shows a sample execution.

Component	Property	Setting
Form	Name	frmDiskExplorer
	Caption	My Disk Explorer
DriveComboBox	Name	drvDiskDrive
	DirList	dirDirName
DirectoryListBox	Name	dirDirName
	FileList	filFileName
FileListBox	Name	filFileName

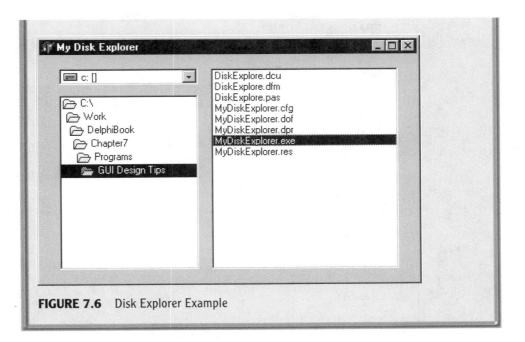

FIGURE 7.6   Disk Explorer Example

• C • A • S • E • S • T • U • D • Y •

Word Counter

Frank's English teacher assigned a 1000-word essay for homework. That is, his final essay must contain at least 1000 words. Frank wrote his essay using Microsoft WordPad, and now he wants to count his total number of words. Rather than count the words by hand, Frank decides to save his essay as a text file and write a program that will count the words for him.

Can you help Frank write this program? The program should allow the user to input a file name and then count the number of words in the file. The result should be displayed in a memo box.

Design your algorithm and write your program. Compare your answer to the following code unit for Frank's word counter program. A sample execution of Frank's program appears in Figure 7.7. It appears that Frank has satisfied the 1000-word requirement for his essay.

```
unit WordCount;

interface

uses
  Windows, Messages, SysUtils, Classes, Graphics,
  Controls, Forms, Dialogs, StdCtrls;

type
  TfrmWordCounter = class(TForm)
    lblInFileName: TLabel;
    edtInFileName: TEdit;
    btnCountWords: TButton;
    memOutput: TMemo;
    procedure CountWords(Sender: TObject);
  private
    { Private declarations }
  public
    { Public declarations }
  end;

var
  frmWordCounter: TfrmWordCounter;

implementation

{$R *.DFM}

{Count the number of words in the user-entered
input data file}
procedure TfrmWordCounter.CountWords(Sender: TObject);

var
  inFile: TextFile;
  words:  Integer;
  ch:     Char;

begin
  AssignFile(inFile, edtInFileName.Text);
  Reset(inFile);

  words := 0;
  while not(Eof(inFile)) do begin

    {Skip whitespace}
    ch := ' ';
    while not(Eoln(inFile)) and
          ((ch = ' ') or (Ord(ch) = 9)) do begin
      Read(inFile, ch);
    end;
```

```
        if Eoln(inFile) then begin
          Readln(inFile);
        end
        else begin
          {Increment the number of words and skip the
           current word}
          Inc(words);
          while not(Eoln(inFile)) and
                not((ch = ' ') or (Ord(ch) = 9)) do begin
            Read(inFile, ch);
          end;
        end;

    end;

    {Display results}
    memOutput.Clear;
    memOutput.Lines.Add(Trim(edtInFileName.Text) +
                        ' contains ' +
                        IntToStr(words) + ' words.');
  end;

end.
```

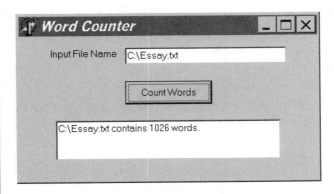

FIGURE 7.7   Word Counter Sample Execution

Summary

Key Terms

access—To read from or write to a data file.

close—To terminate the access of a data file and disassociate it with a file reference variable.

control characters—Nonvisible characters that perform special functions, such as a carriage return or line feed.

data file—A file that contains data.

escape characters—See *control characters*.

file input and output (file I/O)—The part of computer programming concerned with storing information to and retrieving information from data files.

file pointer—A pointer that indicates the current read or write position in an open data file.

file reference variable—A variable that references a data file; for a text file, a variable of the `TextFile` data type.

hidden characters—See *control characters*.

open—To prepare a data file for access and associate it with a file reference variable.

path—A disk drive and subdirectory combination that indicates the location of a file.

personal information manager (PIM)—A program that maintains the user's personal information, such as contacts, appointments, and expenses.

root directory—The main directory.

sequential file—A file that is accessed in order, or sequentially, from the beginning of the file to the end of the file.

whitespace characters—Characters that create empty space in a data file; spaces and tabs.

Keywords

Functions

CreateDir	Eoln
DeleteFile	FileDateToDateTime
DirectoryExists	FileExists
DiskFree	FileGetAttr
DiskSize	FileGetDate
Eof	FileOpen

FileRead	ForceDirectories
FileSearch	GetCurrentDir
FileSeek	RemoveDir
FileSetAttr	RenameFile
FileSetDate	SeekEof
FileWrite	SeekEoln
FindFirst	SetCurrentDir
FindNext	

Procedures

Append	GetDir
AssignFile	Read
AssignPrn	Readln
ChDir	Reset
CloseFile	Rewrite
Erase	SetTextBuf
FileClose	Write
FindClose	Writeln
Flush	

Key Concepts

- Data files provide a means of information storage and retrieval.
- There are three types of data files in Object Pascal: text, typed, and untyped files.
- Text files, the most common of the data file types, are sequential files consisting of ASCII text. A sequential file is a data file that is accessed in order (or sequentially), from the beginning of the file to the end of the file.
- A text file may be created using any text editor or word processor that supports saving files in ASCII format, such as the Delphi Code Editor or the Windows WordPad and Notepad accessories.
- Control (hidden or escape) characters are nonvisible characters in a text file that perform special functions, such as a carriage return or line feed.
- To access a text file in Object Pascal, you must first create a file reference variable of the TextFile data type. This file reference variable contains the file pointer, which indicates the current read or write position in the file.
- The AssignFile procedure associates a file reference variable with a data file.

```
AssignFile(fileRef, fileName);
```

- A text file can be opened for either input or output, but not both simultaneously. The Reset procedure opens or reopens a text file for input, and the Rewrite and Append procedures open or reopen a text file for output. Reset opens an existing data file and sets the file pointer to the beginning of the file. Rewrite creates a new data file and sets the file pointer to the beginning of the file. Append opens an existing data file and positions the file pointer at the end of the file.

```
Reset(fileRef);
Rewrite(fileRef);
Append(fileRef);
```

- Data are read from a text file using the Read and Readln procedures.

```
Read(fileRef, variable1 [, variable2, ...]);
Readln(fileRef, variable1 [, variable2, ...]);
```

- Data are written to a text file using the Write and Writeln procedures.

```
Write(fileRef [, expression[:minWidth[:decPlaces]]]);
Writeln(fileRef [, expression[:minWidth[:decPlaces]]]);
```

- When your program is finished working with a file, you should close the file. The CloseFile statement ends the association between a file reference variable and a data file, returning these resources to the system. For an output file, the CloseFile statement also writes the end-of-file character before it closes the file.

```
CloseFile(fileRef);
```

- Object Pascal contains a variety of built-in text file routines. The Eof (end-of-file) function returns a Boolean value that indicates whether the end of an input file is reached. The Eoln (end-of-line) function returns a Boolean value that indicates whether the file pointer is at the end of the current line.

- Delphi also contains built-in file management routines for performing tasks such as creating directories and renaming files.

Review Questions

1. What is the purpose of a data file?
2. Name the three types of data files in Object Pascal.
3. What is a sequential file? How can you create one?
4. What are control characters? What are some other names for control characters?
5. What is a file pointer?

6. For the text file named `MyData.txt`, write the Object Pascal code necessary to do the following:
   a. Open the file for input
   b. Open the file for output (by overwriting old data)
   c. Open the file for output (without overwriting old data)

7. What is the difference between the following lines of code?

```
Read(inFile, intVar1);
Read(inFile, intVar2);
```

and

```
Readln(inFile, intVar1, intVar2);
```

8. What is the difference between the following lines of code?

```
Write(outFile, intVar1, ' ');
Write(outFile, intVar2, ' ');
```

and

```
Writeln(outFile, intVar1, ' ', intVar2, ' ');
```

9. What does the `CloseFile` procedure do?

10. Describe the purpose and operation of the `Eof` and `Eoln` functions.

Problems

1. Write a program that displays the contents of a text file in a memo box (line by line). This program, known as a "file dump" program, should just "dump" the data from the file onto the screen.

2. Write a program that outputs 10 user-entered numbers to a text file.

3. Write a program that reads 10 numbers from a text file and displays the numbers and their sum in a memo box.

4. Write a program that reads 10 numbers from a text file and outputs these numbers and their sum to another text file in a report format.

5. Write a program that outputs your name and birth date to a text file.

6. Write a program that reads your name and birth date from a text file and displays this information in a memo box.

7. Write a program that outputs your name and birth date to a text file in a report format.

8. Write a program that outputs a user-entered name and address to a text file.

9. Write a program that reads a name and address from a text file and displays this information in a memo box.

10. Write a program that outputs a user-entered name and address to a text file in a report format.

11. Modify the program in Problem 9 from Chapter 6 to output a table of x and $f(x)$ values to a text file in a report format.

Programming Projects

1. Write a program that finds the sum and average of the numbers in a user-specified data file. The first line of the data file contains the number of data items within the file, and this information is not considered part of the data (that is, you should exclude it from the sum and average calculations).

2. Write a program that allows the user to create an input file for the program in Project 1.

3. Write a program that reads student names, course grades, and course credit hours from a text file and then computes grade-point averages (GPAs) for the students. Students can take different numbers of courses, but each student takes at least one course. The student GPAs should be written to a text file in a report format. A sample input file appears below:

```
Smith           John        A 4 B 4 B 4 A 3
Thomas          Mark        C 5 A 5 A 4
Hoffman         Susan       B 3 B 4 C 3 B 4 B 3

          1111111111222222222233333333334444444    Spacing
 12345678901234567890123456789012345678901234545    guide
```

4. Write a program that allows the user to create an input file for the program in Project 3.

Chapter **8**

Structured Programming

Chapter Objectives

In this chapter you will:

- Discover the advantages of modular programming

- Learn about code units in Object Pascal

- Distinguish between the two types of subprograms, procedures and functions, and learn about the appropriate situations for their use

- Understand the difference between arguments and parameters and the relationship between them

- Learn the two methods of parameter passing, pass by reference and pass by value

- Understand the concept of focus in the Windows operating system

- Gain an understanding of Object Pascal events and event handlers, especially for form, focus, and mouse events

So far, our programs have been relatively small and contained within a single block of statements. When designing a large program, however, it is considered undesirable to have only a single block of code perform all processing. This chapter introduces the programming terminology and techniques required to solve larger, more complex problems.

The Modular Design Philosophy

If you own a stereo system, you are probably familiar with the concept of **components.** A typical stereo system, for instance, includes a receiver, a tape deck, a CD changer, and speakers. Manufacturers know that if they provide each component separately, then consumers can mix and match the components as necessary. Component stereo systems are also a more attractive alternative than integrated systems (one-piece systems) because they can be upgraded by simply purchasing a new component. For example, you can easily replace a 3-CD changer in a component system with a 50-CD changer. Additionally, as technology improves and new components become available, they can be added to the system.

A stereo system component is analogous to a **unit** in the world of Object Pascal programming. **Modular programming** refers to computer programming that is based on a modular, or component-based, design that relies on code units. **Structured programs** are programs that contain control structures, such as decision and repetition structures, and execute statements sequentially; they typically contain **subprograms** and may be modular in design. Thus all programs written in Object Pascal are structured programs, because the language itself is highly structured. Furthermore, all Windows applications written with the Delphi IDE are modular programs, because the code for each form appears in a separate unit.

Modular programming offers several advantages. First, it allows the programmer to logically organize a program by dividing the problem into smaller subproblems. Repeatedly using this "divide and conquer" technique to solve a problem is called **stepwise refinement** and is part of the **top-down design** programming methodology. For instance, a programmer may write a program consisting of three subprograms: one subprogram contains the input routine, another performs calculations, and a final subprogram displays the output. Second, modular programming enhances the readability of the code and simplifies the debugging process. Third, as with the components in a stereo system, a module can be easily replaced (or upgraded) to improve the program. Finally, modular programming allows for the reuse of code. **Code reuse** is an important aspect of computer programming. Once a programmer writes a subprogram that performs a certain task, there is no need to rewrite this subprogram in every application that requires it; instead, programmers can simply reuse the existing code. This philosophy of reuse reemphasizes the importance of adequate documentation, which must specify the required subprogram inputs and the type of output.

Subprograms

Procedures and **functions** represent the two types of subprograms (or routines). You have already seen examples of these subprograms and used both in Object Pascal. Let's review one of these routines, the square root finder example from Chapter 4:

> The line numbers are not part of the code but are added for reference.

```
1:    procedure TfrmSquareRoot.SquareRoot(Sender: TObject);
2:
3:    var
4:       value:  Real;
5:       code:   Integer;
6:       result: String;
7:
8:    begin
9:       Val(edtInputNumber.Text, value, code);
10:      value := Sqrt(value);
11:      Str(value, result);
12:      memOutput.Lines.Add('The square root of ' +
13:                          edtInputNumber.Text +
14:                          ' is ' + result);
15:   end;
```

The line numbers in this code are not part of the program, but rather are added just for reference. The user interface for this program consists of the form (frmSquareRoot) and four components on the form: a label (lblInputNum-ber), an edit box (edtInputNumber), a button (btnComputeSqrRt), and a memo box (memOutput). The code computes the square root of a number that the user enters in edtInputNumber and displays the result in memOutput. Further-more, this code is associated with the OnClick event of the btnComputeSqrRt button. In other words, when the user places the mouse pointer over the btnComputeSqrRt button and clicks the left mouse button, this code executes.

Remember, Delphi is designed as a development tool for the Windows operat-ing system. **Events** (key presses, mouse clicks, and so on) occur in Windows, and programmers must write **event handlers** to manage these events. An event han-dler is a special type of procedure that is **invoked** (called or executed) when a specified event occurs on its associated component. An event handler may be as-sociated with several events and components. In the preceding code, line 1 is the declaration (or heading) of the SquareRoot procedure, an event handler for the btnComputeSqrRt component. We can see that it is an event handler rather than a standard procedure because (Sender: TObject) appears in the declaration. This expression indicates that the procedure is invoked by an event occurring on some Sender object of type TObject (the base object class in Delphi). All event handlers in Delphi are procedures, so you have been writing subprograms all along. The code for the `SquareRoot` event handler is delimited by the `begin` and `end` keywords on lines 8 and 15, respectively.

This example also contains procedure and function **calls.** Line 9 invokes the `Val` procedure, and line 11 invokes the `Str` procedure. Line 10 calls `Sqrt`, the built-in arithmetic function that finds the square root of a number. Finally, lines 12 through 14 add a line of text to `memOutput` by calling the `Add` **method** of its `Lines` object. A method is a procedure or function that is associated with a **class** of objects, where the class designates the type of object. Normally, a method alters one or more of its object's properties.

Arguments and Parameters

Can you notice any similarity between procedures and functions just by examining the code in the previous example? In the procedure calls on lines 9 and 11, parentheses follow the procedure names. These parentheses enclose one or more items. Similarly, the `Sqrt` function call on line 10 is followed by parentheses that contain an item. *Parentheses enclose the information passed to subprograms.*

Let's look at another example. This time, the procedure `Adder` sums two numbers.

```
{Add num1 and num2 and store the result in sum}
procedure Adder(num1: Real; num2: Real; var sum: Real);

begin
  sum := num1 + num2;
end;
```

In this code, num1, num2, and sum are the **parameters** of the `Adder` procedure. Parameters act as placeholders for the information passed to a subprogram when it is invoked. The parameter list specified in the `Adder` procedure contains three elements, thereby informing the Delphi compiler that the `Adder` procedure requires three real numbers as input.

A simple **test driver** for the `Adder` procedure appears below. When the user clicks the `btnAdd` button, the `AddNumbers` event handler is invoked. This event handler adds the numbers in the edit boxes `edtNum1` and `edtNum2` by calling the `Adder` procedure, then stores the result in `edtResult`.

```
{Add two user-entered numbers}
procedure TfrmAdderProcedure.AddNumbers(Sender: TObject);

var
  firstNum:   Real;
  secondNum:  Real;
  result:     Real;
  code:       Integer;
```

```
begin
  Val(edtNum1.Text, firstNum, code);
  Val(edtNum2.Text, secondNum, code);

  Adder(firstNum, secondNum, result);

  edtResult.Text := Format('%15.5f', [result]);
end;
```

The variables firstNum, secondNum, and result are the **arguments** of the Adder procedure; these variables contain the values that are **passed** to the procedure. An argument can consist of any expression that is of the same type as its corresponding parameter.

> An **argument** is a piece of information passed to a subprogram. A **parameter** is a placeholder for the information passed to a subprogram when it is invoked. Every argument has a corresponding parameter.

Several important points apply concerning subprogram arguments and parameters:

1. The number of arguments must equal the number of parameters.
2. Order is important. The first argument corresponds to the first parameter, the second argument to the second parameter, and so on.
3. The data type of each argument must match the data type of its corresponding parameter.
4. Names are not important. The name of an argument does not have to correspond to the name of its parameter.
5. Recognize the manner in which data are passed—by reference or by value. These topics are discussed later in this chapter.

Defining and Using Subprograms

Procedures and functions that are not built into Object Pascal are called **user-defined subprograms** because the programmer (the user of the compiler) must define them. As shown in our earlier example, the general form for defining a procedure is

```
procedure ProcedureName(param1: Type1; param2: Type2; ...);

[localDeclarations;]

begin
  [statements;]
end;
```

To invoke a procedure, you state the procedure name along with any required arguments. The general syntax of a procedure call follows:

```
ProcedureName(argument1, argument2, ...);
```

Functions differ somewhat from procedures. A function may take any number of arguments, but it always returns a single value to the **calling routine.** A procedure, on the other hand, does not automatically return a value. *The general rule is to use a function if you need to return exactly one value to the calling routine.* For this reason, our `Adder` procedure is better written as a function:

```
{Return the sum of num1 and num2}
function Adder(num1: Real; num2: Real): Real;

begin
  Adder := num1 + num2;
end;
```

A test driver for the `Adder` function appears below:

```
{Add two user-entered numbers}
procedure TfrmAdderFunction.AddNumbers(Sender: TObject);

var
  firstNum:  Real;
  secondNum: Real;
  result:    Real;
  code:      Integer;

begin
  Val(edtNum1.Text, firstNum, code);
  Val(edtNum2.Text, secondNum, code);

  result := Adder(firstNum, secondNum);

  edtResult.Text := Format('%15.5f', [result]);
end;
```

From this example, we see the general form of a user-defined function:

```
function FunctionName(param1: Type1; ...): FunctionType;
[localDeclarations;]
begin
  [statements;]
  FunctionName := ReturnValue;
end;
```

Notice that the function is defined with a specific data type (*FunctionType*); it gives the data type of the value returned by the function to the calling routine. To return a value to the calling routine, the return value (*ReturnValue*) must be assigned to the function name (*FunctionName*) somewhere within the function's code block, as shown in the line preceding the **end** keyword.

> A **function** is a subprogram that returns a single value to the calling routine. It usually performs a computation. A **procedure** is a subprogram that does not automatically return a value to the calling routine. It is designed to perform a specific task.

Programming Key: Tips

In a function, the function name and **result** variable act as special variables that hold the function's return value. The **result** variable is an implicit variable of every user-defined function. We can rewrite the following general function definition:

```
function FunctionName(param1: Type1; ...):
FunctionType;

[localDeclarations;]

begin
  [statements;]
  result := ReturnValue;
end;
```

Notice that we do not have to declare the **result** variable; it is declared implicitly. Both **result** and the function name always represent the same value. When execution of the function terminates, the last value assigned to **result** or to the function name becomes the function's return value.

Much as with a procedure call, you invoke a function by writing the function name along with any required arguments. Unlike a procedure call, however, a function call returns a single value, and your program should do something with this value (store it in a variable, display it, and so on). The general form of a function invocation with the returned value assigned to a variable follows:

```
variableName := FunctionName(argument1, argument2, ...);
```

To make a subprogram available to other units, a copy of the subprogram heading must appear within the interface section of the code unit that defines it. Such subprograms are **public** in scope; that is, these subprograms may be called

> ### Programming Key: Tips
>
> Parameters that have the same data type and are passed in the same manner may be combined in the parameter list of a subprogram. For instance, we can rewrite the `Adder` function as follows:
>
> ```
> {Return the sum of num1 and num2}
> function Adder(num1, num2: Real): Real;
>
> begin
>   Adder := num1 + num2;
> end;
> ```
>
> When grouping parameters in the parameter list of a subprogram, make sure that you maintain the correct order.

by other units that use the code unit containing the subprogram definition. Normally, all such user-defined subprogram headings are grouped together in the interface section of the unit. For instance, to ensure that you can call the `Adder` function from another code unit, the interface section of the unit in which the `Adder` function is defined must appear as follows:

```
interface

uses
  Windows, Messages, SysUtils, Classes, Graphics, Controls,
  Forms, Dialogs, StdCtrls;
              .
              .
              .
function Adder(num1: Real; num2: Real): Real;
              .
              .
              .
```

In summary, the interface section of a unit must contain the headings of all user-defined subprograms that the programmer desires to call from other units (public subprograms). The entire code unit containing the public `Adder` function and test driver appears below:

```
unit AdderFunc;

interface

uses
  Windows, Messages, SysUtils, Classes, Graphics, Controls,
  Forms, Dialogs, StdCtrls;
```

```
type
  TfrmAdderFunction = class(TForm)
    edtNum1: TEdit;
    edtNum2: TEdit;
    edtResult: TEdit;
    lblPlus: TLabel;
    lblEquals: TLabel;
    btnAdd: TButton;
    procedure AddNumbers(Sender: TObject);
  private
    { Private declarations }
  public
    { Public declarations }
  end;

var
  frmAdderFunction: TfrmAdderFunction;

function Adder(num1: Real; num2: Real): Real;

implementation

{$R *.DFM}

{Add two user-entered numbers}
procedure TfrmAdderFunction.AddNumbers(Sender: TObject);

var
  firstNum:  Real;
  secondNum: Real;
  result:    Real;
  code:      Integer;

begin
  Val(edtNum1.Text, firstNum, code);
  Val(edtNum2.Text, secondNum, code);

  result := Adder(firstNum, secondNum);

  edtResult.Text := Format('%15.5f', [result]);
end;

{Return the sum of num1 and num2}
function Adder(num1: Real; num2: Real): Real;

begin
  Adder := num1 + num2;
end;

end.
```

Those subprograms whose headings do not appear within the interface section but are defined and called in the implementation section are **private** subprograms. A private subprogram can be called only within the unit in which it is defined.

> ### Programming Key: Warning
>
> Object Pascal does place certain restrictions on the ordering of your subprograms. For public subprograms defined within a unit, the subprogram headings may appear in any order in the interface section, and the subprogram definitions may appear in any order in the implementation section, regardless of whether one subprogram calls another. For private subprograms, however, the subprogram definition must appear before the subprogram call. In other words, if one subprogram calls a private subprogram, the private subprogram definition must appear first.

Parameter Passing

Pass by reference is a type of parameter passing in which the memory location (address) of the argument is passed to the subprogram instead of the argument's value, allowing the subprogram to access the actual variable and modify its contents. **Pass by value** is a type of parameter passing in which the value of the argument is passed to the subprogram, allowing the subprogram to access a copy of the variable. Pass by value preserves the contents of the original variable. It is the default method of parameter passing in Object Pascal.

Parameters can be passed either **by reference** or **by value.** Passing a parameter by reference actually passes the memory location (address) of the argument to the subprogram, not the argument's value. This approach allows the subprogram to access the actual variable. As a result, the subprogram can change the variable's value. Passing a parameter by value, on the other hand, passes the value of the argument to the subprogram. This approach means that the subprogram accesses a copy of the variable, so the subprogram cannot change the variable's actual value. Passing by value is the default method of parameter passing in Object Pascal. The following examples illustrate these points.

```
{MyProcedure - pass by value}
procedure MyProcedure(number: Integer);

begin
  frmPassByValue.memOutput.Lines.Add(
                        'Start MyProcedure: ' +
                        '    number = ' +
                        IntToStr(number));

number := 2 * number;
frmPassByValue.memOutput.Lines.Add('End MyProcedure:    ' +
                        '    number = ' +
                        IntToStr(number));
end;
```

```
{Test Driver for MyProcedure}
procedure TfrmPassByValue.TestDriver(Sender: TObject);

var
  value: Integer;

begin
  value := 5;

  memOutput.Clear;
  memOutput.Lines.Add('Start Test Driver:    value  = ' +
                      IntToStr(value));
  MyProcedure(value);
  memOutput.Lines.Add('End Test Driver:    value  = ' +
                      IntToStr(value));
end;
```

The preceding code segment passes the number parameter by value. The output
from this code follows:

```
Start Test Driver:    value  = 5
Start MyProcedure:    number = 5
End MyProcedure:    number = 10
End Test Driver:    value  = 5
```

Notice that value is not affected by the operations of MyProcedure.

Next, let's modify this example and add the **var** keyword before the number
parameter in MyProcedure. The modified code segment follows:

```
{MyProcedure - pass by reference}
procedure MyProcedure(var number: Integer);

begin
  frmPassByReference.memOutput.Lines.Add(
                            'Start MyProcedure: ' +
                            '    number = ' +
                            IntToStr(number));
  number := 2 * number;
  frmPassByReference.memOutput.Lines.Add('End MyProcedure:    ' +
                            '    number = ' +
                            IntToStr(number));
end;

{Test Driver for MyProcedure}
procedure TfrmPassByReference.TestDriver(Sender: TObject);

var
  value: Integer;

begin
  value := 5;
```

> This code is almost identical to the previous example, with the main exception of the var keyword preceding the parameter name in this version.

```
    memOutput.Clear;
    memOutput.Lines.Add('Start Test Driver:    value  = ' +
                        IntToStr(value));
    MyProcedure(value);
    memOutput.Lines.Add('End Test Driver:    value  = ' +
                        IntToStr(value));
  end;
```

This code passes parameters by reference. Its output follows:

```
Start Test Driver:     value  = 5
Start MyProcedure:     number = 5
End MyProcedure:       number = 10
End Test Driver:       value  = 10
```

Because the `number` parameter references the `value` variable, `value` changes as `number` is modified in `MyProcedure`. In a subprogram heading, the `var` keyword must precede each parameter that is passed by reference.

Programming Key: Tips

Object Pascal also supports constant (**const**) parameters. A constant parameter is similar to a pass-by-value parameter, except that its value cannot be reassigned within the body of the procedure or function, nor can it be passed by reference to another routine. You can think of a constant parameter as a local constant or a read-only variable.

GUI Design Tips

A scroll bar may be used as an input device to indicate a desired speed or quantity level. In the following example, the user inputs a number between 0 and 100 with the scroll bar, and the program then calls the `AddOne` procedure this number of times. Figure 8.1 shows a sample execution of this program. Chapter 16 examines scroll bars in greater detail.

Component	Property	Setting
Form	Name	frmGUIScrollBar
	Caption	GUI Design Tips: ScrollBar
Label	Name	lblQuestion
	Caption	How many times should I execute the AddOne procedure?

Component	Property	Setting
	Font	MS Sans Serif
	Size	14
	WordWrap	True
Label	Name	lblInstruct
	Caption	Use the scrollbar below to change the number
Edit Box	Name	edtNumber
	Font	MS Sans Serif
	Size	18
	ReadOnly	True
	Text	0
ScrollBar	Name	sbrNumber
	Kind	sbHorizontal
	LargeChange	10
	Max	100
	Min	0
	Position	0
	SmallChange	1
Button	Name	btnExecute
	Caption	Execute
Memo Box	Name	memOutput
	Lines	*Empty*
	ReadOnly	True

Component Name	Event	Setting
sbrNumber	OnChange	UpdateNumber
btnExecute	OnClick	DoIt

```
unit ScrollBarEx;

interface

uses
  Windows, Messages, SysUtils, Classes, Graphics, Controls,
  Forms, Dialogs, StdCtrls;

type
  TfrmGUIScrollBar = class(TForm)
    sbrNumber: TScrollBar;
    lblQuestion: TLabel;
    edtNumber: TEdit;
    lblInstruct: TLabel;
    btnExecute: TButton;
```

```
      memOutput: TMemo;
      procedure UpdateNumber(Sender: TObject);
      procedure DoIt(Sender: TObject);
    private
      { Private declarations }
    public
      { Public declarations }
    end;

var
  frmGUIScrollBar: TfrmGUIScrollBar;

implementation

{$R *.DFM}

{Update the edit box}
procedure TfrmGUIScrollBar.UpdateNumber(Sender: TObject);

begin
  edtNumber.Text := IntToStr(sbrNumber.Position);
end;

procedure AddOne(var number: Integer);

begin
  Inc(number);
end;

procedure TfrmGUIScrollBar.DoIt(Sender: TObject);

var
  counter: Integer;
  sum:     Integer;

begin
  sum := 0;
  for counter := 1 to sbrNumber.Position do begin
    AddOne(sum);
  end;
  memOutput.Clear;
  memOutput.Lines.Add('The AddOne procedure was called ' +
                      IntToStr(sum) + ' times.');
end;

end.
```

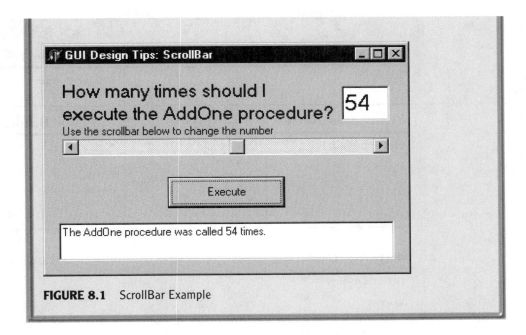

FIGURE 8.1   ScrollBar Example

Events

As mentioned earlier, event handlers are subprograms in Object Pascal, and a user action (such as pressing a key or clicking the mouse) constitutes an event in the Windows operating system. Several events occur upon the initiation and termination of an application, and these events may be used for special processing tasks. When a Delphi application starts, it creates its main form, and the following events occur in the prescribed order: **OnCreate**, **OnShow**, **OnPaint**, and **OnActivate**. OnCreate occurs when the form is created. The OnShow event occurs when the form is displayed (that is, when its Visible property is set to True). OnPaint occurs when the form receives a Windows paint message, and OnActivate occurs when it becomes the active form. When a Delphi application terminates, the **OnClose** and **OnDestroy** events occur, in that order. OnClose occurs before the form closes, and OnDestroy occurs when the form is destroyed. As a matter of good programming practice, you should ensure that any objects created with the OnCreate event are destroyed by the OnDestroy event. The unit that follows on the next page confirms the sequence of these events:

Component	Property	Setting
Form	Name	frmEventOrder
	Caption	Event Order Example

Component Name	Event	Event Handler
frmEventOrder	OnActivate	ActivateForm
	OnClose	CloseForm
	OnCreate	CreateForm
	OnDestroy	DestroyForm
	OnPaint	PaintForm
	OnShow	ShowForm

```
unit EventOrderEx;

interface

uses
  Windows, Messages, SysUtils, Classes, Graphics, Controls,
  Forms, Dialogs, StdCtrls;

type
  TfrmEventOrder = class(TForm)
    procedure ActivateForm(Sender: TObject);
    procedure CreateForm(Sender: TObject);
    procedure PaintForm(Sender: TObject);
    procedure ShowForm(Sender: TObject);
    procedure CloseForm(Sender: TObject; var Action:
TCloseAction);
    procedure DestroyForm(Sender: TObject);
  private
    { Private declarations }
  public
    { Public declarations }
  end;

var
  frmEventOrder: TfrmEventOrder;

implementation

{$R *.DFM}

procedure TfrmEventOrder.ActivateForm(Sender: TObject);

begin
  Application.MessageBox('ActivateForm Event Handler',
                         'OnActivate Event', MB_OK);
end;
```

```
procedure TfrmEventOrder.CreateForm(Sender: TObject);

begin
  Application.MessageBox('CreateForm Event Handler',
                         'OnCreate Event', MB_OK);
end;

procedure TfrmEventOrder.PaintForm(Sender: TObject);

begin
  Application.MessageBox('PaintForm Event Handler',
                         'OnPaint Event', MB_OK);
end;

procedure TfrmEventOrder.ShowForm(Sender: TObject);

begin
  Application.MessageBox('ShowForm Event Handler',
                         'OnShow Event', MB_OK);
end;

procedure TfrmEventOrder.CloseForm(Sender: TObject;
  var Action: TCloseAction);

begin
  Application.MessageBox('CloseForm Event Handler',
                         'OnClose Event', MB_OK);
end;

procedure TfrmEventOrder.DestroyForm(Sender: TObject);

begin
  Application.MessageBox('DestroyForm Event Handler',
                         'OnDestroy Event', MB_OK);
end;

end.
```

In the Windows environment, only one object can receive input (a mouse click or a key press) at any instant in time. This object is said to "have the **focus.**" A form that has the focus, for instance, displays a highlighted caption or title bar. The user can change the focus to another object by clicking that object or by pressing the TAB key to switch between objects. Additionally, program code can change the focus through the **SetFocus** method. For forms, the two focus events are OnActivate and **OnDeactivate**. OnActivate occurs when the form receives the focus, and OnDeactivate occurs when the form loses the focus. For other VCL controls, the focus events are **OnEnter** and **OnExit**. OnEnter occurs when a control receives the input focus, and OnExit occurs when the control loses the focus. The following example illustrates the OnEnter and OnExit events using two memo boxes, memOut1 and memOut2:

Component	Property	Setting
Form	Name	frmFocusExample
	Caption	Focus Example
Memo Box	Name	memOut1
	Lines	*Blank*
	ReadOnly	True
Memo Box	Name	memOut2
	Lines	*Blank*
	ReadOnly	True

Component Name	Event	Event Handler
memOut1	OnEnter	GotFocus
	OnExit	LostFocus
memOut2	OnEnter	GotFocus
	OnExit	LostFocus

```
unit FocusEx;

interface

uses
  Windows, Messages, SysUtils, Classes, Graphics, Controls,
  Forms, Dialogs, StdCtrls;

type
  TfrmFocusExample = class(TForm)
    memOut1: TMemo;
    memOut2: TMemo;
    procedure GotFocus(Sender: TObject);
    procedure LostFocus(Sender: TObject);
  private
    { Private declarations }
  public
    { Public declarations }
  end;

var
  frmFocusExample: TfrmFocusExample;

implementation

{$R *.DFM}

procedure TfrmFocusExample.GotFocus(Sender: TObject);
```

```
begin
  TMemo(Sender).Clear;
  TMemo(Sender).Lines.Add('Got the focus');
end;

procedure TfrmFocusExample.LostFocus(Sender: TObject);
begin
  TMemo(Sender).Clear;
  TMemo(Sender).Lines.
  Add('Lost the focus');
end;

end.
```

TMemo(Sender) typecasts the Sender parameter as a memo box.

Programming Key: Tips

In this example, the `GotFocus` and `LostFocus` event handlers are used by both memo boxes for their `OnEnter` and `OnExit` events, respectively. In these event handlers, the `Sender` parameter is of type `TObject` (the base object class in Object Pascal), but we know that `Sender` is really a memo box. Therefore, we must typecast `Sender` as a memo box (`TMemo`) before we can access its properties and methods. This example demonstrates typecasting and using the same event handler for multiple controls.

Programmers often desire to track mouse events in the Windows environment. The **OnMouseDown** event occurs when the user presses a mouse button over a control. The **OnMouseUp** event occurs when the user releases a mouse button over a control. The event handlers for each of these events contain five parameters: `Sender`, `Button`, `Shift`, `X`, and `Y`. The `Sender` parameter indicates the control over which the mouse button is pressed or released. The `Button` parameter identifies the mouse button that is pressed or released (the button that caused the event). Similar to the `Button` parameter, `Shift` identifies the states of the SHIFT, CTRL, and ALT keys and the mouse buttons. `Shift` consists of a set of flags (bits) that indicate which keys and buttons are pressed. Any combination of these flags may be set, as the user may press more than one key or button at the same time. Figure 8.2 summarizes the Delphi `Button` and `Shift` constants. Finally, the `X` and `Y` parameters indicate the horizontal and vertical positions of the mouse pointer within the `Sender` control, respectively, as measured in pixels.

The **OnMouseMove** event occurs when the user moves the mouse within a control. The event handler for an `OnMouseMove` event has the same parameters as above, except that it lacks a `Button` parameter. The following unit provides an interactive view of mouse events in the `memOutput` memo box:

Button **Constant**	**Mouse Button**	Shift **Constant**	**Meaning**
nbLeft	Left	ssAlt	The ALT key is held down
nbMiddle	Middle	ssCtrl	The CTRL key is held down
nbRight	Right	sDoubles	The mouse was double-clicked
		ssLeft	The left mouse button is held down
		ssMiddle	The middle mouse button is held down
		ssRight	The right mouse button is held down
		ssShift	The SHIFT key is held down

FIGURE 8.2   Delphi Button and Shift Constants

```
unit MouseEventsEx;

interface

uses
  Windows, Messages, SysUtils, Classes, Graphics, Controls,
  Forms, Dialogs, StdCtrls;

type
  TfrmMouseEvents = class(TForm)
    memOutput: TMemo;
    procedure MouseDown(Sender: TObject; Button: TMouseButton;
      Shift: TShiftState; X, Y: Integer);
    procedure MouseMove(Sender: TObject; Shift: TShiftState; X,
      Y: Integer);
    procedure MouseUp(Sender: TObject; Button: TMouseButton;
      Shift: TShiftState; X, Y: Integer);
  private
    { Private declarations }
  public
    { Public declarations }
  end;

var
  frmMouseEvents: TfrmMouseEvents;

procedure DisplayButton(Button: TMouseButton);
procedure DisplayShift(Shift: TShiftState);
procedure DisplayXY(X, Y: Integer);

implementation

{$R *.DFM}

procedure TfrmMouseEvents.MouseDown(Sender: TObject;
  Button: TMouseButton; Shift: TShiftState; X, Y: Integer);

begin
  memOutput.Lines.Add('OnMouseDown Event');
  DisplayButton(Button);
```

Component	Property	Setting
Form	Name	frmMouseEvents
	Caption	Mouse Events Example
Memo Box	Name	memOutput
	Lines	*Blank*
	ReadOnly	True

Component Name	Event	Event Handler
memOutput	OnMouseDown	MouseDown
	OnMouseMove	MouseMove
	OnMouseUp	MouseUp

```
  DisplayShift(Shift);
  DisplayXY(X, Y);
end;

procedure TfrmMouseEvents.MouseMove(Sender: TObject; Shift:
  TShiftState; X, Y: Integer);

begin
  memOutput.Lines.Add('OnMouseMove Event');
  DisplayShift(Shift);
  DisplayXY(X, Y);
end;

procedure TfrmMouseEvents.MouseUp(Sender: TObject;
  Button: TMouseButton; Shift: TShiftState; X, Y: Integer);

begin
  memOutput.Lines.Add('OnMouseUp Event');
  DisplayButton(Button);
  DisplayShift(Shift);
  DisplayXY(X, Y);
end;

procedure DisplayButton(Button: TMouseButton);

var
  lineOut: String;

begin
  lineOut := 'Button = ';
  case Button of
    mbLeft:    begin
                 lineOut := lineOut + 'Left';
```

```
                              end;
          mbMiddle: begin
                      lineOut := lineOut + 'Middle';
                    end;
          mbRight:  begin
                      lineOut := lineOut + 'Right';
                    end;
          else begin
            lineOut := lineOut + 'UNKNOWN';
          end;
        end;
      frmMouseEvents.memOutput.Lines.Add(lineOut);
    end;

    procedure DisplayShift(Shift: TShiftState);

    begin
      if (ssShift in Shift) then begin
        frmMouseEvents.memOutput.Lines.Add('SHIFT key held down');
      end;
      if (ssAlt in Shift) then begin
        frmMouseEvents.memOutput.Lines. Add('ALT key held down');
      end;
      if (ssCtrl in Shift) then begin
        frmMouseEvents.memOutput.Lines.Add('CTRL key held down');
      end;
      if (ssLeft in Shift) then begin
        frmMouseEvents.memOutput.Lines.Add(
          'Left mouse button held down');
      end;
      if (ssRight in Shift) then begin
        frmMouseEvents.memOutput.Lines.Add(
          'Right mouse button held down');
      end;
      if (ssMiddle in Shift) then begin
        frmMouseEvents.memOutput.Lines.Add(
          'Middle mouse button held down');
      end;
      if (ssDouble in Shift) then begin
        frmMouseEvents.memOutput.Lines.Add('Mouse double-clicked');
      end;
    end;

    procedure DisplayXY(X, Y: Integer);

    begin
      frmMouseEvents.memOutput.Lines.Add('X: ' + IntToStr(X));
      frmMouseEvents.memOutput.Lines.Add('Y: ' + IntToStr(Y));
      frmMouseEvents.memOutput.Lines.Add('');
```

> It is necessary to use the **in** operator in the DisplayShift procedure. The in operator is a set operator and will be discussed in Chapter 10.

```
end;

end.
```

Most new mice are "wheel," "browser," or "scroll" devices that contain wheels or some other controls designed for quick vertical scrolling in applications. Many of the Delphi controls support these newer mice. The **OnMouseWheel** event occurs when the user rotates the mouse wheel (in either direction). If no OnMouseWheel event handler exists, then the **OnMouseWheelDown** or **OnMouseWheelUp** event occurs, depending on the direction in which the mouse wheel rotates. The OnMouseWheelDown event occurs when the mouse wheel is rotated downward, and the OnMouseWheelUp event occurs when it is rotated upward.

GUI Design Tips

A static text box is similar to a label control. Unlike a label, however, it can receive the focus (that is, be the active control on the form). Chapter 16 illustrates the static text box control.

Summary

Key Terms

argument—A piece of information passed to a subprogram.

call—To invoke a subprogram.

calling routine—The part of the program (or the routine) from which a particular subprogram is invoked.

class—An object type.

code reuse—A benefit of modular programming derived from using the same source code (or the same units) in different programs.

component—A part of a system.

event—An action that occurs and is detected by the computer, such as a key press or a mouse click.

event handler—A subprogram that is automatically invoked when an event occurs.

focus—The currently active object on the display that can receive input. The currently active object is said to "have the focus."

function—A type of subprogram that returns a single value to the calling routine; usually, a function performs a computation.

invoke—To call or execute.

method—A procedure or function that is associated with a class of objects.

modular programming—Computer programming in a modular or component-based design that utilizes code units.

parameter—A placeholder for the information passed to a subprogram when it is invoked.

pass—To send information to a subprogram by relating arguments to corresponding parameters.

pass by reference—A type of parameter passing in which the memory location (address) of the argument is passed to the subprogram instead of the argument's value, allowing the subprogram to access the actual variable and modify its contents.

pass by value—A type of parameter passing in which the value of the argument is passed to the subprogram, allowing the subprogram to access a copy of the variable and preserve the contents of the original variable. It is the default method of parameter passing in Object Pascal.

private—A scope that extends only to the unit in which the definition appears.

procedure—A type of subprogram that does not return a value to the calling routine; a subprogram that performs a specific task.

public—A scope that extends to all units that use the unit in which the definition appears.

stepwise refinement—A solution method that involves dividing a large problem into smaller subproblems and solving each subproblem to ultimately yield a solution to the large problem.

structured program—A program that contains control structures, such as decision and repetition structures, and executes statements sequentially. Typically, a structured program contains subprograms and is modular in design.

subprogram—A part of a program designed to perform a specific computation or complete a certain task; a procedure or a function.

test driver—A program designed to test the operation of a subprogram.

top-down design—A programming methodology that involves the process of stepwise refinement.

unit—A part of a computer program that occupies its own file (such as a code unit in Object Pascal).

user-defined subprogram—A subprogram that is written by the programmer and not built into Object Pascal.

Keywords

Constants

mbLeft	ssAlt
mbMiddle	ssCtrl
mbRight	ssDouble

ssLeft	ssRight
ssMiddle	ssShift

Events

OnActivate	OnMouseMove
OnClose	OnMouseUp
OnCreate	OnMouseWheel
OnDeactivate	OnMouseWheelDown
OnDestroy	OnMouseWheelUp
OnEnter	OnPaint
OnExit	OnShow
OnMouseDown	

Methods

SetFocus

Statements

const	procedure
function	var

Key Concepts

- Modular programming is programming in a modular or component-based design through the use of units. This technique provides an inherently logical organization of large programs, enhances the readability of code, allows for easier debugging, and promotes code reuse.
- Procedures and functions are the two types of subprograms.
- Parameters are placeholders for the information passed to a subprogram, whereas arguments contain the actual data passed to the subprogram. The number, order, and data types of the arguments must correspond to the parameters of the subprogram, but the names of the arguments and parameters are unimportant.
- A procedure performs some operation but does not automatically return a value to the calling routine. The following general syntax defines a procedure:

```
procedure ProcedureName(param1: Type1; param2:
                        Type2; ...);

[localDeclarations;]

begin
  [statements;]
end;
```

The following syntax invokes a procedure:

```
ProcedureName(argument1, argument2, ...);
```

- A function is usually associated with a calculation and returns a single value to the calling routine. The following general syntax defines a function:

```
function FunctionName(param1: Type1; ...):
                        FunctionType;

[localDeclarations;]

begin
  [statements;]
  FunctionName := ReturnValue;   { or result :=
                                   ReturnValue; }
end;
```

You invoke a function by writing the function name along with the required arguments. The general form of a function invocation where the returned value is assigned to a variable follows:

```
variableName := FunctionName(argument1, argument2,
                        ...);
```

- Passing a parameter by value passes the value of the argument to the subprogram, and the subprogram cannot change the value of the original variable in the calling routine. Passing by value is the default method of parameter passing in Object Pascal.

- Passing a parameter by reference means that the memory location of the argument is passed to the subprogram rather than its value, allowing the subprogram to access and change the value of the actual variable. The var keyword must precede each parameter that is passed by reference in the subprogram definition.

- In the Windows operating system, the object that can receive input at a given instant in time is said to "have the focus." The OnActivate and OnDeactivate events occur when a form receives and loses the focus, respectively. Similarly, the OnEnter and OnExit events may be used to perform operations when a control receives and loses the focus, respectively. Delphi also provides other events associated with forms (creating, showing, painting, closing, and destroying) and the mouse (pressing buttons, releasing buttons, rotating the wheel, and moving).

Review Questions

1. What is modular programming? Describe some of its advantages.
2. Name the two types of subprograms.

3. Define arguments and parameters, and describe the relationship between them.

4. Write the general syntax for a procedure definition and a function definition. Highlight the differences in the syntax.

5. Write the general syntax for a procedure invocation and a function invocation. Highlight the differences in the syntax.

6. When should you use a function as opposed to a procedure?

7. What does it mean to pass a parameter by reference? By value? How do you accomplish each type of paramter passing in Object Pascal?

8. What is "focus" in the Windows operating system?

9. Describe some of the Delphi events for a form, focus, and the mouse.

Problems

1. Write a program that allows the user to input first and last names in two separate edit boxes and then displays the last name, a comma, and the first name (in that order) in a memo box. Use a subprogram to display the output.

2. Write a program that allows the user to input first and last names in two separate edit boxes and then displays the names with the letters in reverse order. Use one subprogram to reverse the letters in the names and another subprogram to display the output. The program should automatically capitalize the first letter of each name. For instance, `Tom Smith` should be displayed as `Mot Htims`.

3. Write a program that reads the account name, account balance, total deposits, and total withdrawals from a data file named `Checkbook.dat` and then computes the new balance. Use three subprograms: one to read the data file, a second to compute the new account balance, and a third to display the output. Sample data appear below:

```
Ima Richman
815.34
312.00
400.00
```

Your program output should be similar to the following output:

```
Account Name:          Ima Richman
-------------------------------------
Previous Balance:      815.34
Total Deposits:        312.00
Total Withdrawals:     400.00
-------------------------------------
New Balance:           727.34
```

4. Write a program that reads a name, address, and phone number from a data file named `Address.dat` and then displays the data in a memo box. Use two subprograms: one to read the data from the file and another to display the data. Sample data appear below:

```
John Doe
1234 Sunshine Drive
Nowhere
AZ
85200
(602) 511-1221
```

5. Write two functions: `DecToHex` to convert a decimal number into its hexadecimal equivalent, and `HexToDec` to convert a hexadecimal number into its decimal equivalent. Write a simple test driver to test these functions.

6. Modify the quadratic formula solver program in Problem 4 from Chapter 5. Use subprograms to perform the input, calculations, and output.

7. The gamma function is defined as follows:

$$\Gamma(n) = (n-1)!$$
$$\Gamma(1/2) = \sqrt{\pi}$$

Write a program that finds the value of the gamma function for a user-entered value of n, where n is an integer or an integer minus 0.5 such that $n > 1$.

8. A continuous random variable x has a gamma distribution, with parameters $\alpha > 0$ and $\beta > 0$, if its probability density function (pdf) is given by

$$f(x) = \frac{1}{\beta^{\alpha}\Gamma(\alpha)} x^{\alpha-1} e^{-x/\beta}$$

for $x > 0$. If $x = 0$, then $f(x) = 0$. Write a program that finds the value of the gamma density function for user-entered values of x, α, and β.

9. Write a program that displays your name, course title, date, and school name in a memo box as soon as the program starts (without any user action). Perform these actions through program code rather than by setting the `Lines` property of the memo box at design time.

10. Write a program that displays the message "`HOORAY! I was tired of the left mouse button.`" in a memo box when the user clicks the right mouse button inside the memo box.

Programming Projects

1. The Lanchester equations can be used to compute force sizes as functions of time in a battle:

a = rate at which one Y using aimed fire destroys X (units are X casualties per Y firer per time period)

b = rate at which one X using aimed fire destroys Y (units are Y casualties per X firer per time period)

Equations for force size as a function of time:

Let $m = (a/b)^{(1/2)}$, $n = (1/m)$, $r = (ab)^{(1/2)}$

$$X(t) = (1/2)(X_0 - mY_0)e^{rt} + (1/2)(X_0 + mY_0)e^{-rt}$$

$$Y(t) = (1/2)(Y_0 - nX_0)e^{rt} + (1/2)(Y_0 + nX_0)e^{-rt}$$

where

X_0 = initial force size of X

Y_0 = initial force size of Y

$X(t)$ = force size of X at time t

$Y(t)$ = force size of Y at time t

Write a program that uses the Lanchester equations to compute force sizes as functions of time. The program should interactively request input from the user and display the results in a memo box. (*Hint:* If you are clever, you can implement the Lanchester equations using only one function.)

2. The officer and enlisted ranks of the U.S. Navy are shown in the accompanying table along with their associated titles. Write a program that allows the user to input a rank and outputs the associated title. Be sure to use subprograms.

Officer		Enlisted	
Officer Rank	Title	Enlisted Rank	Title
O-1	Ensign	E-1	Seaman Recruit
O-2	Lieutenant Junior Grade	E-2	Seaman Apprentice
O-3	Lieutenant	E-3	Seaman
O-4	Lieutenant Commander	E-4	Petty Officer Third Class
O-5	Commander	E-5	Petty Officer Second Class
O-6	Captain	E-6	Petty Officer First Class
O-7	Rear Admiral Lower Half	E-7	Chief Petty Officer
O-8	Rear Admiral Upper Half	E-8	Senior Chief Petty Officer
O-9	Vice Admiral	E-9	Master Chief Petty Officer
O-10	Admiral		

Error-Proofing and Debugging

Chapter Objectives

In this chapter you will:

- Learn the importance of error-proofing programs

- Become acquainted with the three types of errors: run-time errors, syntax errors, and logic errors

- Write error-proofing code and discover the disadvantages of the `goto` statement

- Create exception handlers and understand the types of errors that they handle

- Learn standard debugging techniques, including the data dump and hand-execution of code

- Learn how to use the Delphi Debugger and its associated windows, toolbars, and menus

Unless a computer program is extremely small, rarely does it work as intended the first time that it executes. This chapter discusses two of the most fundamental computer programming skills: error-proofing and debugging programs.

The Importance of Error-Proofing

Error-proofing a program means to make the program as free of errors as possible. When the user enters an unexpected value, for instance, the program should not **crash** (abruptly end program execution and deliver a **fatal error** message). Simple programming errors can be catastrophic in real-world applications. Imagine, for example, a U.S. Navy fighter aircraft uncontrollably flipping upside-down when it crosses the equator due to a flaw in its navigation software. In such instances, the necessity of error-proofing programs becomes all too apparent.

Types of Programming Errors

Three types of errors can occur in a computer program. A **run-time error** occurs at run time, or during program execution. It often results from the user entering invalid input, such as a nonexistent file name. When writing a computer program (that is, at design time), a programmer can make **syntax errors** and **logic errors.** The **syntax** is the structure (spelling, grammar, and punctuation) of a program. The following code segment contains a syntax error. Can you find it?

Syntax refers to the structure of the code. **Semantics** is concerned with the code's meaning.

```
{Syntax error example}
procedure TfrmSyntaxError.DoExample(Sender: TObject);

var
  thisValue: Integer;

begin
  thiValue := 10;
  memOutput.Clear;
  memOutput.Lines.Add('thisValue = ' +
                      IntToStr(thisValue));
end;
```

In the preceding code segment, the variable `thisValue` is misspelled in the assignment statement. As written, this code attempts to assign the value of 10 to an undeclared variable named `thiValue` instead of the intended variable named `thisValue`. Such spelling errors are common syntax errors. Because Object Pascal requires explicit variable declarations, Delphi automatically finds such syntax errors for you at compile time.

Logic errors deal with the **semantics**, or meaning, of the program code. Computers follow the precise instructions of the programmer; they do *exactly* what they are told to do. Sometimes, however, what we (as programmers) think we told the computer to do differs significantly from what we actually told it to do. For instance, consider the following code segment. Can you find a logic error in this code?

> A **syntax error** is an error in the structure (spelling, grammar, or punctuation) of a computer program. A **logic error** is an error in the logic or meaning of the code. A **run-time error** is an error that occurs while the program is executing (or running).

```
{Logic error example}
procedure TfrmLogicError.DoExample(Sender: TObject);

var
  number: Real;

begin
  number := 10.0;
  memOutput.Clear;

  repeat
    memOutput.Lines.Add(Format('%5.2n', [number]));
    number := number - 3.0 / 4.0;
  until number = 0.0;
end;
```

This code segment contains a logic error in the until clause. The variable number never equals 0.0; therefore, we have created an endless (or infinite) loop, a type of logic error. To stop the execution of this endless loop within the Delphi IDE, select Run | Program Reset from the menu or press CTRL+F2 with the Delphi IDE as the active window. To correct this error, replace the until clause with the following line:

```
until number <= 0.0;
```

Typical logic errors include endless loops (like the one in the example) and errors in mathematical formulae.

Error-Proofing

To prevent run-time errors, a programmer should add code to his or her program that validates all user input values. Such **error-proofing code** prevents a user from either accidentally or maliciously crashing the program. One of the most common run-time errors is the divide-by-zero error. For instance, consider the following code segment:

```
procedure TfrmNoErrorProof.ComputeRates(Sender: TObject);
var
  distance1, distance2, distance3: Real;
  time1, time2, time3:            Real;
  rate1, rate2, rate3:            Real;
  code:                           Integer;
begin
  Val(edtDistance1.Text, distance1, code);
  Val(edtTime1.Text, time1, code);
  rate1 := distance1/time1;

  Val(edtDistance2.Text, distance2, code);
  Val(edtTime2.Text, time2, code);
  rate2 := distance2/time2;

  Val(edtDistance3.Text, distance3, code);
  Val(edtTime3.Text, time3, code);
  rate3 := distance3/time3;

  memOutput.Clear;
  memOutput.Lines.Add('Rate 1: ' + Format('%6.2n',
                      [rate1]));
  memOutput.Lines.Add('Rate 2: ' + Format('%6.2n',
                      [rate2]));
  memOutput.Lines.Add('Rate 3: ' + Format('%6.2n',
                      [rate3]));
end;
```

While this code appears to be correct, consider what happens when the user inputs zero in the edtTime2 edit box, for instance. The program assigns zero to time2 and then attempts to compute rate2 by dividing distance2 by time2, resulting in a divide-by-zero error. Also, consider what happens if the user enters a string that does not contain a number in edtTime2. Once again, a divide-by-zero error occurs. On this occasion, the user did not even enter the requested type of information (a number) in the edit box. Your programs should prevent users from entering such erroneous information. This exercise is commonly called "idiot-proofing," but the term "error-proofing" is actually preferable because it does not belittle the intelligence of the user.

In Object Pascal, recall that the Val procedure converts a string to a number. The code argument of the Val procedure may be used to validate user input. If the string cannot be converted to a number, the index of the first offending character is stored in code. Otherwise, code is set to zero. In the preceding code segment and previous examples, we ignored the resulting value of the code argument.

Now we have the necessary tools to validate user input and prevent divide-by-zero errors. The following code segment is an error-proof version of the previous example:

```
procedure TfrmErrorProof.ComputeRates(Sender: TObject);
var
  distance1, distance2, distance3: Real;
  time1, time2, time3:             Real;
  rate1, rate2, rate3:             Real;
  distCode, timeCode:              Integer;
begin
  memOutput.Clear;

  Val(edtDistance1.Text, distance1, distCode);
  Val(edtTime1.Text, time1, timeCode);
  if (distCode <> 0) or (timeCode <> 0) then begin
    memOutput.Lines.Add('Please enter real numbers for ' +
                        'distance and time 1.');
  end
  else if (distance1 < 0.0) then begin
    memOutput.Lines.Add('Please enter a non-negative ' +
                        'distance 1.');
  end
  else if (time1 <= 0.0) then begin
    memOutput.Lines.Add('Please enter a positive time 1.');
  end
  else begin
    rate1 := distance1/time1;
    memOutput.Lines.Add('Rate 1: ' +
                        Format('%6.2n', [rate1]));
  end;

  Val(edtDistance2.Text, distance2, distCode);
  Val(edtTime2.Text, time2, timeCode);
  if (distCode <> 0) or (timeCode <> 0) then begin
    memOutput.Lines.Add('Please enter real numbers for ' +
                        'distance and time 2.');
  end
  else if (distance2 < 0.0) then begin
    memOutput.Lines.Add('Please enter a non-negative ' +
                        'distance 2.');
  end
  else if (time2 <= 0.0) then begin
    memOutput.Lines.Add('Please enter a positive time 2.');
  end
  else begin
    rate2 := distance2/time2;
    memOutput.Lines.Add('Rate 2: ' +
                        Format('%6.2n', [rate2]));
  end;
```

```
  Val(edtDistance3.Text, distance3, distCode);
  Val(edtTime3.Text, time3, timeCode);
  if (distCode <> 0) or (timeCode <> 0) then begin
    memOutput.Lines.Add('Please enter real numbers for ' +
                        'distance and time 3.');
  end
  else if (distance3 < 0.0) then begin
    memOutput.Lines.Add('Please enter a non-negative ' +
                        'distance 3.');
  end
  else if (time3 <= 0.0) then begin
    memOutput.Lines.Add('Please enter a positive time 3.');
  end
  else begin
    rate3 := distance3/time3;
    memOutput.Lines.Add('Rate 3: ' +
                        Format('%6.2n', [rate3]));
  end;
end;
```

As you can see from this example, error-proofing adds a great deal of extra code to a program. To reduce the amount of error-proofing code, many programmers use **line labels**, **goto** statements, and the **Exit** procedure. Let's introduce this technique by rewriting the previous example once more:

```
procedure TfrmGotoErrorProof.ComputeRates(Sender: TObject);

label nonNumber, valueError;

var
  distance1, distance2, distance3: Real;
  time1, time2, time3:             Real;
  rate1, rate2, rate3:             Real;
  distCode, timeCode:              Integer;

begin
  memOutput.Clear;

  Val(edtDistance1.Text, distance1, distCode);
  Val(edtTime1.Text, time1, timeCode);
  if (distCode <> 0) or (timeCode <> 0) then begin
    goto nonNumber;
  end;
  if (distance1 < 0.0) or (time1 <= 0.0) then begin
    goto valueError;
  end;
  rate1 := distance1/time1;
  memOutput.Lines.Add('Rate 1: ' +
                      Format('%6.2n', [rate1]));
```

```
Val(edtDistance2.Text, distance2, distCode);
Val(edtTime2.Text, time2, timeCode);
if (distCode <> 0) or (timeCode <> 0) then begin
  goto nonNumber;
end;
if (distance2 < 0.0) or (time2 <= 0.0) then begin
  goto valueError;
end;
rate2 := distance2/time2;
memOutput.Lines.Add('Rate 2: ' +
                  Format('%6.2n', [rate2]));

Val(edtDistance3.Text, distance3, distCode);
Val(edtTime3.Text, time3, timeCode);
if (distCode <> 0) or (timeCode <> 0) then begin
  goto nonNumber;
end;
if (distance3 < 0.0) or (time3 <= 0.0) then begin
  goto valueError;
end;
rate3 := distance3/time3;
memOutput.Lines.Add('Rate 3: ' +
                  Format('%6.2n', [rate3]));
Exit;

nonNumber:
memOutput.Lines.Add('Please enter real numbers in the ' +
                  'edit boxes above.');
Exit;

valueError:
memOutput.Lines.Add('Please enter non-negative values ' +
                  'for the distances');
memOutput.Lines.Add('and positive values for the times.');
end;
```

Notice that the error-proofing in this code provides only general information regarding an invalid input value; it does not specify which particular values are invalid, as we did in the previous example.

A line label (or simply **label**) is an identifier that marks a particular line of source code. In Object Pascal, a label is any valid identifier or number between 0 and 9999 declared using the **label** keyword as follows:

```
label labelName;
```

To declare several labels on the same line, use the following general syntax:

```
label labelName[, labelName2, …];
```

To mark a particular line of source code, precede the desired statement with the label name and a colon (:), as follows:

```
labelName: statement;
```

The `goto` statement performs an **unconditional branch** (or **jump**) to a specified line label. That is, program execution is transferred to the statement marked by the label. The syntax of the `goto` statement follows:

```
goto labelName;
```

The label declaration, `goto` statement, and marked statement must all be within the same program block (that is, have the same scope). Therefore, it is not possible to perform an unconditional branch into or out of a subprogram. Additionally, each line within a program block must have a unique label. In other words, you cannot mark two lines in a block with the same label.

The `Exit` procedure immediately passes control from the current subprogram to the calling routine. The calling routine then continues execution with the statement following the subprogram invocation. If the current subprogram is the main program, `Exit` causes the program to terminate. As in the preceding example, `Exit` must be used to prevent the unnecessary execution of error-proofing code and display of error messages.

Some early high-level programming languages, such as BASIC, do not contain many of the structured control statements found in the high-level, object-oriented languages of today. As a result, programmers were forced to use the `goto` statement for branching (jumping) operations. This issue prompted the biggest complaint by programmers about these early languages, because `goto` statements make the code more difficult to read, the program logic more problematic to comprehend, documentation more challenging to write, and debugging code a nightmare. Thus you should avoid using `goto` statements; use structured control statements instead. In fact, the `goto` statement is actually unnecessary, because any program can be written using sequential statements, loops, and decision structures.

Given that we avoid the use of `goto` statements in our code, you might think that all of our error-proofed programs will be exceptionally long (as in our first error-proofed example). Fortunately, Object Pascal provides a built-in means of error trapping to catch common run-time errors. Known as **exception handling,** it is the preferred method of error-proofing programs. An **exception** is generated (or raised) by a specific run-time error. When a run-time error occurs, Object Pascal actually creates an instance of an exception object. Because we have not discussed the details of object-oriented programming yet, the discussion of exception handlers here will remain limited to trapping and handling run-time errors.

Programming Key: Tips

Avoid the use of `goto` statements. Using structured control statements, such as loops and decision blocks, instead of `goto` statements promotes cleaner source code.

Exception Handlers

To completely error-proof a program, a programmer must think of every possible contingency that may occur during the program's execution, such as erroneous input values, nonexistent input files, or illegal file names. For large programs, this task is virtually impossible. Commercial programs, for instance, usually undergo months of testing, yet remain error-prone. Serious errors may even crash an entire computer system, requiring the user to **reboot,** or restart, the machine.

Fortunately, Object Pascal provides an easy method to **trap,** or catch, common errors that occur during program execution (run-time errors). In applications that use the `SysUtils` unit, an exception is raised when an error or other event interrupts normal program execution. The exception transfers control to an **exception handler,** which separates normal program logic from error-handling code. Without exceptions and exception handlers, these errors would normally prove fatal and abruptly terminate the application.

An exception handler is code that handles a specific exception or exceptions that occur within a protected block of code. The **try..except** statements designate a protected block of code and its associated exception handler. The general syntax follows:

```
try
   [protected statements;]
except
   [exception-handling statements;]
[else
   [default exception-handling statements;]]
end;
```

The statements following the `try` keyword are **protected statements** that form the normal program logic. If an error occurs while these statements are executing, an exception is raised and the statements following the `except` keyword execute. Thus the `except` part executes only if an exception occurs during the processing of the `try` part. Additionally, the exception handler for the protected statements encompasses the subprograms invoked by these statements. In other words, if a protected statement calls a routine that does not define its own exception handler, execution control returns to the exception handler for the protected statement when an exception occurs.

When a protected statement raises an exception, execution immediately jumps to the `except` part. The application then attempts to locate an exception handler that is relevant for the current exception. Once it finds the applicable exception handler, the application executes the statements and automatically destroys the exception object. If no matching exception handler is found, then the application executes the `else` part containing the default exception handler (if one exists). Execution of the program then continues with the code following the `except` block.

The on statement defines an exception handler for a specific type of exception. Such statements are located in the `except` part of a `try..except` block. The general syntax of the on statement follows:

```
on [exceptionIdentifier:]exceptionType do begin
   [exception-handling statements;]
end;
```

In this syntax, *exceptionType* is the type of exception, where the exception types are listed in Figure 9.1, and *exceptionIdentifier* is an optional identifier used to reference the exception object of *exceptionType*.

Because exceptions are objects, they have associated properties and methods. Two exception properties are `Message` and `HelpContext`. `Message` is a string that describes the exception, and `HelpContext` is an identification number relating to Delphi's context-sensitive online help.

As an illustration of an exception handler, let's rewrite the familiar triple-rate computer example. The exception handler provides the only error-proofing in the following code. A user can therefore enter nonsense data, such as negative distances and times, and the program will not display an error message. The exception handler, however, will trap all divide-by-zero, floating-point math, and run-time errors, preventing the program from crashing.

```
procedure TfrmExceptionHandler.ComputeRates(Sender: TObject);

var
   distance1, distance2, distance3: Real;
   time1, time2, time3:             Real;
```

```
      rate1, rate2, rate3:           Real;
      code:                          Integer;
  begin
    try
      memOutput.Clear;

      Val(edtDistance1.Text, distance1, code);
      Val(edtTime1.Text, time1, code);
      rate1 := distance1/time1;

      Val(edtDistance2.Text, distance2, code);
      Val(edtTime2.Text, time2, code);
      rate2 := distance2/time2;

      Val(edtDistance3.Text, distance3, code);
      Val(edtTime3.Text, time3, code);
      rate3 := distance3/time3;

      memOutput.Lines.Add('Rate 1: ' + Format('%6.2n',
                          [rate1]));
      memOutput.Lines.Add('Rate 2: ' + Format('%6.2n',
                          [rate2]));
      memOutput.Lines.Add('Rate 3: ' + Format('%6.2n',
                          [rate3]));
    except
      on EZeroDivide do begin
        Application.MessageBox('Do not enter 0 for the time.',
                               'Divide-By-Zero Error', MB_OK);
      end;
      on EMathError do begin
        Application.MessageBox('0/0 error.',
                               'Floating-point Math Error',
                               MB_OK);
      end;
      on E: Exception do begin
        Application.MessageBox(PChar(E.Message),
                               'Run-time Error', MB_OK);
      end;
    end;
  end;
```

> Integrated debugging must be inactive for the exception handlers to work within the Delphi IDE. To deactivate integrated debugging, select Tools | Debugger Options... from the menu. Then, uncheck the Integrated debugging box at the lower-left side of the Debugger Options window and click the OK button.

Exception Type	Description
EAbort	Errors that should not display an error message dialog box
EAbstractError	Attempt to call an abstract method
EAccessViolation	Invalid memory access errors
EAssertionFailed	Assert procedure performed on Boolean expression that returned False
EControlC	CTRL+C keypress in a console application
EConvertError	String or object conversion error
EDivByZero	Integer divide-by-zero error
EExternal	Captures Windows exception record
EExternalException	Invalid exception code
EHeapException	Error related to heap-allocated memory
EInOutError	File input/output error
EIntError	Integer math error
EIntfCastError	Interface casting error
EIntOverflow	Result of integer calculation is too large to fit in the allocated register
EInvalidCast	Typecasting error
EInvalidOp	Undefined floating-point operation
EInvalidPointer	Invalid pointer operation
EMathError	Floating-point math error
EOutOfMemory	Unsuccessful attempt to allocate memory
EOverflow	Floating-point register overflow
EPackageError	Package-related error
EPrivilege	Processor privilege violation
EPropReadOnly	Invalid attempt to write to a property using OLE automation
EPropWriteOnly	Invalid attempt to read a property using OLE automation
ERangeError	Integer value is too large for the declared type to which it is assigned
EStackOverflow	Stack overflow
EUnderflow	Value is too small to be represented with a floating-point variable
EVariantError	Error involving variant data type
EWin32Error	Windows error
Exception	The base class for all run-time exceptions
EZeroDivide	Floating-point divide-by-zero error

FIGURE 9.1   Delphi Exception Types

Programming Key: Tips

Use the **try..finally** statement block to ensure that specific parts of an operation are completed, regardless of whether the operation is interrupted by an exception. The finally clause always executes, irrespective of how the try clause terminates. The general syntax of this structure follows:

```
try
  [protected statements;]
finally
  [always executed statements;]
end;
```

As an example, consider the following code segment:

```
procedure TfrmFileDump.DumpFile(Sender: TObject);
var
  inFile: TextFile;
  lineIn: String;
  count:  Integer;
begin
  count := 0;
  AssignFile(inFile, 'C:\MyData.dat');

  try
    Reset(inFile);
    while not(Eof(inFile)) do begin
      Readln(inFile, lineIn);
      memOutput.Lines.Add(lineIn);
      Inc(count);
    end;
  finally
    CloseFile(inFile);
    memOutput.Lines.Add('');
    memOutput.Lines.Add(IntToStr(count) + ' lines.');
  end;
end;
```

This code simply dumps the contents of the file C:\MyData.dat to the memOutput memo box and displays the number of lines in the file. If an error occurs while the file is being processed, the finally clause ensures that the file is closed and the memo box displays the number of lines counted so far.

In large programs, it is not uncommon to find try..finally and try..except blocks nested inside each other.

Debugging

A bug in a computer program may be caused by a syntax error, logic error, or run-time error. It is the programmer's responsibility to test and debug a program, thereby eliminating all types of errors. Syntax errors are more readily apparent to the programmer and often easier to fix than are logic and run-time errors. Furthermore, the Delphi IDE assists the programmer in locating syntax errors. Logic errors are less obvious and sometimes no easy way exists to fix a logic error without recoding part of the program.

Run-time errors are, by far, the most difficult types of bugs to find and correct. Ideally, programmers will find the majority of these errors while testing the program, rather than after the program is released as a commercial product. To prevent all possible run-time errors, programmers must exhaustively test a program using all possible combinations of input values. The dilemma is obviously apparent: A large program may require years, if not a lifetime or more, to test all possible input combinations. As an alternative to carrying out such testing, software companies distribute **beta releases** (test versions of their nearly finished products) to a variety of academic institutions, corporate customers, and end-users. In this manner, a software company can quickly test its product under the most common operating conditions and input values.

The next two sections discuss debugging methods. The first section describes standard techniques that are both language- and platform-independent, whereas the second section is specific to the Delphi IDE.

Standard Debugging Techniques

The two standard debugging techniques are the **data dump** and **hand-execution** of code. They work with any type of computer hardware and programming language.

The data dump is the simplest debugging technique. When a program is not working as expected, the programmer strategically adds lines of code to output the values of selected variables (either to the screen or to an output file). The output of these variables is called a data dump. By tracing through the data dump, a programmer can pinpoint problems in the code (provided that the data dump includes the problematic variables and portions of source code). Consider the logic error example at the beginning of this chapter. This code already performs a data dump—the value of the variable `number` is output during each iteration of the `repeat` loop. Here, the programmer is fortunate and can easily spot the mistake.

In hand-execution of code, the programmer acts as the computer. Hand-executing, or **tracing,** your code is an invaluable computer programming skill. Pencil and paper suffice to mimic the computer's memory space, and you act as the microprocessor, sequentially executing each line of code and performing the necessary operations. This technique is essentially a manual version of the data dump.

Why might a programmer trace code rather than perform a data dump? First, tracing a program by hand does not require a computer. You can debug a program anywhere with just a hard copy of the code, pencil, and paper. Second, programmers can often locate logic errors faster by tracing through their code rather than performing simple data dumps. Let's demonstrate tracing code by using a modified version of the logic error example:

```
{-------------------------------------------------------------
Hand-Execution Example
----------------------
This code is used to illustrate the hand-execution, or
tracing, of code.   The code below contains an infinite
loop.
----------------------------------------------------------}
procedure TfrmHandExecution.DoExample(Sender: TObject);

var
  number: Real;

begin
  number := 5.0;
  memOutput.Clear;

  repeat
    memOutput.Lines.Add(Format('%5.2n', [number]));
    number := number - 2.0;
  until number = 0.0;
end;
```

Hand-Execution		
Iteration	number	memOutput
0	5.0	*Empty*
1	3.0	5.00
2	1.0	5.00
		3.00
3	−1.0	5.00
		3.00
		1.00

At this point, the programmer sees that the value of number is −1.0 and realizes that the code creates an infinite loop. This case is a rather simple example; hand-execution of code is usually more involved and may take longer to locate the error. Try hand-executing the original (unmodified) version of this code, for instance. It takes many more iterations before the value of number becomes negative. Again, the good news concerning hand-execution is that you may find your errors after tracing just a small portion of the code.

The Delphi Debugger

The Delphi development environment contains a built-in debugger to assist the programmer in tracing code and locating errors. To use the Delphi debugger, you must enable the integrated debugging option. Select Tools|Debugger Options... from the menu, check the Integrated debugging box at the lower-left side of the Debugger Options window shown in Figure 9.2, and click the OK button.

The debugger commands are available through the Run menu and the Debug toolbar. To activate the Debug toolbar, click the right mouse button (right-click) on the menu bar or any toolbar to view the Toolbar menu, and then left-click on Debug. Figure 9.3 describes the icons that appear on the default Debug toolbar. Additionally, you can quickly access debugger commands through the Code Editor window. Right-click anywhere inside the Code Editor window to open a pop-up menu. The Debug option on this pop-up menu lists the available debugger commands.

The Delphi debugger provides a semi-automatic method of locating errors. It enables a programmer to simply **watch** specific variables or expressions without requiring a program modification that executes a data dump. Additionally, the debugger can be used to stop the program execution at designated **breakpoints** or to execute the program code step-by-step (**step** through the program). Note that the debugger is a design-time utility; you cannot use the debugger commands in an executable module at run-time outside of the Delphi IDE.

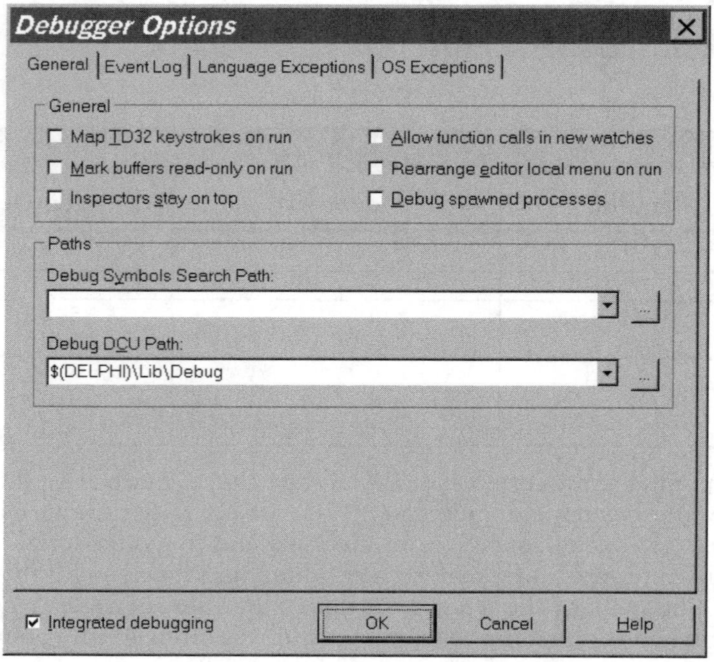

FIGURE 9.2   Debugger Options Window

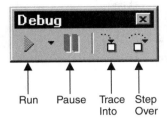

FIGURE 9.3   Debug Toolbar

Breakpoints, stepping, and watches are briefly described in the following paragraphs. For more detailed information, consult the Delphi documentation or online help.

Source breakpoints are toggled on and off at specific lines of code designated by the programmer. Breakpoints can be set only on executable lines of code. Blank lines, declaration statements, and comments cannot include breakpoints. When a program encounters a breakpoint, its execution halts temporarily until the programmer selects Run from the Run menu, presses F9, or left-clicks the Run button on the Debug toolbar. The Delphi debugger also allows address, data, and module load breakpoints; these advanced debugging tools are beyond the scope of this text, however.

While a program is halted, the programmer has the ability to immediately evaluate and modify expressions in the **Evaluate/Modify window.** An expression may also be viewed and changed in the **Inspector window.** The Inspector window provides the programmer with a better view of objects that have advanced data structures.

Programming Key: Delphi Highlight

During interactive debugging, you can use Tooltip Expression Evaluation to display the value of a variable or expression as tooltip text. Simply position the cursor over the variable or expression in the Code Editor; after a one-second (default) delay, Delphi will display the value of the variable or expression as tooltip text.

To enable Tooltip Expression Evaluation, select `Tools|Editor Options...` from the menu bar to open the Editor Properties window, then check the box next to "Tooltip expression evaluation" under the Code Insight page. Note that Integrated debugging must be enabled to use this feature.

The Delphi debugger includes two stepping operations. **Trace Into** executes code one statement at a time. For example, if the statement is a call to a subprogram, the next statement displayed consists of the first statement in the subprogram. **Step Over** executes a subprogram call as a single unit, and then steps to the next statement in the current subprogram. Thus the next statement displayed is the next statement in the current subprogram regardless of whether the current statement is a call to another subprogram (that is, execution of the subprogram called is transparent).

A **watch expression** is a user-defined expression that allows the programmer to observe its behavior. Watch expressions appear in the **Watch window,** and their values are automatically updated in break mode. Furthermore, the **Local Variables window** automatically displays the values of all declared variables in the current subprogram (all local variables).

To practice using the Delphi debugger, follow the steps outlined below:

1. **Fibonacci numbers** are defined by the sequence $a_{n+1} = a_n + a_{n-1}$, where $a_1 = 1$, $a_2 = 1$, and so on. The following program displays the Fibonacci numbers whose values are less than 30,000 and the square of each of these numbers. Enter this program into your computer. The program requires one button (btnFibonacciExample) and one memo box (memOutput). ShowNumbers is the event handler for the OnClick event of btnFibonacciExample.

```
{Display the Fibonacci numbers less than 30,000}
procedure TfrmFibonacci.ShowNumbers(Sender: TObject);

var
   num1:  Integer;
   num2:  Integer;
   sum:   Integer;

begin
   num1 := 1;
   num2 := 1;

   memOutput.Clear;
   memOutput.Lines.Add('Fibonacci #      Squared Value');
   memOutput.Lines.Add(Format('%11d %18d',
                      [num1, Square(num1)]));

   repeat
     memOutput.Lines.Add(Format('%11d %18d',
                        [num2, Square(num2)]));
     sum := num1 + num2;
     num1 := num2;
     num2 := sum;
   until (num2 > 30000);
end;

{Return the square of an integer value}
function Square(value: Integer): Integer;
```

```
begin
  Square := value * value;
end;
```

2. Add a breakpoint on the second line following the `repeat` statement. Move the cursor to this line, click the right mouse button, and select `Debug|Toggle Breakpoint` from the pop-up menu. Alternatively, press the F5 key with the cursor on the appropriate line in the Code Editor window to toggle the breakpoint. Notice that the Code Editor highlights the line and places a red circle next to it (Figure 9.4). Another method to toggle the breakpoint is to left-click in the margin area containing this circle.

3. Run the program. Select Run | Run, press the F9 key, or click the Run button on the Debug toolbar. Click the `btnFibonacciExample` button. Notice that Delphi halts the program execution and displays the Code Editor window (Figure 9.5). The next line to be executed is highlighted and a green pointer (the **instruction pointer**) appears in the left margin.

4. Step through the program by clicking the Trace Into button on the Debug toolbar or pressing F7. Notice that the instruction pointer is now in the `Square` function. Press F7 two more times to return to the `ShowNumbers` event handler.

5. Open the Local Variables window shown in Figure 9.6. Select `View|Debug Windows|Local Variables` or press CTRL+ALT+L.

6. Open the Evaluate/Modify window. Select Run | `Evaluate/Modify...`, press CTRL+F7, or right-click on the Code Editor window and select `Debug|Evaluate/Modify...` from the pop-up menu. Type num1 for the expression and press ENTER. As in Figure 9.7, the Result box shows that the current value of num1 is 1.

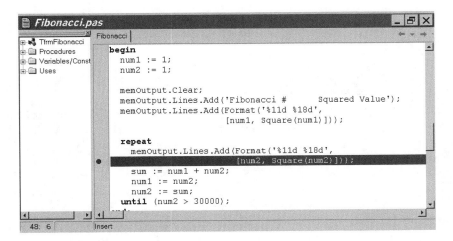

FIGURE 9.4 Add a Breakpoint

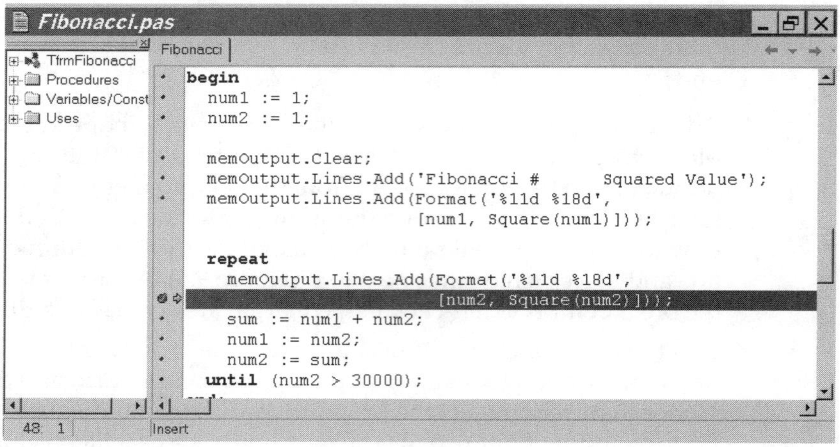

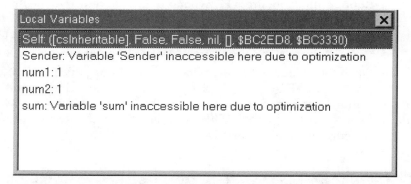

FIGURE 9.5   Execution Halts at the Breakpoint

```
Local Variables                                                    ☒

Self: ([csInheritable], False, False, nil, [], $BC2ED8, $BC3330)
Sender: Variable 'Sender' inaccessible here due to optimization
num1: 1
num2: 1
sum: Variable 'sum' inaccessible here due to optimization
```

FIGURE 9.6   Local Variables Window

7. Change the value of num1 to 5. In the Evaluate/Modify window, type 5 in the New Value box and press ENTER.

8. Open the Inspector window (Figure 9.8). Click the Inspect button in the Evaluate/Modify window. Alternatively, select Run | Inspect..., press ALT+F5, or right-click the Code Editor window and select Debug | Inspect... from the pop-up menu. Left-click the ellipsis button (the three dots) to open the Change window. Enter 1 and press the ENTER key. The value of num1 is now 1 again. Click the Evaluate button in the Evaluate/ Modify window to verify this fact.

9. Close the Local Variables window, Evaluate/Modify window, and Inspector window. Click the X in the upper-right corner of each window to close it.

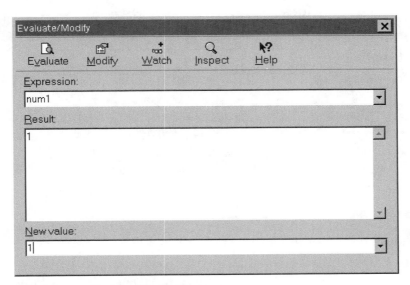

FIGURE 9.7   Evaluate/Modify Window

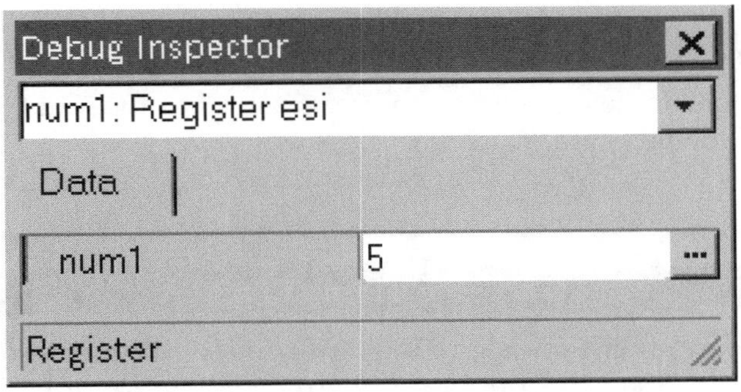

FIGURE 9.8   Debug Inspector Window

10. Add watches for the variables num2 and `value`. Select Run | Add Watch...
    or press CTRL+F5. The Watch Properties window (Figure 9.9) opens on
    the screen. Enter num2 as the Expression and press the ENTER key. Do the
    same for `value`. Alternatively, to quickly add a watch for an expression,
    right-click on the expression in the Code Editor and select Debug | Add
    Watch at Cursor from the pop-up menu.

11. Press F7 five times to trace into the program. Notice that the values of the
    watch expressions change as you trace through the code.

12. Press F7 six more times. The instruction pointer is now at the breakpoint.

13. Press F8 to step over the Square function call. Notice that the instruction
    pointer moves to the next line of code.

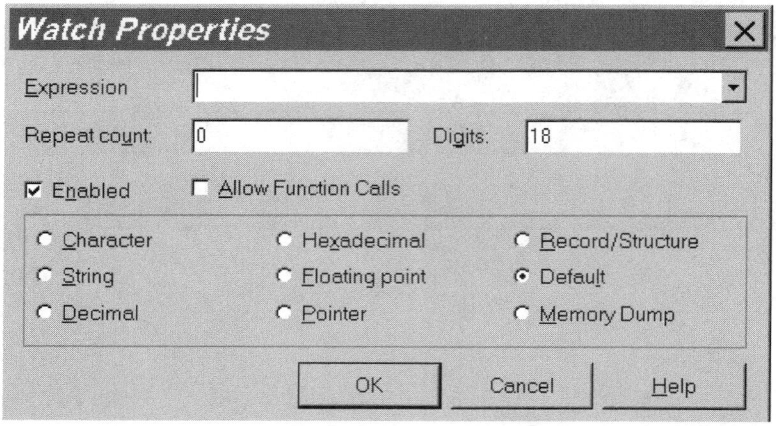

FIGURE 9.9 Watch Properties Window

14. Delete all watches. Right-click in the Watch window and select `Delete All Watches` from the pop-up menu. Close the Watch window by clicking the X in the upper-right corner.

15. Click on the line of code containing the breakpoint in the Code Editor. Press the F5 key to toggle the breakpoint off.

16. Press F9 to complete the program execution. Click the X in the upper-right corner of the program window to close it.

GUI Design Tips

A scroll box control creates a scrolling area on a form, and you may then place other components inside the scroll box. This control provides a clever means of performing data dumps for program testing and debugging. As shown in the following example, the scroll box containing the debug information is visible only when the programmer checks the Show Debug Info check box. Figure 9.10 displays a sample execution of this program.

Component	Property	Setting
Form	Name	frmDebugBox
	Caption	Debug ScrollBox Example
Label	Name	lblInstruct
	Caption	Compute the sum of the squares from the Starting Value to the Ending Value

Component	Property	Setting
	WordWrap	True
Label	Name	lblStart
	Caption	Starting Value:
Label	Name	lblEnd
	Caption	Ending Value:
Label	Name	lblAnswer
	Caption	Answer:
Edit Box	Name	edtStart
	Text	0
Edit Box	Name	edtEnd
	Text	10
Edit Box	Name	edtAnswer
	ReadOnly	True
	Text	*Empty*
Button	Name	btnCompute
	Caption	Compute
CheckBox	Name	chkDebug
	Caption	Show Debug Info
ScrollBox	Name	sbxDebug
	Visible	False
Label	Name	lblStartVal
	Caption	start:
Label	Name	lblFinishVal
	Caption	finish:
Label	Name	lblNumber
	Caption	number:
Edit Box	Name	edtStartVal
	ReadOnly	True
	Text	*Empty*
Edit Box	Name	edtFinishVal
	ReadOnly	True
	Text	*Empty*
Edit Box	Name	edtNumber
	ReadOnly	True
	Text	*Empty*
Memo Box	Name	memDebug
	Lines	*Empty*
	ReadOnly	True

> The lblStartVal, lblFinishVal, lblNumber, edtStartVal, edtFinishVal, edtNumber, and memDebug components are contained within the sbxDebug scroll box.

Component Name	Event	Setting
btnCompute	OnClick	SumSquares
chkDebug	OnClick	ShowDebug

```
unit DebugBoxEx;

interface

uses
  Windows, Messages, SysUtils, Classes, Graphics,
  Controls, Forms, Dialogs, StdCtrls;

type
  TfrmDebugBox = class(TForm)
    sbxDebug: TScrollBox;
    lblStart: TLabel;
    lblEnd: TLabel;
    edtStart: TEdit;
    edtEnd: TEdit;
    btnCompute: TButton;
    lblAnswer: TLabel;
    edtAnswer: TEdit;
    lblInstruct: TLabel;
    lblStartVal: TLabel;
    lblFinishVal: TLabel;
    lblNumber: TLabel;
    edtStartVal: TEdit;
    edtFinishVal: TEdit;
    edtNumber: TEdit;
    memDebug: TMemo;
    chkDebug: TCheckBox;
    procedure SumSquares(Sender: TObject);
    procedure ShowDebug(Sender: TObject);
  private
    { Private declarations }
  public
    { Public declarations }
  end;

var
  frmDebugBox: TfrmDebugBox;

implementation

{$R *.DFM}

procedure TfrmDebugBox.SumSquares(Sender: TObject);
var
  start:  Integer;
  finish: Integer;
  sCode:  Integer;
  fCode:  Integer;
  number: Integer;
```

```
    sumSq:   Integer;
begin
  Val(edtStart.Text, start, sCode);
  Val(edtEnd.Text, finish, fCode);
  if (sCode <> 0) then begin
    edtAnswer.Text := 'Invalid Starting Value';
  end
  else if (fCode <> 0) then begin
    edtAnswer.Text := 'Invalid Ending Value';
  end
  else if (start > finish) then begin
    edtAnswer.Text := 'Starting Value must be' +
                      ' less than Ending Value';
  end
  else begin
    edtStartVal.Text := IntToStr(start);
    edtFinishVal.Text := IntToStr(finish);
    memDebug.Clear;
    memDebug.Lines.Add('number        sumSq');
    memDebug.Lines.Add('——          ——-');

    sumSq := 0;
    for number := start to finish do begin
      sumSq := sumSq + (number * number);
      edtNumber.Text := IntToStr(number);
      memDebug.Lines.Add(Format('%-10d  %d',
                                [number, sumSq]));

    end;

    edtAnswer.Text := IntToStr(sumSq);
    edtNumber.Text := IntToStr(number);
  end;
end;

{Make debug ScrollBox visible if debug check box
 is selected}
procedure TfrmDebugBox.ShowDebug(Sender: TObject);

begin
  sbxDebug.Visible := chkDebug.Checked;
end;

end.
```

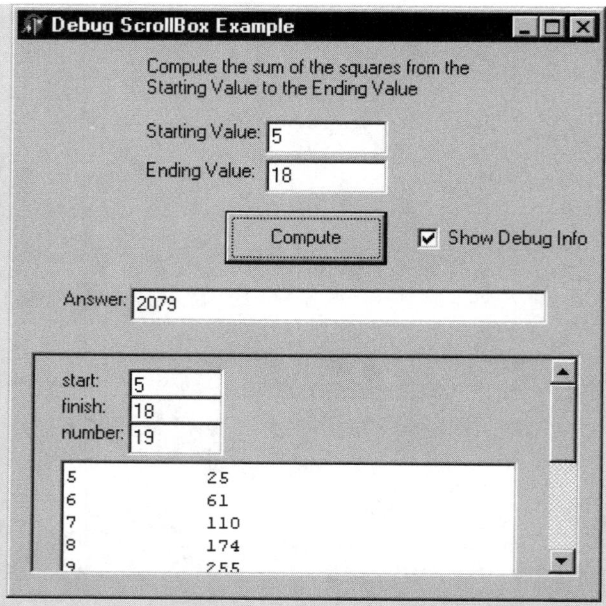

FIGURE 9.10 Debug Scroll box Example

• C • A • S • E • S • T • U • D • Y •

A Failed Space Mission

On July 22, 1962, the Mariner 1 spacecraft was launched from Cape Canaveral, Florida. It was intended to perform a Venus flyby and become the first spacecraft to successfully encounter another planet. Instead, Mariner 1 veered off course, with its guidance system directing it toward a crash, possibly in the North Atlantic shipping lanes or an inhabited area. The spacecraft was destroyed by the Range Safety Officer 293 seconds after launch. Several days later, the cause was isolated to the flight control computer that generated incorrect steering commands due to a flaw in the programming. The Mariner 1 loss was attributed to the omission of a hyphen in coded computer instructions.

On August 27, 1962, Mariner 2 (Figure 9.11), a backup for the Mariner 1 mission, was launched successfully. Mariner 2 became the first spacecraft to encounter another planet, and it is responsible for many scientific discoveries concerning Venus.

New York Times, July 28, 1962, p. 1, col. 4.

FIGURE 9.11   The Mariner Spacecraft
Courtesy of National Aeronautics and Space Administration (NASA).

• C • A • S • E • • S • T • U • D • Y •

The Y2K Problem

The year 2000 (Y2K) problem stems from the use of a two-digit field to represent the year on a computer, either in the software or hardware. For instance, 1900 would be represented by 00 and 1999 by 99. Computer software and hardware that contain this problem are unable to address dates after December 31, 1999. Many appliances and other household devices rely upon computer technology and are susceptible to this flaw. Older mainframes and personal computers, especially those built prior to 1997, are most likely to be affected.

Essentially, the cause of this bug was the shortsightedness of hardware and software engineers. Many years ago, computer memory was expensive. To conserve memory space, programmers and engineers shortened the year to two digits. This practice effectively halved the memory space required to store the year, but created a problem (the Y2K bug) in the long run. Billions of dollars were spent fixing hardware and software afflicted with the Y2K bug.

Summary

Key Terms

beta release—A test version of a nearly finished software product.

breakpoint—A temporary stopping point during the execution of code for debugging purposes at design time.

crash—To end program execution due to a fatal error.

data dump—A debugging method in which variable values are output to the screen or a data file.

error-proofing—To make a program free from errors.

error-proofing code—Code that prevents a user from either accidentally or maliciously crashing the program.

exception—In Object Pascal, an object that results from a run-time error.

exception handler—The code that executes when an exception occurs; error-handling code.

exception handling—Object Pascal's built-in error-trapping capability to catch run-time errors.

fatal error—An unrecoverable error that causes a computer program to halt execution.

Fibonacci numbers—The numbers defined by the sequence $a_{n+1} = a_n + a_{n-1}$, where $a_1 = 1$, $a_2 = 1$, and so on.

hand-execution—The process of a programmer acting as the computer and manually executing the source code with pencil and paper.

instruction pointer—In a microprocessor, a register that contains the address of the next instruction to be executed; a pointer to the next instruction to be executed.

jump—See *unconditional branch*.

line label (or **label**)—An identifier that marks a particular line of source code; in Object Pascal, any valid identifier or number between 0 and 9999.

logic error—An error in the logic or meaning of the code.

protected statements—In Object Pascal, the statements following the `try` keyword; the normal program logic.

reboot—To restart the computer system.

run-time error—An error that occurs during program execution.

semantics—Meaning.

step—To execute program code instruction-by-instruction for debugging purposes at design time.

syntax—Structure.

syntax error—An error in the structure (spelling, grammar, or punctuation) of a computer program.

trap—Catch.

unconditional branch—A "jump" over some program instructions regardless of the condition as executed by the goto statement.

watch—In the Delphi debugger, a method of examining the values of specific variables and expressions.

watch expression—An expression that allows the programmer to observe its value for debugging purposes at design time.

Keywords

Procedures

Exit	Val

Statements

begin	finally
do	goto
else	label
end	on
except	try

Key Concepts

- Error-proofing programs is a fundamental concept in computer science. The possibility of unanticipated inputs causing a catastrophic failure in real-world applications necessitates the error-proofing of code.
- Three types of program errors exist: run-time errors, syntax errors, and logic errors.
- Run-time errors occur during program execution and often result from invalid input from the user. Such errors include divide-by-zero and file-not-found errors.
- Syntax errors affect the code structure (spelling, grammar, or punctuation). Delphi assists the programmer by identifying these errors through its automatic syntax checking and by requiring explicit variable declarations.
- Logic errors occur in the semantics, or meaning, of the code. These errors are often the most difficult to identify and debug. Common logic errors include infinite loops and incorrect mathematical formulae.

- Error-proofing code prevents a user from either accidentally or maliciously crashing the program.

- Using line labels, `goto` statements, and the `Exit` procedure can reduce the length of error-proofing code. The `goto` statement performs an unconditional branch, which is a practice neither highly encouraged nor desired by advanced programmers. Unconditional branches make the code more difficult to read, program logic more problematic to follow, documentation more challenging to write, and debugging very difficult. Thus you should avoid using `goto` statements.

- Object Pascal provides a built-in means of error trapping, known as exception handling, to catch common run-time errors. An exception is an object raised by a specific run-time error.

- An exception handler, designated by the `try..except` statements, separates normal program logic from error-handling code. The general syntax follows:

```
try
  [protected statements;]
except
  [exception-handling statements;]
[else
  [default exception-handling statements;]]
end;
```

- The on statement defines an exception handler for a specific type of exception. Such statements are located in the `except` part of a `try..except` block. The general syntax follows:

```
on [exceptionIdentifier:]exceptionType do begin
  [exception-handling statements;]
end;
```

- Standard debugging techniques work regardless of the computer language being used. They include the data dump and hand-execution of code.

- The data dump requires the programmer to add code to output values of important variables and other information during program execution.

- Hand-executing (or tracing) code is performed by the programmer using a pencil and paper; it is an invaluable computer programming skill.

- Delphi contains a built-in debugger to assist the programmer in finding and correcting errors at design time. This debugger allows the programmer to step through code, add breakpoints and watches, and examine and modify variable values.

Review Questions

1. Why is it important for a programmer to error-proof his or her programs? Give an example.

2. Describe the difference between a run-time error, syntax error, and logic error and give an example of each type of error. What features does Delphi offer to help prevent these errors?

3. What is an exception?

4. What is an exception handler? Write the general syntax for an exception handler within a subprogram.

5. What does the `goto` statement do? What disadvantages does this statement have that make it unattractive?

6. Explain the differences between the data dump and hand-execution debugging techniques. State some advantages of hand-executing or tracing code.

7. Describe the contents of the Debug toolbar.

8. What is a breakpoint? A watch?

9. What is displayed and which operations can be performed in the Local Variables window? The Evaluate/Modify window? The Watch window?

10. Describe the difference between the Trace Into and Step Over commands in the Delphi debugger.

Problems

1. Hand-execute the following code. What is the output?

```
{Chapter 9, Problem 1}
procedure TfrmProblem1.LeftClick(Sender: TObject);

var
  num1: Real;
  num2: Real;

begin
  num1 := 5.0;
  num2 := 10.0;

  Confuse1(num1, num2);
  Confuse2(num2, num1);
  Output(num1, num2);
end;
```

```
{Confuse me once}
procedure Confuse1(x: Real; var y: Real);

begin
  x := x - 1.0 / 4.0;
  y := y * 2.0 + 5.0;
end;

{Confuse me twice, but be nice!}
procedure Confuse2(var val1: Real; val2: Real);

begin
  val1 := val1 / 5.0;
  val2 := val2 - 3.0;
end;

{Output variable values}
procedure Output(num1: Real; num2: Real);

begin
    frmProblem1.memOutput.Lines.Add(Format('%5.2n
                                  %5.2n',
                                  [num1, num2]));
end;
```

2. Type in the code from Problem 1. Trace the code by using a data dump to the screen. What is the output of the code? Check your answer to Problem 1.

3. Use the Delphi debugger to trace the code from Problem 1. Add watches and breakpoints as necessary. Practice using the Trace Into and Step Over commands. What is the difference between these commands?

4. Hand-execute the following code. What is the output?

```
{Chapter 9, Problem 4}
procedure TfrmProblem4.LeftClick(Sender: TObject);

var
  first:  String;
  last:   String;
  target: String;
  result: String;
  pos:    Integer;

begin
  first := 'Humpty';
  last := 'D';

  if (Length(first) > Length(last)) then begin
    target := first;
  end
```

```
    else begin
      target := last;
    end;

    pos := 1;
    result := '';
    repeat
      if (pos <= Length(first)) then begin
        result := result + first[pos];
      end;
      if (pos <= Length(last)) then begin
        result := result + last[pos];
      end;
      Inc(pos);
    until (pos > Length(target));

    memOutput.Clear;
    memOutput.Lines.Add(result);
  end;
```

5. Type in the code from Problem 4. Trace the code by using a data dump to the screen. What is the output of the code? Check your answer to Problem 4.

6. Use the Delphi debugger to trace the code from Problem 4. Add watches and breakpoints as necessary.

7. Write a function named `AveScore` that returns an average exam score. The parameters include `totalOfScores` and `numberOfStudents`. Be sure to use exception handlers to catch run-time errors. Write a driver program to test your function using the following test cases:

totalOfScores	numberOfStudents
500	5
603	7
0	0

8. Find all errors in the following code:

```
{Chapter 9, Problem 8}
procedure TfrmProblem8.LeftClick(Sender: TObject);

var
  count1: Integer;
  count3: Integer;
```

```
begin
  for count1 := 1 to 10 begin
    count3 := 1;
    for count2 := 1 to 20 do begin
      while (count3 + count2 > 0) do begin
        memOutput.Lines.Add(count3);
        count3 := coun3 + 1
      end;
      count1 := count1 + 2;
    end;
  end;
end;
```

9. Find all errors in the following code:

```
{Chapter 9, Problem 9}
procedure TfrmProblem9.LeftClick(Sender: TObject);

var
  a, b, c: Real;
  code:    Integer;
  check:   Boolean;

begin
  Val(edtValueA.Text, a, code);
  Val(txtValueB.Text, b, code);
  Str(txtValueC.Text, c, code);

  check := (a < b);
  if check then begin
    if (a < b < c) then begin
      memOutput.Lines.Add('c is largest');
    else begin
      memOutput.Lines.Add('b is largest');
    end;
  end
  else begin
    if (a > c) then begin
      memOutput.Lines.Add('c is largest');
    end
    else begin
      memoOutput.Lines.Add('a is largest');
    end;
  end;
end;
```

10. Find all errors in the following code:

```
{Chapter 9, Problem 10}
procedure TfrmProblem10.LeftClick(Sender: TObject);

var
  counter: Integer;

begin
  for counter := 1 to 50 do begin
    memOutput.Lines.Add(IntToStr(counter) + ' ' +
                        IntToStr(counter ** 2));
    Inc(counter);
  end;

  for counter := 100 to 1 do begin
    memOutput.Lines.Add(IntToStr(counter) + ' ' +
                        IntToStr(counter div 2));
  end;
end;
```

Data Structures

Chapter Objectives

In this chapter you will:

- Learn the difference between static and dynamic data structures
- Become familiar with enumerated types, sets, and arrays
- Create records and user-defined data types
- Be introduced to pointers and linked lists
- Become acquainted with the operation of lists, stacks, queues, and deques and write Object Pascal code to implement these data structures
- Learn about priority queues, heaps, and trees

A **data structure** is, as its name implies, a structure that contains data. In computer science, entire courses are devoted to data structures and numerous texts have been written concerning the best methods to organize and store data. This chapter describes many of these data structures and serves as a precursor to a formal data structures course.

Static versus Dynamic Data Structures

> **A static data structure** has a fixed type and size. A static data structure cannot be changed unless a programmer modifies the source code. A **dynamic data structure**, however, can change size (and sometimes type) during program execution.

A data structure may be either **static** or **dynamic**. A static data structure has a fixed type and size; it cannot be changed unless a programmer modifies the source code. Conversely, the size (and sometimes type) of a dynamic data structure can change during program execution (that is, dynamically). Some data structures are inherently dynamic and are created and destroyed only at run time. Also, some data structures may be declared as either static or dynamic structures.

Enumerated Types and Sets

Suppose that you want to assign a value to the variable `schoolYear` to indicate the grade level (freshman, sophomore, junior, or senior) of a particular student. In many computer languages, programmers must use either coded values or strings to perform such a task. For instance, a programmer might assign the integer value 1 to the integer variable `schoolYear` to indicate that the student is a freshman. Alternatively, he or she might assign the string `'Freshman'` to a string variable named `schoolYear`. Fortunately, Object Pascal offers a better assignment method—**enumerated types.**

An enumerated type is an ordered set of values defined by the programmer. The values have no inherent meaning, but their ordinality follows the sequence in which they are listed. Thus an enumerated type is a **user-defined data type,** meaning that the programmer (the user of the programming language) defines the data type name and its values.

In Object Pascal, the **type** keyword allows the programmer to define a data type. To declare an enumerated type, you use the following syntax:

```
type
    TypeName = (value1, …, valueN);
```

where *TypeName* and *value1* through *valueN* are valid identifiers. For instance, the declaration

```
type
  Year = (Freshman, Sophomore, Junior, Senior);
```

defines an enumerated type named `Year` whose possible values are `Freshman`, `Sophomore`, `Junior`, and `Senior`.

In an enumerated type declaration, *value1* through *valueN* are declared as constants of type *TypeName*. If these identifiers are used for some other purpose within the same scope, naming conflicts occur. For example, consider the following variable declarations:

```
var
  year1: (Freshman, Sophomore, Junior, Senior);
  year2: (Freshman, Sophomore, Junior, Senior);
```

The variables `year1` and `year2` are declared using enumerated data types without formally defining the type. A compile-time error occurs, however, because the code attempts to redefine the type constants `Freshman`, `Sophomore`, `Junior`, and `Senior` in the declaration of `year2`. We can correct this code as follows:

```
var
  year1, year2: (Freshman, Sophomore, Junior, Senior);
```

Ideally, you should always formally define your enumerated types. Thus the best method of declaring these variables is as follows:

```
type
  Year = (Freshman, Sophomore, Junior, Senior);

var
  year1, year2: Year;
```

Programming Key: Tips

Always formally define enumerated types and user-defined types using the `type` keyword. This ensures type-compatibility between variables, arguments, and parameters and prevents compile-time errors.

A **set** in Object Pascal is very similar to a set in mathematics. That is, a set consists of a group of values of the same ordinal data type. The values have no inherent order, and no value should be included more than once within a set.

Like an enumerated type, a set is a user-defined data type. A set is defined using the **set of** keywords as in the following general syntax:

```
type
  SetName = set of BaseType;
```

SetName is the name of the set and must be a valid Object Pascal identifier. The range of *SetName* is the **power set** of its *BaseType*, a specific ordinal data type. In other words, the possible values of *SetName* include all of the subsets of *Base-Type*, including the empty set, which is denoted by [ ] in Object Pascal. Additionally, Object Pascal limits the size of a set: *BaseType* can include a maximum of 256 values whose ordinalities fall between 0 and 255. Due to this size limitation, sets are usually defined using **subranges,** denoted by two periods (..). For instance,

```
type
   LowercaseSet = set of 'a'..'z';
```

creates a set type named `LowercaseSet` whose values are groups of lowercase letters in the range 'a' to 'z'. We can also assign a data type to this subrange of letters and rewrite the code as follows:

```
type
   LowercaseLetters = 'a'..'z';
   LowercaseSet = set of LowercaseLetters;
```

The two type declarations for `LowercaseSet` are equivalent. Given either of these type declarations, we can now create a set of lowercase letters using a set constructor. In Object Pascal, a set constructor consists of a list of comma-separated values or subranges within square brackets. The general syntax of a set, therefore, is

[*value1*, *value2*, ..., *valueN*]

where *value1* through *valueN* are either values or subranges of *BaseType*. The following code fragment, for example, creates a set consisting of the lowercase letters *a, b, c, m, n, x, y,* and *z:*

```
var
   myLetters: LowercaseSet;

begin
   .
   .
   .
   myLetters := ['a'..'c', 'm', 'n', 'x'..'z'];
   .
   .
   .
end;
```

Just as numeric variables are associated with arithmetic operations that can be performed on them, sets have associated set operations. Figure 10.1 summarizes

Operator	Operation	Operand Types	Result Type	Example
+	union	set	set	set1 + set2
–	difference	set	set	set1 – set2
*	intersection	set	set	set1 * set2
<=	subset	set	Boolean	subSet <= set1
>=	superset	set	Boolean	superSet >= set1
=	equality	set	Boolean	set1 = set2
<>	inequality	set	Boolean	set1 <> set2
in	membership	ordinal, set	Boolean	value in set1

The following rules apply to the +, –, and * operators:
- An ordinal value O is in set1 + set2 if and only if O is in set1 or set2 (or both). O is in set1– set2 if and only if O is in set1 but not in set2. O is in set1 * set2 if and only if O is in both set1 and set2.
- The result of a +, –, or * operation is a set A..B, where A is the smallest ordinal value in the result set and B is the largest.

The following rules apply to the <=, >=, =, <>, and in operators:
- subSet <= set1 is True when every member of subSet is a member of set1; superSet >= set1 is equiv alent to set1 <= superSet. set1 = set2 is True when set1 and set2 contain exactly the same members; otherwise, set1 <> set2 is True.
- For an ordinal value O and set1, O in set1 is True when O is a member of set1.

FIGURE 10.1   Object Pascal Set Operators

the set operators. The **in** operator, for instance, tests set membership: X in $Set-Name$ returns the Boolean value True if the contents of variable X is a member of the set $SetName$.

Arrays

Consider the following problem: The 10 students in computer programming class take an exam. The instructor wants to write a computer program that outputs the average exam score and a phrase describing each student's score relative to the class average (that is, "Above Average," "Average," or "Below Average"). Using the programming techniques presented thus far, you might write a program containing code similar to that shown below:

```
{ ------------------------------------------------------------
Compute and compare student scores to the class average.

NOTE: No error-proofing for user-entered scores.
      Invalid scores are considered 0 by default.
  -----------------------------------------------------------}
procedure TfrmClassAverage.Compute(Sender: TObject);

var
   score1, score2, score3, score4, score5:  Real;
   score6, score7, score8, score9, score10: Real;
```

```
           code:                                    Integer;
           aveScore:                                Real;
       begin
         Val(edtStudent1.Text, score1, code);
         Val(edtStudent2.Text, score2, code);
         Val(edtStudent3.Text, score3, code);
         Val(edtStudent4.Text, score4, code);
         Val(edtStudent5.Text, score5, code);
         Val(edtStudent6.Text, score6, code);
         Val(edtStudent7.Text, score7, code);
         Val(edtStudent8.Text, score8, code);
         Val(edtStudent9.Text, score9, code);
         Val(edtStudent10.Text, score10, code);

         aveScore := (score1 + score2 + score3 + score4 + score5 +
                      score6 + score7 + score8 + score9 + score10) /
                      10.0;

         memOutput.Clear;
         memOutput.Lines.Add('Average Score: ' +
                             Format('%5.2n', [aveScore]));
         memOutput.Lines.Add('');

         Compare(1, score1, aveScore);
         Compare(2, score2, aveScore);
         Compare(3, score3, aveScore);
         Compare(4, score4, aveScore);
         Compare(5, score5, aveScore);
         Compare(6, score6, aveScore);
         Compare(7, score7, aveScore);
         Compare(8, score8, aveScore);
         Compare(9, score9, aveScore);
         Compare(10, score10, aveScore);
       end;

       { -------------------------------------------------------------
       Compare student score to the average score and display
       the result: "Above Average," "Average," or "Below Average"
        ----------------------------------------------------------}
       procedure Compare(student: Integer; score, average: Real);

       var
         lineOut: String;

       begin
         lineOut := 'Student ' + IntToStr(student) + ': ';
         if (score > average) then begin
```

```
      lineOut := lineOut + 'Above ';
    end
    else if (score < average) then begin
      lineOut := lineOut + 'Below ';
    end;
    lineOut := lineOut + 'Average';
    frmClassAverage.memOutput.Lines.Add(lineOut);
  end;
```

Notice that a separate variable must be declared for each student's exam score as well as a variable for the average score. As illustrated by the form in Figure 10.2, 10 edit boxes are needed to input the student exam scores.

Although this programming technique works adequately for a small class of 10 students, what happens when the class size is larger (say, 50 or 100 students)? As you can imagine, writing the variable declarations and mathematical formula (not to mention designing the user interface) would become quite tedious. Fortunately, a better (shorter, simpler, and faster) way is available to write this program using the **array** data structure.

An array is a set of sequentially indexed **elements** of the same intrinsic data type. Each element of an array

> An **array** is a set of sequentially indexed elements of the same intrinsic data type. An **element** is a single location within an array. Each element has a unique identifying index number, and each element acts as a separate variable that can be accessed using this index value.

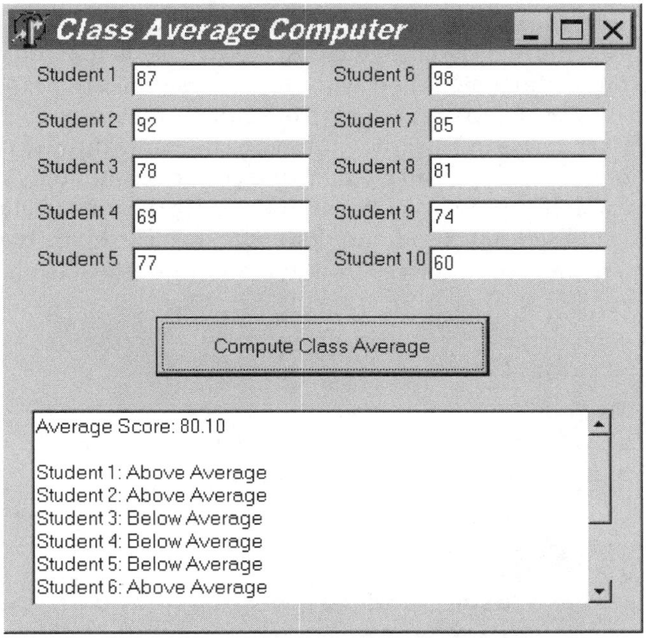

FIGURE 10.2 Class Average Computer

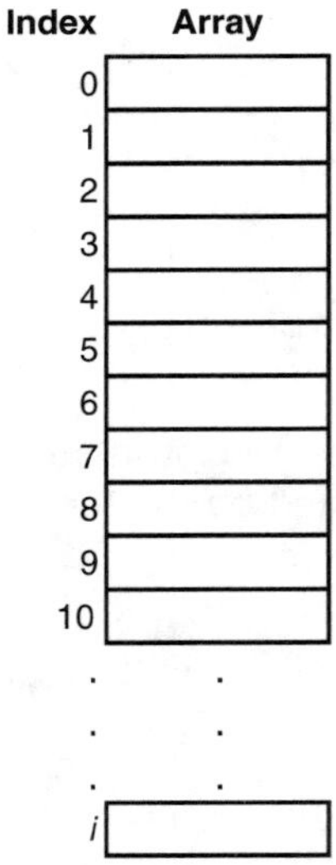

FIGURE 10.3   Physical Diagram of an Array Structure

has a unique identifying index number. Figure 10.3 depicts the physical structure of an array.

An array with one index, like that shown in Figure 10.3, is a **one-dimensional array.** The mathematical equivalent of this array is a *vector*. A **two-dimensional array** is an array with two separate indices; a *matrix* is its mathematical equivalent. Finally, a **multidimensional array** (or **n-dimensional array**) is an array with more than two indices. Figure 10.4 depicts examples of these array structures.

The notation for arrays in most programming languages directly parallels mathematical notation. For example, an element of a vector is commonly denoted by x_i, where x is the variable representing the vector and i is the index value. As we cannot easily write a subscript in a computer program, we use square brackets instead; thus the x_i element of a vector corresponds to the $x[i]$ element of an array.

Static Arrays

In Object Pascal, you declare an array variable using the **array of** keywords. The general syntax to declare a **static array** follows:

```
var
   arrayVariable: array[indexType1, ..., indexTypeN] of
                  BaseType;
```

One-Dimensional Array

```
var myArray: array[1..5] of Integer;
```

Two-Dimensional Array

```
var myArray: array[1..5, 1..4] of Integer;
```

Multidimensional Array

```
var myArray: array[1..5, 1..4, 1..3] of Integer;
```

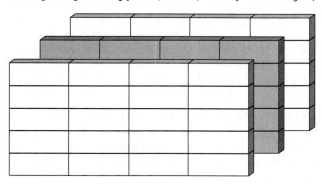

FIGURE 10.4   Examples of Array Structures

Here *arrayVariable* is any valid variable name, and *BaseType* is the data type of each element in the array. Each *indexType* represents a separate index of the array and must be an ordinal data type. The number of elements in the array is the product of the *indexType* dimensions. Usually, the *indexType* values consist of integer subranges.

In the case of a one-dimensional array, only one *indexType* exists. As a consequence, the general syntax to declare a one-dimensional array reduces to

```
var
  oneDimensionalArrayVariable: array[indexType] of BaseType;
```

For instance,

```
var
  sampleArray: array[1..10] of Integer;
```

declares an array variable named `sampleArray` that contains 10 integer elements (in index positions 1 through 10).

The following code fragment contains example declarations of a two-dimensional array and a multidimensional array:

```
type
  Year = (Freshman, Sophomore, Junior, Senior);

var
  smp2DArray: array[1..10, 1..5] of Integer;
  smp4DArray: array[Year, 1..20, 'A'..'F', 1..3] of Char;
```

You can think of a two-dimensional array as an array of an array. Similarly, any multidimensional array is really just an array of arrays. Thus the following declarations are equivalent to the previous code fragment:

```
type
  Year = (Freshman, Sophomore, Junior, Senior);

var
  smp2DArray: array[1..10] of array[1..5] of Integer;
  smp4DArray: array[Year] of array[1..20] of
              array['A'..'F'] of array[1..3] of Char;
```

Regardless of which syntax you use to declare these arrays, `smp2DArray` always contains 50 (10×5) integer elements and `smp4DArray` always contains 1440 ($4 \times 20 \times 6 \times 3$) character elements. The manner in which you choose to declare your array variables is simply a matter of programming style. Note, however, that your chosen programming style should remain consistent throughout a program.

Each element of an array acts as a separate variable that can be accessed using its unique index values. To access a specific array element, use either of the following forms:

```
arrayName[indexValue1, ..., indexValueN]
```

or

```
arrayName[indexValue1] ... [indexValueN]
```

The following statement, for example, assigns the value 10 to the fifth element of sampleArray:

Assign the integer value 10 to the fifth element of sampleArray.

```
sampleArray[5] := 10;
```

As with the array variable declarations, the following array assignment statements are equivalent:

```
smp2DArray[5, 2] := 7;
smp4DArray[Junior, 10, 'A', 1] := 'X';
```

is equivalent to

```
smp2DArray[5][2] := 7;
smp4DArray[Junior][10]['A'][1] := 'X';
```

Now that we know how to create and use array variables, we can rewrite our earlier program. In the following code, the Class Average Computer is simplified by using an array variable:

```
{ -----------------------------------------------------
Compute and compare student scores to the class average.

NOTE: No error-proofing for user-entered scores.
      Invalid scores are considered 0 by default.
---------------------------------------------------------}
procedure TfrmClassAverage.Compute(Sender: TObject);

var
  stNum:    Integer;
  score:    array[1..10] of Real;
  code:     Integer;
  total:    Real;
  aveScore: Real;

begin
  total := 0.0;
  for stNum := 1 to 10 do begin
    Val(InputBox('ENTER SCORE',
                 'Enter the score for student ' +
                 IntToStr(stNum) + ':', ''),
         score[stNum], code);
    total := total + score[stNum];
  end;

  aveScore := total/10.0;

  memOutput.Clear;
  memOutput.Lines.Add('Average Score: ' +
                      Format('%5.2n', [aveScore]));
  memOutput.Lines.Add('');
```

```
    for stNum := 1 to 10 do begin
      Compare(stNum, score[stNum], aveScore);
    end;
  end;

  { ----------------------------------------------------------
  Compare student score to the average score and display
  the result: "Above Average," "Average," or "Below Aver-
  age"
  ----------------------------------------------------------}
  procedure Compare(student: Integer; score, average:
                    Real);
  var
    lineOut: String;

  begin
    lineOut := 'Student ' + IntToStr(student) + ': ';
    if (score > average) then begin
      lineOut := lineOut + 'Above ';
    end
    else if (score < average) then begin
      lineOut := lineOut + 'Below ';
    end;
    lineOut := lineOut + 'Average';
    frmClassAverage.memOutput.Lines.Add(lineOut);
  end;
```

Programming Key: Tips

Use the `type` keyword to create a user-defined type for a static array structure that is the data type of an argument, parameter, or more than one variable. The following code fragment illustrates the reason:

```
var
  intArray1: array[1..10] of Integer;
  intArray2: array[1..10] of Integer;
  count:     Integer;
begin
  for count := 1 to 10 do begin
    intArray1[count] := count;
  end;
  intArray2 := intArray1;
end;
```

Because the Object Pascal compiler uses type name equivalence to determine data type equivalence, `intArray1` and `intArray2` are not type-compatible. Although they have the same physical structure, they are not of the same data type. Therefore, an "Incompatible types" compile-time error occurs due to the assignment statement `intArray2 := intArray1;`. You can correct this code as follows:

```
type
  TenInts = array[1..10] of Integer;
var
  intArray1: TenInts;
  intArray2: TenInts;
  count:     Integer;
begin
  for count := 1 to 10 do begin
    intArray1[count] := count;
  end;
  intArray2 := intArray1;
end;
```

Dynamic Arrays

Next, we will modify the Class Average Computer to allow for an unknown number of students in the class. One way to overcome this problem is to use a static array whose length is the maximum possible class size and to use another variable to specify the exact number of students in the class. Unfortunately, this method wastes memory space for any class smaller in size than the maximum, and it requires modifying the source code if the maximum class size increases. A better solution is to use a **dynamic array**.

To declare a dynamic array, you use the `array of` statement without specifying the indices. The general syntax to declare a one-dimensional dynamic array follows:

```
var
    dynamicArrayVariable: array of BaseType;
```

where *dynamicArrayVariable* is any valid variable name, and *BaseType* is the data type of each element in the dynamic array. Unlike a static array declaration, a dynamic array declaration does not allocate memory space for the array.

Instead, the programmer must allocate memory for the dynamic array and specify its size using the **SetLength** procedure:

```
SetLength(dynamicArrayVariable, length);
```

In the above syntax, *length* is an integer expression. Note that the index values of *dynamicArrayVariable* range from 0 to *length* − 1 after execution of the SetLength procedure. In addition, the SetLength procedure resizes a dynamic array variable while preserving the contents of its memory space. If the length of the dynamic array increases, the contents of the newly allocated memory space are undefined and consist of **garbage**. If the length decreases, the dynamic array is truncated and the contents of the truncated elements are lost.

Because dynamic arrays are dynamic data structures, the programmer must manually remove them from the computer's memory space. The process of eliminating unwanted dynamic variables from computer memory is known as **garbage collection**. Object Pascal provides three methods to dispose of a dynamic array variable:

1. Set the length of the dynamic array variable to zero:

   ```
   SetLength(dynamicArrayVariable, 0);
   ```

   or

2. Assign the value **nil** to the variable. In Object Pascal, nil is the reserved word used to make a **pointer variable** reference nothing. Pointer variables, or simply **pointers**, are discussed later in this chapter.

   ```
   dynamicArrayVariable := nil;
   ```

   or

3. Pass the variable to the **Finalize** procedure:

   ```
   Finalize(dynamicArrayVariable);
   ```

Several other useful functions are available for working with dynamic arrays. The **Copy** function returns a portion of a dynamic array. Its general syntax follows:

```
Copy(dynamicArrayVariable, startIndexValue, numberElements);
```

This function call returns *numberElements* elements of *dynamicArrayVariable* starting at index position *startIndexValue*.

The **High** and **Low** functions return a dynamic array's highest and lowest index values, respectively. That is, High returns length − 1 and Low returns 0. In the case of a zero-length array, High returns –1 with the anomalous consequence that High is less than Low. The general syntax of these functions follows:

```
High(dynamicArrayVariable);

Low(dynamicArrayVariable);
```

In the following modification of the Class Average Computer, a dynamic array is used to allow for any number of students:

```
{ -----------------------------------------------------
Compute and compare student scores to the class average.

NOTE: No error-proofing for user-entered scores.
      Invalid scores are considered 0 by default.
  -------------------------------------------------------}
procedure TfrmClassAverage.Compute(Sender: TObject);

var
   numStudents: Integer;
   stNum:       Integer;
   score:       array of Real;
   code:        Integer;
   total:       Real;
   aveScore:    Real;

begin
   Val(edtNumber.Text, numStudents, code);

   If (numStudents > 0) then begin
     SetLength(score, numStudents);
     total := 0.0;
     for stNum := 0 to (numStudents - 1) do begin
       Val(InputBox('ENTER SCORE',
                    'Enter the score for student ' +
                    IntToStr(stNum + 1) + ':', ''),
           score[stNum], code);
       total := total + score[stNum];
     end;

     aveScore := total/numStudents;

     memOutput.Clear;
     memOutput.Lines.Add('Average Score: ' +
                         Format('%5.2n', [aveScore]));
     memOutput.Lines.Add('');
```

```
      for stNum := 0 to (numStudents - 1) do begin
        Compare((stNum + 1), score[stNum], aveScore);
      end;
    end;
  end;

  { ------------------------------------------------------------
  Compare student score to the average score and display
  the result: "Above Average," "Average," or "Below Average"
  ----------------------------------------------------------}
  procedure Compare(student: Integer; score, average: Real);

  var
    lineOut: String;

  begin
    lineOut := 'Student ' + IntToStr(student) + ': ';
    if (score > average) then begin
      lineOut := lineOut + 'Above ';
    end
    else if (score < average) then begin
      lineOut := lineOut + 'Below ';
    end;
    lineOut := lineOut + 'Average';
    frmClassAverage.memOutput.Lines.Add(lineOut);
  end;
```

Now that we have seen and used a one-dimensional dynamic array, how do we create a multidimensional dynamic array? Remember, a multidimensional array is just an array of arrays. The general syntax to declare a dynamic array containing more than one index follows:

```
var
  multiDimDynArrayVar: array of array of [array of]
                       BaseType;
```

For example, the following code fragment declares and allocates the memory space for a two-dimensional dynamic array. Figure 10.5 depicts the physical structure of this dynamic array. Notice that each row of the array (the first index) does not contain the same number of columns (the second index). As you can see, multidimensional dynamic arrays are extremely flexible data structures.

```
var
  smp2DdynArray: array of array of Integer;
  count:         Integer;
```

Second Index

First Index   0   1   2   3   4   5

FIGURE 10.5   Example Dynamic Array Structure

```
begin
  SetLength(smp2DdynArray, 3);

  for count := 1 to 3 do begin
    SetLength(smp2DdynArray[count - 1], count * 2);
  end;
     .
     .
     .
end;
```

Programming Key: Warning

Dynamic array variables are really pointers. That is, the array variable does not contain the data itself, but rather references (or points to) the first memory location that contains the array data. The indices are used as offsets to reference the appropriate piece of data from this first memory location.

Examine the following code fragment:

```
var
  array1, array2: array of Integer;
  check:          Boolean;

begin
  SetLength(array1, 1);
  SetLength(array2, 1);

  array1[0] := 5;
  array2[0] := 5;

  check := (array1 = array2);
     .
     .
     .
  end;
```

What is the value of check after this code executes? For static arrays, check evaluates to True because it compares the values contained within the arrays. For the dynamic arrays in this code, however, `check` is False because it compares the memory locations contained in (the pointers) `array1` and `array2`. These memory locations are clearly different, as the `SetLength` procedure allocates different memory space to each array. In short, to compare the contents of two dynamic arrays, we must test them element by element.

A problem of a similar nature exists in the following code fragment. Can you find it?

```
var
   array1, array2: array of Integer;

begin
   SetLength(array1, 1);
   SetLength(array2, 1);
   array1[0] := 5;
   array2 := array1;
   array2[0] := 10;

      .
      .
      .

end;
```

What are the values of `array1[0]` and `array2[0]` after this code executes? Notice that `array1` is assigned to `array2`. In other words, `array2` references the same memory location as `array1`. Thus both `array1[0]` and `array2[0]` reference the same memory location, which contains the value 10 (as assigned in the last written line of code).

Programming Key: Delphi Highlight

The `String` data type is essentially a dynamic array of characters. Delphi also provides a string list object data type (`TStringList`) to store and maintain a list of strings. The following code segment demonstrates that these string-related data types consist of arrays of characters:

```
procedure TfrmStrings.TestStrings(Sender: TObject);

var
   bkString: String;
   strList:  TStringList;

begin
   memOutput.Clear;
```

```
      bkString := 'Programming and Problem Solving with
      Delphi';
      memOutput.Lines.Add(bkString[25]);

      strList := TStringList.Create;
      strList.Clear;
      strList.Add('Line 1');
      strList.Add('Line 2');
      strList.Add('Line 3');
      memOutput.Lines.Add(strList.Strings[2][6]);
      strList.Destroy;
   end;
```

The output of this code is:

```
   S
   3
```

Note that the first string in a string list has an index of 0. Thus `strList.Strings[2][6]` refers to the sixth character of the third string, `'Line 3'`.

Passing Arrays to Subprograms

The two previous Class Average Computer examples passed a single array element to the `Compare` procedure. But what if we want to pass an entire array to a subprogram? In the final modification of the Class Average Computer, we pass the entire `score` array to the `Compare` procedure, and this procedure performs the loop instead of the calling routine. The `ClassAve` unit that contains this code appears below:

```
unit ClassAve;

interface

uses
  Windows, Messages, SysUtils, Classes, Graphics, Controls,
  Forms, Dialogs, StdCtrls;

type
  TfrmClassAverage = class(TForm)
    btnComputeAve: TButton;
    memOutput: TMemo;
    procedure Compute(Sender: TObject);
```

```
    private
      { Private declarations }
    public
      { Public declarations }
    end;
    ClassScores = array[1..10] of Real;

var
  frmClassAverage: TfrmClassAverage;

procedure Compare(scr: ClassScores; average: Real);

implementation

{$R *.DFM}

{ ------------------------------------------------------------
Compute and compare student scores to the class average.

NOTE: No error-proofing for user-entered scores.
      Invalid scores are considered 0 by default.
------------------------------------------------------------}
procedure TfrmClassAverage.Compute(Sender: TObject);

var
  stNum:        Integer;
  score:        ClassScores;
  code:         Integer;
  total:        Real;
  aveScore:     Real;

begin
  total := 0.0;
  for stNum := 1 to 10 do begin
    Val(InputBox('ENTER SCORE',
                 'Enter the score for student ' +
                  IntToStr(stNum) + ':', ''),
        score[stNum], code);
    total := total + score[stNum];
  end;

  aveScore := total/10.0;

  memOutput.Clear;
  memOutput.Lines.Add('Average Score: ' +
                      Format('%5.2n', [aveScore]));
  memOutput.Lines.Add('');

  Compare(score, aveScore);
end;
```

```
{ ------------------------------------------------------------
Compare student score to the average score and display
the result: "Above Average," "Average," or "Below Average"
------------------------------------------------------------}
procedure Compare(scr: ClassScores; average: Real);

var
  stNum:   Integer;
  lineOut: String;

begin
  for stNum := Low(scr) to High(scr) do begin
    lineOut := 'Student ' + IntToStr(stNum) + ': ';
    if (scr[stNum] > average) then begin
      lineOut := lineOut + 'Above ';
    end
    else if (scr[stNum] < average) then begin
      lineOut := lineOut + 'Below ';
    end;
    lineOut := lineOut + 'Average';
    frmClassAverage.memOutput.Lines.Add(lineOut);
  end;
end;

end.
```

Programming Key: Warning

Object Pascal does not allow you to use indices as parameters in subprogram declarations. For instance, the following function declaration will generate a syntax error:

```
function Example(inArray: array[1..20] of Real): Real;
```

The syntax error results from specifying [1..20] as the indices of the inArray parameter. Once again, you should declare a user-defined data type to overcome this language restriction. Thus the following code compiles with no errors:

```
type
  RealArray20 = array[1..20] of Real;

function Example(inArray: RealArray20): Real;
```

The `ClassScores` data type is defined in the interface section of this unit. Both the `score` array variable in the `Compute` event handler and the `scr` array parameter in the `Compare` procedure are of this data type. Thus they are type-compatible, and `score` is a valid argument to the `Compare` procedure.

Programming Key: Delphi Highlight

Delphi allows the programmer to use **open array parameters**, or array parameters with no specified indices. For instance,

```
procedure OpenArrayEx(inArray: array of Integer);
```

defines a procedure named `OpenArrayEx` whose only parameter is an integer array of any size. In this way, open array parameters greatly enhance the utility of subprograms. While the syntax of an open array parameter resembles that of a dynamic array, it does not operate in the same manner. A user-defined data type must be used to declare a dynamic array parameter.

Open array parameters are governed by the following rules:

1. Open array parameters are always zero-based. That is, the index of the first element is always 0.

2. The `Low` and `High` functions return 0 and `Length` — 1, respectively. The `SizeOf` function returns the size of the actual array passed to the routine.

3. Open array parameters can be accessed by element only. Assignments to an entire open array parameter are prohibited.

4. Open array parameters cannot be passed to the `SetLength` procedure. They can be passed to other procedures and functions only as open array parameters or untyped `var` parameters.

5. A variable of the open array parameter's base type that is passed into the subprogram as an argument is treated as an array of length 1.

GUI Design Tips

Arrays can store large quantities of information. When working with large arrays, it is often easier for a user to enter data into a data file rather than to edit boxes or input boxes in the user interface. The data file can then be used as an input file for the program. Chapters 7 and 11 discuss Object Pascal data files and file input and output.

• C • A • S • E • S • T • U • D • Y •

Using Arrays

The Del Presto Company manufactures toasters, blenders, and cutting boards. Each toaster sold yields Del Presto a profit of $12, each blender gives a $20 profit, and each cutting board gives a $7 profit. Ralph, the company's accountant, has the sales data for the past three months. He wants to figure out the monthly profit for each of the past three months, the total profit over the past three months, and the average monthly profit. Ralph performs this same computation every quarter (that is, every three months). Can you write a program to help Ralph?

Arrays are very helpful in constructing a program of this nature. This problem involves three products and three sales figures per product, giving a total of nine sales figures. Rather than creating nine edit boxes on a form, Ralph uses an input file named `DelPresto.DAT` to enhance the flexibility of his program. His input file contains the three product names, profit per product sold, and three months of sales figures per product. If Del Presto Company later changes its products, Ralph can modify his input file rather than his program. Ralph's program appears in the code unit below:

```
{ ------------------------------------------------------
Del Presto Company
Quarterly Profit Computer

Input File Name: C:\DelPresto.DAT
Input File Format:

  product1    (String)
  profit1     (Real)
  product2
  profit2
  product3
  profit3
  month1      (String)
  product1Sales product2Sales product3Sales    (Integer)
  month2
  product1Sales product2Sales product3Sales
  month3
  product1Sales product2Sales product3Sales

Example Input File:
```

```
    Toasters
    12.00
    Blenders
    20.00
    Cutting Boards
    7.00
    January
    500 300 150
    February
    620 125 480
    March
    370 165 400
    --------------------------------------------------------}
unit DelPrestoCo;

interface

uses
  Windows, Messages, SysUtils, Classes, Graphics, Controls,
  Forms, Dialogs, StdCtrls;

const
  PRODS  = 3; {3 products}
  MONTHS = 3; {3 months per quarter}

type
  TfrmDelPresto = class(TForm)
    btnCompute: TButton;
    memOutput: TMemo;
    procedure ComputeProfit(Sender: TObject);
  private
    { Private declarations }
  public
    { Public declarations }
  end;
  ProductArray = array[1..PRODS] of String;
  ProfitArray  = array[1..PRODS] of Real;
  MonthArray   = array[1..MONTHS] of String;
  SalesArray   = array[1..MONTHS, 1..PRODS] of Integer;
  MonthlySales = array[1..MONTHS] of Real;

var
  frmDelPresto: TfrmDelPresto;

implementation

{$R *.DFM}

{ -------------------------------------------------------
Read the product and sales data from the DelPresto.DAT
```

```
input file and compute the quarterly profit.  Display the
results in the memOutput memo box.
---------------------------------------------------------}
procedure TfrmDelPresto.ComputeProfit(Sender: TObject);

var
  product:        ProductArray;
  profit:         ProfitArray;
  month:          MonthArray;
  sales:          SalesArray;
  mnthSales:      MonthlySales;
  mnth, item:     Integer;
  totalSales:     Real;
  inFile:         TextFile;

begin
  try
    {Read data from input file, echo data to memo box,
     and compute monthly sales and total sales}
    AssignFile(inFile, 'C:\DelPresto.DAT');
    Reset(inFile);
    memOutput.Clear;

    memOutput.Lines.Add('PROFIT PER PRODUCT:');
    memOutput.Lines.Add('------------------');
    for item := 1 to PRODS do begin
      Readln(inFile, product[item]);
      Readln(inFile, profit[item]);
      memOutput.Lines.Add(product[item] + ': ' +
                          Format('%5.2m', [profit[item]]));
    end;

    memOutput.Lines.Add('');
    memOutput.Lines.Add('MONTHLY PRODUCT SALES:');
    memOutput.Lines.Add('---------------------');
    for mnth := 1 to MONTHS do begin
      Readln(inFile, month[mnth]);
      memOutput.Lines.Add(month[mnth]);
      mnthSales[mnth] := 0.0;
      for item := 1 to PRODS do begin
        Read(inFile, sales[mnth, item]);
        memOutput.Lines.Add('   ' + product[item] + ': ' +
                            Format('%3d', [sales[mnth,
                            item]]));
        mnthSales[mnth] := mnthSales[mnth] +
                          (sales[mnth, item] *
                          profit[item]);
```

```
          end;
        if (mnth < MONTHS) then begin
          Readln(inFile);
        end;
      end;

      {Display monthly sales, total sales, and
       average monthly sales}
      memOutput.Lines.Add('');
      memOutput.Lines.Add('MONTHLY SALES TOTALS:');
      memOutput.Lines.Add('--------------------');
      totalSales := 0.0;
      for mnth := 1 to MONTHS do begin
        memOutput.Lines.Add(month[mnth] + ': ' +
                            Format('%5.2m',
                            [mnthSales[mnth]]));
        totalSales := totalSales + mnthSales[mnth];
      end;
      memOutput.Lines.Add('');
      memOutput.Lines.Add('TOTAL SALES: ' +
                          Format('%5.2m', [totalSales]));
      if (MONTHS > 0) then begin
        memOutput.Lines.Add('');
        memOutput.Lines.Add('AVERAGE MONTHLY SALES: ' +
                            Format('%5.2m',
                            [totalSales/MONTHS]));
      end;
      CloseFile(inFile);
    except
      on E: Exception do begin
        Application.MessageBox(pchar(E.Message), 'ERROR',
                               MB_OK);
        Application.Terminate;
      end;
    end;
  end;

end.
```

A sample `DelPresto.DAT` input file follows:

```
Toasters
12.00
Blenders
20.00
```

```
Cutting Boards
7.00
January
500 300 150
February
620 125 480
March
370 165 400
```

The output of Ralph's program for this input file follows:

```
PROFIT PER PRODUCT:
-------------------
Toasters: $12.00
Blenders: $20.00
Cutting Boards: $7.00

MONTHLY PRODUCT SALES:
----------------------
January
   Toasters: 500
   Blenders: 300
   Cutting Boards: 150
February
   Toasters: 620
   Blenders: 125
   Cutting Boards: 480
March
   Toasters: 370
   Blenders: 165
   Cutting Boards: 400

MONTHLY SALES TOTALS:
---------------------
January: $13,050.00
February: $13,300.00
March: $10,540.00

TOTAL SALES: $36,890.00

AVERAGE MONTHLY SALES: $12,296.67
```

To test your understanding of arrays, modify Ralph's program to compute the total profit per item over the three months. In other words, compute the profits for toaster sales, blender sales, and cutting board sales. What is the total profit? Why?

Records and User-Defined Data Types

Now that you've been introduced to arrays, the next step is to do something useful with them. Consider the design of a simple address book program. The constant, type, and variable declarations for this program appear below. For the sake of simplicity, the code uses static array variables and the program is limited to 50 names and addresses.

```
const
 MAX_RECORDS = 50;

type
 DataField = array[1..MAX_RECORDS] of String;

var
 firstName:    DataField; {First name}
 lastName:     DataField; {Last name}
 address:      DataField; {Street address}
 city:         DataField; {City}
 state:        DataField; {State}
 zipCode:      DataField; {ZIP code}
 phoneNumber:  DataField; {Telephone number}
 number:       Integer; {Number of addresses in address book}
```

Each variable declaration creates an array variable that will hold one of the pieces of data required to form a complete address card (address and telephone number data). There is an array for the first name, last name, street address, and so on. Additionally, the number variable specifies the number of active address cards in the address book program, where the maximum allowable number of active addresses is 50, as specified by the MAX_RECORDS constant.

An address book program using these variable declarations as the underlying data structure relies heavily on proper correspondence of the index values. In other words, the person with firstName[1] and lastName[1] lives at street address address[1] in city[1] and state[1]. Furthermore, all other pertinent information for this individual appears in the first element (index 1) of each of the remaining arrays. Arrays of this form are called **parallel arrays.** Unfortunately, if the data are sorted incorrectly or the index values somehow become misaligned (either through a programming error or file I/O error), all of the address book data will be corrupted. In such a case, the reliability of the entire data set is questionable.

Records provide a safer and more reliable data structure than parallel arrays for implementing the address book program. A **record** is a user-defined data type that encapsulates a group of related data. Each piece of information in a record is called a **field.** The data set consisting of all records forms a **database.** In our address book, for example, each address card is a record. Each record has first name, last name, street address, city, state, ZIP code, and telephone number fields. The database consists of all address cards, or the entire address book.

> A **record** is a user-defined data type that encapsulates a group of related data. A record contains information in one or more **fields**, where a field contains a single piece of information, such as a city within an address. A **database** is the data set consisting of all records.

A record type declaration specifies a record type name as well as a name and data type for each field of the record. The Object Pascal syntax of a record type declaration follows:

```
type
  RecordTypeName = record
                     fieldList1: DataType1;
                     fieldList2: DataType2;
                            .
                            .
                            .
                     fieldListN: DataTypeN;
                   end;
```

In this syntax, *RecordTypeName* must be a valid identifier, and each *fieldList* must be a valid identifier or a comma-delimited list of identifiers. *DataType* denotes a specific data type for each *fieldList*. The final semicolon before the end keyword is optional.

The following type declaration defines the StudentInfo data type. It also declares the static array students of type StudentInfo.

```
const
  MAX_RECORDS = 25;

type
  StudentInfo = record
                  lastName:  String;
                  firstName: String;
                  age:       Integer;
                end;

var
  students: array[1..MAX_RECORDS] of StudentInfo;
```

To access a specific field of a record, you separate the record variable from the field name with a period ("."). Here, the **dot-separator** qualifies the field designator with the record's name. In Object Pascal, dot-separators are also used to separate properties and methods from objects. Thus the form *recordVariableName.fieldName* accesses the *fieldName* field of the record variable *recordVariableName*. Using the preceding declarations, we can assign data to students[1], the first student record, as shown in the following code fragment:

```
students[1].lastName := 'Smith';
students[1].firstName := 'John';
students[1].age := 19;
```

Alternatively, you can use the **with** statement to access the fields of a record. Rewriting the previous assignment statements using the with statement yields

```
with students[1] do begin
  lastName := 'Smith';
  firstName := 'John';
  age := 19;
end;
```

The syntax of the with statement follows:

```
with Object do begin
  [statements;]
end;
```

Programming Key: Tips

When multiple objects or records appear in a with statement, the entire statement is treated as if it consisted of a series of nested with statements. Thus

```
with Object1, Object2, …, ObjectN do begin
  [statements;]
end;
```

is equivalent to

```
with Object1 do begin
  with Object2 do begin

        .
        .
        .

    with ObjectN do begin
      [statements;]
    end;
  end;
end;
```

In this syntax, the program interprets each variable reference or method name within *statements*, if possible, as a member of *ObjectN*; otherwise, it is interpreted, if possible, as a member of the previous object (*ObjectN* − 1); and so on. A similar method applies to interpreting the objects themselves. For example, if *ObjectN* is a member of both *Object1* and *Object2*, it is interpreted as *Object2.ObjectN*.

To conclude this section, let's illustrate the use of records in our Address Book program. Figure 10.6 shows the user interface for this program, and the accompanying code gives the routine used to input the address book records. Additionally, Chapter 11 discusses the use of records for file input and output.

```
{ ------------------------------------------------------------
Address Book Program
--------------------
NOTE: This contains only the code to add an address card
      to the address book
------------------------------------------------------------}
unit Address;

interface

uses
  Windows, Messages, SysUtils, Classes, Graphics,
  Controls, Forms, Dialogs, StdCtrls;

const
  MAX_RECORDS = 50;

type
  TfrmAddressBook = class(TForm)
    edtFirstName: TEdit;
    edtLastName: TEdit;
    edtAddress: TEdit;
    edtCity: TEdit;
    edtState: TEdit;
    edtZip: TEdit;
    edtPhoneNumber: TEdit;
    lblFirstName: TLabel;
    lblLastName: TLabel;
    lblAddress: TLabel;
    lblCity: TLabel;
    lblState: TLabel;
    lblZip: TLabel;
    lblPhoneNumber: TLabel;
    btnAdd: TButton;
    btnClear: TButton;
    procedure AddAddress(Sender: TObject);
    procedure Initialize(Sender: TObject);
    procedure ClearForm(Sender: TObject);
  private
    { Private declarations }
  public
```

```
            { Public declarations }
        end;
        AddressCard = record
                        firstName:    String; {First Name}
                        lastName:     String; {Last Name}
                        address:      String; {Street Address}
                        city:         String; {City}
                        state:        String; {State}
                        zipCode:      String; {ZIP Code}
                        phoneNumber: String; {Telephone Number}
                    end;

    {
    GLOBAL VARIABLES
    These global variables make the coding of this program
    sufficiently easier.  Suffice it to say, this is one
    occasion where global variables are desirable.
    }
    var
      frmAddressBook: TfrmAddressBook;
      {Address book data: array of AddressCard records}
      addressBook: array[1..MAX_RECORDS] of AddressCard;
      {Number of address cards in the database}
      number:       Integer;

    implementation

    {$R *.DFM}

    {Add the address card to the database}
    procedure TfrmAddressBook.AddAddress(Sender: TObject);

    begin
      if (number < MAX_RECORDS) then begin
        Inc(number);
        with addressBook[number] do begin
          firstName := edtFirstName.Text;
          lastName := edtLastName.Text;
          address := edtAddress.Text;
          city := edtCity.Text;
          state := edtState.Text;
          zipCode := edtZip.Text;
          phoneNumber := edtPhoneNumber.Text;
        end;
        ClearForm(Sender);
      end
```

> This code contains only the routine to add an address card to the address book. Also, this code uses global variables to simplify the implementation.

```
      else begin
        Application.MessageBox(PChar(
                            'Cannot add new address card'),
                            'ADDRESS BOOK FULL', MB_OK);
      end;
end;

{Initialize the Address Book database by setting the
number of records to 0}
procedure TfrmAddressBook.Initialize(Sender: TObject);

begin
  number := 0;
end;

{Clear the edit boxes on the form}
procedure TfrmAddressBook.ClearForm(Sender: TObject);

begin
  edtFirstName.Clear;
  edtLastName.Clear;
  edtAddress.Clear;
  edtCity.Clear;
  edtState.Clear;
  edtZip.Clear;
  edtPhoneNumber.Clear;
end;

end.
```

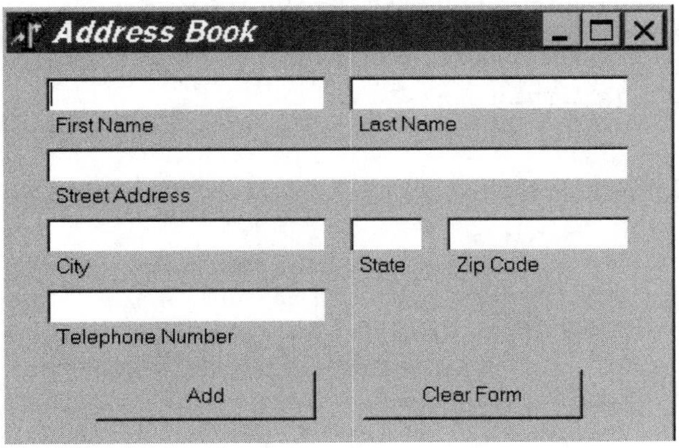

FIGURE 10.6 Address Book Form

Object Pascal allows for the creation of **variant records**, where a variant record is a record type that contains a variant part. A variant record includes fields for different kinds of data, but it never uses all of its fields in a single record instance. Consider the following example:

```
type
  EmployeeData = record
                   firstName:   String[30];
                   lastName:    String[30];
                   birthDate:   TDate;
                   phoneNumber: String[14];
                   case citizen: Boolean of
                      True:  (birthplace: String[30];
                              SSN:        String[11]);
                      False: (country:    String[30];
                              entryPort:  String[20];
                              entryDate:  TDate;
                              workID:     String[20]);
                 end;
```

The `EmployeeData` type allows for different fields within a record based on the value of the Boolean field `citizen`. The following code fragment assigns values to `anEmployee`, a record of type `EmployeeData`:

```
with anEmployee do begin
  firstName := 'Andrew';
  lastName := 'Stallman';
  birthDate := StrToDate('12/31/70');
  phoneNumber := '(205) 925-1363';
  citizen := True;
  birthPlace := 'Skokie, IL';
  SSN := '261-17-9518';
end;
```

The general syntax to declare a variant record appears below:

```
type
  RecordTypeName = record
                     fieldList1: DataType1;
                         .
                         .
                         .
```

```
                     fieldListN: DataTypeN;
                     case tagField: OrdinalType of
                       constantList1: (variant1);
                                  .
                                  .
                                  .
                       constantListN: (variantN);
                end;
```

The first part of the declaration—up to the reserved word `case`—matches that of a standard record type declaration. The remainder of the declaration—from the `case` keyword to the `end` keyword—forms the variant part. The variant part must follow the other fields in the record declaration.

The `tagField` paramater is optional and can consist of any valid identifier. If you omit `tagField`, omit the colon (`:`) that follows it as well. `OrdinalType` is an ordinal type. If `tagField` exists, it functions as an extra field of type `OrdinalType` in the nonvariant part of the record. Each `constantList` is a constant or comma-delimited list of constants of type `OrdinalType`. No single value can be contained in more than one `constantList`.

The arguments `variant1` through `variantN` have the form

```
    fieldList1: DataType1;
          .
          .
          .
    fieldListN: DataTypeN;
```

where each `fieldList` is a valid identifier or comma-delimited list of identifiers, each `DataType` denotes a type, and the final semicolon is optional. The types must not be long strings, dynamic arrays, variant types, or interfaces. Likewise, they cannot be structured types that contain any of these types. They can be pointers to these types.

For each instance of a variant record, the compiler allocates enough memory to hold all of the fields in the largest variant. Thus the record instance contains several variants that share the same space in memory. Furthermore, all fields of a variant record instance are always visible. That is, you can read or write to any field of any variant at any time. Note, however, that if you write to a field in one variant and then to a field in another variant, you risk overwriting your own data. For more information, see "variant parts in records" in the Delphi online help.

Pointers and Linked Lists

A **pointer** is a variable that contains the memory address of another variable instead of the variable's value. In other words, a pointer is a variable that points to the memory location of another variable. In this way, pointers provide indirect references to variable values.

In the real world, a pointer is analogous to a direction (or distance) sign on a freeway. For instance, consider a freeway sign that reads "San Jose 50 miles." The location of the sign is certainly not the location of San Jose but rather "points to" the location of San Jose (50 miles ahead on the freeway). If we follow this sign and travel 50 miles along the freeway, we will reach San Jose. Along a similar vein, consider an integer variable that is allocated memory starting at memory location 5000 and that contains the value 7. A pointer to this integer variable, then, does not contain the value 7 (the value of the variable), but rather the value 5000 (the location of the variable's value in the computer's memory space). The pointer variable says, "Go to memory location 5000 to find the value of the integer variable."

> A **pointer** is a variable that contains the memory address of another variable instead of the variable's value. A **linked list** is a list data structure in which data elements are linked together using pointers.

Using pointers offers an advantage in that a programmer can create **linked lists** of data and other, more complex data structures using dynamic memory allocation (dynamic variables). You can easily add or remove data in any part of a data structure by using pointers. Figure 10.7 shows an example of a linked list.

In Object Pascal, any data type that requires large, dynamically allocated blocks of memory uses pointers. Long string variables and class variables, for instance, are implicitly pointers. Because pointers often operate behind the scenes in code where they do not explicitly appear, an understanding of pointers and pointer operations will improve your understanding of Object Pascal. Furthermore, many advanced programming techniques and data structures require the use of pointers.

Pointers use memory efficiently because they employ dynamic variables. This dynamic memory allocation, however, is also a disadvantage of using pointers. The programmer must remove all broken links (or unused dynamic variables) from memory; otherwise, a **memory leak** occurs. Memory leaks are often difficult to debug, and severe memory leaks can cause the computer to crash.

In Object Pascal, the caret symbol (^) is used to both denote a pointer and **dereference** a pointer. The following syntax declares a pointer type for a specific data type:

```
type
    PointerTypeName = ^DataType;
```

For example,

```
type
  IntPointer = ^Integer;
```

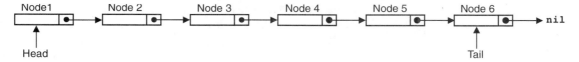

FIGURE 10.7 Linked List Diagram

declares the pointer type `IntPointer` that points to an integer value. In other words, a variable of type `IntPointer` contains the address of a memory location that contains an integer value.

When the caret appears after a pointer variable, it dereferences the pointer variable and returns the value stored in the address contained by the pointer. Thus the syntax

> *pointerVariable*^

dereferences *pointerVariable*. If the variable `ptr` is of type `IntPointer`, for instance, `ptr^` returns an integer value. The `nil` reserved word is a special constant that can be assigned to any pointer variable. When `nil` is assigned to a pointer (that is, *pointerVariable* `:= nil;`), the pointer does not reference anything. Thus pointer variables should be initialized to `nil`.

The **New** and **Dispose** procedures create and destroy dynamic variables of some pointer type. The `New` procedure allocates memory for a new dynamic variable and points the associated pointer variable to it. When an application no longer needs a dynamic variable created with the `New` procedure, it should release the memory allocated for the variable by using the `Dispose` procedure. The general syntaxes of these procedures follow:

> New(*pointerVariable*);
> Dispose(*pointerVariable*);

The value of *pointerVariable* is undefined after a call to the `Dispose` procedure.

In general, pointers are used within records to create linked lists and other complex data structures. For instance, the following code segment creates, prints, and destroys a linked list of integer values from 1 to 10:

```
procedure TfrmIntegerList.CreateList(Sender: TObject);

type
  IntPointer = ^IntRecord;
  IntRecord  = record
```

```
                        value: Integer;
                        next:  IntPointer;
                     end;

var
  top, temp: IntPointer;
  count:     Integer;
begin
  New(top);
  temp := top;

  {Create a linked list of integers from 1 to 10}
  for count := 1 to 10 do begin
    temp^.value := count;
    if (count < 10) then begin
      New(temp^.next);
      temp := temp^.next;
    end
    else begin
      temp^.next := nil;
    end;
  end;

  {Display the linked list of integers}
  memOutput.Clear;
  temp := top;
  while (temp <> nil) do begin
    memOutput.Lines.Add(IntToStr(temp^.value));
    temp := temp^.next;
    if (temp <> nil) then begin
      memOutput.Lines.Add('');
      memOutput.Lines.Add(' |');
      memOutput.Lines.Add('V');
      memOutput.Lines.Add('');
    end;
  end;

  {Destroy the linked list of integers}
  while (top <> nil) do begin
    temp := top;
    top := top^.next;
    Dispose(temp);
  end;
end;
```

As another example, the following code uses pointers to create a linked list of names. This unit contains procedures to initialize the list, add a node to the list, remove a node from the list, display the contents of the list, and destroy the list. Figure 10.8 shows the output of this code.

```
unit LinkedList;
interface

uses
  Windows, Messages, SysUtils, Classes, Graphics, Controls,
  Forms, Dialogs, StdCtrls;

type
  TfrmLinkedList = class(TForm)
    btnDoExample: TButton;
    memOutput: TMemo;
    procedure DoExample(Sender: TObject);
  private
    { Private declarations }
  public
    { Public declarations }
  end;
  NameType    = String[20];
  ListPointer = ^ListType;
  ListType    = record
                  name: NameType;
                  next: ListPointer;
                end;

var
  frmLinkedList: TfrmLinkedList;

procedure InitializeList(var top: ListPointer);
procedure Add(var top: ListPointer; name: NameType);
procedure Remove(var top: ListPointer; name: NameType);
procedure ClearOutput;
procedure DisplayList(top: ListPointer);
procedure DestroyList(var top: ListPointer);

implementation

{$R *.DFM}

{Initialize the linked list}
procedure InitializeList(var top: ListPointer);

begin
  top := nil;
end;
```

```
{Add a node that contains the name to the linked list}
procedure Add(var top: ListPointer; name: NameType);

var
  list: ListPointer;

begin
  if (top = nil) then begin
    New(top);
    list := top;
  end
  else begin
    list := top;
    while (list^.next <> nil) do begin
      list := list^.next;
    end;
    New(list^.next);
    list := list^.next;
  end;
  list^.name := name;
  list^.next := nil;
end;

{Remove the node containing the name from the linked list}
procedure Remove(var top: ListPointer; name: NameType);

var
  list, prev: ListPointer;

begin
  list := top;
  prev := list;
  while (list <> nil) and (list^.name <> name) do begin
    prev := list;
    list := list^.next;
  end;
  if (list <> nil) then begin
    if (prev = list) then begin   {Remove the first node}
      prev := prev^.next;
      top := prev;
    end
    else begin                    {Remove the second or}
      prev^.next := list^.next;   {later node}
    end;
    Dispose(list);
  end;
end;
```

> Notice that the `while` loop in the Remove procedure relies on short-circuit Boolean evaluation, as `list^.name` does not exist when `list` is nil.

```
{Clear the output memo box}
procedure ClearOutput;

begin
  frmLinkedList.memOutput.Clear;
end;

{Display the linked list}
procedure DisplayList(top: ListPointer);

var
  lineOut: String;

begin
  lineOut := '';
  while (top <> nil) do begin
    lineOut := lineOut + top^.name;
    top := top^.next;
    if (top <> nil) then begin
      lineOut := lineOut + ' —> ';
    end;
  end;
  frmLinkedList.memOutput.Lines.Add(lineOut);
end;

{Destroy the linked list}
procedure DestroyList(var top: ListPointer);

var
  temp: ListPointer;

begin
  while (top <> nil) do begin
    temp := top;
    top := top^.next;
    Dispose(temp);
  end;
end;

{Example linked list driver program}
procedure TfrmLinkedList.DoExample(Sender: TObject);

var
  list: ListPointer;

begin
  ClearOutput;
  InitializeList(list);
  Add(list, 'Jack');
```

```
      Add(list, 'Bill');
      Add(list, 'Tom');
      Add(list, 'Harry');
      DisplayList(list);
      Remove(list, 'Jack');
      DisplayList(list);
      Remove(list, 'Harry');
      DisplayList(list);
      Add(list, 'Sally');
      DisplayList(list);
      Remove(list, 'Tom');
      DisplayList(list);
      Add(list, 'Lucy');
      DisplayList(list);
      DestroyList(list);
   end;

   end.
```

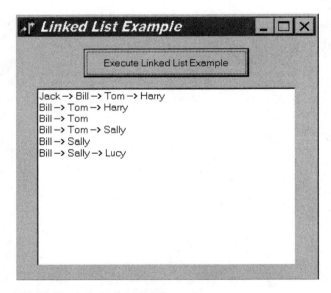

FIGURE 10.8 Linked List Example

Lists, Stacks, Queues, and Deques

A **list** is an ordered set of data to which data can be added or removed. A linked list, as described in the previous section, is a list structure implemented using pointers. Typically, the first node of the list is called the **head,** and the last node of the list is called the **tail**. **Stacks, queues,** and **deques** (pronounced "decks") are specific types of lists, each of which has its own convention for adding and removing data. This section provides sample implementations of these structures using static arrays, dynamic arrays, and pointers. Although the static array structure works well for relatively small amounts of data, the dynamic array is more versatile and can handle a data set of an unknown size. Pointers provide the fastest code and cleanest solutions for working with extremely large data sets, but the programmer must deal with the additional overhead of memory management tasks.

You can think of a stack as being analogous to a stack of plates in a cafeteria. After dirty plates are washed, a cafeteria worker places the newly cleaned plates on top of the previously cleaned plates already in the stack. As customers enter, they remove plates from the top of this stack. Thus the last plate placed on top of the stack is the first one removed. That is, stacks operate in a **last-in first-out, (LIFO)** manner.

The process of adding data to a stack is called **pushing,** and the process of removing data is referred to as **popping.** To see how they work, imagine the cafeteria worker pushing the plates down onto the spring-ejector mechanism of the plate dispenser. The ejector mechanism, in turn, pops a new plate up as plates are removed from the stack. Programmers commonly refer to the **top** and **bottom** of the stack, where the top of the stack indicates the next data item to be removed. Figure 10.9 shows a stack diagram.

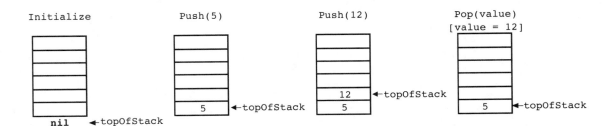

FIGURE 10.9 Stack Diagram Example

The following code unit implements a stack of integers using a static array and demonstrates the Push and Pop routines. Figure 10.10 displays a sample execution of this code. The static array and related variables have global scope. Once again, this code demonstrates an instance where global variables are useful and can greatly reduce the length and complexity of the code.

```
{ -----------------------------------------------------------
Stack Example
-------------
Implement a stack using a static array
-----------------------------------------------------------}
unit StackEx;

interface

uses
  Windows, Messages, SysUtils, Classes, Graphics, Controls,
  Forms, Dialogs, StdCtrls;

const
  STACKSIZE = 50; {Maximum size of the stack}

type
  TfrmStackExample = class(TForm)
    btnTestStack: TButton;
    memOutput: TMemo;
    procedure Test(Sender: TObject);
  private
    { Private declarations }
  public
    { Public declarations }
  end;
  StackType = array[1..STACKSIZE] of Integer; {Stack of
                                               integers}

var
  frmStackExample: TfrmStackExample;
  stack:       StackType;
  topOfStack: Integer;

procedure Initialize;
function IsEmpty: Boolean;
function IsFull: Boolean;
procedure Pop(var value: Integer);
procedure Push(value: Integer);
```

```
implementation

{$R *.DFM}

{Initialize the stack}
procedure Initialize;

begin
  topOfStack := 0;
end;

{IsEmpty returns True if the stack is empty}
function IsEmpty: Boolean;

begin
  IsEmpty := (topOfStack = 0);
end;

{IsFull returns True if the stack is full}
function IsFull: Boolean;

begin
  IsFull := (topOfStack = STACKSIZE);
end;

{Pop an integer value from the top of the stack}
procedure Pop(var value: Integer);

begin
  if IsEmpty then begin
    Application.MessageBox('Illegal Pop operation — ' +
                           'stack empty!', 'ERROR', MB_OK);
  end
  else begin
    value := stack[topOfStack];
    Dec(topOfStack);
  end;
end;

{Push an integer value onto the stack}
procedure Push(value: Integer);

begin
  if IsFull then begin
    Application.MessageBox('Illegal Push operation — ' +
                           'stack full!', 'ERROR', MB_OK);
```

```
    end
  else begin
    Inc(topOfStack);
    stack[topOfStack] := value;
  end;
end;

{Test the stack}
procedure TfrmStackExample.Test(Sender: TObject);

var
  value, count: Integer;

begin
  memOutput.Clear;
  Initialize;
  for count := 1 to 10 do begin
    Push(count);
    memOutput.Lines.Add('Pushed: ' + IntToStr(count));
  end;
  for count := 1 to 5 do begin
    Pop(value);
    memOutput.Lines.Add('Popped: ' + IntToStr(value));
  end;
  for count := 30 to 33 do begin
    Push(count);
    memOutput.Lines.Add('Pushed: ' + IntToStr(count));
  end;
  for count := 1 to 9 do begin
    Pop(value);
    memOutput.Lines.Add('Popped: ' + IntToStr(value));
  end;
end;

end.
```

A queue is the opposite of a stack. Whereas a stack is analogous to a stack of plates in a cafeteria, a queue is like the line of customers in the cafeteria. The first customer in line is the first person served. Thus queues operate in a **first-in first-out (FIFO)** manner. To add data to the end of a queue, we **enqueue** the data. Conversely, we **dequeue** data to remove it from the front of the queue. Programmers refer to the **front** and **rear** of a queue, where the front indicates the next data item to be removed. Figure 10.11 provides a queue diagram.

The code that follows implements a queue of integers and Enqueue and Dequeue routines using a dynamic array; Figure 10.12 displays a sample execution of this program. As before, a global variable is used to simplify the code. This queue implementation has been successfully used in an advanced computer simulation with no noticeable impact on execution speed.

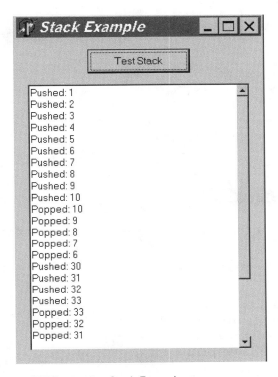

FIGURE 10.10   Stack Example

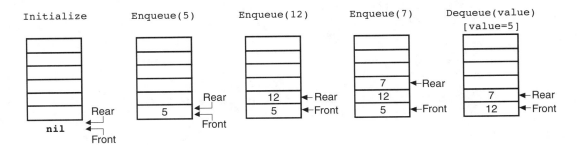

FIGURE 10.11   Queue Diagram Example

```
{ ------------------------------------------------------------
Queue Example
-------------
Implement a queue using a dynamic array
------------------------------------------------------------}
unit QueueEx;

interface
```

```
uses
  Windows, Messages, SysUtils, Classes, Graphics, Controls,
  Forms, Dialogs, StdCtrls;

type
  TfrmQueueExample = class(TForm)
    btnTestQueue: TButton;
    memOutput: TMemo;
    procedure Test(Sender: TObject);
  private
    { Private declarations }
  public
    { Public declarations }
  end;
  QueueType = array of Integer; {Queue of integers}

var
  frmQueueExample: TfrmQueueExample;
  queue:           QueueType;

procedure Initialize;
function IsEmpty: Boolean;
procedure Dequeue(var value: Integer);
procedure Enqueue(value: Integer);

implementation

{$R *.DFM}

{Initialize the queue}
procedure Initialize;

begin
  SetLength(queue, 0);
end;

{IsEmpty returns True if the queue is empty}
function IsEmpty: Boolean;

begin
  IsEmpty := (Length(queue) = 0);
end;

{Remove an integer value from the front of the queue}
procedure Dequeue(var value: Integer);

var
  count: Integer;

begin
  if IsEmpty then begin
    value := 0;
```

```
      Application.MessageBox('Illegal Dequeue operation — ' +
                            'queue empty!', 'ERROR', MB_OK);
    end
    else begin
      value := queue[Low(queue)];
      for count := Low(queue) to (High(queue) - 1) do begin
        queue[count] := queue[count + 1];
      end;
      SetLength(queue, Length(queue) - 1);
    end;
end;

{Add an integer value to the rear of the queue}
procedure Enqueue(value: Integer);

begin
  SetLength(queue, Length(queue) + 1);
  queue[High(queue)] := value;
end;

{Test the queue}
procedure TfrmQueueExample.Test(Sender: TObject);

var
  value, count: Integer;

begin
  memOutput.Clear;
  Initialize;
  for count := 1 to 10 do begin
    Enqueue(count);
    memOutput.Lines.Add('Enqueue: ' + IntToStr(count));
  end;
  for count := 1 to 5 do begin
    Dequeue(value);
    memOutput.Lines.Add('Dequeue: ' + IntToStr(value));
  end;
  for count := 30 to 33 do begin
    Enqueue(count);
    memOutput.Lines.Add('Enqueue: ' + IntToStr(count));
  end;
  for count := 1 to 9 do begin
    Dequeue(value);
    memOutput.Lines.Add('Dequeue: ' + IntToStr(value));
  end;
end;

end.
```

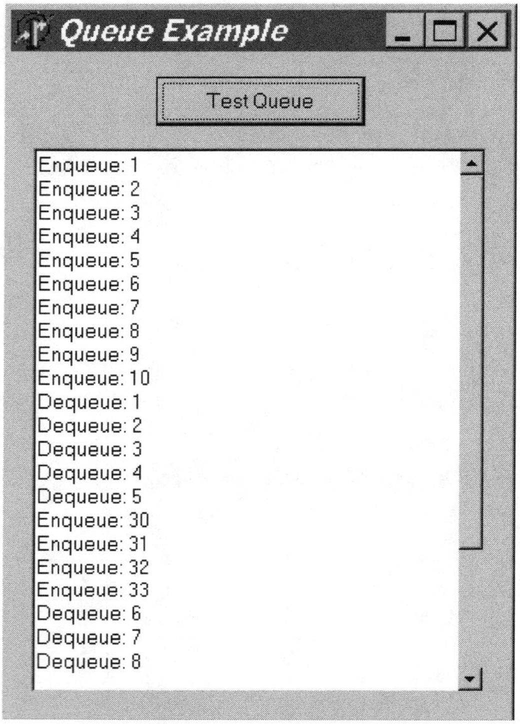

FIGURE 10.12   Queue Example

A deque (double-ended queue) combines the features of a stack and a queue. Data may be added to or removed from either end of the deque. Notice that data may be added to the front of this structure; both stacks and queues add data at the rear. Deques commonly work with `AddFront`, `RemoveFront`, `AddRear`, and `RemoveRear` procedures. Figure 10.13 shows a deque diagram.

An Object Pascal implementation of a deque of integers appears below. This implementation uses a **double-linked list**, a linked list in which each node contains two pointers: one to the next node and one to the previous node. Figure 10.14 displays some of the output of a sample execution.

```
{------------------------------
Deque Example
-------
Implement a deque using a double-linked list
----------------------------}
unit DequeEx;

interface
```

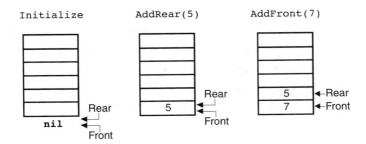

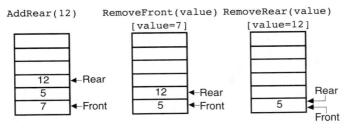

FIGURE 10.13   Deque Diagram Example

```
uses
  Windows, Messages, SysUtils, Classes, Graphics, Controls,
  Forms, Dialogs, StdCtrls;

type
  TfrmDequeExample = class(TForm)
    btnTestDeque: TButton;
    memOutput: TMemo;
    procedure Test(Sender: TObject);
  private
    { Private declarations }
  public
    { Public declarations }
  end;
  NodePointer = ^NodeType;
  NodeType    = record
                  value: Integer;
                  next:  NodePointer;
                  last:  NodePointer;
                end;
  DequeType   = record
                  front: NodePointer;
                  rear:  NodePointer;
                end;
```

```
var
  frmDequeExample: TfrmDequeExample;

procedure Initialize(var deque: DequeType);
function IsEmpty(deque: DequeType): Boolean;
procedure AddFront(var deque: DequeType; value: Integer);
procedure AddRear(var deque: DequeType; value: Integer);
procedure RemoveFront(var deque: DequeType;
                      var value: Integer);
procedure RemoveRear(var deque: DequeType;
                      var value: Integer);

implementation

{$R *.DFM}

{Initialize the deque}
procedure Initialize(var deque: DequeType);

begin
  deque.front := nil;
  deque.rear := nil;
end;

{IsEmpty returns True if the deque is empty}
function IsEmpty(deque: DequeType): Boolean;

begin
  IsEmpty := (deque.front = nil) or (deque.rear = nil);
end;

{Add an integer value to the front of the deque}
procedure AddFront(var deque: DequeType; value: Integer);

var
  temp: NodePointer;

begin
  New(temp);
  temp^.value := value;
  temp^.next := deque.front;
  temp^.last := nil;
  if IsEmpty(deque) then begin
    deque.rear := temp;
  end
  else begin
    deque.front^.last := temp;
  end;
  deque.front := temp;
end;
```

```
{Add an integer value to the rear of the deque}
procedure AddRear(var deque: DequeType; value: Integer);

var
  temp: NodePointer;

begin
  New(temp);
  temp^.value := value;
  temp^.last := deque.rear;
  temp^.next := nil;
  if IsEmpty(deque) then begin
    deque.front := temp;
  end
  else begin
    deque.rear^.next := temp;
  end;
  deque.rear := temp;
end;

{Remove an integer value from the front of the deque}
procedure RemoveFront(var deque: DequeType;
                      var value: Integer);

var
  temp: NodePointer;

begin
  if IsEmpty(deque) then begin
    value := 0;
    Application.MessageBox('Illegal RemoveFront call — ' +
                           'deque empty!', 'ERROR', MB_OK);
  end
  else begin
    temp := deque.front;
    value := temp^.value;
    deque.front := temp^.next;
    Dispose(temp);
    if IsEmpty(deque) then begin
      deque.rear := nil;
    end
    else begin
      deque.front^.last := nil;
    end;
  end;
end;
```

```
{Remove an integer value from the rear of the deque}
procedure RemoveRear(var deque: DequeType;
                         var value: Integer);

var
  temp: NodePointer;

begin
  if IsEmpty(deque) then begin
    value := 0;
    Application.MessageBox('Illegal RemoveRear call — ' +
                         'deque empty!', 'ERROR', MB_OK);
  end
  else begin
    temp := deque.rear;
    value := temp^.value;
    deque.rear := temp^.last;
    Dispose(temp);
    if IsEmpty(deque) then begin
      deque.front := nil;
    end
    else begin
      deque.rear^.next := nil;
    end;
  end;
end;

{Test the deque}
procedure TfrmDequeExample.Test(Sender: TObject);

var
  deque:           DequeType;
  count, value: Integer;

begin
  Initialize(deque);
  for count := 1 to 10 do begin
    AddRear(deque, count);
    memOutput.Lines.Add('AddRear: ' + IntToStr(count));
  end;
  for count := 5 downto 1 do begin
    AddFront(deque, count);
    memOutput.Lines.Add('AddFront: ' + IntToStr(count));
  end;
  for count := 1 to 10 do begin
    RemoveFront(deque, value);
    memOutput.Lines.Add('RemoveFront: ' + IntToStr(value));
```

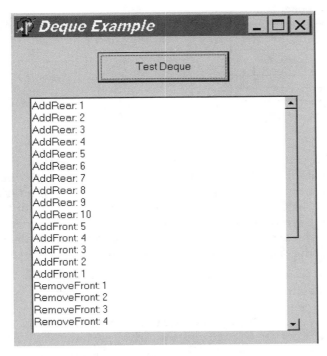

FIGURE 10.14   Deque Example

```
    end;
    for count := 1 to 5 do begin
      RemoveRear(deque, value);
      memOutput.Lines.Add('RemoveRear: ' + IntToStr(value));
    end;
  end;

  end.
```

Priority Queues, Heaps, and Trees

A **priority queue** is a queue in which each element has an associated priority level. For instance, consider Martha's to-do list shown in Figure 10.15. In her to-do list, Martha numbered the tasks in order of decreasing priority. Going to the bank has the highest priority (1) on Martha's list, whereas going to see a movie has the lowest priority (6).

Typically, a priority queue has two operations: `Insert` and `DeleteMin`. `Insert` adds a new element to the priority queue, and `DeleteMin` removes and returns the element with the lowest priority.

Task	Priority
Go to the movies	6
Shop at the grocery store	3
Clean the house	5
Pick up dry cleaning	2
Go to the bank	1
Pay bills	4

FIGURE 10.15 Martha's To-Do List

The following code implements a priority queue using a static array. More precisely, this code implements a circular priority queue; the priority queue has the ability to "wrap around" the endpoints of the static array. The Insert procedure inserts a new element into the priority queue according to its priority level. Thus the elements of the priority queue always appear in ascending order of their priorities. The DeleteMin procedure simply removes and returns the first element of the priority queue. Figure 10.16 displays a partial output of this code.

```
{ ------------------------------------------------------------
Priority Queue Example
----------------------
Implement a priority queue using a static array.  This
implementation uses a circular array; that is, the priority
queue can "wrap around" the ends of the array.
------------------------------------------------------------}
unit PriorityQueueEx;

interface

uses
  Windows, Messages, SysUtils, Classes, Graphics, Controls,
  Forms, Dialogs, StdCtrls;

const
  PQ_MIN  = 1;                      {Starting index}
  PQ_MAX  = 50;                     {Ending index}
  PQ_SIZE = PQ_MAX - PQ_MIN + 1; {Maximum priority queue
                                    size}

type
  TfrmPriorityQueueExample = class(TForm)
    btnTestPriorityQueue: TButton;
    memOutput: TMemo;
    procedure TestPQ(Sender: TObject);
  private
    { Private declarations }
  public
    { Public declarations }
```

```
      end;
    PQRec   = record
                  task:     String[20];
                  priority: Integer;
              end;
    PQArray = array[PQ_MIN..PQ_MAX] of PQRec;
    PQType  = record
                  pq:    PQArray; {The priority queue}
                  front: Integer; {Starting and ending indices}
                  rear:  Integer; {of the priority queue}
                  size:  Integer; {Size of the priority queue}
              end;

var
  frmPriorityQueueExample: TfrmPriorityQueueExample;

procedure Initialize(var pqueue: PQType);
function IsEmpty(pqueue: PQType): Boolean;
function IsFull(pqueue: PQType): Boolean;
procedure Insert(var pqueue: PQType; data: PQRec);
procedure DeleteMin(var pqueue: PQType; var data: PQRec);

implementation

{$R *.DFM}

{Initialize the priority queue}
procedure Initialize(var pqueue: PQType);

begin
  with pqueue do begin
    front := PQ_MIN;
    rear := PQ_MIN;
    size := 0;
  end;
end;

{IsEmpty returns True if the priority queue is empty}
function IsEmpty(pqueue: PQType): Boolean;

begin
  IsEmpty := (pqueue.size = 0);
end;

{IsFull returns True if the priority queue is full}
function IsFull(pqueue: PQType): Boolean;

begin
  IsFull := (pqueue.size = PQ_SIZE);
end;
```

```
{Ensure that the array index is valid}
procedure CheckBounds(var index: Integer);

begin
  if (index < PQ_MIN) then begin
    index := PQ_MAX;
  end
  else if (index > PQ_MAX) then begin
    index := PQ_MIN;
  end;
end;

{Insert a task into the priority queue}
procedure Insert(var pqueue: PQType; data: PQRec);

var
  loc, prev: Integer;
  found:     Boolean;

begin
  if IsFull(pqueue) then begin
    Application.MessageBox('Error in Insert call — ' +
                           'priority queue full!',
                           'ERROR', MB_OK);
  end
  else begin
    Inc(pqueue.size);
    if (pqueue.size = 1) then begin
      pqueue.front := pqueue.rear;
      pqueue.pq[pqueue.rear] := data;
    end
    else begin
      Inc(pqueue.rear);
      CheckBounds(pqueue.rear);
      found := False;
      loc := pqueue.rear;
      repeat
        prev := loc - 1;
        CheckBounds(prev);
        if (data.priority < pqueue.pq[prev].priority) then
          begin
          pqueue.pq[loc] := pqueue.pq[prev];
          loc := prev;
        end
        else begin
          found := True;
        end;
```

This code uses a static array to implement a circular priority queue—a priority queue that can "wrap around" the endpoints of the static array. For a static array with 50 elements (index values of 1 to 50), for instance, `front` may be 46 and `rear` may be 10 when the priority queue contains 15 items. The `CheckBounds` procedure adjusts `front` and `rear` as necessary to implement the circular priority queue.

```
          until found or (loc = pqueue.front);
          pqueue.pq[loc] := data;
      end;
    end;
end;

{Remove the next task from the priority queue — the task
with the lowest priority value}
procedure DeleteMin(var pqueue: PQType; var data: PQRec);

begin
  if IsEmpty(pqueue) then begin
    data.task := '';
    data.priority := 0;
    Application.MessageBox('Error in DeleteMin call — ' +
                           'priority queue empty!',
                           'ERROR', MB_OK);
  end
  else begin
    data := pqueue.pq[pqueue.front];
    Inc(pqueue.front);
    CheckBounds(pqueue.front);
    Dec(pqueue.size);
  end;
end;

{Test the priority queue}
procedure TfrmPriorityQueueExample.TestPQ(Sender: TObject);

var
  pqueue: PQType;
  data:   PQRec;
  count:  Integer;

begin
  memOutput.Clear;
  memOutput.Lines.Add('INSERTING TASKS:');

  Randomize;
  Initialize(pqueue);
  for count := 1 to 20 do begin
    data.task := 'Job ' + IntToStr(count);
    data.priority := Random(10);
    Insert(pqueue, data);
    memOutput.Lines.Add('Insert: ' + data.task +
                        ', Priority ' +
                        IntToStr(data.priority));
  end;
```

> The TestPQ event handler uses random numbers as the task priorities. The Randomize procedure initializes Delphi's built-in random number generator with a value obtained from the system clock. The Random(x) function returns a random number within the range $0 \le returnValue < x$, where x and $returnValue$ are integers.

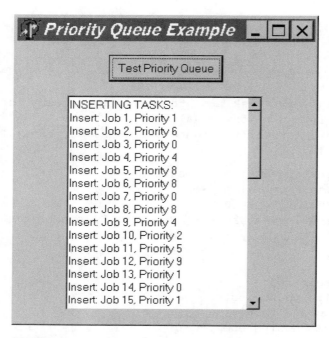

FIGURE 10.16 Priority Queue Example

```
memOutput.Lines.Add('');
memOutput.Lines.Add('REMOVING TASKS:');
for count := 1 to 20 do begin
  DeleteMin(pqueue, data);
  memOutput.Lines.Add('DeleteMin: ' + data.task +
                      ', Priority ' +
                      IntToStr(data.priority));
  end;
end;

end.
```

A **heap** (or **binary heap**) is a priority queue that is structured as a **binary tree.** To understand heaps, therefore, we must first learn about tree structures. A **tree** is a collection of nodes in which a parent–child relationship exists between the nodes. In a general tree structure, each node can have any number of child nodes but only one parent node. Furthermore, each tree contains a distinguished node known as the **root** and zero or more subtrees that are directly connected to the root. Figure 10.17 provides an example of a tree.

The directory structure of a computer disk is often displayed as a tree. Figure 10.18 shows an example directory tree.

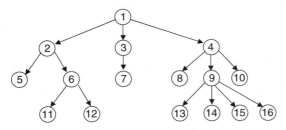

FIGURE 10.17   Tree Diagram Example

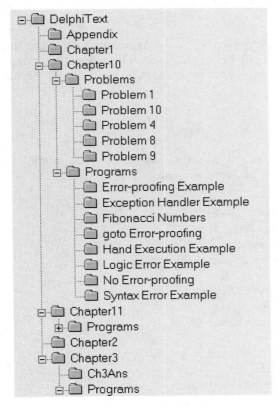

FIGURE 10.18   Directory Tree Example

A binary tree is a tree in which each node has at most two children. An example binary tree appears in Figure 10.19.

The following code example uses pointers to create a binary tree consisting of 20 random integer values ranging from 0 to 99. The program displays the minimum and maximum integer values contained in the binary tree. The tree is organized

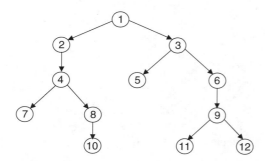

FIGURE 10.19   Example Binary Tree Diagram

such that for any particular node, the left child contains a value less than its parent's value and the right child contains a value greater than or equal to its parent's value. Figure 10.20 shows a partial output from a sample execution of this code.

```
unit BinaryTreeEx;

interface

uses
  Windows, Messages, SysUtils, Classes, Graphics, Controls,
  Forms, Dialogs, StdCtrls;

type
  TfrmBinaryTree = class(TForm)
    btnBinaryTree: TButton;
    memOutput: TMemo;
    procedure Execute(Sender: TObject);
  private
    { Private declarations }
  public
    { Public declarations }
  end;
  NodePointer = ^NodeType;
  NodeType = record
              value: Integer;
              left:  NodePointer;
              right: NodePointer;
            end;

var
  frmBinaryTree: TfrmBinaryTree;

procedure Initialize(var tree: NodePointer);
procedure Insert(var tree: NodePointer; data: Integer);
```

```
function GetMin(tree: NodePointer): Integer;
function GetMax(tree: NodePointer): Integer;

implementation

{$R *.DFM}

{Initialize the tree}
procedure Initialize(var tree: NodePointer);

begin
  tree := nil;
end;

{Insert a node into the tree}
procedure Insert(var tree: NodePointer; data: Integer);

var
  temp, loc, prev: NodePointer;

begin
  New(temp);
  temp^.value := data;
  temp^.left := nil;
  temp^.right := nil;
  if (tree = nil) then begin
    tree := temp;
  end
  else begin
    loc := tree;
    while (loc <> nil) do begin
      prev := loc;
      if (data < loc^.value) then begin
        loc := loc^.left;
      end
      else begin
        loc := loc^.right;
      end;
    end;
    if data < prev^.value then begin
      prev^.left := temp;
    end
    else begin
      prev^.right := temp;
    end;
  end;
end;

{Get the minimum value in the tree}
```

```
function GetMin(tree: NodePointer): Integer;

var
  prev: NodePointer;

begin
  prev := nil;
  while (tree <> nil) do begin
    prev := tree;
    tree := tree^.left;
  end;
  if (prev = nil) then begin
    GetMin := -1;
    Application.MessageBox('Error in GetMin call — ' +
                           'tree empty!', 'ERROR', MB_OK);
  end
  else begin
    GetMin := prev^.value;
  end;
end;

{Get the maximum value in the tree}
function GetMax(tree: NodePointer): Integer;

var
  prev: NodePointer;

begin
  prev := nil;
  while (tree <> nil) do begin
    prev := tree;
    tree := tree^.right;
  end;
  if (prev = nil) then begin
    GetMax := -1;
    Application.MessageBox('Error in GetMax call — ' +
                           'tree empty!', 'ERROR', MB_OK);
  end
  else begin
    GetMax := prev^.value;
  end;
end;

{Test the binary tree}
procedure TfrmBinaryTree.Execute(Sender: TObject);

var
  tree:           NodePointer;
```

```
    count, value: Integer;
begin
  memOutput.Clear;
  memOutput.Lines.Add('CREATING THE TREE:');

  Randomize;
  Initialize(tree);
  for count := 1 to 20 do begin
    value := Random(100);
    Insert(tree, value);
    memOutput.Lines.Add('Insert: ' + IntToStr(value));
  end;

  memOutput.Lines.Add('');
  memOutput.Lines.Add('FINDING MINIMUM AND MAXIMUM VALUES:');
  memOutput.Lines.Add('Minimum: ' + IntToStr(GetMin(tree)));
  memOutput.Lines.Add('Maximum: ' + IntToStr(GetMax(tree)));
end;

end.
```

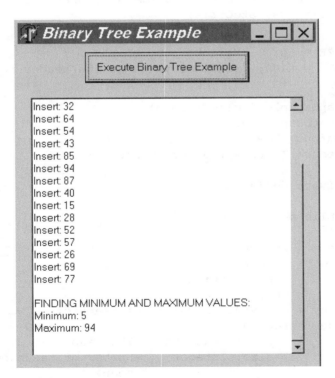

FIGURE 10.20   Binary Tree Example

As noted earlier, a heap is a priority queue that is structured as a binary tree. A heap maintains a "balanced" binary tree, in that every parent node contains a value that is less than or equal to the value of each of its child nodes. Thus the root node always contains the minimum value.

The simplest implementation of a heap requires only a static array. For a parent node located at index i in the array, the child nodes are located at indices $2i$ and $2i + 1$. The following code implements a heap using this structure, and Figure 10.21 shows a sample execution of this program. Tracing this code will help you gain further understanding of the heap `Insert` and `DeleteMin` procedures.

```
{ -----------------------------------------------------------
Heap Example
-----------
Implement a heap using a static array
----------------------------------------------------------}
unit HeapEx;

interface

uses
  Windows, Messages, SysUtils, Classes, Graphics, Controls,
  Forms, Dialogs, StdCtrls;

const
  HEAPSIZE = 50;    {Maximum heap size}
  SENTINEL = -100; {Sentinel value in the header node}

type
  TfrmHeapExample = class(TForm)
    btnTestHeap: TButton;
    memOutput: TMemo;
    procedure TestHeap(Sender: TObject);
  private
    { Private declarations }
  public
    { Public declarations }
  end;
  HeapRec =   record
                task:     String[20];
                priority: Integer;
              end;
  HeapArray = array[0..HEAPSIZE] of HeapRec;
  HeapType  = record
                data: HeapArray; {The heap}
                size: Integer;   {Number of tasks on the
                                  heap}
              end;
```

```
var
  frmHeapExample: TfrmHeapExample;

procedure Initialize(var heap: HeapType);
function IsEmpty(heap: HeapType): Boolean;
function IsFull(heap: HeapType): Boolean;
procedure Insert(var heap: HeapType; data: HeapRec);
procedure DeleteMin(var heap: HeapType; var data: HeapRec);

implementation

{$R *.DFM}

{Initialize the heap}
procedure Initialize(var heap: HeapType);

begin
  heap.size := 0;
  with heap.data[0] do begin
    task := 'HEADER NODE';
    priority := SENTINEL;
  end;
end;

{IsEmpty returns True if the heap is empty}
function IsEmpty(heap: HeapType): Boolean;

begin
  IsEmpty := (heap.size = 0);
end;

{IsFull returns True if the heap is full}
function IsFull(heap: HeapType): Boolean;

begin
  IsFull := (heap.size = HEAPSIZE);
end;

{Insert a task into the heap}
procedure Insert(var heap: HeapType; data: HeapRec);

var
  i: Integer;

begin
  if IsFull(heap) then begin
    Application.MessageBox('Error in Insert call — ' +
                           'heap full!', 'ERROR', MB_OK);
  end
  else begin
    Inc(heap.size);
```

```
      i := heap.size;
      while (heap.data[i div 2].priority > data.priority) do
        begin
          heap.data[i] := heap.data[i div 2];
          i := i div 2;
        end;
      heap.data[i] := data;
    end;
end;
```

{Remove the next task from the heap — remove the task with the minimum priority value}
procedure DeleteMin(var heap: HeapType; var data: HeapRec);

```
var
  i, child:    Integer;
  lastElement: HeapRec;
  done:        Boolean;

begin
  if IsEmpty(heap) then begin
    data.task := '';
    data.priority := 0;
    Application.MessageBox('Error in DeleteMin call — ' +
                           'heap empty!', 'ERROR', MB_OK);
  end
  else begin
    data := heap.data[1];
    lastElement := heap.data[heap.size];
    Dec(heap.size);
    i := 1;
    done := False;
    while (i * 2 <= heap.size) and not(done) do begin
      {Find smaller child}
      child := i * 2;
      if (child <> heap.size) then begin
        if heap.data[child + 1].priority <
           heap.data[child].priority then begin
           Inc(child);
        end;
      end;

      {Move elements in the heap}
      if lastElement.priority > heap.data[child].priority
      then begin
        heap.data[i] := heap.data[child];
```

```
        i := child;
      end
      else begin
        done := True;
      end;
    end;
    heap.data[i] := lastElement;
  end;
end;

{Test the heap}
procedure TfrmHeapExample.TestHeap(Sender: TObject);

var
  heap:  HeapType;
  data:  HeapRec;
  count: Integer;

begin
  Randomize;
  memOutput.Clear;

  memOutput.Lines.Add('INSERTING TASKS:');
  Initialize(heap);
  for count := 1 to 20 do begin
```

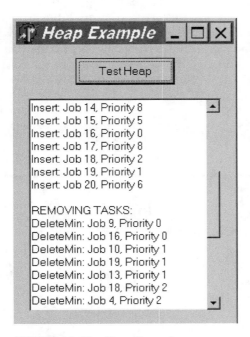

FIGURE 10.21   Heap Example

```
      data.task := 'Job ' + IntToStr(count);
      data.priority := Random(10);
      Insert(heap, data);
      memOutput.Lines.Add('Insert: ' + data.task +
                        ', Priority ' +
                        IntToStr(data.priority));
   end;

   memOutput.Lines.Add('');
   memOutput.Lines.Add('REMOVING TASKS:');
   for count := 1 to 20 do begin
      DeleteMin(heap, data);
      memOutput.Lines.Add('DeleteMin: ' + data.task +
                        ', Priority ' +
                        IntToStr(data.priority));
   end;
  end;

  end.
```

GUI Design Tips

The group box component functionally subdivides a form and groups related controls. Like scroll boxes, group boxes normally contain other controls. The controls found within a group box are accessed through the array entries of its `Controls` property. A radio group box is a special group box that contains only radio buttons and simplifies the tasks involved with their use.

The following example illustrates the use of both group box and radio group box controls. This program allows the user to create and print address labels. Figure 10.22 shows a sample execution.

Component	Property	Setting
Form	Name	frmGUITips
	Caption	Address Label Maker
GroupBox	Name	grpLabel
	Caption	Address Label
	Font	
	Size	12
	Style	[fsBold]
Edit Box	Name	edtLine1
	Font	
	Size	8
	Style	[]

Component	Property	Setting
	ParentFont	False
	Text	*Empty*
Edit Box	Name	edtLine2
	Font	
	Size	8
	Style	[]
	ParentFont	False
	Text	*Empty*
Edit Box	Name	edtLine3
	Font	
	Size	8
	Style	[]
	ParentFont	False
	Text	*Empty*
Edit Box	Name	edtLine4
	Font	
	Size	8
	Style	[]
	ParentFont	False
	Text	*Empty*
RadioGroup	Name	rgpNumber
	Caption	Copies
	Font	
	Size	12
	Style	[fsBold]
	ItemIndex	0
	Items	1; 5; 10; 25
Button	Name	btnClear
	Caption	Clear
	Font	
	Size	10
	Style	[fsBold, fsItalic]
Button	Name	btnPrint
	Caption	Print Labels
	Font	
	Size	12
	Style	[fsBold]
Memo Box	Name	memOutput
	Lines	*Empty*
	ReadOnly	True
	ScrollBars	ssVertical

> The `edtLine1`, `edtLine2`, `edtLine3`, and `edtLine4` components are contained within the `grpLabel` group box.

> The semicolons in the `Items` property indicate that these items appear on different lines in the String List editor (that is, press ENTER after entering each item).

Component Name	Event	Setting
btnClear	OnClick	ClearLabel
btnPrint	OnClick	PrintLabels

```
unit AddressLabelEx;

interface

uses
  Windows, Messages, SysUtils, Classes, Graphics,
  Controls, Forms, Dialogs, StdCtrls, ExtCtrls,
  Printers;

type
  TfrmGUITips = class(TForm)
    grpLabel: TGroupBox;
    edtLine1: TEdit;
    edtLine2: TEdit;
    edtLine3: TEdit;
    edtLine4: TEdit;
    rgpNumber: TRadioGroup;
    btnPrint: TButton;
    memOutput: TMemo;
    btnClear: TButton;
    procedure PrintLabels(Sender: TObject);
    procedure ClearLabel(Sender: TObject);
  private
    { Private declarations }
  public
    { Public declarations }
  end;

var
  frmGUITips: TfrmGUITips;

implementation

{$R *.DFM}

{Print the address labels}
procedure TfrmGUITips.PrintLabels(Sender: TObject);

var
  lineNum: Integer;
  number:  Integer;
  prntr:   TextFile;

begin
  AssignPrn(prntr);
  Rewrite(prntr);
  memOutput.Clear;
```

> This code uses the `AssignPrn` procedure to assign a text file variable to the printer. Output is then directed to the printer via `Writeln` statements.

```
  for number := 1 to
  StrToInt(rgpNumber.Items[rgpNumber.ItemIndex]) do
   begin
     for lineNum := 0 to (grpLabel.ControlCount - 1)
     do begin
       memOutput.Lines.Add(
         TEdit(grpLabel.Controls[lineNum]).Text);
       Writeln(prntr,
             TEdit(grpLabel.Controls[lineNum]).Text);
     end;
     memOutput.Lines.Add('');
     Writeln(prntr, '');
   end;
   memOutput.Lines.Add('DONE!');
   CloseFile(prntr);
end;

{Clear the address label on the form}
procedure TfrmGUITips.ClearLabel(Sender: TObject);
```

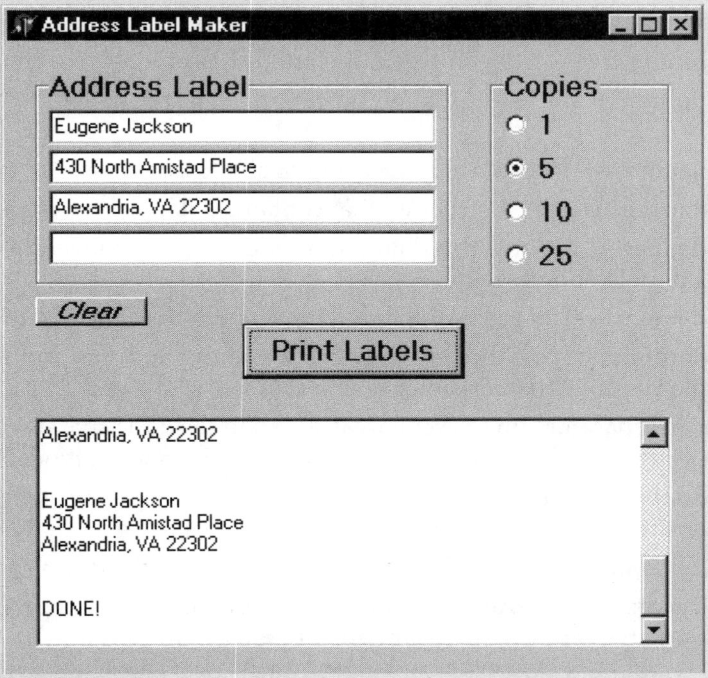

FIGURE 10.22   Address Label Maker Example

```
var
  lineNum: Integer;
begin
  memOutput.Clear;
  for lineNum := 0 to (grpLabel.ControlCount - 1) do
  begin
    TEdit(grpLabel.Controls[lineNum]).Text := '';
  end;
end;

end.
```

Summary

Key Terms

array—A set of sequentially indexed elements of the same intrinsic data type.

binary heap—See *heap*.

binary tree—A tree in which each node has at most two children.

bottom of stack—A pointer indicating the last data item to be removed from a stack.

database—The data set consisting of all records.

data structure—A structure that contains data.

deque—A list in which data can be added to or removed from either end; a double-ended queue.

dequeue—The process of removing an item from the front of a queue.

dereference—To directly refer to the memory location and value (that is, the variable) that a pointer references.

dot-separator—In Object Pascal, a period used to separate record variables from field names and objects from properties and methods.

double-linked list—A linked list in which each node contains two pointers, one to the next node and one to the previous node.

dynamic array—An array that can change in length during program execution.

dynamic data structure—A data structure that can change size (and sometimes type) during program execution (dynamically).

element—A single location within an array. Each element has a unique identifying index number, and each element acts as a separate variable that can be accessed using this index value.

enqueue—The process of adding a new item to the rear of a queue.

enumerated type—An ordered set of values defined by the programmer.

field—A single piece of information within a record.

first-in first-out (FIFO)—The first item added is the first one removed (similar to the line of customers in a cafeteria).

front of queue—A pointer indicating the next data item to be removed from a queue.

garbage—An undefined or "junk" value that occupies a variable's memory space.

garbage collection—The process of removing unwanted dynamic variables from computer memory.

head—The first node in a list.

heap—A priority queue that is structured as a binary tree.

last-in first-out (LIFO)—The last item added is the first one removed (similar to a stack of plates in a cafeteria).

linked list—A list data structure in which data elements are linked together using pointers.

list—An ordered set of data to which data can be added or removed.

memory leak—A decrease in available system memory caused by a failure to remove unused dynamic variables from memory.

multidimensional (*n*-dimensional) array—An array with more than two indices.

one-dimensional array—An array with one index; the equivalent of a vector in mathematics.

open array parameter—An array parameter with no specified indices.

parallel arrays—Separate arrays in which the elements with corresponding index values contain related information.

pointer (pointer variable)—A variable that contains the memory address of another variable instead of the variable's value.

pop—To remove an item from the top of a stack.

power set—A set that includes all of its possible subsets, including the empty set.

priority queue—A queue in which each element has an associated priority level.

push—To add a new item to the top of a stack.

queue—A list that operates in a FIFO manner.

rear of queue—A pointer indicating the last data item to be removed from a queue.

record—A user-defined data type that encapsulates a group of related data. A record contains information in one or more fields.

root—The node in a tree that is the ancestor of every other node.

set—A group of values of the same ordinal data type.

stack—A list that operates in a LIFO manner.

static array—An array of a fixed type and size; an array that is a static data structure.

static data structure—A data structure of a fixed type and size. A static data structure cannot be changed unless a programmer modifies the source code.

subrange—A specified range of values of an ordinal data type.

tail—The last node in a list.

top of stack—A pointer indicating the next data item to be removed from a stack.

tree—A collection of nodes in which a parent–child relationship exists between the nodes. Each node can have any number of child nodes but only one parent node. Each tree contains a root node and zero or more subtrees that are directly connected to the root.

two-dimensional array—An array with two separate indices; the equivalent of a matrix in mathematics.

user-defined data type—A data type defined by the programmer (the user of the compiler).

variant record—A record type that contains a variant part; a record type that never uses all of its fields in a single record instance.

Keywords

Constants

```
nil
```

Functions

Copy	Low
High	

Procedures

Dispose	New
Finalize	SetLength

Set Operators

—	<>
*	=
+	>=
<=	in

Statements

array of	type
record	with
set of	

Key Concepts

- A data structure may be either static or dynamic. Whereas a static data structure has a fixed type and size, a dynamic structure can change size (and sometimes type) during program execution.

- An enumerated type is a data type whose name and values are defined by the programmer. The type consists of an ordered set of values that have no inherent meaning. The ordinality of these values follows the sequence in which they are listed. To declare an enumerated type, use the following syntax:

```
type
    typeName = (value1, …, valueN);
```

- A set is a group of values of the same ordinal data type. The values have no inherent order, and a value should be included only once within a set. A set type is defined using the following syntax:

```
type
    SetName = set of BaseType;
```

A set variable is assigned a value using a set constructor, a list of comma-separated values or subranges within square brackets. The general syntax to assign a value to a set variable is as follows:

```
setVariable := [value1, value2, …, valueN];
```

- An array is a set of sequentially indexed elements having the same intrinsic data type. An element is a single location within an array. Each element has a unique identifying index number and acts as a separate variable. Arrays may be either static or dynamic data structures.

- To declare a static array, use the following syntax:

```
var
    arrayVariable: array[indexType1, ..., indexTypeN] of
    BaseType;
```

- To declare a one-dimensional dynamic array, use the following syntax:

```
var
    dynamicArrayVariable: array of BaseType;
```

To declare a multidimensional dynamic array, use the following syntax:

```
var
   multiDimDynArrayVar: array of array of [array of]
   BaseType;
```

The `SetLength` procedure resizes a dynamic array while preserving the contents of its memory space:

```
SetLength(dynamicArrayVariable, length);
```

The `High` and `Low` functions return a dynamic array's highest and lowest index values, respectively.

- To access an array element, use the form `arrayName[indexValue]`. For instance, `sampleArray[5] := 10;` assigns the value 10 to the fifth element of the one-dimensional array `sampleArray`.

- A one-dimensional array is the computer representation of a vector in mathematics, and a two-dimensional array is the equivalent of a matrix. Arrays with more than two indices are called multidimensional (or n-dimensional) arrays.

- A record encapsulates a group of related data by providing a field to hold each piece of information. A database is the set of all records. The Object Pascal syntax of a record type declaration follows:

```
type
   RecordTypeName = record
                       fieldList1: DataType1;
                       fieldList2: DataType2;

                              .
                              .
                              .

                       fieldListN: DataTypeN;
                    end;
```

- The dot-separator is used to separate a record variable from a field name. The form `recordVariableName.fieldName` accesses the `fieldName` field of the record variable `recordVariableName`.

- The `with` statement can access the fields of a record as well as object properties and methods. The general form of the `with` statement is as follows:

```
with Object do begin
   [statements;]
end;
```

- A pointer is a variable that contains the memory address of another variable instead of the variable's value; it points to the memory location of the other variable and provides an indirect reference to it.

- The caret symbol (^) is used to both denote a pointer and dereference a pointer. The following syntax declares a pointer type for a specific data type:

```
type
  PointerTypeName = ^DataType;
```

To dereference a pointer variable, use the syntax *pointerVariable^*.

- The New and Dispose procedures create and destroy dynamic variables of some pointer type, respectively. The New procedure allocates memory for a new dynamic variable and points the associated pointer variable to it. The Dispose procedure removes the dynamic variable from memory.
- A list comprises a set of ordered data, where data may be added to or removed from any part of the list. A linked list is a list data structure in which data elements are linked together using pointers.
- Data structures in which information is added and removed in a specific order include stacks, queues, and deques.
- A stack operates like a stack of plates in a cafeteria; the last plate in is the first plate out. Thus, a stack is a last-in first-out (LIFO) structure.
- A queue operates like the customers in a cafeteria; the first customer in line is the first person served. Thus, a queue operates in a first-in first-out (FIFO) manner.
- A deque (double-ended queue) is a combination of a stack and a queue where data can be added to or removed from either end. Unlike with a stack or a queue, data can be added to the front of a deque.
- A priority queue is a queue in which each element has an associated priority level.
- A tree is a collection of nodes in which a parent–child relationship exists between the nodes. In a general tree structure, each node can have any number of child nodes but only one parent node. Furthermore, each tree contains a distinguished node known as the root, and zero or more subtrees are directly connected to the root.
- A binary tree is a tree in which each node has at most two children.
- A heap (or binary heap) is a priority queue that is structured as a binary tree.

Review Questions

1. What is the difference between a static data structure and a dynamic data structure?
2. What is an enumerated type? Show an example of one in Object Pascal.

3. What is a set? Show an example of one in Object Pascal.

4. Write variable declarations for a one-dimensional array, a two-dimensional array, a three-dimensional array, and a seven-dimensional array.

5. What is the mathematical equivalent of a one-dimensional array? A two-dimensional array?

6. How do you define your own data type in Object Pascal? Give an example.

7. What is a record? Show an example record type declaration.

8. What is a pointer? A linked list?

9. Describe the operations of a list, stack, queue, and deque. Compare and contrast these data structures (that is, describe their similarities and differences).

10. Describe the priority queue, heap, tree, and binary tree data structures.

Problems

1. Write a simple database program that contains the titles and authors of your textbooks. Your program should use two one-dimensional arrays, one for the book title and one for the author(s). Your program must allow the user to enter a book, remove a book, and find a book's record. Assume that the database can contain a maximum of 20 textbooks.

2. Modify the program from Problem 1 to use dynamic arrays. Allow the database to contain any number of textbooks.

3. Modify the program for Problem 1 to use a static array of records. Assume that the database can contain a maximum of 20 textbooks.

4. Modify the program from Problem 3 to use a dynamic array of records. The database can contain any number of textbooks.

5. Write a code unit that implements a stack of real values using a dynamic array. Also, write a test driver for this code unit.

6. Repeat Problem 5 using a linked list.

7. Write a code unit that implements a queue of real values using a static array. Write a test driver for this code unit. Your program should implement a circular queue, where the queue can "wrap around" the endpoints of the static array.

8. Repeat Problem 7 using a linked list.

9. Repeat Problem 7 using a deque.

10. Repeat Problem 9 using a dynamic array.

Programming Projects

1. Write a program that allows two users to play a game of tic-tac-toe against each other. The computer does not play, but acts as the referee.

2. Write a *matrix algebra package*. This code unit contains subprograms that can add, multiply, scalar multiply, and invert matrices. Write a test driver program to aid in debugging your matrix algebra package.

3. *FlyHigh Airlines Reservation System*. FlyHigh Airlines accepts passenger reservations on a first-come, first-served basis. A single aircraft can carry 40 passengers. Once the aircraft is full, prospective passengers are placed on stand-by (a waiting list). Write a program that accepts reservations and cancellations for a single aircraft. If the aircraft is full and a "ticketed" passenger cancels his or her reservation, the program should give the seat to the first person on the waiting list.

4. *BestBid Online Auctions*. BestBid, Inc., is an online auction house that auctions off a variety of items over the Internet. Bids are prioritized first according to the quantity of the item ordered and second according to the bid price (where a higher bid has higher priority). Write a program for BestBid that accepts and prioritizes the bids for any item.

5. Create a database program that maintains the books in your personal library. The database should contain fields for the book title, author(s), publisher, copyright date, ISBN (International Standard Book Number), and type. The type field categorizes the book, where the possible categories include fiction, romance, mystery, horror, science fiction, fantasy, nonfiction, sports, medicine, games, and self-help. (You may modify these type descriptions to suit your personal library.)

Chapter 11

Binary Files

Chapter Objectives

In this chapter you will:

- Learn the differences between binary files and text files
- Become familiar with the two kinds of binary files, typed and untyped files
- Gain an understanding of binary file (or random-access file) input and output operations
- Learn how to create and use binary files in Object Pascal

Chapter 7 introduced text, or sequential, files. In Chapter 10, we learned about advanced data structures, including record types. Now we turn to a related question: How can we store an entire record in a data file? For a text file, several lines of code are required to store each field of the record. Additionally, accessing a particular record within a text file is an extremely inefficient process. To overcome these problems, we introduce another Object Pascal file type, the **binary file.**

> A **binary file** is a file that can access an entire data structure at a time in any order. Data can be read from or written to any location in a binary file.

Binary Files versus Text Files

Unlike text files, binary files can access data in any order; data can be read from or written to any location in the file. For this reason, binary files are also known as **random-access files.** Furthermore, a binary file accesses an entire data structure at a time. Consequently, it represents a better and faster method of storing and retrieving information contained within a known data structure.

While text files are stored in ASCII format, binary files are not. That is, if a binary file were to be read as a text file, not all of the characters in the file would be meaningful. To correctly access a binary file, a program must know the exact data structure contained in the file.

Kinds of Binary Files

Two kinds of binary files exist: **typed files** and **untyped files.** A typed file is an ordered file of elements of the same data type. You may notice a strong similarity in the definitions of an array and a typed file. Essentially, you can think of a typed file as an array in file form. As you will soon see, instead of using an array index to access a particular piece of data, you use a **record number.**

To define a typed file data type, use the `file of` syntax:

```
type
    FileTypeName = file of DataType;
```

where `FileTypeName` is any valid identifier and `DataType` is a fixed-size data type. Because `DataType` is of a fixed size, both implicit and explicit pointer types are not allowed. In other words, a typed file cannot contain dynamic arrays, long strings, classes, objects, pointers, variants, other files, or structured types that contain any of these types.

As an example, consider the following code fragment:

```
type
  StudentRec = record
                  lastName:   String[30];
                  firstName:  String[20];
                  ID:         String[12];
                  GPA:        Real;
                  crdtHrs:    Real;
               end;
  StudentDB =   file of StudentRec;

var
  studentFile: StudentDB;
```

This code fragment declares the StudentDB data type, a typed file of Student-Rec records. Here studentFile is a typed file variable of type StudentDB, whose associated file contains the names, ID numbers, grade-point averages, and cumulative credit hours for the students at a particular school.

The word **file** by itself indicates an untyped file. Untyped files are low-level input/output (I/O) channels used primarily to provide direct access to disk files regardless of file structure or contents. The following syntax declares an untyped file variable:

```
var
    untypedFileVar: file;
```

The Reset and Rewrite procedures allow you to include an extra parameter that specifies the record size used in untyped file data transfers. The default record size is 128 bytes. Note that a record size of 1 byte can be used with any untyped file.

Instead of the standard Read and Write procedures, two procedures called **BlockRead** and **BlockWrite** are used with untyped files to carry out high-speed data transfers. Otherwise, untyped files use the same standard I/O routines as typed files.

An example application of untyped files is the simple file copier program that appears in the GUI Design Tips at the end of this chapter. The remaining sections of this chapter focus on typed files, the more common of the two kinds of binary files.

Working with Binary Files

As with text files, the AssignFile procedure associates a file variable with an external binary file. The Reset and Rewrite procedures also work in the same way for binary files as they do for text files. By default, a binary file is capable of both input and output operations, regardless of which of these two procedures is used. For a text file, recall that `Reset` accesses the file as read-only (for input) and `Rewrite` sets it to write-only (for output). Both procedures move the file pointer to the beginning of the file. The `Append` procedure is used exclusively for text files; it is not available for use with binary files.

The value of the global variable **FileMode** determines the access mode used when a program opens a binary file using the `Reset` procedure. Valid values of `FileMode` are 0 for read-only access, 1 for write-only access, and 2 for read/write access. The default `FileMode` is 2. Assigning another value to `FileMode` causes all subsequent `Reset` calls to use that mode.

Programming Key: Tips

Use the `Rewrite` procedure to create the initial binary file or clear the contents of an existing binary file. Use `Reset` in all other instances.

The `Read` procedure reads a data element from a binary file into a variable of a compatible data type. Similarly, the `Write` procedure writes the contents of a variable to a binary file of a compatible data type. Both operations (read and write) occur in the current location of the file pointer. After their execution, both `Read` and `Write` automatically increment the file pointer to point to the next data element in the binary file. A simplified syntax for these procedures follows:

```
Read(fileRef, dataVar);
Write(fileRef, dataVar);
```

where `fileRef` is a binary file variable and `dataVar` is a variable of a compatible data type. As with text files, you can combine multiple `Read` statements and multiple `Write` statements. For instance,

```
Read(binFile, data1);
Read(binFile, data2);
Read(binFile, data3);
```

is equivalent to

```
Read(binFile, data1, data2, data3);
```

Similarly, for `Write` statements,

```
Write(binFile, data1);
Write(binFile, data2);
Write(binFile, data3);
```

performs the same operations as

```
Write(binFile, data1, data2, data3);
```

The general syntax of the `Read` and `Write` procedures follows:

```
Read(fileRef, dataVar [, dataVar2, …]);
Write(fileRef, dataVar [, dataVar2, …]);
```

Because binary files are not organized into lines (of text), a syntax error results when you attempt to use the `Readln` or `Writeln` procedure. `Readln` and `Writeln` are used exclusively for text files. Similarly, the `Eof` (end-of-file) function works with binary files, but `Eoln` (end-of-line) does not.

The **Seek** procedure moves the file pointer in a binary file to a specified record or data element. The syntax is

```
Seek(fileRef, recNum);
```

where *fileRef* is a binary file variable and *recNum* is a long integer representing the record number (or element number) in the file, where the first data element has a *recNum* of 0. The **FileSize** function returns the number of records (elements) in a specified binary file. For the binary file corresponding to the file variable *fileRef*, the values of *recNum* range from 0 to `FileSize(fileRef)` — 1. To move the file pointer to the end of the file, use a statement with the following syntax:

```
Seek(fileRef, FileSize(fileRef));
```

Calling a `Write` procedure immediately after this statement expands the binary file by one data element. The **Truncate** procedure deletes all data elements in the binary file at and after the current position of the file pointer; the current file position becomes the end-of-file. When all file operations are complete, the `CloseFile` procedure terminates the association between the binary file variable and external file. Figure 11.1 summarizes the Object Pascal binary file routines.

Function	Purpose
Eof	Tests whether the file position is at the end of a file
FilePos	Returns the current file position (record number)
FileSize	Returns the size of a file (in records for a typed file and bytes for an untyped file)
IOResult	Returns the status of the last I/O operation performed

Procedure	Purpose
AssignFile	Associates the name of an external file with a binary file variable
BlockRead	Reads one or more records from a binary file into a variable
BlockWrite	Writes one or more records from a variable to a binary file
CloseFile	Terminates the association between a binary file variable and an external file
Read	Reads a data element from a binary file
Reset	Opens an existing binary file
Rewrite	Creates and opens a new binary file
Seek	Moves the file pointer to a specified record number
Truncate	Deletes all data elements at and after the current file position
Write	Writes a data element to a binary file

FIGURE 11.1   Object Pascal Binary File Routines

Binary File Example

We can now complete the address book program begun in Chapter 10. This program stores data in a binary file named Address.dat located in the home directory of drive C (C:\). Initialize and Terminate are the OnActivate and OnClose event handlers for the frmAddressBook form, respectively. Figure 11.2 shows the user interface for this program.

```
{ -----------------------------------------------------------
Address Book Program
----------------------------------------------------------}
unit Address;

interface

uses
  Windows, Messages, SysUtils, Classes, Graphics,
  Controls, Forms, Dialogs, StdCtrls;

type
  TfrmAddressBook = class(TForm)
    edtFirstName: TEdit;
    edtLastName: TEdit;
    edtAddress: TEdit;
```

```
      edtCity: TEdit;
      edtState: TEdit;
      edtZip: TEdit;
      edtPhoneNumber: TEdit;
      lblFirstName: TLabel;
      lblLastName: TLabel;
      lblAddress: TLabel;
      lblCity: TLabel;
      lblState: TLabel;
      lblZip: TLabel;
      lblPhoneNumber: TLabel;
      btnAdd: TButton;
      btnClear: TButton;
      btnRemove: TButton;
      btnFind: TButton;
      procedure AddCard(Sender: TObject);
      procedure Initialize(Sender: TObject);
      procedure ClearForm(Sender: TObject);
      procedure Terminate(Sender: TObject; var Action:
                     TCloseAction);
      procedure RemoveCard(Sender: TObject);
      procedure FindCard(Sender: TObject);
    private
      { Private declarations }
    public
      { Public declarations }
    end;
    AddressCard = record
                  firstName:    String[20]; {First Name}
                  lastName:     String[20]; {Last Name}
                  address:      String[30]; {Street
                                             Address}
                  city:         String[20]; {City}
                  state:        String[20]; {State}
                  zipCode:      String[15]; {Zip Code}
                  phoneNumber:  String[20]; {Telephone
                                             Number}
              end;

{
GLOBAL VARIABLES
These global variables make the coding of this program
easier.
}
```

```
var
  frmAddressBook: TfrmAddressBook;
  dataFile:       File of AddressCard;

implementation

{$R *.DFM}

{Return the record number of the address card that matches
 the first and last names.  The search is not case sensitive.
 If a matching address card is not found, Find returns -1.}
function Find(first, last: String): Integer;

var
  addrCard: AddressCard;
  findCard: AddressCard;
  found:    Boolean;

begin
  Reset(dataFile);
  found := False;
  findCard.firstName := Trim(UpperCase(first));
  findCard.lastName := Trim(UpperCase(last));
  while not(Eof(datafile) or found) do begin
    Read(dataFile, addrCard);
    found := (UpperCase(addrCard.firstName) =
                findCard.firstName) and
             (UpperCase(addrCard.lastName) =
                findCard.lastName);
  end;
  if found then begin
    Find := FilePos(dataFile) - 1;
  end
  else begin
    Find := -1;
  end;
end;

{Add the address card to the database}
procedure TfrmAddressBook.AddCard(Sender: TObject);

var
  addrCard: AddressCard;

begin
  with addrCard do begin
```

```
      firstName := Trim(edtFirstName.Text);
      lastName := Trim(edtLastName.Text);
      address := Trim(edtAddress.Text);
      city := Trim(edtCity.Text);
      state := Trim(edtState.Text);
      zipCode := Trim(edtZip.Text);
      phoneNumber := Trim(edtPhoneNumber.Text);
    end;
    Seek(dataFile, FileSize(dataFile));
    Write(dataFile, addrCard);
    Application.MessageBox(PChar('Address card added!'),
                           'ADD', MB_OK);
    ClearForm(Sender);
  end;

  {Remove the address card from the database}
  procedure TfrmAddressBook.RemoveCard(Sender: TObject);

  var
    addrCard: AddressCard;
    pos:      Integer;
    recNum:   Integer;

  begin
    recNum := Find(edtFirstName.Text, edtLastName.Text);
    if (recNum >= 0) then begin

      {Display the address card}
      Seek(dataFile, recNum);
      Read(dataFile, addrCard);
      edtFirstName.Text := addrCard.firstName;
      edtLastName.Text := addrCard.lastName;
      edtAddress.Text := addrCard.address;
      edtCity.Text := addrCard.city;
      edtState.Text := addrCard.state;
      edtZip.Text := addrCard.zipCode;
      edtPhoneNumber.Text := addrCard.phoneNumber;

      {Remove the address card from the database}
      for pos := recNum to (FileSize(dataFile) - 2) do begin
        Seek(dataFile, pos + 1);
        Read(dataFile, addrCard);
        Seek(dataFile, pos);
        Write(dataFile, addrCard);
      end;
      Seek(dataFile, FileSize(dataFile) - 1);
      Truncate(dataFile);
```

```
                  Application.MessageBox(PChar('Address card removed!'),
                                    'REMOVE', MB_OK);
        end
        else begin
          Application.MessageBox(PChar('Address card NOT found!'),
                                    'REMOVE', MB_OK);
        end;
     end;

   {Find and display the address card that matches the first
    and last names}
   procedure TfrmAddressBook.FindCard(Sender: TObject);

   var
      addrCard: AddressCard;
      recNum:   Integer;

   begin
      recNum := Find(edtFirstName.Text, edtLastName.Text);
      if (recNum >= 0) then begin
        Seek(dataFile, recNum);
        Read(dataFile, addrCard);
        edtFirstName.Text := addrCard.firstName;
        edtLastName.Text := addrCard.lastName;
        edtAddress.Text := addrCard.address;
        edtCity.Text := addrCard.city;
        edtState.Text := addrCard.state;
        edtZip.Text := addrCard.zipCode;
        edtPhoneNumber.Text := addrCard.phoneNumber;
      end
      else begin
        Application.MessageBox(PChar('Address card NOT found!'),
                                  'FIND', MB_OK);
      end;
   end;

   {Initialize the program by opening the Address Book
    database -- File Name: c:\Address.dat}
   procedure TfrmAddressBook.Initialize(Sender: TObject);

   begin
      AssignFile(dataFile, 'c:\Address.dat');
      try
        Reset(dataFile);
      except
```

```
      Rewrite(dataFile);
   end;
end;

{Clear the edit boxes on the form}
procedure TfrmAddressBook.ClearForm(Sender: TObject);

begin
   edtFirstName.Clear;
   edtLastName.Clear;
   edtAddress.Clear;
   edtCity.Clear;
   edtState.Clear;
   edtZip.Clear;
   edtPhoneNumber.Clear;
end;

{Close the database file and terminate the program}
procedure TfrmAddressBook.Terminate(Sender: TObject;
   var Action: TCloseAction);
begin
   CloseFile(dataFile);
end;

end.
```

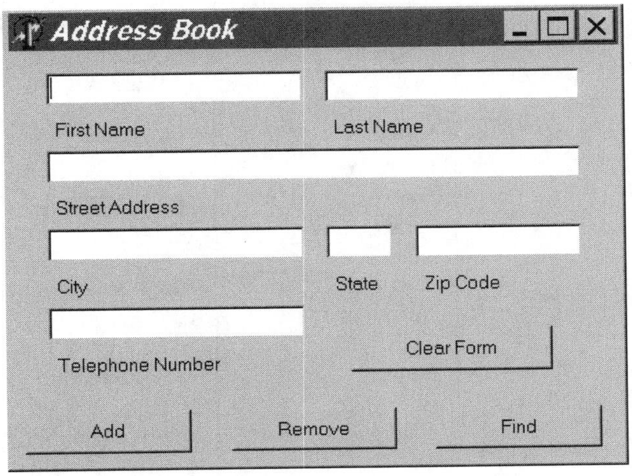

FIGURE 11.2   Form for Address Book Program

GUI Design Tips

Dialog components provide standardized Windows interfaces for frequently performed operations, such as opening a file, selecting a font, or choosing a color. The OpenDialog and SaveDialog components, for example, offer standardized controls to select or enter file names. A dialog component appears as an icon on a form, but it remains hidden from the user at run time. To invoke a dialog component, the program must call its `Execute` method.

Component	Property	Setting
Form	Name	frmFileCopier
	Caption	File Copier
Label	Name	lblSource
	Caption	Source File:
Label	Name	lblDestination
	Caption	Destination File:
Edit Box	Name	edtSource
	Text	*Empty*
Edit Box	Name	edtDestination
	Text	*Empty*
Button	Name	btnSource
	Caption	...
Button	Name	btnDestination
	Caption	...
Button	Name	btnCopy
	Caption	Copy
Memo Box	Name	memOutput
	Lines	*Empty*
	ReadOnly	True
OpenDialog	Name	dlgSource
	InitialDir	C:\
	Title	Source File
SaveDialog	Name	dlgDestination
	InitialDir	C:\
	Title	Destination File

Component Name	Event	Setting
btnSource	OnClick	SetSource
btnDestination	OnClick	SetDestination
btnCopy	OnClick	CopyFile

As an example, the following code implements a simple file copier using untyped binary files. The user can either type in the source and destination file names directly or browse through the directories and files by invoking one of the dialog components. Figure 11.3 shows a sample execution of this program.

```
unit FileCopierEx;

interface

uses
  Windows, Messages, SysUtils, Classes, Graphics,
  Controls, Forms, Dialogs, StdCtrls;

type
  TfrmFileCopier = class(TForm)
    lblSource: TLabel;
    lblDestination: TLabel;
    edtSource: TEdit;
    edtDestination: TEdit;
    btnSource: TButton;
    btnDestination: TButton;
    btnCopy: TButton;
    memOutput: TMemo;
    dlgSource: TOpenDialog;
    dlgDestination: TSaveDialog;
    procedure SetSource(Sender: TObject);
    procedure SetDestination(Sender: TObject);
    procedure CopyFile(Sender: TObject);
  private
    { Private declarations }
  public
    { Public declarations }
  end;

var
  frmFileCopier: TfrmFileCopier;

implementation

{$R *.DFM}

{Set the source file using the OpenDialog}
procedure TfrmFileCopier.SetSource(Sender: TObject);
begin
  if dlgSource.Execute then begin
    edtSource.Text := dlgSource.FileName;
  end;
```

```
end;

{Set the destination file using the SaveDialog}
procedure TfrmFileCopier.SetDestination(Sender:
                                          TObject);
begin
  if dlgDestination.Execute then begin
    edtDestination.Text := dlgDestination.FileName;
  end;
end;

{Copy the file}
procedure TfrmFileCopier.CopyFile(Sender: TObject);
var
  srcFile:  File;
  dstFile:  File;
  numRead:  Integer;
  numWrite: Integer;
  totRead:  Integer;
  totWrite: Integer;
  bufr:     array [1..4096] of Char;
  srcName:  String;
  dstName:  String;
begin
  srcName := Trim(edtSource.Text);
  dstName := Trim(edtDestination.Text);

  memOutput.Clear;
  if (srcName <> '') and (dstName <> '') then begin
    try
      AssignFile(srcFile, srcName);
      AssignFile(dstFile, dstName);
      Reset(srcFile, 1);
      Rewrite(dstFile, 1);

      memOutput.Lines.Add('Copying ' + srcName + ' to '
                          + dstName + '...');
      totRead := 0;
      totWrite := 0;
      repeat
        BlockRead(srcFile, bufr, SizeOf(bufr),
                  numRead);
        BlockWrite(dstFile, bufr, numRead, numWrite);
        Inc(totRead, numRead);
```

```
          Inc(totWrite, numWrite);
      until (numRead = 0) or (numRead <> numWrite);

      memOutput.Lines.Add(IntToStr(totRead) +
                          ' bytes read, ' +
                          IntToStr(totWrite) +
                          ' bytes written.');
      CloseFile(srcFile);
      CloseFile(dstFile);
      memOutput.Lines.Add('Copy complete.');
    except
      memOutput.Lines.Add('ERROR — Can''t copy file.');
    end;
  end
  else if (srcName <> '') then begin
    memOutput.Lines.Add('Please enter a DESTINATION ' +
                        'file name.');
  end
  else begin
    memOutput.Lines.Add('Please enter a SOURCE ' +
                        'file name.');
  end;
end;

end.
```

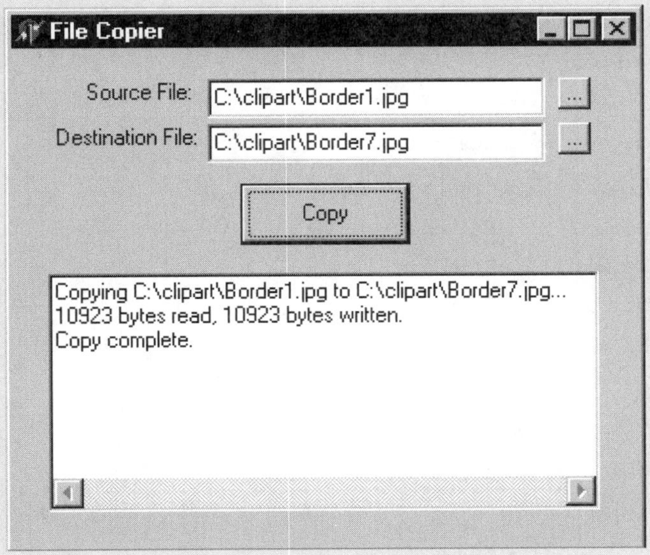

FIGURE 11.3   File Copier Program

Programming Key: Delphi Highlight

File streams provide an object-oriented approach to file handling in Delphi. An object of type `TFileStream` can directly access a file on disk. Chapter 15 introduces object-oriented programming. Refer to "Using file streams" in the Delphi help facility for more information about file streams.

Summary

Key Terms

binary file—A file that can access an entire data structure at a time in any order. Data can be read from or written to any location in the file.

random-access file—See *binary file.*

record number—A long integer value that references a specific data element in a binary file. The first data element is associated with record number 0.

typed file—An ordered file of elements of the same data type.

untyped file—A low-level disk I/O channel used for direct access to a file, regardless of its structure or contents.

Keywords

Functions

Eof	FileSize
FilePos	IOResult

Procedures

AssignFile	Reset
BlockRead	Rewrite
BlockWrite	Seek
CloseFile	Truncate
Read	Write

Global Variables

FileMode

Statements

file of	file

Key Concepts

- Unlike text files, binary files (also known as random-access files) can access entire data structures at a time in any order. Each data element in a binary file has an associated record number, where the first data element is associated with record number 0.

- Two kinds of binary files exist: typed files and untyped files.

- A typed file, the most common kind of binary file, is an ordered file of elements of the same data type. Use the `file of` syntax to define a typed file data type:

```
type
  FileTypeName = file of DataType;
```

- An untyped file is a low-level disk I/O channel that provides direct access to a file, regardless of its structure or contents. The word `file` by itself indicates an untyped file:

```
var
  untypedFileVar: file;
```

- Binary files use the same standard I/O routines as text files, except that the `Readln` and `Writeln` procedures and `Eoln` function are not available because these files are not organized into lines (of text). Additionally, the `Append` procedure is used exclusively for text files.

- The `Seek` procedure moves the file pointer in a binary file to a specified record or data element:

```
Seek(fileRef, recNum);
```

- The `FileSize` function returns the number of records (or elements) in a specified binary file. The `Truncate` procedure deletes all data elements in the binary file at and after the current position of the file pointer, effectively making the current file position become the end-of-file.

- The `BlockRead` and `BlockWrite` procedures are used with untyped files for high-speed data transfers. Otherwise, untyped files use the same standard I/O routines as typed files.

Review Questions

1. What is a binary file? How does it differ from a text file?
2. Name the two kinds of binary files and explain the differences between them.
3. Which kind of binary file is most common?

4. Which standard I/O routines are used exclusively for text files?

5. Which I/O routines are used exclusively with binary files?

6. Name the I/O routines common to both binary files and text files.

Problems

1. Write a program that stores 10 user-entered integer values in a binary file.

2. Modify your code from Problem 1 to store any number of user-entered integer values.

3. Write a program that reads the integer values from a binary file and displays these values and their sum in a memo box.

4. Modify your code from Problem 4 in Chapter 10 to save data to and load data from a user-specified binary file.

5. Modify your code from Problem 5 in Chapter 10 by writing a code unit that implements a stack of real values using a binary file for storage. Also, write a test driver for this code unit.

6. Repeat Problem 5 for a queue of real values. What are some of the technical issues involved with this method?

Programming Projects

1. Modify your code from Project 5 in Chapter 10 to save data to and load data from a user-specified binary file.

2. Write a patient database program for a hospital. The program should be able to add, find, edit, and remove a patient record from the database. Patient information should include first and last names, birth date, Social Security number, doctor's name, hospital room number, date and time of admittance, and date and time of discharge.

Chapter 12

Sorting and Searching

Chapter Objectives

In this chapter you will:

- Learn about the ordering of data, including both ascending and descending order

- Exchange (or "swap") the contents of variables

- Become familiar with sorting techniques, including the bubble sort and Shell sort algorithms

- Understand searching techniques, including the sequential search and binary search

In many of the programs shown in this text, data are stored in the order in which they are entered. In the address book program that appears in Chapter 11, for instance, Ted Johnson may appear before Jill Anderson in the data file, but we know that Anderson alphabetically precedes Johnson. **Sorting** is the process of arranging data in a certain order, either **ascending** or **descending.**

> **Sorting** is a method of arranging data. **Searching** is a method of locating a specific data item quickly.

When data are arranged in ascending order, a particular data item is preceded by a lower-valued data item. If the data are arranged in descending order, the same data item would be preceded by a higher-valued data item. For instance, the digits 1 through 5 are arranged as

$$1, 2, 3, 4, 5$$

in ascending order and

$$5, 4, 3, 2, 1$$

in descending order.

In contrast to sorting, which is used to arrange data, **searching** focuses on finding a specific data item quickly. This task is handled extremely rapidly when we have only 10 data items, but it can be considerably slower when there are 10,000 (or an exceptionally large number of) data items.

Sorting and searching techniques are advanced topics in computer science. Volumes of literature are devoted to these subjects, and most of these texts primarily emphasize the efficiency (speed) of the algorithms involved. As the computation of algorithm efficiency is beyond the scope of this text, we will limit our discussion to a few of the most common sorting and searching algorithms.

Sorting

Let's discuss two sorting algorithms: the **bubble sort** and the **Shell sort.** Both algorithms require exchanging the contents of variables. First, we will think about how to exchange variable values. Examine the following code fragment:

```
var
  value1: Integer;
  value2: Integer;

begin
  value1 := 5;
  value2 := 10;

{Exchange value1 and value2  ???  INCORRECT}
  value1 := value2;
  value2 := value1;
      .
      .
      .
end;
```

Do you see the problem? Both `value1` and `value2` contain the value 10 after this code executes, and the original content of `value1` is lost. We need to temporarily store the content of `value1` in another variable. If we create a variable named `temp` for this purpose, the correct method of exchanging variable values appears in the corrected code fragment:

```
var
  value1: Integer;
  value2: Integer;
  temp:   Integer;

begin
  value1 := 5;
  value2 := 10;

  {Exchange value1 and value2 -- CORRECT}
  temp := value1;
  value1 := value2;
  value2 := temp;
      .
      .
      .

end;
```

The bubble sort compares adjacent data items and swaps them if they are out of order. It repeats this process for each pair of adjacent data items in the list. The sort continues to make **passes** through the list, comparing adjacent data items and swapping values as necessary, until all data items are in order. The methodology of this sorting technique follows:

1. Compare the first and second items. Swap values it they are out of order.
2. Compare the second and third items. Swap values if they are out of order.
3. Continue this process for all remaining pairs of data items in the list.
4. Repeat steps 1 through 3 until the data are ordered correctly (no more swaps are required).

Essentially, small values "bubble" up to the top in an ascending bubble sort. In more general terms, the following pseudocode applies to an ascending bubble sort on a list containing N data items. At most, $N - 1$ passes are necessary to sort a list using this technique. One additional pass is necessary to verify that the list has been sorted.

Bubble Sort Pseudocode

```
repeat
  sorted := True;
  for i := 1 to N-1 do begin
    if data[i] > data[i+1] then begin
      temp := data[i];
      data[i] := data[i+1];
```

```
        data[i+1] := temp;
        sorted := False;
      end;
  end;
until sorted;
```

The following code unit uses a bubble sort to sort an array of 10 user-entered integer values in ascending order. Figure 12.1 gives a sample execution of this code.

```
{ ------------------------------------------------------------
Bubble Sort Example
----------------------------------------------------------}
unit BubbleSortEx;

interface

uses
  Windows, Messages, SysUtils, Classes, Graphics, Controls,
  Forms, Dialogs, StdCtrls;

const
  N = 10; {Number of integers in the data array}

type
  IntArray = array[1..N] of Integer;

  TfrmBubbleSort = class(TForm)
    btnBubbleSort: TButton;
    memOutput: TMemo;
    procedure PrintPass(pass: Integer; data: IntArray);
    procedure BubbleSort(var data: IntArray);
    procedure TestBubbleSort(Sender: TObject);
  private
    { Private declarations }
  public
    { Public declarations }
  end;

var
  frmBubbleSort: TfrmBubbleSort;

implementation

{$R *.DFM}

{Print the data in the array for the current pass}
procedure TfrmBubbleSort.PrintPass(pass: Integer;
                                   data: IntArray);

var
  lineOut: String;
  i:       Integer;
```

```
begin
  lineOut := 'Pass Number ' + IntToStr(pass) + ': ';
  for i := 1 to N do begin
   lineOut := lineOut + IntToStr(data[i]) + ' ';
  end;
  memOutput.Lines.Add(lineOut);
end;

{Sort the data using a bubble sort}
procedure TfrmBubbleSort.BubbleSort(var data: IntArray);

var
  sorted:  Boolean;
  temp:    Integer;
  i:       Integer;
  passNum: Integer;

begin
  passNum := 0;
  repeat
    passNum := passNum + 1;
    sorted := True;
    for i := 1 to (N - 1) do begin
      if (data[i] > data[i + 1]) then begin
        temp := data[i];
        data[i] := data[i + 1];
        data[i + 1] := temp;
        sorted := False;
      end;
    end;
    if not(sorted) then begin
      PrintPass(passNum, data);
    end;
  until sorted;
end;

{Allow the user to enter N integer values and then
 sort these values using a bubble sort}
procedure TfrmBubbleSort.TestBubbleSort(Sender: TObject);

var
  data:    IntArray;
  msg:     String;
  code:    Integer;
  lineOut: String;
  i:       Integer;

begin
  lineOut := '';
```

Note that `data`, the array of integer values, is passed by reference to the `BubbleSort` subprogram. Although the `TestBubbleSort` event handler never uses the sorted array, this step ensures that the original array (and not a copy of the array) is actually sorted.

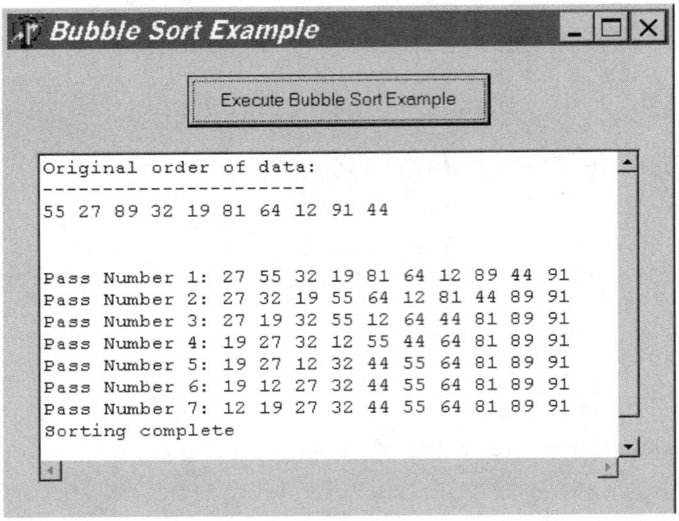

FIGURE 12.1 Bubble Sort Example

```
for i := 1 to N do begin
  msg := 'Enter value #' + IntToStr(i) + ':';
  Val(InputBox('Enter Integer Value', msg, '0'), data[i],
      code);
  lineOut := lineOut + IntToStr(data[i]) + ' ';
end;

memOutput.Clear;
memOutput.Lines.Add('Original order of data:');
memOutput.Lines.Add('----------------------');
memOutput.Lines.Add(lineOut);
memOutput.Lines.Add('');
memOutput.Lines.Add('');

BubbleSort(data);

memOutput.Lines.Add('Sorting complete');
end;

end.
```

The Shell sort (which is named after its creator, Donald L. Shell) is much more efficient than the bubble sort for sorting large lists. This algorithm compares distant data items first and works its way down toward comparing close data items. The **gap** is the interval that separates the data items being compared. Initially, the gap is one-half the number of data items in the list; it is successively halved until eventually each item in the list is compared with its neighbor, as in the bubble sort. The Shell sort algorithm for a list containing *N* items follows:

1. Set *gap* = N div 2.
2. For each item *i* in the list, where *i* ranges from 1 to N – *gap*, compare item *i* and item *i* + *gap*. Swap the items if necessary.
3. Repeat step 2 until no swaps are made for this value of *gap*.
4. Set *gap* = *gap* div 2.
5. Repeat steps 1–4 until the value of *gap* is 0.

By translating the above algorithm into pseudocode, we obtain the pseudocode for an ascending Shell sort on a list containing N items:

Shell Sort Pseudocode
```
gap := N div 2;
repeat
  repeat
    gapDone := True;
    for i := 1 to (N — gap) do begin
      if data[i] > data[i + gap] then begin
        temp := data[i];
        data[i] := data[i + gap];
        data[i + gap] := temp;
        gapDone := False;
      end;
    end;
  until gapDone;
  gap := gap div 2;
until gap = 0;
```

Let's rewrite the previous code unit using a Shell sort instead of a bubble sort. A sample program execution appears in Figure 12.2.

```
{ -----------------------------------------------------------
Shell Sort Example
-----------------------------------------------------------}
unit ShellSortEx;

interface

uses
  Windows, Messages, SysUtils, Classes, Graphics, Controls,
  Forms, Dialogs, StdCtrls;

const
  N = 10; {Number of integers in the data array}

type
  IntArray = array[1..N] of Integer;

  TfrmShellSort = class(TForm)
    btnShellSort: TButton;
```

```
    memOutput: TMemo;
    procedure PrintPass(data: IntArray);
    procedure ShellSort(var data: IntArray);
    procedure TestShellSort(Sender: TObject);
  private
    { Private declarations }
  public
    { Public declarations }
  end;

var
  frmShellSort: TfrmShellSort;

implementation

{$R *.DFM}

{Print the data in the array for the current pass}
procedure TfrmShellSort.PrintPass(data: IntArray);

var
  lineOut: String;
  i:       Integer;

begin
  lineOut := '';
  for i := 1 to N do begin
    lineOut := lineOut + IntToStr(data[i]) + ' ';
  end;
  memOutput.Lines.Add(lineOut);
end;

{Sort the data using a Shell sort}
procedure TfrmShellSort.ShellSort(var data: IntArray);

var
  temp:    Integer;
  i:       Integer;
  gap:     Integer;
  gapDone: Boolean;

begin
  gap := N div 2;
  repeat
    memOutput.Lines.Add('Gap = ' + IntToStr(gap));
    repeat
      gapDone := True;
      for i := 1 to (N - gap) do begin
        if data[i] > data[i + gap] then begin
          temp := data[i];
```

The array of integer values, data, is passed by reference.

```
                data[i] := data[i + gap];
                data[i + gap] := temp;
                gapDone := False;
              end;
          end;

        PrintPass(data);

        if gapDone then begin
          memOutput.Lines.Add('Sorting complete for gap of ' +
                              IntToStr(gap));
        end;
      until gapDone;
      gap := gap div 2;
      memOutput.Lines.Add('');
    until gap = 0;
end;

{Allow the user to enter N integer values and then
 sort these values using a Shell sort}
procedure TfrmShellSort.TestShellSort(Sender: TObject);

var
  data:    IntArray;
  msg:     String;
  code:    Integer;
  lineOut: String;
  i:       Integer;

begin
  lineOut := '';
  for i := 1 to N do begin
    msg := 'Enter value #' + IntToStr(i) + ':';
    Val(InputBox('Enter Integer Value', msg, '0'), data[i],
        code);
    lineOut := lineOut + IntToStr(data[i]) + ' ';
  end;

  memOutput.Clear;
  memOutput.Lines.Add('Original order of data:');
  memOutput.Lines.Add('---------------------');
  memOutput.Lines.Add(lineOut);
  memOutput.Lines.Add('');
  memOutput.Lines.Add('');

  ShellSort(data);

  memOutput.Lines.Add('Sorting complete');
end;

end.
```

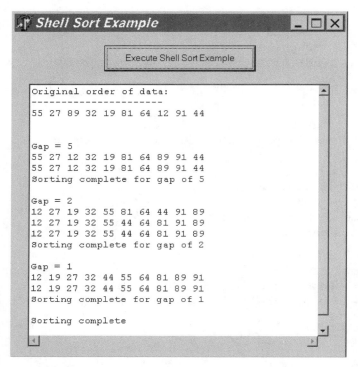

FIGURE 12.2 Shell Sort Example

Programming Key: Tips

Swapping string data in memory is an extremely inefficient process. Rather than sorting the strings themselves, we would prefer to create a parallel array of integer index values. Then we can simply swap the values in the index array in accordance with the correct ordering of the strings. This technique is commonly employed by many commercial applications and database programs.

The following example illustrates this method. This program reads the lines of the text file `C:\Unsorted.dat`, sorts these lines by swapping the values in an index array, and then writes the lines in sorted order to `C:\Sorted.dat`. The program also displays the sorted strings and their associated index values in a memo box.

```
unit IndexExample;

interface

uses
  Windows, Messages, SysUtils, Classes, Graphics,
  Controls, Forms, Dialogs, StdCtrls;

type
  DataArray =  array of String;
  IndexArray = array of Integer;

  TfrmIndexExample = class(TForm)
    btnIndex: TButton;
    memOutput: TMemo;
    procedure SortStrings(Sender: TObject);
  private
    { Private declarations }
  public
    { Public declarations }
  end;

var
  frmIndexExample: TfrmIndexExample;

implementation

{$R *.DFM}

{Sort the data using a Shell sort. Note that this
 subprogram swaps only the indices, not the original
 data.}
procedure ShellSort(data: DataArray; var index:
                    IndexArray);

var
  temp:    Integer;
  i:       Integer;
  gap:     Integer;
  gapDone: Boolean;

begin
  gap := (High(data) + 1) div 2;
  repeat
    repeat
```

```
          gapDone := True;
          for i := 0 to (High(data) - gap) do begin
            if (data[index[i]] > data[index[i + gap]]) then
            begin
                temp := index[i];
                index[i] := index[i + gap];
                index[i + gap] := temp;
                gapDone := False;
              end;
            end;
        until gapDone;
        gap := gap div 2;
    until gap = 0;
end;

{Read the data from the file C:\Unsorted.dat, call the
 Shell sort routine, and write sorted string data to
 C:\Sorted.dat}
procedure TfrmIndexExample.SortStrings(Sender:
                                        TObject);

var
  inFile:  TextFile;
  outFile: TextFile;
  count:   Integer;
  num:     Integer;
  data:    DataArray;
  index:   IndexArray;

begin
  AssignFile(inFile, 'C:\Unsorted.dat');
  AssignFile(outFile, 'C:\Sorted.dat');

  try
    Reset(inFile);
    Rewrite(outFile);

    {Read the input file}
    count := 0;
    SetLength(data, count);
    SetLength(index, count);
    while not(Eof(inFile)) do begin
      SetLength(data, count + 1);
```

```
         SetLength(index, count + 1);
         Readln(inFile, data[count]);
         index[count] := count;
         Inc(count);
      end;

      {Sort the indices, not the original data}
      ShellSort(data, index);

      {Write sorted data to the output file and memo box}
      memOutput.Clear;
      memOutput.Lines.Add('Index  String');
      memOutput.Lines.Add('——  ——');
      for num := 0 to High(data) do begin
         Writeln(outFile, data[index[num]]);
         memOutput.Lines.Add(Format('%5d', [index[num]]) +
                             '  ' + data[index[num]])
      end;

      Application.MessageBox('Sorted data written to ' +
                             'C:\Sorted.dat', 'DONE',
                             MB_OK);
   finally
      CloseFile(inFile);
      CloseFile(outFile);
      Application.Terminate;
   end;
  end;

  end.
```

A sample execution of this program appears in Figure 12.3. In this example, the file `C:\Unsorted.dat` contains the following data items:

```
Scott
Jason
Aaron
Michael
David
Stewart
Pamela
Molly
John
```

After the program executes, C:\Sorted.dat contains the reordered data items:

```
Aaron
David
Jason
John
Michael
Molly
Pamela
Scott
Stewart
```

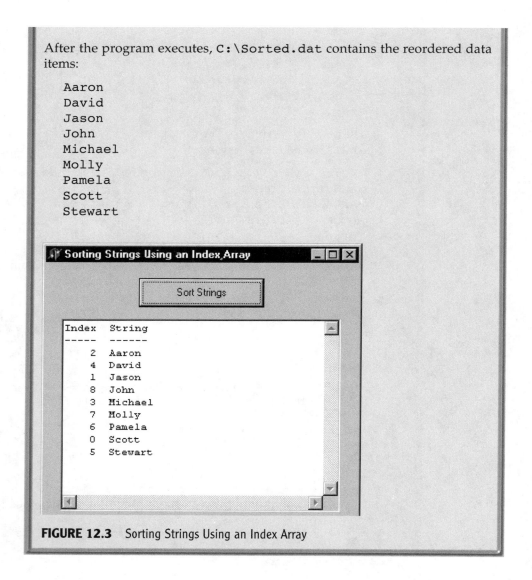

FIGURE 12.3   Sorting Strings Using an Index Array

Searching

This section presents two searching algorithms: the **sequential search** and the **binary search.** The sequential search, as you might expect, starts at the beginning of the data and looks at each data item in sequence until it finds the **target data item.** An example of a sequential search appears in the address book program of Chapter 11. The Find function sequentially searches the data file for a record that contains first and last names that match the user input. If it locates a matching record, Find returns the associated record number; otherwise, it returns –1.

Like the bubble sort, the sequential search is not very efficient in working with large amounts of data. Imagine searching sequentially through a telephone book for the last name "Zugfield"; it could take a long time to find the desired piece of information. A binary search is more efficient than the sequential search for large data sets. *A binary search requires the data to be sorted in a specific order, whereas the sequential search does not.* Once again, the performance of these searches differs very little when dealing with small amounts of data.

To understand the binary search, think of the game of high-low (pick-a-number). In this game, your friend picks a number from 1 to 100, for instance. You then try to guess the number that he picked. If the number that you pick is lower than his number, he tells you "higher." Similarly, if your number is too high, your friend tells you "lower." After a few guesses, you can place upper and lower bounds on your friend's number until you finally "zero in" on the correct number. The binary search operates in much the same way. It continues to split the list of data items in half until it finds the target item or discovers that it is not contained in the data set.

The pseudocode for a binary search on a list of N data items sorted in ascending order follows:

Binary Search Pseudocode

```
target := targetValue;
first := 1;
last := N;
found := False;

while (first <= last) and not(found) do begin
  middle := (first + last) div 2;
  if target < data[middle] then begin
    last := middle - 1;
  end
  else if target > data[middle] then begin
    first := middle + 1;
  end
  else begin
    found := True;
  end;
end;

if found then begin
  {target data found in index position middle}
end
else begin
  {target data not found}
end;
```

Summary

Key Terms

ascending order—Data are arranged in order of increasing value.

binary search—A search algorithm that iteratively splits the list of data items in half until it finds the target data item or discovers that it is not contained in the data set.

bubble sort—A sorting algorithm that compares adjacent data items and swaps them if they are out of order.

descending order—Data are arranged in order of decreasing value.

gap—In a Shell sort, the interval that separates the data items being compared.

pass—One complete iteration through all values of a data set.

searching—A method of locating a specific data item quickly.

sequential search—A search algorithm that starts at the beginning of the data and examines each item in sequence until it finds the target data item.

Shell sort—A sorting algorithm created by Donald L. Shell that compares distant data items first and works its way down toward comparing close data items.

sorting—A method of arranging data.

target data item—The data item of interest in a search.

Key Concepts

- Sorting arranges data in a particular order. Data may be sorted in either ascending or descending order. Ascending order is the arrangement of data by increasing value, and descending order is the arrangement by decreasing value.

- Exchanging the values of variables is a key concept in sorting data. To exchange (or "swap") the contents of two variables, we must create a temporary variable (`temp`) to hold the value of one of the variables during the swap; otherwise, we lose a piece of data and get a redundant value. The proper method of swapping the contents of variables `value1` and `value2` follows:

```
temp := value1;
value1 := value2;
value2 := temp;
```

- The bubble sort and Shell sort are two sorting algorithms. The bubble sort compares adjacent values and swaps data as necessary, allowing small values to "bubble up" to the top of an ascending list. The Shell sort begins by comparing distant items and works its way toward comparing close data items. While both the bubble sort and the Shell sort work well for small amounts of data, the Shell sort is much more efficient for large lists.
- Searching is a method of locating a specific data item (the target data item) quickly.
- The sequential search and the binary search are two searching algorithms. The sequential search starts at the beginning of the data and looks at each item in sequence until it finds its target. The binary search attempts to locate the target data item by iteratively splitting the list in half; it requires the data to be sorted prior to the search. While the performance of these searches differs little when working with small amounts of data, the binary search is much more efficient for large data sets.

Review Questions

1. Write the following numbers in ascending order and descending order.

    88, 76, 94, 52, 37, 29, 100, 92, 67, 48

2. Write the Object Pascal code to swap the values of two integer variables, `variable1` and `variable2`.

3. Write the pseudocode for an ascending bubble sort on a list containing N items.

4. Write the pseudocode for an ascending Shell sort on a list containing N items.

5. Write the pseudocode for a sequential search on a list containing N items.

6. Write the pseudocode for a binary search on a list containing N items. Assume that the list is already sorted in ascending order.

Problems

1. Write a program that sorts a data file created with the address book program of Chapter 11 using a bubble sort.

2. Repeat Problem 1 using a Shell sort.

3. Write a program that finds a specific record and prints an address label. The program should use a data file created with the address book program of Chapter 11. Use a sequential search in this program.

4. Repeat Problem 3 by first sorting the data file using a Shell sort, then using a binary search to find the target record.

Programming Projects

1. Modify the code from Project 3 in Chapter 7 to write the output file in descending order of grade-point average.

2. Assume that you have two output files from Project 1. Write a program that merges (combines) these files in descending order of grade-point average.

3. Write a word frequency counter program. Your program should accept a text file for input and count the number of occurrences of each word in the file. The results should be sorted and stored in a user-designated output file. Your program should not be case sensitive, and it should ignore punctuation marks (that is, it should not count a punctuation mark as part of a word). A sample input file appears below:

```
The quick brown fox jumped over the lazy dog.
```

The output file associated with the above input file follows:

```
Word            Frequency
----            ---------
brown           1
dog             1
fox             1
jumped          1
lazy            1
over            1
quick           1
the             2
```

Databases

Chapter Objectives

In this chapter you will:

- Be introduced to database terminology and concepts
- Gain an understanding of how to efficiently design a database
- Create a database using Borland's Database Desktop
- Use the Structured Query Language to perform data queries
- Create a database application using Delphi's Database Form Wizard
- Become familiar with data source components and data-aware controls
- Create and access a database through Object Pascal source code

Any discussion of Delphi data files and file input and output could hardly be considered complete without some mention of Delphi's extensive database capabilities. A **database program** is designed to provide easy storage, access, and retrieval of data. This chapter describes how to create database files and use these files in your Delphi programs. Additionally, it examines the **Structured Query Language (SQL),** demonstrating how Delphi can harness the power of this language.

This chapter merely touches on some database fundamentals. By no means is it all-encompassing—as a thorough discussion of databases and Delphi database programming would fill several volumes.

Database Fundamentals

A **database file** (or **database**) consists of a set of related information. A school, for example, may use a database to store enrollment information, student transcripts, and financial data. Businesses commonly use databases to hold product inventory, supplier information, customer data, transactions, and personnel data. Many commercial database programs are available, including Microsoft Access, Microsoft FoxPro, Corel Paradox, Oracle Corporation's Oracle, and FileMaker's FileMaker Pro. The word "database" can be used to refer to either the database files or the database program itself; this text adopts the convention of using "database" to refer to a data file and "database program" to refer to the software package.

> A **database** consists of one or more data files that contain a set of related information specifically for use by a database program. A **table**, which is the primary data structure in a database, organizes data into rows and columns. A **record** is a row in a table and encapsulates a group of related data from several fields. A **field** is a column in a table and contains a specific piece of information from each record.

A database consists of one or more tables. A **table** is organized into rows and columns and looks very similar to a spreadsheet. The rows of the table correspond to database records, where a **record** holds a group of related data. Each unique piece of information in a record is called a **field,** and each column of the table represents a different field. Thus a single column contains information from the same field of every record. The terms used here in reference to databases parallel those used in discussing records in Chapter 10.

Chapter 10 also included several example programs that implement "simple" database programs in Delphi using arrays and records. Figure 13.1 shows an example database table created in Microsoft Access. In this table, the three fields include `LastName`, `FirstName`, and `PhoneNumber`. A record consists of a row of data containing information from each database field. For example, the `LastName` field of the first record contains "Andrews," the `FirstName` field contains "Lisa," and the `PhoneNumber` field holds "670-7898." These three pieces of data constitute the first record.

> A **primary key** is a field or set of fields that uniquely identify each record in a table. A **foreign key** is a field or set of fields that references the primary key of another table and links the two tables together.

A well-designed table should contain a field or set of fields that uniquely identify each record. This field or set of fields is called a **primary key.** When a database consists of more than one table, the tables are usually related and the database is called a **relational database.** In a relational database, a **foreign key** links

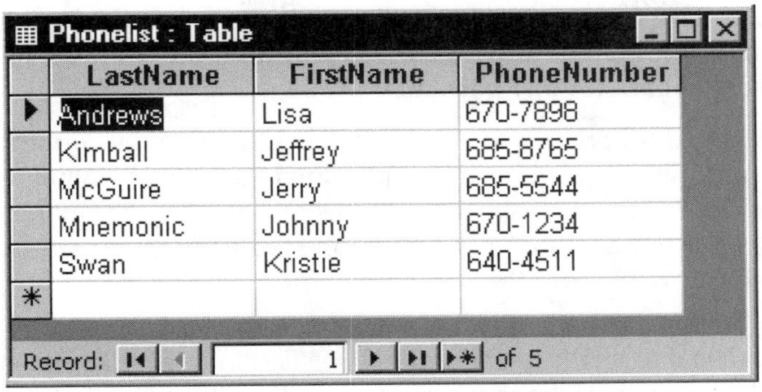

Phonelist : Table

LastName	FirstName	PhoneNumber
Andrews	Lisa	670-7898
Kimball	Jeffrey	685-8765
McGuire	Jerry	685-5544
Mnemonic	Johnny	670-1234
Swan	Kristie	640-4511

Record: 1 of 5

FIGURE 13.1 Example Database Table

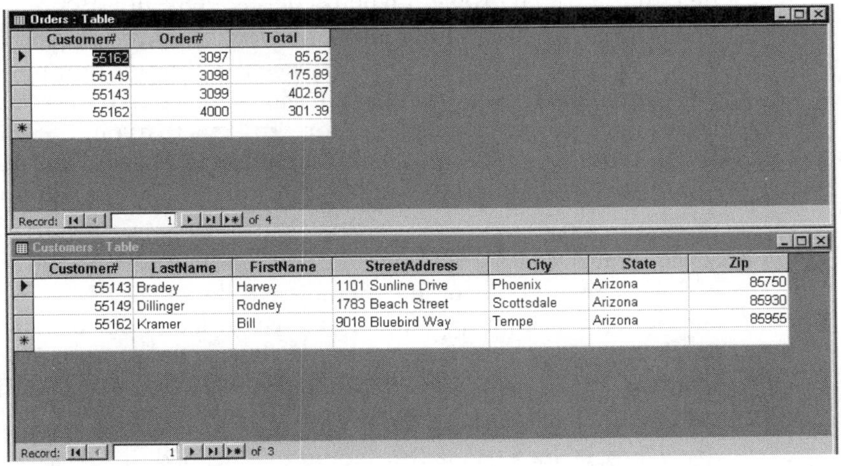

Orders : Table

Customer#	Order#	Total
55162	3097	85.62
55149	3098	175.89
55143	3099	402.67
55162	4000	301.39

Record: 1 of 4

Customers : Table

Customer#	LastName	FirstName	StreetAddress	City	State	Zip
55143	Bradey	Harvey	1101 Sunline Drive	Phoenix	Arizona	85750
55149	Dillinger	Rodney	1783 Beach Street	Scottsdale	Arizona	85930
55162	Kramer	Bill	9018 Bluebird Way	Tempe	Arizona	85955

Record: 1 of 3

FIGURE 13.2 Example Relational Database

data from one table to another. Maintaining the **integrity,** or consistency, of data in a database is of primary concern to both programmers and database designers. To maintain the integrity of the database, a value in a foreign key column of one table must appear as a value in the primary key column of another table as well; this type of linkage is called **referential integrity.** Similarly, it makes sense that no record may have a null value for its primary key, a concept called **entity integrity.**

Figure 13.2 shows an example relational database. In this database, the `Orders` table uses the `Customer#` field as the foreign key that relates to the primary key of the `Customer#` field in the `Customers` table.

No single algorithm can be used to create a relational database design that is suitable for every problem. Much like a well-designed program, a well-designed relational database is a work of art and relies solely upon the logic and creativity of its designers. Nevertheless, you should follow certain guidelines to design the best possible database for any particular problem:

1. *Understand the problem and the customer's needs.* What reports does the customer want generated? What data are available? What are the relationships between the various pieces of data? Does it make sense to logically split the data into more than one table? After you answer these questions, designing the database should be a relatively straightforward task.

2. *Data should generally be stored in the smallest units possible.* In a customer database, you may be tempted to place the city, state, and ZIP code in the same field rather than in three separate fields. While it is relatively difficult to sort the data when all of this information is combined into a single field, it is a trivial problem when separate fields are used.

3. *Avoid redundant, blank, and calculated fields.* Redundant and blank fields waste valuable file space and increase the amount of time required to perform operations on the data. Design your database with enough tables and proper primary and foreign keys to avoid these types of fields. Additionally, avoid using calculated fields, as the values in these fields can be obtained through operations on data in other fields of the database.

4. *Avoid using spaces in field names.* Although Microsoft Access allows spaces in field names, you should generally avoid their use. Many software packages and programming languages have difficulty performing queries on databases whose field names contain spaces. If you want to separate words in a field name, use the underscore character ("_") rather than a space.

5. *Avoid large tables.* Data tables should be "cleaned up" so as not to become unnecessarily large. In other words, records marked for deletion should be deleted. Additionally, tables should be designed with a size limit in mind, because large tables require longer search times.

A **database engine** comprises a set of routines that perform the operations normally associated with a database, such as adding, deleting, sorting, and searching records. Delphi comes equipped with the Borland Database Engine (BDE). Consequently, a programmer using Delphi has the ability to manipulate database files in a variety of formats. Delphi's ability to perform database operations makes it an extremely powerful tool. Unlike the case with the database program examples given in Chapter 10, the programmer need not be concerned with opening or closing files, using loops to search for records, updating counters, or resizing dynamic arrays, among other things. Instead, the database engine automatically controls all file-handling and data functions. For these reasons, Delphi is a popular choice among professional programmers who develop database and data-aware applications.

· C · A · S · E ·   · S · T · U · D · Y ·

Designing a Relational Database

Jim wants to create a database of his personal contacts. He wants to keep important dates, such as birthdays and anniversaries, as well as address and phone number information in this database. After a little thought, Jim writes down the following list of the information he wishes to maintain:

> Contact's first and last names
> Contact's address (including street address, city, state, and ZIP code)
> Contact's phone number
> Contact's birth date
> Spouse's first and last names
> Anniversary date
> Spouse's birth date
> Children's first and last names
> Children's birth dates

Fortunately, Jim has just completed a database course on using Microsoft Access. He designs his database using three tables: one for the contact's information, another for the spouse's information, and a third for children's information. Now Jim must decide how to relate the information in these three tables. Because more than one person can have the same last name, Jim cannot use the last name as the primary key for his database (a primary key must be unique). He decides to use the phone number as the primary key in his design for two reasons:

1. Phone numbers are unique—each address has a different phone number.
2. Jim's database maintains only one phone number per address. Therefore, everyone living at the same address has the same phone number.

Jim now designs the tables and relationships in his database as shown in Figure 13.3. There is **a one-to-one relationship** between the `Contacts` table and the `Spouse` table, as each contact can have at most one spouse. There is **a one-to-many relationship** between the `Contacts` table and the `Children` table, as a contact can have any number of children.

Although you might initially think that the `LastName` fields in the `Spouse` and `Children` tables are redundant and unnecessary, Jim knows that this design gives him the flexibility to account for stepchildren and spouses who keep their last names. Sample data from Jim's database appear in Figure 13.4.

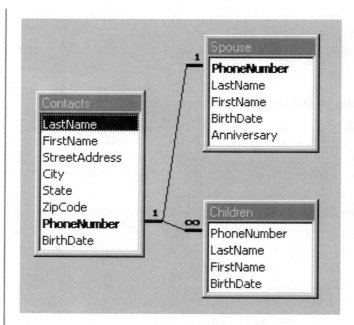

FIGURE 13.3 Jim's Database Design

Contacts : Table

	LastName	FirstName	StreetAddress	City	State	ZipCode	PhoneNumber	BirthDate
▶	Penner	Richard	696 Addler Road	Syracuse	NY	13205	(315) 961-1545	11/4/69
	Patterson	Andrew	1541 Windmill Lane	San Jose	CA	95121	(408) 451-1234	9/15/63
	Fillmore	Linda	854 River Park Place	Richmond	VA	23219	(804) 531-6672	1/11/70
	Williams	Judy	7685 Hope Blvd.	Memphis	TN	38105	(901) 876-5199	3/15/66
*								

Record: 1 of 4

Spouse : Table

	PhoneNumber	LastName	FirstName	BirthDate	Anniversary
▶	(315) 961-1545	Penner	Jennifer	8/15/71	6/15/92
	(804) 531-6672	Fillmore	Bruce	2/5/70	8/3/94
*					

Record: 1 of 2

Children : Table

	PhoneNumber	LastName	FirstName	BirthDate
▶	(315) 961-1545	Penner	Lisa	9/18/93
	(315) 961-1545	Penner	David	4/6/95
	(315) 961-1545	Penner	Mary	7/12/97
	(804) 531-6672	Fillmore	Michael	12/1/96
	(804) 531-6672	Fillmore	Alexandra	1/12/99
*				

Record: 1 of 5

FIGURE 13.4 Sample Data from Jim's Database

Creating Database Files

Database files are easily created in Delphi by using the BDE. You can employ two methods to create a database file with Delphi: you can use the Borland Database Desktop or you can write Delphi source code. Delphi is also capable of accessing database files created with other database programs. Because your database software documentation describes how to create a database file, our discussion will focus on the two Delphi methods. Let's begin by working with the Borland Database Desktop and defer discussion of creating databases through Delphi source code until the end of the chapter.

Even if you do not own database software, you can use the Borland Database Desktop to create database files in a variety of formats. This feature is available only in the Professional and Enterprise editions of Delphi, however, and not in the Standard edition included with this text. A step-by-step example of creating a database file using the Database Desktop is provided below.

1. In Delphi, select `Tools|Database Desktop` from the menu bar. The Database Desktop (Figure 13.5) opens on your screen. (*Note:* You can also start Database Desktop by using the shortcut on the Windows Start menu.)

2. In the Database Desktop, select `File|New|Table...` from the menu bar. Select Paradox 7 as the table type in the Create Table dialog box, and then click the OK button.

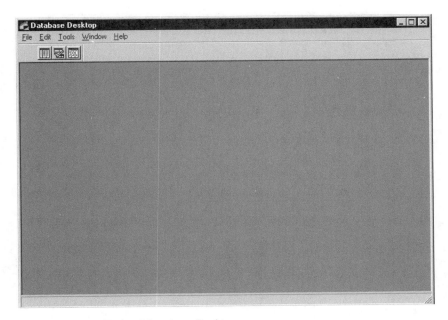

FIGURE 13.5   Borland Database Desktop

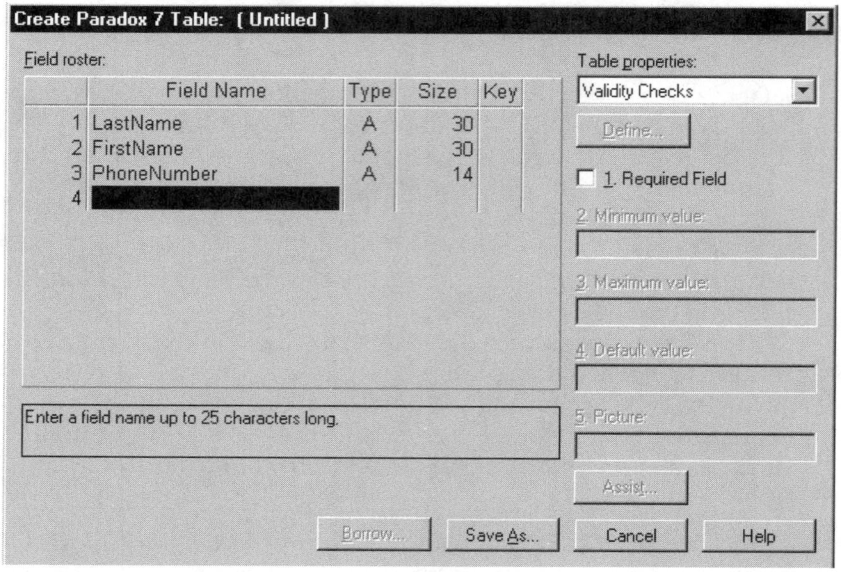

FIGURE 13.6   Create Table Window

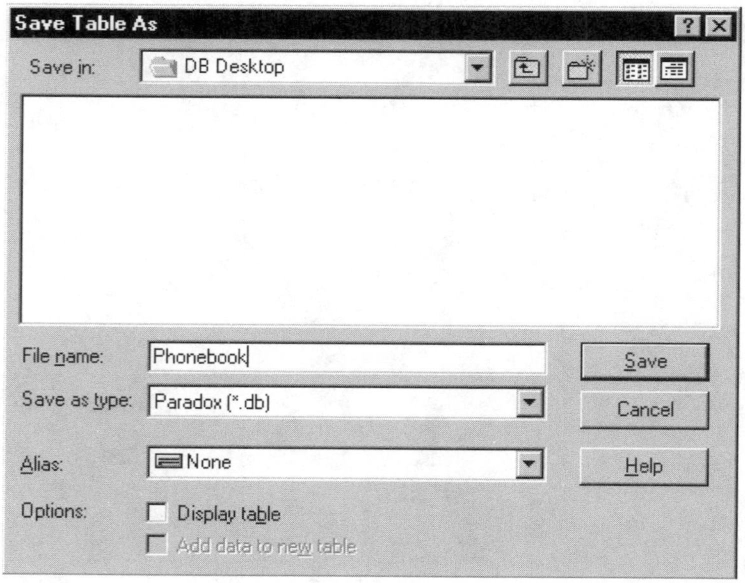

FIGURE 13.7   Save Table As Dialog Box

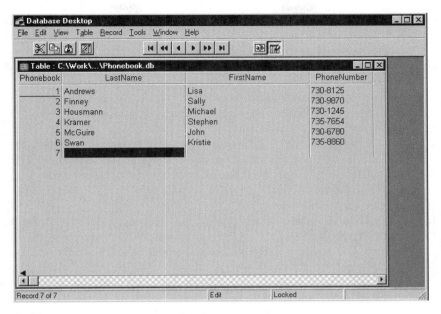

FIGURE 13.8   Phonebook Database

3. The Create Paradox 7 Table window opens on the screen. Complete the field roster with that shown in Figure 13.6.

4. Click the Save As... button. The Save Table As dialog box appears on the screen (Figure 13.7). Select a location in which to save your database file and name the file `Phonebook`. Click the Save button.

5. In the Database Desktop, select `File|Open|Table...` and then select the `Phonebook` file that you created in step 4.

6. Select `Table|Edit Data`, click the Edit Data icon, or press the F9 key. Enter the records shown in Figure 13.8.

7. Select `Table|View Data`, click the Edit Data icon to toggle it off, or press the F9 key to stop editing the data.

8. Experiment with moving around the database using the Record menu and the navigation buttons on the toolbar.

9. Close the `Phonebook` database.

10. Select `File|Exit` to close the Database Desktop.

Structured Query Language

International Business Machines (IBM) Corporation developed the **Structured Query Language (SQL)** in the early 1970s as a relational database language. The language allows a user to request specific information from the database or reorganize information in the database. SQL was first standardized by ANSI in 1986, and both Delphi and Borland's Database Desktop use a version of SQL that complies with the ANSI SQL-92 standards.

SQL provides both **Data Definition Language (DDL)** and **Data Manipulation Language (DML)** commands. Each language's commands overlap in function to some extent, but, in general, DDL commands are used to create new databases, tables, fields, and indexes, whereas DML commands are used to create queries that sort, filter, and extract data from the database.

DDL statements in SQL center around three commands: CREATE, DROP, and ALTER. The CREATE command is used to create new tables, fields, and indexes. The DROP command is used to delete tables and indexes from the database. The ALTER command is used to modify tables by adding fields or changing field definitions.

DML statements are built around four commands: SELECT, INSERT, UPDATE, and DELETE. The SELECT statement is used to query the database for records that meet specific criteria. Batches of data may be loaded into the database in a single operation by using the INSERT command. The UPDATE command records modifications made to records or fields in the database. The DELETE command removes records from a database.

SQL itself would require an entire textbook to describe in detail. Here we will focus our attention on a single SQL command (SELECT) and describe how to create SQL expressions using this command in the Database Desktop.

A simplified form of the SQL SELECT statement follows:

```
SELECT fieldList1 FROM tableExp [WHERE criteria]
[ORDER BY fieldList2 [ASC | DESC]]
```

Statements inside the square brackets [ ] are optional, and statements separated by a vertical bar | indicate that only one of the statements may be selected. For example, if you use the optional ORDER BY statement in the SELECT statement, either or neither—but not both—the ASC keyword or DESC keyword may be used. The *fieldList1* parameter is a field or set of fields to be selected from *tableExp*, where *tableExp* is any expression that evaluates to a table. The asterisk (*) is a **wildcard character** that indicates all fields. Replacing *fieldList1* with an asterisk selects all fields in *tableExp*. The *criteria* parameter must be a Boolean expression and generally involves the fields of the table. The standard Object Pascal relational and Boolean operators can be used in *criteria*. Additional comparison operators include BETWEEN (used to specify a range of values), LIKE (used for pattern matching), and IN (used to test for set membership). The *fieldList2* parameter specifies the field or set of fields by which the resulting records are ordered.

In the syntax, `tableExp` is any expression that evaluates to a table. Thus `tableExp` can be a combination of tables created by joining tables together. The `INNER JOIN` operation combines records from both tables only when the specified field from the first table matches the specified field from the second table. `LEFT JOIN` (or left outer join) combines all records from the first (left) table with records from the second table whose specified fields match certain conditions. Conversely, `RIGHT JOIN` (right outer join) combines all records from the second (right) table with records from the first table whose specified fields match certain conditions. The general syntax for the `JOIN` statement follows:

```
table1 joinType JOIN table2 ON table1Field = table2Field
```

where `table1` and `table2` are the two tables to be joined, `table1Field` is a field from `table1`, `table2Field` is a field from `table2` (specifying the primary and foreign keys), and `joinType` specifies the type of join (`INNER`, `LEFT`, or `RIGHT`).

As an example, let's perform some SQL queries using the Database Desktop. Follow the steps outlined below:

1. In Delphi, select `Tools|Database Desktop` from the menu bar. The Database Desktop (see Figure 13.5) opens on your screen. (*Note:* You can also start Database Desktop by using the shortcut on the Windows Start menu.)

2. In the Database Desktop, select `File|Working Directory...` from the menu bar. The Set Working Directory dialog box (Figure 13.9) opens on the screen. Click the Browse button and change the working directory to the folder that contains the `Phonebook` table created in the previous section. Click the OK button.

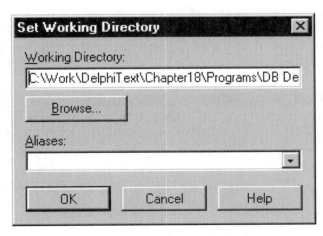

FIGURE 13.9   Set Working Directory Dialog Box

FIGURE 13.10   SQL Editor

3. Select `File|New|SQL File` from the menu bar. The SQL Editor window opens on the screen.

4. Enter the SQL query shown in Figure 13.10.

5. Select `SQL|Run SQL` from the menu bar, click the Run SQL icon, or press the F8 key to execute the SQL statement. Figure 13.11 shows the result of the SQL query.

6. Close the table.

7. Save the SQL query. Select `File|Save As...` from the menu bar. The Save As dialog box opens on the screen. Enter `MyQuery.sql` as the file name and click the Save button.

8. Change the SQL statement to the following:

   ```
   SELECT LastName, PhoneNumber FROM Phonebook
   WHERE LastName IN ('Finney', 'McGuire')
   ```

9. Press the F8 key to execute the SQL query. Examine and then close the resulting table.

10. Change the SQL statement again:

    ```
    SELECT LastName, PhoneNumber FROM Phonebook
    WHERE LastName BETWEEN 'Anderson' AND 'Klein'
    ORDER BY PhoneNumber DESC
    ```

11. Press the F8 key to execute the SQL query. Examine and then close the resulting table.

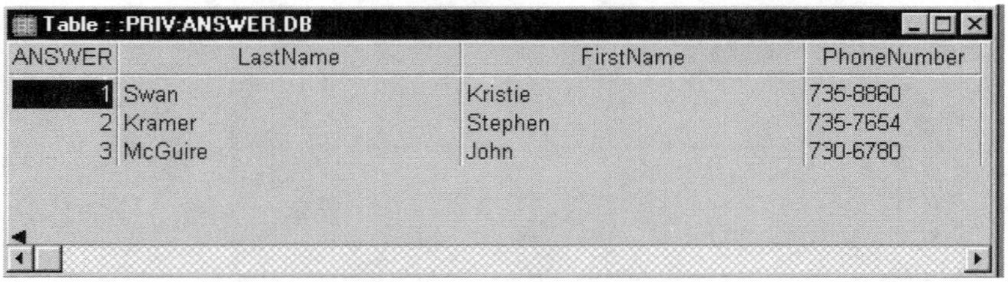

FIGURE 13.11   SQL Query Result

12. Close the SQL Editor window. Do not save the SQL query.
13. Select `File|Exit` to close the Database Desktop.

Query by Example

The Database Desktop also supports Query by Example (QBE), a method of building an SQL query visually. The following sequence of steps provides an example of this feature:

1. In Delphi, select `Tools|Database Desktop` from the menu bar. The Database Desktop (see Figure 13.5) opens on your screen.
2. Make sure that the working directory contains the `Phonebook` table. If it does not, set the working directory using the `File|Working Directory...` option on the menu bar.
3. Select `File|New|QBE Query...` from the menu bar. Choose the `Phonebook` database and click the Open button. An empty Query window (Figure 13.12) appears on your screen.
4. Complete the Query window as shown in Figure 13.13.
5. Press the F8 key to execute the query. Figure 13.14 shows the resulting table. Examine and then close this table.

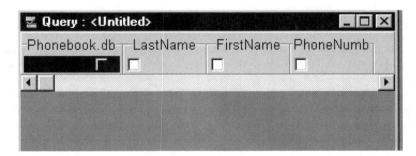

FIGURE 13.12   Query Window

FIGURE 13.13   Completed Query Window

FIGURE 13.14 Query Result

6. Select `File|Save As...` from the menu bar. Enter the file name `MyQuery.qbe` and click the Save button.

7. Select `Query|Show SQL` from the menu bar or click the Show SQL icon. Examine the SQL query.

8. Close the SQL Editor window. Do not save the SQL query.

9. Close the Query window.

10. Select `File|Exit` to close the Database Desktop.

Creating a Database Application

Delphi includes a Database Form Wizard that allows the programmer to quickly develop database applications. This wizard is, by far, the simplest means of integrating a database into a Delphi application. We will first develop a database application using the wizard and then discuss the components used in the application.

Follow the steps below to create the Telephone Book application:

1. Start Delphi. A new, blank application should appear in the IDE.

2. Select `File|New...` from the menu bar. The New Items dialog box opens on the screen. In the Business tab, select the Database Form Wizard and click the OK button. The Database Form Wizard (Figure 13.15) now appears on your screen.

Programming Key: Tips

You can also start the Database Form Wizard started by selecting `Database|Form Wizard...` on Delphi's menu bar.

3. Make sure that the Form and DataSet options are selected (as shown in Figure 13.15) and then click the Next button.

4. The wizard now asks for a table to use with the form. Find and select the `Phonebook.db` database file. Then click the Next button.

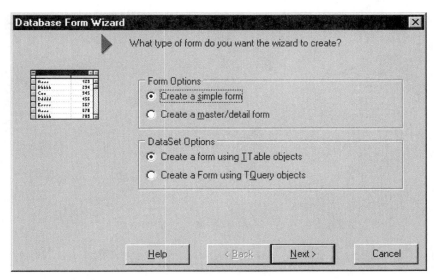

FIGURE 13.15   Database Form Wizard

5. Select all fields in the table by clicking the >> button. Then click the Next button.

6. The wizard presents the form layout options (Figure 13.16). Select the Vertically radio button and click the Next button.

7. Select the Left radio button to place labels to the left of the data fields. Click the Next button.

8. The wizard displays its final screen, the form generation screen. Make sure that the options are selected as shown in Figure 13.17 and click the Finish button to generate the form.

9. The new form (Form2) now appears in your Delphi project. Change the property settings of the components as indicated in the following table:

Component Name	Property	Setting
Form2	Name	frmPhonebook
	Caption	Telephone Book
Label1	Name	lblLastName
	Caption	Last Name
Label2	Name	lblFirstName
	Caption	First Name
Label3	Name	lblPhoneNumber
	Caption	Phone Number
DBNavigator	ShowHint	True

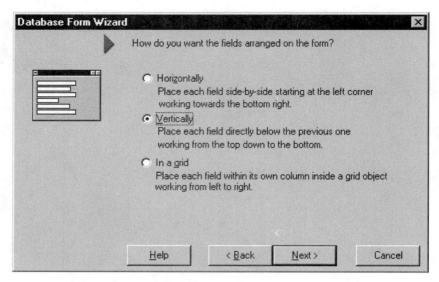

FIGURE 13.16   Database Form Wizard Layout Options

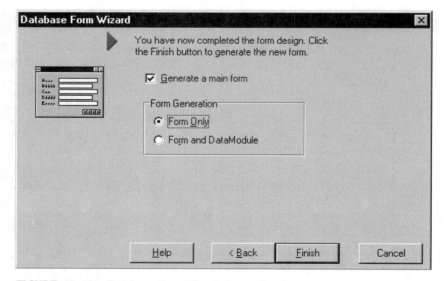

FIGURE 13.17   Database Form Wizard Generation Screen

10. Delete `Form1` from the Delphi project. Select `Project|Remove from Project...` on the menu bar. Highlight `Unit1, Form1` and then click the OK button.

11. Select `File|Save All`. Save the unit as `Phone.pas` and the project as `Phonebook.dpr`.

FIGURE 13.18   Telephone Book Application

12. Select Run | Run from the menu bar to execute the application (Figure 13.18).

13. Experiment with moving around the database using the database navigator icons. Try adding records to and deleting records from the database.

14. Close the Telephone Book application, but keep the project open in the Delphi IDE.

Programming Key: Tips

To create a database form that contains fields from multiple database files, first create separate forms for each database file using the Database Form Wizard. Next, cut and paste the controls onto a single form. Finally, remove the empty forms from your project.

Let's examine the components used by the Database Form Wizard in creating the Telephone Book application. Forms and labels were two elementary components discussed in Chapter 2. We have used these components many times throughout this text, so no further discussion is required here. Chapter 16 examines panels and scroll boxes in more detail.

`Table1` is an object of type `TTable`, an object that accesses data from a single database table using the BDE. This component can also access a subset of records within a database table by using ranges and filters. The `DatabaseName` property specifies the directory location of the table or the name of a `TDatabase` object to associate with this component. The `TableName` property indicates the name of the database table that this component encapsulates. To set `TableName`, the `Active` property must be False. The `Active` property indicates whether the database table is open for access; when it is True, data can be read from and written to the database.

The `Filter`, `Filtered`, and `FilterOptions` properties allow the programmer to create and apply filter criteria to the database. Similarly, sorting criteria may be specified for the database using the index properties—`IndexDefs`, `IndexFieldNames`, `IndexFiles`, and `IndexName`. The `Bof` and `Eof` properties determine whether the **current record** is the first record or last record in the database, respectively. The `First` and `Last` methods reposition the record pointer to the first record and last record in the database, respectively. The `Next` method moves the record pointer to the next record in the database. This component also has `Find` methods (`FindFirst`, `FindLast`, `FindNext`, and `FindPrior`) that reposition the record pointer in a filtered database.

`DataSource1` is a component of type `TDataSource`. The `TDataSource` object provides an interface between a **dataset** (such as a table associated with a `TTable` object) and **data-aware controls** on a form that enable display, navigation, and editing of the data. Each dataset must be associated with a data source component to allow the user to display and manipulate its data within data-aware controls. Similarly, each data-aware control must be associated with a data source component to receive and manipulate data. The `DataSet` property specifies the dataset for which this component serves as a conduit to data-aware controls. The `Enabled` property contains a Boolean value that indicates whether the data-aware controls associated with the data source component can display data.

`EditLastName`, `EditFirstName`, and `EditPhoneNumber` are components of type `TDBEdit`. The `TDBEdit` control can display and edit a single field in a dataset. The `DataSource` property links the edit control to the dataset, and the `DataField` property specifies which field's data are displayed in the control.

`DBNavigator` is a component of type `TDBNavigator`, a database navigator. This component allows the user to move through the data in a dataset and perform operations on the data, such as inserting a blank record or posting a record. The `DataSource` property links the navigator to the dataset. The `VisibleButtons` property lists which buttons appear on the database navigator.

Creating a Database through Object Pascal Source Code

Creating and accessing a database by writing Object Pascal source code is not an especially complex job, but it is a bit more lengthy task. The Address Book application that follows provides an example. This application can either load an existing address book database or create one dynamically at run time. Figure 13.19 displays a sample execution of the Address Book program.

```
unit SourceCode;
interface

uses
   Windows, Messages, SysUtils, Classes, Graphics, Controls,
   Forms, Dialogs, StdCtrls, Grids, DBGrids, DbTables, Db;
```

Component	Property	Setting
Form	Name	frmAddressBook
	BorderStyle	bsSingle
	Caption	Address Book
Button	Name	btnNewDB
	Caption	New Address Book
Button	Name	btnLoad
	Caption	Load Address Book
Button	Name	btnCloseDB
	Caption	Close Address Book
	Enabled	False
ScrollBox	Name	sbxDB
DBGrid	Name	dbgAddress
OpenDialog	Name	dlgOpen
	DefaultExt	adr
	FileName	Address.adr
	Filter	Address Book (*.adr) | *.adr
	InitialDir	C:\
	Title	Load Address Book
SaveDialog	Name	dlgSave
	DefaultExt	adr
	FileName	Address.adr
	Filter	Address Book (*.adr) | *.adr
	InitialDir	C:\
	Title	New Address Book

Place the `dbgAddress` DBGrid control inside the `sbxDB` scroll box.

Component Name	Event	Setting
btnNewDB	OnClick	btnNewDBClick
btnLoad	OnClick	btnLoadClick
btnCloseDB	OnClick	btnCloseDBClick

```
type
  TfrmAddressBook = class(TForm)
    dbgAddress: TDBGrid;
    btnNewDB: TButton;
    btnLoad: TButton;
    sbxDB: TScrollBox;
    btnCloseDB: TButton;
    dlgOpen: TOpenDialog;
    dlgSave: TSaveDialog;
    procedure btnNewDBClick(Sender: TObject);
    procedure btnCloseDBClick(Sender: TObject);
```

```
      procedure btnLoadClick(Sender: TObject);
    private
      { Private declarations }
    public
      { Public declarations }
    end;

var
  frmAddressBook: TfrmAddressBook;
  Table:          TTable;
  DataSource:     TDataSource;

implementation

{$R *.DFM}

procedure TfrmAddressBook.btnNewDBClick(Sender: TObject);

begin
  if dlgSave.Execute then begin
    try
      Table := TTable.Create(Self);
      DataSource := TDataSource.Create(Self);

      Table.DatabaseName := '';
      Table.TableName := dlgSave.FileName;

      {Create the database fields}
      Table.FieldDefs.Add('LastName', ftString, 30, False);
      Table.FieldDefs.Add('FirstName', ftString, 30, False);
      Table.FieldDefs.Add('Address', ftString, 50, False);
      Table.FieldDefs.Add('City', ftString, 20, False);
      Table.FieldDefs.Add('State', ftString, 20, False);
      Table.FieldDefs.Add('ZipCode', ftString, 10, False);
      Table.FieldDefs.Add('Phone', ftString, 14, False);
      Table.FieldDefs.Add('Fax', ftString, 14, False);

      {Index on the LastName field}
      Table.IndexDefs.Add('', 'LastName', [ixPrimary]);
      {Create the table}
      Table.CreateTable;
      {Display the table}
      DataSource.DataSet := Table;
      dbgAddress.DataSource := DataSource;
      Table.Active := True;
    except
      MessageDlg('Error creating table', mtError, [mbOK], 0);
      Table.Free;
      DataSource.Free;
```

```pascal
      Exit;
    end;

    {Set active/inactive buttons}
    btnNewDB.Enabled := False;
    btnLoad.Enabled := False;
    btnCloseDB.Enabled := True;
  end
  else begin
    MessageDlg('No Address Book created', mtInformation,
               [mbOK], 0);
  end;
end;

procedure TfrmAddressBook.btnCloseDBClick(Sender: TObject);

begin
  {Close and free resources}
  Table.Close;
  Table.Free;
  DataSource.Free;

  {Set active/inactive buttons}
  btnNewDB.Enabled := True;
  btnLoad.Enabled := True;
  btnCloseDB.Enabled := False;
end;


procedure TfrmAddressBook.btnLoadClick(Sender: TObject);

begin
  if dlgOpen.Execute then begin
    try
      Table := TTable.Create(Self);
      DataSource := TDataSource.Create(Self);

      Table.DatabaseName := '';
      Table.TableName := dlgOpen.FileName;

      {Display the table}
      DataSource.DataSet := Table;
      dbgAddress.DataSource := DataSource;
      Table.Active := True;
    except
      MessageDlg('Error opening table', mtError, [mbOK], 0);
      Table.Free;
      DataSource.Free;
      Exit;
    end;
```

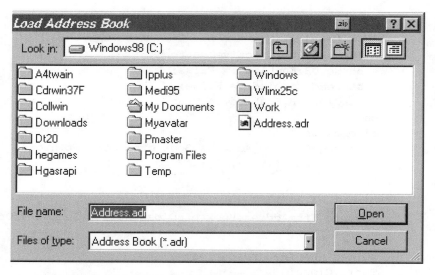

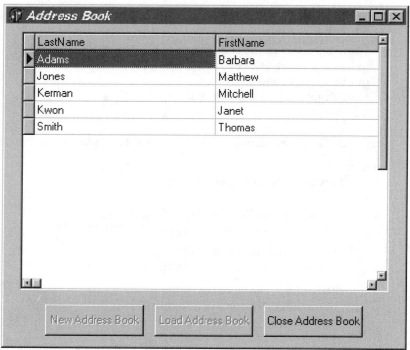

FIGURE 13.19   Address Book Application

```
      {Set active/inactive buttons}
      btnNewDB.Enabled := False;
      btnLoad.Enabled := False;
      btnCloseDB.Enabled := True;
    end
    else begin
      MessageDlg('No Address Book opened', mtInformation,
                 [mbOK], 0);
    end;
  end;

end.
```

Programming Key: Delphi Highlight

The Enterprise edition of Delphi contains **ActiveX Data Objects (ADO)**. ADO components are flexible data objects that allow you to access a database on a local computer system, through a network, or over the Internet.

Summary

Key Terms

ActiveX Data Object (ADO)—A data object that can access a database on a local computer, through a network, or over the Internet.

current record—The record currently being accessed.

data-aware control—A control that enables the display, navigation, and editing of data in a dataset.

database (database file)—A data file consisting of a set of related information intended specifically for use by a database program.

database engine—A set of routines that perform the operations associated with a database, such as adding, deleting, sorting, and searching records.

database program—A program that maintains a database and allows for easy storage, access, and retrieval of data.

Data Definition Language (DDL)—A set of commands used to create new databases, tables, fields, and indexes.

Data Manipulation Language (DML)—A set of commands used to create queries that sort, filter, and extract data from the database.

dataset—The set of data that is being accessed from a database file, such as a table.

entity integrity—No record may have an empty primary key.

field—A column in a table; a specific piece of information from a record.

foreign key—A field or set of fields that references the primary key of another table and links the two tables together.

integrity—Consistency of data.

one-to-many relationship—An association between two tables where the primary key of one table may match the foreign key of any number of records in a second table.

one-to-one relationship—An association between two tables where the primary key of one table may match the foreign key of only one record in a second table.

primary key—A field or set of fields that uniquely identify each record in a table.

record—A row in a table. A record encapsulates a group of related data and consists of a piece of data from each field.

referential integrity—The foreign key of one table must appear as the primary key of another table.

relational database—A database consisting of two or more related tables.

Structured Query Language (SQL)—A language developed by IBM for managing, updating, and querying relational databases.

table—A structure that stores data in rows and columns, where the rows are records and the columns are fields.

wildcard character—A single character used to represent any string of characters.

Keywords
Object Pascal Keywords

Events
OnClick

Methods

FindFirst	First
FindLast	Last
FindNext	Next
FindPrior	

Properties

Active	Filtered
Bof	FilterOptions
BorderStyle	IndexDefs
Caption	IndexFieldNames
DatabaseName	IndexFiles
DataField	IndexName
DataSet	InitialDir
DataSource	Name
DefaultExt	ShowHint
Enabled	TableName
Eof	Title
FileName	VisibleButtons
Filter	

SQL Keywords

* *(wildcard character)*	INNER JOIN
ALTER	INSERT
ASC	LEFT JOIN
BETWEEN	LIKE
CREATE	ON
DELETE	ORDER BY
DESC	RIGHT JOIN
DROP	SELECT
FROM	UPDATE
IN	WHERE

Key Concepts

- A database program allows access to database files and provides for easy access, storage, and retrieval of data.
- A database file (or simply database) contains a set of related information. A database consists of one or more tables; each table contains a set of records; each record contains one or more fields; information is stored in each field.
- A database consisting of two or more related tables is called a relational database. In a relational database, the primary key and foreign key link data from one table to another.

- Maintaining the integrity, or consistency, of data in a relational database is of primary concern to programmers and database designers. With entity integrity, no record may have an empty primary key. With referential integrity, a foreign key must have an associated primary key.

- You can create a database by using the Borland Database Desktop, by writing Object Pascal source code, or by using a database program, such as Microsoft Access.

- The Structured Query Language (SQL) is a relational database language that provides both Data Definition Language (DDL) and Data Manipulation Language (DML) commands. DDL commands include CREATE, DROP, and ALTER. DML commands include SELECT, INSERT, UPDATE, and DELETE.

- A simplified syntax of the SQL SELECT statement is

  ```
  SELECT fieldList1 FROM tableExp [WHERE criteria]
  [ORDER BY fieldList2 [ASC | DESC]]
  ```

- An asterisk (*) is the SQL wildcard character that is used to designate all fields of a table.

- In SQL, tables are combined using the JOIN statement. The general syntax follows:

  ```
  table1 joinType JOIN table2 ON table1Field =
  table2Field
  ```

- Data source components and data-aware controls allow Delphi to access database files. A data-aware control must be bound to a data source component to display specific information contained in the database.

- ActiveX Data Objects (ADO) are flexible data objects that allow a database to be accessed on a local computer system, through a network, or over the Internet. The Enterprise edition of Delphi includes ADO components.

Review Questions

1. Describe the organization of a typical database in terms of tables, records, and fields.
2. What is a relational database?
3. How can you create a database without using Delphi? By using Delphi?
4. Define entity integrity and referential integrity.
5. Summarize the five guidelines for designing an efficient database.

6. What is SQL? Describe the two types of SQL commands.

7. How do a data source component and a data-aware control differ? How do you access a database using these Delphi components?

8. What are ADO components? Which edition of Delphi includes these components?

Problems

1. Honest Joe's Used Cars has a current inventory of nine cars (listed in the table below). Use the Borland Database Desktop to create a database and enter these data.

Make	Model	Year	Mileage	Color	Condition	Vehicle ID
Chevrolet	Camaro	1994	89,546	Black	Fair	IZ90763
Dodge	Stratus	1996	43,128	Black	Good	YL65428
Ford	Escort	1997	27,021	Red	Excellent	IP87654
Ford	Taurus	1993	63,827	Maroon	Good	WB15036
Honda	Accord	1994	87,543	Silver	Fair	VB83921
Honda	Accord	1996	52,371	Blue	Good	ZX58723
Mazda	626	1994	64,180	Yellow	Excellent	PY89045
Toyota	Camry	1991	109,546	Red	Fair	LX45687
Toyota	Celica	1992	101,003	Silver	Good	TV99325

2. Use the Borland Database Desktop to create and execute the following queries on Honest Joe's database in Problem 1. Use the SQL Editor; do not use QBE.
   a. List all silver cars with less than 100,000 miles.
   b. List all cars in good or excellent condition with less than 50,000 miles.
   c. List all 1994 or newer cars.
   d. List all Honda Accords.

3. Repeat Problem 2 using QBE.

4. Write a Delphi program that is a "front end" to Honest Joe's database in Problem 1.

5. The current semester course listings for the Computer Science Department at Western State University appear in the table below. Create a relational database using the Borland Database Desktop and enter these data.

Course Number	Course Title	Instructor	Number of Students
CS100	Introductory Programming	Kerman	29
CS100	Introductory Programming	Brown	28
CS100	Introductory Programming	Perkins	21
CS101	Advanced Programming	Brown	17
CS201	Assembly Language Programming	Perkins	19
CS210	Object-Oriented Programming	Smith	18
CS210	Object-Oriented Programming	Wesson	15
CS220	Data Structures	Finney	11
CS220	Data Structures	Jackson	13
CS300	Computer Architecture	Kerman	14

6. Use the Borland Database Desktop to create and execute the following queries on the database in Problem 5. Use the SQL Editor; do not use QBE.
   a. List the titles of all courses taught by Professor Kerman.
   b. List all course numbers and instructors for courses that have more than 20 students in the course.
   c. List the course number, course title, and instructor for those courses with at most 15 students.
   d. List the course titles of all 200-level computer science courses.

7. Repeat Problem 6 using QBE.

8. Write a Delphi program that is a "front end" to the database in Problem 5.

Programming Projects

1. Create a checkbook register database through Object Pascal source code. The database should contain fields for the check number, date, payee, check amount, and notes.

2. Extend your program from Project 1 to include a graphical "front end" to your database. The interface should contain buttons to add, edit, remove, and search records in the database. In addition, your database should contain a second table that tracks the current checking account balance, and this information should be displayed in the interface.

Chapter 14

Recursion

Chapter Objectives

In this chapter you will:

- Understand how recursion works
- Become familiar with recursive functions in mathematics
- Write recursive subprograms and understand their operation

Some programming problems are difficult to solve using iterative loop structures but are easily solved using implicit loop structures (**recursion**). This chapter explains how recursion works and introduces recursive programming techniques.

Mathematical Recursion

In mathematics, a **recursive function** is a function whose name appears on both the left and right sides of the function equation. Thus recursion provides a method of solving a complex problem by first solving a set of simpler subproblems. Some problems naturally lend themselves to a recursive solution. The factorial function ($n!$), for instance, may be defined recursively:

$$
\begin{aligned}
n! &= n \times (n-1)! &&\text{for an integer } n \geq 1 \\
&= 1 &&\text{for } n = 0
\end{aligned}
$$

Using this definition, we can find 5! as follows:

$$
\begin{aligned}
5! &= 5 \times 4! \\
4! &= 4 \times 3! \\
3! &= 3 \times 2! \\
2! &= 2 \times 1! \\
1! &= 1 \times 0! \\
0! &= 1
\end{aligned}
$$

Then, through backward substitution, we find the value of 5!:

$$5! = 5 \times 4 \times 3 \times 2 \times 1 \times 1 = 120$$

As you can see, recursion forms an implicit loop structure.

Note that we can define the factorial function nonrecursively as well:

$$
\begin{aligned}
n! &= n \times (n-1) \times \cdots \times 1 &&\text{for an integer } n > 1 \\
&= 1 &&\text{for } n = 0, 1
\end{aligned}
$$

From this definition, we immediately find the result of 5!:

$$5! = 5 \times 4 \times 3 \times 2 \times 1 = 120$$

Recursive Subprograms

You can easily implement this definition of the factorial function in Object Pascal by using an `if` statement and a `for` loop. This task is left as an exercise for the reader. To implement the recursive definition, we will use a **recursive subprogram**, or a subprogram that calls itself. A recursive subprogram repeatedly calls itself, each time with a simpler situation, until it reaches the **trivial case**. The recursion then stops. A recursive function that computes $n!$ is shown below. The trivial case occurs when n = 0; then `Factorial = 1`.

```
{
Factorial
---------
```

```
Compute n! recursively.  If n is negative, Factorial
returns a 0.
}
function Factorial(n: Integer): Integer;

begin
  if (n < 0) then begin
    Factorial := 0;
  end
  else if (n = 0) then begin
    Factorial := 1;
  end
  else begin
    Factorial := n * Factorial(n - 1);
  end;
end;
```

Programming Key: Warning

In any recursive routine, you must be absolutely certain that the trivial case is attainable and that the recursion stops when this case is reached. Otherwise, an endless loop will result from recursively calling the routine with no stopping condition. So avoid endless loops when using recursive routines.

For values of n greater than 13 in the preceding function, the Integer data type is **overflowed,** and the function returns an incorrect value. This error occurs regardless of whether the function is written recursively. One way to prevent this error is to use the Real data type:

```
{
Factorial
---------
Compute n! recursively (using the Real data type).
If n is negative, Factorial returns a 0.
}
function Factorial(n: Real): Real;

begin
  if (n < 0.0) then begin
    Factorial := 0.0;
  end
  else if (n = 0.0) then begin
    Factorial := 1.0;
  end
```

```
      else begin
        Factorial := n * Factorial(n - 1.0);
      end;
   end;
```

In this function, the `Real` data type is overflowed for values of n greater than 170, a value approximately 13 times higher than the previous function.

Notice that the `var` keyword does not precede the parameter n in either version of the `Factorial` function. In other words, this function passes parameters by value. Inserting the `var` keyword in either version of this function does not cause the function to perform incorrectly. In many cases, however, a recursive subprogram that passes parameters by reference rather than by value will not operate correctly. Recall that passing parameters by reference allows you to alter the values of the original variables in the calling routine, which is usually not desirable in a recursive subprogram.

The following example demonstrates the difference between passing parameters by value and by reference in a recursive subprogram:

```
unit RecursionEx;

interface

uses
   Windows, Messages, SysUtils, Classes, Graphics, Controls,
   Forms, Dialogs, StdCtrls;

type
   TfrmRecursion = class(TForm)
     btnExample: TButton;
     memOutput: TMemo;
     procedure RunEx(Sender: TObject);
   private
     { Private declarations }
   public
     { Public declarations }
   end;

var
   frmRecursion: TfrmRecursion;

implementation

{$R *.DFM}

procedure RecursionTest(number: Integer);

begin
   if (number <= 0) then begin
     {Trivial case — end the recursion}
   end
```

```
    else begin
      frmRecursion.memOutput.Lines[0] :=
        frmRecursion.memOutput.Lines[0] + IntToStr(number) +
                                          ' ';

      number := number - 1;
      RecursionTest(number);
      if (number < 3) then begin
        RecursionTest(number);
      end;
    end;
end;

procedure TfrmRecursion.RunEx(Sender: TObject);

var
  value: Integer;

begin
  memOutput.Clear;
  value := 5;
  RecursionTest(value);
end;

end.
```

This code passes the `number` parameter by value and outputs 5 4 3 2 1 1 2 1 1 when the user clicks the `btnExample` button. Now, let's insert the `var` keyword in front of the `number` parameter:

```
procedure RecursionTest(var number: Integer);
```

This modified version of the code passes `number` by reference. The output of the code is now 5 4 3 2 1, and the recursion does not work as desired.

Programming Key: Warning

In many languages, a common problem occurring with recursive subprograms is the **stack overflow** error. Each microprocessor has an internal stack structure, and compilers may reserve extra memory to function as a stack and store information during program execution. During program execution, these structures may become overflowed with information. In Delphi, you can change the minimum and maximum size of an application's stack in the Memory sizes frame of the Linker tab under `Project|Options`. Alternatively, you can use the `$M` compiler directive to specify an application's stack size.

C. A. R. Hoare's Quicksort algorithm provides a practical example of a recursive sorting routine. Although computer scientists have devised a variety of algorithms for sorting data, Quicksort is generally regarded as the fastest and most efficient sorting algorithm in the average case.

The Quicksort algorithm operates by first selecting a pivot value. The data are then arranged such that all data items with a value less than the pivot value appear at the beginning of the data structure and all data items with a value greater than or equal to the pivot value are moved toward the end of the data structure. Thus this algorithm partitions the data set into two pieces: those items less than the pivot value and those items greater than or equal to the pivot value.

Neither of the two partitions is sorted as it is built. After the partitioning operation is complete, all we know is that every item to the "left" of the pivot value has a value less than it, and every item to the "right" of the pivot value has a value greater than or equal to it.

Next, the Quicksort routine recursively invokes itself to process the partitions. In each partition, a new pivot value is selected that allows yet another subdivision of the data set. This process of selecting a new pivot value and then subdividing a range of data into two more partitions repeats until the size of a resulting partition becomes small enough that it can be easily sorted. This point usually occurs when two or fewer items remain in a partition, as such ranges can be put in order with very little effort.

The efficiency of the Quicksort depends on the size of the data set and the method used to select a pivot value. In the example that follows, the greater of the first two elements in the data range is selected as the pivot value.

The following program uses the Quicksort algorithm to sort any number of user-entered non-negative integer values. The program outputs both the original order and sorted order of the data as well as the sequence of events that transpires during the Quicksort routine.

```
unit QuicksortEx;

interface

uses
  Windows, Messages, SysUtils, Classes, Graphics, Controls,
  Forms, Dialogs, StdCtrls;

type
  DataArray = array of Integer;

  TfrmQuicksort = class(TForm)
    btnQuicksort: TButton;
    memOutput: TMemo;
    procedure Quicksort(low, high: Integer;
                        var data: DataArray);
    procedure Display(data: DataArray);
    procedure TestQuicksort(Sender: TObject);
```

```
  private
    { Private declarations }
  public
    { Public declarations }
  end;

var
  frmQuicksort: TfrmQuicksort;

implementation

{$R *.DFM}

{Return the index of the selected pivot value}
function GetPivotIndex(low, high: Integer;
                       data: DataArray): Integer;

begin
  {Return the index of the greater of the
   first two values in the range}
  if (data[low] < data[low + 1]) then begin
    Inc(low);
  end;
  GetPivotIndex := low;
end;

{Swap the contents of two integer variables}
procedure Swap(var intValue1, intValue2: Integer);

var
  temp: Integer;

begin
  temp := intValue1;
  intValue1 := intValue2;
  intValue2 := temp;
end;

{Recursive Quicksort routine}
procedure TfrmQuicksort.Quicksort(low, high: Integer;
                                  var data: DataArray);

var
  pivotIndex: Integer; {Index of the pivot element}
  pivotValue: Integer; {Value of the pivot element}
  left:       Integer;
  right:      Integer;
  none:       Boolean;

begin
  {Find a pivot value}
```

```
pivotIndex := GetPivotIndex(low, high, data);
pivotValue := data[pivotIndex];

memOutput.Lines.Add('QUICKSORT(' + IntToStr(low)
  + ', ' + IntToStr(high) + ', data)');
memOutput.Lines.Add('Pivot: data[' + IntToStr(pivotIndex)
                    + '] = ' + IntToStr(pivotValue));

{Partition the data into two parts}
left := low;
right := high;
repeat

  {Move left to the right, bypassing elements already
   in the correct order}
  while ((left <= high) and (data[left] < pivotValue))
  do begin
    Inc(left);
  end;

  {Move right to the left, bypassing elements already
   in the correct order}
  while ((right >= low) and (pivotValue < data[right]))
  do begin
    Dec(right);
  end;

  memOutput.Lines.Add('After bypassing, left=' +
                      IntToStr(left) + '  right='
                      + IntToStr(right));

  {If left <= right, they are pointing to two
   items on the wrong side of the pivot value and must
   be swapped}
  if (left <= right) then begin
    Swap(data[left], data[right]);
    Inc(left);
    Dec(right);

    memOutput.Lines.Add('Swapped left and right data ' +
                        'elements');
    memOutput.Lines.Add('left=' + IntToStr(left) +
                        '  right=' + IntToStr(right));
  end;

until (left > right);

{Recursively call the Quicksort routine on
 each partition that is large enough}
```

```
    none := True;
    memOutput.Lines.Add('Recursive calls:');
    if (low < right) then begin
      memOutput.Lines.Add('  Quicksort(' + IntToStr(low)
        + ', ' + IntToStr(right) + ', data)');
      none := False;
    end;
    if (left < high) then begin
      memOutput.Lines.Add('  Quicksort(' + IntToStr(left)
        + ', ' + IntToStr(high) + ', data)');
      none := False;
    end;
    if none then begin
      memOutput.Lines.Add('  None');
    end;
    memOutput.Lines.Add('');
    if (low < right) then begin
      Quicksort(low, right, data);
    end;
    if (left < high) then begin
      Quicksort(left, high, data);
    end;
  end;

{Display the data}
procedure TfrmQuicksort.Display(data: DataArray);

var
  count: Integer;

begin
  for count := Low(data) to High(data) do begin
    memOutput.Lines.Add(IntToStr(data[count]));
  end;
  memOutput.Lines.Add('');
end;

{Test the recursive Quicksort routine}
procedure TfrmQuicksort.TestQuicksort(Sender: TObject);

var
  value: Integer;
  count: Integer;
  data:  DataArray;

begin
  count := 0;
  SetLength(data, count);
```

```
    repeat
      value := StrToInt(InputBox('ENTER A VALUE',
                'Please enter an integer value (< 0 to quit).',
                ''));
      if (value >= 0) then begin
        Inc(count);
        SetLength(data, count);
        data[count - 1] := value;
      end;
    until (value < 0);

    memOutput.Clear;
    memOutput.Lines.Add('Original order of data:');
    memOutput.Lines.Add('-----------------------');
    Display(data);

    Quicksort(Low(data), High(data), data);

    memOutput.Lines.Add('');
    memOutput.Lines.Add('Sorted order:');
    memOutput.Lines.Add('-------------');
    Display(data);
  end;

  end.
```

The output from a sample execution of this program appears below. You should trace through both this output and the source code by hand. The importance of this activity cannot be overemphasized; tracing this code will increase your understanding of recursion and the Quicksort routine, and ultimately make you a better programmer.

```
Original order of data:
----------------------
5
95
10
90
85
80
15

QUICKSORT(0, 6, data)
Pivot: data[1] = 95
After bypassing, left=1  right=6
Swapped left and right data elements
left=2  right=5
After bypassing, left=6  right=5
```

```
Recursive calls:
  Quicksort(0, 5, data)

QUICKSORT(0, 5, data)
Pivot: data[1] = 15
After bypassing, left=1  right=2
Swapped left and right data elements
left=2  right=1
Recursive calls:
  Quicksort(0, 1, data)
  Quicksort(2, 5, data)

QUICKSORT(0, 1, data)
Pivot: data[1] = 10
After bypassing, left=1  right=1
Swapped left and right data elements
left=2  right=0
Recursive calls:
  None

QUICKSORT(2, 5, data)
Pivot: data[3] = 90
After bypassing, left=3  right=5
Swapped left and right data elements
left=4  right=4
After bypassing, left=5  right=4
Recursive calls:
  Quicksort(2, 4, data)

QUICKSORT(2, 4, data)
Pivot: data[3] = 80
After bypassing, left=3  right=3
Swapped left and right data elements
left=4  right=2
Recursive calls:
  None


Sorted order:
------------
5
10
15
80
85
90
95
```

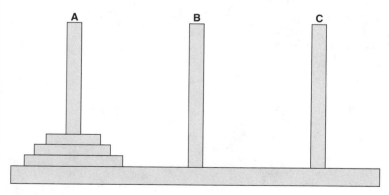

·C·A·S·E· ·S·T·U·D·Y·

The Towers of Hanoi

The Towers of Hanoi is a classic problem that has a simple recursive solution. The game consists of a board with three pegs (A, B, and C) and a certain number of disks. The game begins with all disks on peg A, as shown in Figure 14.1. The object of the game is to move all disks to peg C by following two rules:

1. One disk is moved at a time.
2. A disk can only be placed on top of one that is larger in size.

Take a few minutes and try to develop an algorithm to solve this problem. Think about this problem for one disk, two disks, and three disks. Do you see any patterns?

For one disk, the solution is trivial: Move the disk from peg A to peg C. How about for two disks? Move the first disk from peg A to peg B. Then, move the second disk from peg A to peg C. Finally, move the first disk from peg B to peg C. Note that the first and last steps repeat the solution for the one-disk case. Now, how about for three disks? Obviously the solution is longer, but it contains the solution to the two-disk case: Use the two-disk solution to move two disks from peg A to peg B. Then, move the third disk from peg A to peg C. Finally, use the two-disk solution to move two disks from peg B to peg C. Again, notice the references to the previous solution.

FIGURE 14.1   The Towers of Hanoi

The general solution algorithm follows:

1. Use the $(n-1)$-disk solution to move $(n-1)$ disks from peg A to peg B.
2. Move disk n from peg A to peg C.
3. Use the $(n-1)$-disk solution to move $(n-1)$ disks from peg B to peg C.

This algorithm is implemented in the following Object Pascal program:

```
{Towers of Hanoi}
unit Towers;

interface

uses
  Windows, Messages, SysUtils, Classes, Graphics,
  Controls, Forms, Dialogs, StdCtrls;

type
  TfrmTowers = class(TForm)
    edtNumDisks: TEdit;
    lblNumDisks: TLabel;
    btnSolve: TButton;
    memOutput: TMemo;
    procedure Solve(Sender: TObject);
  private
    { Private declarations }
  public
    { Public declarations }
  end;

var
  frmTowers: TfrmTowers;

implementation

{$R *.DFM}
{
MoveDisk
--------
A recursive procedure to move disks and solve the
Towers of Hanoi problem.
}
procedure MoveDisk(numDisks: Integer; startPeg,
                   endPeg, sparePeg: Char);
```

```
var
  move: String;
begin
  if (numDisks = 1) then begin
    move := 'Move a disk from ' + startPeg + ' to ' +
            endPeg;
    frmTowers.memOutput.Lines.Add(move);
  end
  else begin
    MoveDisk(numDisks - 1, startPeg, sparePeg,
            endPeg);
    move := 'Move a disk from ' + startPeg + ' to ' +
            endPeg;
    frmTowers.memOutput.Lines.Add(move);
    MoveDisk(numDisks - 1, sparePeg, endPeg,
             startPeg);
  end;
end;

{Solve the Towers of Hanoi problem for a number of
disks entered by the user}
procedure TfrmTowers.Solve(Sender: TObject);

var
  disks: Integer;
  code:  Integer;
begin
  Val(edtNumDisks.Text, disks, code);
  memOutput.Clear;
  if (disks > 0) then begin
    MoveDisk(disks, 'A', 'C', 'B');
  end
  else begin
    memOutput.Lines.Add('Number of disks must be > 0');
  end;
end;

end.
```

This code outputs the following solution for the three-disk case:

```
Move a disk from A to C
Move a disk from A to B
Move a disk from C to B
Move a disk from A to C
Move a disk from B to A
Move a disk from B to C
Move a disk from A to C
```

The program gives this solution for the four-disk case:

```
Move a disk from A to B
Move a disk from A to C
Move a disk from B to C
Move a disk from A to B
Move a disk from C to A
Move a disk from C to B
Move a disk from A to B
Move a disk from A to C
Move a disk from B to C
Move a disk from B to A
Move a disk from C to A
Move a disk from B to C
Move a disk from A to B
Move a disk from A to C
Move a disk from B to C
```

For n disks, the solution contains $2^n - 1$ moves. Legend has it that the 64-disk Towers of Hanoi problem was given to monks in an ancient monastery. When all 64 disks were in order on peg C, the world was supposed to come to an end. Applying some mathematics, the 64-disk solution requires on the order of 1.84×10^{19} moves. At the phenomenal rate of moving one disk per second, it would still require 584.9 billion years to solve the 64-disk problem by hand.

Summary

Key Terms

overflow—A run-time error that occurs when a variable's value exceeds the limit specified by its data type.

recursion —An implicit loop structure formed by having a subprogram invoke itself.

recursive function —A function whose name appears on both the left and right sides of the function equation; a function whose definition includes the function itself.

recursive subprogram—A subprogram that invokes itself.

stack overflow—A run-time error caused by the stored stack data exceeding the amount of memory space reserved for the stack structure.

trivial case—The case where the answer is known and the recursion stops.

Key Concepts

- A recursive function in mathematics is a function whose name appears on both the left and right sides of the function equation. That is, the function's definition includes the function itself.

- Recursion forms an implicit loop structure and provides a method of solving a complex problem by solving a set of simpler subproblems.

Review Questions

1. What is recursion?
2. In mathematics, what is a recursive function?
3. Explain how recursion works using the `Factorial` function example.
4. What is a recursive subprogram and how is it used in programming? Give an example.

Problems

1. Modify your program from Problem 7 in Chapter 8 to implement the gamma function as a recursive function in Object Pascal. The recursive definition of the gamma function follows:

$$\Gamma(n) = (n-1)\Gamma(n-1)$$

$$\Gamma(1/2) = \sqrt{\pi}$$

2. Bill works at Crazy Computer Corporation and is leaving on Christmas vacation at the end of the day. He usually receives quite a bit of e-mail, so he programmed his e-mail system to reply to all incoming messages with the following message:

```
I am on vacation.  Merry Christmas and Happy New Year!
I'll talk to you after the New Year.
-- Bill
```

During lunch, Bill told Mary about his clever e-mail setup. Without telling Bill, Mary programmed her e-mail system in a similar fashion, and then she left on vacation. Bill sent a message of holiday cheer to all employees of the company, and then he left on vacation. What is the problem here?

3. Write a program that uses a recursive subprogram to print the following output in a memo box:

```
abracadabra
abracadabr
abracadab
abracada
abracad
abraca
abrac
abra
abr
ab
a
```

4. Modify the program from Problem 3 to print a similar output for any user-entered word or phrase.

5. Write a program that uses a recursive function to sum the integers from 1 to n, where n is a user-specified integer greater than or equal to 1.

Programming Projects

1. Write a program that uses a recursive subprogram to reverse the order of the characters in a user-entered word or phrase. Display the result in a memo box.

2. The Fibonacci numbers are defined by the sequence $a_{n+1} = a_n + a_{n-1}$, where $a_1 = 1$ and $a_2 = 1$. Write a program that uses a recursive subprogram to find a_n, the nth Fibonacci number, for $n > 2$.

3. *The Eight Queens Problem.* A chessboard is an 8×8 board consisting of 64 squares. A queen can move in any direction (horizontally, vertically, or diagonally) until it encounters another piece. The Eight Queens Problem is to place eight queens on a chessboard such that no queen is in the path of another. Write a program that finds all solutions to this problem.

4. *The Knight's Tour Problem.* In chess, a knight moves by jumping two squares horizontally or vertically and then one square to the left or right. The Knight's Tour Problem asks you to find a path for a single knight to visit every square on an empty $n \times n$ board. Write a program that finds a solution to this problem when the knight starts in the upper-left corner of a 5×5 board.

Object-Oriented Programming

Chapter Objectives

In this chapter you will:

- Be introduced to Object-Oriented Programming (OOP) concepts and terminology

- Gain an understanding of Delphi's OOP implementation

- Create and use classes and objects in Delphi

- Become familiar with class operators

Objects are among the most recent advances in representing data on a computer. They first appeared in the more popular high-level languages in the mid-1980s, leading to the widespread adoption of **object-oriented programming (OOP).** While we have already seen and worked with objects in Delphi, such as controls and components, OOP is a vast topic whose full details could easily fill another textbook. Rather than attempt to provide a comprehensive explanation of OOP, this chapter presents common OOP terminology and prepares the student for object-oriented thinking. The following pages describe the main concepts of OOP and discuss their implementation in Delphi.

The Object-Oriented Paradigm

Working with objects requires a slight shift in the way we think about and represent data. Although it may seem convoluted at times, this methodology is designed to make our data structures more closely resemble the real world. Consider the example of a library. A library contains bookcases, bookcases have several shelves, and each shelf contains many books. Furthermore, each book can be described by certain attributes or **properties,** such as a title, author, publisher, and so on. As each of these items is an object in the real world, this problem nicely lends itself to OOP.

In Chapter 10, we learned about records and user-defined data types. Although records could be used to hold the data for the books, shelves, bookcases, and the entire library, this arrangement would require using dynamic array structures of records within records. *As a rule of thumb, whenever a data structure requires records within records and must be dynamic in nature, it is far easier and makes more sense to use OOP.*

Concepts and Terminology

Objects are dynamically allocated structures. An object's type is called its **class;** when we create a new object type, we create a new class. Furthermore, when a new object of a specific class is created, it is **instantiated;** that is, it is a new **instance** of the object class. An object's properties are also called its *instance fields*, *member fields*, or *instance variables*. Although each object contains a unique copy of every instance field defined in its class, all objects of the same class share the same **methods.** In addition, special methods called **constructors** and **destructors** are used to create and destroy objects, respectively.

> A **class** is an object type, whereas an **instance** is an object of a specific class. For example, Crest may be an instance of the object class Toothpaste.

An object variable is actually a pointer that references the object's data in memory. Hence, more than one object variable can reference the same object. Because object variables are pointers, they can contain the value nil (that is, not reference any object). Unlike other pointer variables, however, an object variable does not require an explicit dereferencing operator to access its object. For instance,

```
edtInput.Text := 'Example';
```

assigns the string literal 'Example' to the Text property of the edtInput edit box (remember, controls are objects). We *do not* write this expression as

```
edtInput^.Text := 'Example';     {INCORRECT: ^ not required}
```

Programming Key: Tips

Windows is an event-driven operating system. For instance, the user can click the mouse on a button and cause the program to take some action. Remember that the underlying components and controls in Delphi are really objects, and OOP lies at the heart of GUI programming.

OOP encompasses three fundamental concepts: encapsulation, inheritance, and polymorphism. **Encapsulation** combines the data and behavior of an object in one package. Thus an object contains properties as well as methods that use those properties. The advantage of encapsulation is that it provides a means of **data-hiding;** that is, the way in which the data are stored remains hidden from the user of the object. The user can manipulate an object's properties only by passing messages to the object (using the object's methods). This approach stresses code reuse, as the programmer requires knowledge of only the object's properties and methods rather than its underlying data structure.

Inheritance *extends* a class and supports a *parent–child* relationship between objects. For instance, an employee database program may include an Employee class and a Manager class. The Employee class contains employee information, such as a name and Social Security number. As a manager is simply a higher-level employee, the Manager class must contain the manager's ID number as well as his or her employee information. Thus a logical relationship exists between these classes: the Manager class forms a *superset* of the Employee class. The Manager class (*child class*) inherits all of the properties and methods of the Employee class (*parent class*) but has some additional properties and methods of its own. In summary, inheritance forms an "is a" relationship between objects. In our example, a manager is an employee, but with greater responsibility and pay.

Polymorphism (literally "the ability to appear in many forms") enables a program to process objects differently depending on their class. More specifically, it is the ability to redefine the methods of a parent class for its child classes. For instance, we can define the Shape class as the parent class of Circle, Rectangle, and Triangle classes. Polymorphism enables us to define the Area method for each of these child classes. Regardless of the object's shape, applying the `Area` method will always return the correct result. In this way, polymorphism resembles the overloading of operators, such as the plus sign (+) performing addition for numbers but concatenation for strings in Object Pascal.

Delphi's OOP Implementation

Delphi's object implementation varies slightly from the terminology described previously. As before, a method is a procedure or function associated with a class. In Delphi, most methods operate on objects, but some methods (known as **class methods**) operate on class types. In the last section, we used the terms *field* and *property* synonymously. Delphi, however, does draw a distinction between the two. It defines a **field** as a variable that is part of an object, whereas a property is an interface to the data associated with an object, usually stored in a field. Properties stipulate **access specifiers** that determine how their data are read and modified. From parts of a program outside of the object's methods, a property appears like a field in most respects.

> In Delphi, a **field** is a variable contained in an object, and a **property** is an interface to the data stored in the object's field. A **method** is a procedure or function that is associated with a class and typically alters the fields of an object.

Working with Objects

Let's reinforce these concepts by examining an example. The class definition of `VehicleClass` appears below:

```
type
  VehicleClass = class(TObject)
  private
    Liters: Real;     {Size of engine (in liters)}
    Vx:      Integer; {Number of cylinders (4, 6, or 8)}
    Horses: Integer; {Engine horsepower}
    RPMs:    Integer; {Engine RPM}
    function GetEngineSize: Real;
    procedure SetEngineSize(ltrs: Real);
    function GetCylinders: Integer;
    procedure SetCylinders(cyl: Integer);
    function GetHP: Integer;
    procedure SetHP(hpwr: Integer);
    function GetRPM: Integer;
    procedure SetRPM(revPerMin: Integer);
```

```
public
  function Describe: String;
  procedure SetAll(eng: Real; cyl, hpwr, rev: Integer);
  property EngineSize: Real read GetEngineSize
                            write SetEngineSize;
  property Cylinders: Integer read GetCylinders
                            write SetCylinders;
  property HP: Integer read GetHP write SetHP;
  property RPM: Integer read GetRPM write SetRPM;
end;
```

From this code, we see the general form of a Delphi class definition:

```
type
  ClassName = class(ParentClass)
  private
    {Private fields, methods, and properties}
  public
    {Public fields, methods, and properties}
  end;
```

ClassName is defined as a child class of *ParentClass*. If no *ParentClass* is specified (if you omit its name and the parentheses), then *ParentClass* is `TObject` by default. `TObject` is the base class and ultimate ancestor of all objects and components in Delphi.

The definition of `VehicleClass` contains both private fields and private methods. The fields include `Liters`, `Vx`, `Horses`, and `RPMs`. When an object of type `VehicleClass` is instantiated, it contains its own copy of each of these fields. Typically, the private methods include both **getter methods** and **setter methods** for the class. A getter method retrieves or *gets* a field's value, whereas a setter method modifies or *sets* a field's value. Each getter and setter method accesses only a single field—not multiple fields— and each field has one getter method and one setter method. A getter method must be a function because it returns a value; a setter method, in contrast, is a procedure because it returns no value. As these fields and methods are private, they can be accessed or invoked only through the code contained in the object's methods.

Conversely, public fields, methods, and properties can be accessed or invoked by any part of the program. Most properties are public because we typically desire code from other parts of the program to access them. `VehicleClass` contains two public methods (`Describe` and `SetAll`) and four public properties (`EngineSize`, `Cylinders`, `HP`, and `RPM`). In `VehicleClass`, we see the format of a property declaration. The general syntax follows:

```
property PropertyName: DataType [read GetterMethod]
                                [write SetterMethod];
```

Every property declaration must have at least one read or write specifier.

Let's look at some methods associated with VehicleClass. The getter and setter methods for the EngineSize property follow:

```
function VehicleClass.GetEngineSize: Real;

begin
  GetEngineSize := Liters;
end;

procedure VehicleClass.SetEngineSize(ltrs: Real);

begin
  Liters := ltrs;
end;
```

All objects of type VehicleClass use these methods to get and set the EngineSize property, respectively. That is, each instance of VehicleClass uses these same methods; the methods are not unique for each instance, as in the case of the instance fields.

From this code, we obtain the general forms of getter and setter methods:

```
function ClassName.GetterMethod: DataType;
{Note: DataType is the data type of Field}

begin
  GetterMethod := Field;
end;

procedure ClassName.SetterMethod(value: DataType);
{Note: DataType is the data type of Field}

begin
  Field := value;
end;
```

Data are actually stored in *Field*, an instance field of the object. A property simply provides an interface between an object's data and other code—it is Object Pascal's instrument to ensure data-hiding. *DataType* must be the same for the field, property, getter method, and setter method.

A getter method is invoked when Object Pascal encounters a statement of the form

```
variableName := ObjectVariable.PropertyName;
```

Additionally, *ObjectVariable.PropertyName* invokes the getter method when it appears in a statement other than an assignment. A setter method is invoked by a statement of the form

```
ObjectVariable.PropertyName := expression;
```

Both *variableName* and *expression* must match the data type of *PropertyName*.

The following code segment invokes the setter and getter methods of the EngineSize property for VehicleClass. Additionally, this code shows how to create (or instantiate) and destroy object instances.

```
var
  Vehicle: VehicleClass;   {Declare an object variable of
                            type VehicleClass}
  size:    String;

begin
  Vehicle := VehicleClass.Create;    {Instantiate the
                                      VehicleClass object}
  Vehicle.EngineSize := 2.3;         {Invoke setter method}
  Str(Vehicle.EngineSize:3:1, size); {Invoke getter method}

  memOutput.Lines.Add('Engine size is ' + size +
                      ' liters.');

  Vehicle.Free;                      {Destroy the object
                                      instance}
end;
```

Upon execution, this code displays the following text in a memo box:

```
Engine size is 2.3 liters.
```

As illustrated by the preceding code segment, you instantiate an object of a specific class by using a statement of the form

```
ObjectVariable := ClassName.Create;
```

To destroy an object instance, you use

```
ObjectVariable.Free;
```

These statements invoke the constructor and destructor methods of the object class, respectively. We will write our own constructors and destructors later in this chapter.

> ### Programming Key: Tips
>
> Always invoke the `Free` method rather than the `Destroy` method to destroy an object instance. `Free` automatically calls `Destroy` if the object reference is not `nil`. For a `nil` object, calling `Destroy` results in a run-time error, whereas calling `Free` does not.

Recall that object variables are pointers and memory is dynamically allocated for the object's data. With this idea in mind, can you find the problem with the code segment below?

```
{What is the problem with this code?}
var
  Vehicle: VehicleClass;
  size:    String;
  count:   Real;

begin
  count := 2.0;
  repeat
    Vehicle := VehicleClass.Create;
    Vehicle.EngineSize := count;
    Str(Vehicle.EngineSize:3:1, size);
    memOutput.Lines.Add('Engine size is ' + size +
                        ' liters.');
    count := count + 0.1;
  until count >= 5.0;
  Vehicle.Free;
end;
```

Upon careful examination, we find that this code has a memory leak. The object instantiation appears inside the `repeat` loop, creating a new instance of a `Vehicle-Class` object during each loop iteration. The `Vehicle` variable references the new object instance, leaving the old instance as an **orphaned object,** an object that does not have a reference variable. Thus we cannot reference the older instances, and the computer cannot reclaim the memory space. Although the memory leak is not severe in this example, it can prove catastrophic in large object-oriented programs. To correct this code, we simply move the object instantiation above the repeat statement. There is no reason for this code to have more than one instance of Vehicle-Class:

```
{Corrected code}
var
  Vehicle: VehicleClass;
  size:    String;
  count:   Real;

begin
  Vehicle := VehicleClass.Create;
  count := 2.0;
  repeat
    Vehicle.EngineSize := count;
    Str(Vehicle.EngineSize:3:1, size);
    memOutput.Lines.Add('Engine size is ' + size +
                        ' liters.');
    count := count + 0.1;
  until count >= 5.0;
  Vehicle.Free;
end;         •
```

Inheritance and Polymorphism

Let's extend VehicleClass by creating another class type. As a motorcycle is a type of vehicle, it is natural to define MotorcycleClass as a child class of VehicleClass. The definition of MotorcycleClass follows:

```
type
  MotorcycleClass = class(VehicleClass)
  private      ,
    TankSize: Real;    {Fuel tank capacity (gallons)}
    ExtColor: String; {Exterior paint color}
    function GetCapacity: Real;
    procedure SetCapacity(tank: Real);
    function GetExtColor: String;
    procedure SetExtColor(color: String);
  public
    function Describe: String;
```

```
      procedure SetAll(eng: Real; cyl, hpwr, rev: Integer;
                       tank: Real; color: String); overload;
      property FuelTank: Real read GetCapacity
                              write SetCapacity;
      property Exterior: String read GetExtColor
                                write SetExtColor;
   end;
```

MotorcycleClass has some unique properties and methods, and it also inherits all of the properties and methods of VehicleClass. Notice that the two public methods of MotorcycleClass have the same names as those of VehicleClass. Here, the Describe method of MotorcycleClass hides (or **shadows**) the Describe method of VehicleClass. In other words, when Describe is invoked on an object of type MotorcycleClass, MotorcycleClass's definition of Describe is actually executed. The Describe methods of both classes appear below:

```
{ -----------------------------------------------------------
Method Name: VehicleClass.Describe
Purpose:     Returns a string description of a
             VehicleClass object
-----------------------------------------------------------}
function VehicleClass.Describe: String;

begin
  Str(Liters:3:1, Result);
  Describe := Result + ' liters, V' +
              IntToStr(Vx) + ', ' +
              IntToStr(Horses) + ' HP, ' +
              IntToStr(RPMs) + ' RPM';
end;
{ -----------------------------------------------------------
Method Name: MotorcycleClass.Describe
Purpose:     Returns a string description of a
             MotorcycleClass object
-----------------------------------------------------------}
function MotorcycleClass.Describe: String;

var
  tank: String;

begin
  Result := inherited Describe;
  Str(TankSize:4:1, tank);
  Result := Result + ', ' + tank + ' gallon fuel tank, ' +
            'Exterior color is ' + Trim(ExtColor);
end;
```

MotorcycleClass's Describe method invokes VehicleClass's Describe method by using the **inherited** keyword in the first line of code: Result := inherited Describe;. If inherited is followed by a method name, it performs a normal method invocation, except that the search for the method begins with the immediate ancestor of the enclosing method's class. If inherited is not followed by a method name, it refers to the inherited method with the same name as the enclosing method. In this case, inherited can appear with or without parameters. If no parameters are specified, the same parameters used to call the enclosing method are passed to the inherited method. Thus the reserved word inherited plays an important role in implementing Delphi's polymorphic behavior.

To declare the SetAll method of MotorcycleClass, we use the **overload** directive. In this case, the redeclared method has a different **parameter signature** from its ancestor, so it overloads the inherited method without hiding it. Thus overload is another Delphi reserved word that implements polymorphism. For an overloaded method, calling the method in a descendant class invokes whichever implementation matches the parameter signature (the parameters in the method call). For instance, consider the method calls in the following code:

```
var
   Cycle: MotorcycleClass;

begin
   Cycle := MotorcycleClass.Create;

   {Invoke SetAll of MotorcycleClass}
   Cycle.SetAll(0.25, 4, 60, 2000, 5, 'Black');
   memOutput.Lines.Add('Motorcycle: ' + Cycle.Describe);

   {Invoke SetAll of VehicleClass}
   Cycle.SetAll(0.3, 4, 75, 2500);
   memOutput.Lines.Add('Motorcycle: ' + Cycle.Describe);

   Cycle.Free;
end;
```

The output of this code is as follows:

```
Motorcycle: 0.3 liters, V4, 60 HP, 2000 RPM,  5.0 gallon
fuel tank, Exterior color is Black
Motorcycle: 0.3 liters, V4, 75 HP, 2500 RPM,  5.0 gallon
fuel tank, Exterior color is Black
```

Here Delphi rounds the 0.25 liter to 0.3 liter because we specified only one digit to the right of the decimal point in the Describe method. Note also that methods that correspond to property read or write specifiers cannot be overloaded.

The SetAll methods of both classes appear next. Notice that Motorcycle-Class's SetAll method invokes its inherited method of the same name but with the correct parameter signature.

```
{ ------------------------------------------------------------
Method Name: VehicleClass.SetAll
Purpose:      Sets all properties of a VehicleClass object
----------------------------------------------------------}
procedure VehicleClass.SetAll(eng: Real; cyl, hpwr, rev:
                                  Integer);

begin
  Liters := eng;
  Vx := cyl;
  Horses := hpwr;
  RPMs := rev;
end;
{ ------------------------------------------------------------
Method Name: MotorcycleClass.SetAll
Purpose:      Sets all properties of a MotorcycleClass
              object
----------------------------------------------------------}
procedure MotorcycleClass.SetAll(eng: Real; cyl, hpwr, rev:
                                  Integer; tank: Real;
                                  color: String);

begin
  inherited SetAll(eng, cyl, hpwr, rev);
  TankSize := tank;
  ExtColor := color;
end;
```

Constructors and Destructors

In Object Pascal, we can define our own class constructor and destructor methods. We will examine this capability by introducing another class. Automobile-Class is defined as an extension of MotorcycleClass:

```
type
  AutomobileClass = class(MotorcycleClass)
  private
    PassCapacity: Integer; {Passenger capacity}
    IntColor:     String;  {Interior color}
    function GetNumPassengers: Integer;
    procedure SetNumPassengers(number: Integer);
    function GetIntColor: String;
    procedure SetIntColor(color: String);
```

```
public
  function Describe: String;
  procedure SetAll(eng: Real; cyl, hpwr, rev: Integer;
                   tank: Real; xColor: String; pass:
                   Integer; iColor: String); overload;
  procedure Initialize;
  procedure Free;
  constructor Create;
  destructor Destroy; reintroduce;
  property Passengers: Integer read GetNumPassengers
                               write SetNumPassengers;
  property Interior: String read GetIntColor
                            write SetIntColor;
end;
```

AutomobileClass is a child class of MotorcycleClass, which is itself a child class of VehicleClass. AutomobileClass therefore inherits all of the properties and methods of both MotorcycleClass and VehicleClass. The Describe method hides the Describe method of the parent class, and the SetAll method is overloaded. AutomobileClass also adds two new properties: Passengers and Interior.

Aside from the forementioned properties and methods, AutomobileClass has constructor and destructor methods. Although its use is not required, the **reintroduce** directive following the destructor declaration suppresses compiler warnings about previously declared destructors in ancestor classes. The technical aspects involved with this directive are beyond the scope of our discussion. The Delphi documentation provides more information concerning this and other method directives.

The constructor, destructor, and associated methods of AutomobileClass follow:

```
{ -------------------------------------------------------
Method Name: AutomobileClass.SetAll
Purpose:     Sets all properties of an AutomobileClass
             object
----------------------------------------------------------}
procedure AutomobileClass.SetAll(eng: Real; cyl, hpwr,
                                 rev: Integer;
                                 tank: Real;
                                 xColor: String;
                                 pass: Integer;
                                 iColor: String);

begin
  inherited SetAll(eng, cyl, hpwr, rev, tank, xColor);
```

```
    PassCapacity := pass;
    IntColor := iColor;
  end;

{ ------------------------------------------------------------
Method Name: AutomobileClass.Initialize
Purpose:       Initialize the AutomobileClass object by
               setting all properties to default values
-----------------------------------------------------------}
procedure AutomobileClass.Initialize;

begin
  SetAll(2.2, 4, 135, 5200, 18.5, 'Diamond White Pearl',
         4, 'Ivory');
end;

{ ------------------------------------------------------------
Constructor Name: AutomobileClass.Create
Purpose:          Create and initialize a new
                  AutomobileClass object
-----------------------------------------------------------}
constructor AutomobileClass.Create;

begin
  inherited Create;
  Initialize;
end;

{ ------------------------------------------------------------
Destructor Name: AutomobileClass.Destroy
Purpose:          Destroy the object instance of
                  AutomobileClass
-----------------------------------------------------------}
destructor AutomobileClass.Destroy;

begin
  inherited Destroy;
end;

{ ------------------------------------------------------------
Procedure Name: AutomobileClass.Free
Purpose:         Destroy the object instance of
                 AutomobileClass. If it is nil,
                 displays an error message.
-----------------------------------------------------------}
procedure AutomobileClass.Free;
```

```
begin
  if (Self <> nil) then begin
    Destroy;
  end
  else begin
    MessageDlg('No instance of AutomobileClass to free.',
               mtWarning, [mbOK], 0);
  end;
end;
```

Constructor and destructor methods are syntactically the same as normal methods, except that they are delineated by the **constructor** and **destructor** keywords, respectively. In general, these methods follow the syntax

```
constructor ClassName.Create;

begin
   inherited Create;
   [initialization statements;]
end;

destructor ClassName.Destroy;

begin
   [terminal statements;]
   inherited Destroy;
end;
```

Object Pascal automatically initializes all fields of an object upon instantiation: Numerical fields are set to zero, string fields are assigned the null string, and object fields are assigned `nil`. You may override these default values by defining your own constructor, as we did in the previous code. The `AutomobileClass` constructor calls the `Initialize` method to set the default values for an object instance.

Remember to use the `Free` method to destroy an object instance; Object Pascal's `Destroy` method cannot handle `nil` objects. We will redefine the `Free` method for `AutomobileClass` in the above code. If the object instance is `nil`, the program will display an error message. This method also uses the **Self** variable; `Self` is an inherent variable of every method that refers to the object instance that invoked the method.

Example Program

The complete program for the object-oriented vehicle example appears below. Figure 15.1 shows a sample execution of this code.

```
{ ------------------------------------------------------------
Unit Name: VehicleEx
Purpose:    A test driver for VehicleUnit
------------------------------------------------------------}
unit VehicleEx;

interface

uses
  Windows, Messages, SysUtils, Classes, Graphics, Controls,
  Forms, Dialogs, StdCtrls, VehicleUnit;

type
  TfrmOOPVehicleEx = class(TForm)
    btnTest: TButton;
    memOutput: TMemo;
    procedure TestVehicleUnit(Sender: TObject);
  private
    { Private declarations }
  public
    { Public declarations }
  end;

var
  frmOOPVehicleEx: TfrmOOPVehicleEx;

implementation

{$R *.DFM}

procedure TfrmOOPVehicleEx.TestVehicleUnit(Sender: TObject);
```

```
var
  Vehicle: VehicleClass;
  Cycle:   MotorcycleClass;
  Auto:    AutomobileClass;
begin
  Vehicle := VehicleClass.Create;
  Cycle := MotorcycleClass.Create;
  Auto := AutomobileClass.Create;

  memOutput.Clear;
  memOutput.Lines.Add('Default automobile: ' +
                      Auto.Describe);
  memOutput.Lines.Add('');

  Vehicle.SetAll(2.3, 4, 150, 5700);
  Cycle.SetAll(0.25, 4, 60, 2000, 5, 'Black');
  Auto.SetAll(2.5, 6, 163, 6000, 17.2, 'Brilliant Silver', 4,
              'Beige');
  memOutput.Lines.Add('Vehicle: ' + Vehicle.Describe);
  memOutput.Lines.Add('Motorcycle: ' + Cycle.Describe);
  memOutput.Lines.Add('Automobile: ' + Auto.Describe);
  memOutput.Lines.Add('');

  memOutput.Lines.Add('Let''s paint the car!');
  Auto.Exterior := 'Ruby Red';
  memOutput.Lines.Add('New car: ' + Auto.Describe);

  Vehicle.Free;
  Cycle.Free;
  Auto.Free;
end;

end.

{ -------------------------------------------------------
Unit Name: VehicleUnit
Purpose:   An object-oriented implementation of vehicles in
           Object Pascal.  This unit demonstrates the
           concepts of encapsulation, inheritance, and
           polymorphism.
           ------------------------------------------------------}
unit VehicleUnit;

interface

uses Dialogs, SysUtils;

type
  VehicleClass = class(TObject)
```

```
    private
      Liters: Real;      {Size of engine (in liters)}
      Vx:       Integer; {Number of cylinders (4, 6, or 8)}
      Horses: Integer; {Engine horsepower}
      RPMs:     Integer; {Engine RPM}
      function GetEngineSize: Real;
      procedure SetEngineSize(ltrs: Real);
      function GetCylinders: Integer;
      procedure SetCylinders(cyl: Integer);
      function GetHP: Integer;
      procedure SetHP(hpwr: Integer);
      function GetRPM: Integer;
      procedure SetRPM(revPerMin: Integer);
    public
      function Describe: String;
      procedure SetAll(eng: Real; cyl, hpwr, rev: Integer);
      property EngineSize: Real read GetEngineSize
                                 write SetEngineSize;
      property Cylinders: Integer read GetCylinders
                                   write SetCylinders;
      property HP: Integer read GetHP write SetHP;
      property RPM: Integer read GetRPM write SetRPM;
    end;

  MotorcycleClass = class(VehicleClass)
  private
    TankSize: Real;    {Fuel tank capacity (gallons)}
    ExtColor: String; {Exterior paint color}
    function GetCapacity: Real;
    procedure SetCapacity(tank: Real);
    function GetExtColor: String;
    procedure SetExtColor(color: String);
  public
    function Describe: String;
    procedure SetAll(eng: Real; cyl, hpwr, rev: Integer;
                     tank: Real; color: String); overload;
    property FuelTank: Real read GetCapacity
                             write SetCapacity;
    property Exterior: String read GetExtColor
                               write SetExtColor;
  end;

  AutomobileClass = class(MotorcycleClass)
  private
    PassCapacity: Integer; {Passenger capacity}
    IntColor:     String;  {Interior color}
```

```
      function GetNumPassengers: Integer;
      procedure SetNumPassengers(number: Integer);
      function GetIntColor: String;
      procedure SetIntColor(color: String);
    public
      function Describe: String;
      procedure SetAll(eng: Real; cyl, hpwr, rev: Integer;
                       tank: Real; xColor: String; pass:
                       Integer; iColor: String); overload;
      procedure Initialize;
      procedure Free;
      constructor Create;
      destructor Destroy; reintroduce;
      property Passengers: Integer read GetNumPassengers
                                   write SetNumPassengers;
      property Interior: String read GetIntColor
                                 write SetIntColor;
    end;

implementation

{ ----------------------------------------------------------
Getter and setter methods for VehicleClass
----------------------------------------------------------}
function VehicleClass.GetEngineSize: Real;

begin
  GetEngineSize := Liters;
end;

procedure VehicleClass.SetEngineSize(ltrs: Real);

begin
  Liters := ltrs;
end;

function VehicleClass.GetCylinders: Integer;

begin
  GetCylinders := Vx;
end;

procedure VehicleClass.SetCylinders(cyl: Integer);

begin
  Vx := cyl;
end;

function VehicleClass.GetHP: Integer;
```

```
begin
  GetHP := Horses;
end;

procedure VehicleClass.SetHP(hpwr: Integer);

begin
  Horses := hpwr;
end;

function VehicleClass.GetRPM: Integer;

begin
  GetRPM := RPMs;
end;

procedure VehicleClass.SetRPM(revPerMin: Integer);

begin
  RPMs := revPerMin;
end;

{ -----------------------------------------------------------
Method Name: VehicleClass.Describe
Purpose:     Returns a string description of a VehicleClass
             object
------------------------------------------------------------}
function VehicleClass.Describe: String;

begin
  Str(Liters:3:1, Result);
  Describe := Result + ' liters, V' +
              IntToStr(Vx) + ', ' +
              IntToStr(Horses) + ' HP, ' +
              IntToStr(RPMs) + ' RPM';
end;

{ -----------------------------------------------------------
Method Name: VehicleClass.SetAll
Purpose:     Sets all properties of a VehicleClass object
------------------------------------------------------------}
procedure VehicleClass.SetAll(eng: Real; cyl, hpwr, rev:
                                Integer);

begin
  Liters := eng;
  Vx := cyl;
  Horses := hpwr;
  RPMs := rev;
end;
```

```
{ -----------------------------------------------------------
Getter and setter methods for MotorcycleClass
----------------------------------------------------------}
function MotorcycleClass.GetCapacity: Real;

begin
  GetCapacity := TankSize;
end;

procedure MotorcycleClass.SetCapacity(tank: Real);

begin
  TankSize := tank;
end;

function MotorcycleClass.GetExtColor: String;

begin
  GetExtColor := ExtColor;
end;

procedure MotorcycleClass.SetExtColor(color: String);

begin
  ExtColor := color;
end;

{ -----------------------------------------------------------
Method Name: MotorcycleClass.Describe
Purpose:     Returns a string description of a
             MotorcycleClass object
----------------------------------------------------------}
function MotorcycleClass.Describe: String;

var
  tank: String;

begin
  Result := inherited Describe;
  Str(TankSize:4:1, tank);
  Result := Result + ', ' + tank + ' gallon fuel tank, ' +
            'Exterior color is ' + Trim(ExtColor);
end;

{ -----------------------------------------------------------
Method Name: MotorcycleClass.SetAll
Purpose:     Sets all properties of a MotorcycleClass object
----------------------------------------------------------}
procedure MotorcycleClass.SetAll(eng: Real; cyl, hpwr, rev:
                                      Integer; tank: Real;
```

```
                                              color: String);
begin
  inherited SetAll(eng, cyl, hpwr, rev);
  TankSize := tank;
  ExtColor := color;
end;

{ ------------------------------------------------------------
Getter and setter methods for AutomobileClass
------------------------------------------------------------}
function AutomobileClass.GetNumPassengers: Integer;

begin
  GetNumPassengers := PassCapacity;
end;

procedure AutomobileClass.SetNumPassengers(number: Integer);

begin
  PassCapacity := number;
end;

function AutomobileClass.GetIntColor: String;

begin
  GetIntColor := IntColor;
end;

procedure AutomobileClass.SetIntColor(color: String);

begin
  IntColor := color;
end;

{ ------------------------------------------------------------
Method Name: AutomobileClass.Describe
Purpose:     Returns a string description of an
             AutomobileClass object
------------------------------------------------------------}
function AutomobileClass.Describe: String;

begin
  Result := inherited Describe;
  Result := Result + ', Interior color is ' +
            Trim(IntColor) + ', ' +
            IntToStr(PassCapacity) + ' passengers';
end;
```

```
{ -------------------------------------------------------------
Method Name: AutomobileClass.SetAll
Purpose:     Sets all properties of an AutomobileClass
             object
-----------------------------------------------------------}
procedure AutomobileClass.SetAll(eng: Real; cyl, hpwr,
                                 rev: Integer; tank: Real;
                                 xColor: String;
                                 pass: Integer;
                                 iColor: String);

begin
  inherited SetAll(eng, cyl, hpwr, rev, tank, xColor);
  PassCapacity := pass;
  IntColor := iColor;
end;

{ -------------------------------------------------------------
Method Name: AutomobileClass.Initialize
Purpose:     Initializes the AutomobileClass object by
             setting all properties to default values
-----------------------------------------------------------}
procedure AutomobileClass.Initialize;

begin
  SetAll(2.2, 4, 135, 5200, 18.5, 'Diamond White Pearl',
         4, 'Ivory');
end;

{ -------------------------------------------------------------
Constructor Name: AutomobileClass.Create
Purpose:          Creates and initializes a new
                  AutomobileClass object
-----------------------------------------------------------}
constructor AutomobileClass.Create;

begin
  inherited Create;
  Initialize;
end;

{ -------------------------------------------------------------
Destructor Name: AutomobileClass.Destroy
Purpose:         Destroys the object instance of
                 AutomobileClass
-----------------------------------------------------------}
```

```
destructor AutomobileClass.Destroy;

begin
  inherited Destroy;
end;

{ ------------------------------------------------------------
Procedure Name: AutomobileClass.Free
Purpose:        Destroys the object instance of
                AutomobileClass. If it is nil,
                displays an error message.
------------------------------------------------------------}
procedure AutomobileClass.Free;

begin
  if (Self <> nil) then begin
    Destroy;
  end
  else begin
    MessageDlg('No instance of AutomobileClass to free.',
               mtWarning, [mbOK], 0);
  end;
end;

end.
```

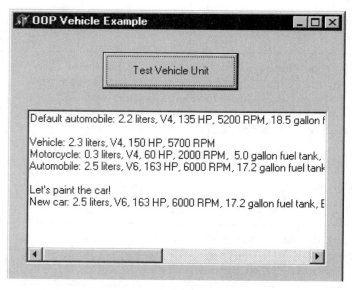

FIGURE 15.1 Object-Oriented Vehicle Example

Class Operators

Object Pascal offers two class operators: **is** and **as.** The is operator performs dynamic type checking and is used to verify the actual run-time class of an object instance. The syntax for its use follows:

> *ObjectInstance* is *ClassName*

This expression returns True if *ObjectInstance* is an instance of the class *ClassName* or one of its descendants; otherwise, it returns False. If *Object-Instance* is nil, then the expression evaluates to False. If the declared class of *ObjectInstance* is unrelated to *ClassName* (that is, the classes are distinct and one is not an ancestor of the other), a compile-time error occurs.

The **as** operator performs a checked typecast. The syntax

> *ObjectInstance* as *ClassName*

returns a reference to the same object as *ObjectInstance*, but with the type given by *ClassName*. At run time, *ObjectInstance* must be an instance of *ClassName* or one of its descendants or must be nil; otherwise, the computer will raise an exception. As with the is operator, if the declared class of *ObjectInstance* is unrelated to *ClassName*, a compile-time error occurs.

The following example illustrates the use of these operators. Figure 15.2 shows the form after executing this code.

```
procedure TfrmClassOperators.TestOps(Sender: TObject);
begin
  if (Sender is TObject) then begin
    memOutput.Lines.Add('Sender is TObject');
  end;

  if (Sender is TButton) then begin
    memOutput.Lines.Add('Sender is TButton');
  end;

  if (Sender is TEdit) then begin
    memOutput.Lines.Add('Sender is TEdit');
  end;

  (Sender as TButton).Enabled := False;
end;
```

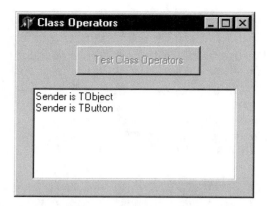

FIGURE 15.2   Class Operator Example

Summary

Key Terms

access specifier—A specifier that determines how a property's data are read or modified.

class—An object's type.

class method—A method that operates on a class type.

constructor—A method that creates a new object instance of a specified class.

data-hiding—The way in which the data are stored remains hidden from the user of the object.

destructor—A method that destroys the object instance of a specified class.

encapsulation—The grouping of the data (properties) and behavior (methods) of an object into one package.

field—A variable that is part of an object.

getter method—A method that retrieves or gets a field's value.

inheritance—The extension of an object class by allowing a parent–child relationship between objects.

instance—An object of a specific class.

instantiate—To create a new object of a specific class; to create a new object instance.

method—A procedure or function that is associated with a class. Typically, a method alters the properties of an object.

object—A structure that groups data and behavior into one entity.

object-oriented programming (OOP)—Computer programming with objects and class types.

orphaned object—An object that does not have a reference variable.

parameter signature—The parameters in the method invocation.

polymorphism—The ability to redefine the methods of a parent class for its child classes. Literally, "the ability to appear in many forms."

property—A value that is associated with an object. In Delphi, an interface to the data associated with an object, usually stored in a field.

setter method—A method that modifies or sets a field's value.

shadow—To hide the parent class's method of the same name.

Keywords

Access Specifiers

read   write

Class Operators

as   is

Directives

inherited   overload
reintroduce

Methods

Create   Free
Destroy

Objects

Self

Statements

class   destructor
constructor   property

Key Concepts

- Whenever a data structure must be dynamic and requires records within records, you should use object-oriented programming (OOP).
- OOP includes three main concepts: encapsulation, inheritance, and polymorphism. Encapsulation combines the data and behavior of an object into a single package. Inheritance extends an object class, allowing a parent–child relationship between objects. Polymorphism allows you to redefine a method for a child class.
- An object variable is a pointer to the memory location of the object data. Unlike other pointers, however, it does not require an explicit dereferencing operator to access its object.

- In Delphi, a field is a variable that is part of an object, whereas a property is an interface to the data associated with an object, usually stored in a field. A method is a procedure or function associated with a class.

- A class is an object's data type. To define a class, use the syntax

```
type
  ClassName = class(ParentClass)
  private
    {Private fields, methods, and properties}
  public
    {Public fields, methods, and properties}
  end;
```

- The `TObject` class is the base class in Delphi; all controls, components, and objects are children of the `TObject` class. If no parent class is specified, the parent class is `TObject` by default.

- To declare a property, use the form

```
property PropertyName: DataType [read GetterMethod]
                                [write SetterMethod];
```

Every property declaration must have at least one read or write access specifier.

- A getter method retrieves or gets a field's value, and a setter method modifies or sets a field's value. The general forms of getter and setter methods follow:

```
function ClassName.GetterMethod: DataType;
{Note: DataType is the data type of Field}

begin
  GetterMethod := Field;
end;

procedure ClassName.SetterMethod(value: DataType);
{Note: DataType is the data type of Field}

begin
  Field := value;
end;
```

A getter method is invoked when Object Pascal encounters `ObjectVariable.PropertyName` on the right side of an assignment statement or in a statement other than an assignment. A setter method is invoked when `ObjectVariable.PropertyName` appears on the left side of an assignment statement.

- You use special methods called constructors and destructors to create and destroy objects, respectively. Constructors and destructors are syntactically the same as normal methods, except that they are delineated by the `constructor` and `destructor` keywords, respectively. In general, these methods follow the syntax

```
constructor ClassName.Create;

begin
  inherited Create;
  [initialization statements;]
end;

destructor ClassName.Destroy;

begin
  [terminal statements;]
  inherited Destroy;
end;
```

Object Pascal automatically initializes all fields of an object upon instantiation: Numerical fields are set to zero, string fields are assigned the null string, and object fields are assigned `nil`. You can override these default values by defining your own constructor.

- Self is an inherent variable of every method that refers to the object instance that invoked the method. It is useful for passing information about the currently executing instance of a class to another subprogram or for invoking another method within a class.

- Object variables are dynamic variables. To declare a new object variable, use the syntax

```
var
  ObjectVariable: ClassName;
```

Before an object variable can be used, it must be instantiated:

```
ObjectVariable := ClassName.Create;
```

- To destroy an object instance, use

```
ObjectVariable.Free;
```

You should invoke the `Free` method rather than `Destroy`, as `Destroy` generates an error if the object is `nil`.

- An orphaned object does not have an associated reference variable and can lead to a memory leak. Remember that objects are dynamic structures. Because they are created by the programmer, they must also be destroyed to reclaim their memory space.

- The `inherited` keyword allows a class's method to invoke a method of its ancestor class. It plays an important role in implementing Delphi's polymorphic behavior.

- The `overload` directive implements polymorphism in Delphi. For an overloaded method, calling the method in a descendant class invokes whichever implementation matches the parameter signature.
- The `reintroduce` directive suppresses compiler warnings concerning previously declared methods of the same name in ancestor classes.
- The `is` operator performs dynamic type checking and is used to verify the actual run-time class of an object instance:

  ObjectInstance is *ClassName*

- The `as` operator performs a checked typecast:

  ObjectInstance as *ClassName*

Review Questions

1. What is an object? How is it different from other computer data structures?
2. What is object-oriented programming (OOP) and when is it useful? Give an example.
3. What is the difference between a class and an object?
4. How does an object differ from a pointer?
5. Define the terms *encapsulation, inheritance,* and *polymorphism* as they relate to OOP. How are these concepts implemented in Object Pascal?
6. What is the purpose of data-hiding? Which OOP concept facilitates it?
7. Write the code necessary to create a new object instance named `MyObject` of the class `MyClass`. Assume that `MyClass` is already defined.
8. Write the code to destroy the object instance named `MyObject` of the class `MyClass`.
9. What are the differences between the `Destroy` and `Free` methods?
10. What are orphaned objects? What problems can they cause?
11. What is special about the variable `Self`?
12. Describe the operation of the `is` and `as` operators.

Problems

1. Write a code unit that defines `DentalClass` as the parent class of `ToothpasteClass`. Properties should include a category name, product ID, product name, quantity on hand, and stock reorder point. Write a simple test driver to test these class definitions.

2. Modify your code from Problem 1 to include `ProductClass` as the parent class of `DentalClass` and `MedicineClass`. Additionally, `ColdMedClass` should be a child class of `MedicineClass`. As in Problem 1, properties include a category name, product ID, product name, quantity on hand, and stock reorder point. Write a test driver program to test the class definitions.

3. Implement a library book class and associated classes, as described in the first example in this chapter, by using objects. Check the class definitions using a test driver program.

Programming Projects

1. Create a `Vector` class that implements three-dimensional vectors. This class should contain methods that perform vector operations, including addition, subtraction, negation, dot product, and cross product. Write a test driver program to aid in debugging this class.

2. Create a simple `Statistics` class. Class properties should include the sum of the observations, the sum of the squared observations, and the number of observations. Include methods to add an observation, compute the mean, compute the variance, and compute the standard deviation.

Additional Delphi Components

Chapter Objectives

In this chapter you will:

- Be introduced to additional Delphi components
- Learn how to add custom frames to the Component Palette
- Learn how to create custom menus and pop-up menus

Chapter 2 introduced the elementary Delphi components required to design a simple GUI and create a program. Although forms, labels, edit boxes, memo boxes, and buttons are sufficient controls for most programs, much of the power and appeal of Delphi stems from the ease with which a programmer can design complex user interfaces by selecting specific components and setting the appropriate properties.

This chapter introduces several additional Delphi components found on the Component Palette, and it is organized according to the Palette pages (or tabs). Simple applications are used to demonstrate these components, and the text explains some of their properties and methods. This chapter is by no means a comprehensive reference; the Delphi documentation and online help provide more detail concerning these controls, and you should consult them as necessary.

Standard Page

☒ CheckBox

A single check box is a toggle that presents the user with two choices. A check mark appears in the box when it is selected, and the box is empty when it is not selected. The user may use either the mouse or the space bar to toggle the state of the check box. When used in groups, check box controls allow the user to select *one or more* items from a list of several alternatives.

The `Caption` property contains the text that appears to the right of the check box. The `Checked` property is a Boolean value that indicates whether the box is checked by default. Setting the `AllowGrayed` property to True means that the check box can have three possible states: checked, unchecked, and grayed. Finally, the `State` property indicates whether the check box is checked (`cbChecked`), unchecked (`cbUnchecked`), or grayed (`cbGrayed`). An example unit that uses check boxes follows, and a sample execution of this code appears in Figure 16.1. Note that the `Name` property for a check box control is prefaced with `chk` in the same manner used for the elementary controls in Chapter 2.

```
unit CheckBoxEx;

interface

uses
  Windows, Messages, SysUtils, Classes, Graphics, Controls,
  Forms, Dialogs, StdCtrls;

type
  TfrmCheckBox = class(TForm)
    btnEvaluate: TButton;
    memOutput: TMemo;
    lblQuestion: TLabel;
```

Component	Property	Setting
Form	Name	frmCheckBox
	Caption	Credit Cards
Button	Name	btnEvaluate
	Caption	Evaluate Answer
Memo Box	Name	memOutput
	Lines	*Empty*
	ReadOnly	True
Label	Name	lblQuestion
	Caption	Which credit cards do you use?
CheckBox	Name	chkVisa
	Caption	Visa
CheckBox	Name	chkMaster
	Caption	Mastercard
CheckBox	Name	chkDiscover
	Caption	Discover Card
CheckBox	Name	chkAmEx
	Caption	American Express

Component Name	Event	Setting
btnEvaluate	OnClick	Evaluate

```
    chkVisa: TCheckBox;
    chkMaster: TCheckBox;
    chkDiscover: TCheckBox;
    chkAmex: TCheckBox;
    procedure Evaluate(Sender: TObject);
    procedure TestCard(chkBox: TObject; var used: Boolean);
  private
    { Private declarations }
  public
    { Public declarations }
  end;

var
  frmCheckBox: TfrmCheckBox;

implementation

{$R *.DFM}

{ ----------------------------------------------------------
Procedure Name: TestCard
Purpose:  Test whether the check box for the credit card is
```

```
                  selected.  If so, display the credit card name in
                  the memo box.
       ------------------------------------------------------------}
       procedure TfrmCheckBox.TestCard(chkBox: TObject;
       .                                var used: Boolean);

       begin
         with (chkBox as TCheckBox) do begin
           if Checked then begin
             memOutput.Lines.Add(Caption);
             used := True;
           end;
         end;
       end;

       { ----------------------------------------------------------
       Procedure Name: Evaluate
       Purpose:  Evaluate which check boxes are selected.
       ------------------------------------------------------------}
       procedure TfrmCheckBox.Evaluate(Sender: TObject);

       var
         used: Boolean;

       begin
         used := False;
         memOutput.Clear;
         memOutput.Lines.Add('You use the following credit cards:');
         TestCard(chkVisa, used);
         TestCard(chkMaster, used);
```

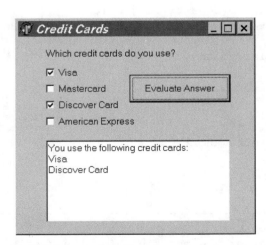

FIGURE 16.1   CheckBox Example

```
      TestCard(chkDiscover, used);
      TestCard(chkAmEx, used);
      if not(used) then begin
        memOutput.Lines.Add('None');
      end;
    end;
  end;

  end.
```

◉ RadioButton

In contrast to check boxes, which allow the user to choose one or more items, radio buttons allow the user to select a *single* item from a list of several alternatives. Radio buttons are grouped by placing them inside a container object, such as a form, group box, panel, or frame. All radio buttons within the same container act as a single group. To group radio buttons within a group box or panel, place the group box or panel on the form first, and then place the radio buttons inside of this container object.

When the user selects a radio button, all other radio buttons in the group are automatically cleared. The `Checked` property describes the state of the radio button; it is set to True when the radio button is selected and False when the radio button is not selected. The `Caption` property contains the text that appears to the right of the radio button. An example program unit containing radio buttons follows, and Figure 16.2 shows a sample execution of this code.

Component	Property	Setting
Form	Name	frmRadioButton
	Caption	RadioButton Example
Button	Name	btnEvaluate
	Caption	Evaluate Answer
Memo Box	Name	memOutput
	Lines	*Empty*
	ReadOnly	True
Label	Name	lblQuestion
	Caption	Do you like programming with Delphi?
RadioButton	Name	radYes
	Caption	Yes
RadioButton	Name	radNo
	Caption	No

Component Name	Event	Setting
btnEvaluate	OnClick	Evaluate

```
unit RadioButtonEx;

interface

uses
  Windows, Messages, SysUtils, Classes, Graphics,
  Controls, Forms, Dialogs, StdCtrls;

type
  TfrmRadioButton = class(TForm)
    lblQuestion: TLabel;
    radYes: TRadioButton;
    radNo: TRadioButton;
    btnEvaluate: TButton;
    memOutput: TMemo;
    procedure Evaluate(Sender: TObject);
  private
    { Private declarations }
  public
    { Public declarations }
  end;

var
  frmRadioButton: TfrmRadioButton;

implementation

{$R *.DFM}

procedure TfrmRadioButton.Evaluate(Sender: TObject);

var
  lineOut: String;

begin
  memOutput.Clear;
  if radYes.Checked then begin
    lineOut := 'I''m glad that you enjoy it!';
  end
  else if radNo.Checked then begin
    lineOut := 'Why not?  It''s fun!';
  end
  else begin
    lineOut := 'Yes or No?';
  end;
  memOutput.Lines.Add(lineOut);
end;

end.
```

FIGURE 16.2   RadioButton Example

ListBox

A list box allows the user to select one or more items from a list. If the number of items in the list exceeds the height of the list box, a vertical scroll bar is automatically added to the list box control. List boxes can dynamically add and remove items from a list.

The `Items` property is of the data type `TStrings`, a list of strings. This property contains the items in the list box. At design time, you use the String List editor to edit the `Items` property. At run time, you can add items to the list box by using the `Add` method of `TStrings` or remove items from the list box by using the `Delete` method. The `ItemIndex` property specifies the ordinal number of the selected item, where the first item corresponds to an `ItemIndex` of 0. `ItemIndex` contains the value –1 if no item is selected. The `MultiSelect` property specifies whether the user may select more than one item from the list. If `MultiSelect` is True, then `ItemIndex` is the index of the selected item that has focus, and its default value is 0. The `SelCount` property contains the number of items that are selected, and the `Selected` property indicates whether a particular item is selected. The `Sorted` property specifies whether the items should appear in alphabetical order. The `Style` property determines how the items are displayed. Although items are displayed as strings by default, changing the `Style` property allows a list box to display items graphically or in varying heights. The following code shows an example use of the list box control. Figure 16.3 shows the form for this example.

```
unit ListBoxEx;

interface

uses
  Windows, Messages, SysUtils, Classes, Graphics, Controls,
  Forms, Dialogs, StdCtrls;
```

Component	Property	Setting
Form	Name	frmListBox
	Caption	ListBox Example
ListBox	Name	lstGrocery
	Items	Milk; Eggs; Cheese; Butter; Apples; Oranges; Pancake mix
Button	Name	btnAdd
	Caption	Add
Button	Name	btnRemove
	Caption	Remove
Button	Name	btnEvaluate
	Caption	Evaluate Answer
Memo Box	Name	memOutput
	Lines	*Empty*
	ReadOnly	True

> The semicolons in the `Items` property indicate that these items appear on different lines in the String List editor (that is, you should press ENTER after entering each item).

Component Name	Event	Setting
btnAdd	OnClick	AddItem
btnRemove	OnClick	RemoveItem
btnEvaluate	OnClick	Evaluate

```
type
  TfrmListBox = class(TForm)
    lstGrocery: TListBox;
    btnAdd: TButton;
    btnRemove: TButton;
    btnEvaluate: TButton;
    memOutput: TMemo;
    procedure AddItem(Sender: TObject);
    procedure RemoveItem(Sender: TObject);
    procedure Evaluate(Sender: TObject);
  private
    { Private declarations }
  public
    { Public declarations }
  end;

var
  frmListBox: TfrmListBox;

implementation
```

```
{$R *.DFM}
procedure TfrmListBox.AddItem(Sender: TObject);

var
  newItem: String;

begin
  newItem := InputBox('Add Item', 'Enter new item:', '');
  if (newItem <> '') then begin
    lstGrocery.Items.Add(newItem);
  end;
end;

procedure TfrmListBox.RemoveItem(Sender: TObject);

begin
  lstGrocery.Items.Delete(lstGrocery.ItemIndex);
end;

procedure TfrmListBox.Evaluate(Sender: TObject);

begin
  memOutput.Clear;
```

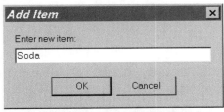

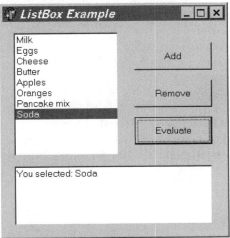

FIGURE 16.3 ListBox Example

```
    if lstGrocery.ItemIndex >= 0 then begin
      memOutput.Lines.Add('You selected: ' +
        lstGrocery.Items[lstGrocery.ItemIndex]);
    end
    else begin
      memOutput.Lines.Add('No item selected.');
    end;
  end;

  end.
```

ComboBox

A combo box combines an edit box with a scrollable drop-down list. A user may either select an item from the list or type directly into the edit box. As a consequence, a combo box has many of the same properties and methods as the edit boxes and list boxes discussed earlier. For a combo box, the Style property determines the type of combo box and indicates whether an edit box is attached.

The previous example is presented here using a combo box rather than a list box. To add an item to the list, the user need merely enter the item in the edit box and press the ENTER key. Figure 16.4 displays a sample execution of this code.

```
unit ComboBoxEx;

interface

uses
  Windows, Messages, SysUtils, Classes, Graphics,
  Controls, Forms, Dialogs, StdCtrls;

type
  TfrmComboBox = class(TForm)
    btnRemove: TButton;
    btnEvaluate: TButton;
    memOutput: TMemo;
    cboGrocery: TComboBox;
    lblInst1: TLabel;
    lblInst2: TLabel;
    procedure RemoveItem(Sender: TObject);
    procedure Evaluate(Sender: TObject);
    procedure AddItem(Sender: TObject; var Key: Char);
  private
    { Private declarations }
  public
    { Public declarations }
  end;
```

```
var
  frmComboBox: TfrmComboBox;

implementation

{$R *.DFM}

procedure TfrmComboBox.AddItem(Sender: TObject; var Key:
                               Char);

var
  newItem: String;

begin
  newItem := Trim(cboGrocery.Text);
  if (Key = Chr(13)) and (newItem <> '') then begin
    cboGrocery.Items.Add(newItem);
  end;
end;
```

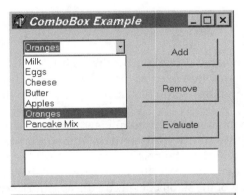

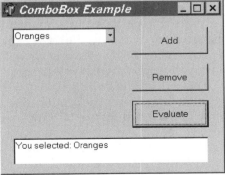

FIGURE 16.4   ComboBox Example

```
procedure TfrmComboBox.RemoveItem(Sender: TObject);

begin
  cboGrocery.Items.Delete(cboGrocery.ItemIndex);
end;

procedure TfrmComboBox.Evaluate(Sender: TObject);

begin
  memOutput.Clear;
  if (cboGrocery.ItemIndex >= 0) then begin
    memOutput.Lines.Add('You selected: ' +
      cboGrocery.Items[cboGrocery.ItemIndex]);
  end
  else begin
    memOutput.Lines.Add('No item selected.');
  end;
end;

end.
```

ScrollBar

Scroll bars provide a rapid means of navigating through long lists of items or large quantities of data. They are often used as input devices to indicate a desired speed or quantity level. Furthermore, scroll bars can be used to provide an analog representation of a position.

While the scroll bar component may be used to view the contents of a window, form, or other control, many Delphi controls contain embedded scroll bars that require no additional coding. For instance, a form has `VertScrollBar` and `HorzScrollBar` properties that automatically configure scroll bars on it.

The `Min` and `Max` properties of the scroll bar specify the appropriate range for the control. The `Position` property reflects the current position of the scroll bar within this range. The `LargeChange` property specifies the amount that `Position` changes when the user clicks the scroll bar. Similarly, the `SmallChange` property specifies the amount that `Position` changes when the user clicks an arrow at the end of the scroll bar. The `Kind` property indicates the orientation of the scroll bar, horizontal (default) or vertical. The code in the `OnScroll` event handler determines the control's behavior when the user moves the scroll bar.

An example use of scroll bars follows, and Figure 16.5 shows the associated form.

```
unit ScrollBarEx;

interface

uses
  Windows, Messages, SysUtils, Classes, Graphics, Controls,
  Forms, Dialogs, StdCtrls;
```

Component	Property	Setting
Form	Name	frmScrollBar
	Caption	ScrollBar Example
ScrollBar	Name	sbrXPosition
	Kind	sbHorizontal
	LargeChange	10
ScrollBar	Name	sbrYPosition
	Kind	sbVertical
	LargeChange	10
Label	Name	lblAirplane
	Caption	Q
	Font	Wingdings
	Size	18
	Left	0
	Top	0

Component Name	Event	Setting
sbrXPosition	OnChange	XPos
sbrYPosition	OnChange	Ypos

```
type
  TfrmScrollBar = class(TForm)
    sbrXPosition: TScrollBar;
    sbrYPosition: TScrollBar;
    lblAirplane: TLabel;
    procedure YPos(Sender: TObject);
    procedure XPos(Sender: TObject);
  private
    { Private declarations }
  public
    { Public declarations }
  end;

var
  frmScrollBar: TfrmScrollBar;

implementation

{$R *.DFM}

procedure TfrmScrollBar.YPos(Sender: TObject);

begin
  lblAirplane.Top := sbrYPosition.Position * 2;
end;
```

FIGURE 16.5 ScrollBar Example

```
procedure TfrmScrollBar.XPos(Sender: TObject);
begin
  lblAirplane.Left := sbrXPosition.Position * 2;
end;

end.
```

GroupBox

A group box provides an identifiable group of related controls and functionally subdivides a form. When a control appears within a group box, the group box becomes its parent. The Caption property contains descriptive text to identify the group box. The Name property of a group box is prefaced with grp. In Figure 16.6, related check boxes are grouped inside of a group box.

GUI Design Tips

Group boxes are containers for other controls. To place controls inside a group box, first insert the group box on the form, and then place the controls inside the group box. For any particular group box at run time, the user may select any number of check boxes but only one radio button.

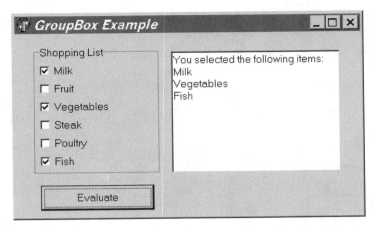

FIGURE 16.6   GroupBox Example

 RadioGroup

A radio group box is a special group box that contains only radio buttons. It simplifies the tasks involved when working with radio buttons. When the user selects a radio button, all other radio buttons in the group automatically become deselected. Thus two radio buttons on the same form can be selected concurrently only if they reside within separate container controls, such as radio group boxes.

Each string in the `Items` property appears as a separate radio button within the radio group box, with the string serving as its caption. The value of `ItemIndex` indicates which radio button is currently selected. To display the radio buttons in a single column or multiple columns, you must set the value of the `Columns` property appropriately. The prefix for the `Name` property of a radio group box is `rgp`. Figure 16.7 shows an example form that uses a radio group box.

 Panel

A panel is a generic container for other controls. Panels have properties to create a beveled border around the control and methods to manage the placement of embedded child controls.

You can align panels with the form so that they maintain the same relative position when the form is resized. The `BorderWidth` property sets the width of the border around a panel (in pixels). Similarly, the `BevelWidth` property sets the width of the bevel.

The panel control in the code unit that follows acts like a special button. A sample execution appears in Figure 16.8.

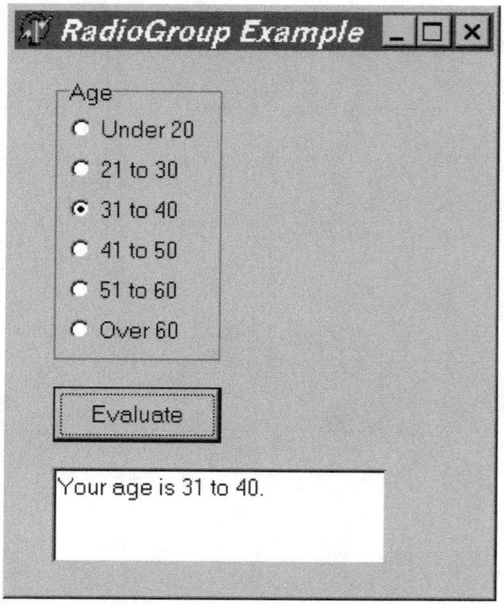

FIGURE 16.7 RadioGroup Example

Component	Property	Setting
Form	Name	frmPanel
	Caption	Panel Example
Panel	Name	pnlTest
	BevelWidth	10
	Caption	Test Panel
Memo Box	Name	memOutput
	Lines	*Empty*
	ReadOnly	True

Component Name	Event	Setting
pnlTest	OnClick	Test

```
unit PanelEx;

interface

uses
  Windows, Messages, SysUtils, Classes, Graphics, Controls,
  Forms, Dialogs, StdCtrls, ExtCtrls;
```

```
type
  TfrmPanel = class(TForm)
    pnlTest: TPanel;
    memOutput: TMemo;
    procedure Test(Sender: TObject);
    procedure FormCreate(Sender: TObject);
  private
    { Private declarations }
  public
    { Public declarations }
  end;

var
  frmPanel: TfrmPanel;

implementation

{$R *.DFM}

var
  number: Integer;

procedure TfrmPanel.Test(Sender: TObject);

var
  lineOut: String;

begin
  number := number + 1;
  memOutput.Clear;
  lineOut := 'You clicked the panel ' +
             IntToStr(number) + ' time';
  if (number > 1) then begin
    lineOut := lineOut + 's';
  end;
  lineOut := lineOut + '.';
  memOutput.Lines.Add(lineOut);
end;

procedure TfrmPanel.FormCreate(Sender: TObject);

begin
  number := 0;
end;

end.
```

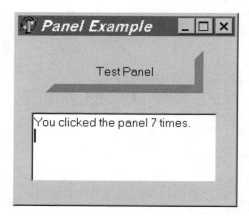

FIGURE 16.8 Panel Example

ActionList

An action list allows you to centralize the response to user actions (events) for different objects. At design time, the programmer specifies actions in the Action List editor. These actions are then connected to client controls via their action links (`Action` properties). A client control triggers an action in response to an event, such as a mouse click. Clients are typically menu items or buttons.

At design time, you can place an action list component on the form. Double-clicking the action list component will open the Action List editor. This editor allows you to add, delete, and rearrange actions. You set the properties for each action in the Object Inspector. The `Name` property identifies the action and should be prefaced with `act`. The other properties correspond to the properties of client controls and usually have the same name. The action list component is visible only at design time; it does not appear on the form during program execution.

The following code presents a simple action list example using two buttons. Figure 16.9 shows a sample execution.

```
unit ActionListEx;

interface

uses
  Windows, Messages, SysUtils, Classes, Graphics, Controls,
  Forms, Dialogs, ActnList, StdCtrls;

type
  TfrmActionList = class(TForm)
```

Component	Property	Setting
Form	Name	frmActionList
	Caption	ActionList Example
ActionList	Name	aclButtons
Action	Name	actClicked
Button	Name	btnLeft
	Action	actClicked
	Caption	Left Toggle
Button	Name	btnRight
	Action	actClicked
	Caption	Right Toggle
Button	Name	btnClear
	Caption	Clear
Memo Box	Name	memOutput
	Lines	*Empty*
	ReadOnly	True
	ScrollBars	ssVertical

To create the `actClicked` action, you must double-click on the `aclButtons` action list in the Delphi IDE. Next, click the New Action button in the Action List editor. Finally, edit its property and event settings in the Object Inspector window.

Component Name	Event	Setting
actClicked	OnExecute	Display
btnClear	OnClick	ClearOutput

```
    btnLeft: TButton;
    btnRight: TButton;
    memOutput: TMemo;
    aclButtons: TActionList;
    actClicked: TAction;
    btnClear: TButton;
    procedure Display(Sender: TObject);
    procedure ClearOutput(Sender: TObject);
  private
    { Private declarations }
  public
    { Public declarations }
  end;

var
  frmActionList: TfrmActionList;

implementation
```

FIGURE 16.9   ActionList Example

```
{$R *.DFM}

procedure TfrmActionList.Display(Sender: TObject);

begin
  memOutput.Lines.Add('You pressed a toggle button.');
end;

procedure TfrmActionList.ClearOutput(Sender: TObject);

begin
  memOutput.Clear;
end;

end.
```

Frames

Like forms, group boxes, and panels, frames serve as containers for other components. Frames can be created and then saved on the Component Palette, however, thereby providing the programmer with an easy means of creating a custom group of components for use in many applications. Each frame functions as a separate unit and inherits changes from the components that it contains. You can also nest frames within other frames or forms.

As an example application, let's design a custom frame and save it on the Component Palette. The NameBox frame appears in Figure 16.10. To create this

FIGURE 16.10   NameBox Frame

frame, first select `File|Close All` and then select `File|New Frame` from the menu. Next, add the components and set the properties as indicated:

Component	Property	Setting
Frame	Name	fraNameBox
	AutoSize	True
Label	Name	lblName
	Caption	Please enter your name:
Label	Name	lblFirstName
	Caption	First Name
Label	Name	lblMiddleInitial
	Caption	MI
Label	Name	lblLastName
	Caption	Last Name
Edit Box	Name	edtFirstName
	Text	*Empty*
Edit Box	Name	edtMiddleInitial
	Text	*Empty*
Edit Box	Name	edtLastName
	Text	*Empty*

Save this frame unit by selecting `File|Save As...` and typing `NameBox` as the file name. The unit is saved as `NameBox.pas`.

Next, add the NameBox frame to the Component Palette. Right-click on the NameBox frame in the Delphi IDE and select `Add To Palette` from the pop-up menu. The Component Template Information window opens on the screen. Enter `NameBox` for the Component name and `Templates` for the Palette page, as shown in Figure 16.11. Click the OK button. The Component Palette now has a new page named Templates, which contains one component, NameBox.

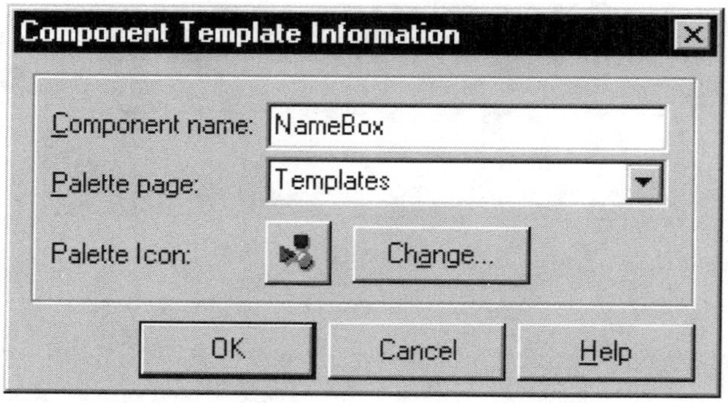

FIGURE 16.11 Component Template Information Window

Let's write a program that uses our new NameBox frame. Select `File|New Application` from the menu bar. Add components and set their properties as indicated:

Component	Property	Setting
Form	Name	frmFrames
	Caption	Frames Example
NameBox	Name	nbxName
Button	Name	btnEvaluate
	Caption	Evaluate
Memo Box	Name	memOutput
	Lines	*Empty*
	ReadOnly	True

Component Name	Event	Setting
btnEvaluate	OnClick	DisplayName

The program code for this example follows, and Figure 16.12 shows a sample execution.

```
{Project File: Frames.dpr}
program Frames;

uses
  Forms,
```

```
  FramesEx in 'FramesEx.pas' {frmFrames},
  NameBox in 'NameBox.pas' {fraNameBox: TFrame};

{$R *.RES}

begin
  Application.Initialize;
  Application.CreateForm(TfrmFrames, frmFrames);
  Application.Run;
end.

{Form File: FramesEx.pas}
unit FramesEx;

interface

uses
  Windows, Messages, SysUtils, Classes, Graphics, Controls,
  Forms, Dialogs, StdCtrls, NameBox;

type
  TfrmFrames = class(TForm)
    nbxName: TfraNameBox;
    btnEvaluate: TButton;
    memOutput: TMemo;
    procedure DisplayName(Sender: TObject);
  private
    { Private declarations }
  public
    { Public declarations }
  end;

var
  frmFrames: TfrmFrames;

implementation

{$R *.DFM}

procedure TfrmFrames.DisplayName(Sender: TObject);

var
  first:    String;
  mi:       String;
  last:     String;
  fullName: String;
```

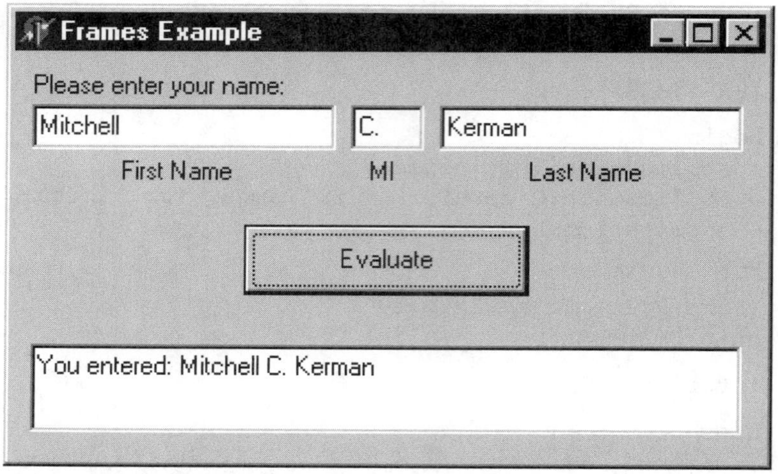

FIGURE 16.12   Frames Example

```
begin
  first := Trim(nbxName.edtFirstName.Text);
  mi := Trim(nbxName.edtMiddleInitial.Text);
  last := Trim(nbxName.edtLastName.Text);
  fullName := Trim(first + ' ' + mi + ' ' + last);
  memOutput.Clear;
  if (fullName <> '') then begin
    memOutput.Lines.Add('You entered: ' + fullName);
  end
  else begin
    memOutput.Lines.Add('Please enter your name.');
  end;
end;

end.
```

MainMenu

The main menu component allows the programmer to design the main menu for a form within the Delphi IDE. A main menu (TMainMenu) consists of a menu bar and its associated drop-down menus. The drop-down menus may contain additional menu items (TMenuItem). To build a main menu at design time, add the main menu component to the form and double-click it, thereby opening the Main Menu editor. Next, add the menu items and set their properties in the Object Inspector window.

Let's demonstrate the use of this component with an example. Create the form described below:

Component	Property	Setting
Form	Name	frmMainMenu
	Caption	MainMenu Example
Label	Name	lblMessage
	Caption	Welcome to the Simple Editor
MainMenu	Name	mmuExample
Memo Box	Name	memEditor
	Lines	*Empty*

Next, double-click the main menu component, `mmuExample`, to open the Main Menu editor window. Create the menus shown in Figure 16.13.

Component	Property	Setting
MenuItem	Name	muiView
	Caption	View
MenuItem	Name	muiMessage
	Caption	Show Message
	Checked	True
MenuItem	Name	muiEditor
	Caption	Show Editor
	Checked	True
MenuItem	Name	muiHelp
	Caption	Help
MenuItem	Name	muiAbout
	Caption	About…

Component Name	Event	Setting
muiMessage	OnClick	DisplayMessage
muiEditor	OnClick	DisplayEditor
muiAbout	OnClick	AboutBox

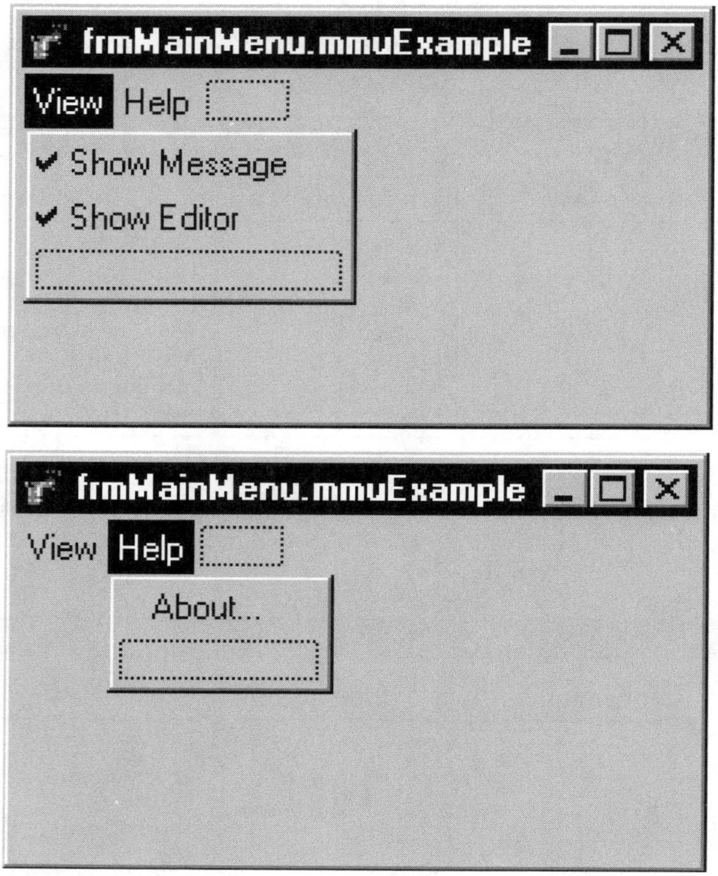

FIGURE 16.13   Main Menu Editor

Finally, add the code shown below. Figure 16.14 demonstrates the execution of this program.

```
unit MainMenuEx;

interface

uses
  Windows, Messages, SysUtils, Classes, Graphics, Controls,
  Forms, Dialogs, Menus, StdCtrls;

type
  TfrmMainMenu = class(TForm)
    mmuExample: TMainMenu;
    muiView: TMenuItem;
```

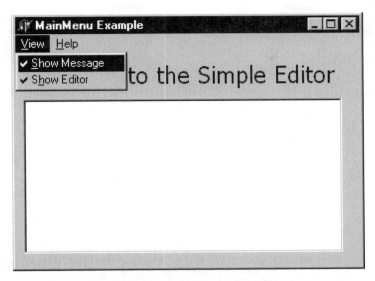

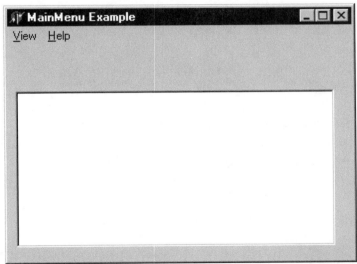

FIGURE 16.14   MainMenu Example

```
muiMessage: TMenuItem;
muiEditor: TMenuItem;
muiHelp: TMenuItem;
muiAbout: TMenuItem;
memEditor: TMemo;
lblMessage: TLabel;
procedure DisplayMessage(Sender: TObject);
```

```
    procedure DisplayEditor(Sender: TObject);
    procedure AboutBox(Sender: TObject);
  private
    { Private declarations }
  public
    { Public declarations }
  end;

var
  frmMainMenu: TfrmMainMenu;

implementation

{$R *.DFM}

procedure TfrmMainMenu.DisplayMessage(Sender: TObject);

begin
  muiMessage.Checked := not(muiMessage.Checked);
  lblMessage.Visible := muiMessage.Checked;
end;

procedure TfrmMainMenu.DisplayEditor(Sender: TObject);

begin
  muiEditor.Checked := not(muiEditor.Checked);
  memEditor.Visible := muiEditor.Checked;
end;

procedure TfrmMainMenu.AboutBox(Sender: TObject);

begin
  Application.MessageBox('This is the Simple Editor ver. 0.01',
                         'ABOUT...', MB_OK);
end;

end.
```

PopupMenu

The pop-up menu component defines the pop-up menu that appears when the user right-clicks a control. To make a pop-up menu available for a control, assign the pop-up menu object (TPopupMenu) to the control's PopupMenu property.

As with the main menu component, you add the pop-up menu component to the form at design time. Next, you double-click on the pop-up menu component to open the Pop-up Menu editor. You can then add menu items to the pop-up menu and set their properties with the Object Inspector.

As an example, let's modify the Simple Editor to include a pop-up menu. First, open the Simple Editor in Delphi (MainMenu.dpr) and add the pop-up menu component to the form:

Component	Property	Setting
PopupMenu	Name	pmuEditor

Now, rename the form and set its `PopupMenu` property to indicate its associated pop-up menu:

Component	Property	Setting
Form	Name	frmPopupMenu
	Caption	PopupMenu Example
	PopupMenu	pmuEditor

Next, double-click the pop-up menu component, pmuEditor. This opens the Pop-up Menu editor window. Add the following menu items:

Component	Property	Setting
MenuItem	Name	pmiMessage
	Caption	Show Message
	Checked	True
MenuItem	Name	pmiEditor
	Caption	Show Editor
	Checked	True
MenuItem	Name	pmiAbout
	Caption	About...

Component Name	Event	Setting
pmiMessage	OnClick	DisplayMessage
pmiEditor	OnClick	DisplayEditor
pmiAbout	OnClick	AboutBox

Finally, modify the code as shown below. A sample execution of this program appears in Figure 16.15.

```
unit PopupMenuEx;

interface

uses
  Windows, Messages, SysUtils, Classes, Graphics, Controls,
  Forms, Dialogs, Menus, StdCtrls;

type
  TfrmPopupMenu = class(TForm)
    mmuExample: TMainMenu;
    muiView: TMenuItem;
    muiMessage: TMenuItem;
    muiEditor: TMenuItem;
    muiHelp: TMenuItem;
    muiAbout: TMenuItem;
    memEditor: TMemo;
    lblMessage: TLabel;
    pmuEditor: TPopupMenu;
    pmiEditor: TMenuItem;
    pmiAbout: TMenuItem;
    pmiMessage: TMenuItem;
    pmiSeparator: TMenuItem;
    procedure DisplayMessage(Sender: TObject);
    procedure DisplayEditor(Sender: TObject);
    procedure AboutBox(Sender: TObject);
  private
    { Private declarations }
  public
    { Public declarations }
  end;

var
  frmPopupMenu: TfrmPopupMenu;

implementation

{$R *.DFM}

procedure TfrmPopupMenu.DisplayMessage(Sender: TObject);

begin
  muiMessage.Checked := not(muiMessage.Checked);
  pmiMessage.Checked := muiMessage.Checked;
  lblMessage.Visible := muiMessage.Checked;
end;
```

FIGURE 16.15   PopupMenu Example

```
procedure TfrmPopupMenu.DisplayEditor(Sender: TObject);
begin
  muiEditor.Checked := not(muiEditor.Checked);
  pmiEditor.Checked := muiEditor.Checked;
  memEditor.Visible := muiEditor.Checked;
end;
```

```
procedure TfrmPopupMenu.AboutBox(Sender: TObject);

begin
  Application.MessageBox('This is the Simple Editor ver. 0.02',
                         'ABOUT...', MB_OK);
end;

end.
```

Programming Key: Tips

In the preceding example, you could use an action list to coordinate the actions of the various objects, such as the main menu and pop-up menu. This modification is left as an exercise for the reader.

Additional Page

 ## Image

The image control displays images or graphics on a form. It supports a variety of graphic file formats, including bitmap, icon, metafile, enhanced metafile, and JPEG files.

You can assign a picture to an image control at either design time or run time. Set the `Picture` property to a `TPicture` object that contains the graphic to be displayed by the image control. At design time, this property opens the Picture editor, which is used to specify the file that contains the image. To assign a picture file to an image control at run time, use the `LoadFromFile` method of the image control's `TPicture` object. For instance, to display the picture file `myPicture.jpg` in the image control `imgExample` at run time, use the following statement:

```
imgExample.Picture.LoadFromFile('myPicture.jpg');
```

The file extension determines the type of picture created. If the file extension is not a recognized graphic file type, the computer will raise an `EInvalidGraphic` exception.

If `AutoSize` is True, the image control will be resized to accommodate the image that it contains. If `AutoSize` is False, the image control will remain the same size, regardless of the size of the image. Thus, the image control is smaller than its image, only the portion of the picture that fits inside the control will be visible.

Rather than resize the control to fit the image, use the `Stretch` property to resize the image to fit the control. If the `Stretch` property is True, the picture will be

FIGURE 16.16   Image Example (Pictured above: Janet and Mitchell Kerman)

resized to fit the image control. Then, when the image control is resized, its image is resized simultaneously. This stretching can distort the image if the control is not the same shape as the image. Note that `Stretch` has no effect on icon images.

The `Name` property of an image control is prefaced with `img`. Image controls respond to click and mouse events; as a consequence, you can use them as graphical buttons. Figure 16.16 shows a form with a picture inside an image control.

Shape

The shape control allows the programmer to draw a simple geometric shape on the form at design time. This control can decorate or highlight specific parts of the form. The shape control can be used to display a circle, ellipse, rectangle, rounded rectangle, square, or rounded square as specified by the control's `Shape` property. The `Name` property of a shape control is prefaced with `shp`. Figure 16.17 displays a form containing several shape controls.

ScrollBox

On many occasions, an application needs to display more information than will fit in a particular area. Some Delphi components contain embedded scroll bars

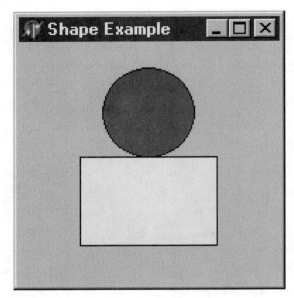

FIGURE 16.17   Shape Example

that are enabled either automatically or manually by setting their `ScrollBars` properties. Other components and even forms full of components may need to be able to scroll, however. The Delphi scroll box component provides a way to create such scrolling regions.

A scroll box contains other components, but normally remains invisible unless it is needed. If all of the components within the scroll box cannot fit inside the visible area, then the scroll box automatically displays the necessary scroll bars, enabling users to move components outside of the visible region into a position where they can be seen and used.

Figure 16.18 shows an example of a scroll box. This example is similar to the NameBox example used for frames. In the code that follows, `DisplayName` is the `OnClick` event handler for `btnDisplay`.

```
unit ScrollBoxEx;

interface

uses
  Windows, Messages, SysUtils, Classes, Graphics, Controls,
  Forms, Dialogs, StdCtrls;

type
  TfrmScrollBox = class(TForm)
    sbxName: TScrollBox;
```

```
        lblFirstName: TLabel;
        lblMiddleInitial: TLabel;
        lblLastName: TLabel;
        lblName: TLabel;
        edtFirstName: TEdit;
        edtMiddleInitial: TEdit;
        edtLastName: TEdit;
        btnDisplay: TButton;
        memOutput: TMemo;
        procedure DisplayName(Sender: TObject);
      private
        { Private declarations }
      public
        { Public declarations }
      end;
  var
    frmScrollBox: TfrmScrollBox;

  implementation

  {$R *.DFM}

  procedure TfrmScrollBox.DisplayName(Sender: TObject);

  var
    first:    String;
    middle:   String;
    last:     String;
    fullName: String;

  begin
    first := Trim(edtFirstName.Text);
    middle := Trim(edtMiddleInitial.Text);
    last := Trim(edtLastName.Text);
    fullName := Trim(first + ' ' + middle + ' ' + last);
    memOutput.Clear;
    if (fullName <> '') then begin
      memOutput.Lines.Add('You entered: ' + fullName);
    end
    else begin
      memOutput.Lines.Add('Please enter a name.');
    end;
  end;

  end.
```

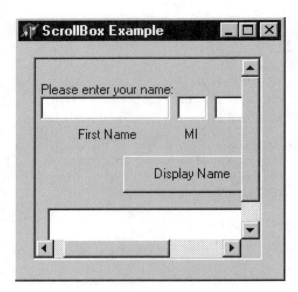

FIGURE 16.18   ScrollBox Example

CheckListBox

A check list box is a scrollable list box in which each item has a check box next to it. Users can check or uncheck items in the list as desired.

The Items property contains the items in the check list box. The ItemIndex property specifies the ordinal number of the currently selected item; it contains –1 if no item is selected. SelCount indicates the number of items selected. The Selected property indicates whether a particular item is selected. Similarly, the Checked property indicates whether a particular item is checked. The Sorted property specifies whether the items are listed in alphabetical order, and the Style property determines how the items are displayed. The following code gives an example of the use of the check list box control. Figure 16.19 shows the form for this example.

```
unit CheckListBoxEx;

interface

uses
  Windows, Messages, SysUtils, Classes, Graphics, Controls,
  Forms, Dialogs, StdCtrls, CheckLst;

type
  TfrmCheckListBox = class(TForm)
```

Component	Property	Setting
Form	Name	frmCheckListBox
	Caption	CheckListBox Example
Label	Name	lblQuestion
	Caption	On what days do you usually go shopping?
	WordWrap	True
CheckListBox	Name	cbxDays
	Items	Sunday; Monday; Tuesday; Wednesday; Thursday; Friday; Saturday
Button	Name	btnEvaluate
	Caption	Evaluate Answer
Memo Box	Name	memOutput
	Lines	*Empty*
	ReadOnly	True
	ScrollBars	ssVertical

> The semicolons in the Items property of the check list box indicate that these items appear on different lines in the String List editor (that is, you should press ENTER after entering each item).

Component Name	Event	Setting
btnEvaluate	OnClick	Evaluate

```
    cbxDays: TCheckListBox;
    lblQuestion: TLabel;
    btnEvaluate: TButton;
    memOutput: TMemo;
    procedure Evaluate(Sender: TObject);
  private
    { Private declarations }
  public
    { Public declarations }
  end;

var
  frmCheckListBox: TfrmCheckListBox;

implementation

{$R *.DFM}

procedure TfrmCheckListBox.Evaluate(Sender: TObject);

var
  day:  Integer;
```

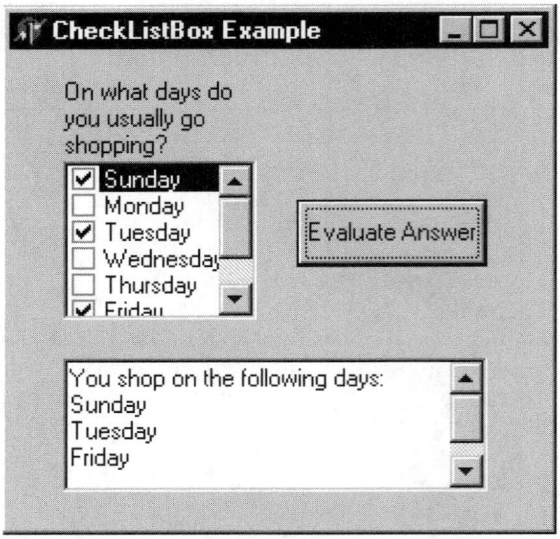

FIGURE 16.19   CheckListBox Example

```
      none: Boolean;
begin
  none := True;
  memOutput.Clear;
  memOutput.Lines.Add('You shop on the following days:');
  for day := 0 to (cbxDays.Items.Count - 1) do begin
    if cbxDays.Checked[day] then begin
      memOutput.Lines.Add(cbxDays.Items[day]);
      none := False;
    end;
  end;
  if none then begin
    memOutput.Clear;
    memOutput.Lines.Add('You don''t shop.');
  end;
end;

end.
```

A StaticText

A static text box functions like a label control, except that it can receive the focus (that is, be the active control on the form). The code that follows illustrates its use, and Figure 16.20 shows a sample run.

Component	Property	Setting
Form	Name	frmStaticText
	Caption	StaticText Example
Label	Name	lblDirections
	Caption	Click on the StaticText Boxes below to change the focus.
	WordWrap	True
StaticText	Name	stxTop
	Caption	StaticText Box
StaticText	Name	stxBottom
	Caption	StaticText Box

Component Name	Event	Setting
stxTop	OnClick	ChangeFocus
stxBottom	OnClick	ChangeFocus

```
unit StaticTextEx;

interface

uses
  Windows, Messages, SysUtils, Classes, Graphics, Controls,
  Forms, Dialogs, StdCtrls;

type
  TfrmStaticText = class(TForm)
    stxTop: TStaticText;
    stxBottom: TStaticText;
    lblDirections: TLabel;
    procedure ChangeFocus(Sender: TObject);
  private
    { Private declarations }
  public
    { Public declarations }
  end;

var
  frmStaticText: TfrmStaticText;

implementation

{$R *.DFM}
```

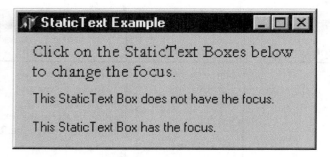

FIGURE 16.20   StaticText Example

```
const
  BEGIN_MESSAGE = 'This StaticText Box ';
  END_MESSAGE = 'the focus.';

procedure TfrmStaticText.ChangeFocus(Sender: TObject);

var
  hasFocus: String;
  noFocus:  String;

begin
  hasFocus := BEGIN_MESSAGE + 'has ' + END_MESSAGE;
  noFocus := BEGIN_MESSAGE + 'does not have ' + END_MESSAGE;
  (Sender as TStaticText).Caption := hasFocus;
  if (Sender = stxTop) then begin
    stxBottom.Caption := noFocus;
  end
  else begin
    stxTop.Caption := noFocus;
  end;
end;

end.
```

System Page

Timer

The timer control allows for the execution of specific code at user-specified intervals by causing the `OnTimer` event to occur. The timer control is transparent to the user, and it is useful for background processing.

The length of time between triggering events is measured in milliseconds and set in the `Interval` property. For the timer control `tmrWatch`, for instance, the `OnTimer` event is automatically triggered each time that `tmrWatch.Interval` milliseconds elapse. To begin timing, the `Enabled` property of the timer must be set to True. To disable a timer control, you can either set its `Enabled` property to False or set its `Interval` to 0.

The code for a stopwatch example follows, and Figure 16.21 shows a sample execution of this program.

Component	Property	Setting
Form	Name	frmTimer
	Caption	Timer Example
Label	Name	lblStopwatch
	Alignment	taRightJustify
	Caption	0.0
	Font	
	Name	Arial
	Size	16
Label	Name	lblSeconds
	Caption	Seconds
	Font	
	Name	Arial
	Size	16
Button	Name	btnToggle
	Caption	Start
	Font	
	Size	12
	Style	[fsBold]
Button	Name	btnReset
	Caption	Reset
	Font	
	Size	12
	Style	[fsBold]
Timer	Name	tmrStopwatch
	Enabled	False
	Interval	10

Component Name	Event	Setting
btnToggle	OnClick	ToggleState
btnReset	OnClick	ResetTime
tmrStopwatch	OnTimer	UpdateTime

```
unit TimerEx;

interface

uses
  Windows, Messages, SysUtils, Classes, Graphics, Controls,
  Forms, Dialogs, StdCtrls, ExtCtrls;

type
  TfrmTimer = class(TForm)
    tmrStopwatch: TTimer;
    lblStopwatch: TLabel;
    btnToggle: TButton;
    btnReset: TButton;
    lblSeconds: TLabel;
    procedure ToggleState(Sender: TObject);
    procedure ResetTime(Sender: TObject);
    procedure UpdateTime(Sender: TObject);
  private
    { Private declarations }
  public
    { Public declarations }
  end;

var
  frmTimer: TfrmTimer;

implementation

{$R *.DFM}

procedure TfrmTimer.ToggleState(Sender: TObject);

begin
  tmrStopwatch.Enabled := not(tmrStopwatch.Enabled);
  if tmrStopwatch.Enabled then begin
    btnToggle.Caption := 'Stop';
  end
  else begin
    btnToggle.Caption := 'Start';
  end;
end;

procedure TfrmTimer.ResetTime(Sender: TObject);

begin
  lblStopwatch.Caption := '0.00';
end;
```

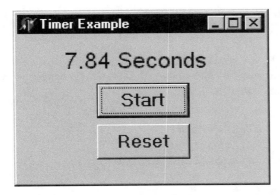

FIGURE 16.21   Timer Example

```
procedure TfrmTimer.UpdateTime(Sender: TObject);

var
  watchTime: Real;
  code:      Integer;
  newTime:   String;

begin
  Val(lblStopwatch.Caption, watchTime, code);
  watchTime := watchTime + 0.01;
  Str(watchTime:6:2, newTime);
  lblStopwatch.Caption := newTime;
end;

end.
```

PaintBox

A paint box is a simple graphic control that provides a canvas for applications to use while rendering an image. Unlike the image control, which displays an image that is stored in a file, a paint box requires an application to draw the image directly on a canvas. It provides a means of limiting drawing on a form to a specific rectangular area and adding custom images to a form.

The `Canvas` object is the drawing surface of the paint box. To draw on the canvas, you must write the appropriate code in the event handler for the `OnPaint` event. The `Name` property of a paint box is prefaced with `pnt`.

Chapter 17 discusses paint boxes and graphics programming with Delphi in greater detail. The code unit that follows demonstrates a simple graphics program. `DrawShapes` is the event handler for the `pntExample` paint box's `OnPaint` event. Figure 16.22 shows the execution of this code.

```
unit PaintBoxEx;

interface

uses
  Windows, Messages, SysUtils, Classes, Graphics, Controls,
  Forms, Dialogs, ExtCtrls;

type
  TfrmPaintBox = class(TForm)
    pntExample: TPaintBox;
    procedure DrawShapes(Sender: TObject);
  private
    { Private declarations }
  public
    { Public declarations }
  end;

var
  frmPaintBox: TfrmPaintBox;

implementation

{$R *.DFM}

procedure TfrmPaintBox.DrawShapes(Sender: TObject);

begin
  with (Sender as TPaintBox).Canvas do begin
```

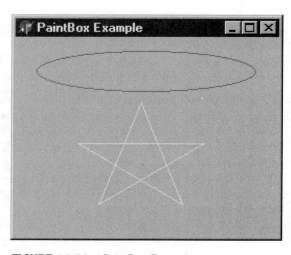

FIGURE 16.22 PaintBox Example

```
    Pen.Color := clYellow;
    Polyline([Point(100, 50), Point(60, 150),
            Point(160, 90), Point(40, 90),
            Point(140, 150), Point(100, 50)]);
    Pen.Color := clRed;
    Ellipse(0, 0, 210, 40);
  end;
end;

end.
```

Win 3.1 Page

    ### DriveComboBox, DirectoryListBox, FilterComboBox, and FileListBox

The drive combo box, directory list box, filter combo box, and file list box access the computer's disk drive information so as to display drive, directory folder, file mask, and file name information at run time. These controls are typically used in combination to allow a user to select a specific file. Consequently, their property settings must be synchronized. For example, when the user selects a specific drive letter from the drive combo box, the information in the directory and file list boxes should change accordingly.

For a drive combo box, the `DirList` property connects the control to a directory list box. The `Drive` property indicates the currently selected drive letter, and `Text` contains the volume name.

For a directory list box, the `Drive` property determines the drive for which the list box will display the directory structure, and `Directory` determines the current directory for the control. The `FileList` property connects the directory list box with a file list box.

A filter combo box provides a set of predefined file filters. The `Filter` property contains all file masks displayed in the filter combo box. Editing this property at design time opens the Filter Editor window. The `FileList` property links the filter combo box to a file list box.

A file list box is a special list box that lists all files in a specified directory. Its `Drive` and `Directory` properties indicate the drive and directory that contain all of the listed files. `FileName` contains the path and file name of the currently selected file. `FileEdit` links the file list box to an edit control that displays the currently selected file.

The following code demonstrates the use of a drive combo box, directory list box, filter combo box, and file list box. Figure 16.23 shows the form for this program.

Component	Property	Setting
Form	Name	frmDrvDirFltFil
	Caption	Drive, Directory, Filter, and File Boxes
DriveComboBox	Name	drvDiskDrive
	DirList	dirDirName
DirectoryListBox	Name	dirDirName
	FileList	filFileName
FilterComboBox	Name	fltFileName
	FileList	filFileName
	Filter	

	Filter Name	**Filter**
	All files (*.*)	*.*
	Text files (*.txt)	*.txt
	Word documents (*.doc)	*.doc
	Batch files (*.bat)	*.bat
	Data files (*.dat)	*.dat

Component	Property	Setting
FileListBox	Name	filFileName
Button	Name	btnEvaluate
	Caption	Evaluate Selection
Memo Box	Name	memOutput
	Lines	*Empty*
	ReadOnly	True
	ScrollBars	ssHorizontal

Component Name	Event	Setting
btnEvaluate	OnClick	Evaluate

```
unit DrvDirFltFilEx;

interface

uses
  Windows, Messages, SysUtils, Classes, Graphics,
  Controls, Forms, Dialogs, StdCtrls, FileCtrl;

type
  TfrmDrvDirFltFil = class(TForm)
    drvDiskDrive: TDriveComboBox;
    dirDirName: TDirectoryListBox;
    filFileName: TFileListBox;
```

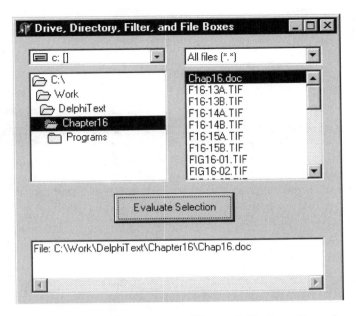

FIGURE 16.23   Drive, Directory, Filter, and File Boxes Example

```
    btnEvaluate: TButton;
    memOutput: TMemo;
    fltFileName: TFilterComboBox;
    procedure Evaluate(Sender: TObject);
  private
    { Private declarations }
  public
    { Public declarations }
  end;

var
  frmDrvDirFltFil: TfrmDrvDirFltFil;

implementation

{$R *.DFM}

procedure TfrmDrvDirFltFil.Evaluate(Sender: TObject);

begin
  memOutput.Clear;
  if filFileName.ItemIndex >= 0 then begin
    memOutput.Lines.Add('File: ' + filFileName.FileName);
  end
  else begin
```

```
        memOutput.Lines.Add('Please select a file.');
      end;
   end;

   end.
```

GUI Design Tips

Rather than create your own file selection interface (as we did in this example), you can use a dialog control (discussed in the next section). Dialog controls provide standardized Windows interfaces for common operations, such as opening a file or selecting a font. The OpenDialog component, for instance, is a standardized control to select a file.

Dialogs Page

Dialog components are dialog boxes that are common to most Windows-based applications. When you save a text file in WordPad, for example, you use the Save As dialog box. When you save a workbook in Microsoft Excel, a similar Save As dialog box appears. Microsoft Windows makes creating such controls easy for us. That is, we need not "reinvent the wheel" each time we want a dialog box to appear when the user saves or opens a file. Instead, we can simply invoke the dialog component to accomplish the desired task.

Delphi provides 10 dialog components: OpenDialog, SaveDialog, OpenPictureDialog, SavePictureDialog, FontDialog, ColorDialog, PrintDialog, PrinterSetupDialog, FindDialog, and ReplaceDialog. Each dialog has its own unique set of properties and events. Like the timer control, a dialog component appears as an icon on a form, but remains hidden from the user at run time. To invoke a dialog, you use its Execute method.

As an example, the following program allows the user to select a file using the OpenDialog component and then displays the name of the selected file in a memo box. SelectFile is the OnClick event handler for btnSelectFile. A sample execution of this code appears in Figure 16.24.

```
   unit OpenDialogEx;

   interface

   uses
     Windows, Messages, SysUtils, Classes, Graphics, Controls,
     Forms, Dialogs, StdCtrls;
```

```
type
  TfrmOpenDialog = class(TForm)
    dlgOpenFile: TOpenDialog;
    btnSelectFile: TButton;
    memOutput: TMemo;
    procedure SelectFile(Sender: TObject);
  private
    { Private declarations }
  public
    { Public declarations }
  end;

var
  frmOpenDialog: TfrmOpenDialog;

implementation

{$R *.DFM}
```

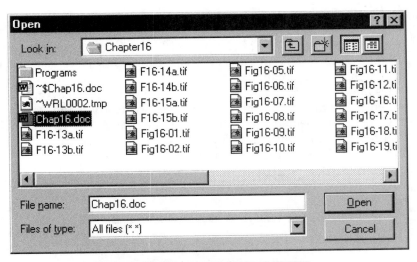

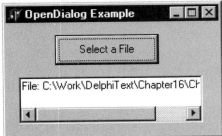

FIGURE 16.24   OpenDialog Example

```
procedure TfrmOpenDialog.SelectFile(Sender: TObject);
var
  selected: Boolean;
begin
  selected := dlgOpenFile.Execute;
  memOutput.Clear;
  if selected then begin
    memOutput.Lines.Add('File: ' + dlgOpenFile.FileName);
  end
  else begin
    memOutput.Lines.Add('No file selected.');
  end;
end;

end.
```

Conclusions

The number and variety of components available in Delphi depends on which edition you use (Standard, Professional, or Enterprise). For instance, the Standard edition includes more than 85 components, whereas the Professional edition provides more than 150 components. The programmer can also create custom components, and many third-party companies sell ready-made Delphi components. This chapter presented a mere fraction of the components available. The best way to become familiar with these and other components is to read the documentation and experiment with them in your own programs.

Summary

Keywords

Constants

cbChecked	fsBold
cbGrayed	taRightJustify
cbUnchecked	

Data Types

TCanvas	TPicture
TMainMenu	TPopupMenu
TMenuItem	TStrings

Events

OnChange	OnPaint
OnClick	OnScroll
OnExecute	OnTimer

Exceptions

EInvalidGraphic

Methods

Add	Execute
Delete	LoadFromFile

Properties

Action	Kind
Alignment	LargeChange
AllowGrayed	Left
AutoSize	Lines
BevelWidth	Max
BorderWidth	Min
Caption	MultiSelect
Checked	Name
Columns	Picture
Directory	PopupMenu
DirList	Position
Drive	ReadOnly
Enabled	ScrollBars
FileEdit	SelCount
FileList	Selected
FileName	SmallChange
Filter	Sorted
Font	State
Font, Name	Stretch
Font, Size	Style
Font, Style	Text
HorzScrollBar	Top
Interval	VertScrollBar
ItemIndex	WordWrap
Items	

Key Concepts

- Although simple controls such as edit boxes and buttons suffice to create most programs, Delphi offers a variety of other controls. These controls greatly reduce the amount of code necessary to perform common tasks. Much of the power and appeal of Delphi stems from the ease with which a programmer can design complex user interfaces using the controls in the Component Palette.

- Check box controls allow the user to select one or more items from a list of several alternatives. Radio buttons allow the user to select only a single item from a list.

- The scroll bar control provides a means of rapidly navigating through long lists of items or large quantities of data. A scroll bar can indicate a speed, quantity, or position.

- A group box groups related controls and functionally subdivides a form. A radio group box is a special group box that contains only radio buttons.

- An action list centralizes the response to user actions for different objects. Action lists are typically used to synchronize the event handlers for menus and buttons.

- Frames are containers for other components that can be saved on the Component Palette for repeated use in many applications. A frame functions as a unit and inherits changes from the components that it contains.

- Main menus and pop-up menus can be easily designed by using the Main Menu editor and Pop-up Menu editor, respectively. Their properties are set in the Object Inspector window. A main menu appears at the top of the form, whereas a pop-up menu is associated with a specific control. Right-clicking a control activates its pop-up menu.

- The image control, which displays images or graphics on a form, supports bitmap, icon, metafile, enhanced metafile, and JPEG formats. To assign a picture file to an image control at run time, use the `LoadFromFile` method of the image control's `TPicture` object.

- A scroll box creates a scrolling region on a form.

- A static text box is similar to a label, except that it can receive the focus.

- The timer control allows for the execution of specific code at user-specified intervals by causing the `OnTimer` event to occur. The timer control, which is transparent to the user, is useful for background processing.

- The drive combo box, directory list box, filter combo box, and file list box access the computer's disk drive information so as to display drive, directory folder, file mask, and file name information at run time. These controls are most often used in combination to allow a user to select a specific file.

- Dialog controls provide standardized Windows interfaces for common operations, such as opening a file or selecting a font. The OpenDialog, for instance, is a standardized control to select a file.

Review Questions

1. Describe the differences between a check box and a radio button.
2. Describe the differences between a list box and a combo box.
3. Give an example of the use of a scroll bar. How does this control differ from a scroll box?
4. What is an action list?
5. How does a pop-up menu differ from a main menu?
6. For each of the following, identify the best control to use in the program interface:
   a. You want the user to select the default disk drive.
   b. The user needs to select several items from a list.
   c. The user interface constitutes an area larger than the form. The user should view specific areas at a time.
   d. You want to use the same set of controls in other programs.
   e. The user can select a title (Mr., Mrs., Dr., etc.) or type in his or her preferred entry.
   f. The user needs to select a font.
   g. A specific piece of code must execute every 10 seconds.
   h. The user can select only one item from a list.
   i. You want to display a graphical indication of position.

Problems

1. Write a distance conversion program that converts units among centimeters, inches, feet, meters, kilometers, and miles. Use list boxes to select the units. (*Note:* There are 3.28 feet per meter and 1.61 kilometers per mile.)
2. Improve the user interface from Problem 1 in Chapter 7. Use a drive combo box, directory list box, and file list box to select the file.
3. Repeat Problem 2 using the OpenDialog component.
4. Create a picture file viewer. The user should be able to select a picture file using the OpenDialog component, and then the program should display the picture in an image control. The user should be given the option as to whether the picture will be resized.
5. Modify Problem 4 so that if the user does not resize the picture, he or she can scroll the image to view different parts of the picture. Note that an image control does not have a `ScrollBars` property. (*Hint:* Use a scroll box and an image control.)
6. Create a program that allows the user to select a date. The interface should include radio buttons to select a month and combo boxes to select the day and year.

7. Repeat Problem 6, placing the necessary controls in a frame. Save this frame on the Component Palette under the name ChooseDate.

Programming Projects

1. Improve the user interface from Project 3 in Chapter 5 by using the ChooseDate frame created in Problem 7.

2. Create your own custom text editor, similar to the Simple Editor example of this chapter. Your editor should include menus and options to cut, copy, and paste text as well as load and save the text file.

Chapter 17

Advanced Delphi Programming

Chapter Objectives

In this chapter you will:

- Gain an understanding of ActiveX technology, ActiveX controls, and ActiveForms

- Create and test an ActiveForm

- Learn about multiple forms programming and Multiple Document Interface (MDI) forms

- Be introduced to random numbers and computer simulation

- Become familiar with Delphi's graphics capabilities and graphics programming

- Learn about Object Linking and Embedding (OLE) and Dynamic Data Exchange (DDE)

- Examine Delphi's Internet capabilities and Internet programming

- Acquire an understanding of compiler directives and conditional compilation

This chapter discusses more advanced Delphi programming topics, including ActiveX controls and forms, multiple forms programming, Multiple Document Interface (MDI) forms, random numbers, graphics, Object Linking and Embedding (OLE), Dynamic Data Exchange (DDE), Internet programming, compiler directives, and conditional compilation. Like Chapter 16, it is not intended to provide a comprehensive reference for these topics, but rather to supply some programming examples that illustrate both the ease and power of Delphi.

ActiveX Controls and Forms

An **ActiveX** control is a software component that integrates into and extends the functionality of any host application that supports ActiveX technology, such as C++Builder, Delphi, Internet Explorer, Netscape Navigator, and Visual Basic. This technology allows programmers to design and develop their own software components for use in programs or Web-based applications. The ActiveX specification is part of Microsoft's Component Object Model (COM), which allows user-developed and off-the-shelf software components to work together seamlessly. Microsoft has led the move toward component-based software design by providing this open, extensible standard for software interoperability. Component-based software development significantly reduces programming time and produces more robust applications.

ActiveX technology is not the same as object-oriented programming (OOP). Whereas OOP supports the creation of object-based software components, ActiveX technology allows the programmer to combine object-based components created using different tools and enables these objects to work together. For instance, you can use Delphi to construct a set of useful objects, which other developers can then use and extend. If your objects are packaged in an ActiveX component, however, they can be used and extended with any programming tool that supports ActiveX technology.

Delphi comes prepackaged with several ActiveX controls, including charting, spreadsheet, and graphics controls. These controls work like any standard VCL component: In the IDE, you select the desired ActiveX control from the Component Palette, place it on the form, and set its properties with the Object Inspector. Each ActiveX control is linked to its application's executable file (or run-time package).

Delphi allows a programmer to create two types of ActiveX components: ActiveX controls and ActiveX forms (ActiveForms). As an aid to the programmer, Delphi includes two wizards for ActiveX development. The ActiveX Control Wizard converts an existing or custom control into an ActiveX control by placing it inside an ActiveX class wrapper. The ActiveForm Wizard creates an ActiveX control from a standard Delphi form for Web deployment. Thus the programmer has ready access to the tools needed for rapidly creating, debugging, and deploying a variety of software components.

Developing custom Delphi components is beyond the scope of this text, so this section will not cover the creation of custom ActiveX controls. Instead, you should consult the Delphi documentation, online help, and Inprise's Web site for information about the development of custom controls. For additional information on ActiveX controls, refer to the Microsoft Developer's Network (MSDN) documentation and Microsoft's Web site.

You can use the ActiveX Control Wizard to easily convert an existing Delphi control into an ActiveX control. This relatively straightforward process is described in the Delphi online help under "Creating an ActiveX control." The remainder of this section lists the steps necessary to create an ActiveForm example. This example requires the NameBox frame from Chapter 16.

1. Start Delphi and select `File|New...` from the menu bar.

2. Select the ActiveForm icon under the ActiveX tab in the New Items window. Click the OK button.

3. Change the names and settings in the ActiveForm Wizard to match those shown in Figure 17.1. Click the OK button.

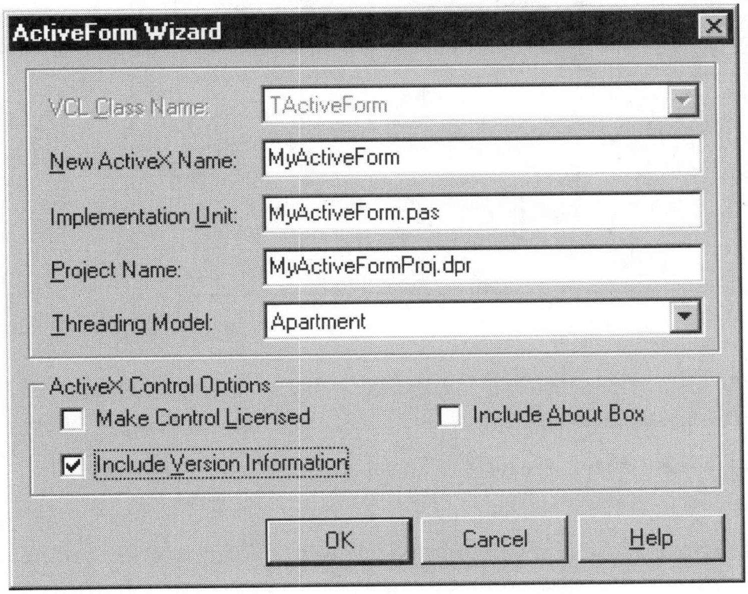

FIGURE 17.1   ActiveForm Wizard

Component	Property	Setting
Form	Name	frmMyActiveForm
	Caption	ActiveForm Example
NameBox	Name	nbxName
Button	Name	btnDone
	Caption	Done
	Font	MS Sans Serif
	Style	Bold
	Size	18
Memo Box	Name	memOutput
	Lines	*Empty*
	ReadOnly	True

Component Name	Event	Setting
btnDone	OnClick	Evaluate

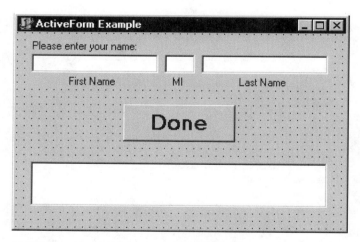

FIGURE 17.2 Form for ActiveForm Example

4. The new ActiveForm named MyActiveForm appears on the screen. Design the form so that it is similar in appearance to the one shown in Figure 17.2. The property and event settings appear in the table above.

5. Add the following event handler to this ActiveForm:

```
procedure TfrmMyActiveForm.Evaluate(Sender: TObject);
var
  first:    String;
  middle:   String;
  last:     String;
  fullName: String;
begin
  with nbxName do begin
    first := Trim(edtFirstName.Text);
    middle := Trim(edtMiddleInitial.Text);
    last := Trim(edtLastName.Text);
  end;
  fullName := Trim(first + ' ' + middle + ' ' + last);

  memOutput.Clear;
  if (fullName <> '')  then begin
    memOutput.Lines.Add('You entered: ' + fullName);
  end
  else begin
    memOutput.Lines.Add('Please enter your name.');
  end;
end;
```

6. Select `File|Save All` to save all files associated with this project.
7. Compile the project into an .OCX (ActiveX component) file. Select `Project|Compile MyActiveFormProj` from the menu bar.
8. Register the new ActiveForm. Select `Run|Register ActiveX Server` from the menu.

Congratulations, you have just created your first ActiveX control, an Active-Form. Now let's complete this example by deploying the control to the Web and testing it in a Web browser:

1. Select `Project|Web Deployment Options...` to open the Web Deployment Options window.
2. Change the Target URL to www.test.url (a "junk" value that is not really used during our testing).
3. Specify target directories for the compiled ActiveX control (.OCX file) and Web page (HTML file).
4. Check the Include file version number box.
5. Click the OK button.
6. Select `Project|Web Deploy` from the menu bar.

Next, let's test this control in a Web browser. By "Web deploying" the control, Delphi automatically generates a test Web page (in HTML format). Follow the steps on the next page to test the ActiveForm:

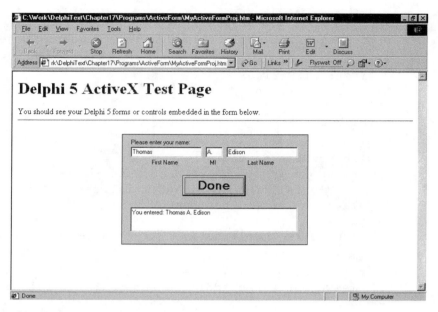

FIGURE 17.3   ActiveForm Example

1. Start Windows Explorer.
2. Locate the target HTML directory that you specified earlier.
3. Double-click the file named `MyActiveFormProj.htm`. Your default Web browser will open and your ActiveForm will appear on a test Web page.
4. Type your name in the form and click the Done button. A sample output appears in Figure 17.3.
5. Close the Web browser and Windows Explorer.

Multiple Forms Programming and Multiple Document Interface Forms

Programming with multiple forms in Delphi is simply a matter of setting the `Visible` properties and calling the `SetFocus` methods of the forms at appropriate times within the program code. The example provided in this section contains two forms: a main form and a sub form. The main form includes a button that displays the sub form. Similarly, the sub form includes a button that returns control to the main form. Notice that the sub form does not contain any border icons to minimize, maximize, or close the form. This format ensures that the user will exit the program from the main form and that the program will terminate properly. Figure 17.4 shows both the main and sub forms.

Main Form

Component	Property	Setting
Form	Name	frmMultipleForms
	BorderStyle	bsSingle
	Caption	Multiple Forms Programming
		Example
Button	Name	btnActivate
	Caption	Activate Sub-form

Component Name	Event	Setting
btnActivate	OnClick	OpenSubform

```
unit MainForm;

interface

uses
  Windows, Messages, SysUtils, Classes, Graphics, Controls,
  Forms, Dialogs, StdCtrls;

type
  TfrmMultipleForms = class(TForm)
    btnActivate: TButton;
    procedure OpenSubform(Sender: TObject);
  private
    { Private declarations }
  public
    { Public declarations }
  end;

var
  frmMultipleForms: TfrmMultipleForms;

implementation

uses SubForm;

{$R *.DFM}

procedure TfrmMultipleForms.OpenSubform(Sender: TObject);

begin
  frmSubform.Visible := True;
  frmMultipleForms.Visible := False;
```

> In this example, each form must be visible to the other form's code unit. This goal is accomplished through the uses clause in the implementation section.

```
      frmSubform.SetFocus;
end;

end.
```

Sub Form

Component	Property	Setting
Form	Name	frmSubform
	BorderIcons	[]
	BorderStyle	bsSingle
	Caption	Sub-form
Button	Name	btnReturn
	Caption	Return to Main Form

Component Name	Event	Setting
btnReturn	OnClick	ReturnToMain

```
unit SubForm;

interface

uses
  Windows, Messages, SysUtils, Classes, Graphics, Controls,
  Forms, Dialogs, StdCtrls;

type
  TfrmSubform = class(TForm)
    btnReturn: TButton;
    procedure ReturnToMain(Sender: TObject);
  private
    { Private declarations }
  public
    { Public declarations }
  end;

var
  frmSubform: TfrmSubform;

implementation

uses MainForm;
```

In this example, each form must be visible to the other form's code unit. This goal is accomplished through the uses clause in the `implementation` section.

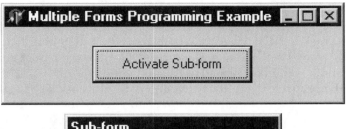

FIGURE 17.4   Multiple Forms Example

```
{$R *.DFM}

procedure TfrmSubform.ReturnToMain(Sender: TObject);

begin
  frmMultipleForms.Visible := True;
  frmSubform.Visible := False;
  frmMultipleForms.SetFocus;
end;

end.
```

MDI versus SDI

A **Multiple Document Interface (MDI)** is an application that allows multiple forms (or windows) to be open within a single container form (or window). The container form (window) is referred to as the *parent*; it provides a workspace for all of the *child* forms (windows) that are open in the application. Many Windows-based programs use MDI forms as their main form. Microsoft Excel, for instance, allows several workbooks to be open simultaneously; each workbook appears in a separate child window.

A **Single Document Interface (SDI)** is the opposite of MDI. In an SDI application, only one file may be open at a time; the user must close the current file before opening another file. Notepad and WordPad are examples of SDI applications that are included with Microsoft Windows.

Clearly, MDI and SDI are different styles of user interfaces. How does the programmer decide which one to use? Quite simply, the choice between MDI and SDI depends on the user's requirements. An MDI is the best choice if the user needs to have several files open simultaneously. MDI is also more flexible than SDI, as the user can control the number of open windows. The disadvantage, however, is that an MDI is slightly more complex and generally takes longer to program than an SDI. Remember that the MDI form is the parent form in your application, and it should control all of its child windows.

All of the programs you have encountered in this book so far have been SDI applications; none of these applications had child windows. To assist the programmer, Delphi includes predesigned MDI and SDI application templates. The Notebook program presents an example MDI application. Follow the steps listed below to create this example program. You may also create an SDI version of the Notebook program using the SDI application template if you like.

1. Start Delphi and select `File | New...` from the menu bar.

2. Select the MDI Application icon under the Projects tab in the New Items window. Click the OK button.

3. The Select Directory window appears on the screen. Select or create the directory where you want to store the files associated with this project. Click the OK button.

4. The predesigned MDI application template is copied, and Delphi opens this copy. The predesigned MDI form shown in Figure 17.5 will appear on your screen.

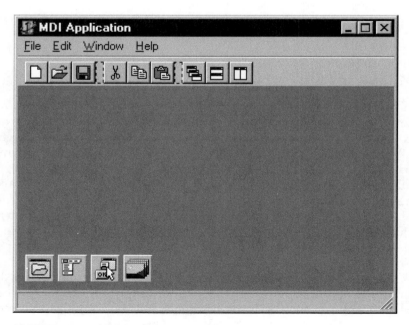

FIGURE 17.5   MDI Application Template

FIGURE 17.6   About Box

5. Press SHIFT+F12 to open the View Form window. Select all of the forms by left-clicking AboutBox and dragging down to MDIChild. Next, click the OK button. All of the forms in the project will appear on your screen.

6. Modify the contents of the labels in the AboutBox so that it appears similar to the one shown in Figure 17.6. Note that the image control is removed and you should use your own name as the programmer.

7. Select the MDIChild form. Set its **Height** property to 250 and its **Width** property to 375. Set **BorderStyle** to bsSingle.

8. Select the Memo1 memo box, and change its properties as follows:

Component	Property	Setting
Memo Box	Name	Memo1
	Align	alNone
	Height	150
	Top	72
	WordWrap	True

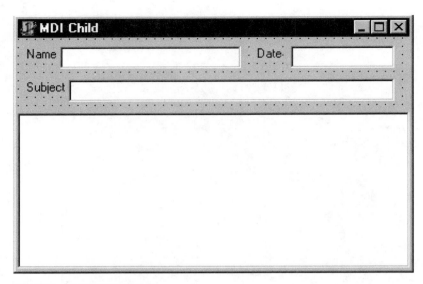

FIGURE 17.7 MDI Child Form

9. Add components to the form and set their properties as indicated in the following table. Figure 17.7 shows the completed form.

Component	Property	Setting
Label	Name	lblName
	Caption	Name
Label	Name	lblDate
	Caption	Date
Label	Name	lblSubject
	Caption	Subject
Edit Box	Name	edtName
	Text	*Empty*
Edit Box	Name	edtDate
	Text	*Empty*
Edit Box	Name	edtSubject
	Text	*Empty*

10. Select the `MainForm` form. Change its `Caption` property to read "Note-book."

11. Modify the `FileNew1Execute` event handler in the unit `Main.pas` as follows:

```
procedure TMainForm.FileNew1Execute(Sender: TObject);

begin
  CreateMDIChild('Notebook ' + IntToStr(MDIChildCount
                 + 1));
end;
```

12. Save all files by selecting `File|Save All` from the menu bar.

Now you can compile and execute the program. Notice that you can use the program's menu bar or toolbar to open multiple notebooks (multiple child windows) within the parent window. Figure 17.8 shows a sample execution of this code. Note that we did not implement the Save and Save As… operations in this program. These operations are left as an exercise for the reader.

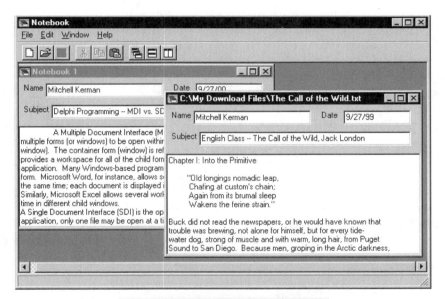

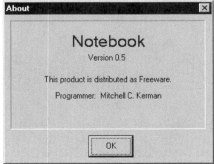

FIGURE 17.8   MDI Application Example

Random Numbers

Random numbers play an important role in games and simulation. In Delphi, the **Randomize** procedure and the **Random** function are used to generate random numbers.

The Randomize procedure initializes Delphi's random number generator. The syntax of this procedure follows:

```
Randomize;
```

This procedure takes a value from the system clock as its **seed value.** The seed value is simply an initial value used by Delphi to generate pseudorandom numbers.

Instead of calling the Randomize procedure, you may specify a seed value directly by assigning a long integer value to the global variable **RandSeed.** RandSeed stores the built-in random number generator's seed value. For each particular value assigned to RandSeed, the Random function generates a unique sequence of random numbers. This capability is useful for applications that require a repeating sequence of random numbers. The following syntax initializes the random number generator by assigning a value to RandSeed:

```
RandSeed := longIntSeedValue;
```

The random number generator should be initialized only once in a program, either by calling Randomize or by assigning a value to RandSeed.

The Random function returns a random number within a specified range. The general syntax is as follows:

```
randomNumber := Random(upperLimit);
```

This statement assigns a random integer value to the integer variable *randomNumber*. This variable will contain an integer value greater than or equal to zero but strictly less than the integer *upperLimit*. Note that *upperLimit* is an optional argument, but the parentheses must be used if it is specified. If *upperLimit* is not specified, the Random function returns a real value greater than or equal to zero but strictly less than 1.

The following program demonstrates the use of random numbers in a **Monte Carlo simulation.** It simulates tossing a die 1000 times, repeating this experiment 10 times. The program then reports the overall percentage of occurrences of each number. Figure 17.9 shows a sample execution of this code. The Simulate procedure is the OnClick event handler for the btnSimulate button.

```
unit RandomNumbersEx;

interface

uses
  Windows, Messages, SysUtils, Classes, Graphics, Controls,
  Forms, Dialogs, StdCtrls;

Const
  TRIALS = 10;    {Number of trials}
  ITERS = 1000;   {Number of rolls (iterations) per trial}
  SIX = 6;        {Max die value}

type
  TfrmRandomNumbers = class(TForm)
    btnSimulate: TButton;
    memOutput: TMemo;
    procedure Simulate(Sender: TObject);
  private
    { Private declarations }
  public
    { Public declarations }
  end;

var
  frmRandomNumbers: TfrmRandomNumbers;

implementation

{$R *.DFM}

{Simulate rolling a die ITERS times, repeat this experiment
 TRIALS times, and report the final results}
procedure TfrmRandomNumbers.Simulate(Sender: TObject);

var
  die:       array [1..SIX, 1..TRIALS] of Integer;
  iteration: Integer;
  trial:     Integer;
  roll:      Integer;
  sum:       Integer;

begin
  {Initialize the array}
  for trial := 1 to TRIALS do begin
    for iteration := 1 To SIX do begin
        die[iteration, trial] := 0;
    end;
  end;
```

```
Randomize; {Initialize the random number generator}

for trial := 1 to TRIALS do begin
  for iteration := 1 to ITERS do begin
    roll := Random(SIX) + 1;  {Roll the die}
    die[roll, trial] := die[roll, trial] + 1;
  end;
end;

{Output final results (overall % of time each number
 occurred)}
memOutput.Clear;
memOutput.Lines.Add('Number  Percentage');
memOutput.Lines.Add('---  -----');
for iteration := 1 to SIX do begin
  sum := 0;
  for trial := 1 to TRIALS do begin
    sum := sum + die[iteration, trial];
  end;
  memOutput.Lines.Add(IntToStr(iteration) +
                  Format('%12.2f',
                  [sum/(TRIALS*ITERS)*100]));
end;

memOutput.Lines.Add('');
memOutput.Lines.Add('In theory, each number should occur');
memOutput.Lines.Add(Format('%f', [(1/SIX)*100]) +
                  '% of the time.');
end;

end.
```

Programming Key: Delphi Highlight

Delphi also provides the **RandG** function, which generates random numbers with a Gaussian (or normal) distribution about the mean. This function is useful for simulating data with sampling errors and expected deviations from the mean.

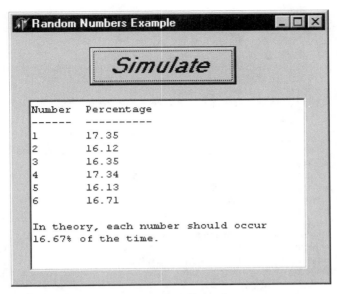

FIGURE 17.9   Random Numbers Example

Graphics

Delphi's graphics components encapsulate the Windows Graphics Device Interface (GDI), providing powerful graphics capabilities and facilitating the addition of graphics to your programs. In particular, you must become familiar with three objects to create graphics in Delphi: **Canvas**, **Brush**, and **Pen**. In this section, we use these objects in reference to an image control. Note, however, that you can use them with any control that contains a canvas, such as a form.

To draw graphics in a Delphi application, you draw on an object's canvas. Canvas is a property of the object as well as an object itself. Its main advantages relate to its efficient handling of resources and device independence. That is, Delphi programs can use the same Canvas methods regardless of whether the program draws on the screen, printer, bitmap, or metafile. An object's Canvas property is available only at run time, however, so all drawings are created through the source code. Figure 17.10 lists the common properties and methods of the Canvas object.

The Brush property of a Canvas controls the manner in which the interiors of shapes and areas become filled. Using a brush to fill an area quickly changes a large number of adjacent pixels in a specified way. Like Canvas, Brush is also an object. The **Color** property of a Brush indicates the color used to fill the area, such as black (clBlack), red (clRed), or green (clGreen). Refer to the TColor type in the Delphi help facility to obtain a list of colors. The **Style** property alters the brush style; possible brush styles include solid (bsSolid), clear (bsClear), forward diagonal (bsFDiagonal), backward diagonal (bsBDiagonal), cross

Property	Description
Brush	Determines the color and pattern that the canvas uses for filling shapes and backgrounds.
Font	Specifies the font to use when writing text on the canvas. The properties of the TFont object indicate the font name, color, size, and style.
Pen	Specifies the pen used for drawing lines and outlining shapes. The properties of the TPen object specify the pen's color, style, width, and mode.
PenPos	Indicates the current drawing position of the pen.
Pixels	Specifies the color of the pixels within the current clip rectangle.

Method	Descriptions
Arc	Draws an arc on the image along the perimeter of the ellipse bounded by the specified rectangle.
Chord	Draws a closed figure represented by the intersection of a line and an ellipse.
CopyRect	Copies part of an image from another canvas into this canvas.
Draw	Renders the graphic object specified by the Graphic parameter on the canvas at the location given by the coordinates (X, Y).
Ellipse	Draws the ellipse defined by a bounding rectangle on the canvas.
FillRect	Fills the specified rectangle on the canvas using the current brush.
FloodFill	Fills an area of the canvas using the current brush.
FrameRect	Draws a rectangle using the brush to draw the border.
LineTo	Draws a line on the canvas from PenPos to the point specified by X and Y and sets the pen position to (X, Y).
MoveTo	Changes the current drawing position to the point (X, Y).
Pie	Draws a pie-shaped section of the ellipse bounded by the rectangle $(X1, Y1)$ and $(X2, Y2)$.
Polygon	Draws a series of lines on the canvas that connect the points and closes the shape by drawing a line from the last point to the first point.
PolyLine	Draws a series of lines on the canvas that connects each of the points using the current pen.
Rectangle	Draws a rectangle on the canvas with its upper-left corner at point $(X1, Y1)$ and its lower-right corner at point $(X2, Y2)$. The rectangle is drawn using the current pen and filled using the current brush.
RoundRect	Draws a rectangle with rounded corners.
StretchDraw	Draws a graphic on the canvas so that the image fits in the specified rectangle. The graphic image may change in size or aspect
TextHeight	Returns the height of a string in the current font, including the leading space between lines.
TextOut	Writes a string on the canvas, starting at the point (X, Y), and then updates the PenPos to the end of the string.
TextRect	Writes a string inside a specified rectangular region. Any portion of the string that falls outside of the region is not visible.
TextWidth	Returns the width of a string in the current font.

FIGURE 17.10 Canvas Object Properties and Methods

(bsCross), diagonal cross (bsDiagCross), horizontal (bsHorizontal), and vertical (bsVertical). The **Bitmap** property specifies an external bitmap image that defines a pattern for the brush. By default, every Brush object is instantiated with a white color, solid style, and no pattern bitmap.

The Pen property of a Canvas refers to an object of type TPen. It controls the appearance of lines, including lines drawn as the outlines of shapes. Like the Brush object, the Pen object has Color and Style properties. Examples of Pen styles include solid (psSolid), dash (psDash), and dot (psDot). The Width property of a `Pen` object contains an integer value that identifies the width of the pen in pixels; the minimum value of this property is 1. The **Mode** property determines how the color of the pen interacts with the color on the canvas.

A `Canvas` object also contains a `Font` property that refers to an object of type `TFont` for writing text. As we have used font objects numerous times throughout this text, we will not discuss them further here.

The following code provides an example of graphics use in Delphi. This program generates two circles in an image control; one circle is drawn using Delphi's prefabricated graphics methods and the other is drawn pixel-by-pixel. Figure 17.11 shows the output of this code.

```
unit GraphicsEx;

interface

uses
  Windows, Messages, SysUtils, Classes, Graphics, Controls,
  Forms, Dialogs, ExtCtrls, StdCtrls;

type
  TfrmGraphics = class(TForm)
    btnDrawExample: TButton;
    imgGraph: TImage;
    procedure DrawExample(Sender: TObject);
  private
    { Private declarations }
  public
    { Public declarations }
  end;

var
  frmGraphics: TfrmGraphics;

implementation

{$R *.DFM}

procedure TfrmGraphics.DrawExample(Sender: TObject);
var
  originX: Integer;
  originY: Integer;
  xVal:    Integer;
  yVal:    Integer;
  loc:     Real;
  radius:  Real;
  rad:     Integer;
begin
  originX := 75;
```

```
  originY := 75;
  radius := 50.0;
  rad := Trunc(radius);

  with imgGraph.Canvas do begin
    Pen.Style := psSolid;
    Pen.Color := clBlack;
    Pen.Width := 1;
    Brush.Style := bsDiagCross;
    Brush.Color := clRed;
    Ellipse(originX-rad, originY-rad, originX+rad,
            originY+rad);

    originX := 75;
    originY := 200;
    loc := -radius;
    while (loc < radius) do begin
      yVal := Round(Sqrt(Sqr(radius) - Sqr(loc)));
      xVal := Round(loc);
      Pixels[originX+xVal, originY+yVal] := clBlack;
      Pixels[originX+xVal, originY-yVal] := clBlack;
      loc := loc + 0.01;
    end;

    TextOut(140, 65, 'Draw a circle the easy way');
    TextOut(140, 80, 'using Delphi''s built-in graphics' +
                     ' methods.');
    TextOut(140, 190, 'Draw a circle the hard way');
    TextOut(140, 205, 'using calculations in program code.');
  end;
end;

end.
```

Programming Key: Delphi Highlight

Delphi includes an **RGB** function with which you can specify a particular color. This function requires three parameters to indicate the intensity of the red, green, and blue colors, respectively. The range of each intensity value is from 0 to 255 (one byte). If all three intensities are 0, the result is black. If all three intensities are 255, the result is white. This function can generate more than 16 million colors.

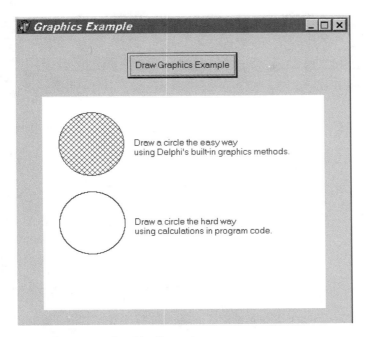

FIGURE 17.11   Graphics Example

Object Linking and Embedding

From our discussion of object-oriented programming in Chapter 15, we know that Delphi components and controls are objects. Documents created with other applications can also be treated as objects within Delphi. This idea underlies the concept of **Object Linking and Embedding (OLE)**.

OLE is a compound document standard developed by Microsoft that allows an object to be created with one application and then linked or embedded in a second application. For instance, you can create a spreadsheet with Microsoft Excel and then link or embed this spreadsheet in a Delphi program. A **linked object** references the original object, so any changes to a linked object also apply to the original object. An **embedded object,** in contrast, is a copy of the original object. Modifications to an embedded object do not alter the original object.

The System tab of Delphi's Component Palette includes the OLE container control (`TOleContainer`). We will describe a few properties of this control here. The **AutoActivate** property determines how the object in the OLE container is activated—by receiving the focus, by double-clicking the control, or manually through code. The **Linked** property contains a Boolean value that indicates

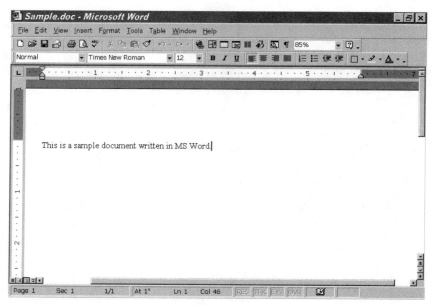

FIGURE 17.12   Sample Document

whether the OLE object is linked or embedded. If `Linked` is True, the object is linked; otherwise, it is embedded. At run time, the **Modified** property contains a Boolean value that indicates whether the object has been modified.

Let's create a program that uses the OLE container control. First, start Microsoft Word and create the document shown in Figure 17.12. Save this document under the name `Sample.doc`.

Next, start a new application in Delphi and create the form described below:

Component	Property	Setting
Form	Name	frmOLE
	Caption	OLE Example — Embedded
Label	Name	lblInstructions
	Caption	Double-click the OLE container below to activate Microsoft Word.
	WordWrap	True
OleContainer	Name	oleDocument

Right-click the OLE container control and select `Insert Object...` from the pop-up menu. The Insert Object dialog box (Figure 17.13) appears on the screen.

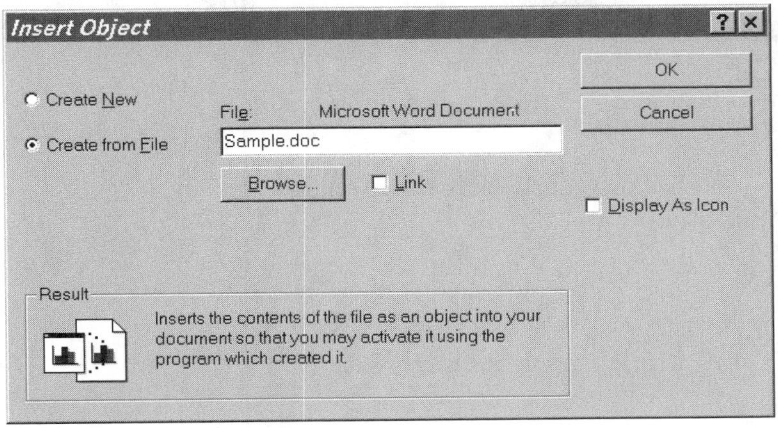

FIGURE 17.13   Insert Object Window

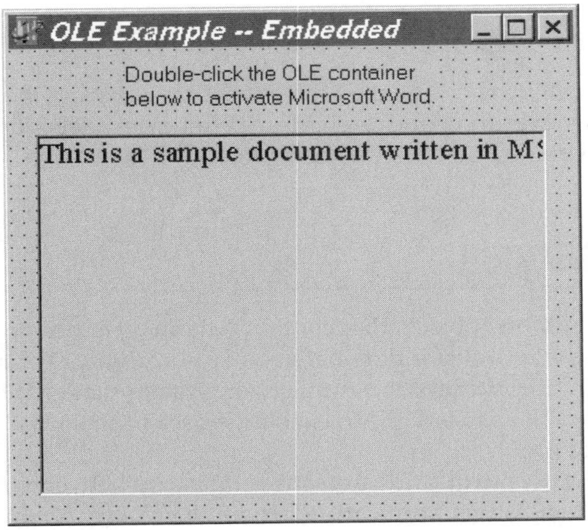

FIGURE 17.14   Form for OLE Example

Select the Create from File radio button, then locate and select the `Sample.doc` Word document that you created earlier. Make sure that the Link check box is cleared, and then click the OK button. The completed form should appear similar to the one shown in Figure 17.14.

Save the project, run the program, and double-click the OLE container control. Your screen should display the form shown in Figure 17.15.

Next, create a new application. Repeat the process described above, but this time set the `Caption` property of the form to "OLE Example — Linked" and link

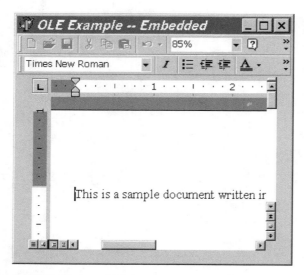

FIGURE 17.15   OLE Example

to the Word document by checking the Link check box. Save and then run the program. How does the execution of this program differ from execution of the previous version when you double-click the OLE container?

Dynamic Data Exchange

Rather than link or embed objects that contain data in a Delphi program, a programmer may choose to transfer data between applications. **Dynamic Data Exchange (DDE)** is an interprocess communication system that enables two active applications to share the same data. To exchange data in this way, both applications must support DDE.

To use DDE, a DDE conversation must be established between the DDE client application and a DDE server application, where the client application requests the data from the server application. Reflecting this relationship, the server application is often called the source and the client is called the destination.

Delphi allows a programmer to create both DDE client and server applications. In fact, a single Delphi application can be both a DDE client and a DDE server. The System tab of the Component Palette contains the components needed to create such applications—namely, the DDE client conversation, DDE client item, DDE server conversation, and DDE server item.

As an example, let's create a DDE client application with Delphi. Microsoft Excel is the server application for this example, so first we must create an Excel spreadsheet. Start Microsoft Excel and create the spreadsheet shown in

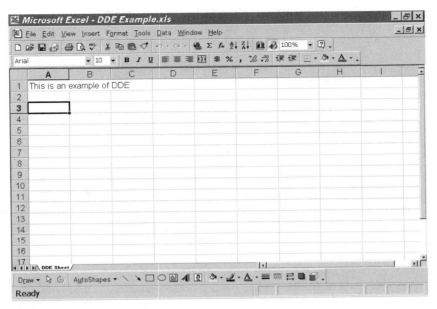

FIGURE 17.16   Microsoft Excel Spreadsheet for DDE Example

Figure 17.16 by typing "This is an example of DDE" in the first cell (cell A1). Save the Excel workbook, but do not close the spreadsheet or exit Microsoft Excel.

Next, create a new application in Delphi and design the form as indicated below:

Component	Property	Setting
Form	Name	frmDDE
	Caption	DDE Example
Label	Name	lblFirstCell
	Caption	First Cell (R1C1):
Edit Box	Name	edtFirstCell
	Text	*Empty*
DdeClientConv	Name	ddcConversation
DdeClientItem	Name	ddiItem
	DdeConv	ddcConversation

Component Name	Event	Setting
ddiItem	OnChange	UpdateDisplay

Now, add the `UpdateDisplay` event handler code:

```
procedure TfrmDDE.UpdateDisplay(Sender: TObject);
begin
  edtFirstCell.Text := ddiItem.Text;
end;
```

Finally, create the link between the two applications (that is, our Microsoft Excel spreadsheet and Delphi program). In Microsoft Excel, select the first cell that contains the text (cell A1). Next, select `Edit | Copy` from the Excel menu bar. In Delphi's Object Inspector window, select the `ddcConversation` component. Click the `DdeService` property, then click the ellipsis button (the three dots) on the right side of the window. The DDE Info window (Figure 17.17) will appear on the screen. Click the Paste Link button to paste in the link to the Excel worksheet data, then click the OK button. Select the `ddiItem` component in the Object Inspector window, then click the `DdeItem` property. Choose `R1C1` from the drop-down list for this property setting.

Save the Delphi project and then run the application. The application window should appear similar to Figure 17.18. Any data that you type into the first cell of your spreadsheet will automatically appear in your Delphi application.

For further information concerning the use and creation of DDE applications, consult "Using DDE," "DDE conversations," "Creating DDE client applications," and "Creating DDE server applications" in the Delphi help facility.

> Microsoft Excel must be open prior to creating and executing this program.

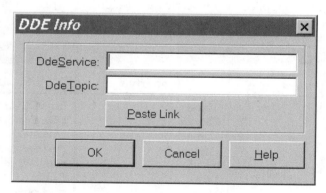

FIGURE 17.17   DDE Info Window

FIGURE 17.18 DDE Example

Programming Key: Tips

Programmers generally prefer to use OLE rather than DDE in Windows programs. Essentially, the use of DDE has been superseded by OLE. Within the past few years, OLE has evolved in COM/DCOM. Microsoft's COM (Component Object Model) is a Windows-based distributed object architecture designed to provide object interoperability using predefined routines known as interfaces. COM applications use objects that are implemented by a different process. The Distributed Component Object Model (DCOM) allows the use of objects that are implemented on a separate machine.

Internet Programming

All Internet-related components are located in the Component Palette's Internet tab. Examining this tab, we find that Delphi offers a variety of components to access the Internet and create Web-enabled programs. These components include Web browsers, client and server sockets, Web dispatchers, page producers, and other components to access and display Web-based data.

An in-depth discussion of each of the Internet components is beyond the scope of this book. Instead, you should refer to the "Internet page components" topic in the Delphi help facility to see a brief description of these components and related information and links. We will focus on the `WebBrowser` component, using it in a sample program.

The Web browser component displays a (HTML) Web page in a Web browser-like viewer. To use this component, Microsoft Internet Explorer 4.0 or later must be installed on the computer. The **LocationURL** property contains the Uniform Resource Locator (URL), or Web address, of the current Web page. Similarly, the **LocationName** property contains the name of the current Web page. The **GoHome** method navigates to the browser's registered home (start) page. The

GoForward and **GoBack** methods navigate to the next and previous Web pages in the history list, respectively. The **GoSearch** method navigates to the browser's registered search page. The **Navigate** and **Navigate2** methods navigate to specific Web pages.

The following code implements a simple Web browser in Delphi using the Web-Browser component. Figure 17.19 displays a sample execution of this program.

Component	Property	Setting
Form	Name	frmWebBrowser
	Caption	Web Browser Example
Label	Name	lblPage
	Caption	Page:
Label	Name	lblLocationName
	Caption	*Empty*
Label	Name	lblAddress
	Caption	Address:
Edit Box	Name	edtAddress
	Text	*Empty*
Button	Name	btnBack
	Caption	<<< Back
Button	Name	btnForward
	Caption	Forward >>>
Button	Name	btnHome
	Caption	Go Home
WebBrowser	Name	WebBrowser

Component Name	Event	Setting
frmWebBrowser	OnResize	ResizeBrowser
frmWebBrowser	OnShow	GoHome
edtAddress	OnKeyPress	GotoURL
btnBack	OnClick	GoBack
btnForward	OnClick	GoForward
btnHome	OnClick	GoHome
WebBrowser	OnNavigate	NavComplete

```
unit WebBrowserEx;

interface

uses
  Windows, Messages, SysUtils, Classes, Graphics, Controls,
  Forms, Dialogs, OleCtrls, SHDocVw, StdCtrls;
```

```pascal
type
  TfrmWebBrowser = class(TForm)
    WebBrowser: TWebBrowser;
    lblAddress: TLabel;
    edtAddress: TEdit;
    btnBack: TButton;
    btnForward: TButton;
    btnHome: TButton;
    lblLocationName: TLabel;
    lblPage: TLabel;
    procedure GoHome(Sender: TObject);
    procedure ResizeBrowser(Sender: TObject);
    procedure GoBack(Sender: TObject);
    procedure GoForward(Sender: TObject);
    procedure DisplayLocation;
    procedure NavComplete(Sender: TObject;
                          const pDisp: IDispatch;
                          var URL: OleVariant);
    procedure GotoURL(Sender: TObject; var Key: Char);
  private
    { Private declarations }
  public
    { Public declarations }
  end;

var
  frmWebBrowser: TfrmWebBrowser;

implementation

{$R *.DFM}

procedure TfrmWebBrowser.DisplayLocation;

begin
  lblLocationName.Caption := WebBrowser.LocationName;
  edtAddress.Text := WebBrowser.LocationURL;
end;

procedure TfrmWebBrowser.GoHome(Sender: TObject);

begin
  WebBrowser.GoHome;
end;

procedure TfrmWebBrowser.ResizeBrowser(Sender: TObject);
```

```
begin
  WebBrowser.Width := frmWebBrowser.Width - 25;
  WebBrowser.Height := frmWebBrowser.Height - 130;
end;

procedure TfrmWebBrowser.GoBack(Sender: TObject);

begin
  try
    WebBrowser.GoBack;
  except
    on E: Exception do ShowMessage('Can''t go back!');
  end;
end;

procedure TfrmWebBrowser.GoForward(Sender: TObject);

begin
  try
    WebBrowser.GoForward;
  except
    on E: Exception do ShowMessage('Can''t go forward!');
  end;
end;
```

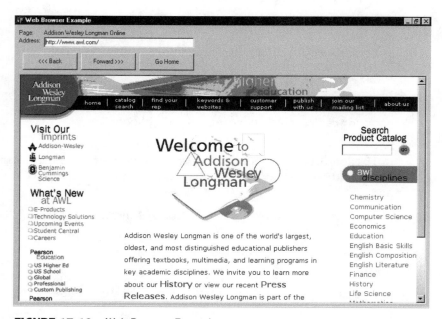

FIGURE 17.19 Web Browser Example

```
procedure TfrmWebBrowser.NavComplete(Sender: TObject;
  const pDisp: IDispatch; var URL: OleVariant);

begin
  DisplayLocation;
end;

procedure TfrmWebBrowser.GotoURL(Sender: TObject;
                           var Key: Char);

begin
  if (Key = Chr(13)) then begin
    WebBrowser.Navigate(edtAddress.Text);
  end;
end;

end.
```

Compiler Directives and Conditional Compilation

In previous chapters, we introduced compiler directives as they became necessary. **Compiler directives** consist of instructions for the compiler; they have no machine language equivalent and, therefore, are not compiled into machine code. In other words, they are **nonexecutable statements.**

> **Compiler directives** are compiler commands within a program's source code. **Nonexecutable statements** are statements that are not compiled into machine code, including comments and compiler directives.

In Delphi, a compiler directive is a comment that follows a special syntax. Delphi allows you to insert compiler directives wherever comments are allowed. A compiler directive consists of the dollar sign ($) as the first character after the opening comment delimiter, immediately followed by a name (containing one or more letters) that designates the particular directive. You may include comments within a compiler directive by placing them after the directive and any necessary parameters.

Each compiler directive may be classified as a switch, parameter, or conditional compilation directive. A switch directive turns a particular compiler feature on or off. A parameter directive specifies a parameter that affects the compilation, such as a file name or memory size. Refer to the "Compiler directives (list)" topic in the Delphi help facility to obtain a list of switch and parameter directives.

Compiler directives may be used to perform **conditional compilation**—that is, to compile specific blocks of code when certain conditions are met. Conditional compilation is typically employed to compile the same program for different computer platforms. Also, it may be used to prevent debugging code from appearing in an executable file. The code excluded during conditional compilation is completely omitted from the final executable file.

Conditional compilation directives include **$DEFINE**, **$UNDEF**, and the **$IF*xxx*-$ELSE-$ENDIF** construct. The $DEFINE directive defines a conditional symbol with the specified name. Its general syntax follows:

{$DEFINE *symbolName*}

where *symbolName* is recognized for the remainder of the compilation of the current module in which it is declared or until it appears in an $UNDEF directive. This directive has no effect if *symbolName* is already defined.

The $UNDEF directive undefines a previously defined conditional symbol. Thus the symbol becomes forgotten while the compilation of the current module continues or until it reappears in a $DEFINE directive. This directive has no effect if the symbol name is already undefined. Its general syntax follows:

{$UNDEF *symbolName*}

The $IF*xxx*-$ELSE-$ENDIF directive conditionally compiles selected blocks of Delphi source code and operates in the same manner as a standard if—then—else statement. Its general syntax follows:

```
{$IFxxx}
  [statements1]
[{$ELSE}
  [statements2]]
{$ENDIF}
```

In this syntax, the $ELSE directive clause is optional, but only one of these clauses may appear in the decision structure. Additionally, three $IF directives may take the place of $IF*xxx* in this syntax: **$IFDEF**, **$IFNDEF**, or **$IFOPT**. $IFDEF compiles the source code that follows it if the specified symbol name is defined. Conversely, $IFNDEF compiles the source code that follows it if the specified symbol name is not defined. $IFOPT compiles the source code that follows it if the indicated compiler switch is currently in the specified state.

The following example uses conditional compilation for debugging purposes. Figure 17.20 shows a sample output.

Component	Property	Setting
Form	Name	frmCondComp
	Caption	Conditional Compilation Example
Button	Name	btnExecute
	Caption	Execute Example
Memo Box	Name	memOutput
	Lines	*Empty*
Memo Box	Name	memDebug
	Lines	*Empty*
	ScrollBars	ssVertical
	Visible	False

Component Name	Event	Setting
btnExecute	OnClick	Execute

```
unit CondCompEx;

interface

uses
  Windows, Messages, SysUtils, Classes, Graphics, Controls,
  Forms, Dialogs, StdCtrls;

type
  TfrmCondComp = class(TForm)
    btnExecute: TButton;
    memOutput: TMemo;
    memDebug: TMemo;
    procedure Execute(Sender: TObject);
  private
    { Private declarations }
  public
    { Public declarations }
  end;

var
  frmCondComp: TfrmCondComp;

implementation

{$R *.DFM}

{$DEFINE Debug}

procedure TfrmCondComp.Execute(Sender: TObject);
```

```
var
  outer: Integer;
  inner: Integer;
  sum:   Integer;

begin

  {Check debug mode and display debug window}
  {$IFDEF Debug}
    memDebug.Visible := True;
    memDebug.Clear;
    memDebug.Lines.Add('DEBUG is on.');
  {$ENDIF}

  {Execute Loops}
  sum := 0;
  for outer := 1 to 5 do begin
    {$IFDEF Debug}
      memDebug.Lines.Add('Begin Outer Loop Iteration: ' +
                         IntToStr(outer));
    {$ENDIF}

    for inner := 1 to 5 do begin
      sum := sum + 1;
      {$IFDEF Debug}
        memDebug.Lines.Add('  Inner Loop Iteration: ' +
                           IntToStr(inner) + '; Sum = ' +
                           IntToStr(sum));
```

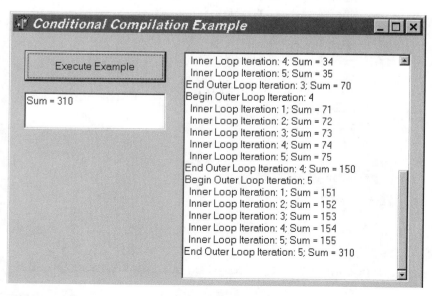

FIGURE 17.20 Conditional Compilation Example

```
        {$ENDIF}
    end;

    sum := 2 * sum;
    {$IFDEF Debug}
      memDebug.Lines.Add('End Outer Loop Iteration: ' +
                         IntToStr(outer) + '; Sum = ' +
                         IntToStr(sum));
    {$ENDIF}
  end;

  memOutput.Clear;
  memOutput.Lines.Add('Sum = ' + IntToStr(sum));
end;

end.
```

·C·A·S·E· ·S·T·U·D·Y·

A Computerized Survey

Allison owns and operates EZ Online, Inc., a small Internet service provider (ISP). She wants to collect customer data concerning Internet use—namely, the primary user's gender, annual income, monthly Internet usage (in hours), and primary reasons for accessing the Internet. Allison decides to design a customer survey as a means of data collection. She wants to computerize this survey by writing it in Delphi and eventually put it on the Internet as a Web page. Can you help Allison design the initial survey program in Delphi?

Figure 17.21 shows the survey form for Allison's program. Note that the Clear and Results buttons are used for testing and administrative purposes. These buttons would not be visible to an Internet customer.

The source code for Allison's survey program and event settings follow.

Component Name	Event	Setting
frmSurvey	OnShow	Initialize
btnSubmit	OnClick	SubmitSurvey
btnClear	OnClick	Initialize
btnResults	OnClick	ShowResults

```
unit SurveyEx;

interface

uses
  Windows, Messages, SysUtils, Classes, Graphics,
  Controls, Forms, Dialogs, StdCtrls, ExtCtrls,
  CheckLst;

type
  TfrmSurvey = class(TForm)
    rgpGender: TRadioGroup;
    rgpIncome: TRadioGroup;
    rgpUsage: TRadioGroup;
    cbxUses: TCheckListBox;
    lblUses: TLabel;
    btnSubmit: TButton;
    btnClear: TButton;
    btnResults: TButton;
    procedure SubmitSurvey(Sender: TObject);
    procedure Initialize(Sender: TObject);
    procedure ShowResults(Sender: TObject);
    procedure ClearForm(Sender: TObject);
  private
    { Private declarations }
  public
    { Public declarations }
  end;

var
  frmSurvey: TfrmSurvey;

implementation

{$R *.DFM}

uses Results;

var
  surveys: Integer;
  gender:  array[0..1] of Integer;
  income:  array[0..4] of Integer;
  usage:   array[0..4] of Integer;
  use:     array[0..7] of Integer;

procedure TfrmSurvey.SubmitSurvey(Sender: TObject);
```

```
var
  count: Integer;
begin
  surveys := surveys + 1;
  gender[rgpGender.ItemIndex] :=
    gender[rgpGender.ItemIndex] + 1;
  income[rgpIncome.ItemIndex] :=
    income[rgpIncome.ItemIndex] + 1;
  usage[rgpUsage.ItemIndex] := usage[rgpUsage.
                                   ItemIndex] + 1;

  for count := 0 to 7 do begin
    if cbxUses.Checked[count] then begin
      use[count] := use[count] + 1;
    end;
  end;

  ClearForm(Self);
end;
procedure TfrmSurvey.Initialize(Sender: TObject);

var
  count: Integer;

begin
  surveys := 0;
  for count := 0 to 7 do begin
    use[count] := 0;
    if (count < 5) then begin
      income[count] := 0;
      usage[count] := 0;
    end;
    if (count < 2) then begin
      gender[count] := 0;
    end;
  end;
end;
procedure TfrmSurvey.ShowResults(Sender: TObject);

var
  cnt: Integer;
```

```delphi
begin
  frmResults.Visible := True;
  frmResults.memOutput.Clear;
  with frmResults.memOutput.Lines do begin
    Add('INTERNET SURVEY RESULTS');
    Add('-----------------------');
    Add('');

    Add('Total Surveys: ' + IntToStr(surveys));
    Add('');

    Add('GENDER');
    for cnt := 0 to 1 do begin
      Add(rgpGender.Items[cnt] + ': ' +
          IntToStr(gender[cnt]));
    end;
    Add('');

    Add('INCOME');
    for cnt := 0 to 4 do begin
      Add(rgpIncome.Items[cnt] + ': ' +
          IntToStr(income[cnt]));
    end;
    Add('');

    Add('MONTHLY USAGE');
    for cnt := 0 to 4 do begin
      Add(rgpUsage.Items[cnt] + ': ' +
          IntToStr(usage[cnt]));
    end;
    Add('');

    Add('USES');
    for cnt := 0 to 7 do begin
      Add(cbxUses.Items[cnt] + ': ' +
          IntToStr(use[cnt]));
    end;
  end;
end;

procedure TfrmSurvey.ClearForm(Sender: TObject);

var
  count: Integer;

begin
```

```
   for count := 0 to 7 do begin
     cbxUses.Checked[count] := False;
   end;

   rgpIncome.ItemIndex := 0;
   rgpUsage.ItemIndex := 0;
   rgpGender.ItemIndex := 0;
   rgpGender.setFocus;
 end;

 end.
```

A sample output for four surveys appears below:

```
INTERNET SURVEY RESULTS
-----------------------

Total Surveys: 4

GENDER
Male: 2
Female: 2

INCOME
Below $20,000: 1
$20,000 to $39,999: 1
$40,000 to $59,999: 0
$60,000 to $79,999: 1
$80,000 or Above: 1

MONTHLY USAGE
0 to 4 hours: 0
5 to 9 hours: 1
10 to 14 hours: 1
15 to 19 hours: 1
20 or more hours: 1

USES
E-mail: 4
Internet Phone: 2
Shopping: 4
Entertainment/Games: 2
News/Weather: 3
Music/Video: 1
Education: 1
Research: 1
```

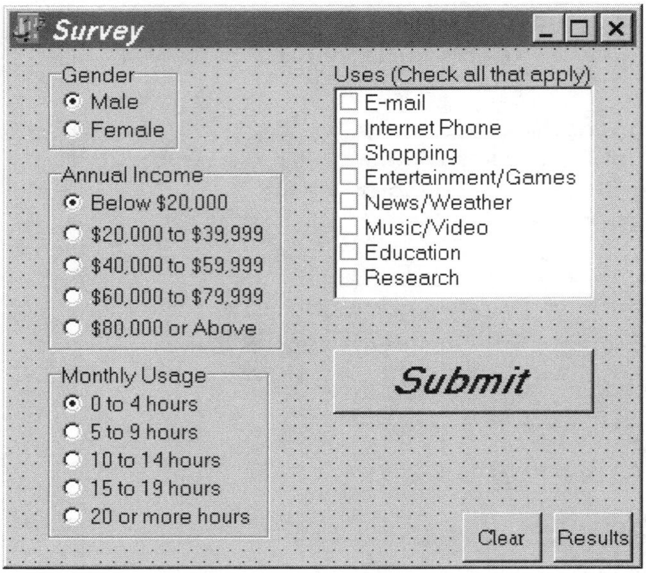

FIGURE 17.21 Form for Survey Program

Summary

Key Terms

ActiveX—A part of Microsoft's Component Object Model (COM) that allows user-developed and off-the-shelf software components to work together seamlessly.

compiler directives—Compiler commands or instructions that are placed in a program's source code.

conditional compilation —Compilation of specific blocks of code when certain conditions are met.

Dynamic Data Exchange (DDE)—An interprocess communication system that enables two active applications to share the same data.

embedded object—An object that is created in an application and then placed in a Delphi program; a copy of the object is contained in the Delphi program.

linked object—An object that is created in an application and then linked to a Delphi program; only a reference to the object is placed in the Delphi program.

Monte Carlo simulation—A type of simulation named after casino-style gambling in Monte Carlo.

Multiple Document Interface (MDI)—An application that allows multiple forms (or windows) to be open within a single container form (or window).

nonexecutable statements—Statements that are not compiled into machine code, such as comments and compiler directives.

Object Linking and Embedding (OLE)—A compound document standard developed by Microsoft that allows an object to be created with one application and then linked or embedded in a second application.

seed value—An initial value used by the Delphi random number generator to produce pseudorandom numbers.

Single Document Interface (SDI)—An application in which only one file may be open at a time; the current file must be closed before another file may be opened.

Keywords

Compiler Directives

$DEFINE	$IFNDEF
$ELSE	$IFOPT
$ENDIF	$UNDEF
$IFDEF	

Constants

bsBDiagonal	bsVertical
bsClear	clBlack
bsCross	clGreen
bsDiagCross	clRed
bsFDiagonal	psDash
bsHorizontal	psDot
bsSolid	psSolid

Events

OnChange	OnNavigate
OnClick	OnResize
OnKeyPress	OnShow

Functions

RandG	RGB
Random	

Global Variables

RandSeed

Methods

Arc	MoveTo
Chord	Navigate
CopyRect	Navigate2
Draw	Pie
Ellipse	Polygon
FillRect	PolyLine
FloodFill	Rectangle
FrameRect	RoundRect
GoBack	StretchDraw
GoForward	TextHeight
GoHome	TextOut
GoSearch	TextRect
LineTo	TextWidth

Objects

Brush	Font
Canvas	Pen

Procedures

Randomize

Properties

Align	Font, Style
AutoActivate	Height
Bitmap	Lines
BorderIcons	Linked
BorderStyle	LocationName
Brush	LocationURL
Caption	Mode
Color	Modified
DdeConv	Name
DdeItem	Pen
DdeService	PenPos
Font	Pixels
Font, Size	ReadOnly

```
ScrollBars      Visible
Style           Width
Text            WordWrap
Top
```

Key Concepts

- Component-based software development significantly reduces programming time and produces more robust applications. Microsoft's ActiveX technology, which is part of the Component Object Model (COM), allows programmers to design and develop their own software components, such as Delphi controls. Using ActiveX technology, a programmer can rapidly create, debug, and deploy a variety of software components. As an aid to the programmer, Delphi includes wizards for ActiveX development.

- Multiple Document Interface (MDI) and Single Document Interface (SDI) are two user interface styles. An MDI application consists of a main form that may contain several child windows. An SDI application contains only a main window; no child windows are permitted in an SDI application. If the user requires several files to be open simultaneously, an MDI is best. MDI is also more flexible than SDI, because the user can control the number of open windows. However, an MDI is slightly more complex and generally takes longer to program than an SDI. To assist the programmer, Delphi includes predesigned MDI and SDI application templates.

- Delphi contains powerful random number features. Random numbers are useful in computer simulations and games. The `Randomize` procedure initializes the Delphi random number generator with a seed value from the system clock:

```
Randomize;
```

Alternatively, you can specify a seed value directly by assigning a long integer value to the global variable `RandSeed`:

```
RandSeed := longIntSeedValue;
```

The `Random` function returns a random number within a specified range:

```
randomNumber := Random(upperLimit);
```

This statement assigns a random integer value to the integer variable *randomNumber*. *randomNumber* will contain an integer value greater than or equal to zero but strictly less than the integer *upperLimit*. *upperLimit* is an optional argument, but the parentheses must be used if it is specified. If *upperLimit* is not specified, the `Random` function returns a real value greater than or equal to zero but strictly less than 1.

- Delphi offers powerful built-in graphics features. To draw graphics in a Delphi application, you draw on an object's `Canvas`. `Canvas` is a property of the object as well as being an object itself. The `Brush`, `Pen`, and `Font` objects are properties of the `Canvas` object. Graphics are useful in games, mathematics, engineering, and business programs.

- Both Object Linking and Embedding (OLE) and Dynamic Data Exchange (DDE) allow Delphi programs to access information from other applications. OLE allows other applications and their objects to be treated as objects in Delphi. For instance, a sheet from a Microsoft Excel workbook may be linked or embedded in a Delphi application. In such a case, OLE does not require Microsoft Excel to be active when the Delphi application is executing. DDE allows information to be passed between active applications. For a DDE link to be established between a Delphi program and a Microsoft Excel spreadsheet, both applications must be active.

- Delphi offers a variety of components to access the Internet and create Web-enabled programs, including Web browsers, client and server sockets, Web dispatchers, page producers, and other components to access and display Web-based data.

- Compiler directives are instructions for the compiler; they are nonexecutable statements. In Delphi, a compiler directive consists of the dollar sign ($) as the first character after the opening comment delimiter, immediately followed by a name (containing one or more letters) that designates the particular directive.

- In conditional compilation, designated blocks of code are compiled only when certain conditions exist. Conditional compilation is typically used to compile the same program for different computer platforms. Also, it may be used to prevent debugging code from appearing in an executable file. The code excluded during conditional compilation is omitted from the final executable file. In Delphi, conditional compilation directives include `$DEFINE`, `$UNDEF`, and the `$IF`*xxx*`–$ELSE–$ENDIF` construct.

Review Questions

1. What is ActiveX? How can you create ActiveX controls and forms in Delphi?
2. Define MDI and SDI. How do you determine which type of interface to use?
3. Write the Delphi code to generate a random number between 1 and 10.
4. Describe the `Canvas`, `Brush`, `Pen`, and `Font` objects. How do you use them to create graphics in Delphi?
5. Describe OLE and DDE. How are they similar? How are they different?

6. In regard to OLE, what are the differences between a linked object and an embedded object?
7. What is a compiler directive?
8. What is conditional compilation? How is it useful?
9. Name the conditional compilation directives.

Problems

1. Convert your application from Problem 6 in Chapter 16 into an Active-Form. Test this ActiveForm with a Web browser.
2. Implement the Save and Save As… operations in the Notebook example from this chapter.
3. Rewrite the Notebook program as an SDI application.
4. In the Random Numbers Example program from this chapter, change the `Randomize` procedure call to read `RandSeed := 768;`. Execute the program five times. Explain why the results are always the same.
5. Write a Delphi program that simulates tossing a coin 1000 times and counts the number of heads and tails. The program should repeat this experiment 10 times and report the percentage of occurrences for each of the two possible outcomes.
6. Write a Delphi program that simulates rolling a pair of dice 1000 times and counts the number of occurrences of the sum. For instance, if one die lands on 4 and the other lands on 3, the sum of the dice roll is 7 and your program should update the counter for "7." The program should repeat this experiment 10 times and report the percentage of occurrences of each sum.
7. Write a Delphi program with a user interface consisting of three scroll bars and a label control. Each scroll bar should control the intensity value (ranging from 0 to 255) of one of the color parameters (red, green, or blue) in the RGB function. The caption color of the label control should change as the user changes the intensity values using the scroll bars.
8. Modify your program from Problem 11 in Chapter 5 to graph the normal density function for user-specified values of μ and σ and for a specified range of x values.
9. Modify your program from Problem 12 in Chapter 5 to graph the cumulative distribution function of the exponential distribution for a user-specified λ and range of x values.
10. Write a Delphi program that contains an embedded Microsoft Word document.
11. Write a Delphi application that is both a DDE client and a DDE server.

Programming Projects

1. Design and program your own custom Web browser. Use conditional compilation to prevent debugging code from appearing in your executable file.

2. Rewrite Project 2 in Chapter 16 as an MDI application.

Computer Arithmetic and Number Systems

Appendix Objectives

In this chapter you will:

- Convert binary numbers to decimal numbers and vice versa
- Perform binary addition and subtraction
- Find the two's complement of a binary number and use it to perform binary subtraction
- Understand the octal and hexadecimal number systems
- Convert numbers between binary, octal, decimal, and hexadecimal formats
- Perform octal and hexadecimal addition and subtraction
- Gain an understanding of the computer representation of real numbers
- Learn about the potential errors in mathematical calculations performed on a computer

Learning about number systems—and particularly the binary number system—promotes a better understanding of mathematics, logic, and computer science. This appendix introduces the number systems and associated mathematics that are essential to every computer scientist.

Binary to Decimal Conversions

Chapter 1 introduced binary numbers. For example, $1001\ 1100_2$ is a binary number, where the subscript 2 indicates the base (base 2 = binary). What is the decimal (base 10) equivalent of $1001\ 1100_2$? Let's examine decimal numbers more closely before making this conversion.

For example, look at the number 1425. Notice that we do not subscript 1425 as 1425_{10} because decimal is our natural number system and the base 10 is implied. We all know that this number is one thousand four hundred twenty-five, but what do the digits and their locations in respect to each other represent? If you think back to when you were introduced to numbers and the decimal number system, your teacher told you that the five is in the ones place, the two is in the tens place, the four is in the hundreds place, and the one is in the thousands place. Mathematically, to get this number from the digits, we perform the following operations:

$$(1 \times 1000) + (4 \times 100) + (2 \times 10) + (5 \times 1) = 1425$$

Because 1, 10, 100, and 1000 are all powers of 10 (the base number in decimal), we can rewrite this expression as follows:

$$(1 \times 10^3) + (4 \times 10^2) + (2 \times 10^1) + (5 \times 10^0) = 1425$$

Notice that the power of 10 starts at zero with the rightmost digit and is incremented by one as we proceed from right to left. This same idea applies to the binary number system, except that powers of 2 are used instead of powers of 10. Thus we translate $1001\ 1100_2$ to decimal as follows:

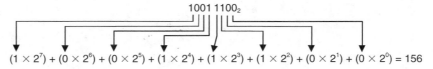

$$(1 \times 2^7) + (0 \times 2^6) + (0 \times 2^5) + (1 \times 2^4) + (1 \times 2^3) + (1 \times 2^2) + (0 \times 2^1) + (0 \times 2^0) = 156$$

Figure A.1 summarizes the methods of converting binary numbers to decimal.

Decimal to Binary Conversions

How about converting decimal numbers to binary? For example, how do you convert 156 back to its binary equivalent? Instead of multiplying by powers of the

We can explicitly write the decimal equivalent of each bit of the binary number $1001\ 1100_2$:

128	64	32	16	8	4	2	1	Value
2^7	2^6	2^5	2^4	2^4	2^2	2^1	2^0	
1	0	0	1	1	1	0	0	Bit

To translate $1001\ 1100_2$ to decimal, we perform the following operations:

$(1 \times 2^7) + (0 \times 2^6) + (0 \times 2^5) + (1 \times 2^4) + (1 \times 2^3) + (1 \times 2^2) + (0 \times 2^1) + (0 \times 2^0) =$
$(1 \times 128) + (0 \times 64) + (0 \times 32) + (1 \times 16) + (1 \times 8) + (1 \times 4) + (0 \times 2) + (0 \times 1)$
$128 + 0 + 0 + 16 + 8 + 4 + 0 + 0 = 156$

As illustrated by the flowchart below, the following algorithm can be used for converting from binary to decimal:

1. Set *RESULT* = the leftmost bit in the binary number (MSB).
2. If there is another bit to the right, multiply *RESULT* by 2 and then add the next bit to *RESULT.*
3. Repeat step 2 until there are no more bits to the right.

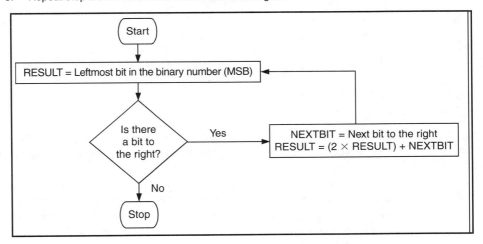

FIGURE A.1 Binary to Decimal Conversion for Integers

base number, we use successive divisions. Again, think back to grade school and use long division with remainders at each step as follows:

$$156 \div 2 = 78\ r\ 0$$
$$78 \div 2 = 39\ r\ 0$$
$$39 \div 2 = 19\ r\ 1$$
$$19 \div 2 = 9\ r\ 1$$
$$9 \div 2 = 4\ r\ 1$$
$$4 \div 2 = 2\ r\ 0$$
$$2 \div 2 = 1\ r\ 0$$
$$1 \div 2 = 0\ r\ 1$$

Our familiar example of 1001 1100$_2$ is used to demonstrate:

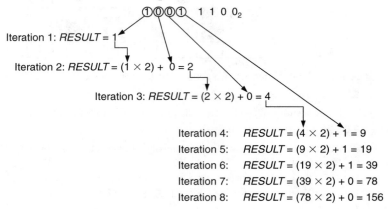

Iteration 1: $RESULT = 1$

Iteration 2: $RESULT = (1 \times 2) + 0 = 2$

Iteration 3: $RESULT = (2 \times 2) + 0 = 4$

Iteration 4: $RESULT = (4 \times 2) + 1 = 9$

Iteration 5: $RESULT = (9 \times 2) + 1 = 19$

Iteration 6: $RESULT = (19 \times 2) + 1 = 39$

Iteration 7: $RESULT = (39 \times 2) + 0 = 78$

Iteration 8: $RESULT = (78 \times 2) + 0 = 156$

The algorithm has performed the following operations:

$2 (2 (2 (2 (2 (2 (2 (1) + 0) + 0) + 1) + 1) + 1) + 0) + 0 = 156$

Notice that this is mathematically equivalent to our original equation:

$(1 \times 2^7) + (0 \times 2^6) + (0 \times 2^5) + (1 \times 2^4) + (1 \times 2^3) + (1 \times 2^2) + (0 \times 2^1) + (0 \times 2^0) =$
$2 (2 (2 (2 (2 (2 (2 (1) + 0) + 0) + 1) + 1) + 1) + 0) + 0 = 156$

FIGURE A.1 *continued*

Where is our binary equivalent of 156? Look at the remainders. Do you notice anything? If you write down the remainders in reverse order, you get 1001 1100, or the binary equivalent of 156.

How do you know when to stop performing the successive divisions? In the first division (156 ÷ 2 = 78 r 0), the base number 2 is the divisor, 156 is the dividend, 78 is the quotient, and 0 is the remainder. We stop the successive divisions when the quotient is 0. If we continued the successive divisions, we would get 0 ÷ 2 = 0 r 0 for all further divisions, and the end result would be the same. The **least significant bit (LSB)** is the rightmost bit in a binary number; it is associated with the lowest value (2^0, or the "ones position") and given by the remainder from the first division. The **most significant bit (MSB)** is the leftmost bit in a binary number; it is associated with the highest value and is equivalent to the remainder from the last division. Therefore, we reverse the order of the remainders to obtain our final answer. Figure A.2 summarizes the method of converting decimal numbers to binary numbers.

Binary Arithmetic

Now that you know about the binary number system and conversions between binary and decimal numbers, you can think about how the computer performs

An algorithm for converting a decimal number to binary:

1. Clear the *RESULT* variable.
2. Let *DIVIDEND* = the decimal number to be converted.
3. Let *DIVISOR* = the base number (= 2 for binary).
4. *QUOTIENT* = *DIVIDEND*/*DIVISOR*, where *QUOTIENT* is an integer value.
5. *REMAINDER* = *DIVIDEND* − (*QUOTIENT* × *DIVISOR*).
6. *DIVIDEND* = *QUOTIENT*.
7. *RESULT* = *REMAINDER* with the old value of *RESULT* appended on the right (which reverses the order of the remainders).
8. Repeat steps 4 through 7 until *QUOTIENT* = 0.

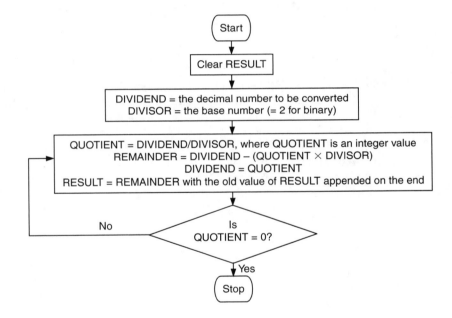

Example

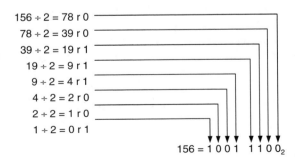

$$156 = 1001\ 1100_2$$

FIGURE A.2   Decimal to Binary Conversion for Integers

math. The computer performs math exclusively in binary. The rules for binary addition are as follows:

$$0 + 0 = 0$$
$$0 + 1 = 1 + 0 = 1$$
$$1 + 1 = 10_2$$

The last addition "carries" a 1 to the twos place. This addition works just like addition in the decimal system: You proceed from right to left, or from the least significant digit to the most significant digit, adding the corresponding digits and "carrying" any excess tens to the next addition operation. When you add 17 to 15, for example, you first add the 7 and 5, giving 12. You then "carry" the 1 to the tens place and add the three 1's, giving 3. The result is 32. Use this same reasoning to add the following binary numbers:

$$1011\ 1000_2$$
$$+\ \underline{1011\ 0111_2}$$

Did you get $1\ 0110\ 1111_2$? Did you correctly reason that $1 + 1 +$ a "carried" $1 = 11_2$?

How about subtraction? Again, think of the decimal system first: You proceed from right to left and subtract corresponding digits. When the subtrahend is larger than the digit from which it is being subtracted, you "borrow" a ten from the next digit to the left. When you subtract 65 from 256, for instance, you first subtract 5 from 6. The result is 1. Next, you need to subtract 6 from 5, but 6 is larger than 5. So you "borrow" a ten from the 2 on the left. The 2 becomes a 1, and 6 is subtracted from 15, giving 9. Finally, nothing (or 0) is subtracted from the 1, and the result is 191. Use this same method to perform the following binary subtraction:

$$1011\ 1000_2$$
$$-\ \underline{1011\ 0111_2}$$

Did you get $0000\ 0001_2$? Did you correctly reason that you needed to "borrow" from the 1 in the eights position (the fourth bit from the right)? Did you perform the sequential "borrowing" operation correctly?

The subtraction method described above does not really explain how computers perform subtraction. The only mathematical operation that most computers can actually carry out is binary addition. How do computers subtract numbers? If you rewrote $256 - 65$ as an addition, you would find that it is equivalent to $256 + (-65)$. That is, computers perform subtraction by adding a negative number.

How do we represent the negative of a binary number? The computer equivalent of the negative of a binary number is the **two's complement** of the number. Once the two's complement has been determined, the desired subtraction can then be completed by adding the negative (or two's complement) of the number. To illustrate, consider the following example: Subtract 36 from 163 in binary.

Step 1

Write the numbers in binary.

$$1010\ 0011_2 \quad 163 \text{ in binary}$$
$$-\ \underline{0010\ 0100_2} \quad 36 \text{ in binary}$$

Step 2

Find the **one's complement** of the subtrahend. For a binary number, the one's complement is found by reversing all of the bits; each 0 becomes a 1, and each 1 becomes a 0.

$$0010\ 0100_2 \longrightarrow 1101\ 1011_2$$
$$36 \text{ in binary} \longrightarrow \text{one's complement of 36 in binary}$$

Step 3

Find the two's complement of the subtrahend by adding a 1 to the one's complement.

$$1101\ 1011_2 + 0000\ 0001_2 = 1101\ 1100_2$$
$$\text{one's complement} + 1 = \text{two's complement}$$

Step 4

Complete the subtraction by *adding* the two's complement of the subtrahend to the first term.

$$1010\ 0011_2 \quad (163 \text{ in binary})$$
$$+\ \underline{1101\ 1100_2} \quad (\text{two's complement of 36 in binary})$$
$$1\ 0111\ 1111_2$$

When added together, the two binary numbers give us $0111\ 1111_2$, or 127. What happened to the "carried" 1 from the leftmost addition? Stated very simply, we ignore it. If you do not ignore it, your answer will be a number larger than 163, which does not make sense for a subtraction operation. The basic rule for binary subtraction is that your answer should always have the same number of bits as your original values.

Octal and Hexadecimal Numbers

Working with binary numbers can be quite tedious, as large decimal numbers are very lengthy when represented in binary. For this reason, computer programmers use two other number systems, **octal** (base 8) and **hexadecimal** (base 16), or hex for short. Binary numbers have two digits, 0 and 1; octal numbers have eight digits, 0 through 7; and hexadecimal numbers have 16 digits. With only 10 digits in the decimal system, 0 through 9, how do we represent the 16 different digits in hexadecimal? The answer is to use a combination of numbers and letters. Hexadecimal digits consist of the numbers 0 through 9 and the letters A through F, where A represents 10 and F represents 15. As you may have surmised, for any

Octal–Decimal Conversions

Convert 234_8 to decimal:

$$234_8 = (2 \times 8^2) + (3 \times 8^1) + (4 \times 8^0)$$
$$= (2 \times 64) + (3 \times 8) + (4 \times 1)$$
$$= 128 + 24 + 4$$
$$= 156$$

Convert 156 to octal:

$$156 \div 8 \quad = 19 \text{ r } 4$$
$$19 \div 8 \quad = 2 \text{ r } 3$$
$$2 \div 8 \quad = 0 \text{ r } 2$$
$$156 = 2\ 3\ 4_8$$

Hexadecimal–Decimal Conversions

Convert $9C_{16}$ to decimal:

$$9C_{16} = (9 \times 16^1) + (C \times 16^0)$$
$$= (9 \times 16) + (12 \times 1)$$
$$= 144 + 12$$
$$= 156$$

Convert 156 to hexadecimal:

$$156 \div 16 \quad = 9 \text{ r } 12$$
$$9 \div 16 \quad = 0 \text{ r } 9 \qquad (12 = C_{16})$$
$$156 = 9\ C_{16}$$

FIGURE A.3   Octal–Decimal and Hexadecimal–Decimal Conversions

base n, the system includes n digits, 0 through the digit or letter representing the value $n - 1$. Similar to subscripting a binary number with 2, octal numbers are commonly subscripted with an 8, and hexadecimal numbers are subscripted with either a 16 or the letter H. Octal–decimal and hexadecimal–decimal conversions follow rules similar to binary–decimal conversions. Figure A.3 shows examples of such conversions.

Binary–Octal–Hexadecimal Conversions

Binary–octal, binary–hexadecimal, and octal–hexadecimal conversions are relatively simple to perform because both 8 and 16 are multiples of 2. It is just a matter of regrouping the bits. One octal digit can be represented with three bits. To convert from binary to octal, start from the right side and group the bits in threes, then write the octal equivalent of each group of bits. Let's revisit our example of $1001\ 1100_2$:

1. Regroup the bits in threes: 10:01 1:100 $010\ 011\ 100$
2. Write the octal equivalent: 2   3   4

$$(0 \times 2^2) + (1 \times 2^1) + (0 \times 2^0) = 2$$
$$(0 \times 2^2) + (1 \times 2^1) + (1 \times 2^0) = 3$$
$$(1 \times 2^2) + (0 \times 2^1) + (0 \times 2^0) = 4$$

Thus $1001\ 1100_2 = 234_8$. Notice that the leading zero is implied when we regroup the bits. In other words, any bit to the left of the MSB in a binary number is inherently a zero. To convert from octal to binary, simply write each octal digit in binary form using three bits per octal digit.

You can use the same method to convert between binary and hexadecimal, except that the bits must be grouped in fours (which is why binary numbers are commonly written as nibbles). Using our example,

1. Regroup the bits in fours: 1001 1100
2. Write the hexadecimal equivalent: 9   C

$$(1 \times 2^3) + (0 \times 2^2) + (0 \times 2^1) + (1 \times 2^0) = 9$$
$$(1 \times 2^3) + (1 \times 2^2) + (0 \times 2^1) + (0 \times 2^0) = 12 \text{ (or } C_{16})$$

Thus $1001\ 1100_2 = 9C_{16}$. Again, converting from hexadecimal to binary is simply a matter of writing each hexadecimal digit in binary form using four bits per hexadecimal digit.

To convert between octal and hexadecimal, translate the number to binary first, then convert the binary number into the desired base. To convert 74_8 to hexadecimal, for instance:

1. Write 74_8 in binary: 111 100
2. Regroup the bits in fours: 11:1 100 $0011\ 1100$
3. Write the hexadecimal equivalent: 3   C

$$(0 \times 2^3) + (0 \times 2^2) + (1 \times 2^1) + (1 \times 2^0) = 3$$
$$(1 \times 2^3) + (1 \times 2^2) + (0 \times 2^1) + (0 \times 2^0) = 12 \text{ (or } C_{16})$$

Thus $74_8 = 3C_{16}$.

Octal and Hexadecimal Arithmetic

Addition and subtraction in octal and hexadecimal are performed in the same manner as their decimal counterparts. Remember to "carry" or "borrow" eights and sixteens instead of tens. Figure A.4 shows several examples of addition and

Octal

$$654_8$$
$$+307_8$$
$$1163_8$$

$$654_8$$
$$-307_8$$
$$345_8$$

Hexadecimal

$$1AC_{16}$$
$$+\ C7_{16}$$
$$273_{16}$$

$$1AC_{16}$$
$$-C7_{16}$$
$$E5_{16}$$

FIGURE A.4   Examples of Addition and Subtraction in Octal and Hexadecimal

subtraction in the octal and hexadecimal systems. Many scientific calculators can perform conversions and mathematics in binary, octal, decimal, and hexadecimal.

Fractional Numbers

We have already seen how computers represent, store, and perform mathematical operations on **integer** values. Of course, not all values are integers—computers must also deal with **fractions** (also known as **fractional numbers**), the **real numbers** between 0 and 1.

Let's consider a fraction in the decimal system first. The fraction 1/8 is equivalent to the decimal number 0.125. During the course of your education, your teacher probably told you that the one is in the tenths place, the two is in the hundredths place, and the five is in the thousandths place. Mathematically, to get this number from the digits, we perform the following operations:

$$(1 \times 1/10) + (2 \times 1/100) + (5 \times 1/1000) = 0.125$$

Because 1/10, 1/100, and 1/1000 are all powers of 10, we can rewrite this expression as follows:

$$(1 \times 10^{-1}) + (2 \times 10^{-2}) + (5 \times 10^{-3}) = 0.125$$

Notice that the power of 10 starts at −1 with the leftmost digit after the decimal point and is decremented by one as we proceed from left to right. This same idea applies to the binary number system, except that powers of 2 are used instead of powers of 10. For instance, we translate 0.1101_2 to decimal as follows:

$$0.1101_2 = (1 \times 2^{-1}) + (1 \times 2^{-2}) + (0 \times 2^{-3}) + (1 \times 2^{-4}) = 0.8125$$

Figure A.5 summarizes the methods of translating a fraction from binary to decimal. You can use the same methods to convert fractions from octal, hexadecimal, or any other base to decimal by using the appropriate base number.

How do we translate 0.8125 back to binary? Recall that for an integer value, we used successive divisions by the base number 2 and then reversed the order of

We can explicitly write the decimal equivalent of each bit of the binary fraction 0.10101101_2:

0.5	0.25	0.125	0.0625	0.03125	0.015625	0.0078125	0.00390625	Value
2^{-1}	2^{-2}	2^{-3}	2^{-4}	2^{-5}	2^{-6}	2^{-7}	2^{-8}	
0	1	0	1	0	1	1	0	1	Bit

To translate 0.10101101_2 to decimal, we perform the following operations:

$(1 \times 2^{-1}) + (0 \times 2^{-2}) + (1 \times 2^{-3}) + (0 \times 2^{-4}) + (1 \times 2^{-5}) + (1 \times 2^{-6}) + (0 \times 2^{-7}) + (1 \times 2^{-8}) =$
$(1 \times 0.5) + (0 \times 0.25) + (1 \times 0.125) + (0 \times 0.0625) + (1 \times 0.03125) +$
$(1 \times 0.015625) + (0 \times 0.0078125) + (1 \times 0.00390625) =$
$0.5 + 0 + 0.125 + 0 + 0.03125 + 0.015625 + 0 + 0.00390625 = 0.67578125$

As illustrated by the flowchart below, the following algorithm can be used for converting

fractions from binary to decimal:

1. Set *RESULT* = the rightmost bit in the binary fraction (LSB).
2. Multiply *RESULT* by 1/2.
3. If there is another bit to the left, add it to *RESULT* and repeat step 2.

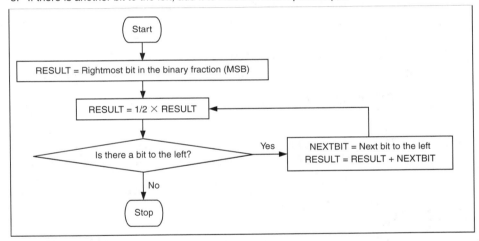

FIGURE A.5 Binary to Decimal Conversion for Fractions *(continued on next page)*

the remainders to find its binary representation. Because fractions appear on the opposite side of the decimal point, we need to use the complement of this procedure: Perform successive multiplications by the base number 2 and then take the integer portions of these products in order. The binary representation of 0.8125 is found as follows:

$0.8125 \times 2 = 1.6250$; fractional part 0.6250 and integer part 1
$0.6250 \times 2 = 1.2500$; fractional part 0.2500 and integer part 1
$0.2500 \times 2 = 0.5000$; fractional part 0.5000 and integer part 0
$0.5000 \times 2 = 1.0000$; fractional part 0.0000 and integer part 1

Our familiar example of 0.10101101_2 is used to demonstrate:

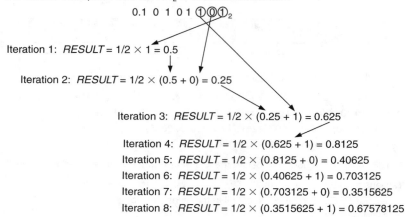

$$0.1\ 0\ 1\ 0\ 1\ 1\ 0\ 1_2$$

Iteration 1: $RESULT = 1/2 \times 1 = 0.5$

Iteration 2: $RESULT = 1/2 \times (0.5 + 0) = 0.25$

Iteration 3: $RESULT = 1/2 \times (0.25 + 1) = 0.625$

Iteration 4: $RESULT = 1/2 \times (0.625 + 1) = 0.8125$

Iteration 5: $RESULT = 1/2 \times (0.8125 + 0) = 0.40625$

Iteration 6: $RESULT = 1/2 \times (0.40625 + 1) = 0.703125$

Iteration 7: $RESULT = 1/2 \times (0.703125 + 0) = 0.3515625$

Iteration 8: $RESULT = 1/2 \times (0.3515625 + 1) = 0.67578125$

The algorithm has performed the following operations:

$1/2\ (1/2\ (1/2\ (1/2\ (1/2\ (1/2\ (1/2\ (1/2\ (1) + 0) + 1) + 1) + 0) + 1) + 0) + 1) = 0.67578125$

Notice that this is mathematically equivalent to our original equation:

$(1 \times 2^{-1}) + (0 \times 2^{-2}) + (1 \times 2^{-3}) + (0 \times 2^{-4}) + (1 \times 2^{-5}) + (1 \times 2^{-6}) + (0 \times 2^{-7}) + (1 \times 2^{-8}) =$

$1/2\ (1/2\ (1/2\ (1/2\ (1/2\ (1/2\ (1/2\ (1/2\ (1) + 0) + 1) + 1) + 0) + 1) + 0) + 1) = 0.67578125$

FIGURE A.5 *Continued*

Thus $0.8125 = 0.1101_2$. Notice that we stop this procedure when the fractional part is 0, as all further multiplications will yield 0, or when we run out of memory space (bits) to store the result. Figure A.6 summarizes the method for converting a fraction from decimal to binary. You can use the same method to convert fractions from decimal to octal, hexadecimal, or any other base by using the appropriate base number.

As before, binary–octal and binary–hexadecimal conversions are simply a matter of regrouping the bits into threes and fours, respectively. For fractions, however, we must group the bits from left to right, starting with the first bit after the binary point. For instance, to convert 0.1011101_2 to octal and hexadecimal, we perform the following steps:

$$0.1011101_2 = 0.101\ 110\ 100_2 = 0.564_8$$
$$0.1011101_2 = 0.1011\ 1010_2 = 0.BA_{16}$$

Thus $0.1011101_2 = 0.564_8 = 0.BA_{16}$. Notice that we added trailing zeros to the binary fraction in these conversions, because any bit to the right of the LSB in a binary fraction is inherently a zero. To convert the fraction from octal or hexadecimal back to binary, simply write the binary equivalent of each digit in order using three or four bits per digit, respectively.

An algorithm for converting a decimal fraction to binary:

1. Clear the *RESULT* variable (*RESULT* = "0").
2. Let *NUMBER* = the decimal fraction to be converted.
3. Let BASE = the base number (= 2 for binary).
4. *NUMBER* = *BASE* $\times$ *NUMBER*.
5. *RESULT* = *RESULT* with the integer portion of *NUMBER* appended on the right.
6. *NUMBER* = the fractional portion of *NUMBER*.
7. Repeat steps 4 through 6 until *NUMBER* = 0 or *RESULT* runs out of space to store digits.

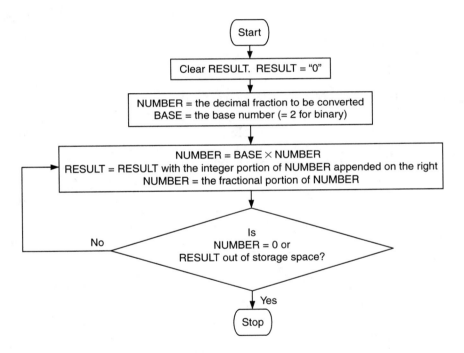

$$0.6328125 = 0.1010001_2$$

Iteration	Operation	Fractional Part	Integer Part	RESULT
				0.
1	$0.6328125 \times 2 = 1.265625$	0.265625	1	0.1
2	$0.265625 \times 2 = 0.53125$	0.53125	0	0.10
3	$0.53125 \times 2 = 1.0625$	0.0625	1	0.101
4	$0.0625 \times 2 = 0.125$	0.125	0	0.1010
5	$0.125 \times 2 = 0.25$	0.25	0	0.10100
6	$0.25 \times 2 = 0.5$	0.5	0	0.101000
7	$0.5 \times 2 = 1.0$	0.0	1	0.1010001

FIGURE A.6   Decimal to Binary Conversion for Fractions

Sign and Modulus Representation

For integers, as noted earlier, we can represent a negative number in binary by taking the two's complement of its positive binary representation. The two's complement form offers advantages when performing arithmetic operations. Another common method of representing negative numbers on a computer is the **sign and modulus representation.** In this representation, the **sign bit** is the leftmost bit in each binary number. By convention, a sign bit of 0 indicates a positive number and a sign bit of 1 indicates a negative number. Thus, if m bits are available to represent an integer, then the integers $-(2^{m-1} - 1)$ to $+(2^{m-1} - 1)$ can be represented because the first bit indicates the sign of the number. Note that this representation contains two zero values, -0 and $+0$. The sign and modulus representation is commonly used in conjunction with the real number representations described in the next section.

Real Number Representations

Two methods are available for representing real numbers on a computer: **fixed-point representation** and **floating-point representation**.

In a fixed-point representation, a specific number of digits is dedicated to both the integer and fractional parts of the real number. The underlying concept is that adding an integer and a fraction results in a real number. Consider such a representation in binary, with three bits dedicated to the integer portion and two bits for the fractional portion, where the leftmost bit is the sign bit. The highest value that can be represented in this system is $+11.11_2$ (+3.75) and the lowest value possible is -11.11_2 (−3.75).

Reviewing this simple example, do you see a problem with representing real numbers on a computer? Consider the number +3.625. How would it be represented in our example? It is given by $+11.10_2$, or +3.5! The error between the actual and represented values is 0.125. This type of error is know as a **round-off error**, and it occurs because we are attempting to express the true value of a real number in a finite amount of space. Gaps are inherent in our numbering system because we use a finite number of bits to store values. In short, we are using a finite memory space to represent the values in an infinite number system. If p bits are used to store the fractional part of a number, the round-off error is at most 2^{-p}. Our example uses 2 bits for the fractional part, so the round-off error has an upper bound of 2^{-2}, or 0.25. Thus we can guarantee the accuracy of any single number stored in our system only within ±0.25. As we cannot store the true values of all real numbers on a computer, we use the term **floating-point numbers** to describe their computer representations.

The floating-point representation uses exponential notation to code real numbers. It is the most common computer representation of real numbers. The form of the floating-point representation is $r = m \times B^e$. The real number r is expressed by three numbers, m, B, and e. The number m is the **mantissa (significand)**, a fractional number between −1 and +1. The number B is the base number, an integer indicating the base used in the exponential notation. In digital computers, B is commonly 2, but sometimes a base of 16 is used. In hand calculators, B is usually 10. The number e is the **exponent (characteristic)** and is usually a signed integer value. The computer needs to store only the values of m and e, as B is a constant whose value depends on the computer's hardware.

Let's examine how the real number 38.96875 is expressed in floating-point notation. For the sake of simplicity, we will use $B = 10$:

$$38.96875 = 0.3896875 \times 10^2 = 0.03896875 \times 10^3 = 0.003896875 \times 10^4 = \ldots$$

Notice that all of the representations on the right sides of the equalities are, in fact, floating-point representations. Also, notice that an infinite number of these floating-point representations exists. Which one should we use? A floating-point number is said to be **normalized** if the highest-order digit of the mantissa is nonzero. In our example, 0.3896875×10^2 is normalized, but 0.03896875×10^3 is not. Computers work with normalized floating-point numbers. In binary, this choice means that the first bit of the mantissa is always 1. Some computers take advantage of this fact and gain an extra bit of precision by not storing the first bit. In this type of system, the suppressed first bit is referred to as a **hidden bit**.

Next, convert 38.96875 to a binary floating-point number ($B = 2$). Did you get $m = 0.10011011111_2$ and $e = 0110_2$? Did you remember to convert the integer and fractional portions separately? Did you remember to normalize the result? The following equalities show how we arrive at the final answer:

$$38.96875 = 100110.11111_2 = 0.10011011111_2 \times 2^6$$

Thus $m = 0.10011011111_2$ and $e = 6 = 0110_2$.

As in the fixed-point representation, we are left with a dilemma. We must decide how many bits of storage to assign to both the mantissa and the exponent. Unfortunately, no standard exists for storing floating-point numbers; the answer depends on the specific computer being used. For a 32-bit floating-point number, for instance, we may assign 23 bits to the mantissa and 8 bits to the exponent, reserving the remaining bit for the sign bit. To determine how floating-point numbers are stored on your machine, consult the programmer's reference manual for your specific microprocessor (or computer system) and the compiler documentation.

Summary

Key Terms

characteristic—See *exponent*.

exponent—The power of a base number.

fixed-point representation—A method of representing real numbers on a computer, in which a specific number of digits is dedicated to both the integer and fractional parts of the real number.

floating-point number—The computer representation of a real number.

floating-point representation—A method of representing real numbers on a computer that uses exponential notation to code the real numbers.

fraction (fractional number)—A quantity less than a whole number; a value that can be expressed as a decimal.

hexadecimal—The base 16 number system, consisting of the digits 0 through 9 and the letters A through F.

hidden bit—A suppressed first bit in a floating-point representation.

integer—A whole number or zero.

least significant bit (LSB)—The rightmost bit in a binary number; the bit that is associated with the lowest value (2^0, or the ones position).

mantissa—The fractional part of a number; a fractional number between –1 and +1.

most significant bit (MSB)—The leftmost bit in a binary number; the bit that is associated with the highest value.

normalize—The process of converting a floating-point number into a form such that the highest-order digit of the mantissa is nonzero.

octal—The base 8 number system, consisting of the digits 0 through 7.

one's complement—The binary number resulting from reversing (or complementing) each bit of a binary number.

real number—A number that exists on the continuous number line; a number that consists of both integer and fractional portions.

round-off error—An error due to the imprecise representation of real numbers on a computer.

sign and modulus representation—A method of storing the sign of a number along with its value by using a sign bit.

sign bit—The leftmost bit of a binary number that is stored in the sign and modulus representation.

significand—See *mantissa*.

two's complement—The binary number resulting from adding one to the one's complement; the computer representation of the negative of a binary number.

Key Concepts

- Binary is the base 2 number system, octal is base 8, decimal is base 10, and hexadecimal is base 16.

- The rules for decimal arithmetic have counterparts in other number bases, such as the rules for "carrying" and "borrowing" values.

- The two's complement of a binary number is useful for performing binary subtraction. The two's complement, which is essentially the negative of a binary value, it is formed by adding one to the one's complement, where the one's complement results from reversing the bits of a binary number.

- Base n to decimal conversions are performed by multiplying each digit in the base n number by n^p, where p represents the position of the digit, and then summing the results. For integer values, the rightmost digit is in position 0, and this conversion is the same as performing successive multiplications by n. Starting with the leftmost digit in the base n number, multiply the value by n and then add the next digit to the right. Continue this process until no more digits are left. For fractional values, the leftmost digit is in position -1, and this conversion is the same as performing successive multiplications by $1/n$. Starting with the rightmost digit in the base n fraction, multiply the value by $1/n$, add the next digit to the left, and then multiply the result by $1/n$. Continue this process until no more fractional digits are left.

- For integer values, decimal to base n conversions are performed using successive divisions. Using long division (with quotients and remainders), divide the original decimal number by n. Continue to divide the quotients by n until the quotient is zero. Reversing the order of the remainders yields the decimal value expressed as a base n number. For fractional numbers, use successive multiplications by n. Continue to multiply the fractional parts of the products by n until the fractional part is zero or you run out of room to store the digits. Taking the integer portions of the products in order yields the decimal fraction expressed as a base n fraction.

- Binary–octal–hexadecimal conversions are performed by regrouping the bits.

- The sign and modulus representation is another method for representing negative numbers on a computer. In this representation, a sign bit indicates the sign of the number, where 0 is positive and 1 is negative by convention. The sign bit is the leftmost bit of the number.

- Real numbers are represented on a computer using either fixed-point or floating-point representation. In fixed-point representation, a specific number of digits is dedicated to both the integer and fractional parts of the real number. Floating-point representation uses exponential notation to code the real numbers.

- Inherent gaps exist in the floating-point number system because it uses a finite number of bits to store the values of real numbers. Round-off errors are the result.

Review Questions

1. Describe how to convert between binary and decimal.
2. What is the one's complement of a binary number?
3. What is the two's complement of a binary number? What purpose does it serve?
4. What are octal and hexadecimal numbers? What are the digits used in each system?
5. Describe how to convert between binary and octal, binary and hexadecimal, and octal and hexadecimal.
6. Describe how to convert between octal and decimal and between decimal and hexadecimal.
7. Describe how to convert fractions into binary, octal, decimal, and hexadecimal numbers.
8. What is the sign and modulus representation?
9. Describe the two methods of representing real numbers on a computer. Which method is most commonly found?
10. What is round-off error? Why does it exist?

Problems

1. Convert the following binary numbers to decimal numbers by multiplying each bit by its respective decimal value and summing the results:
   a. 0011_2
   b. $0011\ 0011_2$
   c. $1010\ 1001_2$
   d. $0110\ 1000_2$
   e. $1100\ 1001\ 0011_2$
   f. $0111\ 1100\ 1001\ 0011_2$

2. Convert the binary numbers in Problem 1 to decimal numbers using the algorithm in Figure A.1.

3. Convert the following decimal numbers to binary numbers:
   a. 13
   b. 42
   c. 125
   d. 255
   e. 300

4. What decimal values can be represented using one bit? One nibble? One byte? One word?

5. Perform the following binary additions:
   a. $0100\ 1101_2 + 1010\ 0011_2$
   b. $0101\ 1101_2 + 0000\ 0011_2$
   c. $1000\ 1101_2 + 0011\ 1111_2$
   d. $1111\ 1111_2 + 0000\ 0001_2$
   e. $1111\ 1111_2 + 1111\ 1111_2$

6. Perform the following binary subtractions using the "borrowing" method:
   a. $0110\ 0010_2 - 0001\ 0011_2$
   b. $1110\ 0011_2 - 0000\ 0011_2$
   c. $0010\ 0110_2 - 0001\ 0011_2$
   d. $1000\ 1111_2 - 0001\ 0101_2$
   e. $1110\ 0000_2 - 0110\ 0011_2$

7. Perform the binary subtractions in Problem 6 using the two's complement method.

8. Convert the following binary numbers to octal and hexadecimal numbers:
   a. 1110_2
   b. $1110\ 1001_2$
   c. $1111\ 1101\ 0110_2$
   d. $0011\ 1001\ 1111\ 0010_2$

9. For each of the following problems, perform the required operation in decimal. Then convert the decimal numbers to binary, octal, and hexadecimal numbers, and perform the same mathematical operation in the different bases. Convert your results back to decimal to check your answers.
   a. $221 + 187$
   b. $221 - 187$
   c. $162 - 137$
   d. $162 + 137$
   e. $198 - 77$
   f. $198 + 77$
   g. $240 - 18$
   h. $240 + 18$

10. Convert the following binary fractions to decimal numbers by multiplying each bit by its respective decimal value and summing the results:
    a. 0.1001_2
    b. 0.0011_2
    c. 0.10101001_2
    d. 0.011010001_2

11. Convert the binary fractions in Problem 10 to decimal numbers using the algorithm in Figure A.5.

12. Convert the binary fractions in Problem 10 to octal and hexadecimal numbers.

13. Convert the following real numbers from decimal to binary using the fixed-point representation. Use 8 bits for the integer portion, 5 bits for the fractional portion, and 1 bit for the sign. What is the maximum round-off error using this representation? Calculate the round-off error in each case.
    a. 240.16425
    b. −167.8125
    c. 87.345
    d. −250.27
    e. 93.45

14. Convert the real numbers in Problem 13 from decimal to binary using floating-point representation. Use 13 bits for the mantissa, 5 bits for the exponent, and 1 bit for the sign. Make sure to normalize the numbers.

ASCII (ANSI)
Character Values

0		32	[space]	64	@	96	'
1		33	!	65	A	97	a
2		34	"	66	B	98	b
3		35	#	67	C	99	c
4		36	$	68	D	100	d
5		37	%	69	E	101	e
6		38	&	70	F	102	f
7		39	'	71	G	103	g
8	BS	40	(	72	H	104	h
9	TAB	41	)	73	I	105	i
10	LF	42	*	74	J	106	j
11		43	+	75	K	107	k
12		44	,	76	L	108	l
13	CR	45	-	77	M	109	m
14		46	.	78	N	110	n
15		47	/	79	O	111	o
16		48	0	80	P	112	p
17		49	1	81	Q	113	q
18		50	2	82	R	114	r
19		51	3	83	S	115	s
20		52	4	84	T	116	t
21		53	5	85	U	117	u
22		54	6	86	V	118	v
23		55	7	87	W	119	w
24		56	8	88	X	120	x
25		57	9	89	Y	121	y
26		58	:	90	Z	122	z
27		59	;	91	[	123	{
28		60	<	92	\	124		
29		61	=	93	]	125	}
30		62	>	94	^	126	~
31		63	?	95	_	127	

128		160	[space]	192	À	224	à
129		161	¡	193	Á	225	á
130		162	¢	194	Â	226	â
131		163	£	195	Ã	227	ã
132		164		196	Ä	228	ä
133		165	¥	197	Å	229	å
134		166	¦	198	Æ	230	æ
135		167	§	199	Ç	231	ç
136		168	¨	200	È	232	è
137		169	©	201	É	233	é
138		170	ª	202	Ê	234	ê
139		171	«	203	Ë	235	ë
140		172	¬	204	Ì	236	ì
141		173		205	Í	237	í
142		174	®	206	Î	238	î
143		175	¯	207	Ï	239	ï
144		176	°	208	Ð	240	∂
145	'	177	±	209	Ñ	241	ñ
146	'	178	²	210	Ò	242	ò
147		179	³	211	Ó	243	ó
148		180	´	212	Ô	244	ô
149		181	µ	213	Õ	245	õ
150		182	¶	214	Ö	246	ö
151		183	·	215	×	247	÷
152		184	ç	216	Ø	248	ø
153		185	¹	217	Ù	249	ù
154		186	º	218	Ú	250	ú
155		187	»	219	Û	251	û
156		188	¼	220	Ü	252	ü
157		189	½	221	Ý	253	ý
158		190	¾	222	ρ	254	ρ
159		191	¿	223	ß	255	ÿ

Blanks indicate characters that are not supported by Microsoft Windows.

Object Pascal Programming Standards

Documentation in the Source Code

D1. Each program must begin with comments that include your name, course and section number, and the date.

D2. Each subprogram must begin with brief comments that describe its purpose. Studies have shown that general descriptions at the beginning of each subprogram are more valuable than comments distributed throughout the code. The comments should describe what the code does rather than how the code does it; a programmer can trace the code to see how it works.

D3. Comments and blank lines that indicate the major sections of the program are useful.

D4. If (and only if) the meaning of a statement or group of statements is not clear from reading the code, brief comments may be included in the body of the program. In general, such comments are not useful. If they merely state what is obvious from reading the code, they detract from it. If these comments are necessary, place them at the beginning of the block of code, thereby reducing the disruption of the structure of the program.

D5. Variable and subprogram names should be chosen to help describe their meaning. A poorly chosen name that misleads the reader is worse than a nondescript name like X or A. Variable names must be written in lowercase letters, except for the first letter of embedded words, which are written in uppercase, such as `taxRate` and `numberOfCars`. A subprogram name must begin with an uppercase letter.

D6. Object classes and variables begin with an uppercase letter. Method names begin with an uppercase letter.

D7. Each component name begins with a lowercase, three-letter prefix that indicates the type of component. For instance, a form begins with `frm`, an edit box with `edt`, and a button with `btn`. The remainder of the name describes the component's purpose or contents. For example, `edtLast-Name` is an edit box containing a last name.

Software Engineering Standards

S1. All real constants must have a decimal point with a digit on each side.

S2. Mixed-mode arithmetic is arithmetic containing variables of different data types. When possible, avoid mixed-mode arithmetic expressions. Use the data type conversion routines as necessary.

S3. When converting a string to an equivalent real value, use the `Val` procedure. When converting a real value to a string, use the `Str` procedure. For integer values, use the `StrToInt` and `IntToStr` functions, respectively.

S4. Expressions containing multiple operators and operators of different types must include parentheses for clarity and to indicate precedence.

S5. Remove unnecessary code. Extra code is particularly important when it appears inside a loop that will execute numerous times. It is not necessary to assign the value zero to a variable or array element before it is assigned a value by another statement. Any such assignment is unnecessary and will be viewed as a violation of this standard.

S6. Avoid global variables. Problems may occur when more than one subprogram uses the same variable; one may change the value of a global variable that would then affect another's use of the variable. Sharing variables by passing them as parameters is preferred because it makes the shared use explicit.

User Interface

U1. Delphi has a variety of ready-made components available for use, including buttons, radio buttons, and drop-down menus. The user interface that you select should reflect the best user control for the task at hand. For example, if the user must select from several mutually exclusive options, the best choice would be radio buttons.

U2. Consistency is a key factor for usability. Use dialog components whenever possible. For example, there is little benefit in inventing your own dialog box to open a file; use the `OpenDialog` component instead.

U3. Plan multiple form interfaces carefully. Group items on a form in a logical and consistent manner. Avoid the extremes of too many forms or a form that is so overpowering that it is difficult to comprehend.

Error Prevention

E1. For each division operation, include either a test to determine that the divisor is not equal to zero or a comment that explains why it can never be equal to zero.

E2. Attempting to dereference a pointer whose value is `nil` generates an error. Thus any pointer whose contents are unknown must be tested before the pointer is dereferenced. For instance,

```
if (intPtr <> nil) then begin
  intPtr^ := 5;
end;
```

Indentation and Blocks

I1. Indentation is an extremely important element of readability. Statements within a subprogram block should be indented at least two spaces. Additionally, statements within decision or repetition structures should be indented at least two spaces. The indentation style should be consistent throughout the source code. An example code segment follows:

```
procedure TfrmIndentExample.DoIt(Sender: TObject);

var
  code: Integer;
  myReal: Real;
  inner: Integer;
  outer: Integer;

begin
  Val(edtNumber.Text, myReal, code);
  if (code = 0) then begin
    for outer := 1 to 20 do begin
      myReal := myReal + 1.0;
      if (myReal > 100.0) then begin
        for inner := 1 to 5 do begin
          myReal := (myReal / 2.0) + inner;
        end; {for}
      end
      else begin
```

```
          myReal := myReal + 5.5;
        end; {if}
      end; {for}
    end; {if}
  end; {DoIt}
```

Repetition

R1. Object Pascal has three repetition constructs: the `while` loop, the `repeat` loop, and the `for` loop. For some repetition situations in a program, only one repetition construct can be used. In most situations, you have a choice. Each repetition construct was designed for a specific situation; therefore, it is possible to develop standards that will dictate the appropriate repetition to use in most programming situations. The following guidelines almost always dictate the appropriate choice:

a. The `while` and `repeat` constructs are called indefinite (or indeterminate) repetition structures because the number of times that the loop executes depends on calculations within the loop. In contrast, the `for` construct is called a definite (or determinate) repetition structure because the number of executions of the loop (if any) is determined before any execution of the loop. When possible, use a definite repetition structure (that is, a `for` loop) rather than an indefinite one.

b. In choosing between the `while` and `repeat` constructs, if the loop must execute at least once, then `repeat` is the appropriate choice because its selection clearly shows that the loop will execute at least once. The `while` loop is used exclusively in situations where the loop may not be executed at all depending on the value of the Boolean expression.

Customizing the Delphi Integrated Development Environment

This appendix briefly describes the menu options and dialogs that allow you to customize the Delphi integrated development environment (IDE). For a more thorough description of these options and dialogs, refer to Delphi's online help.

Customizing Toolbars

To customize the Delphi toolbars, either select View|Toolbars|Customize... or right-click on a toolbar and select Customize... from the pop-up menu. The Customize (toolbars) window shown in Figure D.1 appears on the screen.

The Toolbars page allows you choose which toolbars to display by checking all of the toolbars that appear in the IDE. Selecting one or several toolbars (by holding down the CTRL key while left-clicking the toolbar name) and clicking the Reset button returns the selected toolbars to their default (factory) configurations.

The Commands page allows you to add or remove commands from toolbars through a simple drag-and-drop process. Select a category of commands from the Categories list box; the commands associated with this category then appear in the Commands list box. To add a command to the toolbar, drag the command from the Commands list box and drop it onto the appropriate toolbar. To remove commands from a toolbar, drag the command off of the toolbar.

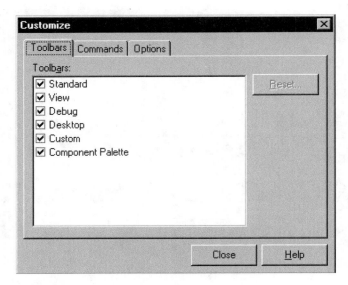

FIGURE D.1   Customize Window

The Options page lets you choose whether to display tooltips for toolbar buttons. If desired, you can also include shortcut keys in the tooltip text.

Environment Options

Choose `Tools|Environment Options...` to display the Environment Options dialog box (Figure D.2). In the pages of this dialog, you can specify IDE configuration preferences and customize the Component Palette. The pages of the Environment Options dialog box include Preferences, Library, Palette, Explorer, Type Library, Delphi Direct, and Translation Tools (in the Enterprise edition).

The Preferences page lets you choose your configuration preferences. The Library page specifies directories, compiler options, and linker options for all packages. The Palette page allows you to customize the Component Palette by renaming, adding, removing, and reordering pages and components. Use the Explorer page to set options for the Code Explorer and Project Browser; the new settings wil take effect when you click the OK button. Use the Type Library page to select options for the Type Library editor; the new settings will take effect when you click the OK button.

Delphi Direct provides access (in your default Web browser) to the latest Delphi news posted on the Internet. Use its page to specify how often Delphi Direct should gather new information from Borland's Web site. Finally, the Translation Tools page is used to configure the integrated translation environment (ITE); it is available only in the Enterprise edition of Delphi.

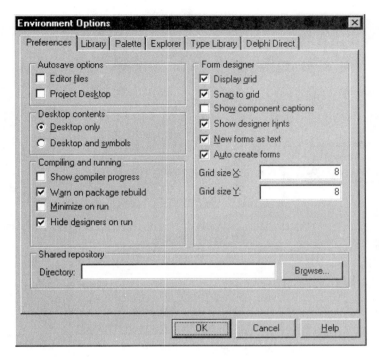

FIGURE D.2   Environment Options Window

Editor Options

Choose `Tools|Editor Options...` from the menu bar or right-click on the Code Editor window and select `Properties` from the pop-up menu to display the Editor Properties dialog box shown in Figure D.3. In this dialog, you can modify your preferences for the Code Editor.

The General page contains options to customize the behavior of the Code Editor for items such as indents and tabs. The Display page allows you to set the editor's display and font options. The Sample area shows an example of the selected font. The Key Mappings page specifies which key mapping to use in the editor, where a key mapping is a set of keyboard shortcuts.

The Color page lets you change the colors of different elements of your code. You can specify both foreground and background colors for any code element that appears in the Element list box, and the sample Code Editor will indicate how your code will appear. Additionally, Color SpeedSettings quickly configure the Code Editor using predefined color combinations.

Finally, the Code Insight page allows you to select and configure the Code Insight options: code completion, code parameters, code templates, tooltip expression evaluation, and tooltip symbol insight.

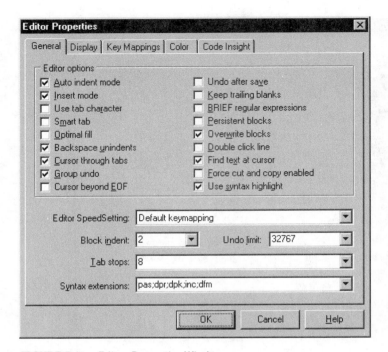

FIGURE D.3   Editor Properties Window

Debugger Options

Select `Tools|Debugger Options...` to display the Debugger Options dialog box containing several tabbed pages of options (Figure D.4). Set the general debugger options for the user interface in the General page. Use the Event Log page to specify event log options, where the event log shows process control, breakpoint, `OutputDebugStrings`, and window messages. The Language Exceptions page indicates how the debugger will handle language exceptions raised by the program currently being debugged. The OS Exceptions page indicates how it will handle operating system exceptions encountered during debugging. The Distributed Debugging page sets debugger options for the remote debugging available in the Enterprise edition of Delphi.

Project Options

You can alter project settings in the Project Options dialog box (Figure D.5). To open this dialog, choose `Project|Options...` from the menu bar, press SHIFT+CTRL+F11, or right-click on the project in the Project Manager and choose

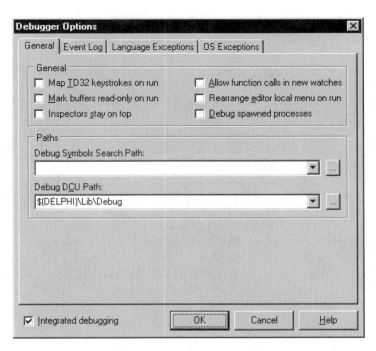

FIGURE D.4   Debugger Options Window

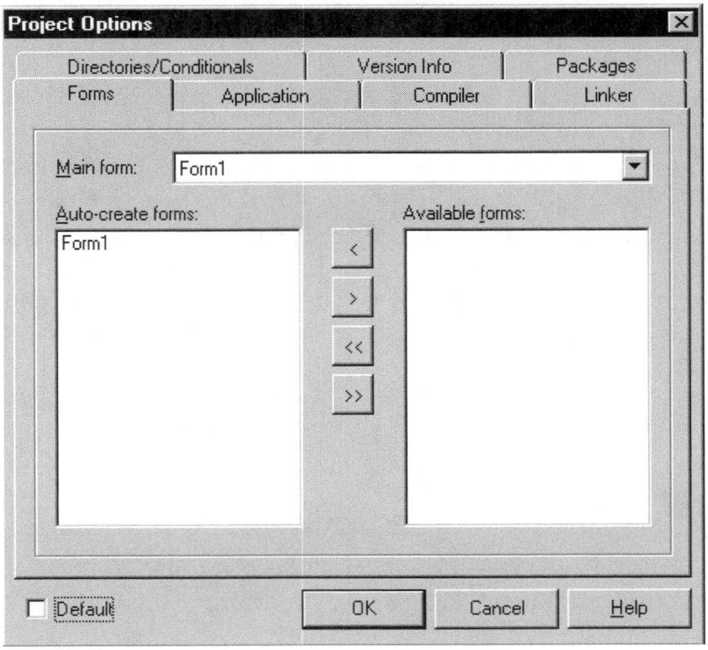

FIGURE D.5   Project Options Window

`Options...` from the pop-up menu. The pages of this dialog allow you to manage project directories and specify form, application, compiler, and linker options for your project.

Your changes well affect only the current project unless you check the Default check box, thereby specifying that these settings should be the default settings for all new projects. If you change a project's default settings, a Delphi options file (*.DOF) is created in the project directory when you save the project.

Select the main form for your project in the Forms page. This page also lets you choose which forms to create automatically when the application begins. The Application page lets you specify a title, help file, icon, and extension for the project. Set compiler options in the Compiler page and linker options in the Linker page. Use the Directories/Conditionals page to identify the locations of any files needed to compile, link, and distribute your application. In addition, you can specify compiler defines on this page. Use the Version Info page to enable the version information option and specify version information for the project. Specify the design-time packages installed in the IDE and the run-time packages required by your project in the Packages page.

Changing the Default Project Type

By default, Delphi displays a blank form when you choose `File|New Application` or `File|New Form` from the menu bar. You can change this behavior by reconfiguring the Object Repository:

1. Select `Tools|Repository...` from the menu bar to open the Object Repository window (Figure D.6).
2. To specify a default project, select the Projects page and choose an item in the Objects list box. Left-click the New Project check box to check it.
3. To specify a default form, select a Repository page (such as Forms) from the Pages list box. Choose a form in the Objects list box. To make it become the default new form, check the New Form check box. To make it become the default main form for new projects, check the Main Form check box.
4. Click the OK button.

Configure Tools

To add, delete, or edit programs on the Tools menu, select `Tools|Configure Tools...` from the menu bar to display the Tool Options dialog box, as shown in Figure D.7.

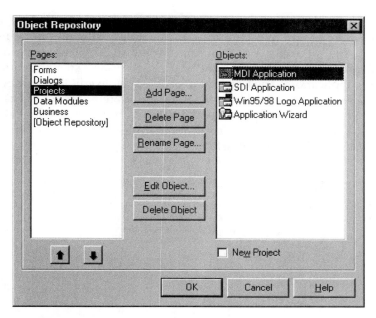

FIGURE D.6 Object Repository Window

FIGURE D.7 Tool Options Window

The Tools list box shows the programs currently installed on the Tools menu. If two or more programs on the Tools menu have conflicting shortcuts, a red star appears to the left of each program name. The Add button allows you to specify a menu heading, executable file, working directory, and startup parameters for a new tool (application). The Edit button enables you to edit these properties for the currently selected tool. Clicking the Delete button removes the currently selected program from the Tools menu. Use the arrow buttons to rearrange the programs in the list. The programs appear on the Tools menu in the same order that they are listed in the Tool Options dialog box.

Distributing Delphi Programs

This appendix discusses how to compile Delphi projects and distribute the final application.

Building Executable Files

Much as in other high-level languages, generating an executable file in Delphi is a two-step process. The first step is to compile the project. The compilation process checks the syntax of each unit in the project and produces an object file for the unit. A unit object file has a DCU (Delphi compiled unit) extension. In the second step, these object files are linked. The linker takes all of the unit object files in the project and combines them to produce a single executable file.

The Project menu in Delphi contains the commands for creating the executable file. The Compile option compiles each unit in the project but does not link them. The Build menu item compiles the units, if necessary, and then links them together, creating the final executable file.

Distributing the Application

If your project does not access a database, third-party dynamic link library (DLL), or ActiveX control, then the executable file that is generated is a stand-alone executable. You can simply copy this executable file to a floppy disk or other removable media and run it on any machine that uses its target operating system. All of the Delphi controls used in the project will be compiled into the resulting executable file. Nothing else needs to be included with the application.

If you use ActiveX controls in a project, the distribution of the application becomes more complicated. You must distribute the OCX file for each ActiveX control used in the project. Be sure to read the documentation for third-party ActiveX controls; some require additional DLLs.

In Windows, an elegant method of deploying an application is to create a Setup program. If you create your own, be sure to register all ActiveX controls used by the application. This task is accomplished by running the `RegSvr32.exe` utility.

The preferred method of creating a Setup program is to use a commercially available installation package. Delphi includes InstallShield Express for this purpose. This menu-driven installation utility allows you to create a Setup program for application deployment, and it is certified by Inprise for use with Delphi and the Borland Database Engine. Other Setup toolkits are available, but you should use only those certified by Inprise to deploy the Borland Database Engine.

InstallShield Express is not automatically installed with Delphi, so you must manually install it after installing Delphi. Run the installation program from the Delphi CD to install InstallShield Express.

Figure E.1 shows the InstallShield Express Setup Checklist. For more information on using InstallShield Express to create installation programs, see the InstallShield Express online help.

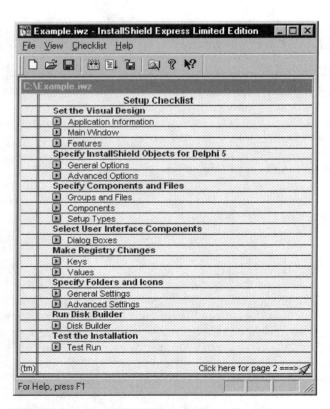

FIGURE E.1   InstallShield Express Setup Checklist

Object Pascal Reserved Words

The following words are reserved in Object Pascal. These words cannot be redefined or used as identifiers.

and	function	property
array	goto	raise
as	if	record
asm	implementation	repeat
begin	in	resourcestring
case	inherited	set
class	initialization	shl
const	inline	shr
constructor	interface	string
destructor	is	then
dispinterface	label	threadvar
div	library	to
do	mod	try
downto	nil	type
else	not	unit
end	object	until
except	of	uses
exports	or	var
file	out	while
finalization	packed	with
finally	procedure	xor
for	program	

Within object type declarations, the words `private`, `protected`, `public`, `published`, and `automated` act as reserved words; otherwise, they are treated as directives. Additionally, the words `at` and `on` have special uses in exception handlers.

Migrating from Visual Basic to Delphi

This appendix is intended for indviduals who are familiar or have programmed with Microsoft Visual Basic (VB) and would like to migrate to Delphi. While it compares product and language features of both packages, it is by no means a complete comparison. It assumes a basic knowledge of RAD, including GUI design concepts, component properties and methods, and event-driven programming. Students, beginning programmers, and experienced programmers alike will benefit from reading the remainder of this appendix.

Benefits of Delphi

Compared to VB, Delphi offers a multitude of benefits, such as the following:

- **Cross-platform development.** Delphi is currently available for the Windows and Linux operating systems (OSs). The same code can be used under both OSs, but it may require minor modifications due to inherent OS differences.

- **Superior development environment.** The Delphi IDE provides all of the functionality expected of a RAD tool and more. The environment is intuitive and easy to use. Furthermore, the IDE is flexible, allowing the programmer to customize the environment to suit his or her needs and preferences.

The material in this appendix has been adapted and reprinted (with permission) from the Borland white paper "Migrating from Visual Basic to Delphi: An Overview for Programmers and Developers" by Mitchell C. Kerman. The full document can be found on Borland's Web site at http://community.borland.com/article/images/26225/vbtodelphi.pdf.

- **Powerful components and controls.** Similar to the VB Toolbox, Delphi contains a Visual Component Library (VCL) of commonly used components and controls. The number and type of components included in this library depend on which edition of Delphi is being used (Standard, Professional, or Enterprise). All library components are written in Object Pascal. Thus the programmer has the ability to modify and extend this library.

- **True object-oriented programming.** While Microsoft claims that VB is object-oriented, we (as educated programmers) know that it is really just object-based. True object inheritance and polymorphism are unavailable in VB. The object model in Delphi is complete, providing encapsulation, inheritance, and polymorphism.

- **Pointers and dynamic variables.** VB does provide for dynamic variables, but it does not allow explicit pointer variables. How many times has this problem come between you and more efficient code or cleaner data structures? "Gee, we really need a tree structure to represent these data properly." While more adept VB programmers can overcome this dilemma by using VB object variables (which are really implicit pointers anyway), many programmers just work around the problem at the expense of algorithm and memory efficiency. Delphi's Object Pascal offers dynamic variables and explicit pointers, effectively dissolving most of your algorithm efficiency and data structure woes.

- **Promotes sound programming practices.** We now come to my pet peeve. As a textbook author and introductory programming instructor, one of my greatest challenges is to teach students to *always* declare their variables. VB gives the programmer the option of not requiring explicit variable declarations (similar to its predecessor, BASIC). "Please make sure that 'Option Explicit' appears at the top of your VB code," I would tell my students. Perhaps you do not agree with me on this point, but try to remember when you first learned how to program. While this option proves extremely powerful and time-saving for expert programmers, it provides just enough rope for novice programmers to hang themselves. Explicitly declaring variables encourages self-commenting variable names, improves code readability, provides greater control over memory space requirements, and avoids confusion between variables of the same name in different portions of the source code. Since Object Pascal always requires explicit variable declarations, it promotes this sound programming practice. Additionally, Object Pascal's syntax encourages structured and modular programming.

- **Strong typing rules.** Akin to sound programming practices, we come to a comparison of the language typing rules. VB is a weakly typed language. For instance, a variable of data type Double (a double-precision floating-point number) can be assigned to a variable of type Integer without repercussion. VB will automatically convert the double-precision value to an integer value. This automatic conversion is not without its problems: Does VB round or truncate the floating-point portion? Do you remember? For positive values, the answer is that VB rounds: It rounds down to the next lowest integer for floating-point portions less than 0.5 (essentially, truncating the floating-point portion), and it rounds up to the next highest integer for floating-point values greater than or equal to 0.5. Of course, we can avoid this problem and simultaneously improve the readability of our code by using a data type conversion function, such as VB's Fix or Int functions. Unlike VB, Delphi's Object Pascal is strongly typed. A double-precision value cannot be assigned to an Integer variable without first performing the necessary data type conversion. Thus the problem is avoided.

The pages that follow further describe the differences and draw parallels between VB and Delphi. This comparison exists at four levels: the IDE, programming language, built-in debugger, and application deployment. Again, rather than act as a complete reference manual, this appendix guides those familiar with VB through the process of learning Delphi by leveraging their existing knowledge.

Integrated Development Environment

VB developers find a comfortable familiarity with Delphi's IDE. Many of the menus, toolbars, and windows have a design and purpose similar to those of VB. Delphi contains all of the tools that are required of modern RAD environments, and it is clear that these tools were created and organized with a great deal of forethought and effort on the part of Delphi's design team.

Both VB and Delphi contain windows with similar names and functionality. For instance, both contain windows in which you can modify control properties. Visual Basic is a multiple document interface (MDI) development environment; all of its windows are fully contained within the main application window. Delphi, however, is a single document interface (SDI) environment, where all windows are free-floating. The following paragraphs introduce the elements of the Delphi IDE and compare and contrast its windows with their VB counterparts.

The default Delphi IDE consists of the following windows:

- A menu bar
- Six toolbars:
  1. Standard toolbar
  2. View toolbar
  3. Debug toolbar
  4. Custom toolbar
  5. Desktops toolbar
  6. Component Palette

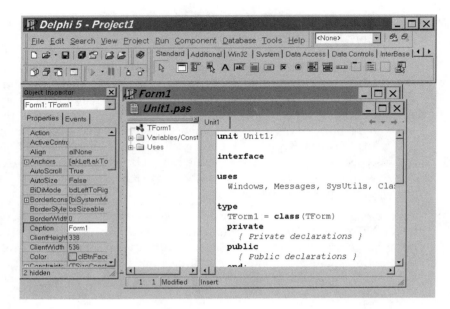

FIGURE G.1   Delphi's Default Integrated Development Environment

- Smaller windows:
  1. Form window
  2. Object Inspector window
  3. Code Editor window
  4. Other windows

Figure G.1 shows the default Delphi IDE layout.

Menu Bar

Like VB, Delphi contains a menu bar. The Delphi menu bar is a typical drop-down menu. Many of the menu options can be accessed directly through the shortcut key combinations that are listed on the right side of the drop-down menu. The menu bar offers all of the functionality required for a developer to create an application. The menu bar and a sample drop-down menu appear in Figure G.2.

Toolbars

Toolbars contain icons that allow quick access to common tasks. VB contains four separate toolbars that divide and organize tasks according to their purpose: the Standard, Debug, Edit, and Form Editor toolbars. By default, VB displays only the Standard toolbar. Delphi has six separate toolbars, all of which are displayed by default.

Both VB and Delphi allow you to toggle the visibility of the various toolbars through the View menu. Alternatively, right-clicking on the Standard toolbar in VB opens a pop-up menu listing the available toolbars. This same action opens a

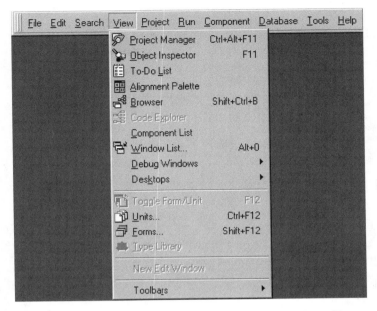

FIGURE G.2   Delphi Menu Bar with an Activated Drop-Down Menu

similar pop-up menu in Delphi. Additionally, both VB and Delphi toolbars are customizable.

Standard Toolbar

The Standard toolbar (Figure G.3) contains icons for common tasks, such as opening, saving, and creating Delphi projects and associated files.

FIGURE G.3   Standard Toolbar

View Toolbar

The View toolbar (Figure G.4) contains icons for creating new forms, viewing forms and code units, and toggling between a form and its code unit. This toolbar allows you to quickly switch between windows in the Delphi IDE.

FIGURE G.4   View Toolbar

Debug Toolbar

As in VB, the Debug toolbar (Figure G.5) is used for interactive testing and debugging of your programs. It provides quick access to several Delphi debugger commands that are available on the Run menu. Like the VB debugger, the Delphi debugger is a design-time utility. It can be used inside of the Delphi development environment only while you are working on the source code.

FIGURE G.5   Debug Toolbar

Custom Toolbar

Figure G.6 shows the Custom toolbar. By default, this toolbar contains a single button to access the Delphi online help facility.

FIGURE G.6   Custom Toolbar

Desktop Toolbar

VB opens with all of its windows and toolbars in their previous positions (that is, the last positions where they were located). The programmer does not have the ability to create several different desktop layouts. Conversely, a programmer can customize Delphi's desktop settings using the Desktop toolbar shown in Figure G.7. This toolbar contains a pick list of the available desktop layouts and allows the programmer to load and save different layouts. A desktop layout includes the display, sizing, docking, and placement of windows in the IDE. A selected layout remains in effect for all projects and is used the next time Delphi is started. Again, VB has no equivalent of this toolbar.

FIGURE G.7   Desktop Toolbar

Component Palette

In VB, the Toolbox houses all of the ActiveX controls that are available to the current project. The equivalent window in Delphi is the Component Palette, shown in Figure G.8.

FIGURE G.8   Component Palette

The first difference between VB's Toolbox and Delphi's Component Palette is that the Component Palette is tabbed. To alter this tab layout, right-click on the Component Palette and select Properties from the pop-up menu. This action opens the Palette Properties window, which allows you to customize the Component Palette. By default, the VB Toolbox is not tabbed. However, a programmer may customize the Toolbox and add tabs to organize the controls for quick and easy recognition, similar to Delphi's Component Palette.

Another difference between the two windows is that the VB Toolbox contains only the controls that are available to or used by the current project. By comparison, the Component Palette always contains all of the controls. Furthermore, when you compile a VB application, each of the ActiveX controls remains separate from the executable file, whereas Delphi compiles the required controls into the executable file.

Delphi also supports the use of ActiveX controls. When an ActiveX control is used in an application, it is "wrapped" in a set of code that allows it to be placed on the Component Palette and used within the Delphi IDE.

Smaller Windows

Smaller windows in Delphi's default IDE include the Form window, Object Inspector window, Code Editor window, and other windows.

Form Window

The Form window in Delphi (Figure G.9) looks and acts like the Form window in VB. The major difference is the unit of measure. Instead of using twips like VB, Delphi uses pixels.

As in VB, the grid dots on the form are used to align and size your controls. To change any of the Form designer's options, select `Tools|Environment Options...` from the menu bar and left-click the Preferences tab. The Form designer frame under this tab allows you to change the options summarized below:

- Display Grid—Controls whether the grid dots are displayed.
- Snap To Grid—Directs the alignment of the controls. When activated, all corners of the controls are aligned to the grid dots.
- Show Component Captions—For nonvisual components, displays the name of the component underneath it on the form designer.
- Show Designer Hints—As you are sizing or moving a control with this option active, the size or position is displayed as a tooltip hint.
- New Forms As Text—Designates whether newly created forms are saved in text or binary format.

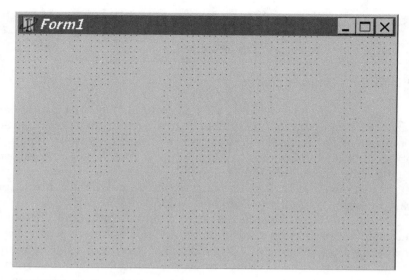

FIGURE G.9 Form Window

- AutoCreate Forms—Determines whether new forms are automatically created when the application executes.
- Grid Size X, Grid Size Y—Determines the number of pixels between the grid dots.

Like VB, Delphi offers several methods of placing a control on a form. The first method, double-clicking the desired control on the Component Palette, places a control of the default size in the center of the form. A second method is to left-click the control on the Component Palette and then left-click on the form; it places a control of the default size on the form with its top-left corner aligned to the location that you clicked. Third, you can single-click the control on the Component Palette and then click and drag to place this control on the form. This method allows the programmer to directly specify the size and position of the control.

You can place multiple controls of the same type on the form by holding down the SHIFT key while selecting the control from the Component Palette. Once the control is selected, you can place controls of this type on the form by using one of the last two methods described above.

Object Inspector Window

Figure G.10 shows the Object Inspector window. Delphi's Object Inspector is closely related to the Properties Window in VB. Both display a list of the available design-time properties for the currently selected object. By default, the Object Inspector displays this list alphabetically. If you are more accustomed to viewing properties by category, Delphi can accommodate you. Simply right-click the Object Inspector window and select Arrange | by Category from the pop-up menu.

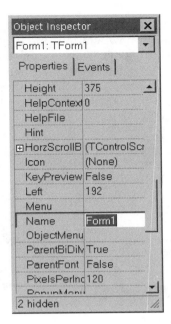

FIGURE G.10   Object Inspector Window

Delphi supports four basic types of object properties: Simple, Enumerated, Sets, and those containing Property Editors. Simple properties allow you to directly enter a property value by using the keyboard. Enumerated properties allow you to select from a valid list of property values. For instance, the BorderStyle property of a form is an Enumerated property. Set type properties are the only properties that allow you to assign multiple values. An example Set type property is the Style property within an object's Font property; possible values for this property include Italics, Bold, Underline, Strikeout, or any combination of these values. As in VB, those properties that use Property Editors appear with ellipses (three dots) on their right side in the Object Inspector. Left-click the ellipses to activate the Property Editor.

The Object Inspector not only displays the available design-time properties for an object, but it also contains a tab listing all of the events to which the object can respond. To see a list of all available events for an object in VB, you must go to the Code Editor, select the object from the Object drop-down list, and then select the event from the Procedure drop-down list.

With Delphi, you can have multiple controls (or even different events) call the same event handler. After writing the event handler, use the Events tab of the Object Inspector to select this same event handler for multiple controls (or different events). The drop-down list in the Object Inspector shows all event handlers that have the same parameter list. You can readily see that Delphi is very flexible and powerful in regard to objects and event handlers. To do something similar in VB, one event handler must call the other.

Code Editor Window

The VB Code Editor opens each module in a new window. In Delphi, the Code Editor is a single window, as shown in Figure G.11. This window contains a tab for each opened unit, or module. A word of caution: All too often, you will be tempted to close the Code Editor window after you finish editing your code. When you close a unit in Delphi, you also close the form that uses it. To close a single unit, and subsequently the form, right-click its tab in the Code Editor and select Close Page from the pop-up menu.

Delphi's Code Editor uses a color-coding similar to that emplyed by the VB Code Editor. The colors can be customized by selecting `Tools|Editor Options...` and clicking the Colors tab. Then, select the element whose color you wish to change. Choose a color with the left mouse button to change the foreground color and with the right mouse button to change the background color. You can also choose to have the element displayed with a bold or an italic font.

The keyboard shortcuts for the Code Editor include the standard Windows navigation keys:

Key	Function
Home	Beginning of the line
End	End of the line
Ctrl+Home	Beginning of the unit
Ctrl+End	End of the unit
PgUp	Previous screen
PgDn	Next screen
Ctrl+PgUp	Top of the screen
Ctrl+PgDn	Bottom of the screen

Similar to VB's IntelliSense technology, Delphi contains a set of five tools known as Code Insight to aid the developer:

1. *Code Completion* displays a list of available data types when you declare a variable or a list of properties and methods when you use an object. As you type the data type, property, or method, Delphi performs an incremental search of the drop-down list. By default, this list is sorted by scope. To display it in alphabetical order, right-click the drop-down list and select Sort by Name from the pop-up menu. Once you have located the desired item, press the ENTER key to select it and place it in your code.

2. *Code Parameters* displays a dialog of the names and types of the parameters for a function, method, or procedure. Thus you can view the required arguments for a function, method, or procedure as you enter it into your code.

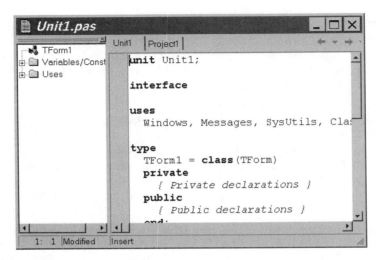

FIGURE G.11   Code Editor Window

3. *Code Templates* is the most useful feature for your migration from VB to Delphi. It provides syntax templates for basic code constructs. Pressing CTRL+J activates this feature and displays a pop-up menu of the available templates. Additionally, you can type in the beginning of a statement and then press CTRL+J. If Delphi can resolve the statement, it will fill in the code with the applicable template. If Delphi is unable to resolve the statement, it displays a list of templates that most closely match the statement. To modify or add code templates, select the Code Insight tab under `Tools|Editor` Options....

4. *Tooltip Expression Evaluation* displays the value of a variable or expression as tooltip text during interactive debugging.

5. *Tooltip Symbol Insight* displays declaration information for any identifier in the Code Editor. A pop-up window shows the kind of identifier (procedure, function, type, constant, variable, unit, and so on) and the unit file and line number of its declaration.

Each open unit in Delphi has a separate tab in the Code Editor. If the unit that you wish to edit is not open, select either `View|Units` or `View|Forms` from the menu. The `View|Units` option displays a list of all available units in the project. Similarly, `View|Forms` lists all available forms in the project. Opening a form opens its corresponding unit.

Another navigation feature in Delphi's Code Editor is bookmarks. Delphi permits 10 bookmarks in the Code Editor, numbered zero through nine. To toggle a bookmark, position the cursor on the desired line of code, and then press SHIFT+CTRL+*number*, where *number* is one of the number keys 0 through 9. To jump to a numbered bookmark, press CTRL+*number*.

Other Windows

In addition to the three windows that are shown by default, Delphi has several other useful windows available. In Figure G.11, the Code Explorer window is located in its default position, inside the Code Editor window to the left of the active editor page tabs. In other words, this window is docked on the left side of the Code Editor window. The Code Explorer allows the programmer to easily navigate through the unit files. It contains a tree diagram that shows all types, classes, properties, methods, global variables, and global routines that are defined in the code unit that is currently being edited in the Code Editor window. It also lists the other units that are used by the unit currently being edited. Select `View|Code Explorer` to open the Code Explorer window if it is not already visible.

The programmer can view the files that compose a Delphi project in the Project Manager window. In this window, Delphi projects may be arranged into project groups, where a project group consists of related projects or projects that function together as part of a multitiered application. In addition, this window allows the programmer to easily navigate among the various projects and each project's constituent files within a project group. Select `View|Project Manager` or press CTRL+ALT+F11 to open the Project Manager window.

To successfully complete a program, especially a large program, the programmer needs to perform many tasks. Delphi's To-Do List provides a built-in notepad for the programmer to organize these tasks. This list is extremely helpful in planning, programming, testing, and debugging large projects that are written by a team of programmers. Select `View|To-Do List` from the menu bar to open this window. You can add, edit, and delete list items by right-clicking on the To-Do List window.

The Alignment Palette window provides a rapid means of aligning components on a form. Select `View|Alignment Palette` from the menu bar to open this window.

The Project Browser lists the units, classes, types, properties, methods, variables, and routines that are declared or used in the current project. The Project Browser arranges this information in a tree diagram. The Project Browser is opened by selecting `View|Browser` or pressing SHIFT+CTRL+B.

The Component List (or Components window) is opened by selecting `View|Component List` from the menu bar. This window shows an alphabetical listing of all of the components that are available in your version of Delphi. You can add a component to your Delphi program by selecting the component from this window with either the keyboard or the mouse. When you use the mouse, the Component Palette provides a more rapid means of selecting components and placing them in your applications because it organizes the components according to their functions. Therefore, we recommend using the Component Palette in lieu of the Components window.

The Window List allows you to quickly switch between windows in the Delphi IDE. If you have many windows open, this option is the easiest way to locate a window and make it active. Open the Window List by selecting `View|Window List` or pressing ALT+0. Then, select the desired window from the list and click the OK button.

Delphi contains several windows that are associated with its built-in debugger. Discussion of these windows is deferred until the debugging section.

Programming Language

This section discusses Delphi file types and the Object Pascal language syntax.

Delphi File Types

Similar to a VB application, a Delphi application (called a project) consists of several file types. The three main file types are project files, unit files, and form files. The project file (.DPR) is the "main program"; it accesses the unit files and form files that compose the Delphi project. Thus the project file ties together the files that are associated with a specific project. Typically, there is a one-to-one relationship between unit files and form files: Each unit file has an associated form file, and vice versa. The form file (.DFM) lists the objects on the form and the object property settings. The unit file (.PAS) contains the source code associated with the form. Recall that VB combines the objects, property settings, and code into just the form file (.FRM).

You must save both the project and the forms for your Delphi application. When you save a form, both the unit file and form file are saved under the same name with the appropriate file extension. To save a form, select File|Save or File|Save As... from the menu bar, click the Save icon on the Standard toolbar, or press CTRL+S. To save the project file, select File|Save Project As... from the menu bar. To rapidly save all files associated with a project, select File|Save All from the menu or click the Save All icon on the Standard toolbar.

Project File

Each application consists of a "main program" in the project file. This file links together all units associated with the application.

The general syntax of a project file is shown below:

```
program Project1;

uses
  Forms,
  Unit1 in 'Unit1.pas' {Form1};

{$R *.RES}

begin
  Application.Initialize;
  Application.CreateForm(TForm1, Form1);
  Application.Run;
end.
```

As in the preceding syntax, a project file consist of three elements:

- A program heading
- An (optional) uses clause
- A block of declarations and statements between `begin` and `end` keywords

The program heading specifies a name for the program. The uses clause lists the unit files used by the program. The block (between `begin` and `end` keywords) contains declarations and statements that execute when the program runs. The Delphi IDE expects to find these three elements in a single project file.

A word of caution: It is best not to manually alter the code generated by the IDE. This warning applies not only to project files but also unit files. In other words, let the IDE do the work for you. For instance, if you want to add a new form to a project, select `File|New Form` or click the New Form button on the View toolbar. Similarly, to add an event handler to a unit file, select the object and event in the Object Inspector for the appropriate form, and then enter a name for the event handler. Delphi automatically generates the heading and block for the event handler.

Units

A Delphi unit consists of data types (including classes), constant and variable declarations, and subroutines (functions and procedures). Each unit exists in a separate unit file.

A unit file contains a heading, interface, implementation, initialization, and finalization sections. The initialization and finalization sections are optional. Like the project file, a unit file must conclude with the `end` keyword followed by a period. The general syntax of a unit file follows:

```
unit Unit1;

interface

uses {List of used units goes here}

const
  {Public constants go here}

type
  {Public types go here}

var
  {Public variables go here}

{Remainder of interface section goes here}

implementation

uses {List of used units goes here}

const
  {Private constants go here}
```

```
type
  {Private types go here}

var
  {Private variables go here}

{Remainder of implementation section goes here}

initialization
{Initialization section goes here}

finalization
{Finalization section goes here}

end.
```

The interface section begins with the reserved word `interface` and continues until the beginning of the implementation section. The interface section declares constants, data types, variables, and subroutines that are available to clients (other units or programs) that use the unit where they are declared. Therefore, any entity that appears in the interface section has a public scope, because a client can access it as if it were declared in the client itself.

The implementation section begins with the reserved word `implementation` and continues until the beginning of the initialization section (if one exists) or the end of the unit. The implementation section declares constants, data types, variables, and subroutines that are private to the unit; that is, these entities have a private scope and are inaccessible to clients.

The interface declaration of a procedure or function includes only the routine's heading. The block of the routine follows in the implementation section. Thus procedure and function declarations in the interface section act like forward declarations.

The interface and implementation sections may include their own uses clauses, which must appear immediately after the section headings (the `interface` and `implementation` keywords). The uses clause specifies the units that are used. The `System` unit is used automatically by every Delphi application and cannot be listed explicitly in the uses clause. This unit implements routines for file input and output, string handling, floating-point operations, dynamic memory allocation, and so on. Other standard library units, such as `SysUtils`, must be included in the uses clause. In most cases, Delphi places all necessary units in the uses clause when it generates and maintains a source file.

Unit names must be unique within a project. Even if the unit files are located in different directories, two units with the same name cannot be used in a single program.

Elements of Programming

Now that you are familiar with the purpose and organization of the Delphi file types, it is time to focus on the elements of programming—those elements that are common to most high-level languages.

Comments

VB has two kinds of comment statements: the remark statement (Rem) and the apostrophe ('). Both are ignored by the VB compiler. In Object Pascal, comments are also ignored by the compiler, except when they function as separators (delimiting adjacent tokens) or compiler directives. There are three ways to construct comments:

- `{Text between a left brace and a right brace consti-tutes a comment}`
- `(* Text between a left parenthesis followed by an asterisk and an asterisk followed by a right paren-thesis constitutes a comment *)`
- `// Any text between a double forward slash and the end of the line constitutes a comment`

A comment that contains a dollar sign ($) immediately after the opening { or (* is a compiler directive. Compiler directives are non executable statements within the code that alter compiler options. For instance, `{$WARNINGS OFF}` tells the Object Pascal compiler not to generate warning messages. In VB, the Option statement signifies a compiler directive.

Statement Termination

In VB, the end of a line terminates a statement unless the line continuation character (underscore) is used to continue the statement on the following line. Object Pascal does not require a line continuation character; that is, a statement may span several lines. The semicolon (;) is the statement separator and terminator; it separates one statement from the next.

Identifiers

An Object Pascal identifier denotes a constant, variable, field, data type, property, procedure, function, program, unit, library, or package. An identifier can be of any length, but only the first 255 characters are significant. The first character of an identifier must be either a letter or an underscore. Any number of letters, digits, and underscores may follow the first character. Identifiers cannot contain spaces, and reserved words cannot be used as identifiers.

Object Pascal is case insensitive, meaning that an identifier named `FindItem` can be written in a variety of ways, such as `finditem`, `findItem`, `Finditem`, and `FINDITEM`.

Data Types

A data type specifies the kind of data that a variable can contain. Table G.1 summarizes the predefined (built-in) data types for Object Pascal. This table shows the valid range of values for each data type and their memory space requirements. Note that these data types apply to the Windows version of Delphi; the Linux version does not contain a Variant data type, as this data type is a Windows anomaly.

TABLE G.1   Object Pascal Data Types

Logical and Numeric Data Types

Data Type	Range	Format or Size	Significant Digits
Shortint	−128 to +127	signed 8-bit	
Smallint	−32768 to +32767	signed 16-bit	
Integer (or Longint)	−2147483648 to +2147483647	signed 32-bit	
Int64	-2^{63} to $+2^{63}-1$	signed 64-bit	
Byte	0 to 255	unsigned 8-bit	
Word	0 to 65535	unsigned 16-bit	
Longword (or Cardinal)	0 to 4294967295	unsigned 32-bit	
Boolean (or ByteBool)	True or False	1 byte	
WordBool	True or False	2 bytes	
LongBool	True or False	4 bytes	
Real48	2.9×10^{-39} to 1.7×10^{38}	6 bytes	11 to 12
Single	1.5×10^{-45} to 3.4×10^{38}	4 bytes	7 to 8
Real (or Double)	5.0×10^{-324} to 1.7×10^{308}	8 bytes	15 to 16
Extended	3.6×10^{-4951} to 1.1×10^{4932}	10 bytes	19 to 20
Comp	$-2^{63}+1$ to $+2^{63}-1$	8 bytes	19 to 20
Currency	−922337203685477.5808 to +922337203685477.5807	8 bytes	19 to 20

Character and String Data Types

Data Type	Maximum Length	Memory Required
Char (or AnsiChar)	1 ANSI character	1 byte
WideChar	1 Unicode character	2 bytes
ShortString	255 ANSI characters	2 to 256 bytes
Strin (or AnsiString)	2^{31} ANSI characters	4 bytes to 2 gigabytes
WideString	2^{30} Unicode characters	4 bytes to 2 gigabytes

Constants

A constant is a named item that retains the same value throughout the execution of a program. It may be defined by any mathematical or string expression. At compile time, the compiler simply replaces the constant name with its associated value. A numeric constant refers to a number, or numeric literal, and a string constant is a string literal. The number 7, for example, is a numeric constant, and "days per week" is a string constant.

In Object Pascal, the `const` statement is used to define constants. Like its VB counterpart, the `const` statement can declare a group of constants. The general form of this statement appears below:

```
const
  constantName = Expression;
  [constantName = Expression;]
```

In this syntax, square brackets ([...]) are used to designate optional items that can appear any number of times. For instance, the following code fragment defines three constants:

```
const
  MINS_PER_HR = 60;
  HRS_PER_DAY = 24;
  DAYS_PER_WK = 7;
```

In VB, these same constants are defined using the following statement:

```
Const MINS_PER_HR = 60, HRS_PER_DAY = 24, _
      DAYS_PER_WK = 7
```

Variables

A variable is a named location in memory where values are stored. These values can be changed throughout a program's execution.

While VB uses the Dim (dimension) statement to declare variables, Object Pascal uses the `var` statement. The general syntax of the `var` statement follows:

```
var
  variableName[, variableName]: DataType;
  [variableName[, variableName]: DataType;]
```

where `DataType` is any predefined or user-defined data type.

As an example, consider the following VB variable declarations:

```
Dim dollars As Integer, cents As Integer
Dim cost As Double
Dim myMessage As String
```

The equivalent variable declarations in Delphi follow:

```
var
  dollars: Integer;
  cents: Integer;
  cost: Real;
  myMessage: String;
```

Operators

In VB, the equals sign (=) is an overloaded operator; it functions as both the assignment operator and the comparison operator for equality. The equals sign is only the comparison operator for equality in Object Pascal, however; it always compares the contents of the variables to determine equality. The Object Pascal assignment operator is a combination of two characters, the colon (:) immediately followed by the equals sign (=), or :=.

Consider the following VB code fragment:

```
Dim value1 As Integer, value2 As Integer
Dim check As Boolean
```

```
value1 = 5
value2 = 7
check = (value1 = value2)
```

In this code, `value1` and `value2` are assigned different values—5 and 7, respectively. The Boolean variable `check` is assigned a value based on whether `value1` equals `value2`. In this case, `check` is assigned False because the variable values are unequal. The equivalent Object Pascal code appears below:

```
var
  value1: Integer;
  value2: Integer;
  check: Boolean;

begin
  value1 := 5;
  value2 := 7;
  check := (value1 = value2);

end;
```

Object Pascal's arithmetic and relational operators are presented in this appendix in two tables. Table G.2 shows the arithmetic operators, and Table G.3 displays the relational operators. The relational operators are the same as those used in VB.

TABLE G.2   Object Pascal Arithmetic Operators

Operation	Operator	Operand Types	Result Type	Example
Sign Identity	+ (unary)	integer, real	integer, real	+x
Sign Negation	– (unary)	integer, real	integer, real	–x
Multiplication	*	integer, real	integer, real	x * y
Division	/	integer, real	real	x / y
Integer Division	div	integer	integer	x div y
Modulo Division	mod	integer	integer	x mod y
Addition	+	integer, real	integer, real	x + y
Subtraction	–	integer, real	integer, real	x – y

TABLE G.3   Object Pascal Relational Operators

Relational Operator	Object Pascal	Mathematics
Less than	<	<
Less than or equal to	<=	≤
Greater than	>	>
Greater than or equal to	>=	≥
Equal to	=	=
Not equal to	<>	≠

The arithmetic operators are also the same as those used in VB, except for integer division, modulo division, and exponentiation. In Object Pascal, integer division and modulo division have built-in operators, but exponentiation does not. To perform exponentiation, the programmer must call a function from the math library.

Logical operators in Object Pascal include `and`, `or`, `not`, and `xor`. By default, Object Pascal performs short-circuited evaluations of `and` and `or` operations. That is, it evaluates only as much of the expression as is required to determine the final value. To force complete evaluation of these expressions, select `Project |` `Options...` and then click on the Compiler tab. Next, click `Complete` `boolean eval` under the Syntax options frame. Alternatively, you can put the `{$B+}` compiler directive in your code.

As in VB, the only string operation in Delphi is string concatenation (which combines strings). VB has two interchangeable operators that perform string concatenation, the ampersand (&) and the plus sign (+). In Object Pascal, only the plus sign (+) is used for string concatenation. Thus the plus sign (+) is an overloaded operator in Object Pascal; it is used for sign identity, addition, and string concatenation.

While we are on the subject of strings, another difference between VB and Object Pascal relates to the string delimiter character. VB uses double quotes (") to delimit strings, whereas Object Pascal uses single quotes ('). An example line of code that uses strings and the string concatenation operator follows:

```
myName := 'Mitchell' + ' ' + 'Kerman';
```

This line of code is equivalent to

```
myName := 'Mitchell Kerman';
```

Decision Structures

As in VB, Delphi's Object Pascal has two types of decision structures: `if` statements and `case` statements. These constructs are similar in both languages.

`if` Statements

Nearly every high-level language includes some form of the `if` statement. The main difference between VB and Delphi `if` statements is that Object Pascal requires multiple lines of code under a condition to be in the form of a compound statement, where a compound statement is delimited by `begin` and `end` keywords. To ensure that you use this construct correctly, *always* use a compound statement, even if the compound statement consists of only one statement. This approach avoids several syntax problems in the long run. For instance, you will not inadvertently forget to add the `begin` and `end` keywords when you increase the number of statements under one of the conditions, as these keywords are already in place.

The general form of the Object Pascal `if` statement follows:

```
if condition1 then begin
  [statements1;]
end
```

```
else if condition2 then begin
  [statements2;]
end
    .
    .
    .
else if conditionN then begin
  [statementsN;]
end
else begin
  [statementsX;]
end;
```

An if statement may have any number of else if clauses, but may contain at most one else clause. In evaluating this if statement, we find that it operates in the same manner as its VB counterpart. statements1 executes when condition1 is True; statements2 executes when condition1 is False and condition2 is True; statementsN executes when conditionN is True and all other preceding conditions (condition1 through condition{N-1}) are False. statementsX executes only if all conditions (condition1 through conditionN) are False.

The following example code computes a golf handicap for a friend based on your difference in scores:

```
difference := yourAverageScore —
              myAverageScore;
if (difference >= 10) then begin
  handicap := 5;
end
else if (difference >= 7) then begin
  handicap := 3;
end
else if (difference >= 4) then begin
  handicap := 2;
end
else begin
  handicap := 0;
end;
```

The VB equivalent of this code follows:

```
difference = yourAverageScore - myAverageScore
If (difference >= 10) Then
  handicap = 5
ElseIf (difference >= 7) Then
  handicap = 3
ElseIf (difference >= 4) Then
  handicap = 2
```

```
Else
   handicap = 0
End If
```

There are some important syntax differences to note here. In VB, `ElseIf` is a keyword, but the Object Pascal equivalent is two separate words, `else` followed by `if`. Also, Object Pascal has no equivalent to VB's `End If` statement; it is not required because we use a semicolon (;) to terminate program statements. Notice the locations of the semicolons in the Delphi syntax shown above. No semicolon directly precedes an `else` statement, as it would cause a syntax error.

case Statements

Delphi's `case` statement is very similar to the `Select Case` statement in VB. The main difference is that the VB `Select Case` statement can test strings and real numbers. Delphi's `case` statement is restricted to testing only ordinal data types, including integers and characters. If you need to test strings or real values, then you must use an `if` statement in Delphi.

The syntax of the Object Pascal `case` statement follows:

```
case selectorExpression of
   caseList1: begin
                  statements1;
              end;
   caseList2: begin
                  statements2;
              end;

              .

              .

              .

   caseListN: begin
                  statementsN;
              end;
   else begin
      statementsX;
   end;
end;
```

In this syntax, `selectorExpression` is an expression that is compared to each `caseList` expression. `selectorExpression` must be an expression of an ordinal type, where the ordinal types include Integer, Char, and Boolean. Furthermore, each expression in a `caseList` must be an ordinal expression that can be evaluated at compile time. For instance, 12, True, $4 - 9 * 5$, 'X', and Integer('Z') are valid `caseList` expressions, but variables and most function calls are not. A `caseList` may also be a subrange having the form `firstExpr..lastExpr`, where `firstExpr` and `lastExpr` are ordinal expressions with $firstExpr \leq lastExpr$. Finally, a `caseList` may be a list in the form `expr1, expr2, ..., exprN`, where each `expr` is an ordinal expression or a subrange as described above.

A case statement may have any number of caseList expressions, but at most one else clause. The execution of a case statement parallels that of the if structure. If selectorExpression matches any expression in a caseList, then the statements following that caseList execute, and control passes to the code following the case statement. If selectorExpression matches an expression in more than one caseList, only the statements following the first matched caseList expression execute. If selectorExpression does not match an expression in any caseList, then the statements following the else clause, statementsX, execute. Although an else clause is not required in a case statement, using one allows your code to handle unforeseen selectorExpression values. If selector-Expression does not match any caseList expression and there is no else clause, execution continues with the code following the case statement.

The golf handicap example is converted to a case statement in the code below. This code assumes that the maximum difference between your score and your friend's score is 126 strokes.

```
difference := yourAverageScore —
              myAverageScore;
case difference of
  4, 5, 6: begin
              handicap := 2;
           end;
  7, 8, 9: begin
              handicap := 3;
           end;
10..126: begin
              handicap := 5;
           end;
  else begin
    handicap := 0;
  end;
end;
```

For comparison purposes, the VB equivalent of this code follows:

```
difference = yourAverageScore - myAverageScore
Select Case difference
  Case 4, 5, 6
    handicap = 2
  Case 7, 8, 9
    handicap = 3
  Case 10 To 126
    handicap = 5
  Case Else
    handicap = 0
End Select
```

Repetition Structures

Repetition structures (also known as loops) may be either definite or indefinite. A definite repetition structure is one in which the number of times that the loop executes is known or can be computed. An indefinite repetition structure is one in which the number of times that the loop executes is not necessarily known.

In VB, the For loop is a definite loop structure, whereas the Do loops are indefinite loop structures. VB's Do loop structures include Do While...Loop, Do...Loop Until, Do Until...Loop, and Do...Loop While. Similarly, Object Pascal's for loop is a definite loop structure, and the while and repeat loops are indefinite loop structures. The following paragraphs discuss each of these loop structures.

for Loops

In VB, the loop control variable of a For loop may be any numerical data type, including integers and real numbers. In Object Pascal, the loop control variable of a for loop must be of an ordinal data type. Additionally, no step value may be specified in Object Pascal; a for loop always increments (or decrements, depending on the syntax) to the next ordinal value.

The following VB code uses an incrementing For loop to compute the sum of the integers from 1 to 100:

```
Dim counter As Integer, sum As Integer

sum = 0
For counter = 1 To 100
   sum = sum + counter
Next counter
```

The general syntax of an *incrementing* for loop in Object Pascal follows:

```
for counter := start to finish do begin
   [statements;]
end;
```

Translating the VB code into Object Pascal syntax, we get

```
var
   counter: Integer;
   sum: Integer;

begin
   sum := 0;
   for counter := 1 to 100 do begin
      sum := sum + counter;
   end;
end;
```

We can just as easily compute the sum of the integers from 1 to 100 using a decrementing `For` loop as opposed to an incrementing one. The necessary VB code follows:

```
Dim counter As Integer, sum As Integer

sum = 0
For counter = 100 To 1 Step -1
  sum = sum + counter
Next counter
```

The general syntax of a *decrementing* `for` loop in Object Pascal follows:

```
for counter := start downto finish do begin
  [statements;]
end;
```

Rewriting our decrementing loop structure in Object Pascal, we get

```
var
  counter: Integer;
  sum: Integer;

begin
  sum := 0;
  for counter := 100 downto 1 do begin
    sum := sum + counter;
  end;
end;
```

`while` and `repeat` Loops

Delphi's `while` and `repeat` loops are indefinite loop structures. The `while` loop is the equivalent of VB's `Do While...Loop`, and the `repeat` loop is equivalent to VB's `Do...Loop Until`. Note that Delphi does not provide equivalents for VB's `Do Until...Loop` and `Do...Loop While` structures, but these structures may be easily converted to one of the other forms by negating the logical condition.

The `while` loop has the following general syntax:

```
while condition do begin
  [statements;]
end;
```

The `while` loop executes the body of the loop as long as `condition` evaluates to True. This type of loop is a top-tested loop; if `condition` evaluates to False before the first loop execution, then the body of the loop never executes.

The following code sums the integers from 1 to 100 using a `while` loop:

```
sum := 0;
count := 1;
```

```
while (count <= 100) do begin
   sum := sum + count;
   count := count + 1;
end;
```

The VB equivalent of this code follows:

```
sum = 0
count = 1
Do While (count <= 100)
   sum = sum + count
   count = count + 1
Loop
```

The `repeat` loop has the following syntax:

```
repeat
   [statements;]
until condition;
```

The `repeat` loop executes a block of code until `condition` becomes True. It is a bottom-tested loop; the body of the `repeat` loop is guaranteed to execute at least once. Notice that no `begin` and `end` keywords are needed for this loop structure; the body of the loop is delimited by the `repeat` and `until` keywords.

The following code sums the integers from 1 to 100 using a `repeat` loop:

```
sum := 0;
count := 1;
repeat
   sum := sum + count;
   count := count + 1;
until (count > 100);
```

The VB equivalent of this code follows:

```
sum = 0
count = 1
Do
   sum = sum + count
   count = count + 1
Loop Until (count > 100)
```

break and continue Statements

VB allows a program to unconditionally exit out of a loop structure through the use of either the `Exit Do` or `Exit For` statement. Both statements transfer control to the statement following the loop structure. To accomplish this same task in Delphi, use the `break` statement. Delphi has another statement that is not available in VB, the `continue` statement. It transfers control to the beginning of the loop, skipping the remainder of the loop body.

Subprograms

Like most other high-level languages, Object Pascal supports two types of subprograms: procedures and functions. Procedures and functions that are not built into Object Pascal are called user-defined, because the programmer (the user of the compiler) must define them. A `procedure` in Delphi is analogous to a `Sub` procedure in VB. Similarly, a `function` in Delphi operates in the same manner as a VB `Function`.

In VB, event handlers are actually `Sub` procedures. Similarly, event handlers in Delphi are procedures that are automatically called when an event occurs on its associated object. For instance, the following VB event handler finds and displays the square root of a user-entered value:

```
Private Sub cmdComputeSqrRt_Click()
Dim value As Double

   value = Sqr(Val(txtInputNumber.Text))
   picOutput.Print "The square root of " & _
                   txtInputNumber.Text & _
                   " is " & CStr(value)
End Sub
```

This event handler is written in Delphi as follows:

```
procedure TfrmSquareRoot.SquareRoot(Sender: TObject);

var
   value: Real;
   code: Integer;
   result: String;

begin
   Val(edtInputNumber.Text, value, code);
   value := Sqrt(value);
   Str(value, result);
   memOutput.Lines.Add('The square root of ' +
                       edtInputNumber.Text +
                       ' is ' + result);
end;
```

The user interface for the Delphi code consists of the form (`frmSquareRoot`) and four components on the form: a label (`lblInputNumber`), an edit box (`edtInputNumber`), a button (`btnComputeSqrRt`), and a memo box (`memOutput`). This code computes the square root of a number that the user enters in `edtInputNumber` and displays the result in `memOutput`. Furthermore, this code is associated with the `OnClick` event of the `btnComputeSqrRt` button. In other words, when the mouse pointer is on the `btnComputeSqrRt` button and the user clicks the left mouse button, this code executes.

Procedures

The general form for defining an Object Pascal procedure follows:

```
procedure ProcedureName(param1: Type1;
                        param2: Type2; ...);

[localDeclarations;]

begin
  [statements;]

end;
```

You invoke a procedure by stating the procedure name along with any required arguments. The general syntax of a procedure call follows:

```
ProcedureName(argument1, argument2, ...);
```

As an example, the procedure `Adder` sums two numbers:

```
{Add num1 and num2 and store the result in sum}
procedure Adder(num1: Real; num2: Real;
                var sum: Real);

begin
  sum := num1 + num2;
end;
```

In this code, num1, num2, and sum are the parameters of the `Adder` procedure. Parameters are merely placeholders for the information passed to a subprogram when it is invoked. The parameter list specified in the `Adder` procedure contains three elements, thereby informing the Delphi compiler that the `Adder` procedure requires three real numbers as arguments. Note that the var keyword precedes the sum parameter. It will be discussed later.

A simple test driver for the `Adder` procedure follows. When the user clicks the btnAdd button, the AddNumbers event handler is invoked. This event handler adds the numbers in edit boxes edtNum1 and edtNum2 by calling the `Adder` procedure and then stores the result in edtResult.

```
{Add two user-entered numbers}
procedure TfrmAdderProcedure.AddNumbers(Sender: TObject);

var
  firstNum: Real;
  secondNum: Real;
  result: Real;
  code: Integer;

begin
  Val(edtNum1.Text, firstNum, code);
```

```
Val(edtNum2.Text, secondNum, code);

Adder(firstNum, secondNum, result);

edtResult.Text := Format('%15.5f',
                         [result]);
```

end;

The variables firstNum, secondNum, and result are the arguments of the Adder procedure; these variables contain the values that are passed to the procedure. Note that an argument can be any expression that is of the same type as its corresponding parameter.

Functions

A function may take any number of arguments, but it always returns a single value to the calling routine. A procedure, on the other hand, does not automatically return a value. The general rule is to use a function if you need to return exactly one value to the calling routine. For example, the Adder procedure is better written as a function:

```
{Return the sum of num1 and num2}
function Adder(num1: Real; num2: Real): Real;

begin
  Adder := num1 + num2;
end;
```

A test driver for the Adder function appears below:

```
{Add two user-entered numbers}
procedure TfrmAdderFunction.AddNumbers(Sender: TObject);

var
  firstNum: Real;
  secondNum: Real;
  result: Real;
  code: Integer;

begin
  Val(edtNum1.Text, firstNum, code);
  Val(edtNum2.Text, secondNum, code);

  result := Adder(firstNum, secondNum);

  edtResult.Text := Format('%15.5f',
                           [result]);
end;
```

From this example, we see the general form of a user-defined function:

```
function FunctionName(param1: Type1; ...):
  FunctionType;

[localDeclarations;]

begin
  [statements;]
  FunctionName := ReturnValue;
end;
```

Notice that a function is defined with a particular data type (*FunctionType*); it specifies the data type of the value that the function returns to the calling routine. To return a value to the calling routine, the return value (*ReturnValue*) must be assigned to the function name (*FunctionName*) somewhere within the function's code block, as shown in the line preceding the end keyword. Alternatively, the return value can be assigned to the parameter `Result`, an implicit parameter of every Object Pascal function. `Result` and *FunctionName* refer to the same value.

Much as with a procedure call, you invoke a function by writing the function name along with any required arguments. Unlike a procedure call, however, a function call returns a single value, and your program should do something with this value (store it in a variable, display it, and so on). The general form of a function invocation with the returned value assigned to a variable follows:

```
variableName := FunctionName(argument1,
                             argument2, ...);
```

Parameter Passing

An argument is a piece of information passed to a subprogram. A parameter is a placeholder for the information passed to a subprogram when it is invoked. Each argument has a corresponding parameter. With regard to arguments and parameters, several important points apply to most high-level languages, including Object Pascal:

1. The number of arguments must equal the number of parameters.

2. Order is important. The first argument corresponds to the first parameter, the second argument to the second parameter, and so on.

3. The data type of each argument must match the data type of its corresponding parameter.

4. Names are not important. The name of an argument does not have to correspond to the name of its parameter.

5. It is important to recognize the manner in which data are passed.

In Object Pascal, parameters that have the same data type and are passed in the same manner may be combined in the parameter list of a subprogram. For instance, we can rewrite the `Adder` function as follows:

```
{Return the sum of num1 and num2}
function Adder(num1, num2: Real): Real;

begin
  Adder := num1 + num2;
end;
```

When grouping parameters in the parameter list of a subprogram, make sure that you maintain the correct order.

Object Pascal, like VB, permits passage of parameters either by reference or by value. Passing a parameter by reference actually passes the memory location (address) of the argument to the subprogram instead of the argument's value. This apporach allows the subprogram to access the actual variable. As a result, the variable's value can be changed by the subprogram. Passing a parameter by value, on the other hand, passes only the value of the argument to the subprogram. The subprogram accesses a copy of the variable, and the variable's actual value cannot be changed by the subprogram.

Passing by value is the default method of parameter passing in Object Pascal. To pass a parameter by reference, the parameter must be preceded by the `var` keyword in the subprogram heading. In VB, however, the default method of parameter passing is by reference, and the programmer must specify those parameters to be passed by value by preceding them with the `ByVal` keyword in the subprogram heading.

VB does not have the ability to pass parameters as constants, unlike Object Pascal. This method of parameter passing uses the least amount of resources. When a parameter is passed as a constant, the subprogram is not allowed to alter its value. Any attempt to do so will result in a compiler error. To pass a parameter as a constant, precede the parameter name with the `const` keyword in the subprogram heading.

Data Structures

Object Pascal contains a variety of built-in data types for storing data structures. Additionally, a programmer can define his or her own data types (that is, create user-defined data types).

Arrays

An array is a set of sequentially indexed elements of the same intrinsic data type. In Object Pascal, you declare an array variable by using the `array of` keywords. To declare a static array, use the following syntax:

```
var
   arrayVariable: array[indexType1, ...,
                        indexTypeN] of BaseType;
```

where *arrayVariable* is any valid variable name, and *BaseType* is the data type of each element in the array. Each *indexType* represents a separate index of the array and must be an ordinal data type. These are normally integer subranges.

To declare a dynamic array, use the `array of` statement without specifying indices. For instance, to declare a one-dimensional dynamic array, use the following syntax:

```
var
   dynamicArrayVariable: array of BaseType;
```

Use the `SetLength` procedure to allocate memory for the dynamic array and set its size:

```
SetLength(dynamicArrayVariable, length);
```

Each element of an array acts as a separate variable that can be accessed using its unique index values. To access a specific array element, use either

```
arrayName[indexValue1, ..., indexValueN]
```

or

```
arrayName[indexValue1] ... [indexValueN]
```

For instance, the following statement assigns the value 7 to the fourth element of myArray:

```
myArray[4] := 7;
```

Short Strings

A short string is a string whose length does not exceed 255 characters. To dimension a short string, use the following syntax:

```
var
   stringName: String[n];
```

where *n* is the length of the short string in characters. Note that the variable *stringName* occupies *n*+1 bytes of memory (from 0 to *n*), where bytes 1 through n contain the characters in the string, the zeroth byte contains the size of the string, and *n* is less than or equal to 255. The `ShortString` data type is equivalent to `String[255]`.

In Object Pascal, any string is just an array of characters. To access a particular character within a string variable, use the syntax *stringName[i]*, where *i* is the index of the character within the string (that is, you want to access the *i*th character of the string), and the first character in a string has an index value of 1. Note that *stringName[i]* is of the Char (character) data type.

Enumerated Types

An enumerated type is an ordered set of values defined by the programmer. The values have no inherent meaning, but their ordinality follows the sequence in which they are listed. In Object Pascal, the `type` keyword allows the programmer to create user-defined data types. To declare an enumerated type, use the following syntax:

```
type
    TypeName = (value1, ..., valueN);
```

where `TypeName` and `value1` through `valueN` are valid identifiers. Consider the following example:

```
type
Days = (Sunday, Monday, Tuesday, Wednesday,
            Thursday, Friday, Saturday);
```

This code defines an enumerated type named `Days` whose possible values include the days of the week.

Sets

A set consists of a group of values of the same ordinal data type. The values have no inherent order, and it is not meaningful for a value to be included more than once within a set.

A set is defined using the `set` `of` keywords. The syntax follows:

```
type
    SetName = set of BaseType;
```

where `SetName` is the name of the set and must be a valid identifier. The possible values of `SetName` include all subsets of `BaseType`, including the empty set (denoted by [ ] in Object Pascal). Object Pascal restricts the size of `BaseType` to no more than 256 possible values.

Sets are usually defined using subranges, denoted by two periods (`..`). A set constructor consists of a list of comma-separated values or subranges within square brackets. Consider the following code fragment:

```
type
    LowercaseLetters = 'a'..'z';
    LowercaseSet = set of LowercaseLetters;

var
    myLetters: LowercaseSet;

begin
    myLetters := ['a'..'c', 'm', 'n', 'x'..'z'];
        .
        .
        .
    end;
```

This code creates the `LowercaseSet` data type and the `myLetters` variable of this data type. The code block assigns `myLetters` the set consisting of the lowercase letters a, b, c, m, n, x, y, and z.

Records

As in VB, a record type declaration must specify a record type name as well as a name and data type for each field of the record. The Object Pascal syntax of a record type declaration follows:

```
type
  RecordTypeName = record
                      fieldList1: DataType1;
                      fieldList2: DataType2;
                               .
                               .
                               .
                      fieldListN: DataTypeN;
                   end;
```

Object Pascal, like VB, uses the dot-separator to access the fields of a record. Use the `recVarName.fieldName` format to access the `fieldName` field of record variable `recVarName`.

Pointers

A pointer is a variable that "points" to the memory location of another variable. Thus a pointer is an indirect variable reference. VB does not allow explicit pointer variables, but Object Pascal supports them. In Object Pascal, the caret symbol (^) is used to both denote a pointer and *dereference* a pointer. The following syntax declares a pointer type:

```
type
  PointerTypeName = ^DataType;
```

For instance, to declare a pointer type named `IntPointer` that points to an integer value, use the following code:

```
type
  IntPointer = ^Integer;
```

A variable of type `IntPointer` contains the memory address of a variable that contains an integer value.

When the caret appears after a pointer variable, it dereferences the pointer variable and returns the value stored in the address contained by the pointer. The syntax `pointerVariable^` dereferences `pointerVariable`. For the variable `ptr` of type `IntPointer`, for instance, `ptr^` returns an integer value or `nil`; `nil` is a reserved word and special constant that can be assigned to any pointer variable to reference "nothing," similar to VB's reserved word `Nothing` for objects.

The New and Dispose procedures create and destroy pointer variables, respectively. New allocates memory for a new dynamic variable and points the associated pointer variable to it. When an application finishes using a pointer, it should release the memory allocated for it using the Dispose procedure. The syntax follows:

```
New(pointerVariable);
Dispose(pointerVariable);
```

The value of *pointerVariable* is undefined after a call to the Dispose procedure.

File Input and Output

VB provides two file types for file input and output (file I/O): sequential files and random-access files. Text files are the Delphi equivalent of VB sequential files, and binary files serve the same purpose as random-access files.

Text Files

To access a text file in Object Pascal, we must first create a variable capable of referencing a text file. Declaring a variable of the TextFile data type creates such a file reference variable. A file reference variable contains a file pointer. A file pointer is similar to the cursor in a text editor; that is a cursor indicates the position within a file in a text editor, whereas a file pointer indicates the position in an open file. For an input file, the file pointer indicates the next data item to be read from the file. For an output file, the file pointer indicates the position of the next data item written to the file.

Next, we must associate the file reference variable with a data file using the AssignFile procedure. The syntax follows:

```
AssignFile(fileRef, fileName);
```

where *fileRef* is a file reference variable and *fileName* is a string expression containing any valid Windows file name. *fileName* can specify the path of the file, where the path indicates the disk drive and subdirectory where the file resides.

Finally, before we can access a data file, we must open it. A text file can be opened for either input or output, but not both simultaneously. The Reset procedure opens or reopens a text file for input, and the Rewrite and Append procedures open or reopen a text file for output. The syntax for these procedures follows:

```
Reset(fileRef);
Rewrite(fileRef);
Append(fileRef);
```

where *fileRef* is the file reference variable. Reset opens the existing data file whose name is associated with *fileRef* and sets the file pointer to the beginning of the file. If the file is already open, it is closed and then reopened. A "file not found" run-time error results if no data file with the given name exists.

The `Rewrite` procedure creates a new data file whose name is associated with *fileRef* and sets the file pointer to the beginning of the file. If a data file of the same name already exists, it is deleted and a new, empty file is created in its place. If the file is already open, it is closed and then recreated. In summary, the `Rewrite` procedure either creates a new file or overwrites an existing one.

To add data to the end of a file, you use the `Append` procedure. `Append` opens the existing text file whose name is associated with *fileRef* and positions the file pointer at the end of the file. If the file is already open, it is closed and then re-opened. If no data file with the given name exists, a "file not found" run-time error results.

Once a `Reset` statement opens a text file for input, data can be read from the file using the `Read` statement:

```
Read(fileRef, variable);
```

This statement reads the next piece of data indicated by the file pointer from the input file associated with *fileRef*, stores this information in *variable*, and then moves the file pointer to the next character in the input file. The data type of *variable* should match the type of data being read from the input file. If the data file consists of integers, for example, the data should be read into Integer variables. Whitespace characters (spaces and tabs) delimit numerical data in text files.

Multiple variables can be read using one `Read` statement. The general syntax of the `Read` statement follows:

```
Read(fileRef, variable1 [, variable2, ...]);
```

Whereas the `Read` statement reads data item by item from a text file, the `Readln` statement reads only a specified number of data items per line. The syntax to read one data item into a variable follows:

```
Readln(fileRef, variable);
```

This statement reads the next piece of data indicated by the file pointer from the input file associated with *fileRef*, stores this information in *variable*, and then moves the file pointer to the beginning of the next line of the input file.

The general syntax of the `Readln` statement follows:

```
Readln(fileRef, variable1 [, variable2, ...]);
```

When a file is opened for output with the `Rewrite` or `Append` statement, data may be written to the file using the `Write` procedure. The general syntax appears below:

```
Write(fileRef[, expression[:minWidth[:decPlaces]]]);
```

where *fileRef* is the file reference variable, *expression* is an expression of any simple or string data type, and *minWidth* and *decPlaces* are integer expressions. The optional *minWidth* parameter specifies the minimum number of characters in the output of expression. If the length of expression is less than *minWidth*, then the *Write* procedure pads the left side of the output with blank spaces. All characters in expression are output when its length exceeds *minWidth*. For a real type expression, the optional *decPlaces* parameter specifies the number of digits following the decimal point. Any number of expressions may be output with a single *Write* statement (including no expressions) by separating the expressions with commas. For example,

```
Write(myFile, 10:5, 10.47589:8:2);
```

outputs the following text to the file associated with `myFile`:

```
10 10.48
```

The `Writeln` statement operates in much the same way as `Write`, except that it outputs a carriage return/line feed combination (<CR><LF>) after all of its expressions are output. For instance,

```
Write(myFile, 'Hello ');
Write(myFile, 'and Good-bye');
Writeln(myFile); {Skip to next line}
Writeln(myFile, 'Hello ');
Writeln(myFile, 'and Good-bye');
```

outputs the following text:

```
Hello and Good-bye
Hello
and Good-bye
```

As with `Read` and `Readln`, `Write` statements can be combined but `Writeln` statements cannot. Thus we can rewrite the previous example as follows:

```
Write(myFile, 'Hello ', 'and Good-bye');
Writeln(myFile); {Skip to next line}
Writeln(myFile, 'Hello ');
Writeln(myFile, 'and Good-bye');
```

Finally, when your program has finished working with a file, you should close the file. The `CloseFile` statement ends the association between a file reference variable and a data file, returning these resources to the system. For an output file, the `CloseFile` statement also writes the end-of-file character before it closes the file. The syntax of the `CloseFile` statement follows:

```
CloseFile(fileRef);
```

Two extremely important functions are available for working with text files: `Eof` and `Eoln`. As in VB, the `Eof` (end-of-file) function returns a Boolean value that indicates whether the end of an input file has been reached. `Eof(fileRef)` is True when the file pointer is beyond the last character of the file associated with *fileRef*. This function is useful in an indefinite loop structure for reading data from an input file until the end of file is reached. The `Eoln` (end-of-line) function returns a Boolean value that indicates whether the file pointer is at the end of the current line. For an input file associated with *fileRef*, Eoln(*fileRef*) is True when the file pointer is at the end of the current line or Eof(*fileRef*) is True. The Eoln function is also useful in an indefinite loop structure for processing an input file character by character. VB does not contain a built-in function similar to Eoln.

Binary Files

Unlike text files, binary files can access data in any order; that is data can be read from or written to any location in the file. For this reason, binary files are also known as random-access files. Furthermore, a binary file accesses an entire data structure at a time. For that reason, binary files present a better and faster method of storing and retrieving information contained within a known data structure.

While text files are stored in ASCII format, binary files are not. That is, if a binary file were to be read as a text file, not all of the characters in the file would be meaningful. To correctly access a binary file, a program must know the exact data structure contained in the file.

Object Pascal supports two kinds of binary files: typed files and untyped files. Our discussion concentrates on typed files, the more common of the two. A typed file is an ordered file of elements of the same data type. You may notice a strong similarity between the definitions of an array and a typed file. Essentially, you can think of a typed file as an array in file form. As you will soon see, instead of using an array index to access a particular piece of data, you use a record number.

To define a typed file data type, use the file of syntax shown below:

```
type
   FileTypeName = file of DataType;
```

where *FileTypeName* is any valid identifier and *DataType* is a fixed-size data type. Because *DataType* has a fixed size, both implicit and explicit pointer types are not allowed. In other words, a typed file cannot contain dynamic arrays, long strings, classes, objects, pointers, variants, other files, or structured types that contain any of these types.

As an example, consider the following code fragment:

```
type
   StudentRec = record
                   lastName: String[30];
                   firstName: String[20];
                   ID: String[12];
                   GPA: Real;
                   crdtHrs: Real;
                end;
   StudentDB = file of StudentRec;

var
   studentFile: StudentDB;
```

This code fragment declares the `StudentDB` data type, a typed file of `StudentRec` records. `studentFile` is a typed file variable of type `StudentDB`, whose associated file contains the names, ID numbers, grade-point averages, and cumulative credit hours for the students at a particular school.

As with text files, the `AssignFile` procedure associates a file variable with an external binary file. The `Reset` and `Rewrite` procedures also work in the same way for binary files as they do for text files. By default, a binary file is capable of both input and output operations regardless of which procedure is used. For a text file, recall that `Reset` accesses the file as read-only (for input) and `Rewrite` sets it to write-only (for output). Both procedures therefore move the file pointer to the beginning of the file. The `Append` procedure is used exclusively for text files; it is not available for use with binary files.

The value of the global variable `FileMode` determines the access mode used when a binary file is opened using the Reset procedure. Valid values of `FileMode` are 0 for read-only access, 1 for write-only access, and 2 for read/write access. The default `FileMode` is 2. Assigning another value to `FileMode` causes all subsequent `Reset` calls to use that mode.

The `Read` procedure reads a data element from a binary file into a variable with a compatible data type. Similarly, the `Write` procedure writes the contents of a variable to a binary file with a compatible data type. Both operations (read and write) occur in the current location of the file pointer. After execution, both `Read` and `Write` automatically increment the file pointer so that it points to the next data element in the binary file. As with text files, you can combine multiple `Read` statements and multiple `Write` statements. The general syntax of the `Read` and `Write` procedures appears below:

```
Read(fileRef, dataVar [, dataVar2, ...]);
Write(fileRef, dataVar [, dataVar2, ...]);
```

As binary files are not organized into lines (of text), a syntax error results when you attempt to use the `Readln` or `Writeln` procedures. In short, `Readln` and `Writeln` are used exclusively for text files. Similarly, the `Eof` function works with binary files, but `Eoln` does not.

The `Seek` procedure moves the file pointer in a binary file to a specified record or data element. The syntax follows:

```
Seek(fileRef, recNum);
```

where `fileRef` is a binary file variable and `recNum` is a long integer representing the record number (or element number) in the file, where the first data element has a `recNum` of 0. The `FileSize` function returns the number of records (or elements) in a specified binary file. For the binary file corresponding to file variable `fileRef`, the values of `recNum` range from 0 to `FileSize(fileRef)`−1. To move the file pointer to the end of the file, use a statement of the form

```
Seek(fileRef, FileSize(fileRef));
```

Performing a `Write` procedure immediately following this statement expands the binary file by one data element. The `Truncate` procedure deletes all data elements in the binary file at and after the current position of the file pointer; the current file position becomes the end of file. When all file operations are complete, the `CloseFile` procedure terminates the association between the binary file variable and external file.

As an example, the following code unit implements an address book program using records and binary file I/O. This program stores data in a binary file named `Address.dat` located in the home directory of drive C (C:\). Figure G.12 displays the user interface for this program.

```
{---------------------------------------------------------
Address Book Program
---------------------------------------------------------}
unit Address;

interface

uses
  Windows, Messages, SysUtils, Classes,
  Graphics, Controls, Forms, Dialogs,
  StdCtrls;

type
  TfrmAddressBook = class(TForm)
    edtFirstName: TEdit;
    edtLastName: TEdit;
    edtAddress: TEdit;
    edtCity: TEdit;
    edtState: TEdit;
    edtZip: TEdit;
    edtPhoneNumber: TEdit;
    lblFirstName: TLabel;
    lblLastName: TLabel;
    lblAddress: TLabel;
    lblCity: TLabel;
    lblState: TLabel;
    lblZip: TLabel;
    lblPhoneNumber: TLabel;
    btnAdd: TButton;
    btnClear: TButton;
    btnRemove: TButton;
    btnFind: TButton;
    procedure AddCard(Sender: TObject);
    procedure Initialize(Sender: TObject);
    procedure ClearForm(Sender: TObject);
    procedure Terminate(Sender: TObject;
              var Action: TCloseAction);
```

```
   procedure RemoveCard(Sender: TObject);
   procedure FindCard(Sender: TObject);
private
  { Private declarations }
public
  { Public declarations }
end;
AddressCard = record
                firstName: String[20];
                {First Name}
                lastName: String[20];
                {Last Name}
                address: String[30];
                {Street Address}
                city: String[20];
                {City}
                state: String[20];
                {State}
                zipCode: String[15];
                {Zip Code}
                phoneNumber: String[20];
                {Telephone Number}
                end;

{
GLOBAL VARIABLES
These global variables make the coding of this .
program sufficiently easier.
}
var
  frmAddressBook: TfrmAddressBook;
  dataFile: File of AddressCard;

implementation

{$R *.DFM}

{Return the record number of the address card
that matches the first and last names. The
search is not case sensitive. If a matching address card
is not found, Find returns -1.}
function Find(first, last: String): Integer;

var
  addrCard: AddressCard;
  findCard: AddressCard;
  found: Boolean;
```

```
begin
  Reset(dataFile);
  found := False;
  findCard.firstName :=
    Trim(UpperCase(first));
  findCard.lastName := Trim(UpperCase(last));
  while not(Eof(datafile) or found) do begin
    Read(dataFile, addrCard);
    found := (UpperCase(addrCard.firstName) =
              findCard.firstName) and
             (UpperCase(addrCard.lastName) =
              findCard.lastName);
  end;
  if found then begin
    Find := FilePos(dataFile) - 1;
  end
  else begin
    Find := -1;
  end;
end;

{Add the address card to the database}
procedure TfrmAddressBook.AddCard(Sender: TObject);

var
  addrCard: AddressCard;

begin
  with addrCard do begin
    firstName := Trim(edtFirstName.Text);
    lastName := Trim(edtLastName.Text);
    address := Trim(edtAddress.Text);
    city := Trim(edtCity.Text);
    state := Trim(edtState.Text);
    zipCode := Trim(edtZip.Text);
    phoneNumber := Trim(edtPhoneNumber.Text);
  end;
  Seek(dataFile, FileSize(dataFile));
  Write(dataFile, addrCard);
  Application.MessageBox(
    PChar('Address card added!'),
    'ADD', MB_OK);
  ClearForm(Sender);
end;

{Remove the address card from the database}
procedure TfrmAddressBook.RemoveCard(Sender: TObject);
```

```
var
  addrCard: AddressCard;
  pos: Integer;
  recNum: Integer;

begin
  recNum := Find(edtFirstName.Text,
             edtLastName.Text);
  if (recNum >= 0) then begin

    {Display the address card}
    Seek(dataFile, recNum);
    Read(dataFile, addrCard);
    edtFirstName.Text := addrCard.firstName;
    edtLastName.Text := addrCard.lastName;
    edtAddress.Text := addrCard.address;
    edtCity.Text := addrCard.city;
    edtState.Text := addrCard.state;
    edtZip.Text := addrCard.zipCode;
    edtPhoneNumber.Text :=
      addrCard.phoneNumber;

    {Remove the address card from the
      database}
    for pos := recNum to (FileSize(dataFile) -
                          2) do begin
      Seek(dataFile, pos + 1);
      Read(dataFile, addrCard);
      Seek(dataFile, pos);
      Write(dataFile, addrCard);
    end;
    Seek(dataFile, FileSize(dataFile) - 1);
    Truncate(dataFile);

    Application.MessageBox(
      PChar('Address card removed!'),
      'REMOVE', MB_OK);
  end
  else begin
    Application.MessageBox(
      PChar('Address card NOT found!'),
      'REMOVE', MB_OK);
  end;
end;

{Find and display the address card that
matches the first and last names}
procedure TfrmAddressBook.FindCard(Sender: TObject);
```

```
var
  addrCard: AddressCard;
  recNum: Integer;
begin
  recNum := Find(edtFirstName.Text,
             edtLastName.Text);
  if (recNum >= 0) then begin
    Seek(dataFile, recNum);
    Read(dataFile, addrCard);
    edtFirstName.Text := addrCard.firstName;
    edtLastName.Text := addrCard.lastName;
    edtAddress.Text := addrCard.address;
    edtCity.Text := addrCard.city;
    edtState.Text := addrCard.state;
    edtZip.Text := addrCard.zipCode;
    edtPhoneNumber.Text :=
      addrCard.phoneNumber;
  end
  else begin
    Application.MessageBox(
      PChar('Address card NOT found!'),
      'FIND', MB_OK);
  end;

end;

{Initialize the program by opening the Address
Book database -- File Name: c:\Address.dat}
procedure TfrmAddressBook.Initialize(Sender: TObject);

begin
  AssignFile(dataFile, 'c:\Address.dat');
  try
    Reset(dataFile);
  except
    Rewrite(dataFile);
  end;
end;

{Clear the edit boxes on the form}
procedure TfrmAddressBook.ClearForm(Sender: TObject);

begin
  edtFirstName.Clear;
  edtLastName.Clear;
  edtAddress.Clear;
  edtCity.Clear;
```

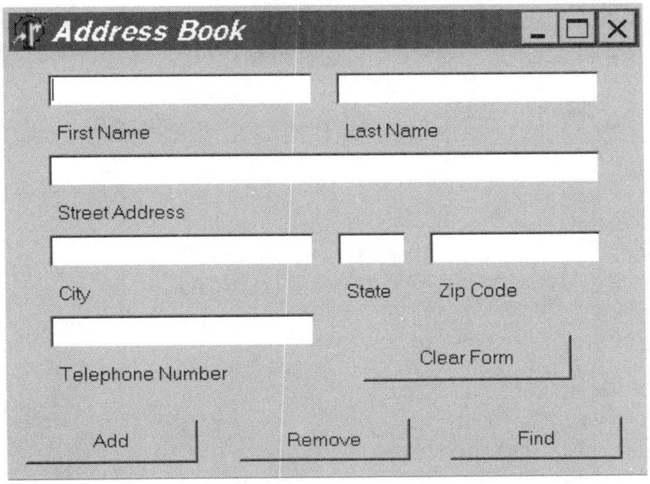

FIGURE G.12   User Interface for Address Book Program

```
    edtState.Clear;
    edtZip.Clear;
    edtPhoneNumber.Clear;
end;

{Close the database file and terminate the program}
procedure TfrmAddressBook.Terminate(Sender: TObject;
    var Action: TCloseAction);
begin
    CloseFile(dataFile);
end;

end.
```

As a final note, Delphi contains a `TFileStream` class for object-oriented file I/O. This class offers the programmer a portable, high-level approach to file I/O. The next section introduces object-oriented programming in Delphi.

Object-Oriented Programming

As previously discussed, Delphi has a complete object model. All components and controls are ancestors of `TObject`, the base object class. Thus all components and controls are fully extensible through object-oriented programming (OOP). VB, however, does not include a complete object model. Consequently, it does not offer true object inheritance and polymorphism like Delphi.

Rather than extol the virtues of OOP and detail its syntax in Object Pascal, this appendix will simply provide an example of its use. The following Delphi unit file defines two classes, `Employee` and `Supervisor`. The `Supervisor` class is a descendant of the `Employee` class. A sample execution of this code appears in Figure G.13.

```
unit OOPEx;

interface

uses
  Windows, Messages, SysUtils, Classes,
  Graphics, Controls, Forms, Dialogs,
  StdCtrls;

type
  TfrmOOPEx = class(TForm)
    btnTest: TButton;
    memOutput: TMemo;
    procedure DoTest(Sender: TObject);
  private
    { Private declarations }
  public
    { Public declarations }
  end;

type
  NameStr = String[25];
  IDStr = String[10];
  DivType = (Operations, Production,
             Maintenance);
  Employee = class
    lastName: NameStr;
    firstName: NameStr;
    division: DivType;
    procedure SetAll(lname, fname:
                  NameStr; dv: DivType);
    procedure SetLastName(lname: NameStr);
    function GetLastName: NameStr;
    procedure SetFirstName(fname: NameStr);
    function GetFirstName: NameStr;
    procedure SetDivision(dv: DivType);
    function GetDivision: DivType;
  end;
  Supervisor = class(Employee)
    managerID: IDStr;
    procedure SetAll(lname, fname: NameStr;
                     dv: DivType;
                     id: IDStr);
    procedure SetID(id: IDStr);
```

```
    function GetID: IDStr;
  end;

var
  frmOOPEx: TfrmOOPEx;

implementation

{$R *.DFM}

procedure Employee.SetLastName(lname:
                                NameStr);
begin
  lastName := lname;
end;

function Employee.GetLastName: NameStr;
begin
  GetLastName := lastName;
end;

procedure Employee.SetFirstName(fname:
                                  NameStr);

begin
  firstName := fname;
end;

function Employee.GetFirstName: NameStr;
begin
  GetFirstName := firstName;
end;

procedure Employee.SetDivision(dv: DivType);
begin
  division := dv;
end;

function Employee.GetDivision: DivType;
begin
  GetDivision := division;
end;

procedure Employee.SetAll(lname, fname:
                             NameStr;
                          dv: DivType);

begin
  Self.SetLastName(lname);
  Self.SetFirstName(fname);
  Self.SetDivision(dv);
end;
```

```
procedure Supervisor.SetID(id: IDStr);
begin
  managerID := id;
end;

function Supervisor.GetID: IDStr;
begin
  GetID := managerID;
end;

procedure Supervisor.SetAll(lname, fname:
                            NameStr; dv:
                            DivType;
                            id: IDStr);

begin
  Self.SetLastName(lname);
  Self.SetFirstName(fname);
  Self.SetDivision(dv);
  Self.SetID(id);
end;

procedure TfrmOOPEx.DoTest(Sender:
                           TObject);

var
  emp: Employee;
  mgr: Supervisor;

begin
  emp := Employee.Create;
  mgr := Supervisor.Create;
  emp.SetAll('Thompson', 'James',
            Operations);
  mgr.SetAll('Stewart', 'Linda',
            Operations, '003685');
  memOutput.Clear;
  memOutput.Lines.Add('OPERATIONS DIVISION');
  memOutput.Lines.Add('Supervisor: ' +
                      mgr.GetLastName + ', '
                      + mgr.GetFirstName);
  memOutput.Lines.Add('Employee: ' +
                      emp.GetLastName + ', '
                      + emp.GetFirstName);
  emp.Free;
  mgr.Free;
end;

end.
```

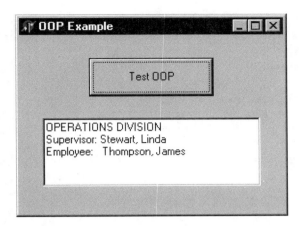

FIGURE G.13   Object-Oriented Programming Example

Built-in Debugger

Like VB, Delphi contains a built-in debugger to assist the programmer in tracing code and locating errors. To use the Delphi debugger, you must enable the integrated debugging option. To enable integrated debugging, select `Tools | Debugger Options...` from the menu, check the Integrated debugging box at the lower-left side of the Debugger Options window, and click the OK button.

The debugger commands are available through the Run menu and the Debug toolbar. Additionally, debugger commands can be quickly accessed through the Code Editor window. Right-click anywhere inside the Code Editor window to open a pop-up menu. The Debug option on this pop-up menu lists the available debugger commands.

The Delphi debugger provides a semi-automatic method of locating errors. It enables a programmer to watch specific variables or expressions without modifying the program code. Additionally, the debugger can stop the program execution at designated breakpoints or execute the program code step by step. Note that the debugger is a design-time utility; none of the debugger commands may be used in an executable module at run time outside the Delphi IDE.

Source breakpoints are toggled on and off at specific lines of code as designated by the programmer. Breakpoints can be set only on executable lines of code. Blank lines, declaration statements, and comments cannot include breakpoints. When it encounters a breakpoint, the program's execution is temporarily halted until the programmer selects Run from the Run menu, presses F9, or left-clicks the Run button on the Debug toolbar. The Delphi debugger also supports address, data, and module load breakpoints.

While a program is halted, the programmer can immediately evaluate and modify expressions in the Evaluate/Modify window (Figure G.14). An expression may also be viewed and changed in the Debug Inspector window (Figure G.15). The Debug Inspector window provides the programmer with a better view of objects that have advanced data structures.

The Delphi debugger uses two stepping operations. Trace Into executes code one statement at a time. For example, if the statement is a call to a subprogram, the next statement displayed is the first statement in the subprogram. Step Over executes a subprogram call as a single unit, then steps to the next statement in the current subprogram. Thus, in every situation, Step Over moves to the next statement in the current subprogram.

A watch expression is a user-defined expression that allows the programmer to observe its behavior. Watch expressions appear in the Watch List window (Figure G.16), and their values are automatically updated in break mode. Further-

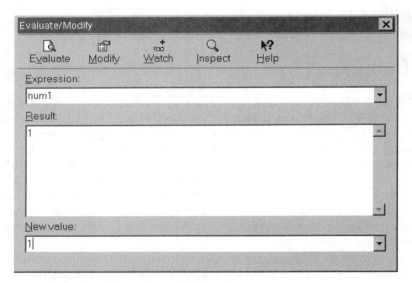

FIGURE G.14   Evaluate/Modify Window

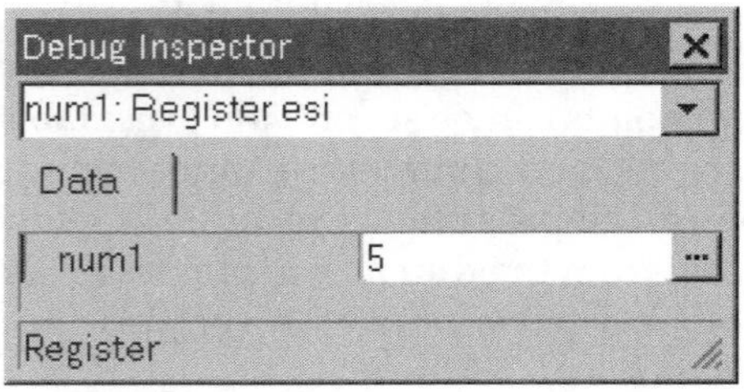

FIGURE G.15   Debug Inspector Window

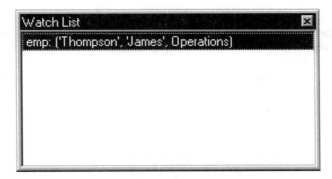

FIGURE G.16   Watch List Window

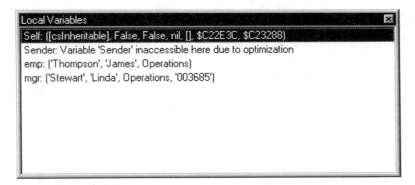

FIGURE G.17   Local Variables Window

more, the Local Variables window automatically displays the values of all declared variables (all local variables) in the current subprogram, as shown in Figure G.17.

Application Deployment

This section discusses how to compile Delphi projects and distribute the final application.

Building Executable Files

Much as in C, C++, and other high-level languages, generating an executable file in Delphi involves a two-step process. The first step is to compile the project, which checks the syntax of each unit in the project and produces an object file for the unit. A unit object file has a DCU (Delphi compiled unit) extension.

The second step is to link these object files. The linker takes each of the unit object files in the project and combines them to produce a single executable file.

The Project menu in Delphi contains the commands for creating the executable file. The Compile option compiles each unit in the project but does not link them. The Build menu item compiles the units, if necessary, and then links them together, creating the final executable file.

Distributing the Application

If your project does not access a database, third-party dynamic link library (DLL), or ActiveX control, then the executable file that is generated is a stand-alone executable. You can simply copy this executable file to a floppy disk or other removable media and run it on any machine that uses its target operating system. All of the Delphi controls used in the project will be compiled into the resulting executable file. Nothing else must be included with the application.

As with VB, if you use ActiveX controls in a project, the distribution of the application becomes more complicated. You must distribute the OCX file for each ActiveX control used in the project. Be sure to read the documentation for third-party ActiveX controls; some require additional DLLs.

For Windows, an elegant method of deploying an application is to create a Setup program. If you create your own, be sure to register all ActiveX controls used by the application. This task is accomplished by running the `RegSvr32.exe` utility.

The preferred method of creating a Setup program is to use a commercially available installation package. VB includes the Package and Deployment Wizard for this purpose. Similarly, Delphi ships with InstallShield Express, a menu-driven installation utility that allows you to create a Setup program for application deployment.

Additional References

In addition to writing this Delphi book, Mitchell Kerman is the lead coauthor of a VB textbook. Although both of these texts are designed for introductory programming courses, they are also invaluable references for advanced programmers. Both textbooks are published by Addison Wesley Longman (AWL). See the AWL Web site (www.awl.com/cs) for more information regarding the texts.

Computer Programming Fundamentals with Applications in Visual Basic 6.0, by Mitchell C. Kerman and Ronald L. Brown

Programming and Problem Solving with Delphi, by Mitchell C. Kerman

Conclusions

Delphi is a fully capable RAD tool that harnesses the power of the Object Pascal language. It offers a variety of readily available components and tools, a hierarchical component design, true object-orientation, and an intuitive IDE.

Although no single document can truly expound the benefits of Delphi, this appendix shoud have at least intrigued you with the ease with which you can migrate from VB to Delphi and become a proficient Delphi developer.

Enjoy your future with Delphi. Borland has truly let the genie out of the bottle: its name is Delphi, and you are granted an infinite number of wishes.

Index